Edmonton In Our Own Words

Edmonton
In Our Own Words

Linda Goyette

Carolina Jakeway Roemmich

The University of Alberta Press

Published by

The University of Alberta Press

Ring House 2   Edmonton, Alberta, Canada   T6G 2E1

ISBN 0–88864–428–0

Library and Archives Canada Cataloguing in Publication Data

Goyette, Linda, 1955–

   Edmonton in our own words / Linda Goyette, Carolina Jakeway Roemmich.

   Includes bibliographical references and index.

   ISBN 0–88864–428–0

   1. Edmonton (Alta.)—History. I. Roemmich, Carolina Jakeway, 1974– II. Title

FC3696.4.G69 2004   971.23'34   C2004–904059–6

Printed and bound in Canada by Kromar Printing Ltd., Winnipeg, Manitoba.

First edition, first printing, 2004

   The University of Alberta Press is committed to protecting our natural environment. As part of our
efforts, this book is printed on stock produced by New Leaf Paper: it contains 100% post-consumer
recycled fibres and is acid- and chlorine-free.

   The University of Alberta Press gratefully acknowledges the support received for its publishing
program from The Canada Council for the Arts. The University of Alberta Press also gratefully
acknowledges the financial support of the Government of Canada through the Book Publishing
Industry Development Program (BPDIP) and from the Alberta Foundation for the Arts for our
publishing activities.

To those who had a story to tell
and no one to listen.

Contents

List of Maps

Foreword

THE EDMONTON PUBLIC LIBRARY has a mission "to connect the people of Edmonton to the knowledge and cultures of the world" and we treasure the rich stories of our own community.

This book is one part of an ambitious exploration of urban history, the education project for Edmonton's centennial in 2004. The *Edmonton: A City Called Home* project began in an unusual way. In 1999 Mayor Bill Smith asked a group of city archivists, librarians, educators from the city's school districts and the University of Alberta as well as academic and community historians to consider a proposal for two new books and an online resource that would explore the city's past in a new way. The mayor asked for a collaboration that would honour the contributions of Edmonton's citizens over time, reflect their diverse points of view and capture the city's creative spark and character.

Linda Cook, the Director of Libraries, stepped forward to offer the library as the project headquarters. City Archivist Leslie Latta-Guthrie and her staff delivered the substantial expertise and resources of the City of Edmonton Archives. In the summer of 2002 Alva Shewchuk of Edmonton Public Schools pulled together dedicated volunteers from the city's school districts and post-secondary institutions to support the project. Community organizations and individuals volunteered countless hours of hard work to the endeavour.

By the spring of 2002, writer Linda Goyette and researcher Carolina Jakeway Roemmich were working in an office in the library, and travelling around the city in search of fresh stories and recent scholarship in urban history. For the next two years they invited citizens to monthly gatherings at the Stanley Milner Library. Some days 60 or more people gathered to share their knowledge, and to talk about the city. Many of their stories were new and unknown outside of immediate families because, as they put it, "nobody ever asked us before." Hundreds of their stories will be published on the web site, and preserved in a special collection at the City of Edmonton Archives.

When I became the project's administrator, I had been a faithful reader of Linda Goyette's columns in the *Edmonton Journal* for years, but I did not know her. My appreciation grew—for her ideas, her strong work ethic, her sense of humour and her absolute respect for the people she was working with and whose stories she was collecting. Carolina Jakeway Roemmich had an equal commitment to a project that will endure long after Edmonton celebrates its 100th birthday as a city.

The Edmonton Public Library respected the independence of the authors, as did every individual and organization that contributed funds to the project. We are especially grateful to Ernie Ingles, Associate Vice President [Learning Services] and Chief Librarian of the University of Alberta Libraries, and to Linda Cameron, Mary Mahoney-Robson, Cathie Crooks, Alan Brownoff and Yoko Sekiya at the University of Alberta Press for their expert collaboration. Copy editor Peter Midgley, designer Kevin Zak, cartographer Wendy Johnson and photographer John Ulan also deserve special thanks for their fine contributions.

Listen to the voices on these pages. This book honours Edmontonians from all walks of life, people who did their best with what they had, who raised their children, experienced hardship and joy—people who were and are just like us. They are not romanticized, nor are their tales whitewashed. They are real. And that is what makes *Edmonton In Our Own Words* so exceptional.

Keith Turnbull
Associate Director
Edmonton Public Library

The City and The University

THE UNIVERSITY OF ALBERTA IS DELIGHTED to participate in the centenary celebration of the City of Edmonton. For most of the past 100 years the University has been a key participant in the economic, cultural and social development of the City. We pride ourselves in the role we played in past, continue to play and will play in future in the daily lives of Edmontonians.

The University of Alberta Press (UAP) and the University of Alberta Libraries (UAL) are pleased to be part of the Edmonton: A City Called Home centennial project. *Edmonton In Our Own Words* is one of three inter-related products of the project that also includes a children's book and an interactive website. Included in *Edmonton In Our Own Words* are the collected stories of many people who have called Edmonton home. They lived and live in a community—a community that itself evolved from a gathering place, to a small town and then to a larger town, to a major urban centre. This evolution was a result of their contributions made and by way of the relationships they nurtured.

Over the course of the Edmonton: A City Called Home project the UAP and the UAL have reinforced and nurtured their respective relationships with Edmonton Public Library (EPL) as well as other municipal departments. At this time we particularly congratulate the EPL on their leadership role in the successful completion of this historic project, and in particular applaud the work of Linda Cook, Director of Libraries, and Keith Turnbull,

Associate Director, as well as writer Linda Goyette and researcher Carolina Jakeway Roemmich. We look forward to future collaborative undertakings that will, in the best traditions of Edmonton, contribute to the quality of life in our City.

Also, we thank all the volunteers associated with the project, and in particular Alva Shewchuk of Edmonton Public Schools. As Chair of the steering committee, Alva's dedication was instrumental in seeing the project through to conclusion.

Edmonton In Our Own Words epitomizes the spirit of the individuals whose stories it celebrates. It is a co-operative endeavour that relied on the energy and commitment of numerous individuals. It brought together in partnership and common cause two great organizations, the City of Edmonton and the University of Alberta. And, in terms of the latter, it showcases one of Canada's preeminent University presses. Most importantly, it was and will remain a lasting recognition that the history of the City walks by us and talks to us each and every day as represented by the people with whom we interact. It is to these residents we dedicate our labours.

Ernie Ingles
Associate Vice-President (Learning Services)
and Chief Librarian

How a City Remembers

YOU HAVE TO LIVE IN EDMONTON to know about our riverbank walks. When we need to talk to one another about something important—or listen—we find a trail beside the North Saskatchewan River and start walking. This city is a conversation with a river running through it.

I like to walk along the river and talk to Samuel, Ellen and Laura. Samuel is a coal miner. Ellen plants a garden every spring. Their daughter Laura is a young nurse at the University of Alberta Hospital. I ask them about their lives in Edmonton. Why did you immigrate here? What do you think of this city? Can you tell me about your lives in that tiny house in Beverly? They never answer—they died long ago—so I have to imagine their replies. The Depression drove them out of town. Samuel lost his job when the Bush Mine shut down. Ellen sold the house, and followed her husband back to Britain. Laura's family moved east to find work, and never returned. Laura died before I retraced her steps to a city she loved. I remember only vague fragments of my grandmother's Edmonton stories. You would not call it history.

Is your family like mine? Samuel, Ellen and Laura left no memoirs, diaries or letters to describe their arrival here after the First World War, or their departure in the 1930s. You will not find their personal papers in an archival collection because, like most people, they left no personal papers. Published histories of Canada, Alberta and Edmonton do not describe their gifts to this place—digging coal, planting gardens and comforting the sick. I can only try to hear their voices as I walk beside the river, wondering about them.

Care to go for a walk? All of the people who ever lived at this bend in the North Saskatchewan took part in creating the city we know as Edmonton. They have plenty to tell us.

This city was born with a rich storytelling tradition. Passing on their inheritance from their ancestors, Edmonton's aboriginal elders continue to preserve First Nations and Métis history by telling stories from one generation to the next. They are the recognized historians of the city's founding peoples. Some of their stories have been written down; most have not. Their descendants are researching and publishing their own histories of Edmonton and more of these books will appear in the future.

A surprising number of people in early Edmonton left behind historical clues in their writing, drawings, photographs, early film and sound recordings. Far more people left spoken stories, or fragments that need to be collected from families, compared, and pieced together to be understood. The great majority of inhabitants left nothing at all—not a word, nor a whisper—to help us comprehend the city we inherited, or adopted as our own.

In any conversation, no matter how hard we listen, we will misunderstand spoken words and the silences in between. The only remedy is to ask another question and think about the answer.

Every city is an act of imagination. Can we imagine a conversation between a city's past inhabitants and its living citizens? What would we ask one another if we could? What would we argue about? If we could write Edmonton's collective memoir—assembling the written record, the spoken stories and the vast silences—what would we tell the rest of the world about our place on the map? What stories would we hide? What stories would we exaggerate? What stories would we tell with laughter, or pride or tears in our eyes?

What stories have we lost? What stories have we forgotten? Why have we forgotten them?

•~

I AM A JOURNALIST BY TRAINING and inclination—not an historian—so I am better at asking questions than answering them. To begin this assignment I read the published histories of Edmonton, and I asked myself what else I wanted to know about my hometown. I made long lists of the people

I wanted to meet—the living and the dead—and the unfamiliar stories they might share. I made longer lists of contentious issues. A reporter soon learns that three different people will tell three different versions of the same event. I kept a notebook of contradictions and contested history. Twenty years at the *Edmonton Journal* also taught me that people prefer to speak for themselves. I looked for first-person accounts in diaries, letters, court testimonies and memoirs. I asked people to sit down over a cup of coffee and tell me exactly what happened in their own words. They talked and talked into a tape recorder and later corrected their own transcripts for the record.

Academic historians can sift through the same clues and reach different conclusions. I interviewed them to understand their differences of opinion, and examined recent scholarship that challenges local certainties. As Edmonton's history is intertwined with its surrounding communities—past and present—I looked beyond city limits for missing accounts that would complete an urban picture.

One day the telephone rang and a stranger said she had heard about the centennial project on the radio, and she was coming to work with me as a researcher. There was no arguing with her. Carolina Jakeway Roemmich has two passions—western Canadian history and crossword puzzles—and do not try to stand in front of her bicycle when she is on the way to the City of Edmonton Archives. For a year she cycled all over the city in an intrepid search for overlooked stories. She filled in empty squares, hundreds down, and hundreds across, knowing the infinite puzzle could never be completed.

We searched for three kinds of people: eyewitnesses, descendants and interpreters. Their contributions are in this book. Eyewitnesses tell a story about Edmonton from first-hand knowledge. Descendants describe their families' experiences to break a silence in the published record. Interpreters are informed elders—and academic and community historians—who place these stories in historical perspective and help us to understand differences of opinion.

Personal stories are intriguing but how much can we trust them as factual accounts of Edmonton's history? Qualified historians—and most people with common sense—remind us that storytellers have imperfect memories and personal reputations to protect. They are not impartial observers of their own lives. They distort our understanding of an event through their choice of words and through their omissions. Some of

Edmonton's best-known storytellers acknowledge these limitations. Albert Lacombe, the Oblate priest who founded St. Albert, tried to write a memoir in his old age, but he stopped after a few dozen typed pages: "To speak of one's self is a delicate task. One will relate with complacency certain facts and circumstances where vanity will shine; and we will ingenuously keep silence on other facts and events the narration of which would be humiliating." Lacombe is honest about the shortcomings of any memoir. Open his soft leather notebook in the Provincial Archives of Alberta. Carefully touch his crumbling letters and you will feel only too grateful he kept a pencil in his pocket. You can walk along the North Saskatchewan with him, too, and ask a thousand questions.

Secrets hide between the lines of every story. "If history, in small and large matters, were truly written without gloss, and just as the facts occurred, what a commotion would be created, and how many would want it suppressed!"[1] said William Newton about Edmonton in the 1870s and 1880s. His own reticence is exasperating. Newton hints at the harsh truths he would like to reveal about local land speculators. Why did he not write down what he meant? Perhaps he suspected that future readers would dissect his words and judge him. Storytellers protect themselves from judgement. Sometimes they camouflage an event in unexamined nostalgia and civic boosterism; sometimes they pass on inaccurate information disguised as fact.

Many people refuse to share what they know, protecting a truth with silence. This is their right.

So what do we do about these problems? Consider each story a map. A story can help us find our way through an unknown land, but as historian Barbara Belyea reminds us, the map is not the territory.[2]

We should not confuse a story with historical fact but we should not dismiss a personal memoir as meaningless either. Compelling stories engage us more easily than a dry recitation of facts or a cautious analysis of urban development. Diaries and letters light a match to our imaginations. Family stories fill gaps in the published historical record. We can learn a little about people who did not read or write and did not speak English. We can honour their rightful place in history. We can enter the past with our senses, our emotions and our intellect.

Edmonton is a city that destroys its architectural heritage each time it reinvents itself. Consequently, it is not always possible to touch the past as we walk along the sidewalk. I used to smile at an old plaque on the wall at City Centre. It explained that a stately courthouse on the site had bowed to progress. The old courthouse, the old downtown post office, the old railway stations are all gone, regrettably, and even the bowed-to-progress plaque disappeared for a time. This city continues to neglect its architectural legacy as hundreds of younger buildings bow and scrape their way to oblivion. Strangers in town think we built the place yesterday—and we did—but I am not as concerned about the danger of urban amnesia as other people seem to be.

Stories are stronger than buildings. The city's cultural memory survives in dozens of fine books; in museums and historical parks; in libraries and archives. More importantly, it endures in the formal and informal stories we tell one another every day. Pamela Cunningham and her team members bring tobacco to aboriginal elders, and carefully record a strong oral history of a Fort Edmonton cemetery on the Rossdale Flats. Philip Coutu publishes his own theories about the location of early trading posts. Young descendants of the Papaschase band meet on Saturday mornings in the Sacred Heart church basement to check 1880 band lists on Joyce Bruneau's laptop computer. Veterans of the Loyal Eddies gather for beers and conversation at the Norwood Legion. Velma Logan brings a beautiful story to the library about her mother who read tea leaves in a Jasper Avenue café. Edith Stone Sutton describes her years on the Edmonton Grads to a room full of people who spontaneously applaud the 85-year-old champion in their midst. Bob Davies creates a homemade book with intricate neighbourhood maps and illustrations of the homemade toys, games and exploring places of an Edmonton childhood. Mary Kur, an immigrant girl from Sudan, tells her arrival story and her first impressions of snow. Is all of this not a kind of historical preservation?

The people of this city have not forgotten their history. They live and breathe it. The conversation between past and present continues.

It is true that children can be born and raised in Edmonton without encountering an engaging account of their urban heritage at school. They hear the generic buffalo hunt story, and the generic homesteaders' story, so frequently they can recite test answers in a coma. What is a sod house made of? Sod. Who opened the West? The stalwart pioneers. Where did aboriginal people live? On the plains. They hear too many rural generalizations and safe clichés and too few gritty urban details and contradictions.

Cities rarely get a word in edgewise in the everyday discussion of western Canadian history. This is not just a school curriculum problem; it is a mystifying blind spot in our regional culture. More than five million people live in Canada's prairie provinces and three million of them live in five major cities. If you count the population of smaller cities the size of Red Deer or Lethbridge, 70 per cent of citizens in the West live in cities. Albertans live in one of the most urbanized provinces in the country. Even in the celebrated period of western Canadian settlement, between 1901 and 1911, the rural population of the Prairies rose 2.7 times; in contrast the urban population increased 4.6 times, from 103,000 people to 500,000 people. In 1911, 38 per cent of the West's populations lived in towns and cities. Yet urban historical questions are rarely considered inside or outside Edmonton's classrooms. When did aboriginal people begin to live in the territory we now call Edmonton? Were they not the ones who opened this corner of the West? What were their names? How many of Edmonton's current citizens are their descendants? How many rural homesteaders moved into town after one brutal winter? How many stayed because they liked the city better? Who built the factories and apartment buildings, the sewer trenches and telephone lines? Why are urban westerners never called pioneers? These questions beg answers.

The West's dominant myths continue to transmit a vague rural identity to the world, to the rest of Canada, and, oddly, to the people who live here. George Melnyk, an Alberta writer, explored the contradiction with the rigour it deserves. "All my childhood and youthful memories are urban, and all my adult experience is likewise urban," he writes in *New Moon At Batoche*. "I see the West through urban eyes: the eyes that see brick and concrete towers, imposing mansions and clapboard row housing, diesel buses and freeways, and ubiquitous suburban lawns."[3] Melnyk asks why we continue to search for the true meaning of the West's wide, open spaces as if they expressed everything about our daily lives: "We have been obsessed with the land and its meaning for us for over a century. Perhaps it is time to reflect on the cities we have built, and seek to understand how our identity is expressed through them."

How do we do that? We tell one city story after another.

❧

THIS BOOK IS NOT A CONVENTIONAL URBAN HISTORY. It does not offer one author's single narrative of Edmonton's unfolding story. It is not an anthology of oral history in the usual sense. Each section opens with a commentary on a time period. Here, interpreters guide us through

Edmonton's historical record: warning us of stumbling places, and reminding us of potential bias. Then the eyewitnesses and descendants begin to speak for themselves: explaining, arguing, crying, scolding, laughing and interrupting one another in a city's evolving conversation with itself.

Enjoy your walk along the river with all of Edmonton's storytellers. They never left us. They live in our midst.

Edmonton Through Time

A Bend in the River

to 1700

2,500 million years ago ⤳ A rugged mountain range covers the Edmonton area during the Precambrian era.

570 to 245 million years ago ⤳ A tropical sea covers Alberta in the Palaeozoic era.

245 to 67 million years ago ⤳ The sea retreats to the west. ⤳ Volcanic ash descends on the region and a cooler climate and abundant rainfall prevail. ⤳ Dinosaurs dominate the tropical jungle in the Mesozoic era.

67 million years ago ⤳ Dinosaurs disappear as the Cenozoic era begins. ⤳ The climate cools. The Edmonton area becomes dry grassland.

1.6 million years ago ⤳ The Arctic ice cap expands.

21,000 years ago ⤳ A 1.5 km layer of ice covers the Edmonton region. This ice carves hills above the valley, and deposits the Saskatchewan Sands and Gravels in the channel of an ancient river.

13,000 to 11,000 years ago ⤳ Aboriginal people leave evidence of their camps in the area we now know as Alberta. **Creation Stories** ⤳ They hunt for large game such as mammoths, bison, bears and moose. Mammoths become extinct over the next 1,000 years. **Exploring an Ancient Past**

12,000 years ago ⤳ Melt water from glacial ice creates a deep lake, covering much of what is now the Edmonton area.

8,000 years ago ↦ Aboriginal people leave lasting evidence of their camps, hunting practices and quarries in the Edmonton area. They may have been here earlier.

6,800 years ago ↦ Volcanic eruption of Mount Mazama in present-day Oregon leaves a layer of ash in Edmonton's river valley.

4,000 years ago ↦ Northern peoples leave evidence that they have had contact with southern civilizations in the Americas through the trade of corn and decorative objects.

2,800 years ago to 1640 AD ↦ Tribal groups move across the western plains in seasonal rounds for hunting, gathering, trading and war, and return to this territory regularly. ↦ Aboriginal peoples of the western plains camp in the Beaver Hills and pass through Edmonton's river valley.

1670 ↦ King Charles II of England grants to the newly-formed Hudson's Bay Company (HBC) a vast territory in North America, to be called Rupert's Land. The territory includes the North Saskatchewan river valley.

1690 ↦ Henry Kelsey of the HBC begins exploring of the West with Cree guides.

1700 to 1869 **The Meeting Place**

1700s ↦ The Cree, Blackfoot and Nakoda peoples form a trade and military alliance and push enemy tribes across the mountains. **Trails to a New Home** ↦ The Beaver Hills region becomes a trading centre.

1730s ↦ The Shoshoni people are the first aboriginal peoples of the north-western plains to acquire horses from the Comanches to the south.

1724 to 1753 ↦ Pierre Gaultier de Varennes, sieur de La Vérendrye, and his family explore the plains, and establish small trading posts to buy furs, and negotiate with aboriginal peoples in the West.

1740 to 1750 ↦ British entrepreneur Arthur Dobbs suggests that the western plains of North America have considerable agricultural and settlement potential.

1755 ↦ Anthony Henday and his guides, Attikosish and Connawapa, and their families arrive.

1770 to 1820 ↦ Rise of the Métis people, the descendants of indigenous women and European fur traders.

1776 ↦ The North West Company (NWC) is founded.

1778 ↦ Traveller Peter Pond finds evidence of oil sands at the confluence of the Athabasca and Clearwater Rivers; northern aboriginal peoples use the material to repair canoes.

1780 to 1782 ⤳ A smallpox epidemic claims thousands of lives on the western plains.

1795 ⤳ James Hughes of the NWC establishes Fort Augustus near present-day Fort Saskatchewan. A few months later, William Tomison of the HBC builds the first Edmonton House near the fort of his rivals. **Rivals on the River**

1800 ⤳ Louis Kwarakwante, Michel Callihoo's Iroquois father, signs on with the NWC in Montreal and arrives later at Fort Augustus.

1802 to 1806 ⤳ Fort Augustus and Edmonton House are moved upstream to the present-day Rossdale Flats.

1803 ⤳ John Rowand signs on as an apprentice clerk with the NWC, working out of Fort Augustus.

1808 to 1810 ⤳ David Thompson visits Fort Augustus on several occasions. **The Dance of Spikanoggan**

1808 ⤳ Marie-Anne Gaboury Lagimodière and her husband, Jean-Baptiste, arrive at Edmonton House. **Buffalo and Babies**

1810 ⤳ Warfare intensifies among Cree, Nakoda and Blackfoot tribes. ⤳ Fort Augustus and Edmonton House are relocated to the Smoky Lake area. **Battles on the Prairies**

1813 ⤳ Fort Augustus and Edmonton House are moved back to the present-day Rossdale Flats, near the 1802 site.

1816 ⤳ The Métis people win a victory in their fight against the colonization of Red River during the Battle of Seven Oaks.

1818 to 1820 ⤳ A measles epidemic strikes the Cree, killing thousands. ⤳ Half the Nakoda population dies in a whooping cough epidemic.

1821 ⤳ The NWC amalgamates with the HBC; two posts are combined to become Edmonton House.

1823 ⤳ John Rowand assumes charge of the Saskatchewan district in and becomes and becomes Chief Factor of Edmonton House in 1826. **Country Marriages**

1830 ⤳ The North Saskatchewan River floods for the second time in five years. ⤳ Edmonton House is moved up the riverbank to the location below the present-day Alberta Legislature. **Joys and Sorrows**

1831 ⤳ John Rowand sends Jimmy Jock Bird south to promote trade with the southern tribes. **Jimmy Jock**

1832 ⤳ John Rowand builds the Big House at Fort Edmonton. Nicknamed Rowand's Folly, it is the largest structure on the western plains. **Queen of the Plains**

1837 to 1838 ⟶ A smallpox epidemic strikes the people of the western plains. Two-thirds of the Nakoda people perish.

1838 ⟶ The Roman Catholic missionaries François-Norbert Blanchet and Modeste Demers stop briefly at the Fort, the first missionaries to do so. They erect a cross.

1840 ⟶ Traders using Red River carts begin to use the overland Carlton Trail between Winnipeg and Edmonton. ⟶ Methodist missionary Robert Rundle arrives, and opens a school for the fort's children. **Competing for Converts**

1841 ⟶ Local coal is used in a blacksmith's forge.

1842 ⟶ Missionary Jean-Baptiste Thibault arrives. He establishes the first Roman Catholic mission west of Winnipeg on the shores of Lac Ste. Anne in 1844.

1845 ⟶ A scarlet fever epidemic hits Edmonton.

1846 ⟶ The artist Paul Kane visits. He returns to Edmonton House the following year. ⟶ A new windmill begins grinding local flour.

1849 ⟶ Michel Callihoo and his wife Marie Savard arrive at the fort. **"It Was Slavish Work"**

1850s ⟶ The Papaschase band moves to the south side of the river, opposite Edmonton House, and makes a camp at the Two Hills. ⟶ Despite rivalry among the traders and the missionaries of different denominations, people of the region come together to celebrate. **"The Noise Was Terrific"** ⟶ **Mixed Messages**

1852 ⟶ Roman Catholic Oblate missionary Albert Lacombe arrives. **"I Felt Sorry for Them"**

1854 ⟶ John Rowand dies in a fistfight at Fort Pitt. **The Strange Journey of John Rowand's Bones**

1856 ⟶ Peter Erasmus, a young Métis guide, interprets for Rev. Thomas Woolsey at Edmonton House. **The Ceremony of the Trade** ⟶ Trade flourishes despite regional hardships. **Ripe for Business** ⟶ Lapotac assists the Fort community.

1857 to 1859 ⟶ John Palliser and a team of investigators explore the western plains with the assistance of Peter Erasmus. The Palliser Report changes outsiders' perception of the Prairies, and suggests the potential for settlement.

1859 ⟶ Sisters Emery, Adèle Lamy, and Alphonse establish a Grey Nuns mission at Lac Ste. Anne. **Les Soeurs Grises** ⟶ Visitors note the lively children of Fort Edmonton and their health, but the HBC shows a growing impatience with the financial burden of looking after the children of employees. **The Company's Children**

1861 ⇝ Lapotac is buried at Fort Edmonton. His descendants found the Enoch Cree band. **Lapotac, the Hunter** ⇝ Albert Lacombe establishes a mission at St. Albert. **The Founding of St. Albert**

1862 ⇝ The Overlanders—gold prospectors bound for British Columbia— pass through Edmonton. ⇝ Prospectors begin working the river valley near Edmonton. **Fortune Seekers** ⇝ Roman Catholic missionary Constantin Scollen starts a school. ⇝ Methodist missionaries George and Elizabeth McDougall establish a mission at Fort Victoria, now Pakan. They move to Edmonton in 1871.

1867 ⇝ The British North America Act creates the Dominion of Canada.

1869 ⇝ Canada purchases Rupert's Land from the HBC. The area, which includes much of what is now Alberta, is renamed the North-West Territories. ⇝ The Buffalo herds are disappearing. **"The Buffalo Entered the Earth"**

The Manitou Stone   1870 to 1891

1862 ⇝ Tribes negotiate a tentative peace treaty between The Plains Cree and the Blackfoot Confederacy and its Tsuu T'ina allies at Fort Edmonton. The peace holds until November 1863. **Peace Negotiations**

1866 ⇝ Thunderchild, a Cree youth, witnesses a battle on the Plains. Albert Lacombe, a Catholic missionary, visits the Blackfoot camp at the same time. **Battlegrounds**

1869 to 1870 ⇝ The peace negotiator Maskipiton, or Broken Arm, is killed in a Blackfoot ambush while on a peace mission. His death brings the final wave of warfare between the Cree and the Blackfoot to the gates of Fort Edmonton. **"Bullets Are Falling"** ⇝ A smallpox epidemic strikes the western plains and kills thousands of people, including hundreds in the Fort Edmonton region. **Omikiwin/Smallpox**

1870 ⇝ Elizabeth Chantler McDougall and her husband move from Victoria to open a new Methodist Church near Fort Edmonton. **"I Tried to Speak"** ⇝ The Métis in Red River resist the Canadian government's purchase and control of Rupert's Land. **Trading the Land** ⇝ On behalf of the Canadian government, Captain William Francis Butler visits Fort Edmonton to report on conditions. ⇝ The last tribal battle near Fort Edmonton occurs. ⇝ American whiskey traders arrive at the fort.

1871 ⤳ Sweetgrass leads a delegation of chiefs to Fort Edmonton to send a message to Canada. The chiefs object to the sale of their land without their consent, and request a treaty. **"Come and See Us"** ⤳ Edmonton is incorporated as a village. ⤳ George McDougall and his family run a day school for local children at their mission.

1872 ⤳ The Canadian government grants free homesteads to settlers under the Dominion Lands Act; provisions are made for railroads, schools, and HBC land.

1873 ⤳ The HBC surveys its Edmonton Reserve; land is set aside for the company. ⤳ The North-West Mounted Police (NWMP) is established. ⤳ Edmonton's first resident physician, Dr. Verey, arrives.

1874 to 1879 ⤳ With the disappearance of the buffalo, the First Nations and Métis of the plains begin to endure famine.

1874 ⤳ The NWMP arrive in Edmonton under Inspector William Jarvis. They run the first postal service and found Fort Saskatchewan. **Founding of Fort Saskatchewan**

1875 ⤳ The *Northcote* is the first steamboat to reach Edmonton. ⤳ The Anglican missionary, William Newton, arrives. Eliza Newton, his sister, joins him in 1886 to treat patients at their residence, the Hermitage.

1876 ⤳ The Plains Cree sign Treaty 6 at Fort Carlton and Fort Pitt. **Treaties and Talks** ⤳ Donald Ross builds the first hotel in Edmonton. ⤳ Sweetgrass, Little Hunter, Pakan; Kehewin and others negotiate for many of the western Cree. ⤳ The Dominion telegraph line reaches Hay Lakes, southeast of Edmonton. Canada introduces the Indian Act.

1877 ⤳ Cree and Nakoda chiefs in the Edmonton area sign an adhesion to Treaty 6 near Fort Edmonton, bringing their bands into treaty. **Treaty 6** ⤳ In the south, the Tsuu T'ina, Siksika, Blood, Nakoda and Piikani sign Treaty 7. ⤳ Widespread famine strikes the First Nations of Western Canada. **Festivities and Famine**

1878 ⤳ Edmonton's population is 148. Michel Callihoo signs an adhesion to Treaty 6 in Edmonton on behalf of 178 band members. ⤳ The first post office opens. ⤳ The Dominion telegraph line reaches Edmonton from Hay Lakes.

1879 ⤳ The Canadian government passes a new National Policy, promising protective economic tariffs, a transcontinental railway, and incentives for settlement in the West. ⤳ Edmonton holds its first Agricultural Fair.

1880s ⤳ The Humberstone Mine and Ross Mine begin operating. Edmonton area mines will eventually employ thousands of people and produce an estimated 13 million tons of coal between 1880 and 1970. ↝ The HBC starts selling off its land holdings in Edmonton. **"A Surging Mass of Humanity"** ↝ Judges and lawyers visit Edmonton intermittently for trials. **Called to the Bar**

1880 ↝ The Canadian government surveys a 104-square kilometre reserve for the Papaschase band under Treaty 6 in what is now south Edmonton. Frank Oliver leads an opposition to Cree settlement of this land. ↝ The *Edmonton Bulletin* begins publication, becoming the first newspaper in the area now known as Alberta.

1881 ↝ Edmonton's population is 263. ↝ Canadian Pacific Railway (CPR) is founded. The government decides to build the railway through Calgary, not Edmonton. ↝ William Humberstone opens first brickyard. ↝ The first public school opens and serves as an early courthouse and meeting hall.

1882 ↝ Old-timers evict newcomers in a struggle over land tenure. ↝ John Walter launches the first cable ferry. **Walter's Ferry** ↝ The Jasper House Hotel opens. ↝ The first public library opens. ↝ The Edmonton Cricket Club is formed.

1883 ↝ The CPR reaches Calgary. ↝ The McPherson and Coleman stagecoach makes the first stagecoach run from Edmonton to Calgary. ↝ In January, local chiefs meet to send a letter of protest to the Canadian government, claiming that treaty promises for emergency relief had been broken. **"If we must die by violence…"**

1884 ↝ Tricycles are the latest arrival to Edmonton. ↝ A local baseball game makes the news for the first time. ↝ Edmontonians play the first local ten-pin bowling game.

1885 ↝ A Métis and First Nations uprising begins and creates panic and confusion in the Edmonton district. **Edmonton and the North-West Rebellion** ↝ Major-General Strange commands the Alberta Field Force. ↝ Canada imprisons Big Bear and Poundmaker and executes Louis Riel. ↝ Ottawa sends a scrip commission to Edmonton in an attempt to resolve outstanding land issues with local Métis. **Scrip and Speculators** ↝ The CPR drives in the last spike of the transcontinental railroad. ↝ Alex Taylor makes Alberta's first telephone call between Fort Edmonton and St. Albert. The cost for a local business call is 15 cents; telegrams are free.

1886 ↝ January 19 is the coldest day ever recorded in Edmonton. The thermometer reads -49.4° C.

1887 ↜ Edmonton's population is 350. Canada's first long distance telephone call is placed between Edmonton and Battleford, Saskatchewan.

1888 ↜ The Papaschase band in Edmonton is the first in Canada to lose its full reserve after signing a treaty. Many families take Métis scrip and disperse to the Enoch reserve and beyond. **The Papaschase Story** ↜ Local chiefs Alexis, Alexander and Michel return to Edmonton to demand treaty rations because of hunger on their reserves. **War of Words** ↜ Heavy pressure begins on Cree bands around Edmonton to surrender more land. ↜ The first Roman Catholic school opens.

1889 ↜ The Edmonton Board of Trade is established. ↜ The HBC imports the first bicycle to Edmonton.

1891 ↜ Establishment of South Edmonton. ↜ The Calgary and Edmonton Railway opens, allowing the CPR to bring the first train into the settlement. ↜ The first local electric light is switched on. ↜ An early theatre group, the Edmonton Amateur Society, is formed.

1892 to 1913 Newcomers

1890 ↜ Large-scale immigration to the Canadian West begins. **This New Land of Ours**

1891 ↜ Sixty-five French-speaking immigrants in 12 wagons arrive in Abbé Jean-Baptiste Morin's colony. They homestead north of St. Albert in a district they call Morinville. ↜ The first German Settlers arrive by ox-wagon to homestead around Stony Plain, at Breuderfeld on the old Papaschase reserve, as well as at Rivière Qui Barre and Josephsburg.

1892 ↜ Edmonton's population is 700. ↜ Edmonton is incorporated as a town with Matthew McCauley as the first mayor. ↜ In an unruly clash, Edmonton residents prevent the removal of the Land Titles building to the south side of the river. **Rival Cities: Edmonton vs. South Edmonton** ↜ The Board of Health is established. ↜ The first Immigration Hall welcomes newcomers.

1893 ↜ Ukrainian immigrants began to arrive on the encouragement Ivan Pylypiw. ↜ Abraham and Rebecca Cristall are the first Jewish immigrants to settle permanently in Edmonton.

1894 ↜ The Edmonton Thistles play the first recorded hockey game in Edmonton. ↜ The local curling club competes in the first covered rink in the province.

1896 ↝ Edmonton Golf and Country Club is established. ↝ Wilfrid Laurier is elected prime minister.

1897 ↝ Edmonton's population is 1,638. ↝ The Klondike gold rush begins. **Klondike Days** ↝ John A. McDougall is elected mayor.

1897 to 1913 ↝ New immigrants arrive in great numbers to claim homesteads, buy farms or settle in Edmonton. **More Arrivals**

1899 ↝ North Saskatchewan River floods. **The Flood of 1899** ↝ South Edmonton is incorporated as a town and renamed Strathcona. ↝ Bob Edwards, the hard-drinking satirist, lampoons Edmonton's gentry in *The Alberta Sun*, which he had wanted to call *The Strathcolic*. He departs for Wetaskiwin within a few months before going to Calgary, where he starts the *Eye-opener*. **Community News** ↝ Fort Saskatchewan, St. Albert and Leduc become villages. ↝ Local soldiers leave for the Boer War in South Africa.

1900 ↝ The Low Level Bridge opens as the town's first bridge.

1901 ↝ The Cameron Mine collapses triggering a massive landslide on Grierson Hill.

1902 ↝ Carpenters organize Edmonton's first union local; they are followed by bricklayers, plumbers and typesetters. ↝ The Enoch band loses 37 square kilometres of its reserve. ↝ John A. McDougall and Richard Secord buy 70 per cent of the land parcel from Ottawa below market price. ↝ The Edmonton, Yukon, and Pacific Railway train crosses to the north side of the river. **"Muchias"**

1903 ↝ The Michel band loses the first portion of its reserve west of Edmonton. ↝ The first edition of the *Edmonton Journal* rolls off the press. ↝ The Thistle Rink opens. ↝ Photographer Ernest Brown arrives. He employs a young assistant, Gladys Reeves, who later catalogued his collection. **Pioneer Photographers**

1904 ↝ Edmonton's population is 8,350. ↝ Edmonton is incorporated as a city. ↝ Five bands in the Edmonton area petition Ottawa to remove the Indian agent for letting land go on sale well below market value. ↝ The city purchases Edmonton and District Telephone Company. ↝ John Morris brings the first car to town. ↝ The Edmonton Operatic Society stages *Les Cloches de Corneville*, its first performance. ↝ Students begin to attend Alberta College. ↝ Fort Saskatchewan and St. Albert become towns.

1905 ↝ Alberta and Saskatchewan become provinces. ↝ Wilfrid Laurier visits Edmonton and addresses a crowd on the Rossdale Flats. **A New City, a New Province** ↝ Alexander Rutherford becomes the first Premier of Alberta. Edmonton is named the temporary capital. ↝ The Alexander band loses 39 square kilometres of land without seeing the proceeds. ↝ The Canadian Northern Railway reaches Edmonton; it consolidates with others to form the Canadian National Railway (CNR). ↝ One-fifth of Edmonton residents have running water. ↝ Gertrude Balmer Watt arrives to edit the *Saturday News*, and becomes a founder of the Canadian Women's Press Club. Her husband, A.B. Watt, later becomes the editor of the *Edmonton Journal*. **"The Dearest Place in All the World"**

1906 ↝ The first sitting of the Alberta Legislative Assembly opens at the Thistle Rink. ↝ Thousands of acres of Michel land are sold in a four-hour sale at the Empire Theatre; the band does not receive the proceeds. ↝ The University of Alberta is founded, but classes only begin in 1908. ↝ Hyman Goldstick, Edmonton's first rabbi, arrives. ↝ Leduc becomes a town. ↝ The Edmonton Trades and Labour Council is founded.

1907 ↝ Six miners die in a fire at the Strathcona Coal Company. ↝ William Griesbach is elected mayor. ↝ Strathcona is incorporated as a city. ↝ Spruce Grove and Stony Plain become villages. ↝ Construction begins on the Alberta Legislature building. ↝ The Penn mine opens on Grierson Hill. ↝ Mail carriers make their first deliveries.

1908 ↝ Edmonton's population is 18,500. ↝ Henry Marshall Tory tells the university's first convocation: "The people demand that knowledge shall not be the concern of scholars alone. The uplifting of the whole people shall be its final goal." **A Pioneering University** ↝ Edmonton installs the first automatic dial telephones in North America. ↝ The first music festival in Canada is held in Edmonton. ↝ The city's first motion picture theatre, the Bijou, opens. Diamond Park opens as the city's first permanent baseball field. ↝ Riders pay five cents to ride on the city's first streetcar. ↝ The Edmonton Eskimos hockey team makes the city's first appearance at the Stanley Cup finals. ↝ Impatient hockey fans wait at the CNR station for the telegraph operator to decipher the play-by-play. **The Telegraph Playoffs** ↝ Stony Plain becomes a town.

1909 ↝ The Grand Trunk Pacific railroad reaches Edmonton. ↝ John Walter launches the *City of Edmonton* steamer. ↝ Sun Yat-sen, the revolutionary Chinese leader, visits Alberta. Morris Cohen, a gun-toting gambler from Edmonton, is later hired to be his bodyguard. **A Friendship in Chinatown**

1910 ⌁ The Villages of North Edmonton and West Edmonton are incorporated. **"All five of us slept in a double bed"** ⌁ The Young Men's Christian Association (YMCA) opens. ⌁ New exhibition grounds open at the current Northlands Park site. ⌁ Edmonton's football team is officially named the Eskimos.

1911 ⌁ Edmonton's population is 24,900. **The African-Americans from Oklahoma** ⌁ Real estate boom begins. By 1914 new structures in Edmonton include the Civic Block, Court House, Tegler and McLeod buildings; the University of Alberta; the Royal Alexandra Hospital and numerous schools and bridges.

1912 ⌁ Edmonton's population is said to be 53,611. ⌁ Strathcona and Edmonton amalgamate. **Gunfire at the Commercial** ⌁ North Edmonton is annexed. ⌁ The HBC sells its local land holdings. ⌁ The local branch of the Women's Canadian Club is organized. ⌁ The first ski tournament is held on Connor's Hill. ⌁ Annie Jackson becomes the first female police officer in Canada. ⌁ Cree athlete Alex Decoteau competes at the Stockholm Olympics, the only Albertan at the Games.

1913 ⌁ The Edmonton Arena, later named the Edmonton Gardens, opens to replace the Thistle Rink, which was destroyed by fire. ⌁ Beverly is incorporated as a village. ⌁ The first train crosses the newly completed High Level Bridge. **The High Level Bridge** ⌁ The Pantages Theatre opens with live theatrical performances. ⌁ The Strathcona Library welcomes its first visitors. ⌁ John Hougan sets a new Canadian ski-jumping record of 33 meters at Connor's Hill.

1913 to 1915 ⌁ Recession strikes, leaving 4,000 Edmontonians unemployed. **The Boom Goes Bust**

The Emerging City   1914 to 1946

1914 ⌁ Edmonton's population is 72,516. ⌁ The First World War begins, and Edmonton's first soldiers leave for the front. **"This Inferno of War"** ⌁ **"Noi siamo qui"** ⌁ Canada passes the War Measures Act and imprisons 8,000 "enemy aliens." ⌁ The Turner Valley Gas Field is discovered. ⌁ Golfers tee off at the Victoria Golf Course, the first municipal course. ⌁ The Edmonton Newsboys Band is organized. **Mike's News** ⌁ The new Edmonton Arena opens.

1915 ⌁ The North Saskatchewan River floods. **The Great Flood of 1915** ⌁ Enlistment begins in the 49th Battalion. ⌁ The Edmonton Commercial Graduates Basketball Club plays its first game. Over its 25-year history the Grads record 502 wins—including all 27 Olympic matches—and only 20 losses. ⤳ The city dismantles Fort Edmonton. ⤳ The Hotel Macdonald opens. ⤳ The Princess Theatre opens.

1916 ⤳ Prohibition begins. ⤳ Emily Murphy and Alice Jamieson become the first female magistrates in the British Empire. ⤳ Alberta women win the right to vote in provincial elections. **Votes for Women**

1917 ⤳ Edmonton's population is 56,000. ⤳ Edmonton annexes Calder. ⤳ Edmonton's first Community League is organized in Crestwood. ⤳ Printer Elmer Roper arrives and organizes labour slates for city council.

1918 ⤳ The First World War ends. **The Miseries of War** ⤳ The Spanish Flu epidemic kills 614 Edmontonians. **The Spanish Influenza** ⤳ Katherine Stinson makes Canada's first airmail delivery to Edmonton.

1919 ⤳ Dissatisfied citizens in Winnipeg begin a general strike on May 15. ⤳ One week later a sympathy strike begins in Edmonton. **The 1919 Strike** ⤳ The 49th Battalion returns. ⤳ Edward, Prince of Wales visits. ⤳ "Fightin'" Joe Clarke elected mayor. ⤳ Edmonton teachers walk off the job for six days in Alberta's first teachers' strike. ⤳ Provincial civil servants organize a staff association, which evolves into a union.

1919 to 1924 ⤳ Near drought conditions on the prairies.

1920 ⤳ The Edmonton Symphony holds its first performance.

1921 ⤳ Edmonton's population is 58,821. ⤳ The Edmonton Federation of Community Leagues organizes. ⤳ David Duggan is elected mayor. ⤳ The United Farmers of Alberta win the provincial election and remain in power until 1935. **Rebuilding the Community**

1922 ⤳ CJCA begins broadcasting as Edmonton's first radio station. ⤳ The Grads win the Canadian Basketball Championship.

1923 ⤳ A natural gas pipeline reaches Edmonton from Viking. ⤳ Coal industry begins its decline. ⤳ Prohibition is repealed. ⤳ The Grads win the World Basketball Championships. ⤳ Waitresses strike to stop deep wage cuts.

1924 ⤳ Kenneth (Kenny) Blatchford is elected mayor.

1925 ⤳ Leona McGregor graduates with the first medical degree granted at the University of Alberta. ⤳ John Brownlee becomes premier of Alberta.

1926 ⤳ Edmonton's population is 65,163. ⤳ Elephants escape from a visiting circus.

1927 ⤳ Blatchford Field becomes the first licensed municipal airport in Canada. ⤳ CKUA begins broadcasting. ⤳ Canada amends the Indian Act to make it illegal for First Nations to hire lawyers to pursue land claims.

1928 ◦ Edmonton's first neon sign shines above Darlings Drug Store.

1929 ◦ Stock market collapses. ◦ Wop May and Vic Horner fly on a mercy mission to deliver vaccine to the remote northern community of Little Red River. **Mercy Mission** ◦ Due to the efforts of Alberta's Famous Five, women are declared "persons" and become eligible for membership in the Senate. ◦ John J. Maloney organizes a local branch of the Ku Klux Klan. In the early 1930s, the Klan had between 5,000 and 7,000 members in Alberta.

1930 ◦ Alberta wins control of its oil and gas reserves when Canada passes the Natural Resources Transfer Act. ◦ The Conservatives win the federal election under Calgarian R.B. Bennett. "Bennett Buggies"—cars pulled by horses because gas was unaffordable—are soon seen in Edmonton.

1931 ◦ Edmonton's population is 79,059. ◦ Local economy collapses in a decade of depression, drought and severe unemployment.

1932 ◦ About 10,000 unemployed Albertans and labour activists begin a Hunger March to the Alberta legislature that ends violently in Market Square. **The Great Depression: The Hunger March** ◦ Alberta's first province-wide aboriginal rights organization, L'Association des Métis des Alberta et des Territoires de Nord Ouest is established; Malcolm Norris of Edmonton is one of its early leaders. ◦ Daniel Knott elected mayor, leading one of the first labour-socialist urban governments in North America. ◦ The first traffic light is installed on Jasper Ave. and 101st Street.

1933 ◦ The first baseball game is held in Renfrew Park. ◦ Margaret Crang, at age 23, becomes the youngest member ever to be elected to City Council. **Pulling Through the Thirties** ◦ **The Dreamland and Other Diversions**

1934 ◦ Premier Brownlee goes on trial in a civil lawsuit, accused of seducing his assistant Vivian McMillan. ◦ Local Métis leaders call for a secure land base for Alberta's Métis at the Ewing Commission hearings.

1935 ◦ Offering hope to Depression-weary voters, William Aberhart and the Social Credit Party sweep Alberta. The Socreds win 56 of 63 seats in the election, but Edmonton elects four Opposition MLAs. Social Credit remain in power in Alberta for 36 years. ◦ Mackenzie King becomes prime minister of Canada.

1936 ◦ Edmonton's population is 85,470. ◦ The Canada Packers plant is built.

1937 ⌁ Edmonton's hottest temperature is recorded as 37.2°C on June 29. ⌁ Men's bathing trunks are approved as suitable for public pools. **Two Lonely Children**

1938 ⌁ *The Edmonton Journal* and other Alberta newspapers receive a special Pulitzer prize for opposing the Social Credit *Accurate News and Information Act* of 1937, a law designed to gag the press. ⌁ Clarke Stadium opens. ⌁ The Al-Rashid mosque, the first mosque in Canada, opens on 101st St. and 108th Ave.

1939 ⌁ King George VI and Queen Elizabeth visit Edmonton. ⌁ The Second World War begins. **World War II** ⌁ Some German and Italian immigrants are interned, or are ordered to report regularly to the Royal Canadian Mounted Police. ⌁ Alberta's First Nations bands with treaty status organize the Indian Association of Alberta, under the leadership of Johnny Callihoo.

1941 ⌁ Edmonton's population is 93,924. ⌁ The Edmonton Public Library establishes the first travelling library in North America; the book-filled streetcar serves the Calder area.

1942 ⌁ A record-breaking snowfall of 39.9 centimetres hits Edmonton on November 15, bringing the city to a halt. ⌁ US soldiers pour into the city to begin construction of the Alaska Highway and CANOL pipeline.

1943 ⌁ Ernest Manning becomes the premier of Alberta after the death of William Aberhart.

1945 ⌁ The Second World War ends; Edmonton records the death of 666 soldiers. **The Loyal Eddies**

1946 ⌁ Edmonton's population is 114,976. ⌁ The Trocadero Ballroom opens in the renovated Empire Theatre. ⌁ Harry Ainlay is elected mayor.

1947 to 2004   **The New City**

1947 ⌁ Edmonton's population is 118,541. ⌁ Oil is discovered at Leduc. **Leduc No. 1** ⌁ Alberta's first popcorn machine appears at the Empress theatre. **Edmonton's Oilpatch Kids**

1948 ⌁ Atlantic No. 3 well blows out near Leduc. **Atlantic No. 3** ⌁ The first oil refinery opens in Clover Bar. ⌁ CBC radio begins to broadcast from the Hotel Macdonald. ⌁ The Edmonton Flyers hockey team wins the Allan Cup. ⌁ Parking meters appear on city streets. **City Snapshots**

1949 ⌁ Edmonton's first drive-in theatre, The Starlite, opens.

1950 ⌁ Jasper Place is incorporated as a village. ⌁ The town of Devon is established. ⌁ The first inter-provincial pipeline from Edmonton to

Ontario is completed. ⌁ Edmonton's Waterloo Mercurys win the hockey World Championships; they go on to win the Olympic gold medal in 1952. **Sporting City** ⌁ Walter Kaasa performs in *Anna Christie*, his first lead role at Studio Theatre.

1951 ⌁ *The Edmonton Bulletin* closes after 71 years.

1952 ⌁ Edmonton's population is 169,196. ⌁ The Paramount Theatre opens. ⌁ William Hawrelak becomes mayor.

1953 ⌁ In a nationwide epidemic, 319 Edmontonians contract polio; 16 people die. ⌁ Canada's largest oilfield, the Pembina field, is discovered west of Edmonton. ⌁ The Clover Bar bridge opens.

1954 ⌁ CFRN television is launched. ⌁ The Edmonton Eskimos win the first of three straight Grey Cups. The team wins twelve championships in total, including five straight titles in the late 1970s. **Praying for Touchdowns**

1955 ⌁ The first resident moves into the community now known as Sherwood Park. ⌁ Edmontonians park underground for the first time. ⌁ Groat Bridge opens. ⌁ Westmount Centre opens as the city's first shopping mall.

1957 ⌁ Edmonton's population is 238,353. **New Voices** ⌁ The city welcomes visitors to a new City Hall. ⌁ The Jubilee Auditorium opens. ⌁ John Diefenbaker becomes prime minister of Canada.

1959 ⌁ Mayor Hawrelak resigns. ⌁ Chester Kuc founds the Ukrainian Shumka Dancers. He establishes the Cheremosh Dance Ensemble a decade later. ⌁ The city zoo, eventually named the Valley Zoo, opens.

1960 ⌁ The first planes take off from the Edmonton International Airport. ⌁ Queen Elizabeth Planetarium opens. ⌁ Elmer Roper becomes mayor. ⌁ Ottawa gives aboriginal people with treaty status the right to vote in federal elections.

1961 ⌁ Edmonton annexes Beverly. ⌁ The last horse-drawn milk wagon goes out of service.

1962 ⌁ Edmonton's population is 294,967. ⌁ The city launches the Klondike Days exhibition. ⌁ The first students enrol at the Northern Alberta Institute of Technology (NAIT). ⌁ Strathcona County is established.

1963 ⌁ The Edmonton Oil Kings win the first Western Hockey League Memorial Cup. **City of Champions** ⌁ The Edmonton Professional Opera Company stages *Madame Butterfly* as its first performance.

1964 ⌁ Edmonton annexes Jasper Place.

1965 ⤳ The re-elected Mayor Hawrelak is ousted from office. ⤳ The Citadel Theatre, the city's first professional stage, opens with *Who's Afraid of Virginia Woolf?*

1966 ⤳ The Edmonton Indian Residential School closes in St. Albert after 43 years. ⤳ The CN Tower, with 26 storeys, is the city's highest skyscraper.

1967 ⤳ Edmonton's population is 393,593. ⤳ The Centennial Library welcomes its first visitors. ⤳ The Provincial Museum of Alberta opens. ⤳ Albertans with treaty status vote for the first time in a provincial election.

1968 ⤳ Ivor Dent becomes mayor. ⤳ Pierre Trudeau becomes prime minister of Canada.

1969 ⤳ Edmontonians become the first Canadians to dial 911 in emergencies. ⤳ Canada introduces the White Paper on Indian Affairs, hoping to end the collective rights and special status of aboriginal people. Harold Cardinal and Alberta chiefs lead national opposition; the plan is withdrawn in 1971.

1970 ⤳ Fort Edmonton Park opens. ⤳ The town of Spruce Grove is established.

1971 ⤳ The city begins to develop Mill Woods. ⤳ The first students enter Grant MacEwan Community College. ⤳ The James MacDonald Bridge opens. ⤳ Peter Lougheed leads the Progressive Conservatives to an election victory, and the Social Credit era ends in Alberta.

1972 ⤳ Edmonton's population is 441,530. ⤳ The Alberta Oilers join the Western Hockey Association. They are renamed the Edmonton Oilers in 1973. ⤳ The new Law Courts building opens. ⤳ Cec Purves becomes mayor.

1973 to 1974 ⤳ International energy crisis begins. ⤳ Rapid price increase creates another economic boom in Edmonton.

1974 ⤳ William Hawrelak is re-elected as mayor. ⤳ The Edmonton Coliseum opens. It is renamed Northlands Coliseum in 1978.

1976 ⤳ The Heritage Days Festival begins at Mayfair Park. ⤳ Muttart Conservatory opens.

1977 ⤳ Edmonton's population is 471,474. ⤳ St. Albert becomes a city.

1978 ⤳ Edmonton's Light Rail Transit (LRT) carries its first passengers. ⤳ Edmonton hosts the Commonwealth Games at the newly constructed Commonwealth Stadium. **How We Won the Commonwealth Games** ⤳ Kinsmen Centre opens. ⤳ The *Edmonton Sun* begins publication.

1979 ↝ The Edmonton Oilers join the National Hockey League.

1980 ↝ The Great Divide waterfall flows from the High Level Bridge for the first time. ↝ Ottawa introduces the National Energy Program, with severe economic consequences for Edmonton. ↝ The Edmonton Folk Music Festival and the Jazz City International Music Festival are launched.

1981 ↝ The Edmonton Food Bank begins operation. ↝ West Edmonton Mall opens as the largest shopping centre in the world.

1982 ↝ Edmonton's population is 551,314. ↝ After a general annexation, Edmonton nearly doubles in land area. ↝ Voters defeat bid to annex Sherwood Park and St. Albert. ↝ The first Edmonton Fringe Theatre Festival attracts 7,500 visitors to Old Strathcona. **Edmonton on the Fringe**

1983 ↝ Edmonton hosts the World Universiade Games. ↝ The Edmonton Convention Centre opens. ↝ Laurence Decore becomes mayor. ↝ Leduc becomes a city. ↝ The Hotel Macdonald closes after falling into disrepair; the Mac reopens in 1991 after significant restorations.

1984 ↝ The Edmonton Oilers win its first Stanley Cup; the team goes on to win the trophy five times in the next seven years. **"Welcome to the Big Time" "For the Fans, It Was Paradise"** ↝ The Edmonton Trappers win the first of four Pacific Coast League championships. ↝ Edmonton hosts the Canadian Football League Grey Cup game for the first time. ↝ The Space Sciences Centre opens; it is later renamed Odyssium. ↝ Brian Mulroney becomes prime minister of Canada.

1985 ↝ Fort Saskatchewan becomes a city. ↝ Don Getty becomes Alberta's premier.

1986 ↝ Three people die when the Mindbender roller coaster at West Edmonton Mall derails. ↝ The North Saskatchewan River rises to 11.5 metres, the worst flood since 1915. ↝ A strike at the Gainers meatpacking plant becomes the most divisive labour dispute in Edmonton's history. **The War on 66th Street** ↝ Oil prices plummet, and over 50,000 Albertans lose their jobs. ↝ The Works Art and Design Festival is launched. ↝ Spruce Grove becomes a city.

1987 ↝ Edmonton's population is 576,249. ↝ A tornado strikes Edmonton. Twenty-seven people die in Edmonton's deadliest natural disaster. **Black Friday**

1988 ↝ Edmonton Oiler's owner Peter Pocklington trades Wayne Gretzky to the Los Angeles Kings.

1989 ↝ Jan Reimer becomes Edmonton's first female mayor. ↝ Kurt Browning wins his first men's world figure skating championship; he wins four titles in five years. ↝ Randy Ferbey leads the Edmonton rink to win the Men's World Curling Championships; and wins again in 2002 and 2003.

1992 ↝ Edmonton's population is 618,195. **Where Are You From?** ↝ A new City Hall opens. ↝ Ralph Klein becomes Alberta's premier.

1994 ↝ EdTel, the city's publicly owned telephone company is privatized after 91 years of service. ↝ Edmontonian Scotty "Bulldog" Olson wins the International Boxing Organization world championship.

1995 ↝ The Municipal Airport closes to scheduled air service after a city-wide plebiscite. ↝ CFB Edmonton, the army base at Namao, becomes the Edmonton Garrison. ↝ Bill Smith becomes mayor.

1997 ↝ Edmonton's population is 626,500. ↝ The Winspear Centre holds its first performance.

2001 ↝ Descendants of the Papaschase band and the Michel band sue the federal government, alleging illegalities in the loss of their reserves. ↝ Edmonton hosts the IAAF World Championships in Athletics. ↝ Jamie Salé and David Pelletier win the World Pairs Figure Skating Championship.

2002 ↝ Edmonton's population is 676,293. ↝ Four soldiers from the Edmonton base are killed on duty in Afghanistan.

2003 ↝ Commonwealth Stadium is transformed into an ice arena for the first outdoor NHL game.

2004 ↝ Edmonton celebrates its 100th year as a city.

Note: Sources for information noted in the timeline appear in the main text where relevant and in the bibliography.

Edmonton In Our Own Words

A Bend in the River

to 1700

A BOY ON A SNOWBOARD leans into the arc of a fresh snowdrift and begins his descent.

He is a trespasser here, but not the first. After school he hitched a ride toward the oil refineries on the eastern edge of his city, then turned up 17th Street toward a crowded ski hill. Looking for a steep slope of his own, he hiked past the *No Tobogganing* sign, dragging his snowboard behind him, sinking to his knees with every step. Nobody stopped him.

Now he carves a semi-circle on the hillside, down and down and down. Below him the North Saskatchewan River pushes ice chunks between overhanging cliffs and under city bridges. He can hear the sounds of commuters on the nearby freeway. It is dusk and very cold. The refineries breathe cloud-shapes into the winter sky. The boy keeps his eyes on his feet. Beneath his heavy boots, beneath his snowboard and the squeaking crust of snow, a secret is buried.

He glides over ancient fire pits, skilfully chipped stone tools and weapons, fragments of ancient pottery and the leftovers of thousands of fossilized dinners. This is Edmonton's richest archaeological find, the Strathcona site—known to the experts as FjPi-29. Human beings have camped on this hill, at intervals, in every season, for at least 4,000 years.[1] The boy finds no signpost, no plaque, to describe the significance of the buried treasure beneath his feet.

A Bend in the River

Ancient peoples are known to have arrived in what is now Alberta at least 11,000 years ago, perhaps earlier. Archaeologists have identified 780 occupation or quarry sites through the Edmonton region and another 225 in Elk Island Park, but they caution that they have explored only a small fraction of the possible locations. Campfires on this map mark the largest and best-known sites of the earliest visitors.

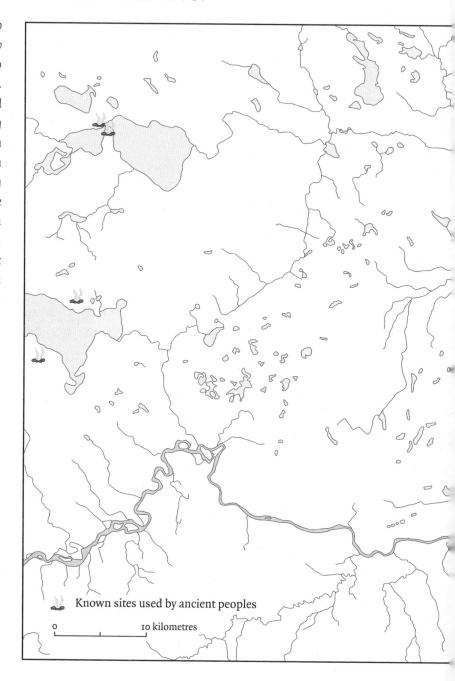

Known sites used by ancient peoples

0   10 kilometres

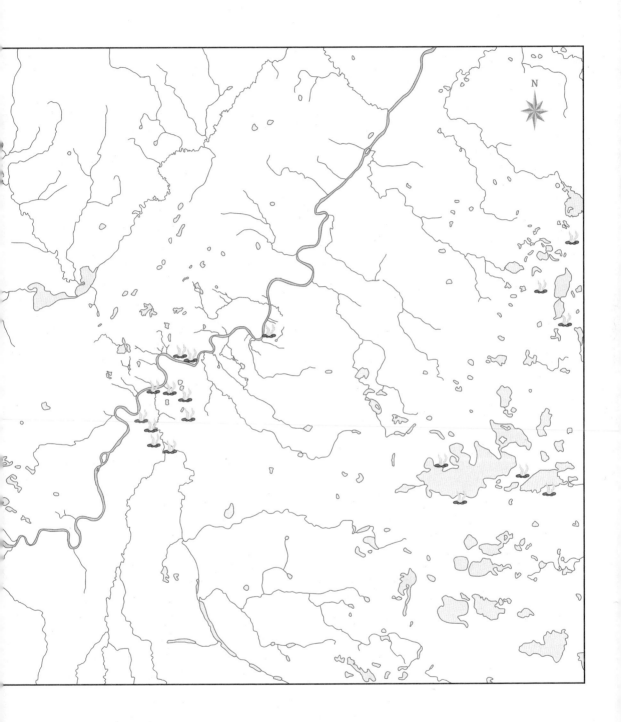

People in Edmonton assume, incorrectly, that their city is young. If they think about the origins of the community, they talk about a fur-trading fort on a riverbank, recreated at Fort Edmonton Park; or a rugged frontier town in the old Northwest, celebrated during Klondike Days. They might suggest that travelling aboriginal families camped occasionally at this bend in the North Saskatchewan River before the first fur-trading post was established in 1795. They imagine these migrating families packed up after a brief stay and moved on to the southern plains or the northern forest, with no thought of return. It is easier to think of this particular place on the map—near the 53rd parallel, the 113th meridian—as empty for an eternity. It is simpler to mark Edmonton's lifespan from known days in the recent past—200 years from the founding of a fur-trading fort or 100 years from the first city proclamation—and ignore more complex questions about the city's origins.

A snowboarder slides down an ancient hill with the wind in his face. The challenge is to think about the city's past with imagination.

Edmonton is as old as Jerusalem at the time of Christ; Mecca at the time of Mohammed; northern India at the time of the Buddha; Beijing at the time of Lao Tzu; Rome at the time of Julius Caesar; or Cairo at the time of Cleopatra. Warehouses around the city contain hard stone evidence of early human occupation.

Archaeologists know the limits of the proven record in Edmonton. They have never unearthed the ancient rock paintings, medicine wheels, buffalo jumps or fortified earth lodge villages discovered elsewhere in Alberta. There are no local remnants of an early Plains city to compare with Cahokia, east of present-day St. Louis, Missouri, which had 30,000 citizens in 1000 AD—more inhabitants than London, England had at the time. Not one microscopic flake of evidence suggests continuous human settlement in Edmonton's river valley since the end of the Ice Age, but archaeologists do know that this bend in the river has been a camping place, a favoured place, for 500 generations of human beings.

The snowboarder's hill hides a buried story. In *Edmonton: Beneath Our Feet*, Alberta's geologists have carefully traced the chronology of events before the arrival of human beings. Far below this surface of snow and ice, beneath four kilometres of rock, lies Edmonton's Precambrian cellar. Nature created the city's rock foundation 2,500 to 3,500 million years ago.[2] Geologists deduced from nature's layering that a tropical sea covered

Alberta between 350 and 245 million years ago.[3] Closer to the surface is the lingering evidence of a dense rainforest where dinosaurs roamed.[4] After the dinosaurs became extinct, roughly 67 million years ago, the Edmonton region cooled and became a grassland savannah for the ancestors of camels and hyenas.[5] Alberta's ice age began about 21,000 years ago, burying the Edmonton area under an ice sheet more than a kilometre deep.

The most dramatic event in Edmonton's history happened toward the end of the Ice Age. Around 12,000 years ago a gigantic ice dam created Glacial Lake Edmonton.[6] Geologists believe that for about a century the melt water covered the area from present-day Morinville to Leduc and Stony Plain to Fort Saskatchewan. This huge lake emptied in a sudden, crashing torrent through the Gwynne Outlet, a narrow valley that can still be seen southeast of the Edmonton International Airport.[7]

Did a human family witness this terrifying event? Possibly. No one knows for certain.

Glacial ice carved four terraces into the North Saskatchewan riverbank.[8] About 6,800 years ago Mount Mazama in Oregon exploded, sending volcanic ash to blanket Edmonton's river valley. A white band of this ash is exposed on the south bank of the North Saskatchewan, just upstream from the LRT Bridge.[9]

Slowly, animals returned to the valley as the climate warmed again. Woolly mammoths, mastodons, lions, sabre-toothed cats, musk ox, camels, bison, ground sloths and wolves wandered through the new river valley and its ravines. Catherine Reininger and her sons found the evidence, a mastodon tooth, one day in 1984 when they were walking along Whitemud Creek. On a similar ramble, Gene Seal was exploring a gravel pit in Clover Bar in 1989 when he found another rare specimen, the fossilized leg of a giant bear.[10] Excavation workers in Fort Saskatchewan discovered most of the skeleton of a woolly mammoth all in a day's work.[11]

So much for ancient animals. Who were the first human visitors? When and why did they stop here? The answer lies buried under the ground.

"Reconstructing the early history of the people of the northwestern plains of North America has been so difficult for the historian that the task is still far from completed," acknowledges Olive Dickason. With no written record of the arrival story, Dickason says, Canadian historians have relied mainly on unwritten archaeological evidence, "but the plains have not been kind to archaeologists either, especially in Alberta and south-western Saskatchewan where the record has been particularly difficult to decipher."[12]

The aboriginal oral tradition suggests that human beings have lived in the Americas since the world began. "When we were placed on earth, there was plenty of food and resources for our livelihood," Plains Cree elder Lazarus Roan told an elders' gathering in 1977: "Animals were abundant in the mountains and also on the plains. They were placed on the earth by the Great Spirit, our Father. They were even placed underwater for our sustenance, and our children's sustenance."[13]

Traditionally, archaeologists have argued that the first North Americans migrated here from the north, the descendants of Asians who crossed the Bering Land Bridge. Archaeologists and anthropologists continue to investigate the estimated arrival dates; the travel routes; and the ancestral links between the ancient newcomers and aboriginal peoples who live on the continent today. They offer fewer certainties about the arrival story and far more strenuous debate than they did even a decade ago.

It was once widely accepted that the first North Americans travelled south through an ice-free corridor near the eastern slopes of the Rockies sometime between 12,000 and 11,200 years ago. Now some researchers suggest it is more likely the first newcomers travelled south along the Pacific coast, then moved inland.[14] Some doubt an ice-free corridor ever existed. Intriguing evidence unearthed near the Athabasca tar sands outside Fort McMurray suggests that early people used boats on vast inland lakes there about 13,000 years ago, perhaps earlier. Radiocarbon-dated evidence confirms that people have lived in Alberta, from the Peace River district to the Bow River, for at least 11,000 years. It has been more difficult to put precise dates on the origins of human habitation in the Edmonton region. Much of the evidence has been destroyed or mixed up in a jumble of sedimentary layers—not just by busybody humans when they were building a prairie city, but also by nature itself.[15]

That does not mean the secret will be buried forever. For more than a decade, Edmonton archaeologist Heinz Pyszczyk has searched for the clearly stratified layers that could put an accurate date on the first arrival of human beings here. Pyszczyk and his colleagues have identified 780 archaeological sites spread evenly throughout the Edmonton region: from the Rossdale Flats in the heart of the city, north to Redwater, west to Morinville, south to Calmar and east to New Sarepta. Another 225 sites have been recorded just east of the city within Elk Island National Park, part of the traditional Beaver Hills territory of aboriginal peoples. Pyszczyk suggests that Europeans built fur-trading posts near here because hunters and trappers gathered at the Beaver Hills and had done so for many thousands of years.[16]

Archaeologists cannot be certain how many important sites they have missed inside Edmonton's present city limits because they have not explored every centimetre of ground, but they have gleaned some information about ancient preferences. Edmonton's earliest families preferred staying on the flats along the lower terraces of the North Saskatchewan River to camping places further back in the ravines, since fish spawned at the mouths of the creeks in the spring. They returned to pry rocks and stones from the glacial gravels along the riverbank and to carve tools and weapons on the spot. At the smaller camping sites, they left behind a few stone flakes or spear points as enduring proof of their hard work and inventiveness.

Edmonton is usually described as a flat city. The sprawl of neighbourhoods, freeways, shopping malls, parks and industrial areas can blind newcomers to the gentle rise and fall of the natural landscape and the occasional hills. The earliest inhabitants had a better view. When they were searching for a safe refuge from giant bears or for a lookout from which to spot approaching wolves or human enemies or even a windy refuge from mosquitoes and summer heat, they climbed nearby hills formed by the melting glaciers. The evidence of their camps lies buried under the townhouses at the intersection of the Calgary Trail and Whitemud Freeway; under the graves of generations of Edmonton's citizens in Mount Pleasant Cemetery; at the crossing at 50th Street and Whitemud Freeway; and elsewhere along south and west-facing hills throughout the city.

Archaeologists explored two large and significant sites on opposite sides of the city during the construction boom of the late 1970s and early 1980s. The Strathcona site is located on the highest terrace, about 60 metres above the North Saskatchewan River directly across from Rundle Park. After exploring the area for decades, two amateur archaeologists, Val Diederich and Nick Sheptycki, began to report on their private collections. In 1976 the city assigned a team of researchers to investigate the archaeological, historical and palaeontological resources in the chain of parks along the North Saskatchewan River. Tom Head returned with promising news about the Strathcona site. For the next five years a series of provincial archaeologists excavated the land, searching and sifting with trowels and screens, checking finds with radiocarbon dating and asking and answering their own persistent questions.[17] The 10 per cent of the site they explored revealed 25,000 artifacts from every era in Edmonton's history—including, oddly, a 1901 coin from Malaysia.[18]

The archaeologists knew they had found more than an ancient camping place, more than a safe refuge on the hill: it was an ancient quarry and workshop. Once again team members reported the intermingled evidence of repeat visits from aboriginal peoples over thousands of years. They discovered tremendous quantities of leftover debris from early tool manufacturing, as well as a cluster of fire-broken rock, a hammerstone, scrapers and the pointed tips of the finished tools. The remains of a family hearth hid in one lower depression of earth. Nearby lay the butchered hindquarters of a bison. It was at least 2,000 years old.

The Strathcona Science Park opened in 1980, becoming the first archaeological site in Canada to invite the public to join the scientific investigation. For a decade, tour guides led visitors around the excavation and the Archaeological Service of Alberta began a field school for students and other volunteers interested in Edmonton's history. When Edmonton's citizens drive to the Clover Bar landfill these days, they see only a private ski park on the riverbank, some empty buildings and an old metal fence. Nothing tells them that ancient peoples also left their garbage here.

On the other side of the city, a large deposit of ancient evidence lies buried under the basements of family homes in suburban Riverbend. Children playing in the small Bulyea Park, near the corner of Rabbit Hill Road and Terwilligar Drive, are standing on it. Like the modern families who love southwest Edmonton, ancient families camped in this high area because they liked the view.

Ted Prosser was an amateur archaeologist who reported his fascinating discoveries in this area to the province. A professional team explored about 10 per cent of the Prosser site before construction crews arrived to build a new neighbourhood. The archaeologists found a treasure trove: 1,700 artifacts deposited in a 40-centimetre layer of soil. Early families sharpened tools made of quartzite, chert, petrified wood and mudstone here. Fortunately, they did not clean up after themselves. In layers jumbled together by farmers' ploughs, digging rabbits and gophers, and by nature's crazy whims, archaeologists found tools used by people who lived thousands of years apart.[19]

Neither the Strathcona site nor the Prosser site answered the confounding riddle of the first humans' arrival in the Edmonton area. An unexplored hilltop on 23rd Avenue may yet pry open the mystery.

In the late 1950s, archaeologist William Mulloy became the first person to consider the possibility that people camped on this hill, at intervals, perhaps for as long as 12,000 years. He suggested that the earliest visitors would prefer the high, protected lookout with its excellent view of the prairie. Preliminary tests did not begin until 2003 when Heinz Pyszczyk and his colleague, Jack Ives, stooped to the ground on a summer visit and picked up projectile points on the surface of the field. Pyszczyk suggests that the Prosser site may have the clear stratification necessary to tell us exactly when people began to camp in the Edmonton area. "I think it will add greatly to the aboriginal story," he says. "Hopefully there will be very old projectile points that can be dated."[20]

The archaeological evidence does not identify specific aboriginal ethnic groups in the Edmonton area before the first contact with Europeans, although one artifact discovered at the Strathcona site offers a hint: a fragment of South Saskatchewan Basin pottery was left here at some point in the last 1,000 years by the Plains people—ancestral to the people in the Blackfoot Confederacy.[21] This evidence is consistent with aboriginal oral tradition, which suggests that the Blackfoot, the Cree, the Nakoda and their ancestors had known of and had visited this place long before the people from Europe and colonial North America began trading in furs.

Can we say Edmonton is an old city if human occupation here, though sparse and intermittent, was steady over the ages? The answer depends on the expert you ask and the worldview you accept. Aboriginal elders say their ancestors moved across an immense prairie often enough and long enough to call every bend in the river an enduring home. The European tradition is to measure the age of a city in the uninterrupted years of human occupation at one spot on the map and in the kinds of activities that happen in a permanent settlement.

Edmonton's people have their own definitions, their own creation stories, and their own imaginations. They can picture another boy or girl, 4,000 years ago, sliding down the snowy banks of the North Saskatchewan, reaching the bottom, and throwing both hands to the sky with the delight of a young snowboarder. Human beings have inhabited this territory for a long time in many of the same ways. This is an ancient place, built of water and stone, snow and ice.

In Our Own Words

Spirits of the World ⤳ Cree

When light first came to the earth, Omâmâmâ, the earth mother of the Cree people, gave birth to the spirits of the world. The first born was the thunderbird who protects the animals from the sea serpent. Thunderbirds shout out their unhappiness or anger with black clouds, rain and fire flashes in the sky. The second born was the lowly frog who heightens the sorcerer's powers and helps to control the insects in the world. The third born was the trickster Wîsahkecâhk, who can change himself into many forms or shapes to protect himself. The fourth child was Wîsahkecâhk's little wolf brother. They travel together with Wîsahkecâhk on his back. The fifth born was Amisk the beaver, who is greatly respected because he is an unfortunate human from a different world. Fish, rocks, grasses, and trees all came from the womb of the great earth mother Omâmâmâ. The earth was inhabited a long time by only animals and spirits because Wîsahkecâhk had not yet made any people.[22]

How the Land Was Made ⤳ Nitsitapii

Our Napi, the old man, he inhabited this land a long time ago, before there were human beings. When the world was still covered with water, Napi needed some mud to make the land. He asked beaver, loon and otter to dive to the bottom, and bring up some mud. They all tried, but failed. Napi then asked little muskrat Nisopski to try. Nisopski was gone for a long time, but when he finally returned he had some mud in his paws. Napi took the mud and formed the land and forests, animals and birds. And then he formed a woman and a child from the mud. On the fourth morning, they rose and followed him.[23]

Our Beautiful Earth ⌁ Dene

When the Earth was first made, the Creator's servants took a giant moose hide and spread it over the earth's surface. They covered it completely and when they lifted it up, the earth had become more beautiful. They did this six times. Each time they did it, the earth became more and more beautiful. That is how the world was made.[24]

The Sun and the Moon ⌁ Eleanor Brass, Cree storyteller

A long, long time ago there was no moon, but there was a sun. The Great Spirit had lesser spirits working for him, and one of these was in charge of the sun. He had two children, a son and a daughter, and all three of them lived together in the sky and were very happy. The daughter looked after the camp and kept it clean and tidy, shaking out the bedding and making the feathers fall to the earth as snow. The son hunted and fished; when he hung up his fish nets to dry, the dripping creating rain on the earth.

The father spirit was always busy keeping the great fire burning on the sun. He was away all day long and came home only at night. One day, after becoming very old he decided to speak to his children about taking over the important task of looking after the fire. "My son and daughter," he began, "you know that I'm getting old and can't tend the sun's fire much longer. I'll be leaving you in a little while and then it will be up to you to keep the fire burning. If you let it out, the people and animals on earth will die."

A short time later, when the fire was getting low on the sun, the old man came home and told his children he must leave them and would never return. They mourned for most of the night but when it came time to start the sun's fire in the morning, they began to quarrel over who had the task. The girl said she should do it as she was the oldest, but the boy said that he was now the man of the camp and that he should be the one to watch over the fire.

By this time, those on earth were becoming frightened, wondering why the sun was so late in coming up. At last, Wesuketchuk went to see what was the matter and found the brother and sister fighting. He became very angry with them and after rebuking them severely he said to the boy, "You being a man, it will be up to you to keep the fire burning during the day; henceforth your name will be Pesim." Then he said to the girl, "Since you are so anxious to keep a fire burning, too, yours will never have flames and will only shine at night. But you will have to work just as hard to keep the coals glowing so they won't go out. After this, your name will be Tippiskawepesim. And because you cannot get along together your punishment will be that you will only see one another once a year and for the rest of the time you will only look at each other across the sky.[25]

EXPLORING AN ANCIENT PAST

Heinz Pyszczyk, archaeologist

When we look at the North Saskatchewan River valley today it is difficult to imagine when it did not exist. But approximately 12,000 years ago there was only a flat lake bottom here. Prior to that date, the Edmonton area was covered by glacial ice—the last in a series of glacial events that have profoundly altered Alberta.... No one is exactly sure when the last ice sheet melted, but by 12,000 years ago the Edmonton area was becoming ice-free and was covered by water from the melting glaciers. The melt water formed Glacial Lake Edmonton—a short-lived body of water, which drained rapidly away through a channel south of Edmonton, setting the stage for the appearance of the North Saskatchewan River. Water flowing over the old glacial lakebed eventually established a preferred channel, and thousands of years of erosion formed the river valley we see today.

The river valley walls are composed of unstable sands, silts and gravels that periodically collapse in large and small landslides. Some of these landslides were caused when old coalmines that once lined the river valley collapsed. Today the river snakes between wide valley walls, eroding former flood plain deposits within the valley. Because the valley was carved out from top to bottom, the earliest archaeological sites will be found on the highest river terraces. Occupations dating after 8,000 years ago can be found on the lowest terrace, but also on the highest terraces as well.[26]

Catherine Reininger

I was a university student with young sons, living at Michener Park student housing on a limited income, so we used to go exploring in the river valley together for our adventures. Michael was 14. James was eight years old.

One day in 1984 we were walking through the Whitemud Creek ravine, and we found some petrified wood in the dirt under a pipeline. At first I had no idea what we'd found. I discovered some large teeth, about three inches long, and I thought they were probably dinosaur teeth. My son James picked up something bluish that looked like old fungus. I wrapped everything carefully in a tea towel, and put it inside a cardboard box, to take it to the Provincial Museum on the bus. I didn't want anything to break. When I showed the teeth to Jim Burns, the palaeontologist, he said: "Yes they're teeth—horses teeth, perhaps 600 years old—but what I'm really interested in is the blue thing." That fungus turned out to be the milk tooth of a mastodon. They said it was between 22,000 and 40,000 years old. James was amazed. Talk about cheap toys.[27]

The Meeting Place

1700 to 1869

HERE IS A BRAID OF SWEETGRASS, LISETTE, a gift on a spring morning.

It will be rush hour soon. Drivers will approach this corner with their eyes on the day ahead, not the days behind, and they will not see you in their rear-view mirrors. They will listen to the familiar hum and rattle of the Walterdale Bridge as they cross the North Saskatchewan River along 105th Street. Perhaps they will be thinking about an overdue marketing report, a child's cough, or a trip to the mountains. Were your morning thoughts so different? You squinted into the same sunlight when you crossed the river, a little upstream, with an infant on your back, and another child in your arms. Did you wonder about the unknown ones who lived on this riverbank generations before you? Or were you thinking about a *pimikan* shipment, a child's cough, or a trip to the mountains?

This is a trail you could not imagine. Thousands of suburban commuters follow the route every morning to jobs in downtown office towers. Once off the bridge, they steer right across the Rossdale Flats and circle past the power plant, the baseball stadium and the homemade crosses planted on an island in the middle of the traffic. Newcomers to the city ask: "What's with those crosses?" They are told that men, women and children are buried under this road in an unmarked cemetery from the fur trade era. Descendants pound crosses into the ground, in remembrance, and as a reproach to the rest of the city for forgetting. When the crosses fall down, or vandals push them over, a few men come back and build new ones. One cross is for you, Lisette. You are buried here, too.

Your full name was Louise Umfreville and you spoke Cree. You were the daughter of a Cree woman whose name has been lost and a fur trader and author, Edward Umfreville—a man who abandoned his family to return to England when you were five.[1] Your descendants believe you were living in a tipi on this riverbank with your sister Marie-Anne and six children when you met a young clerk of the fur trade, John Rowland, around 1809. In 1810 his horse returned to Edmonton House without its rider. You searched the prairie and found him lying on the ground with a broken leg.[2] You brought a herd of horses to him as your dowry to a country marriage. According to one family story, he adopted three children in your family. You gave birth to seven more of his children—John, Sophia, Alexandra, Nancy, Henry, Marguerite and Adelaide—and they, in turn, began large western Canadian families.

Some commuters on the road this morning could be your descendants, Lisette. What would you tell them if you could?

⁘⁓

EDMONTON DID NOT BEGIN as a European trading place on the Rossdale Flats, nor did it begin at two earlier fur-trading posts downstream near the mouth of the Sturgeon River in 1795. The Orkney Islanders, English, Métis and French Canadians who built Fort Augustus for the North West Company (NWC)—and their fierce competitors who built Edmonton House for the Hudson's Bay Company (HBC) a few months later—were not the founders of the city.

The true founders of Edmonton gathered at a meeting place on the river flats and on higher terraces in the valley near a beautiful bend in the river. Today the area is called Rossdale, but it has had many other tribal names. "Pehonan is the Cree word for the waiting place, the gathering place," says Buff Parry, who has researched the history of the flats for the Confederacy of Treaty 6 First Nations, and still lives in the area. He says the city barely knows that indigenous peoples used this place in a continuous way for many thousands of years: "What we're not doing is

The Meeting Place 1808

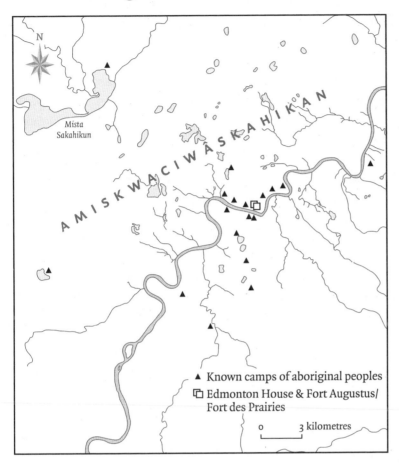

Tribal peoples had their own names for their traditional territory in the Beaver Hills and for two trading posts on the river flats in 1808. The Cree majority called the place amiskwâciwaskahikan or Beaver Hills House. The Nakoda Sioux, known then as the Assiniboines, said ti oda, meaning Many Houses. The Blackfoot called the trade forts omahkoyis, which means Big Lodge. The North West Company and the Hudson's Bay Company forts were located in the area now known as Rossdale.

Aboriginal trails through the territory had not yet been mapped. Siksika headman Old Swan, Ak ko mokki, drew two maps of the western plains for fur trader Peter Fidler in 1801 and 1802. Fidler collected two other drawings from unnamed aboriginal travellers, but none of these maps are specific about local trails. Aboriginal oral history and Edmonton House records suggest these trails established the routes of future roads and railways.

getting the pattern of the use of the North Saskatchewan River by Cree and Ojibway people before contact, and understanding the roots of that use beneath the cemetery." In his interview with the Rossdale Flats Aboriginal Oral Histories Project, Parry echoed the words of aboriginal descendants who believe this is a sacred place, worthy of more respect. He called these river flats the womb of the community, the place that "gave birth to the city of Edmonton."[3]

Tribal peoples who camped on the Rossdale flats lived in the larger territory of the Beaver Hills.[4] The sloping hills and wooded trails around Cooking Lake, Hastings Lake, Miquelon Lake, Astotin Lake and Beaverhill Lake have beckoned people for thousands of years. Archaeologists have examined the artifacts gathered by early amateur collectors who explored the area on summer rambles. Local farmers Mary and Bill Teidemann found an Agate Basin dart dated at 8,000 years old, as well as ancient spear heads, arrow heads, axe heads, scrapers and pounders from later periods.[5] The assembled evidence suggests the parkland was a gathering place for hunting and gathering, inter-tribal trade, war councils and warfare, religious ceremonies and family life for perhaps as long as 10,000 years.

Among the first aboriginal bands known to have entered the Beaver Hills were the Tsuu T'ina.[6] They once belonged to the Beaver people of the Peace River country, but separated from them to move steadily south. "The environs of the Beaver Hills are generally their station," wrote the trader Alexander Henry the Younger in 1811. Henry counted 90 lodges, with 150 men and many more women and children in the hills that year. He remarked of them: "These people have the reputation of being the bravest tribe in all the plains, who dare face ten times their own numbers; and of this, I have convincing proof during my residence in this country."[7] A northern branch of the Blackfoot Confederacy considered the region its territory before 1800. The Nakoda gathered here, too.

This place was known as the Beaver Hills in several languages, but thousands of buffalo also roamed the forests. Hunters created buffalo pounds to capture the huge animals in large, frequent, slaughters. They also hunted deer, moose, elk, bear and otter and smaller game. Wildfowl, fish and berries were in abundance. Bands travelled away from the Beaver Hills, and returned, at seasonal intervals. They were here for the Goose dances and medicines lodges; for the sundance ceremonies and feasts in the early summer; for the buffalo chase and berry picking of midsummer; for the elk and deer hunting and the buffalo pounds of the autumn and for trapping in the woods in the long winter.

The Cree, or the *nehiywak* as they called themselves, were living west of Hudson's Bay by the mid-1700s. Canadian historians have traditionally suggested that the eastern Cree moved west with the Europeans, or just ahead of them.[8] Recent scholarship challenges that interpretation, suggesting that a western branch of the Cree-speaking peoples could have lived on the Plains at an earlier period, arriving some time during the 1600s or perhaps earlier.[9] Aboriginal elders, researchers and academic historians differ in their understanding of tribal boundaries, but they agree that the Cree were familiar with the Beaver Hills before the European traders arrived here.

The indigenous inhabitants did not know that a foreign nation claimed authority over their territory. Far from the Beaver Hills, and across the Atlantic Ocean, an English king signed a royal charter in 1670 that gave the HBC exclusive trading rights to a vast inland region that would be called Rupert's Land. The London company built York Factory on Hudson's Bay. It was soon competing for western furs with the NWC, founded at Montreal in 1776, and with independent French-Canadian traders who paid no attention to the English monopoly.

Early Cree traders brought provisions from the trading posts at York Factory to trade for furs with bands in the Beaver Hills. They were middlemen—traders who brought strangers together—as well as interpreters, guides, labourers and canoeists for the English and French-Canadian traders.

Here the Cree called themselves *amiskwaciwiyiniwak*, the Beaver Hills People, one of several groups belonging to the *natimiwiyiniwak*, the Upstream People. They lived on the western edge of a much larger territory of Cree-speaking bands. Aboriginal trading patterns were complex. The Cree relied on the Blackfoot and Nakoda for horses after the 1740s; the Blackfoot and Nakoda needed the European guns and ammunition they could obtain from the Cree. All tribes trapped beaver to obtain what they needed from one another, but also to barter with the rival traders who were already fighting over their business.

Tribal boundaries shifted through the eighteenth and nineteenth centuries. The Cree in the parkland and plains camped along the upper North Saskatchewan River, from the present site of Edmonton through the Beaver Hills, Saddle Lake and Whitefish Lake; and at the Maskwachees or Bear Hills and Buffalo Lake area near present-day Hobbema. All travelled across the territory according to the season. The Cree, Blackfoot and Nakoda formed a trade and military alliance in the 1700s to push other tribes, like the Shoshoni, the Flathead and the Kootenay, out of the southern Plains and the foothills.[10]

Further east, aboriginal women started families with the Orkneymen, English and French Canadians who worked at isolated posts throughout the West. Their extended Métis families were moving toward Edmonton by the 1700s. Their descendants still live in the Beaver Hills.

WAS ANTHONY HENDAY THE FIRST EUROPEAN to visit what is now Alberta? Possibly not. Pierre Gaultier de Varennes, sieur de La Vérendrye, and his family explored the plains, searching for the western sea, beginning in the 1730s. His extended family established small trading posts to buy furs and negotiated agreements with aboriginal peoples in the West. His family members could have visited the Edmonton area before Henday began his journey across the plains.

Henday was the first European to document a journey to an unnamed place where he could see the mountains. Does his journal confirm that he visited the Edmonton region at all, as has been suggested for decades? Not definitively. Two Cree men, Connawapa and Attitckosish, brought the HBC labourer from York Factory to meet the tribes of the West in 1755. Several historians who have examined four different versions of Henday's journals reach different conclusions about his route.[11] Some conclude that the three men, nine women and their children dragged sleds along the frozen river, walking below present-day Edmonton to a camping place just below the mouth of the Sturgeon River where Fort Saskatchewan is today.[12] These historians say the visitors camped with Nakoda families and waited for the ice to melt so they could continue their journey by canoe. Other scholars suggest that Henday's journals are not so precise about the location of the spring camp.[13]

Henday tried to convince western hunters to come to York Factory to trade directly. Many declined the offer, for they saw no need. So the eager companies came to them. The NWC concocted an elaborate plot to keep the rich resources of the Athabasca country to itself. It lured the HBC to the upper Saskatchewan River to distract the English traders from the greater treasure to the north.

The two companies raced to this riverbank. Peter Fidler, William Flett and John Ward explored the shoreline on horseback for the HBC in 1793, looking for a site, but they turned around.[14] Two years later, James Hughes, John MacDonald of Garth and about 20 unnamed men built Fort Augustus for the NWC on the west bank of the river, about two miles north of present-day Fort Saskatchewan.[15] Their exasperated rivals were right behind them. William Tomison, Peter Pruden and a work crew arrived to build Edmonton House "within a musket shot"[16] of Fort Augustus.

Oh, the comforts of home. Their first winter was coming. In "thick, rimy weather,"[17] the HBC traders at Edmonton House built two log buildings—one 18 by 7 feet, the other 10 by 5 feet—with parchment on the windows and turf on the roof.[18] Up to 17 men, and presumably some of their family members, lived for long periods in these buildings behind a partial log stockade and the Union Jack. All men came from the Orkney Islands and spoke Gaelic and Cree. Their aboriginal wives and children spoke Cree and other aboriginal languages.

Rival traders at Fort Augustus and Edmonton House were rarely friends. They lived side by side for mutual security in a land where they were intruders. Servants of the two fur-trading companies worked hard, in considerable danger and deprivation, and with few rewards for their labour. They recorded small pleasures. At Edmonton House, William Tomison wrote to thank a friend for a parcel of tea, sugar and coffee in 1796: "Thank God for health, when I want to get merry I go to the River, and when I want to drink Tea I go to the Bushes."[19] If the competitors had one common enemy it was the independent traders in the nearby XY Company shanty "who like the Locusts of Egypt bring Devestation and Ruin along with them wherever they Winter."[20] All traders brought liquor to trade for furs and to buy peace and compliance.

In a perpetual quest for the perfect location, traders at Fort Augustus and Edmonton House relocated their fur-trading posts often. Sometime between 1802 and 1806, the two companies moved upstream to the riverbank that would later be called Rossdale Flats.[21] They moved downstream to a site near present-day Smoky Lake in 1810.[22] "Stop moving Edmonton about,"[23] the company complained from London, but nobody listened. They moved upstream again in 1813, probably reconstructing the forts near what is now Victoria Park.[24] The HBC and NWC amalgamated in 1821, forcing old rivals to live together despite the reported "strife and hatred"[25] between their labourers. Plagued by fire and flood, the traders moved to an impressive post on higher ground near the present-day Alberta Legislature in 1830.[26] Here, thankfully, they stayed put.

The gentlemen at HBC Headquarters in London sent another firm order to the distant traders: "Changing the Names of dependant Settlements not only misleads but often times perplex us when referring to the Maps, let it therefore be avoided."[27] They wasted their breath. The Cree called this place, *Amiskwaciywaskahagen*, or Beaver Hills House. The Chipewyan said *sawyah-thay-koi*. When John Rowand built the three-story log house inside the fort in 1831, the Blackfoot called it *omukoysis*, or The Big House. The Tsuu T'ina called it *nasagachoo*. The Nakoda called it *ti oda*, Many Houses. French-speaking Métis and French-Canadian voyageurs said *Forts des Prairies*, a name also used for other posts on the upper Saskatchewan. Nor'Westers said Fort Augustus until they were forced to stop. At first the HBC traders said Edmonton House, and later Fort Edmonton, probably because trader William Tomison wanted to impress the deputy governor of the HBC, James Winter Lake, by naming the post after his birthplace in England.[28] Fur traders tried to float the name Fort Sans Pareil for a short time, but it was a dud without equal.[29] Edmonton was the name that stuck.

What was the great purpose of this trading enterprise? The soft underfur of the beaver was perfect for the construction of felt hats for English gentlemen. This Canadian city owes its existence to a hat.

❧

THE OLD ALLIANCE between the Blackfoot and the Cree was breaking down just as the English, Scottish and French-Canadian traders arrived here in 1795. Newcomers found themselves in the middle of a war zone. The Blackfoot no longer needed to trade horses to the Cree for guns because they could trade directly with the two companies. The Cree and Nakoda needed more horses to hunt buffalo on the Plains and they sent raiding parties into enemy territory to increase their supply.

The Beaver Hills Cree and Nakoda steadily launched attacks and withstood counter-attacks after 1810. These horse wars included raids on the fur-trading posts. Chiefs travelled to Edmonton House and Fort Augustus to negotiate truces and smoke the pipe together in ceremonies, but warfare resumed, season after season. Company traders did everything to keep the warring tribes apart, setting up distant posts to separate them for the benefit of their business transactions, but the Blackfoot bands continued to come north to trade.

To the consternation of the company traders the beaver supply diminished along the North Saskatchewan, but the aboriginal peoples already preferred the magnificent buffalo hunt and the expanding culture it created. The tribes formed a confident majority, riding a crest of their history in the early 1800s. They did not see a few outsiders as a threat to their superior position.

"They are numerous and almost independent of us," observed Chief Factor James Curtis Bird at Edmonton House in 1807. "We are often obliged, in favour of the Trade, and for our own Subsistence, to disperse ourselves, and travel in such small numbers, as to be often in their power."[30] The great achievement of the era was that the aboriginal peoples and company traders rarely fought with one another. There were occasional breaches, but both sides worked to preserve a profitable relationship. When John Rowand sent the intrepid Jimmy Jock Bird to live among the Blackfoot, or sent his Métis sons to hunt with the Cree, he acted in the company's interest to protect the local trade from American competition. These new allegiances and intermarriages were the first hints of a future city.

⌣

Come to trade. Bring us beaver pelts, wolves, lynx, martens. We want black bear, fox, muskrats, otter. Bring us elk, deer, goose and swan quills. We want buffalo robes, buffalo skins, buffalo meat and pemmican to feed the voyageurs in the brigades.

Let the ceremony begin. Smoke the pipe, offer speeches. We will exchange gifts to honour the trade. Teach us your languages. Explain where trails will take us through the wall of mountains. Tell us who is at war. Tell us why.

Take these wooden tokens. Each one stands for the value of a beaver pelt on the London market. Come to the wicket. Exchange the tokens for the treasures of the Trade Room.

Take away hunting guns and musket balls, knives and axes. Here are copper kettles and cast-iron pots, red ribbons and ostrich feathers. Run your fingers through the pony beads and seed beads made of blue Italian glass. Take these striped point-blankets for your hooded capotes; these Assomption sashes, ceinture flechée, to wrap around your waist. Here is Irish Roll tobacco for your ceremonies. We'll trade a nine-gallon keg of rum for your beaver pelts to keep you away from the traders on the Missouri. Come back soon. We have more.

Come to work. Pack your fiddle. We'll take you at fourteen, make you into a man.

Can you take this country's punishment without complaint? Tie this sash to your forehead and under an 80-pound fur bale. Run along the shore with the bale on your back on a day's portage. We need trackers—eight men harnessed with ropes to a boat—who can pull heavy loads through cold water. We need men who can run dog teams for 50 miles a day through blizzards and hack trails through northern forests in a summer haze of mosquitoes.

We need labourers to stack fur bales and haul buffalo carcasses. We need carpenters to make furniture, windows, dog sleds and oars; coopers to build kegs for the trade liquor; and millers to grind barley and wheat. We need literate clerks to count fur shipments and recopy letters and journals. We need Orkneymen to build ten York boats a year.

Sign up here. Your shoulders look strong. We'll pay you 10 pounds for the first two years, a fortune for a boy like you.

Welcome to Edmonton House. Here's a bunk in the Bachelor's Quarters where you'll sleep with 20 men. If you take a local woman and have children, you can share a room with three families. When your shoulders give out, you can retire to Red River, go north to the Athabasca country, or stay on this riverbank with your family. Build yourself a cabin. Make this place a home.

TAKING A MAGNIFYING GLASS to the slanted script of the Fort Edmonton journals requires patience. "Wind and weather as yesterday," the clerk's entry began on December 16, 1796. "Men employed as before."[31] Gerhard Ens teaches students at the University of Alberta how to find more revealing information in HBC journals, reports and correspondence. A specialist in the history of western Canada, Ens recently introduced the university's first course on Fort Edmonton. The documentary record, available on microfiche at the Rutherford Library, offers rich detail about First Nations and Métis history around Edmonton, as well as the economic, social and cultural life of the isolated fur trade post in the first half of the nineteenth century. "But you have to be willing to read carefully and read widely," says Ens, "to get at this kind of material."[32]

How do you read carefully? First, remember that Fort Edmonton journals are not personal diaries, but cautious business reports to an employer. "I suspect the Fort Edmonton journals are not the originals,"[33] Ens adds. Clerks at York Factory recopied the huge books and perhaps omitted or changed information. The journals are missing from 1834 to 1854, perhaps lost, for unknown reasons.

Turning to the personal correspondence, Ens cautions readers to consider the natural bias. Fur traders wrote scathing descriptions of early Roman Catholic and Protestant missionaries, for example, because they resented interference in their exclusive domain. Missionaries wrote harshly about one another, balking at religious differences and competing for converts after 1840. Some clergymen—like Robert Rundle and Thomas Woolsey—abandoned the region after a few frustrating years. Others, like Albert Lacombe and the McDougall family, began their own communities in the 1860s, negotiated treaties and wrote letters and memoirs that promoted their reputations. Their personal biases continue to shape western Canada's understanding of its history to this day. Early adventurers who visited Fort Edmonton in the nineteenth century gave their travel notebooks to ghostwriters in London or Toronto, who in turn transformed their experiences into entertaining pulp fiction about the Canadian wilderness. Eyewitness accounts cannot be accepted as truthful reporting, says Ens, but each piece can offer useful clues. Read with an open mind; remember the filters of diverse perspectives; consider the possible viewpoints of those who did not write at all and you can glimpse through the gaps in the stockade, in both directions.

~

WHAT ABOUT LOST FAMILY STORIES? Literate men at Edmonton House wrote thousands of pages in post journals, reports and letters about their own hard work; the quality of the traded furs; their profits and losses; their relationships with chiefs, warriors and hunters; company gossip; the wars, floods, prairie fires and diseases of their century. They wrote so much about the weather that at one point their bored superiors in London begged them to stop. "Diaries of Winds & Weather are to us useless and need not be Kept,"[34] they complained. Weather reports continued. Yet through a full century the fur traders rarely wrote a syllable about their growing families, perhaps in fear of the Company's disapproval. They slipped occasionally, scribbling gems about a newborn baby or a child's pet rabbits, before returning to a recitation of beaver pelt tallies.

Traders had private lives, though, and wives after a fashion. They gave names like Jane, Julia or Cecile—often their mothers' names—to aboriginal women and daughters who rarely spoke the English language.

Chief Factor James Curtis Bird had a large family with an aboriginal woman he called Mary, with a Métis woman, Elizabeth Montour, and with other indigenous women, but he returned to England to marry an English wife and left most of his money to English children.[35] This was the usual pattern for senior officers at Edmonton House in the early years, but company servants with less status had fewer restrictions. Kenneth McDonald, for example, married Emma Rowland, raised seven children with her, and settled permanently on the riverbank with his Métis in-laws.

John Rowand and Louise Umfreville lived together for almost 40 years. Entering the trade at Edmonton House in his early teens, Rowand grew up to be one of the most powerful traders in his generation. One Pound One, the men called him, nicknaming him after the sound of his shuffling footsteps after his early leg injury. Aboriginal hunters called him Big Mountain or Iron Shirt.[36] Rowand did not formally marry Umfreville when the first missionaries, François-Norbert Blanchet and Modeste Demers, arrived in 1838, although he made certain the priests baptized four of their children. He considered leaving his country wife to find a wife of a lighter colour in Red River. "If I get a wife below, or in England, or elsewhere, the Columbia [River] shall not see me, it shall be as she may think proper,"[37] he wrote to a colleague in 1840. When Louise died at the age of 66 at Fort Edmonton in 1849, he wrote that he had lost his "old friend, the Mother of all my children."[38] A handful of half-loving words.

"The women here work very hard," Rowand acknowledged in a rare tribute, "if it was not so, I do not know how we would get on with the Company work."[39] Women and children outnumbered men by a large margin at every fur-trading post in Edmonton's early history and in surrounding aboriginal camps due to heavy casualties in tribal warfare. Historians Sylvia van Kirk and Jennifer Brown have explored the historical records for documented evidence of women's labour in the fur trade. They conclude that women's work was as critical as the hunting, trapping, trading and freighting of the men. Country wives and daughters scraped and prepared furs. They were the central suppliers of pemmican—the breakfast, lunch and supper of the fur trade—for all brigades along the Saskatchewan. For weeks at a time, they cut buffalo meat, dried it on racks over slow fires, and pounded the mixture into a fine powder. They mixed this powder with dried berries and melted buffalo fat, bundled it, and packed the food staple into 40-kilogram sacks. They manufactured thousands of these sacks for export from Edmonton House every year and yet pemmican production was only the beginning of their work.

They were Alberta's first farmers. With many men away through the summer, they planted, hoed and harvested 1,600 bushels of potatoes on the river flats annually. They cultivated wheat and barley. They dried fish, butchered fresh meat, hunted small game, gathered thousands of baskets of berries, made lye soap from ashes and buffalo fat. They constructed snowshoes for an industry that relied on winter travel through deep snow. They created the shirts and the moccasins, the hooded coats and the leggings with intricate beadwork and ribbon decoration. They healed the sick with medicinal herbs in a community without doctors; they were the midwives who delivered the babies. They ate in separate quarters from the men, after they had fed them. Once a year, on New Year's Day, the chief factor acknowledged each woman's contribution to the trade with a small drink and a kiss on both cheeks. The women called it Kissing Day.

Only a few hundred people lived at Fort Edmonton at any time through the first half of the 1800s, but their little society was perhaps more stratified than our own: the chief factor was on top, the senior servants and clerks, skilled tradesmen in the middle, and labourers and hunters down below. Senior company men—William Tomison, James Curtis Bird, Francis Heron, and John Rowand—claimed supreme authority within the stockades of Edmonton House, but they had no authority in the tribal territories beyond their horizon. They wrote second-hand reports of distant wars and epidemics and changes in tribal boundaries, but their understanding was limited to what the indigenous hunters and trappers chose to tell them.

Company traders remained a small minority in the region. Their aboriginal neighbours were travelling people, coming and going in great numbers. By 1857 the visiting Captain Palliser counted 300 lodges with 1,900 people in the Beaver Hills alone. Many families maintained a long association with Fort Edmonton as "freemen," or independent traders, for generations. Company employees referred to nearby bands and local hunters on contract as the Home Guard. Aboriginal people of mixed lineage who lived a traditional way of life were often known by family names that appear to be French or English, sometimes after Christian baptisms, or for the convenience of traders who were unable to pronounce their names.

Consider the Callihoo family: Two Mohawk parents, Marie Ann Tekonwakwehni and Thomas Anatoha had a baby in Ganawake, near Montreal, on October 17, 1782. This son, Louis, used the surname Kwarakwante. "He went north, married there, had a family there and never came back," local Jesuits recorded. [40] When Louis signed a contract as a voyageur in November 1800, the Montreal clerk recorded his name as Caliheue. By 1805 Louis was working as a steersman at Fort Augustus, and he may have travelled with David Thompson on an expedition through the Rockies in 1810. His family worked in the Athabasca region and Jasper but visited Fort Edmonton often.

In 1824 Louis and his third wife, Marie Patenaude, had a son named Michel Callihoo. Michel and his Métis wife Marie Savard moved to Fort Edmonton around 1849 with four children. Michel worked on contract as a steersman, guide, hunter, carpenter and labourer. When he left the company, the family settled near Lac Ste. Anne. [41] In 1878 Michel Callihoo signed an adhesion to Treaty 6 and claimed a reserve for his extended family. Michel's many descendants in Edmonton today include the Chalifoux and Calliou families.

The Papaschase band moved to the south shore of the river opposite Fort Edmonton from the Lesser Slave Lake area. The chief Papaschase, or Papastayo, appears to have arrived in 1856; his six brothers and their large families followed in 1858 or 1859. These brothers were the children of John Quinn, or Kwenis, and Lizette Gladu. The band joined other families like the Bruneaus, Cardinals, Daigneaults, Decoynes, Bernards and Batoches at the Two Hills on the south side of the river. [42] The community included former hunters and labourers for the HBC who were too old to work, as well as the widows or abandoned wives of Company employees and their children. The Papaschase band spoke Cree and maintained traditional beliefs and frequently hosted sundances and other ceremonies, to the frustration of local missionaries. Chief Papaschase would later sign an adhesion to Treaty 6 on behalf of his band and for a time his band settled on a large reserve on the south side of the river. Traders mentioned his brother Tahkoots frequently in Fort Edmonton journals and letters. They regarded him as a local villain for his participation in Cree raiding; the band's tradition is that he was a war leader. The Papaschase story was just beginning in the 1850s.

Lapotac and the families of Alexander and Alexis were also associated with the company in different roles. They led Cree and Nakoda bands that eventually settled in the lake district northwest of the fort toward Lake Wabamun and Lac Ste. Anne. To the south, Kiskyo, known as Bobtail, and his brother Ermineskin, would lead Cree bands with camps at Maskwachees, or the Bear Hills. Bobtail, too, signed the adhesion to Treaty 6. He visited Fort Edmonton often to negotiate with other Cree leaders, including Pakan and Blue Quills from Saddle Lake and Whitefish Lake and the influential Plains Cree leaders, Sweetgrass and Maskipiton. Together these chiefs and their headmen would petition future governments on behalf of the Cree people.

Métis settlements were well-established at Buffalo Lake and Lac Ste. Anne by the mid 1800s, but many Métis families like the Birds, the Donalds, Brelands, Delormes, Laderoutes, Andersons and Belleroses, Belcourts, Rowlands, Savards and Cunninghams would soon settle on river lots around the Hudson's Bay Post, or in the new Métis community of St. Albert.

Arriving from the south, Siksika, Tsuu T'ina, Bloods, Piikani and hunters from more distant tribes camped on the river flats and nearby hills when trading. With the exception of a few dozen HBC employees, a half-dozen missionaries and about 50 gold prospectors who drifted through the territory, the Fort Edmonton district was a First Nations and Métis community until the late 1870s.

⁓

ONE VICTORIAN PAINTER shaped the image of life at Fort Edmonton for successive generations. It is difficult to escape Paul Kane in our imagined West. He put a lock on the city's memory, creating a shared image of fur-trade life, with beautiful paintings and a famous memoir, *Wanderings of an Artist Among the Indians of North America*. Kane visited Fort Edmonton twice on his two-year trip—in September 1846 and December 1847. He produced four paintings based on his experiences here, but it was the book that offered the small details people seem to crave.

Edmonton clings to Kane to this day. At Christmas local newspapers reprint his irresistible story about the holiday feast at Fort Edmonton in December 1847: "boiled buffalo hump...dried moose nose...boiled buffalo calf...taken from the cow by the Caesarean operation long before it attains its full growth...white fish, delicately browned in buffalo marrow... buffalo tongue...[and] beavers' tails."[43] Local history buffs re-enact the festive dinner. Kane's portrait of a Fort Edmonton Métis girl hangs in the

Provincial Museum of Alberta, identified as in his book, as Cunne-wa-bum or "One Who Looks at the Stars." Who can forget the author's description of dancing with another beautiful Métis girl? "I was so much struck with her beauty that I prevailed upon her to promise to sit for her likeness, which she afterwards did with great patience, holding her fan, which was made of the tip end of swan's wing with an ornamental handle of porcupine quills, in a most coquettish manner."[44] These passages continue to be cited, creating the Fort Edmonton of local fantasies.

The awkward problem is that Kane was not the author of the book. Historian Ian MacLaren has investigated the riddles of Paul Kane's western tour in exhaustive scholarship for more than a decade.[45] He compared Kane's surviving field notes to the surviving versions of *Wanderings of an Artist* and concludes that the gifted painter had little to do with the famous book. The manuscript was revised at least three times after Kane turned over his notebooks and the final book probably had several authors. Kane's field notes say nothing about the Christmas dinner; or about a dancing maiden and her fluttering fan. Instead Kane wrote in pencil: "Edmunton is a large Fort witch has about 50 men it supulies to other Forts about a 1000 bags of pimecon. they cilled this winter 700 Buffalo for thare one cunsumtion which are cept in ise all summar."[46]

In his quirky phonetic spelling, Kane recorded his encounters with real people in the region—the Brosseau family, Francois Lucier, John Rowand Jr. and Margaret Harriott, Colin Fraser, the Cree chief, Maskipiton, or Broken Arm and his family—but no Cunne-wa-bum. A shivering Kane was preoccupied with the "cake of ise" in his "mockisen's," not romance. "Fell through the ise to day and traveled all day in my frosen cloths," he says. "Dare not stand still for feere of freesing anchious to get on would not stop to dry my selfph."[47]

Kane is less condescending about aboriginal people in his notebooks than the authors who later wrote the book under his name. He writes with admiration of the canoeists who waded in cold water to their waists, their coats hardened with ice. Distant ghostwriters transformed this scruffy Canadian artist into a snobbish English sporting gentleman with perfect diction. They invented a Fort Edmonton, too, a wilderness castle full of gentrified men and women. "Consider that the audience for travel writing was the cosmopolitan London book reader," advises MacLaren. "Hang on to that idea, and you'll be less frequently waylaid by the illusion that Edmonton was like its descriptions in narratives published in the Imperial centre."[48]

━◦━

PEOPLE IN EDMONTON cling to other illusions about the fur-trade era, often by accident.

Archaeologists excavated the remaining ruins of the last Fort Edmonton south of the Alberta Legislature in 1992.[49] They assigned university students to talk to curious bystanders and show them artifacts. The students reported that a majority of visitors were surprised to learn that a Hudson's Bay Post was ever located on the site. Many people thought the original location of the fur trading post was in Fort Edmonton Park, a popular historical theme park tucked in the south-western corner of the city. Some people believed the huge replica of Fort Edmonton, carefully constructed in the park in 1974 according to the 1846 specifications, was the original fort.

Look for the truth in a room on the third floor of St. Stephen's College on the University of Alberta campus. Pull down the filing boxes from the shelves. Examine the drawings, maps and photographs and the pages of archaeologists' reports to the province over the past five decades.

Here is the report on excavations at the Alberta Legislature grounds in 1992. Archaeologists discovered more than 6,000 artifacts of the fur trade period on a small portion of the site, dating between 1830 and 1915.[50] They found palisade walls, a log foundation, a cellar of the fort, and abundant evidence of everyday life: the fragments of clay tobacco pipe, game dice, bits of dishes, musket balls and gun cartridges, metal arrowheads and iron nails, a brass broach in the shape of a ribbon. They also found the stone flakes of ancient toolmakers who camped on this hill at an unknown time in the distant past.

Dig through the box on the table. These reports come from excavations of an earlier fort site on the Rossdale Flats.[51] Here is the evidence of at least four ancient occupations, aboriginal campsites beside the river. Radiocarbon dates on butchered bison bones reveal that people camped here 5,500 years ago. Here are pictures of artifacts from the early Fort Augustus and Edmonton House. Long after the first forts fell down, and tipis disappeared from the flats, the Edmonton Exhibition built a racetrack and a grandstand on the land in 1888; Prime Minister Wilfrid

Laurier declared Alberta a province on this place in 1905; here the city built a waterworks and power generating station and a sewage treatment plant after 1909. Archaeologists even found an American League baseball from an early game at the park. Every layer of the city's existence is mingled in the dirt.

Look closer. Here are the descriptions of the old Fort Edmonton cemetery, the one under the road in Rossdale, and under the power plant. Construction workers discovered the first human remains near the power plant in 1943. More surfaced in 1957 and 1964. They dug up four human skeletons in 1966 and seven in 1967.[52] Here is a photograph of two researchers in shorts, talking in a trench, with a full skeleton in the foreground. Archaeologists discovered more remains in 1973 and more in 1981. They reported their findings with scientific precision: "*Individual #81–1 was an adult male Caucasian, in his 40s at time of death, and standing about 5'6' tall. He was a pipe smoker, habitually holding his pipe on the left side of his mouth between his canine and first premolar. The cause of his death is unknown. He was buried in the Old Fort Edmonton Cemetery sometime between 1802 and 1880, probably in a coffin, and some kind of copper artifact was included in the grave with him, resting against his left forearm.*"[53] Some bodies were left where they were found, "or otherwise permanently disposed of"[54] in known and unknown places. Human remains of six individuals, including an infant, were moved to vaults at the University of Alberta in 1967 without ceremony or family or tribal notification; here the skeletal material was tested and the bone analysis published in a scientific journal.

Much older Canadian cemeteries are treated as sacred ground, and protected by law from interference, yet one of Alberta's first fur trade cemeteries has been desecrated seemingly at will. As early as 1977 an Edmonton archaeologist wrote that the Rossdale site had "high historic value... the unmarked graveyard must be treated as a major historic site... [and] approached in a very cautious manner."[55] In 2000, the university offered to return the human remains and accompanying artifacts—a medicine bundle, a bird bone whistle and buffalo horns—for reburial.[56] Yet in early 2004—after years of emotional public hearings, difficult negotiations, two comprehensive historical studies and a promise from the city to build a respectful memorial and repatriate the human remains—cars, buses and trucks continued to rumble over the bodies of Edmonton's founding families. The city has recently approved reburial, permanent road closure and a memorial.

Gerald Delorme voices the frustration of many other descendants at the delay: "This desecration of our burials has to stop. It has gone on too long. Please respect our ancestors' resting place."[57] He has asked the city to honour its promise before 2005.

~~

WHEN ARCHAEOLOGISTS EXCAVATED the Rossdale Flats site in 1999, they found fragments that spoke of the existence of the silent ones in the fur-trade era: one Mother-of-Pearl button, 130 glass beads, white and peacock blue; a single silver bead; a silver broach and the loops of two earrings; two brass rings; a scrap of black wool. Beneath these personal belongings they found the stone tools and flakes that proved aboriginal families lived here as early as 8,000 years ago.[58]

Could this silver earring hoop have belonged to Louise Umfreville, the woman John Rowand called Lisette? Did it belong to Jane MacDonald who buried her three boys, Donald, James and Joseph, on higher ground during the scarlet fever epidemic in 1845? Did it belong to Julie Daigneault or Marie Katis or Waysitkawaykis or Julia Batoche or Ellen Petite Couteau or Saskatchewan or Louise Onakos or Agatha, known as Cat, or Archange Nipissing or Cacoosis or Angelique Bruneau or Isabelle, daughter of Mistikomin and Miyanam, or Sarah Bird, or Betsy Brass? Each woman knew this meeting place, camped here, worked here and walked here. So many stories are missing from Edmonton's documented record of the fur trade because the words of known grandmothers, mothers and daughters were not written down. These women gave birth to the city's first children.

We leave this braid of sweetgrass, Lisette, to tell you we remember.

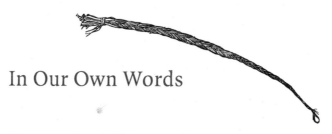

In Our Own Words

TRAILS TO A NEW HOME

How the Nakoda Arrived Here ⌁ Francis Alexis, descendant

OUR GREAT, GREAT GRANDFATHER WHITE BEAR was a young man. He had a dream about a lake. It had life in abundance. There were a lot of berries and a lot of animals. But there was something about this lake that bothered him about this dream, and he went to the old people and the old people said you have to go out and search for that dream and find it.

At that time I guess, our people were scared. They did not want to be kept like the black people who were made slaves. There were not too many of our people left and there were a lot of little kids around that were orphans. Their parents either were killed or they died in some massacre. After many years of fighting, there were not too many men.

I guess it was at this time, our grandfather had a dream and the old people told him to take these orphans. So he gathered a whole bunch of orphans together and he searched for the lake. He went to a lake north of here, went around it, but it wasn't the lake he saw in his dream. So he went looking south. I guess they looked for three years. They camped at Lake Isle, which wasn't it. While they were camped there, he went looking and he came upon Wabamun. He went around it; it wasn't the lake that he dreamt about.

So on his way back, he came here and camped. Early in the morning, they say just before sunrise, a morning star came up and my grandfather heard singing. He got up and he listened and said this is one of our songs. Our people used to sing that song a long time ago. He listened, and as soon as he got his things ready, he started heading that way. As he got closer, the song kept getting louder and louder. Pretty soon he came by the shore of this lake. The singing was coming from the lake. He got some logs together and he built a raft, and he went to the rock island, where the singing was coming from. There was singing but when he looked around, there was nobody. There were just a whole bunch of rocks.

Our grandfather looked around and something clicked, "I have seen this place before," he said. "This is the lake I saw in my dream. This is where our people will have life." He named it "Wakãmne," meaning a holy lake. I guess he pulled out his pipe, they say, and he prayed. After he prayed, he came back and put his raft on the shore and he looked towards the rock. The singing was starting to go faint and he saw a lady walking on the water. She had a hide coat; it was not tan but it was white. It had shells on it and porcupine stuff decorated on it and she had a bundle. It was a lady walking on the water. The woman spirit that represents Mother Earth, like a mother provides for us everything we need. Not only for us but also the animals and the birds; all the living things. Our people still sing songs about it at sundance.

The singing disappeared after that. While he was walking around, he saw a whole bunch of berries. He looked at the ground and he saw that the ground can produce a lot of strawberries. Also, there was an abundance of animals—ducks, beavers, and fish. Everything they needed to depend on was there. He went back and got his people.[59]

The "Musketoes" Were Plenty ⌐ Anthony Henday, traveller and diarist

7 MARCH Indians pitched different ways in search of food. Myself and Tent mates are to continue here if we can procure food. We are twelve in number; three men, Nine women & Children. What Ammunition I had I gave to those I hope will join me, and proceed to York Fort in May next.

8 MARCH Men & Women repairing Snow Shoes and Sleds.

14 MARCH Indians hunting, very good success. Myself hath been out of order with a Head-ack.

Anthony Henday was the
first European to leave a
written record of his visit to
Alberta and the Edmonton
region. He travelled with
his guides Attitckosish and
Connawapa, nine women
and their children in 1755.

18 MARCH I went a hunting with my Companions; Saw many Waskesew but could not come at them; the Snow so hard makes a noise under our Snowshoes. Ten tents came & pitched along side of us in order to build Canoes.

17 APRIL This morning see 4 Swans, my partner went to get a Shott att them killed two, and I was Standing att a distance, I saw a moose Coming Right to me. I was to Leeward of him, but had no Gun, but it being so nigh that I with my bow & arrow prick't him thro' the throat and with another Arrow in his broad side, so that he soon Lay down, my partner Come with his 2 Swans, and I was a Skinning My Moose, now we have plenty of provisions, and a great way to our tent, this Evening we went about 10 M on our Journey homewards.

21 APRIL Came Connawappa to our tents, being the first time I have seen him Since the fall of the year when he went away he Left his Wife, Bob and An Earchithinue Girl for me to keep, he has made an Exceeding Good use of his time having gave his and Bob's Gun away, and all his powder & Shott, he said he had Eat nothing for 2 days, I told him I had nothing for to Eat myself, when he went to his own tent I gave him Some dryed Meat, and 4 Loads of Shott.

23 APRIL Displayed my Flag in Honour of St. George; and the Leaders did the same, after acquainting them and explaining my reason. In the Afternoon the ice in the River broke up. A great many Geese and Swans were seen flying to the Northward. In the Evening we had a grand feast with Dancing, Drum. Drumming, Talking &c.

27 APRIL Musketoes plenty and bites without Mercy, they are worse than cold weather.[60]

William Flett and Saskatchewan ⌁ Vern Wishart, descendant

In 1793, William Flett and
his wife, Saskatchewan,
accompany Peter Fidler
in a search for a site on
which to build a trading
post for the HBC.

We discovered quite by accident in about 1964 that we had ancestry that went back to the Orkney Islands and to Canada's indigenous people. William Flett, an Orkney man, came west to work for the Hudson's Bay Company in 1782. He married a Cree woman named Saskatchewan....

Without their native wives I think these men would have had a hard time surviving and meeting native people....

Saskatchewan would accompany him on inland trips. She would do the things like repair moccasins, speak to the other native people, and open up dialogue. In that way she helped him to facilitate trade with the native people.

I have no idea where they met. I think that she may have been part of a home guard. These were native people who were close to the fort. The fort relied on them for guidance and so forth.

They were married *a la façon du pays*—according to the custom of the country. There were certain formalities that they went through and that was recognized as a marriage. They likely came to the Edmonton area in 1793. William Flett came with Peter Fidler who was a well known English surveyor. The Hudson's Bay Company wanted to set up a fort closer to their rival the North West Company. Flett, Fidler, and another fellow called Thomas traveled for 130 miles from Buckingham House near Elk Point. They arrived at the mouth of the Sturgeon River to complete a survey to determine the possibility of building a Fort Edmonton. In 1795 William Tomison, building on their expedition, went a little further and set up Edmonton House....

With Saskatchewan's help, and also because he was literate, William was promoted. The Hudson's Bay Company was strong on record-keeping and that is great if you are tracing your family history. We know Flett became a master and a canoe-man at Edmonton House from 1814 to 1820 and again from 1822 to 1823. "Master" meant that he could go out from the fort and trade with Indians. He would take some company men with him and they could trade outside the fort. "Canoe-man" meant that he was in charge of constructing canoes. And there Saskatchewan would be a big help. This is the story of my great-great-great-grandparents.[61]

John MacDonald of Garth worked as a labourer at Fort Augustus for the North West Company in the 1790s.

RIVALS ON THE RIVER

John MacDonald of Garth, NWC

Riding a swift horse in the fine valley of the Sascatchewan, abounding with buffaloes, deer and game of all sorts, was I've thought, the most pleasant part of our lives: we rode all day, following the progress of the brigade against a current of four knots.... I was ordered to join Mr. Hughes at Fort Augustus, with a complement of men and goods for the trade....

The canoes proceeded on the river while I did so with a couple of men by land. All was got ready for a long traverse, when there appeared on the opposite (the south) side of the river, a large band of Indians with horses in number, women, and all other accompaniments. Who were they? was the question. We were not picketed nicely, log houses in a square shape, with a gate between the houses. Shortly some chiefs came to the bank of the river to hold a parley, saying they came to sue for peace—they were the Mississouri Indians who had nearly cut off Mr. Finlay, and had destroyed the Hudson's Bay establishment, on the Bow River....

The Hudson's Bay Fort at the head was my old friend Mr. Tomison. The Forts were within musket shot of one another. As we required all the help we could give one another, Mr. Hughes and myself held a council of war with Mr. Tomison. He told us that after destroying their establishment and killing their men, he could not receive them as friends. Mr. Hughes and myself resolved that we should and accordingly I took my best horse, rode to their camp, and with an interpreter told them of Mr. Tomison. They loaded me with kindness and buffaloes fur robes. They had by this time pitched their tents—they told me they willingly made peace and would not molest the Hudson's Bay establishment—but would trade all they had with me. I was glad that I met them without any fears of any harm since I placed confidence in them.

They accordingly came on, and we made a good trade. Mr. Tomison biting his fingers at the result. He thought that they should not be allowed to trade as a punishment and I gained more of his ill-will, but I saved his life afterwards by seizing upon an Assiniboine's gun, while in the act of shooting him.[62]

William Tomison, HBC

12 MARCH 1798 Sent four men to fetch meat, and the rest employed within doors. Traded with the Indian and he went away, and at noon the Blood and Muddy River Indians arrived, eight-three able men and about 300 women and children, also two of the Cuttencha tribe which I sent for. Those have not brought any furs of any kind but by their account their country abounds with all kinds, but far off. Those that went for meat on Friday returned, brought the flesh of sixteen buffalo.

17 MARCH The men employed as on the preceding day, finished tying up the skins now brought, the quantity as follows: whole parchment beaver 20, wolves 940, foxes red 22, grey 3212, badgers 13, wolverenes 6, bears old grizzle 2, cub 2 and provisions of sorts 200 lbs. This band traded no less than 34 guns besides two given to the principal men. I have been

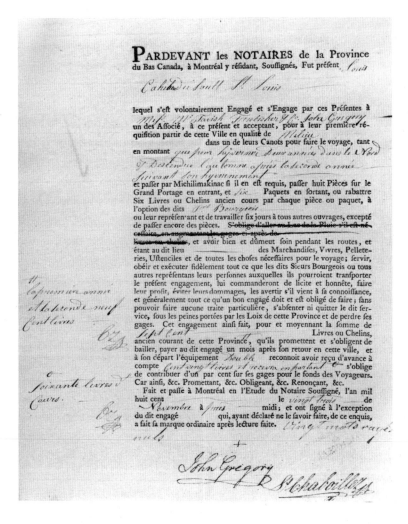

Louis Callihoo, a Mohawk from Ganawake, signed this contract in Montreal on November 23, 1800. He promised to serve the North West Company as a voyageur for two years in exchange for 1,600 pounds in hard currency. He spent the rest of his long life in the West with three wives, Marie Katis, Josephte Patenaude and Marie Patenaude. One of his sons, Michel Callihoo, signed an adhesion to Treaty 6 on behalf of the extended family in this area.

obliged to dress several of them with the best hats, for want of common ones, and had not hatchets for half of them and now more than three kegs of powder and three rolls of tobacco now in the house which would be little enough two months hence.[63]

THE DANCE OF SPIKANOGGAN

David Thompson

[The visitors from the eastern tribes] saw plainly the Natives of these countries had no great opinion of them, and giving up all thought of revenge, as they were about to separate for the winter, agreed to make a feast and perform all their dances, to which the Nahathaways were invited.

David Thompson, Canada's great explorer and mapmaker, witnessed the arrival of eastern aboriginal voyageurs at Fort Augustus and their first encounter with the people he called the Nahathaways.

The next day they all appeared in their best dresses; and the feast took place about noon of the choice pieces of the Bison and Red Deer; at which as usual, grace was said and responded to by the guests.

The feast being over the dances began by the Iroquois and their comrades. After a few common dances, they commenced their favorite dance of the grand Calumet, which was much admired and praised, and they requested the Nahathaways to dance their grand Calumet, to which they replied, they had no smoking dance. This elated the Iroquois and they began their War dance, from the discovery of the enemy to the attack and scalping of the dead, and the war hoop of victory. The Nahathaways praised them. The Iroquois, being now proud of their national dances, requested [to see] the Nahathaways'...War dance, and intimating they thought they had none, which was in a manner saying they were not warriors.

I felt for my old friends, and looking round, saw the smile of contempt on the lips of Spikanoggan (the Gun Case), a fine, stern warrior of about fifty years of age, with whom I had been long acquainted, and whom I knew excelled in the dance. I asked if he intended to take up the challenge, he said, he had no wish to show himself off in dancing before these strangers; "You certainly do not wish them to return to their own country and report of you as so many women. You Spikanoggan, your eye never pitied, nor your hand ever spared an enemy, is the fittest man to represent your country men in the War dance; and show these strangers what you are."

Somewhat nettled, he arose, put on a light war dress, and with his large dagger in his right hand he began the War dance: by the Scout, the Spy, the Discovery, the Return to Camp, the Council, the silent march to the ambuscade, the war whoop of attack, the tumult of the battle, the Yells of doubtful contest and the war whoop of victory; the pursuit, his breath short and quick the perspiration pouring down on him his dagger in the fugitive, and the closing war whoop of the death of his enemy run through our ears. The varying passions were strongly marked in his face, and the whole was performed with enthusiasm.

The perfect silence, and all eyes rivetted on him, showed the admiration of every one, and for which I rewarded him. The Iroquois seemed lost in surprise, and after a few minutes said, "Our dances please ourselves and also the white people and Indians wherever we go, but your dance is war itself to victory and to death." It was evident they were much mortified and at length one of them remarked that he did not scalp his enemy. To which Spikanoggan replied in contempt; "any old woman can scalp a dead man." I was much pleased with the effect this dance had on the Iroquois, it seemed to bring them to their senses, and showed them that the Indians of the interior countries were fully as good Warriors, Hunters, and Dancers, as themselves. They lost all their self conceit and arrogance but became plain well behaved men, left off talking of war, and turned to hunting.[64]

BUFFALO AND BABIES

Remembering Marie-Anne ⤳ **Liliane Coutu-Maisonneuve, descendant**
They worked here at Fort Edmonton for four years. Well, they lived here during the winter. I have the records where my great-great-great grandmother paid for her lodging with 60 beaver pelts. Jean-Baptiste Lagimodière was a voyageur, in trapping, so she would stay the winter months....He was with the first group that were free traders....She had come with one small child, Reine, who was born in Winnipeg, Pembina, and she had her second child here, Jean-Baptiste, too. His nickname was La Prairie, because he was born on the prairie about an hour out of here, near Battle River, south of Edmonton. Then they came back into the fort, and her third child was born in southern Alberta.... I would like this to be more recognized. Aboriginal and Métis and French-Canadian history has always been overlooked.

The Birth of La Prairie ⤳ **Georges Dugas, priest and family friend**
The day following J.B. Lagimodière and his companions struck their camp and started on the return trip to the Fort. It was then the month of August. Madame Lagimodière followed her husband on horseback, carrying her child with her in a moss bag which hung from one side of the saddle, while on the other side she carried a bag of provisions which by its weight counterbalanced the child and kept it from falling.

Madame Lagimodière was a good horsewoman and could ride nearly all day without resting when she was returning to take up winter quarters at the Fort. They often spent the summers at long distances from the Fort, and this year they had camped for some time in the neighborhood of Battle River. Two or three days after their adventure with the Indians they found themselves on a large prairie frequented by innumerable herds of buffalo and suddenly a band of these animals crossed their path. The presence of a herd of buffalo produces an astonishing effect on the horses. Without being urged by his rider a horse will often start off in pursuit of them with a fervor that it is impossible to check. A hunter thus carried into the midst of these animals, rushing in a mad race, runs the very greatest danger.

Unfortunately on this occasion Madame Lagimodière was mounted on a horse accustomed to this mode of procedure and as soon as he caught sight of the animals, without a thought of his burden, he took the bit in his teeth and galloped after the herd. Burdened with the two bags which hung on either side of the horse, in one of which was her child, the poor woman every instant expected that she would be thrown to the earth and trampled under foot by the buffalo. She commended herself to God and clung with all her strength to the horse's mane. She could not calculate how long the race lasted, she was only certain that it was horribly long. When her husband by wheeling and cutting across the horse's path succeeded in stopping his flight she was on the point of succumbing to fear and fatigue. This was about three o'clock in the afternoon. They pitched their tents on a rising piece of ground near some trees and it was there, some hours after the race that Madame Lagimodière gave birth to her second child, who they nicknamed La Prairie because he was born in the middle of the prairie.[65]

Marie-Anne Gaboury Lagimodière's journey is captured in this fanciful engraving published in 1902. She and her voyageur husband Jean-Baptiste Lagimodière and their baby, Reine, arrived at Edmonton House on 30 September 1808. She was the first known Quebec woman to travel this far West and lived on the prairies until her death at the age of 96.

BATTLES ON THE PRAIRIES

A War Party at Fort Augustus ⌐ Alexander Henry the Younger, 1809
This morning early Le Boeuf qui Bois, a chief of the Blood Indians, made his appearance on the South side of the River and called to be crossed over, which was done accordingly. This was something uncommon for a great Chief to arrive ahead and without sending in for Tobacco by the young men, but the cause was this. The Tribe during the Summer had formed a War Party to search for the Crees and had crossed the River below this Place for that purpose, but failing in their undertaking, they appear'd desirous of wreaking their vengeance upon our people at this Establishment but

fortunately their tracks were discovered in the course of the day, and our people kept a good watch during the night. The fellows actually came near the Fort but observing our people had received the alarm and were upon their guard, they dare not attempt an attack, but contented themselves in taking away all the horses they could find, which was only twelve.[66]

A Vicious Attack of Measles ⤳ Francis Heron—HBC, Edmonton House, 1821

All the different tribes of indians who inhabit the plains and thickwoods in this quarter are at present at variance with each other, and in this hostile state have lost all their former respect for the traders, whom they rob of their property, insult in their Forts, and even menace their lives without provocation, and what is most mortifying that we must bear the whole, having it not in our power to chastise them for their crimes. But if there are not some measures adopted soon, for the purpose of punishing them for their offenses, the traders cannot attempt coming to this part of the Country unless at the risk of their lives and property.[67] ...

One day's march from the Forts... they were attacked with the Measles which disease proved fatal to great numbers of them, and those who survived through grief for the loss of their relatives, gave over all thoughts of hunting furs, and resigned themselves to mourning for the rest of the Winter.

This dreadful disease (for so it was at that Season of the Year) as well as the hooping Cough prevailed during the great part of the Winter among all the different tribes of Indians who trade with us at this District and proved equally fatal to all. It is impossible to describe, or for any person (except those who were eye witnesses) to form any idea of the state of wretchedness which these diseases reduced the unfortunate natives. The North West Company on the first appearance of these diseases tried every means to exasperate the Natives against us, as well as against the Settlers at Red River, by imposing upon their minds that it was the Settlers who first brought these diseases to Red River, and that it was the English (as we are called) who brought them from there to this part of the Country, and notwithstanding every argument has been used to convince them to the contrary, yet, many of them are still of opinion that it was the Colonists who first introduced these diseases into this Country for the purpose of destroying the Natives, however through time I hope we will be able to convince them of the error into which they have been led by the false representations of our inveterate foes.[68]

Raid at Fort Edmonton ⌁ John Rowand, chief factor, HBC

12 OCTOBER 1826 Early in the morning the alarm was again given that more Stone Indians had attempted to steal the horses....

All went off in a band in search of the Thieves, which they found, when collected together to consist of about 30 armed men. Their hiding place was in our haystacks, but finding themselves discovered and closely pursued they turned about to give battle when directly several shots were exchanged almost in sight of the Fort & 3 Stone Indians killed near the spot. The [gun]fire began when John Welch the Interpreter was severely wounded in the breast and arm, who made for the Fort, and seeing the Stone Indian that had been a little before brought into the Fort trying to make his Escape, he had still strength enough to rush

John Rowand, chief factor at Fort Edmonton, was the most powerful Hudson's Bay Company trader on the North Saskatchewan River for three decades. Local people knew him by his nicknames— One-Pound-One or Iron Shirt—and his fiery reputation.

upon him and stab him with a bayonet and the Indian [Forcier] Expired almost Instantly, and himself Welch who dropped down as if Dead and was given over as such, however a little while after he came to again after vomiting a quantity of blood and after Examination found his wound not to be mortal, but very near it. The Stone Indians during this time continued to fly across the Point of the Fort to the Edge of the River, where it is supposed they had previously made holes in the ground as the last resource in case of being pursued where they kept firing for some time, & we had the mortification to see 2 of our men and 2 Indians (Sinam and the little Assiniboine) brought home wounded, one of the men Breland got an arrow in the Breast which I fear will kill him, Pepin our Blacksmith, a ball in the haunch, Sinam the Cree, one of our hunters, got a Ball through the left shoulder, the little Assiniboine a Ball through his Neck and one arm broken.[69]

COUNTRY MARRIAGES

My Wife as Long as We Lived ⌁ John Harriott, HBC

When I say married, I mean according to the custom of the country, which was by an agreement between the father of the girl and the person who was going to take the girl for wife.... I consider it as binding as if celebrated by an archbishop. I was married this way myself.... The marriage according to the custom above described, was considered a marriage for [life]. I considered it so. I know of hundreds of people living and dying with the woman they took in that way without any other formalities....

A servant of the company is obliged to obtain permission of a superior officer before he takes a wife. A superior officer acts from his own sense of propriety; he may do what he likes. When I took a wife as above mentioned, I made a solemn promise to her father to live with her and treat her as my wife as long as we both lived. I kept this promise until her death which occurred in the North West in 1830. Had I come to civilized community, I believe I should have married according to the civilised form of solemnising marriage. I should have done so to please

people and to conform to the custom of society. I would not consider myself more strongly bound to that woman as before.[70]

Tragedy in the Rockies ⟿ Edna Rowand Cramer and E.J. Don Rowand, descendants

Mr. Harriott, who retired, wanted to bring his wife and children back to see her father Mr. Pruden. They had a boy two years old and a nursing baby. The Indian wife of one of Astor's chief traders made the trip with them as a nurse for the children. They were crossing the Rocky Mountains on horseback and on foot with an escort of about 60 to 80 men. One night they camped in the Miette area.... During the night Mrs. Harriott, who was a large woman, rolled over in her sleep and accidentally smothered her son. Momentarily crazed by the loss of her baby she rushed out of the tent and wandered off into the night. This area abounded in hot springs and canyons; no trace of her was ever found. The nurse took charge of the little baby and kept her alive until the party reached Fort Edmonton. John Rowand had imported the first cows and here the baby was able to

Born in 1830, Margaret Harriott arrived at Fort Edmonton as a baby rescued after the tragic death of her mother, Margaret Pruden. She grew up to marry John Rowand's eldest son at Edmonton House. The artist Paul Kane accompanied the couple to Fort Pitt by dog sled, and created a painting of the honeymoon trip in 1847.

5 | Fine weather, early in the morning the Cree went off Valle and Smith weeding the potatoes, Pepin & Pag as usual — a circumstance somewhat uncommon took place on thursday last, the Children having caught two small hares of about four days old brought them to our Room, and a Cat that had kittens of about fifteen days old ran from under the Closet and carried off one of them, some time after she came forward very shy, and bore away the other one, and our endeavours to extricate them proved ineffectual, a few days since we however observed that the Cat was

June.

giving them suck and has nourished them in common with her young — what the result would have been we cannot conjecture for unluckily they both fell through a hole in the corner of the flooring this evening, and were killed

get milk. They kept the baby in Edmonton for a year until she was old enough to eat solid food and then they brought her to Winnipeg to her grandmother. The baby's name was Margaret Harriott.[71]

JOYS AND SORROWS: FAMILY LIFE AT EDMONTON HOUSE

Edmonton House Post Journal

2 APRIL 1824 The Fall Indians...have given us the opportunity of relating a curious instance of maternal affection. One of their women had a young and only child, that had died in the early part of the winter, and ever since that time, as a token of her affection for it, carrys its remains in a frozen state wrapped up in a piece of embossed blanket, along with her, where ever she goes, and occasionally lets up groans and cries over it, with the

usual ceremonies of inflicting wounds upon herself and cutting her hair. But we should suppose as the warm weather is now coming on, that she must part with the beloved objects, and consign it to the earth, where it should have been. But this is not their general way of burying the dead. They erect a temporary scaffold, where the remains of the dead are laid, wrapped up in Buffaloe Skins, and are thus left & exposed to be devoured by Wolves and other rapacious animals.[72]

Edmonton House Post Journal

5 JUNE 1828 A circumstance somewhat uncommon took place on Thursday last, the children having caught two small hares of about four days old brought them to our Room, and a Cat that has kittens of about fifteen days old ran from under the [closet] and carried off one of them, some time after she came forward very sly, and bore away the other one, and our endeavouring to extricate them proved ineffectual, a few days since we however observed that the Cat was giving them suck and has nourished them in common with her young—what the result would have been we cannot conjecture for unluckily they both fell through a hole in the corner of the flooring this evening and were killed.[73]

Alexander Ross, visitor

An abominable custom is very prevalent among the traders on this side the mountains, and Edmonton is entitled to its own share of odium—the keeping so many starving dogs about the establishment in summer for their imaginary services in winter. There were no less than fifty-two snarling and growling curs; and they are said to be very useful and profitable animals....[T]he nuisance of their presence in a fort is beyond endurance: they are the terror of every woman and child after dark. Nor can a stranger step from one door to another without being interrupted by them; and, worst of all, the place is kept like a kennel: in wet weather the horrid stench is intolerable....

Adjoining the cultivated fields is a very fine level race-ground, of two miles or more in length; horse-racing being one of the chief amusements of the place during the summer season: and here we may observe that Fort des Prairies is not only celebrated for fine women, but for fine horses. Mr. Rowand, a man of active habits, good humour, and fond of riding and racing as a pastime, keeps some of the best horses the country can produce, and we were favoured with a specimen of them. I rode round the race-ground a chestnut sixteen hands high, and very spirited. I must not fail to observe, after what has been already stated on the subject of horses, that many of them, both for size and muscle, were as fine animals as ever I had seen in the country.[74]

Edmonton House Post Journal

1 JANUARY 1828 God forbid this Year to terminate with us in the manner it commences; lamenting over the mangled Body of a Poor sufferer. This morning the men and half Breeds anxious to salute the rising Sun assembled before the hall Door for that purpose....Our Interpreter Welsh (poor man) went to one of the Bastions to fire a small Iron piece as a signal for those at the Door. The dirty and rejected Instrument was heard and an immediate volley from the men ensued, without even the faintest Idea of what had so unfortunately happened therein. The Cannon had bursted and literally carried away the miserable man's limbs. Two larger Pieces entered his body, the one through the collar bone and the other through the Breast. He lay in the Bastion in this condition either dead or suffering the most excruciating Pains and agony of mind as not a soul went to sooth his dying moments, nor did we know of this wretched Catastrophy until later. Mr. Rowand—after the people were all collected in the hall—made several enquiries respecting the absence of Welsh who, having taken an Oath never to drink any more liquor, was one thought such was the cause and that he had hidden himself until the ceremony would be over.

After a dismissal of the People Mr. Rowand observed to me while standing out at the Front Fort Gate the derangement of the Bastion which the report of the Cannon had created and Himal our Boat builder being near...was called to examine it. He immediately went up into it when—awful to relate—he descried the bloody Body of Poor Welsh. God Almighty what an object!... the Iron pieces were strewn in every corner of the Bastion and the very flesh of the unfortunate man hanging to the Roof—oh spectacle for a poor young woman and 2 sweet Babes (his family). What a lesson? Man in the midst of mirth and gaiety is in one moment cut off and launched into eternity.

2 JANUARY 1828 This morning two carpenters were ordered to make a coffin for the remains of the poor deceased. Mr. Rowand and myself with [Delorme] and [Robidoux] attended the dead body during the night and the whole of the People during the day joined in supplicating the Almighty to receive his departed Spirit and towards evening he was laid in the

ground interred in the most decent manner our means afforded. He was followed by many of our People who had tears of pity over his grave at the deplorable conclusion of his existing.[75]

JIMMY JOCK

"Always at Liberty and Ready for Mischief" ⌐ **A.D. Pambrum, visitor, 1835**

His name was James Bird, alias Jimmy Jock, who was educated in England, and a large finely built man, very fair for a halfbreed. His beautiful raven hair hung down in ringlets to his shoulders. He was undoubtedly the finest specimen of a man I ever saw. Disagreeing with the Hudson's Bay Company, he left and joined his Cree relations, then one tribe and another. There were Cree, Blackfoot, Sioux and Assiniboine. He boasted families in each.

His stay with one tribe depended on his whims, imaginary injuries or a desire to revenge supposed injuries. If Cree, he would join the Blackfoot; if Blackfoot, the Sioux and so on, and whichever tribe he headed was always victorious. I do not know that he did much fighting himself, but he planned and the warriors executed. The association with his name was enough to ensure success. He was therefore courted by all, even by the Company, who paid him annually a certain amount in goods, to secure his goodwill. His wants were therefore supplied without any effort on his part, and was consequently always at liberty and ready for mischief. His movements were therefore closely watched by all inimical tribes and by trappers as well, for none knew when and where he was going to strike. He has even been known to go as far south as the Snake River in the vicinity of Fort Boise. Booty he wanted, and would have, and it was no doubt that led to his visit to the [American] emigrant highway. In fact one man who knew Jimmy Jock well, told me he saw him on a butte watching the Snakes attack an emigrant train. The man was travelling in the same train and lost his horses.[76]

Jimmy Jock Bird was the legendary son of Oomenahowish, a Cree woman and Chief Factor James Curtis Bird of Edmonton House. He married Sally Peigan and lived among the southern tribes, visiting Edmonton House frequently during his lifespan of almost 100 years.

"Quite a Character" ⤙ Fran Gosché, descendant

Jamie Jock is kind of my hero. He's my great-great uncle. When I first started doing genealogical research I went to the City Archives at the Prince of Wales Armouries, and I asked if they had anything on the Birds. They told me they had one article, and said it wasn't very complimentary. I told them I was interested. Anyway it wasn't complimentary because he was quite a character alright....

One of my lowest points in doing this research was when I found out the truth about what happened to the First Nations people and the Métis in the river valley. For some reason I had a real problem coping with the realization of what these people went through, the same persecution as the people of the Red River.... A few months later I was still trying to decide whether or not to go on with my quest. It was late one night and I went into my kitchen for a glass of water before going to bed. I noticed the northern lights in the sky. I put on my jacket and went out into the backyard and stood there, watching them. I couldn't remember ever seeing them so beautiful before. I thought of my great-great uncle Jamie Jock....Tears filled my eyes, and I cried. I couldn't believe how good it made me feel. The next day I felt so much better. I decided not to give up. I have to finish this project. Since then there are other similar incidents that have happened to me. I won't go into it now but I feel Jamie Jock is trying to encourage me.

Jamie Jock didn't like how the new settlers were changing the country, and how they were treating his people. He also knew it couldn't be stopped. He made a decision how he wanted to live his life, and he did exactly that. He did what he believed was right for him, and he was true to himself. That is why he's one of my heroes and I admire him. I think he was one of the most colourful people in our history, and he grew up at Fort Edmonton....

I also think all of the women who lived in and around that fort were a major part of the history of this area. Without them I don't think the men would have survived. It's a shame that there isn't anything—anything at all—in this city, saying they even lived here. They are completely ignored. I would like something written in the history book about these people. I would like any pictures, any information anybody has, to be displayed somewhere. I think there should be a monument down in that river valley dedicated to all those people, who worked so hard.... I know some of their relatives from there, as well as white people who lived in the fort, their family

members are buried in that cemetery where the power plant is. Maybe they could have a little park there, especially for this remembering. [77]

QUEEN OF THE PLAINS

John Rowand

My son John went to the place reported to be ritch in Beaver, but it is not so.... John met face to face with a war party of 1000 men and upward of 200 women with them, and at their head the Queen of the Plains—the latter with her army were very kind indeed to John he was two days with them....[78]

Composed of Crees, Saulteaux and Stone Indians from far and near, the best of it they had another Queen Victoria at their head, who had the command of the party an army, her face was as with a nail. She was to do wonders when they would see the Black feet tribes, the many which vanished in disappointments, they fell in with a small party of black feet who was all killed but the latter fought the like a devil to the last they killed as many Crees as was killed themselves and wounded a great many besides. A party of Kootonnees, the band and free men from Columbia who came out to hunt Buffaloe the Piegan lands had a Battle with the Black feet and killed twenty four of the latter. But it is enough about Indian war.... The war party he saw was very kind to him even the Queen of the Plains.[79]

In the early nineteenth century, the Cree, Blackfoot, Nakoda and Métis majority built a regional economy and a vibrant culture around the buffalo hunt. They hunted the herds on the plains through the summer and set up buffalo pounds in the late fall for mass harvesting in December. Lt. George Back published this fanciful depiction of a Cree buffalo pound on the western plains in 1823.

Robert Rundle, Methodist missionary

22 FEBRUARY 1841 Started in the morning for the Fort & the scenery increased in interest as I approached it. After some time we saw Indian Boys & a young man & were told that a party of Black Feet were near. I must confess I felt much quaking when I thought of encountering these savages but this was nature & thanks to a kind Providence was only short lived. On the present occasion the following passage of Scripture was powerfully applied to my mind, "Fear not for I am with thee." When near the Fort a few Indians were seen coming towards us, one of whom, by his dress appeared to be a chief. My man said they were Crees. When they drew near nothing could exceed the delight which they expressed on seeing me. "They are the [Rocky Mountain] Crees," thought I, "& are thus expressing their delight at my coming amongst them." But who in reality were they who welcomed me so warmly & cordially? Who? Why the terrible Black Feet about whom I had felt a shuddering only a few moments before.[80]

Jean-Baptiste Thibault, Oblate missionary

8 JULY 1842 I left the Red River on April 20, with one man to guide me across the prairies that I had to traverse. I was on one horse and the other carried my luggage. I arrived here on June 19, happily enough though after many little difficulties. Thanks to God, my ministry was useful enough on my way wherever I met people, here especially, in spite of the efforts of a protestant minister, who spares nothing to hinder me from succeeding. The weapons he uses to fight against me are those ordinarily made use of by people of his sort, that is to say, lies and slander. The Indians to whom I have been able to speak have come to me, and I think they will persevere. They seem well disposed.... I am to spend the rest of the summer among very wicked nations, who could very well scalp me one of these days. I have but one man to accompany me and to guide me on my journeys.[81]

John Rowand

20 JUNE 1843 The worse thing for the trade is those ministers & Priests—the natives will never work half so well now—they like praying & singing. If Mr. Thingheaute [Thibeault] is allowed to go back again to the Saskatchewan we shall all be Saints after a time. Rundle says that all the

Catholics will go to [hell], as for himself he is sure of going straite to heaven when he dies.[82]

Sweetgrass, speaking to a missionary
Leave me be, when my time comes, I will tell you.[83]

"IT WAS SLAVISH WORK"

"Pretty Tough Grub..." ⌐ **William Gladstone, labourer, 1850**
Soon we had nothing to eat but buffalo meat which had gone bad in the ice house. It was pretty tough grub but it was that or nothing.

We planted plenty of potatoes, but they would not let us have any to eat until the return of the boats. As a treat we were allowed a few on Sundays and some of us managed to steal a few between times but when we were caught they made us feel that it was hardly worth the price. There was a lot of smutty wheat in the stores and once a week we were allowed some of that. After washing it several times at the river, we ground it in a steel coffee mill and made a cake of the meal. We also had some barley which we used to pound in a basin hollowed out of a log, making the hulls into a kind of soap.

The other men kicked a good deal about their grub, but as for me, I had the digestion of a goat and I don't think that tin tacks or strychnine could have killed me at that time....

A bit of dog meat, or owl or horse, was a luxury to us and although there were plenty of cows at Edmonton, we were not allowed any of their milk. It was all used for butter-making, but we occasionally got the leavings of the churn.

We used to comfort ourselves by talking of the tea and flour and good times we would have when the boats returned.[84]

William Gladstone's lively account of his life at Fort Edmonton in the 1850s was published in the Rocky Mountain Echo later in his life. Here he appears with his granddaughter Nellie.

Hitched to a Boat ⌐ John Norris, tracker, 1850

Eight men were hitched to each boat and it was slavish work....We were practically transported: it was of no use to rebel....But you've no thanks for us for opening up the country, though I believe if we hadn't opened up the cart trail to Winnipeg there would not be as many settlers on the prairies today....We found the work "tracking" pretty hard. Some men used to be so tired they could not eat. They would roll themselves in a blanket after a day's work and roll in like dead men....The first time I was on, we had no rest all day.

We would eat the pemmican we carried in our pockets. But in case of a head wind we got some rest. We had to rush through the trip to get the goods in to the posts on time. Half the time we were wet to our belts....In winter our work was hard too—running dogs. We would make 40 to 50 miles a day if the trail was light and good—if there were no snowdrifts.[85]

Frank Norris, descendant

John Norris was my great-grandfather. He was born in 1826 in Caiphness Scotland....At age sixteen my great-grandfather went to sea and spent six years at sea on a trading schooner. He made a number of trips to Greenland, I believe. He didn't like the sea—although it paid reasonably well.

In 1846, John boarded the Hudson's Bay steamer "Prince Rupert" from Caiphness in the Orkney Islands. He landed in York Factory near the close of summer, spent three weeks in York Factory and then set out with the Saskatchewan Brigade. Norris was attached to Fort Pitt for eighteen years, first as a labourer and then as a boat man. He made yearly trips between Edmonton and York Factory. They tracked the boats, with eight men per boat. He said it was sluggish work. In the winter they would run dogs, 40 or 50 miles per day.

He was married in Fort Pitt in 1852 to Mary Pelletier, a Métis woman, with whom he had thirteen children. Later he married Bella Fraser at Edmonton—she was the daughter of Colin Fraser and she was also Métis. She had no children and died quite young of cancer. Then he married Frazine Laplante and had seven children.

John Norris and George Flett were in charge of the first brigade of Red River carts coming from Winnipeg. It was 1864. They had 200 carts. The trip took three and a half months to travel from Winnipeg to Edmonton. They made annual trips with this brigade of ox-carts....

His first home outside the fort was near the place where 109th Avenue and 123rd Street are today, which was on the St. Albert Trail at that time. There was eight blocks of bush between it and the fort. It became a stopping house and it wasn't uncommon to have 30 or 40 people for meals.

There is one story told about a time when they were sitting down to a meal and they had a black man at the table. Someone spoke up and said, "We can't associate with a black person." So John Norris got up and said, "Anyone who is unhappy with the situation, pick up your pay and leave." And that was the end of it....He was a very astute businessman, although he was illiterate....They say his estate was worth about three-quarter of a million dollars when he died in 1916.[86]

"I FELT SORRY FOR THEM"

Albert Lacombe, Oblate missionary

SUMMER 1852 One might say that the way of life of these men, during the summer months, was as hard as that of the African slave.

At night they camped on the river bank. There, crushed with fatigue, and constantly tormented by the terrible mosquitoes, they were obliged to prepare their miserable meal of pemmican and dry meal with river water as a beverage. I who enjoyed the company of the bourgeois and clerks was better provided with food, and had a tent to protect me for the night and in bad weather. Looking at these poor men to who I could give no relief, I felt sorry for them....

Think of it! At three in the morning, after a few hours rest on the bare ground, to hear the cry: "Get up! Get up!" Then to be yoked to the cable to haul the barge, all in walking in the water, over stones, in mud holes, along precipices, and at times in the water up to their necks, and that, beneath a burning sun or in a drenching rain till nightfall, that is, till nine o'clock at night. Those who have not witnessed such can have no idea of the cruel fatigue of these voyages which they called "going out to sea."

It was a monotonous two month journey. I was constantly facing Mr. Rowand, a few clerks who slept or passed their time reading or smoking,

Albert Lacombe was born of mixed heritage in St-Sulpice, Lower Canada. Arriving at Fort Edmonton in 1852, the Oblate priest served the families of Lac Ste. Anne and founded St. Albert in 1861 before moving south to work among the Blackfoot tribes. The Father Lacombe Chapel in St. Albert, believed to be the oldest surviving building in the province, commemorates his life. When Lacombe died in Midnapore, Alberta, in 1916, he left behind detailed letters, notebooks, a short memoir, as well as dictionaries, grammar texts and translated religious works in the Cree and Blackfoot languages.

and our workmen, who spoke but little. It was a matter of French, English and Cree. As for myself, after my spiritual exercises, I tried to spend my time doing all the good possible. I undertook a serious study of English, but especially of Cree. During their free moments the Métis very willingly taught me all they could of their beautiful tongue. A knowledge of the Saulteux idiom was of great help since these two tongues have so many analogies and similarities, especially with regard to rules of grammar. I continue to thank God for having given me this strong liking for the study of the Indian languages. Though not gifted with a good memory, I never became discouraged. And, though this type of work could be boresome, I easily caught on to the accent, and my desire to be able to express myself, helped me overcome all difficulties. It was then that I took the resolution that with time and patience I would compile a Cree dictionary and grammar, having as basis the data already given by Father Thibault....

Finally, on the afternoon of September 19, we arrived at Fort Edmonton, where the crew was awaited with impatience. Métis, mostly women, and Indians, covered the shore and the hillsides to cheer our arrival. The English flag with the honorable Company's coat of arms, floated over one of the bastions. The canon and gunfire announced to all that we had tobacco, munitions, and booty for another year. I hurried to shake hands with each of the Christians making up that crowd, for, that day, they became my children and parishioners. There are moments and circumstances ever to be remembered in the life of a missionary when he reaches the land of his apostolate. I met Mr. Rowand's three daughters, true Métis, who knew only the Cree language. The only learning they had was the religious instruction Father Thibault had given them. These excellent Christians were very devoted in giving the missionary priest a most agreeable hospitality, whenever he came to the Fort.[87]

THE CEREMONY OF THE TRADE

Peter Erasmus, as told to Henry Thompson

A week had passed since quiet had again settled on the fort. Then two Blackfoot arrived at the gate and were given admittance. They were envoys who had been sent ahead to notify the factor of the arrival of their band the next day. It was customary for any band of Indians to send word ahead and receive tobacco to smoke the peace pipe the night before their arrival. This was an indication of their intentions for a trade mission.

The next forenoon a big band arrived. The men were all mounted on good horses. The horsemen came in sight first as they were strung along a deep ravine that enters the Saskatchewan on the south side. They were followed by a long line of dogs and loaded pack horses. They followed the flat upriver until they were about opposite the fort, then crossed over the river. A number of other horsemen now appeared above the flat; these I presume were guards to protect their rear.

It was a picturesque sight to watch from the heights of the bastion where I had gone to get a better view. The Blackfoot took up a position

west of the fort, on a flat up from the river. I was somewhat worried for the Pigeon Lake Crees who were stationed near the south stockade of the fort, but apparently they were to enjoy immunity because they were under protection of the fort.

The next morning I was again on the bastion where the men had been stationed in preparation for the reception of the Blackfoot. A horse was led up to a teepee where we could plainly see that he was being loaded with all kinds of tanned hides and furs. We could not see exactly what was placed on the horse but the men told me what the pack would probably contain.

The chief held the line as they made their way towards the fort, followed by a bodyguard and a troop of singers whose voices could be heard quite distinctly from where we stood. As they advanced towards the fort they continued what I thought was a weird but melodious tone, till they almost reached the gate. The chief and his bodyguard all held their guns towards the sky and discharged them. The first bastion gun

Born of Cree and Danish ancestry, Peter Erasmus worked as an interpreter and guide at Fort Edmonton in the 1850s. He was an influential translator for the Palliser expedition; at the Treaty 6 negotiations at Fort Carlton and Fort Pitt; and in the adhesion talks at Fort Edmonton that brought local First Nations into the treaty in 1877 and 1878. A trader and trapper in later life, he died at Whitefish Lake in 1931.

Peter Erasmus was a young Métis interpreter for Rev. Thomas Woolsey at Edmonton House in 1856. He described the local fur trade and his recollections of treaty negotiations when he dictated his memoir, *Buffalo Days and Nights,* at the age of 87.

was fired, and at a signal flashed back from the gate, a second volley was fired from the other cannon. Then the gate was swung open. The firing of Indian guns was an indication of peaceful purposes, as their guns were empty and could do no harm.

The factor was standing at the gate to welcome the visitors. The chief then handed the line to him and he passed the line to the chief clerk, who walked with the chief towards the trading house where the door opened at a signal from the factor.

The Indian house where the actual trading was done was a special building, extremely long, divided in the middle and containing two chimneys, one at each end. A door giving entrance for the traders was fastened with a heavy bar similar in construction to the outer gate, and opened inwards. Bill showed me where the guards would be stationed for the whole of the trading. This was a precautionary measure in case of treachery. From where we lay above we could through portholes command a view of every part of the room.

The room was divided in such a manner that any goods handed out would pass through a small opening about breast high. A ledge on the inside wall allowed the display of any goods asked for. Too large a display at one time excited the Indians and made them difficult to handle.

A clerk appeared from behind the small door and handed out a black suit of clothes with brass buttons, a stove pipe hat that had a red feather attached to the band in front, and a special medal with the coat of arms of the Hudson's Bay Company. The medal was fastened to the chief's new coat with a great display of ceremony.

A ninety-pound roll of tobacco was shoved out of the window and also a ten-gallon keg of rum. This latter, of course, had been heavily diluted with about two-thirds water. A quantity of ammunition, shot, powder, and bullets—not a large amount but I thought a quite generous amount— made a fairly well-balanced exchange for the chief's horseload of skins and furs.

The Blackfoot chief then gave an oration which I presumed indicated his appreciation of the generosity of the factor and a promise of good fellowship for him and his people in their trade with the Company.

The factor made a return speech, translated back to Blackfoot language by his interpreter, in which he spoke of his high regard for the chief and his admiration for the fine braves accompanying him. On behalf of the great Hudson's Bay Company he hoped that these fine Blackfoot people would continue their trade in good fellowship and friendliness with the Company to their own mutual benefit. Referring to himself as but a poor servant, he expressed his personal feeling for the whole Blackfoot people as the finest examples of all the native people.

The singers, who had been patiently waiting outside the door while all this was going on, were now summoned by one of the chief's guards. They all came inside in an orderly manner, picked up the presents, and were ready to depart. The chief, who had stood waiting, now strode towards the door, followed by the two guards a pace behind, and the singers swung in behind, two abreast. When they passed the door they again started to sing...their voices blended together with a thrilling penetration that affected me with something of fear and dread. Perhaps my memory of the massacred Crees at Saddle Lake was still heavy on my mind. If this singing was intended for good will and friendliness then I wanted none of their war songs. The careful precautions in the loaded guns held in readiness for any eventuality were to my mind well justified.

None of the usual work was carried on during the Blackfoot visit as the men were all assigned to garrison duty and alerted to the necessity of extreme care. I was greatly impressed with the efficiency with which this was accomplished. Each man assumed his task and was relieved of duty without any apparent orders from any particular officer.

The exchange of goods for tanned hides, fur, pemmican, fresh meat, or any other article of Indian make was done by barter. Lead bullets were used to signify the value of approximately fifty cents. A pile of furs, skins, or other articles was valued by the trader and an equal number of bullets pushed towards the seller as an estimate of his valuation. From there on they bargained to an agreement, and the final sale completed. It was a cumbersome procedure and took up a great deal of time, but a system that had become a custom and was satisfactory to native understanding. In my opinion the quality of the goods offered for sale were good value when one considers the tremendous labour and cost entailed in the transportation, especially upriver by hand as the boats were towed against the current.

The Blackfoot departed as soon as they had traded all their products of the hunt. Five or more riders started out ahead. The chief led the main body with his personal bodyguard of a half-dozen mounted riders, the women and children following. I noticed that a number of riders took up positions at the rear and flanked the main body of the band on both sides.[88]

Paul Kane painted this scene of Fort Edmonton and the nearby camps on the river flats from a sketch he made in September 1846.

RIPE FOR BUSINESS

"Those Desiring It Might Purchase Kegs" ⟶ Henry Moberly, labourer, Fort Edmonton

After 9 o'clock in the morning the Indians, a limited number at a time, were admitted to the Indian room. This was reached through a narrow palisaded passage from the small gate in the stockade surrounding the fort. No liquor could at this time be bought for consumption on the premises, though those desiring it might purchase kegs to be carried away with them. The rule that these kegs must not be broached except in camp was never violated. There, the purchasers often traded with the others.

Besides liquor, their purchases in those days were limited almost entirely to ammunition, guns, tobacco and vermilion in small buckskin bags. The latter was often mixed with flour—one of paint to five of flour. The liquor, Jamaica rum, was first mixed in the ratio of one part rum and seven water. As the trade progressed it was diluted more and more until little was left but the smell....

Before the speeches began each Indian was given a drink. The head chief then rose and made his talk, asking the master to pity and favour them, proclaiming that they had done their best and would try to do better in the future. The master followed, saying he was well pleased that they had striven to make good hunts and had no doubt, as they had said, that their next visit would prove even more satisfactory. The speeches ended, each Indian received another drink and they were turned out of the fort. All gates were closed. The trade, meaning the barter in rum, then began and might be kept up all night and until nine next morning, when it ceased summarily....While a liquor trade was in progress the fort was closed tight; every door and gate in the stockade firmly locked and secured, and no Indian was admitted within the walls of the fort.[89]

"...And the Fun Commenced" ⌐ William Gladstone

About the 20th of July a band of Indians came to the Fort to trade. I had never seen any of them before and I was told that this was their first visit to Edmonton. Some of them were South Peigans. Some were Big Butte Indians from the valley of the Arkansas. An advance party came to tell us that the main body would soon follow, then commenced great preparations to receive them, in which we all shared. Some of us hauled water and mixed it with the rum, and others got out the Blunderbusses (most alarming looking affairs with great bell mouths) and mounted loaded them on the walls and our one canon was dragged out and loaded in case of trouble. We took care to lay in a good supply of water, in case of emergencies.

On the fourth day they came and there were 1,000 of them and when they had made camp, each chief, at the head of his tribe, marched up to the gate, where the boss and his interpreter and all the rest of us stood, with guns in our hands. The chiefs shook hands with the boss, and by way of salute, the Indians discharged their firearms and we returned the compliment.

Then the red men filed into the Indian House and the fun commenced. Each of us was in charge of a kettle of mixed rum and every Indian was given a dram of firewater, by way of a starter. Speech-making followed, washed down by another dram, then some more talkee-talkee, and another drink until every man jack of them had absorbed five drams and was ripe for business.[90]

One-Pound-One's Last Fight ⌐ William Gladstone

Our boss was an incarnate fiend, the harshest man, at that time, in the whole service. He was a Mr. Rowand, one of the old bourgeois of the North-West Company and would curse you blind if you looked sideways. We were careful to keep our eyes straight.[91] ...

Old One-Pound-One kept us all on the jump. He was one of the most fluent swearers I ever met. His language then was a continuous flow of red hot explosives and the man who happened to be nearest him when he was busy, used to get the worst scorching. I avoided him during his periods of verbal eruptions as carefully as if he had been a volcano on duty.[92] ...

In a few days, the York boats left, and One-Pound-One went with them, but he only got as far as Fort Pitt, where he kicked the bucket.

I think his death gave more genuine pleasure to us than anything he could have done for us.[93] ...

A son of One-Pound-One came from Fort Pitt to take charge for the summer at Edmonton. He told us of the particulars of his father's death.

It seems that when the men arrived at Fort Pitt they got into a general fight and raised a row that reached the old man's ears. He hastened to the scene of the fight, fuming with rage and frothing at the mouth. He got himself worked up to a great pitch, trying to stop the fight and swore like a mad man.

Suddenly he dropped in his tracks and when lifted up was found to be stone dead. When the men who were on the river bank heard the news there was great rejoicing and all around the country, wherever that news went, all that knew him and had suffered from his brutal tyranny was glad to hear that his day was done. He had not a single friend in the whole country.

His son threatened to kill the man who was the innocent cause of his father's death, but that man escaped to the woods...fled from pursuit. One night they camped at Vermilion River. The fugitive, whose name was Paul, took his axe to cut timber for a raft and the half-breed with his gun, left the camp to hunt game for supper.

While Paul was engaged in felling a tree he was shot dead by the Frenchman who claimed that seeing him dimly through the underbrush, he mistook him for a wild animal and fired. We all believe that the truth of the matter was that Paul had been murdered by the half-breed and that

One-Pound-One's son had bribed him to follow Paul and killed him. The poor fellow was buried where he fell and nothing further was heard about the matter....

One-Pound-One was buried at Fort Pitt. Next spring his body was taken up and an old Cree boiled all the flesh off his bones which were sent to St. Boniface for burial.

The women say that long before the water boiled in the cauldron they heard groans and hisses issuing from it. It did not take much to make the old man hot when he was alive and perhaps even his inflammable old carcass resented being boiled in a pot like beef. Women are always a trifle superstitious and I don't put much faith in that story.

Perhaps it grew some since for there was also a yarn about them making a by-product of soap from his remains, so that on wash days, the old man, in the form of soap, became a blessing to the fort. But I don't believe that story either, for he was too far from godliness when alive, to become an agent of cleanliness after death.

So good-bye to old One-Pound-One and I hope he is not in that hot place to which he was always sending us, but if he is Satan must have given him a place among his advisors, for he certainly had all the qualifications to make a first-class devil. His son was a chip off the old block and when we got rid of him too, a year later, there was not one of us who did not bear his grief like a man and if we needed our handkerchiefs, it was to hide our smiles.[94]

A Handsome Monument to Their Father's Memory ⌐ Sir George Simpson, Hudson Bay House, Lachine, Quebec

29 JULY 1856

My dear Doctor [Alexander Rowand],

It was one of the last instructions your father gave John, on the day preceding his death, that his bones were not to be left in the Indian Country but removed to Canada and interred near those of his own father. I accordingly directed that the body should be disinterred last winter and brought out to Norway House, from whence I conveyed it this summer in my own canoe to Red River, but some of the crew having discovered the contents of the package, I was afraid they might, from superstitious feeling, drop it overboard at some time. I therefore had it repacked and sent to York Factor for transmission to England by the ship, from whence it will be forwarded to this place.

The wish of the family at Red River is to erect a handsome monument to their father's memory in Montreal, by subscription among themselves and I have undertaken to see the design carried out. You will, no doubt, be happy to join your sisters & brothers in showing this mark of regard for so kind and worthy a parent, on which point I shall be glad to hear from you.[95]

LAPOTAC, THE HUNTER

The Death of Our Greatest and Best Chief ⌐ Edmonton House Post Journal

The Enoch Cree on the city's western boundary trace their history to a leader named Lapotac. The Fort Edmonton journals reveal the hunter's importance to the trading post in the hard times of the late 1850s. Lapotac's sons were chiefs on the Enoch reserve after the signing of Treaty 6.

6 OCTOBER 1856 The Chiefs [Lapitugue] & Maskepetoon with their respective bands came this afternoon on a trade they were received with a salute of 3 Guns each—Lapitugue has been recognized as a chief of the first rank—after the customary speechifying and smoking the Calumet was gone through the chiefs got a present of a suit of clothes & a keg of mixed Rum each—they appear to be well satisfied with their treatment & Lapitugue has promised to be one of our Hunters.[96]

2 JULY 1859 Lapatac came in with the meat of one moose, Borwick came in from the gard he tells us that several horses are sick and some dead.

3 JULY Men and Women all out for Berries, Eggs, and sap. The fort in a state of desolation.

4 JULY A great many horses sick at the gard. No less then fifteen have died of late we had to kill [an] other animal this evening. No news of our men that are gone to the plains, buffalo must be far.

6 JULY Lapatac sent the meat of one moose this morning.

8 JULY Abram Lalois returned from the plains they went a great distance for Buffalo. The carts will be here in the morning Abram brought us a little dried meat in advance as he knew we had nothing to eat.

9 JULY Some starving Crees crossed the river.

11 JULY More half starved Crees crossed.

14 JULY Lapatac sent in the meat of two Moose and one red deer.

15 JULY James Ward returned from Lapatac's hunting place with the meat of one red deer.

16 JULY Lapatac himself came in with the meat of one Moose. More Starving Indians crossed the river this day.

18 JULY James Ward returned from the horse Gard and says that the horses are dying every day he could tell the number that died since the boat

left us....More Starving freemen and Crees are crossing the river. They have the common complaint.

20 JULY Lapatac our fort hunter returned sick he killed nothing this hunt.

23 JULY The men [stopped] work early this evening on account of our not having provisions to give them.[97]

9 FEBRUARY 1861 Mr. John Cunningham & party who left this last Tuesday for George Ward's Camp arrived today with heavy loaded sleds. They brought the melancholy news of the death of our greatest and best chief "Lapotack" his body was brought to here for burial—he fell down dead suddenly, it is supposed by the Crees that he had been poisoned by some of the Ft. Pitt Crees, but upon this hand we can't give an opinion, the general opinion here of the old Freeman is that he was not poisoned, but died from the bursting of a blood vessel, as he bled a great deal from the mouth. He was a good man in every way and always did his best for the whites, he was a sober man, never tasted a drop of Liquor, his loss to Edmonton House is irreparable. His Family are left for the charity of the HBC and right well do his children deserve to be taken care of.[98]

"THE NOISE WAS TERRIFIC"

Christmas at Fort Edmonton, 1856 ⟿ Peter Erasmus, as told to Henry Thompson

It was the custom of Hudson's Bay officials to meet at Fort Edmonton during Christmas week, staying for New Year's Day. They discussed business concerned with the trade, and prepared their orders for the following year. The conference had developed into a week of social activities commemorating the Christmas period.

Fort Pitt, Slave Lake, Chipewyan, Fort Assiniboine, Jasper House, Rocky Mountain House, and Lac La Biche were all represented. The two days before Christmas was a bedlam of noise as each new dog team arrived. Every arrival was a signal for all the dogs of the fort and those of the Crees camped nearby to raise their voices in a deafening uproar of welcome or defiance as their tempers dictated.

The noise was terrific, yet none of the regular inmates paid any attention or made any effort to silence any dog within reach. The drivers of the dog teams and the factors were assigned quarters as quickly as they arrived; the arrangements for the guests was a wonderful example of organized planning.

On Christmas Eve, Father Lacombe drove in to conduct Midnight Mass. I was somewhat surprised that the priest and my employer were on such friendly and cordial terms. Woolsey went out to meet him and immediately invited him to his room, where they spent several hours of congenial conversation. Of course I was on hand to take care of his dogs, as the man drove his own team....

It was some time before I was able to get to sleep, then suddenly it was morning. I was aroused from a deep sleep by a tremendous bloodcurdling noise that actually seemed to vibrate the room. For a moment I was shocked motionless, then the notes of music sounded into my senses. I was out of bed and scrambled for my clothes. Bill was already half dressed.

John Graham, a Scottish employee, burst into the room, almost incoherent with excitement and fairly dancing in his joy. Finally he shouted at the top of his voice, "The Pibroch! The Pibroch!" Tears coursed down his cheeks as he motioned for Bill and me to come. We dressed in seconds that morning and followed him out as he turned and dashed for the door.

Striding back and forth on the walk that surrounded three sides of the factor's three-storied building was a man by the name of Colin Fraser playing a set of bagpipes. The long droning notes that precede the actual music were what awakened me so suddenly. He made a striking figure, dressed in all the gay regalia of tartan and kilt, his knees exposed to the elements. He seemed quite indifferent to the weather that was at least thirty degrees below zero. The deep notes of his instrument echoed back from the high hills of the ice-covered Saskatchewan River. It was beautiful even to my unfamiliar ear; never till then had I heard the bagpipes played.

I turned to watch the face of our old friend and felt some of the deep loneliness that marked the features of this old man, whose life ambition had been to return to his native land; he now realized he was too late ever to attain it. He stood with his hand on Borwick's shoulder; unashamed tears flowed down his cheeks. That night Bill and I carried him to his room, too inebriated to manage his own way....

There was very little rest for the musicians between dances, and there were plenty of fiddlers among the French Métis people from Lac Ste. Anne. Having too good a time dancing I did not offer my services that night, but later on I happened to mention to Bill that I liked playing the fiddle, and thereafter on Borwick's insistence I had to do my share.

The settlement guests all left for their homes at broad daylight. After dancing all night they had to run behind dogs for another forty miles before they would have any rest or sleep. The men were tough athletes to stand a grind like that and I did not envy their trip under those conditions....

The more serious business of the post leaders was of course not neglected for any of the social events at the fort or at the settlements. The conference was brought to a final grand finish with New Year's Day sports. There were foot races, toboggan slides on the North Saskatchewan River hill, some competitions for the women, and the big dog-train race of three miles on the river. Every team from each post competed in this race. Each factor contributed a share to this prize; the winner took all, which was a choice of any clothes in stock to the amount of approximately twenty-five dollars....

At daylight the next morning the far-distant post managers had pulled out for another long year of isolated wilderness where their duties held little of entertainment and no social life whatever, until the following gathering a year hence at Edmonton. No wonder the Chief Factor had put so much effort and attention for their comfort and entertainment while they were in Edmonton. Their dogs still were dressed in all the ribbons, tassles, and bells of the previous day, but at noon the dogs would be stripped of the decorations which were carefully put away for the next year.[99]

MIXED MESSAGES

Albert Lacombe

It was not so much the privations, fatigue and work that were in these missions, but above all, the isolation to which the missionary is abandoned, especially in their first years of apostolate. One must have experienced it to understand.[100]

Thomas Woolsey, Protestant missionary

25 OCTOBER 1855 I visited the Crees at their camp, about a mile from the fort, taking a gentleman with me as interpreter. Our arrival was speedily announced to the Crees by a good old Indian named Stephen, who at once introduced us to the best tent, where a large buffalo robe was spread for our accommodation. The chief men of the camp then took their seats around us. The sacred pipe, or calumet, was speedily passed, each one taking a whiff. I then addressed them at some length, and answered questions relative to baptism, the Lord's Supper, the observance of the Sabbath, &c. One of them, who appeared to have been at the priest, was very inquisitive about the cross, beads, saints' days, & etc. I told them that

Two English adventurers published colourful books about their visit to Fort Edmonton and the West in 1862. Viscount Milton, 23, and his physician friend Walter Cheadle, 27, hired local guides to take them across the Rockies. An artist's engraving in Cheadle's travel narrative identified the individuals as, left to right: Assiniboine's son, Milton, Cheadle, Battenotte the Assiniboine, and Assiniboine's wife.

the teaching of the priests, in most cases was nothing more than their old paganism, under another name, and that what I did now wished to stand by in a coming day. They all listened very attentively, and this man said he was satisfied, and would not go near the priest again.[101]

Dr. Walter B. Cheadle, visitor

17 MAY 1862 Hardisty told us of contest between priest and Methodist minister, Mr. Wolsey. Priest catches a convert and baptizes him. Wolsey hears of it and baptizes him over again, and so on *ad infinitum*, it being with great difficulty that convert knows whether he was made Papist or Protestant last. Quarrelled very fiercely at table about saying grace at dinner when both staying at the fort. Mr. Brazeau, who was in charge at the time, told them if they did not behave better they should neither of them be allowed to say it at all. Whereupon they compromised and agreed to say it alternately. The priest did not understand English, and Wolsey not French. Priest tried Latin; Wolsey at fault. They were therefore driven

to Cree, of which they neither knew much. Their, "Keya Margastun, niya mirvarsin," "keya a rascal," "keya crapeau," intensely amused Brazeau and Macaulay who were the spectators.[102]

"My Guardian Spirit Helped Me" ⟿ Suzette Piche, as told to Anne Anderson

All the women were given time to think this over and when I told them of my intentions no one believed me. They said, "You will not be able to leave your husband and sisters. You are endangering yourself and you will be scalped." But I had made up my mind to do it. I felt a superior being above me who was giving me courage....

I spoke to my husband and told him of my decision to leave, taking my three children with me, along with what I owned, and headed north to Beaver Hill House (Edmonton) and Big Lake (St. Albert). My sisters all gathered around me and said how foolish I was to venture out alone. But I was not afraid. I could not forget the Lacombe sermon. When I saw Father Lacombe I told him of my decision and immediately began to prepare for my hazardous trip....

When I started out I knew I would arrive.... My guardian spirit helped me. [My Red River cart turned over in a river.] One by one I picked up my children and the bedding and pemmican, then righted the cart and loaded everything back on. We crossed the ravine with me leading the horse. One of the kids was on my back and the other two were hanging on to my skirts. We finally made it to the top of the bank. We were all safe and once more I was ready to continue on my journey....

It took four more days before I sensed that our trip was coming to an end. I watched for the big river (North Saskatchewan) and when we saw it we were all happy. I was told there would be someone to help me ford the big river. The crossing is where the High Level Bridge now stands. The day before I reached the big river, all I thought about was the crossing and hoped that help would be there. My prayers were answered. As we approached, I could see someone already there.[103]

Suzette Piche, as she became known, was a young Blackfoot woman, one of four wives of a Cree chief. After hearing Albert Lacombe preach against bigamy, she decided to travel to St. Albert mission with her three children. Later she described her journey to Métis historian and linguist Anne Anderson.

LES SOEURS GRISES

Sister Alphonse

24 SEPTEMBER 1858 The thought that this day would mark the end of our long journey instilled in us a new ardor. The Fathers went ahead to

Three Quebec nuns travelled
for 51 days to reach Lac Ste.
Anne mission in 1858. Sister
Emery, born Zoe Leblanc,
served as a surgeon, doctor and
dentist for the Fort Edmonton
district. Sister Alphonse, born
Marie Jacques, taught at the
mission school. Sister Adele
Lamy looked after the chapel.

announce our arrival. As we approached the goal where henceforth, our days would be spent, and where we most likely would be laid to rest in our graves, our pleasure abated and serious reflections replaced it. However, our trust in God soon dissipated the clouds which the future seemed to hold in store for us.

At last we had but to cross the Priests' Creek when the church bell started ringing out its welcome and the Fathers, with some thirty people—the only ones around since all others were out on the Prairie—stood almost at arm's length on the other side. No one could have foreseen the great difficulty we had in reaching them as our vehicles sank deeply in the mud. The men had to strain for a long while before freeing them.

After a ceremony of thanksgiving in the church decorated as on festive days, Fr. Lacombe led us to our house. It was three o'clock. After partaking of a lunch we went over to the rectory to express our gratitude to Fr. Rémas for his great sollicitude for us during the whole trip. Getting back to our abode we fell to our knees. We wanted the protection of the Blessed Virgin and of Mother d'Youville, our Foundress.[104]

Sister Emery

24 SEPTEMBER 1858 The mission is in possession of fifteen horses, seventeen heads of cattle, ten dogs and ten cats each with its particular name. We cannot raise either sheep or hogs because the dogs would devour them.

This year the barley and potato crops have been good. As to wheat... let's forget about it; we have already lost our taste for bread. The garden has furnished its share of cabbages, onions, turnips, carrots, etc. We eat fresh meat, pemmican, fish, and rabbit in Winter. Fish constitutes more than half our total fare. Many families have but fish boiled without salt and without sauce of any kind. We have as many potatoes as we desire, sometimes too some barley bannock. We never suffer from indigestion! Sisters Lamy and Alphonse have never been as plump; I am the only one to remain slim.[105]

Sister Alphonse

Although I am very lonesome, I feel quite happy in my new position, because I see much good to be done. I will have to learn to twist my tongue to succeed in learning Cree, a language Fr. Lacombe teaches us one hour a day in the evening when he is here. He is not only a father to us but also a mother. He is not satisfied with taking care of our material needs; he enriches our spiritual life through wonderful instructions.

In my classroom, the second largest of the house, I have anywhere from 42 down to 24 [children] according to the presence or the absence of the families. It is a real medley of nations. Only one understands French; the others only Cree and I know so little as yet of that language. This makes for great difficulties of communications.[106]

Sister Emery

3 APRIL 1860 Father Lacombe is at the same time a father and a mother to us. He believes always that we will do something that will be too tiring, too injurious to our health, and all the same this is a bit annoying. He treats us like little children. Almost every day, he finds out if we are eating well, if we have taken our snacks and so on. He follows us like little children.[107]

We have much privations to endure...famine is great....Many times we feel the pangs of hunger without anything to eat.[108]

THE COMPANY'S CHILDREN

James Carnegie, Earl of Southesk

15 AUGUST 1859 Again I had cause to admire the fine riding of the boys. Little fellows ten or twelve years old would jump on the back of any horse they could lay hands on, and gallop him about the place, with no saddle at all, and with no better bridle than a cord round his lower jaw. They were perfectly fearless, and sat their horses with a firmness, spirit, and grace very beautiful to see, guiding them at their will by movements scarcely discernible.[109]

Thomas Woolsey

12 JANUARY 1858 Twenty scholars under instruction, most of whom are the children of Romanists. No ragged school can be more trying than mine. Inkstands are upset, slates broken, books torn, and cursing and swearing most alarmingly indulged in. They often rush from their seats to fight or wrestle with each other, and when interfered with, threaten to revenge themselves on me.[110]

Dr. Walter B. Cheadle

23 MAY 1862 Mr. Christie's little girl, who had an attack of remittent fever when I arrived, is now quite well; a pretty little child of three.

25 MAY Three women and six children suffering from secondary syphilis. The fort will be in a nice state eventually....

31 MAY Numerous patients with syphilis improving. Nine children and four women with syphilis ulcers and eruption.[III]

Colin Fraser, Jr.

My father died suddenly on April 1867 and with his death came a breakup of our happy family circle. But before this occurred, I had led the life usual among the fur traders of that day. There was not much that I could not do around the Post. Early in life I had become used to handling horses and dogs, and familiarity with the latter got me much work in life. Of course, as my mother was a Cree Indian, I was almost born to the use of the Cree tongue and this too had been a wonderful asset to me....

After my father's death in 1867, my mother, myself and the younger children went to Long Lake, six miles west of Edmonton, where we built a log house and lived upon such produce as we raised ourselves. After a time I went into Edmonton and worked under Chief Factor Christie. One of my principal duties was to care for and drive his team of dogs which he was very proud and I still boast of the skill with which I handled his team. I often went with a dog team eastward across the prairie, trading for furs and buffalo robes, and one task for which I often was selected was to out-manoever the fur traders who came into the county with whiskey. On one such occasion, I

raced Don Noyes, a celebrated character, to Rocky Mountain House and all he could secure on his arrival was a couple of cayuses—I had everything else....One vivid recollection is of a fight outside the palisades of Fort Edmonton between marauding Blackfeet and Crees from the North; the Crees killed two and wounded two of their enemy and the conflict was ended by the intervention of Mr. Brazeau and John Cunningham.[112]

Julie Daignault was the second of 13 children born to Julie Larance and Isaac Daignault, who was later a Papaschase band member. She was born in 1846 and married three times. This picture may have been taken about the time she married Louis Charland.

THE FOUNDING OF ST. ALBERT

"What a Lovely Place for a Mission" ∽ Albert Lacombe

APRIL 1861 In my travels from Edmonton to Saint Anne, when I'd stop on a hillside to have my dogs rest, I'd gaze towards a certain hill with a lake in the distance, and just opposite a forest. As I'd gaze, I'd murmur to myself: "What a lovely place for a mission."

At the beginning of April, accompanied by Michel Norman, his wife, Rose Plante, and a young orphan named Nancy, I went to the large lake I was to name Saint Albert. We camped at night and then reached the hill. We had with us four oxen, some horses, a plow and the tools we needed. A beautiful large shelter made of hides served us as residence. It was a Saturday. The next day, Sunday, after mass in the tent, I had plenty of time to consider and admire the extent and beauty of my new domain. What dreams I made as I sat near the rough cross I had erected in place of the stick Mgr. Taché had stood there....

On Monday we began our work. With Michel and two Métis I set out for the forest, our vast spruce grove which covers the hillside across the river and lake. Once in the midst of these deep-rooted giants, I spoke to my companions: "My children, we are about to fell these beautiful trees which will serve as lumber to build the Fathers' residence and the House of God. Let us kneel and say a prayer and ask the Master to help us and bless us." Leaning on our axes, we made the sign of the cross, and recited the Our Father and the Hail Mary. "Yes, that God's holy will be done." With the pride and daring of a pioneer of Christ I began felling a majestic pine. My companions followed my example. In no time, three beautiful trees fell to the ground with a crash. During ten days my men continued preparing the necessary wood for our first buildings. Our beasts of burden hauled this material to the chosen site. But another field of action was ready. The snow was gone. The earth was no longer frozen and was drying. It was time to do the plowing. Having but one plow I set my oxen to work each their turn. During the day one man did his plowing with two beasts, and at night another man took over and carried on the same work. This set up made it possible for us to seed a large field in a few days. At the same time the women who were as courageous as we were busy preparing their garden plots in which they sowed cabbage, carrots, turnip, onions etc. All in cooking our meals. A certain number of Métis joined us with their families. As Lord over this land, I divided the land and gave to each his share, all in keeping a few thousand acres on each side of the river.[113]

By Solemn Midnight Mass ⤳ Hippolyte Leduc, Oblate missionary

On the 25th of December, 1867, the celebration of Christmas day began, as was usual at St. Albert, at 12 a.m. by solemn midnight mass, in a kind of log house 30 x 20 feet, only half finished, which was however destined to become, a few years later, the first Cathedral of St. Albert. People from all quarters within a radius of 40 miles came in sleds drawn by horses or dogs to assist at Divine service. On such an occasion Fort Edmonton was almost deserted, as Catholics and Protestants alike went to Midnight Mass at St. Albert. On that special night Christmas hymns were sung in the Cree language by the majority of the congregation during almost the whole service, and a sermon was also given in the Cree language by the

A Pemmican Recipe
Louisa Bellcourt, Métis descendant

Take Moose meat. Slice and cook over a fire to dry in strips.

Smoke it slowly, combining the sun and smoke. Put it away at night for protection.

Boil it in grease, add currants and a bit of sugar. Cook and stir until completely cooked.

One pound dried meat, three pounds of grease, about 1 cup of sugar (not too sweet), 5 cups of currants.

Grind up the meat or pound it until the dried meat is very soft and fine.

Saskatoon berries were used in the early days instead of currants. Saskatoons were placed on a shelf on a clean cloth, and dried by the sun; it takes four to five days to dry them.

officiating priest. The religious part of the Christmas Night celebration was over about 2 a.m., and then the home and social celebration began by a feast—a banquet which lasted more or less all morning, all day, and even into the night. From 2 a.m. until 10 p.m. the kettle was kept continually boiling in the house of our dear half-breeds, and the tables were kept constantly set for the benefit of strangers and visitors. No invitation was necessary, and everyone who called was perfectly welcome. Pemmican (dried meat), splendid white fish, and in some cases fresh buffalo meat and strong black tea, to which the luxury of a little sugar was added on that day, were offered gratis to all applicants....

There was nothing to dampen the real enjoyment of my first Merry Christmas under the shadow of the Rockies in 1867. There seemed to be no sickness. There was not a single doctor in the whole country. People died of old age or accident only. There were no law suits, no lawyers, no crimes, no policemen, no gaols, no party division, no voting, no politicians, no taxes, and, in fact, no government. In those times, on that Blessed Day, every man seemed to be the other man's brother; and there was no such thing as coldness of reserve in the celebration of Christmas in that truly good old time, which has disappeared before the coming of what is proudly called "Higher Civilization."

Christmas was freer and happier in 1867.[114]

FORTUNE SEEKERS

Archibald Thompson, visitor

FORT EDMONTON, 23 JULY 1862

Dear Brother, I am happy to inform you that we have all arrived here safe and in good health. It is a nice place. I think I could live here contented if I could get provision but they do not raise enough for themselves. They live the most of the time on pemmican and potatoes.

There are some pretty girls here, some of the boys say, as they have ever seen, but I have not seen them yet, as I have not been over the river but I will go over this afternoon....We have seen no Indians at all since we left only what few we have seen about the forts, and no wild animals except three antelope and a few wolves. We saw any quantity of dead buffalo lying on the prairie starved to death. We passed over the battle ground where the Blackfeet and Crees fought a battle some twenty days ago and there were three killed on each side. There is gold in the river, as I washed some out myself, but it is very fine. I have no time to wash any more or I would send you a few specks to let you see it, as my letter has to leave here in the morning by our guide that came up with us. We will leave here on Monday morning for Cariboo.[115]

"THE BUFFALO ENTERED THE EARTH"

The Hunt ⌐ Victoria Belcourt Callihoo

I was thirteen years old when I first joined in a buffalo hunt. We left Lac Ste Anne after the leaves were out on the poplar trees and our small fields and gardens were seeded or planted. Before making the journey, there would be a meeting among the leading men as to the exact day of leaving. After this was decided on all the families who wanted to join the hunt would prepare for the trip. Our main transportation, the Red River cart, would be overhauled. These vehicles at that time did not have any metal in their construction. Large wooden pegs were used where bolts would be used now, while small pegs answered for screws or nails. Cart harness was made of hides from the buffalo.

I always used to accompany my mother on these trips. She was a medicine woman who set broken bones and knew how to use medicinal herbs. The riders who chased the buffalo were often thrown, sometimes by the bulls charging the riders' horses or by the horses getting their feet in badger holes.

We usually took three carts along. We had no axle grease and tallow was used instead to lubricate the wooden axles. The carts were very squeaky and they could be heard from a long way off.

We, from Lac Ste. Anne, would be the first to start as we were the furthest north. The Métis of St. Albert settlement would join us on the way. Usually, there would be about one hundred families going on the hunt. All streams were forded as there were no bridges. The Saskatchewan River was the largest and most dangerous and it was a relief after it was crossed. We used to cross at a good ford about where the High Level Bridge is now. About a day's travel south from Saskatchewan River we usually found the herd. Riders, young men they were, would scout on ahead to see we did not run into any enemies. There were no police, no law. We always had a leader in our caravan and his orders were respected. He always had a flag flying on the top of his cart. He led his people ahead and we followed him.

When the herd was startled it was just a dark solid moving mass. We, of those days, never could believe the buffalo would ever be killed off, for there were thousands and thousands. We took firewood and poles for tipis and for tripods, on which we hung our thin sliced slab meat to dry in the sun. We had no matches, but got fire from flint and birch punk. It seems no one was anxious to start their morning fire, as we would wait and see if any smoke would come out of the tipis, and when smoke was seen then there was a rush to get a flame or coal to start one's own fire.

The riders of the chase all had guns, single barrel flint locks—some muzzleloaders with caps. Bows and arrows were used before my time but the Crees and Blackfeet still used them then. Powder horns and ball bags were slung on each shoulder. At close range the guns would kill the animal. Some riders rode bareback while others had homemade saddles. They were almost flat and were stuffed with the hair of the buffalo. They were beaded on the corners and stirrups were of dry rawhide. When the kill was over, the women would go out to help bring the meat in, and then the slicing of meat began. We girls would then keep a little smoke going all day to keep the flies away from the meat. The meat would be hung on rails that rested on two tripods at each end.

Often we would run short of wood. Then a pony would be hitched to a cart and we go out on the plain and pick chips (buffalo dung). On a warm day this was very dry and burned readily. Only old ones were used for fuel. The buffalo was a very useful animal, for we ate the meat, we used its hide for robes, ropes, shelter for our lodges, foot wear, clothes and bags. The meat was cooked and sun-dried and also made into pemmican. We always camped close to water. We set our tipis in a large circle outside the cart circle. A few of the fastest horses were kept in this enclosure and the others were herded all night by a night herder, for horse thieving was a very common occurrence. A fast horse was the best possession. A hunter on a fast horse would kill more buffalo than others with less speedy ponies. There was no money; no one knew what it was.

We made pemmican out on the plains, as the dried meat was too bulky to take home. A large green hide would be hung on six posts, three on each side, so the hide would form a U-shape. When it was dry the slabs of meat would be dumped in the U-shaped hide and two men on each end would then pound the dry meat into a pulp. Then sun-dried saskatoons would be mixed and grease would be poured on and stirred to make an even mixture. When this was done it would be packed in robes, sewn with sinew all around, the hair part outside to keep the pemmican in good condition regardless of the weather. These bags were heavy and it usually took two men to load one on a cart. Hides would be put on top of the loads. Nothing would be wasted from the buffalo but the bones, hoofs and horns. The fall hunt, the last before winter, which would start after haying, was the most important one, for we had to get enough dried meat and pemmican to last all winter. At this time, the buffalo would be fat and calves grown up. Calves were not killed as no one cared for veal anyway.

The homeward journey was slow, but who cared? The nice sunny days in the fall, Indian summer, made travelling rather fascinating. Occasionally we would run into bad weather, but we were accustomed to it and did not mind as long as we had plenty of the best and most nourishing food I ever ate. In all I made four trips to the plains hunting the buffalo. Each was further, away toward south.[116]

"When the Land Was Taken Over" ↝ John Buffalo, descendant, as told to Richard Lightning

This land had herds of buffalo; they were all over the prairies. During mid-summer, the land looked as if there was a prairie fire with the amount of dust made by the buffalo. The elders said that if a person was to put his ear to the ground by a hole, he would hear the loud rumbling of the buffalo. That was the Indians' source of food. The hides were tanned for clothing, blankets and shelter. During the winter they used buffalo jumps. One old man in a few was given this power to be able to attract the buffalo towards the jumps. They would eventually get them in the jump by riding circles around the buffalo....

The elders said that the buffalo just left when the land was taken over, that is when they moved towards the southwest. The Indians moved camps as the buffalo migrated. They were in search of food. During the night they could hear them, but the following day they would move again until night fell, never reaching the buffalo. Some old men said that the buffalo entered the earth somewhere but I do not know. It must be true, as there are none left.[117]

The Manitou Stone

1870 to 1891

A MYSTERIOUS STONE lies in the heart of the city. Look for it on a pedestal in a dark room.

A child touches it one morning, tracing the mottled surface with her fingertips, then races to catch up with her classmates. Their teacher warns them to Slow Down Right Now and Listen Up because this is the Provincial Museum of Alberta, not a Playground! The kids keep running. No one tells the girl of the power of the stone or of its significance in the life of her city. It is just a big rock to her, something cool to the touch.

People in Edmonton call it the Manitou Stone, the Iron Stone, or *Papamihaw Asini*, the Flying Rock, if they know about it at all. The meteorite is round and black, too heavy to lift; yet it was lifted once. It was stolen to proclaim the superiority of Christianity and never returned to its true place of honour. The theft in 1866 inspired a prophecy of calamity. The prophecy came true, every word of it.

Museum curators are cautious in their description of Alberta's sacred places, spiritual objects and the puzzling match between predictions and events. They avoid the trap of true and false. They sidestep the word theft and they do not name the thieves. Historians prefer to use the story of the Manitou Stone as a metaphor for wrenching events that transformed life in western Canada between 1870 and 1890. The stone is symbol for them, not an explanation. They take a detour around judgment.

Beyond the museum and the university lecture theatres, there are no rules of interpretation—only a story to ponder and a stone to touch.

If you listen to one of the original stories, you will know that Nanabozho, the Great Spirit or Manitou, placed the stone on a hill near the Battle River at Piwapiskoo, or Iron Creek, after the great flood. The elders said it had the power to protect the people of the Plains and the buffalo herds that sustained them. They said the rock had once been small but kept growing until no human being could move it. The stone existed to remind the Cree, the Nakoda and the Blackfoot of the presence of *manito*, or spirit, in their lives. For generations it beckoned hunters, families and bands in a pilgrimage before and after the buffalo hunt. People left offerings in hope and gratitude. Tribal leaders in the mid–nineteenth century recognized the spiritual power of this place.[1]

Many of Alberta's earliest written texts mention the importance of the Manitou stone, too. At Fort Augustus, Alexander Henry the Younger reported on September 10, 1810 that four Cree families had arrived from a camp "on the south side of the Battle River at the Iron Stone."[2] Thomas Woolsey asked a chief to take him to see the stone in 1860. "This, after three or four hours ride from the camp, was at length submitted to my inspection, with the assurance of my being the first white man who had ever seen it,"[3] he noted in his diary on August 24. Woolsey made a note to himself to inquire about the stone's scientific value in a letter to Dr. Hector of the recent Palliser Expedition, carefully recording his Edinburgh address. He added: "The pagans regard this metallic substance as a mun-e-to and have placed sundry offerings under it, such as beads, buttons, broken earthenware, arrow-shods, tobacco, red cloth and feathers."[4]

Could the meteorite have fallen closer to Edmonton earlier? In 1862, the Métis guide Baptiste Supernault told a story about the Manitou Stone's travels to the doctor-adventurer, Walter Cheadle, who recorded it: "Many years ago, but within the memory of people still living, an Indian found a piece of native iron in the neighbourhood of Edmonton, which he carried out to the plains, and placed on the top of a hill. Since that time it had regularly increased in size and was now so large that no man could lift it!"[5]

The Cree, Nakoda and Blackfoot looked at the Manitou stone in appreciation as a guardian spirit, but a newcomer named George Millward McDougall could only see a pagan idol. McDougall arrived in 1862 and with his wife Elizabeth and their children, opened a Methodist

The Manitou Stone 1884

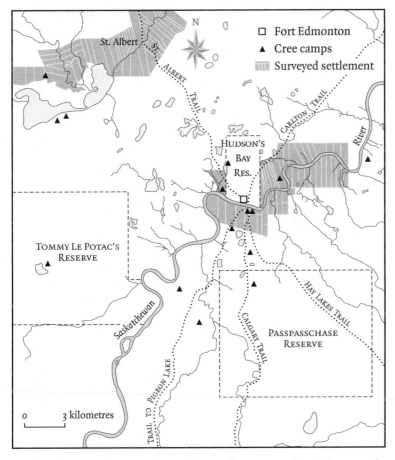

The shaded area on this map suggests a large settlement around Fort Edmonton, the Hudson's Bay Company post located near the present-day site of the Alberta Legislature Building. In truth one or two families occupied each of the surveyed river lots and some lots were empty. The federal government set aside development lands for the Hudson's Bay Company and large reserves for the Papaschase and Enoch bands to meet the obligations of Treaty 6. The Michel and Alexander bands settled on large reserves west of St. Albert, just off the edge of this map. Trails were well-established and mapped, but there were no roads.

mission at Victoria, about 100 kilometres north-east of Fort Edmonton.[6] In photographs, he looked like a Moses of the Prairies, the unyielding patriarch of a large family that defined the region, and sometimes invented it through best-selling books and tracts, public speaking tours, missionary work and government service. McDougall observed the people he had come to convert and the beauty of their homeland in an early diary entry. "From these majestic scenes the untutored Indian paints his future paradise," he wrote, "Alas for him his religion makes his heart no better."[7] McDougall believed his duty was to convince the inhabitants to "look from nature, to nature's God."[8] His God.

In the summer of 1866, the Manitou stone disappeared.

McDougall did not try to hide what had happened. On his instructions, the meteorite was brought to his mission by ox cart. For three years it sat in McDougall's yard, a captive symbol of the beliefs he had come to erase. "This roused the ire of the conjurers," he told readers of the Wesleyan magazine. "They declared that sickness, war and decrease of buffalo would follow the sacrilege. Thanks to a kind Providence, these soothsayers have been confounded."[9]

McDougall spoke too soon. Captain William Francis Butler picked up the story in 1870 after visiting the missionary and touching the stone himself: "When the Indians found it had been taken away they were loud in the expression of their regret. The old medicine men declared that its removal would lead to great misfortunes, and that war, disease and dearth of buffalo would afflict the tribes of the Saskatchewan." Butler noted that their predictions predated the tragedy: "A few months later brought all the three evils upon the Indians; and never, probably, since the first trader had reached the country, has so many afflictions of war, famine and plague fallen upon the Crees and Blackfoot as during the years which succeeded the useless removal of their Manito-stone from the lone hilltop upon which the skies had cast it."[10]

Hardships descended on the North Saskatchewan River valley between 1870 and 1890: the buffalo disappeared, tribal warfare erupted; a devastating smallpox epidemic broke out; famine, economic collapse, political and social upheaval and an armed insurrection befell the people of the region. The Manitou stone was crated and shipped to Toronto.[11] The prophecy was fulfilled.

MORE PEOPLE LIVE in downtown Edmonton today than lived across the Canadian Prairies in 1870. That year the entire West was home to an estimated 25,000 to 35,000 people of numerous First Nations, 10,000 Métis and fewer than 2,000 people of strictly European origin.[12]

Edmonton was the largest and most important trading centre between the Red River settlement and the Pacific coast. The First Nations bands, local Métis families and Fort Edmonton employees of European and French-Canadian origin depended on each other and by 1870 they were often related. Their descendants take care to describe the mingled lineage: Gilbert Anderson, who grew up among Cree relatives in the Enoch band, inherited his name from a Métis great-grandfather who was an HBC employee; but he was also great-grandson of Chief Michel Callihoo and a nephew of the early gold prospector Jimmy Gibbons. "These people were contemporaries in a small community," said Anderson. "The families intermarried in the early years and that's how Edmonton began."[13]

In 1878, the official HBC census counted 148 people in Edmonton, 178 in St. Albert and 59 in Fort Saskatchewan. It included HBC traders and labourers, their aboriginal or Métis wives, a few missionaries and gold prospectors, and some Métis families—but not the First Nations people who lived in the immediate vicinity of Edmonton and who formed the majority of the district's population at any given time. The Cree who camped at the Beaver Hills, Saddle Lake and Goodfish Lake, and at Maskwachees or Bear Hills near present-day Hobbema were also frequent visitors to Fort Edmonton. Trading parties from more distant places camped along Edmonton's river flats or in the Beaver Hills at intervals throughout the year. Many members of Cree, Iroquois and Nakoda bands in the Edmonton region, including those living an entirely aboriginal way of life, could count an Orkneyman or a Quebec voyageur as a grandfather.

Increasingly, the HBC's chief factor assigned middlemen to trade with hunters on the plains to avoid tribal conflict at the post. Fort Edmonton also hired local Cree leaders and Métis freemen on contract to supply pemmican, fresh meat and fish to feed the growing number of families at the post. Yearning for land and privacy, HBC employees like John Norris, Malcolm Groat and John Walter, along with their Métis wives, left the service and built log homes for their families—and successful businesses—beyond the shadow of the Big House. Lured by dreams of earning $10 a day, prospectors like Jim Gibbons and his pal English Charley lived in a cluster at Miners' Flats, near the present-day location of the Valley Zoo; or downstream near Tom Clover's sandbar. About 50 prospectors came and went, also marrying into local Métis families.

Edmonton's everyday working language was Cree. French, Michif, Blackfoot, Gaelic and Nakoda were all heard along with English. A second and third generation of Fort Edmonton's Métis children began to take positions as local freighters, labourers, guides, interpreters and traders. Fur trade families—such as the Donalds, Groats, Birds, Callihoos, the Bruneaus, Letendres, Belcourts, Frasers, Gladues, Rowlands, McDonalds, Gullions, Daignaults, Andersons and Cunninghams—put down roots to create a community. The changes that uprooted their lives were sudden and largely unexpected.

ABORIGINAL ELDERS KNEW the buffalo were disappearing long before the Manitou stone vanished in 1866. The herds declined in northern plains and parklands first. Warfare accelerated largely because the Cree and Nakoda were forced to follow the declining buffalo herds south into Blackfoot territory. Tribes were soon competing for the remnants of the diminishing herds. The Cree peace negotiator Maskipiton died in a Blackfoot ambush in 1869 as he was attempting to stop the fighting, as he had done at the Peace Hills earlier. The death of this influential man devastated not only the Cree, but missionaries and traders at Fort Edmonton. Born around 1807, Maskipiton is believed to have travelled widely in the United States, where he witnessed treaties; he wrote letters to missionaries in Cree syllabics as early as the 1840s.[14] Perhaps his murder provoked Tahkoots, the brother of Papastayo, to attack a Tsuu T'ina hunting party outside the gates of Fort Edmonton the following spring. Predictably, the Blackfoot confederacy launched counterattacks. Fort Edmonton was briefly under siege.

The Cree and Métis around Fort Edmonton were also concerned about a more distant intruder. The HBC sold its vast western territory to the Canadian government for £300,000 in 1869 without consulting the people of the West.[15] The Métis of Red River and the Cree of the Qu' Appelle

Valley acted quickly to assert their right to their homeland.[16] Frustrated by the failure of the Red River rebellion, Laurent and Eleanor Garneau and many other Manitoba families moved west to join the Métis in the Edmonton area. The new Dominion sent messages to Fort Edmonton to reassure local inhabitants of its fair intentions. Chief Factor W.J. Christie, the McDougalls and Albert Lacombe tried to calm the local population. They assumed the worst when they heard that 15 Cree bands had gathered at the Hand Hills. George McDougall's son, John, rode out to talk to them. The Plains leader, Weekaskookeeseyin, or Sweetgrass, explained to him that the gathering was not a war council, but an attempt to survive the winter. "In sorrow and in hunger, and with many hardships, we have gathered here, where we have grass and timber," the chief told McDougall, "and since we came, buffalo in the distance, few, though still sufficient to keep us alive."[17] McDougall may not have heard the full story and there is evidence from the Cree oral history tradition that there was talk of war.

Smallpox struck the First Nations camps and the Métis settlements with the greatest ferocity in the summer and fall of 1870. The disease swept in from the south and afflicted thousands across the Plains. It killed the young hunters and pemmican makers who fed families and sustained the fur trade, disfigured the survivors, and left small orphans wandering along the riverbank. Antoine Jibeau of Moose Lake, near present-day Bonnyville, later recalled how he watched his father, mother, a sister and three brothers die in the space of a few days, then searched for his relations in the cold, "wearing a piece of canvas tied with a string."[18] Over days and weeks, smallpox infected 600 of St. Albert's 900 people, killing 320 of them;[19] it raced through the Cree camps around Fort Edmonton. Downstream at the Victoria mission, the McDougalls did not escape its cruelty, losing two daughters and a daughter-in-law to the disease.[20]

After a season of death, angry delegations arrived in Fort Edmonton from the Plains to challenge the HBC's transfer of Rupert's Land without their consent. In April 1871, Sweetgrass led a party of chiefs and headmen, including Kehewin, Onchamanihos (Little Hunter), and Kiskyo (Bobtail) to Fort Edmonton. The chiefs dictated and signed a letter to Governor Archibald at Red River. They asked for treaty negotiations and assurances about the limitations on white settlement. "We heard our lands are sold, and we do not like it," said Sweetgrass. "We don't want to sell our lands; it is our property, and no one has a right to sell them."[21] In an accompanying letter, Christie urged Canada to send a police force and to negotiate a treaty before mass starvation could begin.

The emergency was real, yet the people of the Edmonton district waited another three years for the arrival of the North West Mounted Police, and six years for the treaty commissioners.

⁓

THERE IS NO SINGLE VERSION of the terms of Treaty 6. One account is written, many are told.

Most First Nations of the North Saskatchewan River region negotiated Treaty 6 with representatives of the Queen at Fort Carlton and Fort Pitt in August and September of 1876. Sacred pipe ceremonies and displays of horsemanship added to the significance of the gatherings. Difficult negotiations continued for days within the Cree camps, and with Canada's treaty commissioner. Interpreters attempted to communicate for both sides, with mixed results. Stories of the treaty signing have been preserved for generations in the oral tradition of aboriginal peoples and in the published text of the Government of Canada.

The chiefs of the Edmonton district did not enter treaty immediately, but many chiefs, interpreters and witnesses at the Fort Pitt negotiations had strong links to Fort Edmonton. Sweetgrass, Little Hunter, Pakan and Kehewin negotiated for many of the western Cree, with Chief Factor Christie of Edmonton assisting the treaty commissioner and Peter Erasmus acting as interpreter. John Chantler McDougall and Constantin Scollen, as well as Eliza McDougall Hardisty, signed as witnesses.

Most bands of the Fort Edmonton district entered Treaty 6 on August 21, 1877, signing in a ceremony near the riverbank. Michel Callihoo signed for his band on September 18, 1878.

With their X-signatures, Papastayo [Papaschase as it was recorded in the treaty], Alexander, Alexis and Michel and their headmen agreed to the terms as they understood them through their interpreters. On paper, Treaty 6 promised each band one square mile of land for each family of five, or about 128 acres per capita, in a permanent reserve; hunting and fishing rights; farming implements and seeds; rations during times of famine; a school, should they request it; a medicine chest; annual payments of $25 to the chief and five dollars to each member of the band; a new suit of clothes for the chief every three years; and a treaty medal.

In return, the written treaty required the chiefs of the North-West Territories to "cede, surrender, release and yield up to the Government of the Dominion of Canada for Her Majesty the Queen and her successors forever, all their rights, titles and privileges whatsoever"[22] to 313,400 square kilometres of their traditional territory. Later, the chiefs and their descendants asserted that they understood the agreement as a peace treaty and an agreement to share the land. Many said they did not surrender the territory to outsiders in the way the written text suggests. The Canadian government considered the deal done.

•••~

YOUNG NEWCOMERS BEGAN to trickle into the Fort Edmonton district in the late 1870s and early 1880s. They were neither HBC traders nor missionaries. They were adventurers, looking for a reliable income, a sharp deal or two, and a chance to start over in a new place.

The Lamoureux brothers—Joseph and François—were among the first agricultural settlers. Born in Quebec, they traveled west through the United States on the Oregon Trail, then wandered north to search for gold in the Cariboo country. There they met railroad workers who told them about farming opportunities along the North Saskatchewan. They crossed the mountains on horseback to see for themselves before returning to Quebec for their large families. In 1873, they built log cabins near present-day Fort Saskatchewan. The McKernan brothers and the Ottewells were not far behind.

Soon, early settlers would be called "Old Timers": the aristocracy of early Edmonton; the founding fathers of a prairie city. The city's first historians would repeat their yarns so often that future generations could be forgiven for assuming that a few dozen men were the first inhabitants of the river valley. Their names would cling to neighbourhoods and schools. Their likenesses would appear on downtown statues. In time Edmonton's collective memory would render their distinct personalities into one indistinct blur.

Today, the city's citizens remember that Donald Ross opened the first hotel between Manitoba and the Cariboo and the first commercial coal mine in Edmonton, but they forget his passion for rhyming elocution and vegetable gardening. They remember that Alex Taylor brought the first telephones and electricity to Edmonton, but they forget the gentle genius of this inventor and meteorologist who swept through the hamlet in a black cloak, partly to cover his paralysed arms. They remember that Matt McCauley was the first mayor and founder of the first public school, but they forget that he led an armed citizens' revolt in downtown Edmonton in June 1892. They remember Laurent Garneau as successful homesteader and renowned fiddler on the south shore, but forget that the Métis patriarch was locked up at Fort Saskatchewan jail for six weeks on suspicion of treason during the North-West Rebellion. They remember John A. McDougall and Richard Secord as the settlement's most successful merchants, the founders of the Jasper Avenue commercial district, but they forget that the partners made much of their fortune through land speculation and that they specialized in the cheap acquisition of Métis land scrip certificates and First Nations reserve land.

People also forget that these men had wives with names and influence of their own—Olive Ross, Eleanor Taylor, Eleanor Garneau, Mathilda McCauley, Annie McCauley, Lovisa McDougall and Annie Secord. Some women left letters and diaries describing their isolation and loneliness, their hopes and adventures, their tiny children. There are no statues, no neighbourhoods, named for them.

Edmontonians remember Frank Oliver as the fiery founder of Edmonton's first newspaper, The Bulletin, and as an ambitious politician on a steady rise through the North-West Council in 1883; the Legislative Assembly of the North-West Territories in 1888; and the House of Commons in 1896.[23] People remember him as the influential Minister of the Interior and Superintendent-General of Indian Affairs in Sir Wilfrid Laurier's government. They forget his relentless pressure on First Nations across the West to surrender reserve lands and the careful way in which he acquired 26 quarter-sections of Cree land in the Edmonton district for himself for half their appraised value.

Today the city remembers Oliver and his contemporaries as they appear in tintype portraits—jovial old fellows with handlebar moustaches, swapping tall tales around the billiard table at the Edmonton Hotel.

Edmonton forgets they arrived on the riverbank when they were young, with nothing in their rumbling ox carts except ambition.

•~

THE FINAL BUFFALO HERDS disappeared in 1879, some say into the earth.

Along the North Saskatchewan River, several hundred people died of apparent starvation in the first year. Hundreds more arrived at Fort

Edmonton's gates from distant places, looking for food. Three years after signing the Treaty 6 adhesion at Fort Edmonton, the bands in this district were still waiting for their reserve lands.

Ken Tyler, a graduate student at the University of Alberta in the late 1970s, was one of the first non-aboriginal historians to interview local elders for their oral history and to examine government documents in an effort to determine what happened to the Cree and Nakoda bands in the Edmonton district in this period. His painstaking research remains a valuable source of information.

Treaty 6 First Nations have documented a more complete story since then through a comparison of government documents and oral history. In 1879, Commissioner Edgar Dewdney promised Tommy Lapatac, son of the deceased chief, that Canada would grant a reserve to the Cree "living about Edmonton" if he organized the families into a band. New settlers and local Métis families had already staked claims around Edmonton when a government surveyor finally arrived in 1880. The surveyor calculated that the 241 members of the Papaschase band were entitled to 124 square kilometres on the south side of the river. Chief Papastayo selected the area surrounding the Two Hills, opposite Fort Edmonton. On the day the surveyor began his work, Papastayo argued with the local Indian Affairs Inspector Timothy Wadsworth. The next day Wadsworth transferred 84 Papaschase band members to a new band he called the "Edmonton Stragglers" on the north side of the river. This new band included the families of Lapatac and Mahminawatow; 24 orphans at St. Albert mission; and the aboriginal wives, widows and children of fur traders around Fort Edmonton. Wadsworth told the government surveyor the Papaschase reserve would have to be smaller in consequence and that the "Edmonton Stragglers" could not expect land for their benefit because they were not a recognized band.

In response, Papastayo ordered the surveyor to stop his work. When the surveyor refused, the chief removed his instruments. Wadsworth tried to fire Papastayo as chief. His superior, Commissioner Dewdney, reinstated the chief and recognized the Enoch band. By 1882, Lapatac had assembled 57 families in what was known as Enoch's band and had selected a reserve west of Edmonton that stretched over 115 square kilometres. But the Papaschase reserve survey was not finished until 1884.

The emerging Edmonton had its eye on Papaschase land, which was well supplied with water, timber and hay. On January 13, 1881, a crowd of settlers held a meeting at the Edmonton Hotel to demand that the Papaschase band be removed 20 miles south of the river. They sent two petitions to Prime Minister Sir John A. Macdonald, advising against any Cree reserves close to "a great central point"[24] like Edmonton. "Now is the time for the Government to declare the reserve open, and show whether this country is to be run in the interests of the settlers or the Indians,"[25] Frank Oliver wrote in The Bulletin. Settlers began to build cabins and cut timber on the Papaschase claim.

Tensions rose as hard times deepened. In January 1883, chiefs in the Edmonton district appealed directly to the Canadian prime minister. Papastayo, Kiskyo, Samson and Ermineskin dictated their grievances to Constantin Scollen, an Irish missionary with a fiery reputation who had agreed to write the letter. The chiefs charged that the government had broken its treaty promises, that Canada was trying to exterminate them slowly by starvation, and that the Blackfoot in the south could count on fair rations because they were well-armed. "If we must die by violence, let us do it quickly,"[26] they said. Scollen added his own rhetorical flourishes. Indignant at his tone, William Anderson, the government's Indian agent in Edmonton, and Captain Severe Gagnon of the NWMP prepared to arrest the missionary for inciting the chiefs, but they later backed down.

The Cree leaders of the Maskwachees Hills returned to Edmonton in July to demand emergency assistance, as Treaty 6 had promised.[27] They brought with them Papastayo and representatives of the Enoch and Paul bands to ask for food. At first company agent Anderson refused; then he gave them a small quantity of flour. The next day the Cree returned and Anderson told them he had no more food. The Cree replied that there was food in the HBC warehouse and one Cree leader pulled Anderson by the collar to Fort Edmonton. There company traders advanced the food to the bands on credit against the next year's treaty money, while a frightened Anderson sent for the Mounties in Fort Saskatchewan. New rations calmed the situation in Edmonton, but across the prairies, hungry people without a secure land base or a livelihood were preparing to act on their grievances.

The Plains Cree leader, Big Bear, still refused to sign Treaty 6 and attempted to organize a Cree-Blackfoot council and a Treaty 6 council to discuss common difficulties. The Mounties arrested his emissaries. He kept trying. On a freighting trip to Fort Edmonton, Big Bear urged the influential Pakan at Whitefish Lake to press forward his own demand for a much larger reserve for the Cree of the North Saskatchewan country so bands could live together with strength in numbers.

A Thirst Dance on the Papaschase land in Edmonton on June 5, 1884 attracted a large crowd from every corner of Cree country.[28] A band member, the Pound, hosted the ceremony in thanksgiving for his daughter's recovery from a serious illness. A stranger named Papastis and 12 young men from Big Bear's band joined the crowd. Five days later Papastayo's brother, Tahkoots, sent a warning letter to William Anderson across the river. Big Bear had invited the Papaschase band "to join him in war path,"[29] he said, but the band had refused. Did Tahkoots invent the story to win a favour, or to alarm an old adversary, or was the message real? Anderson could not decide. He forwarded the letter to Ottawa, where it remains to this day.

The inevitable confrontation finally began near Batoche. Historians Bob Beal and Rod Macleod describe the complex series of events in their book, *Prairie Fire: The 1885 North-West Rebellion*: "The rebellion was essentially an incident in the occupation of the North-West Territories by white settlers, and the imposition of their institutions of government on the indigenous population," they conclude. "A little more flexibility, generosity and attention to the special problems of the region on the part of those who were administering the territory would have prevented the bloodshed that occurred."[30] This would be the last time Canadians took up arms against other Canadians in a serious challenge to the federal government. The rebellion's consequences endure in Canada.

In Edmonton, there was panic but no bloodshed. A telegram arrived in Alex Taylor's telegraph office on March 27, 1885: "Métis attacked at Duck Lake yesterday. Ten police killed. Louis Riel and Gabriel Dumont victorious."[31] Then, a shattering silence. The telegraph wire was cut. Settlers and traders gathered at Kelly's Saloon to consider the emergency. North West Mounted Police Inspector, Arthur Griesbach, hurried in from Fort Saskatchewan. The men elected a defence committee and after arguing for hours about who should pay to send a messenger to Calgary, an exasperated settler, James Mowat, offered to ride for free. Leaving at midnight, Mowat galloped south and arrived in Calgary two days later with an alarmist message from the defence committee: "Have wired Sir John. Indians on the war path. Send us men and arms immediately. Can't you help us at once?"[32]

For one long month the isolated settlers of Edmonton lived on wild rumours and panic. All but four families took refuge within the walls of the HBC post or the St. Albert Catholic mission. About 30 men formed the Edmonton Volunteer Company, dusted off three old brass cannons, their muskets, and their hunting rifles. Men cleared the riverbanks to allow clear sight lines from the fort. Women filled small bags with gunpowder. Three snipers were assigned to guard duty. Many settlers looked at their Cree, Nakoda and Métis neighbours with suspicion.

Some chiefs had strong connections with the leaders of the rebellion. Chief Ermineskin was married to Poundmaker's sister.[33] Local Cree witnessed the heightened panic of their neighbours in an atmosphere of mutual confusion. Receiving a message from Big Bear, Bobtail contacted the bands in the Edmonton district to ask their position. He received initial messages of support from the Nakoda at Lac Ste. Anne and Rivière Qui Barre. Samson travelled south to talk to the Blackfoot and the Nakoda in the Rockies. The Cree had all but decided to go to war at a gathering at Maskwachees on April 12, when Bobtail and Ermineskin rejected the idea after consulting with Constantin Scollen and John McDougall. Some Cree men from the Edmonton district are reported to have joined Poundmaker and Big Bear.

The Métis of Edmonton, St. Albert and Lac Ste. Anne found themselves in a frustrating position. Many had relatives and friends in the war zone, and also resented the arrival of new settlers who did not acknowledge their land tenure. Nevertheless, few of the founding families of Fort Edmonton had any interest in the revolt. Some settlers accused them of guilt by association and the agent at Fort Edmonton questioned their loyalty in a telegram to Winnipeg. Seven Métis community leaders voiced the indignation of the St. Albert Métis in a letter in the Edmonton Bulletin of April 21, 1885: "Do you think we have no feelings? We feel these wrongs deeply." Samuel Cunningham and Dan Maloney organized the St. Albert Mounted Rifles to prove their loyalty. The great majority of its members were Métis, including Felix Dumont, a cousin of Louis Riel's lieutenant, Gabriel Dumont. The militia travelled north to protect Lac La Biche from a rumoured attack that never came.

Edmonton's panic subsided in May. Hastily answering the settlers' call for help, Sam Steele's Scouts crossed the river on John Walter's ferry after a difficult 10-day march from Calgary. To the east, General Middleton took Louis Riel prisoner, ending the uprising at Batoche.

Eight Cree were hanged at Battleford. Riel was hanged after a stormy trial, Gabriel Dumont went into exile, and Big Bear and Poundmaker were imprisoned. Poundmaker's young son, Jean-Marie, wrote to his jailed father from St. Albert: "I have been much troubled, but I am glad to know you were not killed."[34]

⁘

THERE WAS NO FIGHTING in Edmonton, not a drop of blood spilled, yet the North-West Rebellion had its casualties here, too.

The Canadian government sent a commission to Edmonton on June 3, 1885 with authority "to satisfy any claims existing in connection with the extinguishment of the Indian title."[35] The commission offered scrip—a government certificate that could be redeemed in Crown land, or in money to purchase private land—to people of mixed ancestry, including band members with treaty status. Scrip coupons could be exchanged for up to 240 acres of land or $240. Canada processed scrip applications for more than 24,000 Métis in the West and North between 1870 and 1925 in transactions with a land value of 5.4 million acres. Historian Frank Tough, who has investigated the scrip process across western Canada, estimates that less than one per cent of these applications resulted in Métis property ownership.[36] Almost all of the scrip coupons ended up in the hands of land speculators, who often travelled from place to place with the government commissioners. Tough concludes that the Canadian government used scrip as a way to transfer public Dominion lands to private owners and increase the property value along the way. In Edmonton, as elsewhere, the scrip program poured thousands of dollars into the local economy and into family bank accounts.

Most First Nations and Métis people in the Edmonton district qualified for scrip because of fur trade intermarriages in the early years. Pierre Rowand, for example, was a grandson of Chief Factor John Rowand and Louise Umfreville and a Cree-speaking member of the Papaschase band when the scrip commission arrived. These were hard times. Canada had failed to deliver the Treaty 6 promises of adequate farm supplies and famine relief. Many First Nations members and Métis families applied for scrip, but most sold the coupons for a small amount of immediate cash.

Speculators were eager for their business. The government commission took 1,000 scrip applications in Edmonton in the first summer. Land speculators from as far away as Winnipeg, Calgary and Montreal, as well as local merchants like McDougall and Secord, offered 40 to 60 cents—or less—on the dollar on the spot, often through Métis middlemen.[37] Business was so brisk in town that some speculators returned to Calgary to retrieve more cash for the swaps. Frank Oliver estimated the transactions put $50,000 in circulation in the Edmonton district in July 1885,[38] a windfall for the local economy. Federal government agents processed the withdrawal of 202 people from treaty status in one summer.[39] Each scrip applicant forfeited treaty rights for all descendants.

Ottawa knew what was happening in Edmonton. The Deputy Super-intendent-General of Indian Affairs, Lawrence Vankoughnet, wrote to the prime minister in April 1886 that land speculators were applying pressure to the local Cree to apply for Métis scrip, offering them "a trifle" in exchange for their money coupons.[40] He recommended that the government forbid scrip transfers to land dealers for five years, but the prime minister rejected the suggestion. The government offer divided aboriginal families into legislated racial categories that often had little to do with their ancestry. One brother would take Métis scrip while another maintained "Indian" treaty rights for future generations. When the scrip commissioner returned to Edmonton and St. Albert in July 1886, he set up shop on a fairgrounds with a dozen beer tents, according to *The Bulletin*.[41] Preferring to live on their chosen land without government interference, Chief Papastayo applied for scrip, as did many people from local reserves; others refused the scrip offer. In confusion, Anderson wrote a frantic telegram to his superiors: "What action am I to take? Answer quick."[42] The government tried to slow down the withdrawals from treaty. Chief Papastayo objected in a telegram to the prime minister, and Ottawa chose to supply the scrip. In the end, more than half of the Papaschase band members received small cash payments from speculators for their scrip certificates.

The Papaschase people—those who had taken scrip and those with treaty status—refused to leave their cabins, tipis and cultivated fields on the Two Hills reserve. They needed rations to survive two hungry winters when the scrip money ran out. People in Edmonton, including both candidates for Edmonton's first seat in Parliament, urged Ottawa to throw open the reserve to settlement. Assistant Indian Commissioner Hayter Reed visited in 1887 to tell scrip recipients they would have to leave; those with treaty status could join Enoch's band. On August 12, 1887, the remaining Papaschase people left the reserve, but the land still belonged to them.[43]

The Papaschase band lost its entire reserve in south Edmonton under highly questionable circumstances when three men signed a document on November 19, 1888, at a meeting called at four days' notice by government agents. They surrendered the reserve to "such person or persons and upon such terms as the Government of the Dominion of Canada may deem most conducive to our welfare, and that of our people."[44] Ottawa subsequently sold the land to seven speculators: four from Calgary, two from Quebec and one from Ontario. The government credited $98,000 to the Enoch account but band members never saw the benefits.[45] The Papaschase people moved to the Enoch reserve, Hobbema, Kehewin, Fishing Lake, Onion Lake and beyond. Chief Papastayo moved to the Beaver Hills briefly, then moved north with his family. He died in the northern bush country near Elinor Lake in 1918.

Almost a century later, Margaret McGilvery sits at a kitchen table in a small north Edmonton apartment, holding a treasured item. The faded photograph of a group of Cree men standing in a field has been passed from hand to hand for generations. McGilvery believes it is the only existing photograph of Treaty 6 chiefs in the Edmonton area, standing together sometime in the 1890s or early twentieth century. McGilvery is a member of the Saddle Lake Cree Nation and a great-granddaughter of Chief Papastayo—although she was an adult before she traced her family roots to the Edmonton band through baptismal records and scrip certificates. "It bothers me that so many people don't know their lineage," she says. "Their history was taken away from them through this loss." She was disappointed to learn that the only identified photograph of Papastayo in Alberta's archives—a handsome portrait in the Glenbow Museum and Archives collection—is probably a picture of the wrong man. Edmonton's pioneer photographers, Charles Mathers and Ernest Brown, only rarely named the aboriginal and Métis people in their photographs. Mathers' notes were lost in a fire and Brown was casual about the authenticity of his studio portraits and local aboriginal scenes, often transposing images for commercial effect. The search for photographs, documents and family stories that will reveal the full aboriginal perspective of local historic events continues across Alberta.[46]

In Edmonton, racial categories hardened into rigid law after 1885. For a time, federal regulations confined band members to reserves unless they had a permission paper from a government agent. Intermarriage slowed down as white women arrived from eastern Canada with Victorian assertions about racial purity and British superiority. Many First Nations and Métis families moved away from Edmonton to farm in the Beaver Hills around Cooking Lake and Hastings Lake; some used scrip to acquire homestead land elsewhere; others moved to reserves and settlements across the West. Many of their children and grandchildren would eventually return to reclaim their rightful place in a new city.

⁓

DREAMING OF THE NEW RAILWAY and abundant farms, land booms and bustling commercial districts, Edmonton's new settlers concluded they were the victors after the Rebellion. They behaved as if they owned the place, and in time, they did.

Yet the newcomers, too, endured harsh disappointments. Their dreams depended, not on the buffalo, but on the Iron Horse. The new Canadian government promised a national railway and sent large parties of surveyors to determine the best routes through the Rockies to British Columbia. Local people assumed with complete confidence that the railway would be built through the Yellowhead Pass, bringing thousands of settlers and unimagined prosperity. They waited for their windfall. Then the CPR decided on the southern route through Winnipeg, Regina, Medicine Hat and Calgary, through the impossible Rogers Pass, and on to Vancouver. Soon thousands of settlers were pouring into the West on the new trains— 100,000 people arrived in 1882 alone—and the startled population of Edmonton realized they would not be coming here. This was betrayal.

The CPR probably chose the southern route for short-term financial reasons: the company could raise more money by shipping high-volume cargo across the continent in the early years before mass agriculture. They could also compete with the American railways if the line were located closer to the border. Local people understood the consequences: "Railways were the great generators of wealth," says Rod Macleod, a specialist in the history of the nineteenth-century West.[47] Settlers wanted to be near railways so that they could transport their crops to the larger markets; without a railway people would not come to the district. Edmonton would not only miss out on the construction of the early mansions and commercial buildings that are landmarks in Winnipeg and Calgary, it would forfeit population growth. Cut off from the economic development in the region, Edmonton became "a little forgotten fur trade place, with a very little bit of agricultural settlement, but not very much."[48]

Edmonton lost its head start. It had no real roads linking the settlement to distant places, only mud trails through the bush and prairies. Stern wheel steamboats inched along the North Saskatchewan, striking rocks and sandbars along the way. In a good year, the steamboats made two trips between Edmonton and Prince Albert. That made stagecoach travel seem speedy. Stagecoaches began to run between Calgary and Edmonton in 1883. Passengers paid $25 to sit opposite one another on benches, their knees bumping, their bodies thrown back and forth as horse teams pulled them through mud holes and over logs. The stagecoach left Edmonton on alternate Mondays and arrived in Calgary the following Friday. Passengers slept in farmhouses along the way. Edmonton waited weeks for mail and cargo—and years for a second chance.

Early settlers held on through the discouraging period. The Lamoureux family and the Ottewells kept farming. John Walter and his family kept the ferry running. William Bird and his family ran the flourmill at Mill Creek. John Norris and Ed Carey and their families kept their store going. John A. McDougall and Richard Secord resisted the urge to take their merchant trade and investment savvy to a more prosperous settlement. Frank Oliver promoted the town tirelessly in the *Bulletin*, a lively if sometimes vituperative newspaper. Somehow Edmonton endured its setbacks and returned to what it knew. The fur trade was in decline in other western cities, but it sustained the population here despite the disappearance of the buffalo. Waiting for the railway and the prosperity it would deliver, the disappointed traders and settlers looked north to the Peace River and Athabasca Country. As always, the north would sustain Edmonton.

⌐⌐~

THE MANITOU STONE was far away by 1890. George McDougall shipped the meteorite to Victoria University, the Methodist College in Toronto, after the first sign of trouble. In 1889, George Maclean wrote that the western Plains people still resented the sacrilege of the theft: "Science and superstition wage war against each other," he wrote, "and the evident conclusion in this matter is that the red man's ideal must pass through the crucible, in order that they may minister to the advancement of the nobler civilization of the white race."[49]

The Manitou stone stayed at the Royal Ontario Museum for another half-century. In the early 1950s Martin Jacobs, a farmer near Killam, Alberta, told a little girl in a grocery store about the meteorite that once sat on a hill on his farm. Sharleen Chevraux grew up to be a local high school teacher. She wrote an article about the Manitou stone in the *Western Producer* and retold the story in public speaking engagements around rural Alberta in the late 1960s.[50] Suddenly the lost meteorite became a symbol of Alberta's rising sense of its new place in Canada. Conservative politicians stood in the legislature to demand its return from Ontario.

The Manitou Stone was set up at the Provincial Museum of Alberta in Edmonton on June 10, 1973, where it has been ever since. It may be moving soon. A sign on the wall says the museum is "currently exploring how to care for this extraordinary object in a way that respects both its spiritual and scientific value."[51] In 2004 the exhibit did not name George McDougall as the man who took it away. Difficult questions linger. Does the Manitou Stone belong in the museum, or on a hill on the prairies? Who are the rightful owners? The Cree sculptor Stewart Steinhauer created a sculpture he calls *Papamihaw Asini*, which is installed near the meteorite. "Even though 133 years have passed since the Flying Rock was taken prisoner, the song the elders sing contains his memory," Steinhauer writes. "Each generation learns this song and keeps the memory alive."[52]

A child touches a stone in a dark room. She runs into the sunlight with a memory on her fingertips.

In Our Own Words

PEACE NEGOTIATIONS

Edmonton House Post Journal

8 DECEMBER 1862 Sent Mr. Brazeau off to meet the Blackfeet with Tobacco from the Crees to make peace. Condition of coming: all arms—Guns & knives—to be delivered up by both parties before meeting. If the Blackfeet won't agree to this, [they are] not to come here until the Crees are done Trading & away. Crees [are to] agree to give up above & do nothing if the Blackfeet will make peace & do the same. If not, Crees agree to go off home quietly for the present, & not to molest the Blackfeet at Fort or going off.

9 DECEMBER Mr. Brazeau arrived with the Band of Blackfeet, Slave Indians Piegans & Circees 50 men besides women & children.... Received them in the Indian House took all the Guns from them, and then introduced the Crees with their chiefs to them. All passed over well and the Peace made, a great deal of speeches made on both sides and no want of promises to keep the peace well. Took all the Blackfeet & Horses into the back square of Fort, and kept a strong Guard on watch all night.

10 DECEMBER The Peace was finally ratified today in the next room the chiefs of each of the Tribes being present, delivered a paper to each chief confirming the Peace made, signed with the name of all the chiefs present. Tobacco exchanged & sent to Slave Indian camps & Cree camps, all parties saluted each other with a kiss, shook hands...long may it last.[53]

Cree leaders Sweetgrass and Maskipiton led 50 warriors to Fort Edmonton for peace talks in late 1862. The Blackfoot Confederacy delegation arrived two days later with Tsuu T'ina allies. The peace held until November 1863.

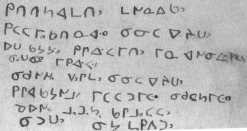

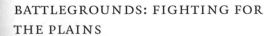

Born around 1810, Maskipiton travelled widely across North America and negotiated a Cree truce with the Blackfoot at Wetaskiwin, or the Peace Hills. He corresponded with missionaries in Cree syllabics. In the letter above he promised Rev. Woolsey 160 buffalo to pay for English lessons for his son, Benjamin: "I give my word. My friend. I Maskipiton." The negotiator walked into a Blackfoot ambush in 1869 while on another peace mission. His death brought a final wave of warfare to the gates of Fort Edmonton.

BATTLEGROUNDS: FIGHTING FOR THE PLAINS

Thunderchild, as told to Edward Ahenakew

One winter, when it was very cold, the Crees came from all over the plains to meet near the place where high platforms had been built for the bodies of their dead. They gathered there to take revenge against the Blackfoot who had killed fifteen women of the Crees that past summer, when they went for water. One of these women was Broken Wing and another was her sister...their father had gone through all the camps of the Crees, crying for his daughters and stirring up the people to avenge them.

It was January when all the people gathered in a great encampment, and there were women there and many young boys. I was one of these. It was my first expedition and I felt like a man, but the men said to us, "You are not old enough to fight, and if the Blackfoot surprise us, you must run away."

The northern lights were bright above the encampment and for three nights the people danced, before we moved out in long, long lines through the deep snow. Scouts went out before us, on both sides, and there was a general shout when three riders appeared. Two were scouts, the third was a Blackfoot woman, very pretty. The scouts had killed her husband, and they gave her to Short Tail, [Kiskyo or Bobtail], the brother of Ermine Skin. They warned us that one Blackfoot had escaped and would give the alarm ... there might be an attack that same night. We would have to be ready.

It was cold, cold. Everyone was running, some of them on snowshoes; everyone was watchful. Some went ahead of the main body, and those who reached the Blackfoot camp stole horses and brought them back to our encampment late in the night. We camped in the centre of wooded hills, and across the creek there were stands of poplar, and the Blackfoot camp.

With all the other boys, I was made to take my place well back in the circle of our encampment....

By now the Blackfoot had fled back to their camp, and there were war yells, and the cries of women and children. I ran forward to the line of Crees facing the Blackfoot camp....

They began to cut the tents open and pull them down, but the Blackfoot had run in amongst the trees, where there were more tents, and they were digging pits in the soft ground of the fire places. They shot and killed some of the Crees at the edge of the bush.

I saw one man rush forward, and when he was hit, he shouted, "Come for me. I am killed." Two of our men went forward while the others covered them, and they dragged him back. Those two were As-ka-chas and Ka-ya-sa-yis, a Stoney. Ka-ya-sa-yis said to me, "Come, boy, and bid me good-bye." He had been hit in the stomach. He was a man who had always been kind to me, and I felt sad....

Again there was much noise, for someone had found Father Lacombe's robes in a tent. His horse was taken too, as it was known later. No one would tell where the priest was, and A-chim put on the robes, and called out, "Here is the priest." Then there was a cry that a Cree was being scalped, and men rushed to the rescue.

The battle raged all that night; Crees were killed and wounded; the women wailed for their dead.

One of the Crees—he was Mi-sa-ti-mois—had been looking for horses all night, and he called out, "Cover me, and I will try to get them from the corral at the centre." He moved slowly towards it, and he had a hard time lifting one big log. At last it was off, and he led out three horses, one of them a beautiful grey racer.

The morning was coming, and the wounded and dead were carried back to our encampment, though the dead who were close to the Blackfoot tents we had to leave. I walked beside my wounded friend and wet his lips with snow. The Blackfoot followed us, but they were afraid to come near, and their shots fell short.

Mi-sa-ti-mois raced part way back on the grey horse that he had taken, crouched low on its back, his robe flying; the Blackfoot shot at him again and again, but they could not hit him. Then a Blackfoot did the same, and was not hit; as he rode, he sang, shouting out to us, "Crees, go back home quickly. We have two other camps close by, and we will fight you to them." But the Crees shouted back that he was lying, and we went on to our camp.

These eyewitness accounts depict a winter encounter between the Cree and Blackfoot in a period of renewed warfare. Thunderchild related the Cree side of the story to Edward Ahenakew. Albert Lacombe said he was camping with the Blackfoot when a skirmish began on December 3, 1866.

There my friend died of his painful wound. His father said, "My son has been in the games, and has been beaten. We will leave his body here." And we dressed him in his finest clothes and stood him up to face the Blackfoot proudly.

The Cree who had been scalped and stabbed also died at the camp. Before he died, he gave his three horses to his aunt and he asked her to care for his dog which had waited at the camp for him and had stayed beside the dying man. Then the woman sang of her nephew, of his manliness and of the love that his dog had for him. She wept for him and the women mourned aloud. And the dog searched the camp for the man he had followed faithfully.

We returned the way we had come, having taken our revenge and killed many Blackfoot.[54]

Albert Lacombe

In the year 1866, the third day of December, at one o'clock in the morning, at a place called by the Indians The Three Pounds, a war-party of Crees, Saulteaux, and Stoneys, about eight hundred in number, fell suddenly, without any warning, upon a small camp of Blackfoot, whose Chief was *Natous* (The Sun).

I was at the time in the camp, receiving the hospitality of *Natous*. I had been sent by my superiors to pass the winter with the Blackfoot, to study their language and character, and to ascertain their disposition towards Christianity. On my way from Edmonton and Rocky Mountain House, I had joined a party of travelling Indians, and, after visiting many camps, had arrived at the last encampment, where it was intended to unite into one all the dispersed little camps, and so to pass the winter with the whole nation, that they might protect themselves against their enemies. The snow was pretty deep. The day before, Crowfoot, who was yet under the command of his old father (*A-kow-int-kas-tiw*, The Many Names), was visited, and he promised to join *Natous* as soon as possible; and so also did the Chiefs of other camps.

Exhausted by fatigue, I was quietly sleeping in the tent of the Chief, and, when no thought of a war-party of lurking enemy was entertained, suddenly a dog put his head into the lodge. It was a Cree dog (*assinow emita*). The alarm was given. In one second, the Crees, who were watching about a hundred yards off, opened fire. In an instant some score of bullets came crashing through the leather lodge, and the wild war whoop of the Crees broke forth through the sharp and rapid detonation of many muskets.

It is not my intention to give the awful details of that fearful night, when the groans of the dying, the yelling of the warriors, the harangues of the Chiefs, and the noise of dogs and horses all mingled, formed a kind of hell.

I have only to say that at the most critical moment, when our little camp was half-taken by the Crees, and when the scalping and butchering were going on, the voice of Crowfoot was heard. He was rushing to our rescue. "Take courage (Ekakimak)," he cried out as he came with a large party of warriors. We were saved. Crowfoot, alongside *Natous*, fought like a bear.[55]

"BULLETS ARE FALLING ALL AROUND THE FORT"

Harrison Young, trader, 1870

In the spring of that year, Edmonton was in a state of siege for a few days. A big party of Blackfoot came in to wipe out Takoots and his friends, but unluckily the river was breaking up and they could not get across, so they contented themselves with firing at the fort and robbing the Hudson's Bay trader from Pigeon Lake who had just got in and was camped on Walter's flat. He and his men and David McDougall of Morley, who was also trading at Pigeon Lake, had a narrow escape with their lives, just getting across the river in a skiff in time. The [musket] balls was falling thick around their boat before they got ashore. There was great excitement inside the fort. Arms and ammunition were issued, bastions were manned and the cannon loaded. Mr. Groat and I loaded them and I really do not know which of us knew least about the job. Mr. Groat said he knew how much powder was required and I said if he knew that I would warrant the right charge of [cannon] ball, but I found out Mr. Groat was not quite sure whether it was one pound or five of powder that should go in, and as I had equal doubts of the quantity of ball, we did not weigh either but guessed at both.

We erected a barricade of carts before one of the gates and behind that placed the cannon. If the Blackfoot got across and stormed the fort and burst in at that particular gate, we were to fire our cannon. I am not of a blood thirsty disposition, and I never wished to kill anyone except the Indians who shot my dog "Don" in 1885, but I must confess I have always had a feeling that I would have liked to have seen the effect of one shot out of these cannons.[56]

The Cree around Fort Edmonton avenged the death of Maskipiton with a raid on an enemy trading party on April 8, 1870. The Blackfoot arrived to retaliate. Traders raced into the fort as bullets flew behind them. Three people—Harrison Young, James Gibbons and an aboriginal child named Saynis—left three very different accounts of the same event.

James Gibbons, prospector

As the Blackfeet were unable to cross the river at this place the pursuit came to an end. Four hundred Blackfeet came in and camped on Walter's Flat opposite the Hudson's Bay fort.... Beaupre, who subsequently farmed at Fort Saskatchewan, rode up to us and gave us the alarm. The fort at Edmonton had been closed and the garrison was standing ready to repel an attack. The Blackfeet were firing from the south side of the river and bullets were falling all around the fort.

Dave McDougall, who was trading at Pigeon Lake, and William Rowland of the Hudson's Bay Company, just managed to get in ahead of the Blackfeet. Dave McDougall had been shot through the coat. While they escaped with their lives they left their goods behind them, which fell into the hands of the Blackfeet and were promptly seized and destroyed.

There were in the Hudson's Bay fort in Edmonton at that time two small brass cannon. A man named Zeb Hariner, who had formerly been in the American artillery service, offered to bring these guns into action against the Blackfeet. Mr. Christie, who commanded the fort, would not allow it, giving as his reason that while we might succeed in driving the Blackfeet away from Edmonton they would probably wreak vengeance upon the other forts of the Company elsewhere.[57]

Saynis, a child witness

After four days a band of Blackfeet came; they had heard that their chief had been killed. A whole tribe. Must have been about four thousand. Hudson's Bay had a lot of stuff in their wheel wagons. There were about ten wagons full of blankets. There were about one hundred wagons full of goods, all kinds of goods. It was on the Saskatchewan. The Blackfeet came there. It was in the spring. The river was in flood, very high. Then one of the Hudson's Bay drivers took a boat and ran over to where the goods were on the other side. There were, in all, six drivers. They put the goods into the boats and crossed the river to the store with the baggage, leaving six wagons of goods on the other side. Must have cost lots of money. The Blackfeet could not ford the river, because it was flooded and high. Lots of wood and ice floating downstream. Then the Blackfeet burnt all the goods in the wagons, burnt all that was there, and spoilt the whole Hudson's Bay's goods....

After about six months, the Blackfeet got [smallpox]. Some of them said, "We have [smallpox] because we burned the Hudson's Bay's goods.

That is why white people gave us sickness." The Blackfeet then were about ten thousand. But now there are just a few left. There used to be a lot of tribes. Some Blackfeet got shot. Others died of [smallpox].[58]

OMIKIWIN/SMALLPOX

Victoria Belcourt Callihoo, child witness

All my sisters, brothers and I went along with our mother then to the Plains for the hunt. We heard about a disease on our way out. Not knowing its dreadfulness, we moved on. The bison were getting further South. The journey was now two days longer than usual. Father stayed home, tending the chores and gardening the small crop we had.

People began to act sick before the herd was caught up, but no deaths had occurred. When the chase camp was set, the sickness got worse, people dying fast. The illness started with a fever. Some people not knowing how to treat smallpox, would wade in the water. These never survived. Towards fall when nights were frosty, the plague got worse, for people did not stay in bed as they would now. Inoculation was unknown—almost everyone caught it, young and old. Families were wiped out. My aunt and four children died from smallpox. Her husband was thrown from a horse on a buffalo hunt and was killed from the fall. My mother never caught the sickness, although she worked day and night attending the sick and slicing the [buffalo] meat. Riders would tell of seeing teepees full of dead. These were Crees and Blackfeet.

This was the saddest hunt: no horse races, no merriment, only death. A pall fell on the people. Some of the corpses were buried there on the Plains, others were brought home. Those buried out were wrapped in cotton (we always had cotton with us to make dresses and shirts). We got the material from the Hudson's Bay Company. A hide would be wrapped around the body and it was then buried in a shallow grave. We had spades. A Roman Catholic priest would always accompany the hunting trips, providing for the spiritual needs of the Métis. His vehicle had four wheels and was the first four-wheeled vehicle I saw. He was provided with food by the people. Father Lacombe, Father Andre, and Father Lestanc were the

In her old age Victoria Belcourt Callihoo offered vivid descriptions of Métis history and traditions in Lac Ste. Anne, St. Albert and Fort Edmonton. Born in 1861, she accompanied her parents on some of the last buffalo hunts to leave the district. Victoria was a great-granddaughter of Chief Factor John Rowand and Louise Umfreville and a niece of Chief Michel Callihoo. She and her husband raised 13 children. She danced at her 100th birthday party in St. Albert and died in 1966.

priests who took part in the hunts. We brought back the bodies of my Aunt and her children, and Mother bought lumber (whipped sawed) and got coffins made. They were all buried at St. Albert. My Father, hearing of this terrible sickness that had fallen on us, met us at St. Albert. We were greatly consoled when we saw him. Without exaggeration, fully fifty percent of the Métis and seventy-five percent of the Indians succumbed to smallpox in the seventies.[59]

Angelique Nault, widow

I, Angelique Nault, nee Brabeuf, of St. Albert declare and say, first, that my husband took up what is now Lot Number 30, St. Albert, about the year 1860 and died three years before this, of smallpox, leaving eight children.... The eldest, Alexis, died of the smallpox, leaving a widow and one child. The latter has since died, immediately after the father's death. The second is named Julie, married first to Benjamin Bellerose...who died of the smallpox, leaving a widow and one child. The third, Justine, who is the wife of Felix Dumont, is still living. The fourth, named Abraham, died.... The fifth son is Edward, still living. The sixth, Madeleine, died of the smallpox.... The seventh, Josephine, also died of the smallpox.... The eighth Francis, also died of the smallpox....

And I make this solemn declaration, consequently believing this same to be true....

Angelique (her X mark) Nault[60]

George McDougall, Methodist missionary, Victoria mission

16 AUGUST 1870 Surrounded by circumstances that cannot be described, I sit down to pen you a few lines. The evening we left Red River I learned that the smallpox had reached the Saskatchewan. Anxious to be with our people we crossed the plains in nineteen days, and at Canton we met the destroyer of the poor red man. One hundred had died at Fort Pitt, and along the road we encountered bands flying from the plague, yet carrying death with them.

On reaching Victoria I found my worst fears more than realized. My son had induced the Crees to scatter, but many, already struck down with the small-pox, were incapable of helping themselves. Two days after my arrival John was taken very ill, and is now in a critical state. For weeks my dear boy has had very little rest. Day and night he has waited on the sick and the dying. Many of our best members have passed away....

> The smallpox epidemic of 1870 killed half of all the First Nations people in Alberta, according to some estimates. More than 300 people died in St. Albert alone, a third of the population. Aboriginal people along the North Saskatchewan River had no physical immunity to European diseases. Through the eighteenth and nineteenth centuries, smallpox, influenza, measles, diphtheria and scarlet fever struck Cree camps and Métis settlements in deadly waves.

Friends of suffering humanity, pray for us. Verily the judgments of a just God are now upon this land of blood and idolatry; and yet, of how many of these suffering creatures, it may be truly said "they know not their right hand from their left."

25 SEPTEMBER The disease first appeared in my own family, and on the 13th of October our youngest daughter, aged eleven years, died. How precious to our bleeding hearts her dying words! Flora loved the Saviour.[61]

21 OCTOBER I have just received a letter from Mr. Hardisty, of Fort Edmonton. Two hundred of the St. Albert people are reported dead. There will be great distress this winter, the fall hunt being a failure.[62]

23 OCTOBER We are now passing through deep waters, all prostrate with the fearful disease, except Mrs. McDougall, and she exhausted with watching.

1 NOVEMBER At five o'clock this afternoon our Georgiana breathed her last. The last intelligible words she uttered were prayer.... My kind neighbors, Messrs. Hardisty and Tait, brought the coffin and placed it at the gate, and my son and self carried her mortal remains to the grave. When we were filling in the earth, he uttered an expression which found an echo in my poor heart, "Father, I find it hard to bury our own dead;" but just then the words of the apostle were applied with such force to my mind that I could not restrain myself from shouting them aloud: "O, death, where is thy sting? O, grave, where is thy victory? Thanks be to God, who giveth us the victory through our Lord Jesus Christ."[63]

George McDougall and his wife Elizabeth Chantler McDougall founded the Methodist mission at Victoria, now known as Pakan, in 1862. After the smallpox epidemic, the McDougalls established missions outside Fort Edmonton, at Pigeon Lake, and among the Nakoda at Morley. George McDougall died of exposure in a blizzard in 1876.

Albert Lacombe, to Archbishop Alexandre-Antonin Tache

12 SEPTEMBER 1870

Monseigneur...

Day and night I was constantly occupied, barely had time to say mass. I had to instruct and baptize dying infidels, confess and anoint our neophytes at the point of death, minister to the different wants, give a drink to one and food to another, kindle the fire during the cold nights. This dreadful epidemic has taken all compassion from the hearts of the Indians. These lepers of a new kind are removed at a distance from the others and sheltered with branches. There they witness the decomposition and putrefaction of their bodies several days before death....

The patient is at first very feverish, the skin becomes red and covered with pimples, these blotches in a few days form scabs filled with infectious matter. Then the flesh begins to decompose and falls off in fragments. Worms swim in the parts most affected. Inflammation of the throat impedes all passage for meat or drink. While enduring the torments of this cruel agony the sufferer stops breathing, alone in a poor shed with no other help than what I can offer.

The hideous corpse must be buried, a grave must be dug and the body borne to the burial ground. All this falls on me and I am alone with Indians disheartened and so terrified that they hardly dare approach even their own relatives.

God alone knows what I have had to endure merely to prevent these mortal remains being devoured by dogs....

Of Your GRACE

the affectionate and devoted missionary

Alb. Lacombe ptre

OMI[64]

Suzette Piché, as told to Anne Anderson

I had a very close call with death. It was during the time of the smallpox epidemic. Not having any help, my whole face became infected and so I decided to do what I thought was best. I made a mild solution of lye, which is wood ashes and water, strained. This liquid was then diluted and I washed my face with it. The solution was still too strong. It got into my eyes and nearly ruined my sight. Yes, the infection cleared up but the heavy pox marks remained.[65]

Sister Emery to Mother Slocombe, Youville Home of St. Albert

JANUARY 6, 1871

My dear Mother...

This year, we have passed a very sad New Year's Day. As in the past, we received many visitors, but mostly very sad visitors, pain written all over their faces. Each one seemed to understand today, his or her loss. Poor

Dr. William Todd, an HBC surgeon, was sending smallpox vaccines to John Rowand at Fort Edmonton before 1850, but the quality was often suspect and many Cree, Nakoda and Métis in the region were not vaccinated.

people! In fact, there is much to be sad about—there is cause enough when one sees families nearly all dead; and those who have escaped the disease cannot rejoice. Lately, we received a little orphan girl—seven years old, blind and all scarred by smallpox; that poor child is the only one left from a family of seven. There are still a few cases of illness amongst those who haven't had it yet. In mid-December, two young persons (they were sisters) became ill with smallpox....

How sad it was to see, that afternoon, first day of the year, two bodies without casket, in a sleigh being driven to the cemetery.... No wonder joy was tempered by such circumstances. But that's not all. The next day, a new scene was reserved for us: we saw two corpses deposited on our doorsteps.... I've already told you dear Mother, in another letter, how many persons had died in the St. Albert Mission alone. The number is augmented—two hundred eighty four victims nearly and twenty-nine in Lac Ste. Anne. There has been also a great number of dead amongst the Blackfoot; the Sarcis have practically all died.... It is said that in that nation there are only 4 or 5 tents left. For other Nations, ravages have not been as bad as for the Sarcis.[66]

In an unsigned account, another Grey Nun described the terror of a local child who had wandered alone for 20 days after watching a pack of dogs attack the dead bodies of his parents and brothers. "This poor child still remembers his many hardships, and relates his tale of woe with such visible innocence as to bring forth a tear from many a listener's eye."

Captain William Francis Butler

Only three white persons appear to have fallen victims to the disease one, an officer of the Hudson's Bay Company service at Carlton, and two members of the family of the Rev. Mr. McDougall, at Victoria. Altogether I should be inclined to estimate the entire loss along the North Saskatchewan, not including Blood, Blackfeet or Peagin Indians, at about 1,200 persons.... With regard to the supply of medicines sent by direction of the Board of Health in Manitoba to the Saskatchewan, I have only to remark that I conveyed to Edmonton the portion of the supply destined for that station. It was found, however, that many of the bottles had been much injured by frost, and I cannot in any way favourably notice either the composition of general selection of these supplies.[67]

"I TRIED TO SPEAK"

Elizabeth Chantler McDougall

We moved from Victoria; my husband and self, and two of our neighbors, started on our journey to Edmonton. The roads were very bad, the banks of every stream we came to flooded. The two first were crossed without very

great difficulty; the third, called Sucker Creek, was raging, the waters rushing and foaming with swiftest speed. When I first saw it, I wondered how we were to cross it, and turning round to speak to Mr. McDougall, I saw he was preparing to cross by moving the luggage from the buckboard and placing it on the cart; and when ready he drove down the bank of the stream, and at the same time spoke to the boy who was driving the cart to follow.

Scarcely had the horse struck the current when he was thrown on his side, and horse and buckboard, with Mr. McDougall standing on the buckboard seat, were carried down the river. There were trees projecting from the bank into the stream on either side, and presently all were carried under one of these trees, and

Still grieving for her daughters and daughter-in-law, Elizabeth Chantler McDougall began a terrifying trip with her husband to Fort Edmonton in 1871. In her lifetime she gave birth to eight children and adopted others, but saw several children meet untimely deaths. She assumed nursing and teaching duties at the Methodist missions and died at Morley in 1904.

horse, buckboard and driver were tangled up together by the force of the current. This was repeated several times, and very soon all disappeared around the point out of my sight. All this happened, as it seemed to me, in a moment.

I tried to speak, but could not. I turned to the men, but I saw them running through the bushes down along the bank of the river, and my first thought was to follow, and I was going to do so, when the boy with the cart drew my attention.

He had been directed to follow, and had just got down the bank of the stream, and the horse had stopped, with the water above the shafts, and I went to see if I could do anything to help him.

I found that it was impossible, the steep bank shoving the horse and cart towards the current. We could not possibly back the cart out. I told the boy to sit still, and I spoke a few words to the noble animal, and he stood perfectly quiet, bracing against the current as if he knew both life and property were at stake. In the meanwhile I was continually looking to God, and praying that my dear husband's life might be saved from a

watery grave, and while doing so, I realized all would be well. I had only to wait, but the time seemed very long before anyone came, and how my heart leaped for joy when I heard his voice, calling to me, and I ran to meet him.

His first words were: Let us praise the Lord for the preservation of my life.[68]

Charles G. Horetzky, an Ontario survey photographer from a Ukrainian family in Scotland, is believed to have taken the first photographs of Fort Edmonton on March 10, 1871. The man in the bowler hat in the foreground is Samuel Trott.

TRADING THE LAND

William J. Christie

26 APRIL 1871 On the 13th instant I had a visit from the Cree Chiefs, representing the Plain Crees from this place to Carlton, accompanied by a few followers.

The object of their visit was to ascertain whether their lands had been sold or not, and what was the intention of the Canadian Government in relation to them. They referred to the epidemic that had raged throughout the past summer and the subsequent starvation, the poverty of their country, the visible diminution of the buffalo, their sole support, ending by requesting certain presents at once and that I should lay their case before Her Majesty's representative at Fort Garry. Many stories have reached these Indians through various channels, ever since the transfer of the North-West Territories to the Dominion of Canada and they were most anxious to hear from myself what had taken place.

I told them that the Canadian Government had as yet made no application for their lands or hunting grounds, and when anything was required of them, most likely Commissioners would be sent beforehand to [make a treaty] with them, and that until then they should remain quiet and live at peace with all men. I further stated that Canada, in her treaties with Indians, heretofore, had dealt most liberally with them, and that they were now in settled houses and well off, and that I had no doubt in settling with them the same liberal policy would be followed.

As I was aware that they had heard many exaggerated stories about the troops in Red River, I took the opportunity of telling them why troops had been sent; and if Her Majesty sent troops to the Saskatchewan, it was as much for the protection of the red as the white man, and that they would be for the maintenance of law and order....

At a subsequent interview with the Chiefs alone, they requested that I should write down their words, or messages to their Great Master in Red River. I accordingly did so, and have transmitted the messages as delivered....

The buffalo will soon be exterminated and when starvation comes, these Plains Indian tribes will fall back on the Hudson's Bay Forts and settlements for relief and assistance....

I think that the establishment of law and order in the Saskatchewan District, as early as possible, is of most vital importance to the future of the country and the interest of Canada, and also the making of some treaty or settlement with the Indians who inhabit the Saskatchewan District.[69]

"Come and see us"

1. The Chief Sweet Grass, The Chief of the country

GREAT FATHER,—I shake hands with you, and bid you welcome. We heard our lands were sold and we did not like it; we don't want to sell our lands; it is our property, and no one has a right to sell them.

Our country is getting ruined of fur-bearing animals, hitherto our sole support, and now we are poor and want help—we want you to pity us. We want cattle, tools, agricultural implements, and assistance in everything when we come to settle—our country is no longer able to support us.

Make provision for us against years of starvation. We have had great starvation the past winter, and the small-pox took away many of our people, the old, young, and children.

We want you to stop the Americans from coming to trade on our lands, and giving firewater, ammunition and arms to our enemies the Blackfeet.

We made a peace this winter with the Blackfeet. Our young men are foolish, it may not last long.

We invite you to come and see us and to speak with us. If you can't come yourself, send some one in your place.

We send these words by our Master, Mr. Christie, in whom we have every confidence. That is all.

2. Kehewin, The Eagle

GREAT FATHER, Let us all be friendly. We never shed any white man's blood, and have always been friendly with the whites, and want workmen, carpenters and farmers to assist us when we settle. I want all my brother, Sweet Grass, asks. That is all.

3. The Little Hunter

You, my brother, the Great Chief in Red River, treat me as a brother, that is, as a Great Chief.

4. Kis-ki-on, or Short Tail

My brother, that is coming close, I look upon you, as if I saw you; I want you to pity me, and I want help to cultivate the ground for myself and descendants. Come and see us.[70]

Sweetgrass, also known as Abraham Wikaskokiseyin, was an influential leader of the Plains Cree. In 1871 he led a delegation of chiefs to Fort Edmonton to object to the HBC sale of Cree traditional territory to the Canadian government. He posed for this portrait in St. Boniface, Manitoba, the following year.

Sgt.-Major Sam Steele

The North West Mounted Police arrived at Fort Edmonton in November 1874. Sergeant-Major Sam Steele later described why Inspector W.D. Jarvis decided to build a headquarters at Fort Saskatchewan over the protests of local people.

The site selected was a good one, but very inconvenient at that time, being quite out of the line of travel by trail. The ground opposite Edmonton was equally good and in other respects better, but at that time, one must remember, the preliminary survey of the C.P.R. passed 40 miles south, at a point known as the Hay Lakes, and crossed the Saskatchewan many miles west of Fort Edmonton, thus giving the impression that the main line would not touch Edmonton. Inspector Jarvis had quite a different opinion, however. He knew that Edmonton had a name already, and had large quantities of coal beneath the fort, in veins which extended and improved all the way up the river for many miles, but he knew that the crossing at the new site was easier and believed that a good town would spring up there in the future....

In April, 1875, we set to work to build our new quarters.... In July the Company's steamer Northcote arrived on her maiden trip, the first steamer to navigate the Saskatchewan. She brought great quantities of mails for our division, the first mail of any consequence since we left our camp at Dufferin more than a year before.[71]

TREATIES AND TALKS AT FORT EDMONTON

Lazarus Roan, Papaschase descendant, as told to Louis Rain and Richard Lightning

This is the story they always related to us, the manner by which the chief was dealt with. He would indicate with his hands approximately one foot in depth: "That is the depth that is requested from you, that is what the deal is, nothing below the surface, that will always belong to you. Only land where agriculture can be viable; other areas where nothing can grow, that will always belong to you. You will always be the owner of that land." That is what they were promised. That is why they were agreeable to treaty because the promises were so good. The government official was always making references to a woman (Queen) who had sent them. The Indians sympathized with the woman, the Queen, through her representatives....

The only thing which was included in the bargaining was those portions of land where something could be sown by the white man. "The area where nothing will grow, that will always be yours.... And when the negotiation has been concluded, and settlers begin to homestead, it will only be their property that will be fenced off, that you will not be allowed to enter. Other areas which are not homesteaded and remain open will belong to you as long as the sun shines." These are the promises that were made to our forefathers and our fathers.[72]

John Brown, Cree descendant

This is my father's story.... A meeting was held in Edmonton at some location between the High Level Bridge and Low Level Bridge on the north side of the Saskatchewan river. Michel Callihoo and Pagan Kachistawaiskum were negotiating with the governor. These were the Queen's representatives. They were sent here to make an agreement on the land....

At this very moment when the actual discussion took place, Michel Callihoo was told that the whole country to be bought by the white man was only to depth of one foot and no further. He was told that anything further down after the one foot depth was theirs. It is only the dirt that is to be bought from you by the white man. He is not going to buy anything that flies up in the air nor any wild animal. All of these things are to be yours for your own use. This is what was said. I have already said that there are many things that I don't remember of what my father used to say. I only wish that the gathering of information was done long before...when the older people were still living. My father would have had much to tell of what took place at the time of negotiations because he was an observer. He was about ten feet away from the main spokesman....

As the discussion of the treaties went on, the Indian people were told that any wild game was lawfully theirs at all times. Michel Callihoo was asked, "If a fire started up in the mountains, would you be willing to fight it?" Without a reply, he was told, "Some day you will be distributed some firearms." Surprisingly he jumped up, saying, "If you want to do this to me you might just as well blot off what's written in the documents or else I will clean your body right out. Do you see all these people sitting all around us?" The distribution of guns was disregarded in the signing of treaties. A Hudson's Bay spokesman spoke up, and said: "I have looked after the Indian people for four hundred and fifty years in the past. I am now going to turn these people to the white man and see what treatment he will be able to give them. I am going to put up a stake into the ground across the river and after seventy years from this time on, if the white man fails to give these people proper treatment I shall take them back." As he was standing

The aboriginal peoples of the North-West negotiated the terms of Treaty 6 with representatives of the Queen at Fort Carlton and Fort Pitt in August and September of 1876. Many chiefs, interpreters and witnesses at the first signing ceremonies had strong links to this region. Weekaskookeeseyin, or Sweetgrass; Onchamanisos, or Little Hunter; Pakan and Kehewin negotiated for many of the western Cree at Fort Pitt. W.J. Christie was a treaty commissioner; Peter Erasmus was the interpreter. Missionaries John McDougall and Constantine Scollen, as well as Eliza McDougall Hardisty signed as witnesses.

there, [someone said] "the south shore of the Saskatchewan river shall become my boundary line. Any land south of it is mine. Someday in the future you shall have your own land. No white man will ever be allowed to make money on it."[73]

Treaty 6, as it is written

Chiefs and headmen in the Fort Edmonton district brought their bands into Treaty 6 when they signed this adhesion document on August 21, 1877. The treaty had been negotiated and signed at Fort Carlton and Fort Pitt the preceding year. Chief Michel Callihoo signed the treaty adhesion in 1878.

The Plain and Wood Cree Tribes of Indians and all other the Indians inhabiting the district hereinafter described and defined, do hereby cede, release, surrender and yield up to the Government of the Dominion of Canada for Her Majesty the Queen and her successors forever, all their rights, titles and privileges whatsoever, to the lands included within the following limits...that is to say:

Commencing at the mouth of the river emptying into the north-west angle of Cumberland Lake...continuing westerly along the said shore to the western limit thereof, and thence due west to the Athabaska River, thence up the said river, against the stream, to the Jasper House, in the Rocky Mountains...to the mouth of the said Red Deer River on the South Branch of the Saskatchewan River; thence eastwardly and northwardly....

And also all their rights, titles and privileges whatsoever, to all other lands, wherever situated, in the North-West Territories, or in any other Province or portion of Her Majesty's Dominions, situated and being within the Dominion of Canada;

The tract comprised within the lines above described, embracing an area of one hundred and twenty-one thousand square miles, be the same more or less;

To have and to hold the same to Her Majesty the Queen and her successors forever....

And Her Majesty the Queen hereby agrees and undertakes to lay aside reserves for farming lands, due respect being had to lands at present cultivated by the said Indians, and other reserves for the benefit of the said Indians, to be administered and dealt with for them by Her Majesty's Government of the Dominion of Canada, provided all such reserves shall not exceed in all one square mile for each family of five, or in that proportion for larger or smaller families....

Signed at Edmonton, this 21st day of August, in the year above-written, by the Chiefs and head men hereto, the whole having been first read and explained by Peter Erasmus, in the presence of the following witnesses.

(Signed)

ALEXIS KEES-KEE-CHEE-CHI,	His X mark.	Chief.
OO-MUO-IN-AH-SOO-WAW-SIN-EE,	X	Head man.
CATSCHIS-TAH-WAY-SKUM,	X	Chief.
KOO-SAH-WAN-AS-KAY,	X	Head man.
PAHS-PAHS-CHASE.	X	
TAH-KOOTCH.	X	
BOBTAIL	X	Signed at Blackfoot Crossing
MICHEL CALLIHOO	X	Signed at Plain Stony[74]

FESTIVITIES AND FAMINE

Samuel Steele, NWMP at Fort Saskatchewan, 1874

On the approach of Christmas Inspector Jarvis gave me permission to get up a ball in the fort, as it was thought to be a good thing to introduce ourselves to the people in the settlement and to return some of the hospitality which we had received. A meeting was held and all voted a month's pay towards the dance. Chief Factor Hardisty gave us the use of a large store-house, in which there was an enormous fire-place, and loaned all the crockery and other table necessaries required for the feast. Large quantities of fresh buffalo tongues, humps (or "boss ribs," as they were called), buffalo hind quarters, venison, prairie chickens and wild geese were purchased and the chef, Sam Taber, with his assistants, was set to work to make plum-puddings and mince-pies, for which there was an ample supply of material in the Company's store.[75]

Vital Grandin, missionary, St. Albert

21 MARCH 1876 The Natives and starving people overwhelm us.

18 MARCH 1877 In the evening M. Joly sings several amusing little songs and Brother Leriche amuses the children with the marionettes which he handles.

22 MARCH We no longer know how to furnish food for the starving people. It is truly desolating and disquieting; each day there are more cases. This evening opening of the Retreat; sermon on Death by Father Lestanc.

18 APRIL We are overwhelmed by the starving Assiniboines who come to join the Métis in asking us for food.

The Grey Nuns and students at the St. Albert mission in 1885. Sister Emery sits to the left of the kneeling child.

19 APRIL A poor Native woman, second wife of the same man, is abandoned by her husband who wants to beg; this woman having four children beseeches me to take one. I have accepted conditionally while waiting the assent of the Sisters who have refused; I then had to dismiss the poor mother. In the evening we were horrified by a prairie fire; a watch had to be kept all night.[76]

James Stewart, Edmonton Indian agent

REPORT TO OTTAWA, 1881 The unusual destitution of the Indians, all over this Agency, obliged us to assist them to a large extent; indeed, large as it may appear, it was by no means what it looks at first sight. If you divide the amount distributed by the number of recipients, you will find it but a small portion to each sufferer. I may well call them sufferers, for I have never seen anything like it since my long residence in this country. It was not only the want of buffalo, but everything else seemed to have deserted the country; even fish were scarce. Fur-bearing animals, from which the Indians might have supplied themselves with clothing etc., were not to be had. In some cases some hunting might have been done, but the poor people were naked, and the cold was intense, and remained so during the whole winter; under these circumstances they behaved well, and no raids were made on anything here. They ate many of their horses and all the dogs were destroyed for food; in fact, everything was tried and failed. In our assistance the strictest economy was practised, and unless the Indians had been allowed to die, or to help themselves to the settlers' cattle (neither of which ways would have brought much credit to anybody concerned), we could not have got through with less. We fully hoped that in the spring, wild fowl and fish would have been plentiful, but owing to the continued bad weather, few of either of these sources of provisions were available.[77]

A Grey Nun, unidentified, St. Albert

We have not seen or smelled anything like this for at least ten years. Could these be APPLES? And there are enough for a generous sharing with the whole family at the Youville Asylum! God of surprises, you know when we need this kind of novelty in our isolated life![78]

LOCAL ENTERTAINMENT:
FROM HOCKEY TO PUBLIC EXECUTIONS

John Chantler McDougall

The next day being Saturday, we organized a big game of shinty on the ice before the Mission, and announced meeting for Sunday in the church. Hardisty rode one way and I the other to bring the people together, and the satisfaction of all was sublime. The old and the young came to the game on Saturday afternoon, and all took sides, some on skates and others on foot. Away went the ball, and some one "swiped" it across the river under the towering and almost perpendicular bank which cast a deep shade over the ice, and in lily rush after the ball I did not see the open hole and swift, silent current until too late.

I sheered off, but only to cut through the thin ice, and in I went. I grabbed the stronger ice as I took the plunge, feet foremost, and with most vigorous swimming with both legs and one hand I managed to keep from going under. I knew I could not hold out very long, but presently was aware that Hardisty, who had been at the other end of the field, was now stretched out on the ice and was holding his shinty stick to me. This I gripped for life, and felt I was saved from present drowning. It was now my turn to take command, and I called to Charles Whitford to lie down and take Mr. Hardisty by the feet; then I shouted to others to take hold of Charles and pull us out, all of which was done in a minute. I ran off up to the house and changed my clothes, and was in the game again in a little while.[79]

Jean D'Artigue, visitor

In February of this year I was invited to attend a play and ball given by the inhabitants of Edmonton. My readers will naturally ask how, in a wild country like this, theatrical representations could be given. Nevertheless these plays are of frequent occurrence, and this is how the matter is arranged.

First, a managing committee is formed, whose duty it is to make all necessary preparations and to invite the guests. Invitations are frequently sent to a distance of fifty miles and thus the guests are sometimes reckoned by hundreds. As these balls sometimes last five or six days, an abundance of provisions must be prepared. It was to a ball of this character, that I was invited, and both the play and the ball took place within the Fort itself. I arrived at five p.m., and very soon the hall was crowded.

On the platform, in front of the curtain, was seated a half-breed, a very passable violinist, who played a few military marches, followed by different national anthems, and ended with the "Marseillaise," amid the hearty applause of all present. The curtain rose, and then began the representation of a rustic scene composed for the occasion, and entitled "Hard Times." It would take up too much space and time to give an analysis of the play; suffice it to say that it lasted three hours, the different characters were well sustained throughout, and the hall resounded with merited applause from the spectators. The play ended, a bountiful supper was disposed of, and the play-room cleared for the dance. Here the white guests danced by themselves, and after the usual fashion, while the half-breeds, who formed the largest part of the assembly, retired to another apartment, and organized a dance of their own, and one more suited to their tastes and habits.[80]

James Gibbons

I remember that in 1875 we introduced candle moulds and made our own candles from any fat we could get hold of. Prior to that time tallow dips were used which were very bad for the eyes. We were very short of reading matter, and I remember that in the winter of 1875–76 I read Josephus' *History of the Jews* and Macaulay's *History of England*. These books belonged to Malcolm Groat, and I think that everybody who could read for fifty miles around read these books.[81]

Lovisa McDougall, wife of trader John McDougall

We had a party New Years Eve at Mr. Hardesties. It was splendid. All the "Elate" of the country was their, but I was the only lady except Mrs. Hardistie and her sister Mrs. Wood. They and Mrs. Whitesides are the only wemon here I associate with. The rest are not much.

We have company nearly every evening. T[he] organ is as good as ever. Mr. Little burry came up one day & took it all to pieces. He was from 10 o'clock in the morning until 12 at night fixing it. Some part inside had come unglued. He took the back out first & then took it all to pieces. There are lots of nice young fellows up here, all nearly professionall. Mr. Littleury is an engineer. I had Mr. Brearden and Mr. Trail calling on me yesterday. Mr. Brearden came down from Jasper House in the Mountains to spend his holiday, and Mr. Trail is from Lac La Biche, 180 miles north of us.

That Indian was hung on the 20th of dec., Johnnie sold the rope, blach gound and C. for the occasion. We had an invitation to spend Xmas at Mr. Taber but it was to cold to go. Colonel Garvis got a telegram from Toronto New Years morning. It is $3.50 to Toronto. Their was races New Years Day down to the Fort. S[n]ow shoe race, old wives race & dear knows what all. I must close now as my paper is full....[82]

Jean D'Artigue

On the day before the execution took place a gallows was erected within [Fort Saskatchewan], the rope tested, and everything made in readiness. The priest passed the whole night with the condemned, and also breakfasted with him. Finally the Sheriff, attended by Inspector Jarvis and the executioner, entered the jail and announced to the prisoner that his hour had come. The executioner tied his hands, the guards entered and conducted him to the scaffold, attended by the priest and the officers. Being placed on the trap, the opportunity was given him to address the large crowd which had gathered to witness the execution. After saying a few words, in which he again acknowledged his guilt and thanked those who had charge of him during his incarceration for their uniform kindness, the bolt was drawn and Kakisikutchin launched into eternity.[83]

Descendants of the Papaschase First Nation are researching the correct identities of the couple in this photograph; the man is believed to be either Chief Papaschase or his brother Batteau. Born in 1845 in Fort Assiniboine, Chief Papastayo (also spelled Papaschase or Passpasschase), was sometimes known by his English name John Gladu Quinn. He and his five brothers, Batteau, Tahkoots, Satooch, George Meecham, and Abraham moved to the district with their parents, John Kwenis and Lizette Gladu in the 1850s. The family worked for the HBC and hunted in the Beaver Hills with other Cree families. Papastayo signed an adhesion to Treaty 6 and claimed a large reserve on behalf of the band before accepting scrip.

THE PAPASCHASE STORY

Calvin Bruneau, descendant

I'm glad the history of the Papaschase band is being brought out. It will show the people of Edmonton, and also the aboriginal people of Alberta, what happened here to our ancestors, and the injustices that took place.

This is our motivation today. We want to bring the truth out, and by revealing injustices, take the necessary steps to correct the situation. By holding Aboriginal Day at the Rossdale cemetery, by repatriating the bodies to the cemetery, we will commemorate our history out of honour and respect for our ancestors.

By bringing out the history of the Papaschase we can reveal what happened to the band. It was the government that took our land and

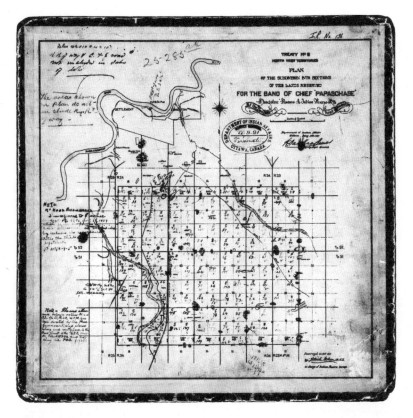

The federal government survey map shows the boundaries of the Papaschase reserve in south Edmonton. Treaty 6 promised one square mile for every five people. Chief Papastayo was originally promised 48 sq. miles [78 sq. km.], but federal authorities later reduced the reserve to 40 square miles [64 sq. km.] The land was located around the Two Hills—these can still be seen, one north and one south of 51st Avenue. When the Papaschase band lost the land and dispersed, the federal government subdivided the reserve and sold much of the land at auctions in 1891 and 1893.

rights away. We are trying to rectify that situation now, with the public and through the courts.[84]

George A. Simpson, Canadian government surveyor, 1880

Shortly after my arrival at Edmonton, I was instructed by the Indian Agent to survey a reserve for Chief Pay-pa-tays (The Woodpecker), located opposite Fort Edmonton, and two miles from the south side of the Saskatchewan. As this would materially interfere with the "claims" of the settlers, I prevailed on the chief to move two miles further south, and commenced the survey on the 2nd of August. On the 16th instant, the chief ordered my party to stop work, giving as a reason that he was not satisfied with the area of the reserve....

I at once instructed [the crew] to pay no attention to mere talk of the chief, but complete the survey, unless he (the chief) resorted to actual force; in that case, to bring the party to Edmonton. With these instructions I enclosed a letter from Mr. Wadsworth, advising him if he had any complaints, to make them to him on his return, and in no way to interfere with the progress of the survey, upon the pain of the utmost displeasure of the Government. This letter was presented to the chief; who asked for its interpretation, and then refused to accept it. He stopped the survey by removing the instruments and said he was prepared to prevent further work.

The number given me as being paid in this band in 1879, was 241, and upon this basis I informed them that they would get 48 square miles, but the number in the band at the time of payment this year was only 189, and on this account Mr. Wadsworth notified me to give them not more than 40 square miles, or the allowance for 200 souls. I may also state that the present number (189) is made up of Indians, half-breeds, and a lot of "absentees," old women living at Fort Edmonton, who declare they will not move across the river to the reservation.

Before the survey was commenced, in answer to a demand of the chief for 60 square miles, I plainly explained to him that the treaty allowance was one square mile for every five souls, and upon no consideration would he get more.[85]

Frank Oliver, citizens' petition

The petition against the Indian reserve at the Two Hills, gives as reasons why it should not be granted there: First—because the Indians are not satisfied with it, and ordered the survey to be stopped. Second—because they have no right to it, not being natives of this part of the country. Third—because it will oblige the neighboring settlers to leave their claims, as it takes in their hay ground and wood land. And fourth— because it is disadvantageous to all parties to have an Indian reserve so close to a business centre. A fifth reason might be added—because the land is needed by better men.[86]

Jerry Quinn, as told to Richard Lightning

My name is Jerry Quinn, I was born in 1911 on November 23.... What I want to talk about is my grandfather's reserve.... That is what I wanted to straighten out because my grandfather didn't give away his reserve, he did not sell it. They left the reserve when the soldiers first arrived here. He just loaned it out, that is what I was told by the old people. He said, "In the future when my grandchildren inquire about the reserve you may turn it over to them...that is how I want to leave it for them." So that is why I made a trip to Edmonton, I've worked on this for quite awhile now, but today I am talking about it here. Many Indians know about it, I think all the people on the surrounding reserves know about it.... that I have family ties there, he was my grandfather. Passpasschase was my grandfather. That is all I can tell you today....

I did see a map, Passpasschase reserve was almost 40 square miles in area. I had that map but now I don't. There was a lawyer who was looking at it and I asked for it but I never got it back. I was going to show it to you people....

That is my story to prove my point I have for keepsake a pipe which belonged to my grandfather Passpasschase, I still have it, it used to belong to his dad. That pipe still exists, now I will in turn give it to my sons so they too can pass it down so it will always exist. That is how we protected it, that is how it was protected in the past. Those are the words of honesty as I have the pipe to prove it and everybody knows it, that pipe is very old. That is all I can say for now....

They never came back here [to Edmonton] and they never received any more money. They just moved away.[87]

BUYING FEVER

"A surging mass of humanity" — Charles John Brydges, HBC employee in Winnipeg

17 APRIL 1882 I cabled you on Saturday about the sales at Edmonton. We got the plan out not very long ago & of which I sent you copies. About a fortnight ago the agent I sent up there returned and gave in his list of sales at Edmonton, amounting to 349 lots for about $11,300, being an average of about $32 a lot. As soon as he wired what he was doing, I stopped him by wire & told him to come down with full reports....

It was soon known that our agent had returned and the enquiries again became numerous. I found that there was a feeling to buy at about $75 a lot, which I thought too low. So I held off for a few days. The result was that a Syndicate offered to buy about 300 lots & I finally agreed to sell that number at $110 a lot.

As soon as that was known a great desire arose to get lots and I had numerous telegrams from Toronto, London, & Hamilton. I put the price up to $150 a lot & 30% more for corners, and the following day to $200 & $250 in choice positions, and sold about 500 lots at those prices. The Syndicate put their lots on the market and they were sold out in 24 hours.

The HBC began selling its land holdings in Edmonton in the 1880s. Speculators and bankers transferred the property into private hands in a whirlwind of buying and selling. A Winnipeg employee, Charles John Brydges, reported to head office about the buying fever in Edmonton.

I then announced that we would begin selling at the counter in our office at 2 o'clock on Thursday last....

People began to come long before 2 o'clock & at that hour it was impossible to reach the office door. The place was perfectly jammed with a surging mass of humanity. Only about 10 people can stand round the counter & well packed at that. The hall was completely full, the office opposite was also crammed, the people crowded up the staircase—and extended through the street door & out on the sidewalk. Everyone shouted that he had been there first, and the pressure of the crowd, trying to reach the counter threatened to tear the place to pieces. Bedlam let loose was a mere incident to the scene in our office. After making sales to men who were tightly jammed against the counter & could not get out when they had paid their money, I saw it was hopeless to attempt to go on and after getting the crowd quiet, I told them it was impossible to sell under the circumstances and that to give everyone a fair chance, we would then close the office & would hold an auction the next day at 2 o'clock in the largest room we could get in the city. This pleased everyone and the crowd gradually dispersed.

The next day at 2 o'clock there were nearly 500 people present and the bidding was most spirited and active. The sale as far as I can tell at present reached somewhere about $130,000 in 2 hours, and the prices went considerably beyond what we were ready to sell for the day before in our office. I have no doubt some of the purchasers will forfeit their deposits as at the auction they were perfectly wild. But the total sales during the week at Edmonton will be somewhere between $250,000 and $300,000....

The whole affair took place between Monday morning and Friday afternoon, and I never saw Winnipeg in such a state of frantic excitement. In some of the brokers' offices, lots were sold 3 or 4 times over & each time at a considerable advance.[88]

"If we must die by violence, let us do it quickly"

7 JANUARY 1883, Fort Edmonton

To the Minister of the Interior,

Honorable Sir,—We, the undersigned chiefs and representatives of the different Indian bands in the district of Edmonton, Treaty No. 6, humbly beg to submit the following statements to your earnest and immediate consideration....

Chief Kiskayo, called Bobtail or Kiskion in English documents, was born in 1827. He signed an adhesion to Treaty 6 at Blackfoot Crossing in 1877. Convinced that treaty promises had been broken, he led local chiefs to Fort Edmonton in 1883 to send a strong protest to the Canadian government through the Oblate missionary Constantin Scollen. After a period of hardship, Bobtail settled with his brother Ermineskin on the reserve at Hobbema, where he died in 1900.

Nothing but our dire poverty, our utter destitution during this severe winter, when ourselves, our wives and our children are smarting under the pangs of cold and hunger, with little or no help and apparently less sympathy from those placed to watch over us, could have induced us to make this final attempt to have redress directly from headquarters. We say final, because if no attention is paid to our case now we shall conclude that the treaty made with us six years ago was a meaningless matter of form and that the white man has indirectly doomed us to annihilation little by little. But the motto of the Indian is "If we must die by violence let us do it quickly...."

Now, honorable sir, this is our great complaint. We have never yet been supplied with one-half of what was promised in the treaty. We who send you this letter, represent seven different bands. One article promised to us was one plow to every three families. Three of the bands have received only one-half the number each—the others less than one-half, and in one case, none at all. Harrows, the same way. Axes, hoes, and all other instruments promised have been denied us in the same ratio. Some of us have received all their cattle, some only a portion, and some none at all. Of course, those who have received only a portion or none at all will lose the increase for so many years. We were promised during four years, all the seed we could put in the ground, and although many of us have been forced to break the ground with hoes, yet we have on no occasion received more than one-half what we could plant....

We are reduced to the lowest stage of poverty. We were once a proud and independent people and now we are mendicants at the door of every white man in the country; and were it not for the charity of the white settlers who are not bound by treaty to help us, we should all die on government fare. Our widows and old people are getting the barest pittance, just enough to keep body and soul together, and there have been cases in which body and soul have refused to stay together on such allowance. Our young women are reduced by starvation to become prostitutes to the white man for a living, a thing unheard of before amongst ourselves and always punishable by Indian law. What then are we to do? Shall we not be listened to...?

We hope, sir, you will pay quick attention to this letter. One great complaint we have is that the government interpreters of this country, with few exceptions, will scarcely or never tell our exact words to the agents, when they fear that the agent, who is very often a man of peevish disposition, would be offended, and so we seldom can say what we desire. But in this letter we have given you in plain talk a short sketch of our position, which we beg you to attend to at once, and we conclude by saying that the half is not told yet.

Your humble servants,

Chief Bob Tail	his X mark	Agowastin	X	
Chief Samson	X	Siwiyawiges	X	
Chief Ermine Skin	X	Iron Head	X	Stoney.
Chief Papaschase	X	William	X	Stoney.[89]
Maminonatan	X			

NEW CHILDREN AT FORT EDMONTON

By 1883, when this picture was taken, the missionary McDougalls had a strong family connection with leading HBC traders through several marriages. Left to right: [Front] William Young, Birdie, Nellie McDougall Wood, Percy Hardisty, George Young, Clara Hardisty, Leslie Wood, Edith Young, Fred Young.

Anna Laura Robertson Harrison, arrived 1883

We reached Edmonton, population then between two and three hundred, October the third, 1883. Here there was a ferry to take us over the Saskatchewan River (Though have forded it many times since), but our camping days were not over as the house, which was to have been ready, was without doors and floors. A big marouse was put up and a floor laid. In this we lived until the house was ready. Again it was the mother who did the pioneering. The next excitement was the arrival of our furniture. The day the piano arrived ice was running in the river, the ferry had been taken out, so the first piano that crossed the Saskatchewan River was forced to ford it, anxiously watched by the inhabitants of the town from the river bank. Though dangerously near upsetting many times, it finally reached the north side. By this time the house was finished and the piano was promptly unloaded and taken out of its case. My brother Harry, who played very well, immediately sat down and played it to the delight of the freighters and others who had gathered about....

It was at about this time that I had an experience that not many little girls had even in those days. I was "sliding" on McCauley Hill with the McCauley children when a young man who lived a few miles down the river drove up with two moose hitched tandem to a "carry-all" the kind that generally was drawn by sleigh dogs. Imagine my delight when he asked me if I would like to ride up the hill. I would and I did! The moose had been caught when young, and trained. The "carry-all" was like a toboggan with a shoe-shaped canvas or hide covering, very comfortable once you crawled into it. The driver stood up at the back....

The man who gave me the ride with the moose took the mail to St. Albert every Saturday. He always drove beautiful horses and very often asked mother if I might go for the drive. There was always a bag of candy along, very often frozen stiff before we had gone far. We always stopped on the way back at a half-way house, owned by a Mr. Norris. Here there were a number of children who always made us welcome and didn't scorn the frozen candy. Many years later nothing was left to mark the spot but the remains of a fireplace, a sad reminder of those happy days.[90]

Clare Casey Matthews, arrived 1887

The ice had just broken up in the Saskatchewan River which we had to cross. A man by the name of John Walter ran a ferry, but couldn't run it with the great chunks of ice flowing down, so were loaded into a big scow run by cable and taken across the river, with a couple of men with long poles pushing the large pieces of ice from bumping the boat. We were taken down to the scow on the south side by a ladder and when landed on the north side just below the Fort were taken up a ladder to safe land and taken on up the steep hill to the Hudson Bay Fort which was to be our home for two and a half years.

The Fort was enclosed by a high stockade with four bastions built for protection. Our quarters was a log building facing the square just behind the Hudson Bay store; a sitting room, dining room, and kitchen, and Father's and Mother's bedroom and Father's office. There was a large room upstairs with an outside stair and a ladder off Father's office. We children slept up there, using the ladder and closed the outside stairs....

In the spring great balls of garter or water snakes were washed down by the high water from their homes just above the fort and were washed ashore at the bend of the river just below the Fort, and used to swarm up the banks of the river and nest in the sawdust trenches in the warm sun and would pop their heads out. I was a bit of a tomboy and my special friend was Henry LaRoche, whose Father was an employee of the Fort. He taught me to catch the snakes by the tail and snap them like a whip and snap their heads off (nice sport for a little girl).

Percy Hardisty and Willie Young were also my special friends and we used to climb up on the top of the high stockade and run around on top. The stockade had been levelled off to eight or ten feet high and a flat narrow board nailed on the top. Mr. Kinnaird (who was Ken Kinnaird's Father) and head accountant in the H.B. office used to try to get me down off the stockade, declaring some day I would fall and break my neck. He always called me "Thomas" but I lived to tell the tale.[91]

Matt McCauley, Jr.

The first school had homemade wooden desks and seats. An iron box stove, using long billets of wood, heated the room.

Mr. Richard Secord, who recently passed away, was our first teacher. He was very strict and made liberal use of heavy willow switches to keep our minds on our work.

One of the lessons taught the beginner was: "Is it an ox?—It is an ox." The teacher taught us numbers by moving coloured pieces of wood on wire attached to a wooden frame. Old Ontario readers were used by the classes. For writing we used slates and slate pencils. Scribblers were then unheard of.

Some of the games we played out of school were Pom-Pom-Pull-Away, Pussy Wants a Corner, Drop the Handkerchief, ball, as well as jumping and running. We made our own balls by wrapping a piece of rubber with yarn and covering it with deer skin. With this ball we played ante-over and catch. Percy Hardisty used to win all the running races. As the people of Edmonton know, Percy afterwards became famous as a football player, cricketer and oarsman.

In the winter we had a toboggan slide right behind the school. Only one or two had toboggans; most of us used barrel staves. At times we would choose sides for a rabbit drive through the bush below the school; whichever side produced the most rabbits at the finish was declared the winner. Some winters the rabbits were very thick, so it was not a difficult matter to kill one. In the summer we went to the river quite often to fish and swim, if the water was low. One day some of us visited the North-East tower or bastion of the Fort; while there we uncovered a stock of coloured beads, which the Hudson's Bay Company used to trade with the Indians. The towers, or bastions, had loop-holes for riflemen to shoot through.[92]

CALLED TO THE BAR

William Griesbach, son of Lt.-Col. Arthur Henry Griesbach

Three or four times a year a judge of the Supreme Court visited Edmonton and held criminal and civil court. Three lawyers had made their way to Edmonton and hung out their shingles. The holding of Court was quite

an event and caused a good deal of excitement which was too much for the lawyers, who invariably were drunk when Court opened. Since one of them was the Crown Prosecutor and prisoners of various sorts charged with various offences relied on one of the other two lawyers to defend him, it was my father's responsibility to see that justice was done to everybody.

He believed in direct action. It was, therefore, his practice to arrest the whole of the Edmonton Bar (three lawyers) a few days before Court sat and have them before him on a charge of vagrancy, which enabled him to sentence them to, say, ten days in the Police Guard Room.

In this way he was able to produce the whole of the Bar, sober, properly dressed and ready to discharge their duties, either in the prosecution or the defence.

This was considered eminently proper and I would like to say for the record that never in a single case did any of the three offer any defence to the charge of vagrancy.... As time passed lawyers became more respectable, they arrived at Court to discharge their various duties under their own steam.[93]

John Walter, a boat builder from the Orkney Islands, arrived at Fort Edmonton in 1870 at the age of 21. Six years later the Walter family decided to build a home on the opposite shore. They ran a profitable ferry and built scows and river boats. The family also opened a successful lumber business and a coal mine. Strathcona's first millionaire lost his fortune through fire, embezzlement and the flood of 1915. The family home is now a museum.

Walter's Ferry

NOTICE. The undersigned is now prepared to ferry passengers across the river at the landing above the Edmonton Mills. The scow will be ready for teams shortly. Rates 10 cents for foot passengers, 20 cents for horse and rider, 25 cents for cart and 50 cents for wagon. Hours: from sunrise to sunset. Free on Sundays from 10 to 2 o'clock, for parties attending religious services.

Any person unauthorized by me found ferrying passengers across will be prosecuted.

J. Walter, Proprietor.[94]

THE telephone line was completed to St. Albert on Saturday at 4 p. m. The following are the first messages transmitted : " Edmonton, 3rd January, 1885 Rev. Father Leduc, St. Albert We wish you all a very happy new year. Alex. Taylor." " St. Albert, 3rd January, 1885. Edmonton The people of St. Albert congratulate the people of Edmonton on telephone communication being established between the two places, and wish the clergy and people a happy new year. Narcisse St. Jean, Chairman."

EDMONTON AND THE NORTH-WEST REBELLION

J.R. McPhaden, Edmonton

[On a] lovely spring Sunday morning in 1885 in McDougall's church while John McDougall was preaching, a messenger (a scout) came suddenly with a written note for the minister. McDougall read it and paled then raised his hand and asked them all to pray as he had got word that 2000 Indians were marching on to the post from Wetaskiwin and Fort Saskatchewan. It was a tense and dramatic moment—we were all keyed up and all prayed very fervently for our safety and then scattered to our homes to do what we could for defence. Actually it was only a false rumor.[95]

Métis families of St. Albert

21 April 1885

To the Editor of *The Bulletin*,

The Hudson's Bay Company [in Winnipeg] received a telegram from their agent at Edmonton last night stating that the half-breeds were holding secret meetings for some time, and are now organizing for action of some kind....We cannot adequately express the indignation we feel at the reading of such a dispatch. Undoubtedly we have many reasons for complaining against the government, and those who accuse us cannot say we are wrong. They know best the rights that we have to the lands of the country. We are aborigines as well as Indians and have the same

Alex Taylor ordered the settlement's first two telephones from England in 1884. Once the telephone poles and wires had been built, he asked H.W. McKenny to become the keeper of the St. Albert telephone. People in Edmonton crowded into Taylor's office on January 3, 1885 to listen to the first conversations. They were astonished to hear the sound of meat sizzling in a frying pan in McKenny's kitchen 14 km away.

Sam Cunningham, a leader of the Métis in St. Albert, served as a captain of the St. Albert Mounted Rifles during the Rebellion. He was later elected to the North-West Territories Council and became the first mayor of Grouard.

rights as they. Before any of those foreigners, whom the government today prefers to us, saw the country, we had begun to cultivate it. The company who are reported to have sold our country would willingly have sold us as well. Had they more rights than we? The government understood that the Indians had rights in this country, and consequently made treaties with them but with us half-breeds what treaties have been made...?

Far from receiving favours, we have not been accorded fair play. Last summer a government agent came here to settle a local land question and had it been his aim to provoke the halfbreeds to rebellion he could not have devised better means than his decisions, which were always so manifestly unjust to them.... In many cases half-breeds who were long settled in their homes of their own, have seen their lands taken from them, and portioned out to newly arrived strangers, and those men are thus forced to make requests of foreigners, locating again to be very probably dispossessed later in the same way.

Do they believe we have no feelings? We feel those wrongs deeply. Our complaints heretofore have not found expression beyond ourselves. We ask you today to publish them in your column for the first time. We have never thought of rebellion or inciting a rebellion.... As a rule no Half-Breed ever treats a stranger with injustice, contempt or even incivility. The treatment he gives to a stranger, has he not a right to demand from the stranger? There are in this district many strangers who have deservedly earned our good will and who are as indignant as we are at the injustice of the malignant accusation we are complaining of. In conclusion we ask all newspapers who are friends of justice to publish this, our protest, against the above slander dispatched to Winnipeg by the agent of the Hudson's Bay Company at Edmonton.

Signed,

Samuel Cunningham, Octave Bellerose, John Cunningham, Baptiste Courtepatte, John Rowland, Adophus Rowland, Louis Chastellaine, Lawrence Gurness, on behalf of the Half-Breeds of St. Albert, Alberta, April 21, 1885.[96]

Harry Long, settler, near Fort Saskatchewan

9 APRIL 1885 I went to Edmonton for the mail. Took Lizzie and the baby. We found everyone very excited about the hostile Indians. Have formed a company of volunteers, and are fixing up and fortifying the Hudson's Bay Fort; fixing up all the arms that can be found. Telegraph wires are down. Indians have made a general outbreak around Battleford. Mrs. Sanderson and Mrs. Kelly are going to Roman Catholic Mission at St. Albert for safety. They think Lizzie and the baby should go too. I consented as danger seems very near. A courier has been sent to Calgary for help. All help that can be found in Canada is needed, I came home alone, very tired and excited.

18 APRIL 1885 Nearly everyone is moving home, still excitement is very great. News from Victoria that people at [Fort] Pitt are all massacred. Victoria people are moving to Edmonton for safety. We feel danger is near and no way to prevent it. I went and brought the baby and Lizzie home. Little Bert is looking fine. Roads are bad. War and bloodshed staring us in the face. Do not know the day or the hour we will have to fly. No hope, only trust in Jesus.

19 APRIL Is a very long sad uncertain afternoon. Nick came in, no one can look cheerful or smile, I am glad when night comes.

20 APRIL About 10 o'clock Murdock Sutherland brought news that 600 soldiers are on the road from Calgary for here. They are expected in this week. Everyone's countenance changes instantly. Now we feel safe, which we have not done for two weeks.

25 APRIL Plowing again. Feel very thankful that the soldiers are so near.

1 MAY The first soldiers arrived to-day, everyone is rejoicing.[97]

Kate Maloney, St. Albert

I well remember seeing the Brother, early one morning, coming along a foot-path through the brush between our house and the mission. Feeling something unusual was astir, my father hurried over to the mission and found the old Bishop in tears over the murder of his priests. "I wrote to Sir John", said the Bishop "warning him of danger, and he would not heed. Now we must do something ourselves."

The outcome of this interview was that the Bishop sent a telegram to Ottawa to the Department of Militia and Defense, asking leave to organize a Local Corps of Volunteers [St. Albert Mounted Rifles]....

Most of the People of Edmonton and surrounding country moved their wives and children to the Hudson Bay Company's Fort. This was soon

The Métis and Cree uprising of 1885 created panic in the small settlement near Fort Edmonton, but there was no fighting here. Shortly after Louis Riel and Gabriel Dumont and their compatriots announced a provisional government at Batoche on March 19, 1885, the telegraph wire to Edmonton was cut. Settlers hurried to Fort Edmonton and the St. Albert mission amid false rumours of an impending attack. Riel was executed at Regina in November 1885 on an order from the federal Cabinet, a decision that had enduring consequences across the country.

Hannah Catherine "Kate" Maloney arrived in St. Albert with her family at the age of six in 1881 after 98 days en route in an ox cart caravan. She was one of the first graduate nurses at the Misericordia Hospital and worked all her life as a practical nurse and midwife. She died in 1947.

filled. Bishop Grandin offered sanctuary to any and all who cared to come to the Mission. Accordingly the schoolhouse, carpenter shop and every other available shelter were soon filled with women and children. Some of the nearby farm houses were also filled. Many of the Namao settlers came for safety to the Mission. Our house had its share, four families with twenty-seven children lodged with us. Among these families was the Homestead Inspector's wife and children. There was in addition a bride from Ontario, who brought her wedding presents along with her....

About ten days after this panic news came that the troops were coming from Eastern Canada. This calmed the fears of most people, who returned to their own homes after a period of mortal terror. These were memorable ten days.

From being an asylum of refuge, our house became a recruiting office, it being chosen on account of its central location. Every volunteer was a self-appointed recruiting officer. Not all present would join however, Finally forty-five signed: two Oblate lay brothers, four trusty Irishmen, the remaining thirty-nine all Halfbreeds. The officers, excepting the first Lieutenant, were also Halfbreeds, being chosen according to their ability.

These men were furnished with 40:70 repeater Winchester Rifles. Each man furnished his own mount. There was no standard of height or measurement, thus there were tall and short, fat and lean. Most of them wore moccasins and moved silently. They were all fearless, keen eyed, unerring shots and expert horsemen, being able to lie flat on a horse and rise instantly....

Next came word of the pillaging of Lac La Biche by some of Big Bear's scouts and some local Indians. The St. Albert detachment were ordered to go there, six of the local men being left as home guards under Mr. N.

Christine Lacombe and her husband Leon Harnois endured a family tragedy in April 1885 when their neighbours in Fort Edmonton and St. Albert were preoccupied the North-West Rebellion. Christine, the sister of missionary Albert Lacombe, came West at the age of 17 to teach at Lac La Biche and later married a farmer in the St. Albert area. Christine and Leon buried all five of their children—aged between 14 months and eight years old—on a single day. The children had died of diphtheria. Eleven months later, Christine gave birth to the first child of their second family. She died in 1920.

Beaudry, who was looked up to by the others. It was felt that there might be need for a few home men here....

It is characteristic of the times that the women were as courageous as the men. When the Volunteers left, the little children were forbidden by their mothers to weep when their fathers said farewell.[98]

Annie McKernan Turnbull, settlers' child
We children thought it was a great lark, actually we had no fear of Indians. We knew them as peaceable, friendly people, though they were touchy and easily offended. There was about seven of us children then.

We got to John Walter's place very late and we stayed over night there until the next morning and then crossed in the ferry. The Fort was filled with tents that had been put up, and most crowded, for temporary

shelter of settlers. It was the busiest place you ever saw.... My brother had to go back to our farm every day to milk. He brought back the milk and mother churned and carried on much the same as at home. We remained in the Fort for about three weeks and all the while men picketed the place.

One night there were shots fired over from the south side of the river and it stirred up suspicion against Lawrence Garneau, and he was subsequently locked up for a period of time.[99]

Matthew McCauley, Edmonton's first mayor, with Chief Ermineskin in 1884.

Jean-Marie Lestanc Poundmaker, son of imprisoned Cree chief, St. Albert

2 JULY 1885

Dear father,

Learning that there has been fighting in your lands I have been much troubled, but I am glad to know that you were not killed.

Be grateful father to the Great Spirit who has protected you. I also thank him for having spared my father, whom I love. I have heard the priests; that is why I am glad now. Believe me, father, do as I do, hear the priests and their teachings. God grant that you may be baptised. If you do that, I shall be glad; the Great Spirit will love you and bless you on earth and still more in heaven. I desire also that all my relations may be praying people, as well all the Indians who are upon your lands.

I wish to be a carpenter. I am learning the trade. When I know it well I shall be able to earn a little money to provide for my subsistence and to be useful to my father.

If everything turns out thus, I shall be happy but I shall be more so if you will give yourselves to prayer. I embrace all my relatives and especially you, my beloved father.

Your loving son.[100]

In 1874 Laurent and Eleanor Garneau joined an exodus of Métis families that left Red River to settle across the West. The Garneaus farmed opposite Fort Edmonton on the land that still bears the family name. A popular fiddler in the district, Laurent Garneau was briefly jailed at Fort Saskatchewan during the North-West Rebellion of 1885 on a suspicion of sympathies with Louis Riel. The couple posed for this photograph while on holiday in Niagara Falls, N.Y. a year before before Laurent Garneau's death in 1911.

A charge of treason, an act of friendship ⌐ James Brady, grandson of Laurent Garneau

My maternal grandfather Lawrence Garneau had been a follower of Louis Riel during the rebellion at the Red River in 1870 and, as a consequence of the persecution which followed the episode, joined the exodus to the West. He settled at [what is now] Strathcona, south of Edmonton, in 1874. This land adjoined on the north a small Indian camp, known as Papasschayo's Reserve, and my grandfather was on very good terms with this band. Papasschayo was a rare combination of band chief and medicine man....

During the 1885 rebellion Canadian troops arrived at Fort Edmonton and declared martial law. All local residents were ordered to retire within the fort. But my grandfather and another French Metis, Benjamin Vandal, ignored the order to abandon their farms as they felt they were in no

Edmonton Bulletin

July 1, 1882

Sir,

A letter written from Edmonton which I have seen lately in the *Toronto Daily Globe* where in Laurent Garneau is stigmatized as a Red River rebel is both false and cowardly and I consider the writer no better than an assassin that will stab a man in the back without giving him a chance to defend himself. This reply I think is as much as the coward and sneak is entitled to.

Laurent Garneau

P.S. Please Mr. Coward next time you write to the *Toronto Daily Globe* state your name and address that the rustics of Edmonton may know what kind of snake in the grass you are.

danger from the Indians. Vandal, who lived on the White Mud Creek about eight miles above Edmonton, had also been a soldier in the Manitoba Metis army of 1870....

Riel and his council had sent letters to my grandfather and Vandal enquiring as to the local situation and the degree of support that could be expected from the local Metis. My grandfather kept this letter to read to some of the Metis sympathizers who were illiterate.

My grandmother was in the kitchen when she heard a sudden clatter of hooves. A sergeant and four constables of the North West Mounted Police galloped into the yard and dismounted. The sergeant entered. He asked my grandmother: "Mrs. Garneau where is your husband? We have a warrant for his arrest and a search warrant for these premises."

"He is sleeping upstairs," she replied. My grandfather was an excellent musician, much in demand in social affairs. The night before he had gone across the river to the fort to play the violin at a dance, and had returned shortly after daylight to ensure a few hours sleep before returning to the field to work.

The sergeant bounded up the stairs.... The other police immediately ransacked the house. One policeman went to the actual spot where the letter had been hidden. It was evident they were acting on information from an informer. But they found nothing. My grandmother had acted with great presence of mind. She had been laundering when they came into the yard, and she reached up, placed the letter and other incriminating material in the wash tub, and calmly destroyed them by rubbing them on the washboard until they were completely disintegrated.

The death sentence caused great excitement in Fort Edmonton. The more responsible White residents, particularly the Hudson's Bay Company people, free traders and the earlier White settlers, even the Protestant clergy, protested the severity of the sentence.

Inspector Griesbach of the North West Mounted Police made a personal appeal to the military commander. All agreed [Garneau and Vandal] had erred in not complying with the military order, but they felt the death sentence was harsh and vindictive. A delegation of white citizens led by Hon. Frank Oliver...went to Col. Ouimet, the military commander, and interceded on their behalf. But to no avail...

As a last measure Bishop Grandin requested that an appeal from the Committee be transmitted to Ottawa by military telegraph. This was a reasonable request which the commander could not refuse. Bishop

Agathe, Archange and Charlotte Garneau with Placide Poirier in Strathcona. Their father was elected to the territorial assembly in 1894 but he was not allowed to take his seat because of his association with Louis Riel in his Red River days. The family left Strathcona for St. Paul des Métis in 1901.

Grandin added an appeal to the Minister of National Defence, Sir Adolphe Caron, who was a personal friend, urging a stay of execution.

A few hours later the Committee [was] informed that the Minister had reversed the verdict of the court martial. However the prisoners were held in custody until after the rebellion. Then they were tried in a civil court and sentenced to six months imprisonment.

Here Papasschayo entered the scene. After the rebellion considerable animosity and an attitude of revenge appeared among the Anglo-Saxons against the defeated Metis. In those days social aid and other amenities of the welfare state were unknown. My grandmother and eleven children were left destitute to shift for themselves. The Whites, it seemed without thinking about it, punished them for my grandfather's rebellious spirit.

They would have starved but for the enduring friendship, compassion and generosity of Papasschayo [and his band].... For during this period of imprisonment, they fed both the Garneau and Vandal families. My grandfather never forgot this....

Years passed. My grandfather and related families moved to [St. Paul des Metis] in 1901.

Three years later, and nearly twenty years after the rebellion, my grandfather heard that Papasschayo was old and in straitened circumstances. So he journeyed to the foothills and brought the chief back to St. Paul des Metis. The Cree band of earlier days had broken up, it now existed only in the memories of the old timers. A comfortable cabin was built for Papasschayo across a small lake near our trading post, and here Papasschayo lived with his two wives...."[101]

The Bulletin's coverage of the Garneau case did not mention a death sentence. G.A. Ouimet, the Speaker of the House of Commons reported in 1888 that Garneau was jailed for "over two months."

Lazarus Roan, Papaschase descendant, as told to Eric Stamp

Elizabeth Brass Donald was a well-known midwife in the late nineteenth century. Born in 1836, she married George Donald at the age of 17 and raised 11 children. Her descendants believe she posed in front of Frank Oliver's house to leave behind a message about the loss of Métis and Cree land in the Edmonton area.

My father and uncles told us the truth about it, why the reserve got broken up. My grandfather Papastayo, wanted to sell some cattle or horses but was not allowed to sell. I don't quite remember, if they did not want to give him a permit to sell the stock. That is when he got angered, because he thought that whatever he owned did not belong to him or to us treaty Indians. The way the white people are, they told them about the scrip, which they took. But they did not get much money, although the larger families got more than the smaller families. My grandfather was the oldest and then came Papastayo and Mitchim and Pato and Wasates and the youngest I don't recall for he was named in an English name. All these grandfathers of mine [great-uncles] took the scrip, and the others followed. Their relations followed, because they bribed them into taking the scrip because they said we will never own anything in our future lives. The white people had a lot to say about this....

My father was about the last to leave the reserve, but as you know how cunning the white man is, for talking to the people who took the scrip. My father had the intention of taking the scrip also, so he went to the store, and that is where the clergy talked him into not taking it: "You just watch and see how poor these people are going to be. There will be a road lower, and that is where these people will be staying. Do not do that for you will suffer, your children in the future to come. Stay on the reserve for you will know where to go home to, like a bird who has finished her nest, they too know where to go. You will see your brothers who took the scrip, that they will someday not have any shelter to go to. These people were promised to be given homesteads alright. But they will never finish paying for the homestead, and if they cannot pay for the land, it will be taken away from them. Then they will not be given any more homesteads and they will try to come back to the reservation but they cannot stay there." That is what the storekeeper told my dad.

That is where he changed his mind, and he got hell for not taking the scrip, from his brothers and uncles also. That is how the reserve got broke. My father was the last to go, although he stayed and yet the white people told him that some day a big town or city will arise here, and that you will be right in the midst of a white society. That is when he left the reserve, and came here to live [Hobbema]. That is what my father told me before he died....

The white people just took them away... the land was not given to them. They took the land, and never told anyone. That is how much pride they had. They did not pay for the land they took. That is how the reserves got lost....

My father died in 1919, May 22nd.... My father was 76 years old when he passed. I was 16 years old when he passed. That is why I can clearly remember the stories he has told me.[102]

The Canadian government sent a commissioner to Edmonton in the summers of 1885 and 1886 to offer scrip (certificates that could be exchanged for land or cash) to local Métis in an attempt to extinguish their remaining aboriginal title. Land speculators travelled with the government agents and paid cash on the spot for scrip—at a discounted rate.

WAR OF WORDS

A. Blanchet, priest and translator

Mr. Reed said he had come in pursuance of his promise of the day before to hear what the Indians had to say.

Alexander said he spoke as it might be for God and for the government on behalf of the poor people who could not speak for themselves.

Alexander—"I don't depend on what you are doing here—both of you." (Messrs. Reed and de Balinhard) "Everything has been going badly since you two came here. We consider that you have acted against the law. It is you who have caused the government cattle to be killed. You knew last fall the game and fish had failed in this country. You have come from far and you have seen no track of anything to kill and eat. You see how miserable the Indians are here, and when you go back you will tell them all is well."

Mr. Reed—"You told me all this when I spoke to you before, and I gave you your answer then. The government is pretty well aware of the facts of the case. My business here is to report the facts to the government which I will do."

Alexander—"What I say is truth, as everyone who is here knows. Because it is true I sent the telegram to Sir John. I have waited for an answer, but have got none. I am not as wise as you. I look like a dog before

Local chiefs Alexis, Alexander and Michel return to Edmonton in the winter of 1888 to request treaty rations because of hunger on their reserves. They speak to government agents Hayter Reed and William de Balinhard. Rev. A. Blanchet takes notes at the meeting. His report remains in the Oblate Archives.

Chief Michel Callihoo brought his Cree-Iroquois band into Treaty 6 in 1878 and settled a large reserve west of St. Albert. He is seen here with family, left to right: Philomene Callihoo, Sévère Callihoo, Michel Callihoo, unknown priest, Jean Baptiste Callihoo, and three unidentified women.

you, but I have a mind to think of these things. I follow the track of the law, and I am not ashamed. White men would do as we have done. We killed our cattle from hunger. Hunger might make us kill each other.

It is you were pushing us to do evil. That we have eaten our horses and the cattle that the government gave us should be blamed on you. What the poor people are saying every day rings in my ears. We do not depend on you."

Mr. Reed—"Does he mean that the promises I made him yesterday won't be kept?"

Alexander—"I am talking not of what is ahead, but of what is behind, since last fall."

Michel—"When we were forced with hunger we went to the agent here. He spoke well to us, but that did not fill us. When matters did not improve we said: Let us see how it is farther away. We got no answer from the telegram we sent. We see that nothing is going right from Regina. You knew that it was a hard year with us. If you wanted to save us why did you not send the food while the roads were good? The agent had asked for 500 sacks of flour this winter. He heard that only 300 sacks had been sent."

Mr. Reed said that the total number of sacks of flour asked for was 500 but the government was using its judgment about the time of delivery....

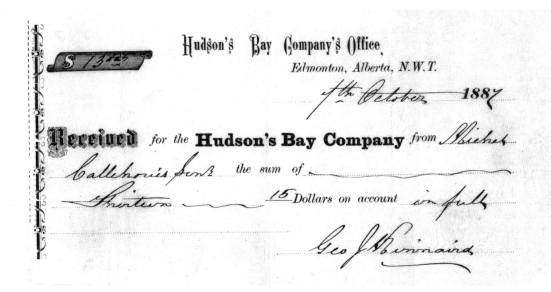

Hudson's Bay Company's Office,
Edmonton, Alberta, N.W.T.

7th October **1887**

Received _for the_ **Hudson's Bay Company** _from Michel_

Callihou's Junr _the sum of_

Thirteen 15 _Dollars on account_ _in full_

Geo J Kinnaird

Alexander—"I understand that the government said, if you help yourselves we will help you not; if you help yourselves, we will leave you off. You know it is deep snow and a hard season. You knew these things before. If you had opened your eyes before, things would not be as they are. But you did not wish to see you want to do nothing but gather money. Your name is neither good with Indians or whites—neither of you."

Another councillor (Attikusis)—"I am a coward, but when I hear my children cry from hunger, I kill cattle. I think of you as the cold. You want to kill all on the reserves."

Alexander—"You were sent word last spring about sickness on the reserves. On my own Reserve many have died of sickness and hunger. Medicine is no use without food. Thirty have died on my own Reserve, and fifteen besides. Five of my children have died, most of them grown up. I sent word every day, but you would do nothing for me. You think what I say of the sickness is not true. I tell you in your ears, you lie when you say you take the part of sick children. Mr. Juin had been used to working for the whites. This winter he could get no work. There was no game and no fish, and he had nearly starved to death depending on the Indian Department. He did not go to the whites to sell his country. They came to him to buy it, and now they would not pay the price."

Mr. Reed ordered dinner to be provided for the Indians and answered them that they would receive the Increase of rations promised....

[Blanchet's _concluding note:_] The Indians are not satisfied.[103]

Tucked in a file at the Musée Heritage in St. Albert, this HBC receipt carries the names of two well-known Fort Edmonton families: the Callihoos and Kinnairds.

Land dealers made substantial profits from the cheap acquisition of land and money scrip certificates from Métis and Cree families. Richard Secord faced a lawsuit for some of this activity; other businessmen were sometimes criticized by the clergy and lampooned in the gossip press. Photographer Ernest Brown sent this cartoon from an issue of The Eye-Opener to Robert Gard, a folklorist at the University of Alberta, with the comment: "The Eye-Opener, Jack Canuck and Hush have each at times increased their circulation by printing some homely truths that certain members of Edmonton's '400' thought it not wise that others should see, and therefore bought up every available copy in the City."

PUZZLE PICTURE FOR EDMONTON.

Here is an insurgent, who insurged on a question of conscience. Who is he? And why? Also wherefore?

Frank Oliver

During the four days of the scrip issue about the land office was like a fair ground, from the number of men, women and children, horses and buggies of all descriptions, standing leaning or lying around. The proceedings were enlivened by an occasional horse race and on Wednesday by one or two small fights, but as a general thing everything was very quiet and orderly.

The scrip was bought principally by acquaintances of the parties receiving it, who turned it over to the Winnipeg buyers at a stated figure, leaving the person buying whatever difference there was for profit. The town had flush times during these four days. The stores and saloons reaped a regular harvest, horses and cattle changed hands at lightening rate and at good figures, and the inspiring horse race absorbed whatever money could not conveniently be blown in any other way. The large amount of scrip that is being issued in this district will have a good effect on business during the current year. The price paid is considered fair value, being within a few cents of the Winnipeg market price, and is a great improvement over that of last year, when some was sold at forty cents on the dollar. The commission left for St. Albert on Friday and will probably commence the issue of scrip there to-day....[104]

The cause of the desire of the Indians to leave the treaty is no doubt a mystery to people at a distance who are led to suppose, according to the treaty, that they are supplied with cattle, implements and seed, and food in times of scarcity.

In this district since the treaty was made matters have been nearing that point gradually, but have not yet reached it, while with the Indians remain the memory of how their efforts have been balked, their requests denied, the promised made to them broken and themselves allowed to starve in past years, so that although matters have improved they have no confidence in the good intentions of the department and desire to leave its control and take their chances.[105]

William Newton, Anglican missionary, about the 1880s

It is a curious part of the local history which records that these lots were conveyed to other persons, and helped to make the fortunes, in one case, of two persons....

While these uncertainties were occurring, about the land claims of natives and settlers in the Edmonton district, land speculators were busy, and very successful, in their greed for spoils. A company was set going with a grand name, ostensibly patronized by the Ottawa Government supporters. It proposed to colonize, and bring both settlers and capital into the country. Large tracts of fine land were entrusted to the company, but they brought no settlers, and to-day their buildings are in ruins, and most of their lands are waste.

Meanwhile, honest settlers were compelled to go far into the wilderness for homesteads, and business and civilization were hindered in order that these speculators might make money by the labour and enterprise of neighbours who were cursed by their presence.

A poor man is sharply looked after if he does not fulfil his engagements on his land claim, and his titles are cancelled. How is it, then, that fraudulent companies can hold their own, or, rather, the lands that should belong to other people?

Governments in these days are, in theory, governments for the people by the people. As population increases here, some of these questions may receive stern answers.[106]

Frank Oliver was an irascible Edmonton newspaperman who became the most powerful politician in the West. At 23, he arrived at Fort Edmonton in an ox-cart brigade and with the help of Alex Taylor, founded Alberta's first newspaper, the Edmonton Bulletin in 1880. Oliver rose steadily through the Legislative Assembly of the North-West Territories to the House of Commons and eventually became Minister of the Interior. He is remembered not only as the man who ensured that Edmonton became the capital of Alberta and as a strong advocate for western homesteaders, but also as the Superintendent-General of Indian Affairs who put pressure on First Nations communities to surrender their land. He died in Edmonton in 1933.

THE GREAT DISAPPOINTMENT

Frank Oliver

In 1881 it was decided to switch the projected railway from the northern to the southern route, leaving the Edmonton settlements 200 miles off the line. The pioneers were licked but they did not quit. They had faith in the country and confidence in themselves.

They knew the railway had to come; but they could not tell when. They only could wait and hope. But while they waited, they worked.

For 24 years hope was met by disappointment. These years of disappointment included the usual chances of frost and hail and drought and hard winters, with the Rebellion of 1885 thrown in for good measure. But it was during that quarter of a century that the work of the pioneers demonstrated the possibilities of the district.[107]

Charles John Brydges

There is no railway projected at present to Edmonton, and until that is done the sale of lots will not amount to anything. There is no doubt a very good Country round Edmonton, but it is so far away from any line of railway, and so distant from any market, that it will be some considerable time before any activity can arise at that point....

What the future of Edmonton may be depends upon circumstances upon which it is entirely useless to speculate at present.[108]

Newcomers
1892 to 1913

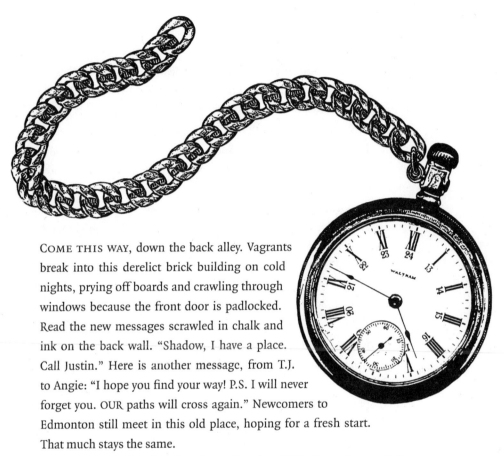

COME THIS WAY, down the back alley. Vagrants break into this derelict brick building on cold nights, prying off boards and crawling through windows because the front door is padlocked. Read the new messages scrawled in chalk and ink on the back wall. "Shadow, I have a place. Call Justin." Here is another message, from T.J. to Angie: "I hope you find your way! P.S. I will never forget you. OUR paths will cross again." Newcomers to Edmonton still meet in this old place, hoping for a fresh start. That much stays the same.

Welcome to the abandoned Immigration Hall, the only remaining one in the city. Thousands of foreign-born newcomers began their lives in Edmonton in this red brick building. They climbed down from a transcontinental train, holding a child's hand, and walked wearily north across the railway tracks. The reception centre gleamed like a new school when it opened in 1931 and it was so much larger than the earlier Immigration Hall that had opened down the street in 1906. Exhausted families registered at the front desk, ate a meal, and fell into bunks. They rested for a few days until they found a small apartment or a room of their own. They did their laundry. They made halting telephone calls in an impossible, new language. They asked their children to pose on the front sidewalk for a photograph that could be mailed home to Poland or Italy, Ukraine or Holland, England, Greece or Germany, to say: "We are here. We're fine." Every day people arrived to collect unfamiliar cousins, or to leave messages for the new arrivals from the old country. "Anna, I have a place. Call Nick." This is a city where we can begin again.

❧

THE FIRST IMMIGRATION HALL was a small shed at the end of the Calgary and Edmonton Railway tracks on the south side of the river.[1] In the late summer of 1891, twelve weary passengers climbed down to the platform just before midnight after a 12-hour trip from Calgary.[2] They were the vanguard; more train immigrants followed. If they had money in their pockets, newcomers found a room in Hotel Edmonton (later the Strathcona Hotel), or in a cheaper boarding house around the corner. If they had empty pockets and no one to meet them, they peered through the darkness for a place to lie down until morning. The station man pointed to a shack behind the freight shed. Full tonight? He pointed to two canvas tents beside the shack. Also full? The station man shrugged. Try the bench on the platform, or the hard ground.

Edmonton waited for the multitudes to make their way to the Last, Best West. Thousands of settlers began to arrive after Interior Minister Clifford Sifton announced a new homestead policy in 1896.[3] To populate a wide country, Canada was willing to offer free land to those who would farm it. Families answered this call from small farms in eastern Canada and the United States and from distant European seaports. Seasick in the lower bunks of the immigrant ships, staring out train windows at northern forests and the infinite prairies, the homesteaders travelled toward the miracle of 160 free acres of land in northwestern Canada. Most of the quarter-sections within 65 kilometres of Edmonton had already been settled; and the land on both sides of railway lines to Calgary and Lloydminster was also claimed, so the new homesteaders searched for land farther away from the city, or decided to stay in town.

By 1906, hundreds of newcomers were arriving every month on the homesteader trains. Immigrants filled the new hotels, boarding houses, attics of stores, porches of livery stables, and the Exhibition Grounds to overflowing. The old immigration shed was torn down. Lucky newcomers found a bed at two new Immigration Halls—both rambling three-storey boarding houses with verandas—built to accommodate this startling

Newcomers 1904

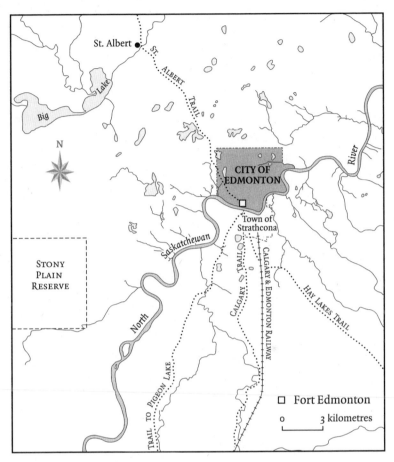

Edmonton declared itself a city in 1904 with 8,350 citizens. The bustling railway town of Strathcona across the river had about 1,600 citizens. City boundaries on the map do not reflect the settlement of the area, as many lots had no occupants. By 1904 the federal government had subdivided and sold the entire Papaschase reserve and large portions of the Enoch and Michel reserves. The Hudson's Bay Company had developed and sold much of its land to settlers, but owned a remaining parcel in the centre of the city.

influx of humanity. One was just east of the Strathcona railway station, at 80th Avenue and 101st Street; the second opened on the north side of the river at 101st Street and 105th Avenue. Both places were infested with bed-bugs and lice, but they were safe havens for the weary and starting places for the adventurous.

In 1910—in the single month of June—more than 400 families entered the two Immigration Halls.[4] Did they lie awake in dormitory bunks, wondering whether the homestead or the coal mine would live up to expectations, whether to stay in this Edmonton or keep moving north?

If they spoke English they could tell their travel story to the newspaper reporters who came by every morning to inspect them as if they were exotic birds. "Last Saturday a colored gentleman from Oklahoma with a B.A. after his name, arrived in search of a school," wrote the *Edmonton Bulletin* reporter on June 13th. "Thomas John Sydes, a steeplejack from Ireland and Joseph Mesler a German musician with flowing locks, are some other arrivals," he continued. More rare birds in June? The *Bulletin* listed an 89-year-old American who wanted a homestead while he was still alive and kicking; a Quebec rock driller who lost a poker game on the train and had 10 cents to his name;[5] a Cornell University student;[6] 21 men who described themselves as "gentlemen" rather than farmers or labourers;[7] four generations from the same German family,[8] and four wanderers from Brazil.[9] Reporters offered careful nationality counts in every story: English, 91; Irish, 5; Scotch, 30; Germans, 50; Scandinavians, 36; French, 16; Americans, 72; Canadians, 6; Other Nationalities, 94.[10] Almost all of the Other Nationalities were Ukrainians and Poles, known in this era as Galicians and Bhukovinians.

Both the Liberal *Bulletin* and its new Conservative rival, the *Journal*, communicated the Otherness of eastern Europeans in every column inch of newsprint. "The idea of the West is not only greatness, but greatness achieved under the British Flag, and stamped and molded by the genius of race,"[11] the *Bulletin* explained to its readers. The established society shared a vertical order of racial preference. The new gentry preferred English-speaking Protestant Canadians, then newcomers from the British Empire, then American farmers and French Canadians with frontier experience, then Germans, Scandinavians and farmers from Holland and Belgium, especially if they were Protestant. It looked askance at newcomers from Eastern Europe, the Balkans or Mediterranean countries; Jews from any place got a raised eyebrow; Arab Muslims, Chinese labourers and African-American farmers were at the bottom of the list. Go home, the old town muttered quietly to some. You are not wanted.

And yet in June of 1910 and for generations after that summer, this mingled crowd walked through Edmonton's front door. When it was time to leave the Immigration Hall, settlers shook hands with strangers they had met on the ship or on the train. Good luck, they said as they picked up suitcases. I hope you find your way. I will never forget you. Our paths will cross again.

⌁

MISUNDERSTANDINGS LINGER about the newcomers who arrived in Edmonton between 1891 and the First World War: pioneers were all poor; they wore sheepskin coats because they were from eastern Europe; they were all farmers who passed through Edmonton on their way to rural homesteads; they came without coaxing; they found a better life here than the one they left behind; they all stayed.

Inspector Beeven's records for the Immigration Hall in the summer of 1910 reveal part of the complicated truth. Poor? Yes, and no. Some newcomers were destitute when they saw Edmonton for the first time. Many homesteaders brought modest assets: a suitcase of clothes, a steamer trunk full of household belongings, a letter with a friend's address, and whatever money was left after the expensive journey. However, thousands of new settlers were well-established farmers from Ontario, Britain or the United States who preferred to buy choice agricultural land near Edmonton rather than claim a free homestead at a distance from a railway line. Poverty is not a word that can be associated with the 55 settlers who arrived over two days in the summer of 1910, bringing with them "in hard, cold cash $238,000."[12] Mr. Higgins from North Dakota, Mr. Wade from Oregon, and Mr. Carter from Arkansas came here as land scouts for well-to-do neighbours back home. Affluent farmers located the land, bought it from realtors, and then sent a telegram to call for their families. In July of 1910, 365 settlers from Michigan and Ohio sent word ahead from Minneapolis that they were on their way to Edmonton.[13] Many new families brought boxcars full of livestock, farm equipment, house-building supplies, rosewood pianos, hardwood maple bedroom suites, and cash to spend in new commercial districts on Jasper and Whyte. English gentlemen brought remittance income and inheritances. Many newcomers were far better off than the old-timers who smoked cigars with them at the long bar of the

Edmonton Hotel. They had big plans that did not include breaking sod on a lonely prairie homestead.

Canada was home to five million people in 1900, and with its beckoning immigration policy, it absorbed 3.3 million new immigrants in the first two decades of the century. Howard and Tamara Palmer analysed the ethnic background of the newcomers in their book *Alberta: A New History* and found that by 1914 more than half of the population could trace family roots to Britain.

Nearly 600,000 Americans came to the Canadian West between 1898 and 1914 because the best land at home was already claimed, and expensive. Many families had lived in the United States for only a generation or two after leaving Europe and still spoke a European language. By 1911 Americans were the largest immigrant group in Alberta, accounting for 22 per cent of Alberta's population. They were clustered in the southern ranchland and in Calgary, but many settled on the superb farmland around Edmonton, too. Newcomers from Ontario, Britain and the United States created a large and confident English-speaking majority in Edmonton throughout the homestead era.[14]

They did not have the place to themselves. With the promise of Catholic schools, a new wave of French-Canadian homesteaders from overcrowded areas of Quebec and New England, as well as French-speaking Métis from across the West, arrived in Edmonton, St. Albert and Morinville.[15] In 1894 Edmonton already had a Saint-Jean-Baptiste Society and a newspaper called *L'Ouest canadien*. By 1913 five MLAs in the Alberta Legislature spoke French and francophone neighbourhoods were growing.[16]

German newcomers settled northeast of the city and in Strathcona, opened businesses along Whyte Avenue and spoke their language at Lutheran and Catholic services. Gustave Koermann even published the *Alberta Herold* in German. One in 10 Albertans was German by 1914.[17]

When Ivan Pylypiw and Wasyl Eleniak arrived at the southside railway station in the summer of 1893, they were experienced travellers in Canada. They had already inspected land in Manitoba and Saskatchewan and in Calgary before returning to western Ukraine to urge other landless farmers to try their luck on the new territory. Pylypiw was soon arrested in his country of origin and imprisoned for encouraging people to emigrate to western Canada.[18] As soon as he was released he brought his family to homestead northeast of Edmonton. The first year was cruel. A fire destroyed the Pylypiw homestead and the family started again. On Easter

Sunday 1897, the Pylypiws invited the first Ukrainian priest in Canada, Nestor Dmytriw, to conduct Alberta's first religious service in Ukrainian.[19] The Edna-Star settlement, 60 kilometres east of Edmonton, was the first of many Ukrainian communities in a block settlement of 8,000 square kilometres between Edmonton and the Saskatchewan border. Within a decade this aspen parkland was home to the largest concentration of Ukrainians outside Europe. Edmonton was their first stopping place and their enduring regional capital.

Michael Gowda was one of the thousands who followed Pylypiw and Eleniak from western Ukraine. He was a 23-year-old bachelor with an education and a smattering of English when he arrived in May 1898. Instead of filing for a homestead, he decided to make a new life in the town. He found a job as an interpreter with a farm equipment company on Jasper Avenue. He started the first Ukrainian reading society in Edmonton, directed the first Ukrainian play and wrote poetry about his new home:

> We are not reared within thy broad domains,
> Our fathers' graves and corpses lie afar,
> They did not fall for freedom on thy plains,
> Nor did we pour our blood beneath thy star,
> But Canada, in Liberty we work till death,
> Our children shall be free to call thee theirs,
> Their own dear land.[20]

Contemporary writers Yar Slavutych and Jars Balan suggest Gowda may have been the first Ukrainian poet anywhere to see his verse published in an English translation, a few years before the famous Taras Shevchenko.[21] Gowda helped many Ukrainians through their first difficult days in Edmonton. Some were headed for homesteads in the bloc settlements east of town; others stayed. By 1911 one in nine Albertans could trace roots to Slavic, Hungarian or Romanian communities in Europe.[22] The hardships of homesteading eventually drove many Ukrainians back to town, where they created a rich urban culture.

Chung Gee is believed to be the first Chinese immigrant to settle in Edmonton, although it is impossible to know for certain: A 21-year-old Chinese man named John Kee was listed in the 1891 census, but he could be possibly be Chung Gee. More than 18,000 Chinese men immigrated to Canada to construct the Canadian Pacific Railway and any one of them could have travelled here to begin a business or prospect for gold. Sam Sing and Charles Yeo are known to have lived here before 1894. Historian Brian Evans has compiled a database with 4,000 names of Chinese immigrants to Alberta. He has compared the names from immigration records and registrations to contemporary newspaper accounts and other local documents. He cannot find the evidence to support the familiar story that the early Chinese settlers came to Edmonton to escape mob violence after an outbreak of smallpox in Calgary in 1892. Nor can he substantiate or refute the local story that Chung Yan was threatened with mob action in Edmonton in March 1983 when he threw ashes into an alley and inadvertently started a minor fire.[23]

Racial hostility was a fact of life in the era. *The Edmonton Bulletin* proclaimed in an editorial on August 25, 1892 that Canada should feel no obligation to "furnish asylum, sympathy or support any number or kind of foreign heathens who may chose to engage in the distribution of opium, leprosy, smallpox and diabolism"; the editor also described the immigrants as "Chinese dirt." Aside from finding such repulsive references, Evans notes that his research suggests the newcomers fared better in Edmonton than in Calgary and Lethbridge and that "by the beginning of the 20th century Edmonton's Chinese population was beginning to increase with Ma [or variations Mah, Mar, Maar] and Lee [Li] becoming the most prominent surnames."[24] Other newcomers included the Sing, Pon and Quan families. For generations, Canada's discriminatory immigration laws kept Chinese women and children away from working husbands, fathers, brothers and sons. "It was a lonely time for me when I first came to Edmonton," Henry Wah Hein Mah later recalled, "I was never happy."[25] Yet by 1901, 235 Chinese immigrants had settled in the territory; a decade later, they numbered 1,781. Many made Edmonton their permanent home.

African-American farmers and ranchers came north to escape racial segregation after Oklahoma became a state in 1907. An advance party inspected the district in 1910 and returned to the United States with enthusiastic reports of a safe haven. Oklahoma newspapers printed headlines such as "Alberta, Home for the Coloured Race"[26] and encouraged a mass emigration to the Canadian West: "Within the next few months it is estimated that at least one thousand Negroes will leave from the northern and central part of this state for Alberta," said one Oklahoma report, "where they will form colonies in the vicinity of Edmonton."[27]

Both the Edmonton Board of Trade and the Edmonton Trades and Labour Council passed resolutions opposing the migration, alleging that "an unlimited influx of negroes into the province would invariably lower the standard of living."[28] In 1911, 3,400 people in the Edmonton district signed petitions asking the prime minister to block the migration;[29] Fort Saskatchewan and Strathcona citizens sent their own petitions to Ottawa. Petition papers were posted in the windows of the Union Bank, the Windsor Hotel, the King Edward Hotel, Merchants' Bank and the Board of Trade office. "We Want No Dark Spots in Alberta" echoed the *Edmonton Journal*.[30] The Hotel and Restaurant Employees Union demanded only white labour in city hotels and many commercial establishments said they would refuse service to the unwanted immigrants. Intimidation did not work. The first Oklahoma settlers included 94 adults, some of them former slaves, and 24 children. Their belongings and livestock filled seven railway cars. Hundreds followed them north. Many Oklahomans decided to stay in Edmonton and they quickly formed a strong-knit community around the sustaining Shiloh Baptist Church. The Canadian government effectively cut off African-American immigration to the West after 1911, but the Edmonton community endured.

Abe and Rebecca Cristall are believed to be the first Jewish immigrants to settle permanently in Edmonton in 1893,[31] but they were not the first to arrive. Jewish fur traders, merchants, miners and prospectors had passed through during the nineteenth century. Later Jewish immigrants arrived from all parts of Canada, particularly Winnipeg, as well as from Europe and the United States.

The new Edmonton welcomed more farmers than anyone else between 1891 and 1914, but it also beckoned urban settlers. Arriving on every train were skilled tradesmen, bankers, unskilled labourers, clerks, domestic servants, lawyers, doctors, railway workers, merchants, coal miners, nurses, seamstresses, surveyors, civil servants, midwives, preachers and undertakers. There was no free land for urban pioneers; they faced the risks and opportunities on their own.

None of the foreign-born immigrants arrived at this remote place by accident. Government agents and local business promoters recruited settlers at their point of origin with a fair bit of false advertising. To hear the agents tell it you could grow grapevines in March in this part of the world.[32] Once they learned the truth, many newcomers felt stung. A farm worker named Louis Pintz sent this warning home to a South Dakota newspaper in April 1892: "There is no work here," he wrote, "Wages are nothing as compared with the Dakotas. It is false that wages are higher in the Canadian northwest. Farmers offer from $15 to $16 per month."[33] The government and railroads did not care about immigrants once they lured them here, he said, and the real estate sharpies emptied a young man's pockets. Pintz saved his fury for Edmonton's April weather: "The weather is very cold and backward here yet...I can tell you right here that I stood on the platform with overcoat and mittens on, and my advice to the people of South Dakota is to stay there."

The Ukrainian priest, Nestor Dmytriw, wrote a blunt warning back to his homeland in 1897 about the hardships he was witnessing:

Let none come to Canada without a cent. Let such stay in Galicia, for it is easier to be a beggar there than here. There, a beggar is handed a piece of black bread, but here none will give away anything gratuitously. They may pay for work done, but work is not to be found on the farms, except on your own farm. And how can you work your own farm if you do not have oxen and a plough, even if you are dying of hunger, and die you surely will. To start farming, and to last out until you can enjoy the fruits of your labour, you must have not less than $300 in your pocket on arrival at the site. Without that modest capital, a person will either perish or forever be a pauper. A grave error was committed by those of our people who arrived in Canada towards winter. It is certainly obvious that, in wintertime, you will not get bread from under the snow. Your money will all be spent for food in the course of a long and hard winter, and in the spring, you will be left without a cent—and then try beating your head against a wall.[34]

To survive, many homesteading families sent their sons to work for the railways, coal mines, brickyards and lumber yards, often in Edmonton. They sent their daughters into town to work as domestic servants. Poverty of the cruellest kind—children who died of malnutrition, hungry adults who walked into the city from failed homesteads—existed alongside Edmonton's prosperity and confidence through the pioneer era. There were always two Edmontons, but they seldom saw each other.

Some young immigrants returned to distant families, disappointed and defeated. Others would have left in a minute if they could find the money. Those who disliked wearing overcoats and mittens in April departed promptly for the United States or for warmer British Columbia.

Sometimes even the most successful newcomers moved on for reasons of their own. Photographer Charles Mathers sauntered into Edmonton in 1893, an ambitious newcomer from rural Ontario. He built a studio, darkroom and gallery to exhibit his portraits and scenic views of the area. His clientele was instantly impressed. Mathers published his creative work in pamphlets and postcards and organized special exhibitions. He travelled through the remote North, promoting the hinterland to the business people of Edmonton with beautiful pictures. His healthy income allowed him to build a brick home for his family and hire an eager assistant named Ernest Brown. Mathers created most of our lingering impressions of pioneer Edmonton—the horse races on the river flats, the Cree sundances, the Klondike prospectors in transit, the proud merchants and their storefronts in the mud—and he worked hard to promote the town he clearly loved. In his last pamphlet, Mathers praised the "People of Destiny" who lived in a "delightsome land that lies on the sunny slopes of the eastern side of the Great Rockies where Alberta's sparkling fountains roll down their golden sand. With its prairies and its mountains, its forests and fertile fields, and a healthy, invigorating climate with perennial youth in the very air, there is avenue and opportunity for every kind of effort and enterprise."[35]

And then in 1904, at the click of a shutter, he left for British Columbia.

···

FOR EVERY WANDERER who left town, a crowd arrived on the next train. What kept them here? Who could define it without sounding like Charles Mathers in full flight? We only know that a little town with muddy streets, and a less than delightsome winter, expanded at a steady pace.

Edmonton had an upstart competitor on the south side of the river. Invented by a railway company with speculative ambitions, the town of Strathcona declared itself a city in 1907. Within four years it had a bustling market, a city hall, library, hospital, impressive railway stations, fire hall, public streetcars—and a distinct sense of superiority that exasperated people in Edmonton. "The rivalry was very keen between the two towns, especially in sports," wrote Anna Laura Robertson, recalling a hockey game of the era. "On one occasion I was standing watching as our Edmonton players came on the ice. They were wearing new sweaters, each displaying a big "E." A Strathcona girl standing near me, said: "Yes, 'E' for idiot!'"[36]

People stay in remote cities if they find a welcoming community and an urban culture. Long winters nurtured Edmonton's enduring love for the arts. Early citizens invited world-renowned opera singers, actors and circus troupes to their remote northern town, even luring the Divine Sarah Bernhardt in the frigid January of 1913.[37] The Edmonton Public Library opened its first tiny lending library in 1913—in cramped quarters at Jasper Avenue and 104th Street.[38] Booklovers could buy their sausages in the butcher shop and their whisky in the liquor store before climbing the rickety stairs to find a book. Local authors began to write novels, travelogues and memoirs. Journalist Katherine Hughes became Alberta's first provincial archivist in 1908; she immediately began to interview Edmonton's old-timers to preserve their stories. "I should like to get from them, if possible, portraits of the early settlers, buildings, fairs, banquets or any striking incident connected with the old times,"[39] she wrote in her advertisement. She began a biography of Albert Lacombe the following year. Vernon Barford created the Edmonton Operatic Society in 1903; he dreamed of developing "our own singers, instrumentalists, orchestras, choirs, choruses...and above all, our deep love for that greatest of all the arts—music."[40] Edmonton could boast its own theatrical groups and a music festival by 1908. At night, Métis fiddlers continued to play the tunes their grandparents had played at Fort Edmonton. Cree elders preserved drum songs and spiritual ceremonies despite legislated restrictions. Ukrainian immigrants organized their first chytalnia, or reading society, in 1901, and staged the first Ukrainian play in 1907[41]—all signs that creative people were exploring the spirit of the place. They brought warmth and light to a cold riverbank.

Edmonton declared itself a city on October 8, 1904, but it did not become an influential provincial capital the following year because of the growth of its population, its proud fur trade history or its emerging culture. The embarrassing truth is that Edmonton won the prize because it steadfastly supported Prime Minister Wilfrid Laurier's Liberal party at a critical time in the city's development. In 1896, voters elected the irascible

Bulletin publisher Frank Oliver to represent them in Ottawa.[42] He argued, cajoled, bargained and bullied on behalf of Edmonton's business leaders and settlers. The new citizens of the North-West Territories were soon demanding provincial status. Laurier doubted Alberta and Saskatchewan were ready to become provinces, but his government eventually bowed to the pressure from Frederick Haultain's territorial legislature in Regina. Edmonton, Calgary, Red Deer and Banff all hoped to be the capital of the new province. When Clifford Sifton resigned as Minister of the Interior in April, 1905, Frank Oliver took the job that gave him full control over patronage in the West. Every cabinet decision turned on partisan politics. A favour was bestowed if a favour was returned. At the dawn of the century, Conservative Calgary was out of luck.

A Liberal domino game began. Prime Minister Laurier appointed a Liberal, George Bulyea, as Alberta's first lieutenant-governor. Bulyea appointed Alexander Rutherford, a Strathcona lawyer and Liberal party president, as interim premier. Prime Minister Laurier came to Edmonton, not Calgary, to declare the birth of Alberta. "I see everywhere calm resolution, courage, enthusiasm to face all difficulties, to settle all problems,"[43] he told the cheering crowd. He also saw Liberals. Behind the scenes Frank Oliver had already won a promise that Edmonton would be the interim provincial capital, pending a final decision in the Alberta legislature after the first election. The Liberals created new electoral boundaries that gave Edmonton and northern Alberta an advantage during the first provincial election. Rutherford led a Liberal landslide—and surprise, surprise—the first Alberta legislature named Edmonton the permanent capital.[44]

If Calgary was miffed in 1906, it was apoplectic in 1907 when Premier Rutherford located the new University of Alberta in his own constituency. "The day will come when the outraged citizens of Alberta will tear down the university and cast it brick by brick into the North Saskatchewan River!"[45] Calgarian R.B. Bennett exclaimed in the legislature. Edmonton's leaders could reply without lying that the new university was not in the capital at all. Why it was practically in southern Alberta—in the independent city of Strathcona.

Every duel needs a starting pistol. The eternal rivalry between Edmonton and Calgary may have begun when the CPR transcontinental ran through Calgary, but it deepened when Edmonton used its Liberal connections to win two promising assets. Alberta's entire civil service earned just

$127,800 in 1906 and oversaw a $1.7 million budget.[46] In 1908 the new-born university had only four professors and 45 students who paid $20 a year for tuition and fees. Yet both institutions grew rapidly and in prosperous times they became roaring engines for Edmonton's economy. Both shaped the city's cultural identity, too. Edmonton's voters experimented with every kind of politics, but citizens who worked and studied at the university and found employment in the civil service would be one reason the city remained more liberal in outlook than its southern neighbour. Other Canadians saw the two cities as bickering siblings, but Edmonton and Calgary were never, ever identical twins.

Insults flew back and forth between the two cities for decades. Edmonton heard endless accusations that it lacked an entrepreneurial spirit; that it was too dependent on the public purse for its bread and butter; that its people were not self-starters, not risk-takers, not venture capitalists.

John Walter was the living contradiction of this Calgary stereotype—one of thousands, of course, but perhaps the finest. Born in the Orkney Islands, he arrived in Edmonton on a dog sled to build York boats for the HBC in 1870. He left Fort Edmonton later to build a home on the southern riverbank. He operated a profitable ferry, built riverboats and scows, and opened sawmills and a large lumber operation. He built the first carriage in Alberta. He opened the Strathcona Coal Mine with a partner in 1905. He established the *City of Edmonton* steamboat to take pioneer townspeople to their beloved Big Island for picnics. As Strathcona's first millionaire, he encountered the triple disasters of an embezzling manager, a deadly mine fire, and a flood that destroyed his businesses. His wealth floated away. He started again.[47]

Edmonton's earliest business leaders invested the profits of their small endeavours in larger ones, steadily building local industries and employing new immigrants. Butcher Wilhelm Vogel built one of the first meatpacking plants in 1901; John Gainer followed in 1903 and meat processing soon became one of Edmonton's dominant industries. Hotel-keeper William Sheppard built a large brewing company. The J.B. Little and Pollard Brothers brickyards, the Humberstone mine and the Bedard tannery were all locally-owned family businesses that grew steadily before the First World War. Edmonton's early public ownership of utilities and telephones—far ahead of other Canadian cities—supported economic development in a period of rapid expansion. Pioneer traders like John A. McDougall and Richard Secord were becoming wealthy men.

WATCHING THE TRAINS ARRIVE, day after day, were the descendants of Edmonton's first families. What did they think as they saw home-steaders lining up at the land office to claim a piece of their ancestral territory? Frank Oliver argued in the *Bulletin* that local aboriginal people should live "in a more congenial setting" than Edmonton. "It would be for the benefit of the Indians to remove them from civilization, as too close communication with whites is not conducive to making them good agriculturalists," he wrote. He suggested they belonged somewhere near "northern lakes."[48]

Oliver continued to call for the expulsion of Cree people from the Edmonton area and the surrender of their land to local commercial and agricultural interests. He was also antagonistic to non-Anglo Saxon immi-gration. "He was certainly a racist, but so was everybody else in his era,"[49] cautions Rod Macleod, adding that the *Bulletin* was more even-handed than many newspapers at the time. Whatever his attitudes, Oliver helped to sustain the morale of new settlers before the arrival of the railway and promoted the city's commercial interests throughout his life. His personal papers have been destroyed so it is difficult to piece together every detail of his political career, but his legacy is clear enough. "It's because of Frank Oliver that Edmonton is the capital of Alberta," says Macleod, "and no one else."[50]

With Oliver's encouragement, Stony Plain settlers and Edmonton busi-nessmen asked the federal government for the full surrender of the Enoch reserve in 1898 and 1899. Enoch band members refused with a petition of their own and the support of the local Indian agent. Oliver saw to it that a new agent was hired: his Edmonton pal, the old prospector and liquor merchant, James Gibbons. Under pressure, Enoch members surrendered 37 square kilometres of their reserve in 1902 in exchange for fencing and farm equipment they could have claimed under treaty. John A. McDou-gall and Richard Secord bought 70 per cent of this land.[51] "The Indians are masters in what they have to sell," Oliver wrote to McDougall, "as we are masters in what we wish to buy."[52]

Bands under treaty had no direct access to revenue earned on their land at this time. The local Indian agent held the purse strings on trust accounts tightly. The Michel band badly needed horses and farm equip-ment in 1903 and agreed to surrender 32 square kilometres to raise money for the purchases.[53] The sale was marked by corruption in Ottawa. In one case, Maria Allison, a cleaning lady in the Department of Indian Affairs, bought three quarter-sections of Michel land for $1 an acre, then gave it to her boss. The surveyors had estimated the value at $4.20 an acre. No money was available to the Michel band for its purchases. Angry about the surrender, five bands in the Edmonton area petitioned Ottawa for a new Indian agent in 1904. Their request was refused.

Chief Alexander was deposed in 1903 by government order; he was reinstated after the Alexander band surrendered 39 square kilometres at Rivière Qui Barre in 1905.[54] The neighbouring Michel band again refused to sell. In Ottawa that year Frank Oliver was appointed the Minister of the Interior. To encourage more surrenders, he introduced legislation to offer bands direct access to 50 per cent of land sales and to make the tendering process more flexible for speculators.

Eager buyers appeared at the Empire Theatre on Jasper Avenue on December 5, 1906 to bid on all unsold Michel land. Surveyors had estimated the value at between $9 and $15 an acre. It went for $9 an acre, but almost none of the 17 buyers paid their bills. Four years later, Ottawa had collected $900 on the $48,000 due to the Michel band's account. In 1910, while Oliver was still Minister of the Interior and Superintendent-General of Indian Affairs, J.J. Anderson, the manager of the Union Bank on Jasper Avenue, approached one of the indebted Manitoba speculators with an offer to purchase his portion of Michel land. The deal was done and in 1914 Anderson transferred the title of 14 square kilometres of Michel land and another parcel of Alexander land to his father-in-law, Frank Oliver.[55] Altogether Oliver acquired 26 quarter-sections of Cree land around Edmonton for $34,771—half the appraised value at the time of the transaction.[56]

Newcomers who came to town rarely heard this story. The elders in Edmonton's first families watched the trains arrive and remembered.

⌁

HIGH ON THE RIVERBANK old Fort Edmonton stood diminished in the shadow of the new Alberta Legislature Building. Although fur prices soared between 1895 and 1911, the HBC no longer monopolized the fur trade. Canada's first corporation reinvented itself as a major real estate developer and landowner, but retained an interest in the flourishing fur trade. In 1899, a well-established French company, Revillon Frères, opened a small warehouse in Edmonton where traders paid cash for furs.[57] Two years later Revillon opened a large wholesale business to supply a network of small posts through the fur-rich Athabasca region and across the north.

A new generation of trappers brought muskrat, beaver, lynx, red fox, ermine and rabbit pelts into the city. Independent buyers and traders, often Jewish or Lebanese immigrants, opened fur businesses along 101st Street and travelled north on buying trips. Métis business families pursued the trade as actively as their ancestors. Fur trade historian Arthur Ray has traced the small city's importance in the international fur markets in the early industrial era. By the end of the First World War, Edmonton ranked second to Montreal as a fur-marketing centre, with a hinterland that stretched from The Pas in Manitoba to interior British Columbia and up to the Arctic coast. This territory was yielding $4 to $5 million worth of raw fur every year by 1920.[58]

The citizens of Edmonton hauled, baled, counted and exported much of the fur, in part, because Edmonton had become a railway hub. Transcontinental trains arrived at last in 1905, thanks to the entrepreneurship of William Mackenzie and Donald Mann who founded the Canadian Northern Railway against considerable odds. A surprising number of railway companies carved rail lines through the bush and muskeg, west to Edson, north to Athabasca Landing, later into the rich Peace Country, and toward Fort McMurray. The Edmonton, Yukon and Pacific Railway struggled to link Strathcona with the Klondike, but the tracks stopped dead on the Rossdale Flats. Was this the little engine that couldn't?

Larger railways hired thousands of surveyors, construction workers, railway yard and train employees who regarded Edmonton as their home base. Soon homesteaders and independent traders were pouring through Edmonton to explore the potential of a northern frontier. A few curious geologists were investigating the oil sands near Fort McMurray. Could the tar be extracted to pave the city's muddy streets? Was it good for anything else? Edmonton was strengthening its connection to a vast territory and its unknown resource wealth.

Coal ruled in Edmonton's river valley and by the early 1900s labourers were working in more than two dozen mines. One Saturday night in the summer of 1907, pit boss George Lamb found the Strathcona Coal Mine in flames and climbed down an airshaft in a brave attempt to rescue five trapped miners. He failed to get them out and like the other young men, he died from smoke inhalation and severe burns in Edmonton's worst-ever industrial accident. The Penn mine on Grierson Hill was named for the penitentiary that operated with prisoners as the unpaid miners.[59] New mines opened in Riverdale, Ottewell, Beverly, Clover Bar, south along Whitemud Creek and up in Namao. Edmonton families heated their homes with local coal—in hard times, they defied the law and dug it from the riverbanks for their own use—and every local business depended on coal until the advent of natural gas in 1923.

The labyrinth of underground mine tunnels and shafts created trouble for the people up above. Hillsides, houses, roads, sidewalks, sewer and water lines collapsed or shifted because of subterranean upheavals. The city tolerated the danger and aggravation because the industry was a critical employer and energy supplier. At its peak in the early 1920s, the Edmonton coal mines produced 533,000 tons of coal a year and employed 3,600 miners and many more wholesalers and truck drivers. Business profits were considerable in the good years, yet it was only in 1922 that miners began to earn five dollars a day.

⌐⌐◡

FIVE DOLLARS A DAY was no fortune, even in 1922, but as writer Warren Caragata suggests in *Alberta Labour: A Heritage Untold*, unskilled labourers in 1900 would have considered the wage a ticket to heaven. The first industrial workers in Edmonton had no concept of child labour laws, minimum wages, overtime pay or safe working conditions. They had no recourse when a boss refused to pay them, or mistreated them, and no compensation if they were injured on the job. Boys as young as 12 could work at Edmonton's coal mines, sorting coal at the screening tables, for ten hours a day, then brought home $1.25 to parents who needed it.[60] Girls worked as domestic servants.

Edmonton's rapid growth at the turn of the century, particularly in construction, gave skilled workers an opportunity to insist on collective agreements and enforced labour laws. Carpenters and joiners were the first to organize a union local in 1902, followed six months later by bricklayers and typesetters. In 1904 Edmonton plumbers were working six days a week for as little as 35 cents an hour; they formed the Plumbers and Pipefitters local in 1905 and negotiated the miracle of an eight-hour day and 64 cents an hour. Blacksmiths, hotel waiters, railway workers, tailors, barbers and teamsters organized soon after. The Edmonton Trades and Labour Council could count 33 union locals by 1911 and began to elect labour candidates to city office in 1914.[61]

Women in Edmonton were among the earliest unionized female workers in Canada when the Great Western Garment Company opened in 1911 and they were the first to win the eight-hour day. Eight seamstresses walked through the factory on opening day. They sewed men's work clothing at piece work rates. Alexander Rutherford was a co-founder with an initial investment of $10,000. The company was so successful that 100 employees were working at the plant within the year. Thousands of immigrants found their first jobs at the 97th Street factory, learning English as they manufactured farmers' overalls, soldiers' uniforms and denim jeans for generations of Canadians. The firm continued to expand until GWG was a nationally-known brand name and an Edmonton trademark.

Unskilled labourers and female domestics had the lowest wages. Labourers who installed Edmonton's underground telephone lines in 1907 earned 25 cents an hour. They worked for ten hours a day, six days a week, collecting a grand sum of $15 a week. What did that money purchase in 1907? A single man could rent a room for $4.50 a week, eat for $4 a week, and buy a shirt for a quarter. Raising a family on the same income was a tougher challenge in a town where small houses rented for $40 a month by 1911. The International Workers of the World, the radical Wobblies, tried to organize unskilled labourers in Edmonton in 1912. About 250 labourers with no union were digging the new sewer line in September when they went on strike for higher pay. They earned 25 cents an hour and asked for a nickel-an-hour raise. Strikers marched behind brass bands to other city works sites, holding signs that said: "Come out of the ditch." Alarmed, the city called out the militia and arrested the leader, Gus Larsen. The employer refused to raise the ditch-diggers' wages, but allowed them to work nine hours a day, instead of eight, with 45 cents for the extra hour. After five days without pay, the labourers accepted the offer. It was a living.[62]

Many unskilled labourers struggled to read and write their own names and heard snickers of ridicule at their heavy foreign accents, yet their contributions endured. They built the first bridges across the river. They put up the first telephone lines. They laid down streetcar tracks. They dug the foundations of every hospital, house, office building, store, factory and hotel. They dug out sewers and mine tunnels, streets and avenues with their shovels and their picks. They constructed every street and avenue. They loaded the coal, packed the fur bales, built the meatpacking plants, cut the ice blocks from the river, shovelled the snow. Female domestics cooked, cleaned and cared for Edmonton's merchant families as they raised their own children. Women worked in market gardens, bakeries, small factories, dressmaking shops, restaurants, hotels, laundries and hospitals as cleaners and cooks. Together they constructed a Canadian city from the ground up.

Edmonton grew because it remembered its birth ties to the fur trade, and to the north, and because it learned how to serve farmers and townspeople in the surrounding district. Business profits were reinvested at home. These are the admirable reasons for the city's expansion, but Edmonton also grew for less commendable reasons. In the early years, a powerful Liberal clique in the city manipulated the Liberal political establishment in Ottawa at the expense of southern Albertans. Merchants indulged in highly profitable and exploitative land speculation at the expense of local farmers and townspeople. Local speculators acquired large amounts of First Nations and some Métis land at discounted prices, often with questionable legality. These actions had consequences, but not immediately. By the time Edmonton and Strathcona voted to create a single city in 1911, their combined population was 31,064 and the city's confidence was growing.

Can you hear the train whistle blowing? Here comes a short but sweet miracle. The 1912 Boom.

New in town? Let me help you with them suitcases. The name's Charlie. Got a place to stay? Tried the King Eddie? The Cecil? The Royal George? You're in a tent, I bet, down on the flats. I read in the paper 2,600 people are living down there this summer. Been to the land office yet? Speaking of land, need some?

I'm a curbside broker, a lot man, and my office is right out here on the corner of Jasper and 101st under the wild, blue yonder. I don't rent a roof over my head, so I can pass on the bargains to you. What? Sure, it's legal. What kind of land are you after, anyway? Homestead land? Forgive me saying so, sir, but you should consider city land. This place is hopping. Over a few blocks they're constructing Edmonton's tallest building—the McLeod Building—and it's going to be nine storeys tall! Then there's the Tegler and the Civic Block. We've got three new bridges across the river this year alone, and that includes the High Level Bridge. Four men died building it. A real Duke and Duchess opened it in September. We've got streetcars that go down to McKernan Lake, and new neighbourhoods that go up to Inglewood and Calder. You don't know about those places? Why, I guess you wouldn't, but why not invest your hard-earned money in a going concern?

Our fine city is going to be the new Chicago. Last May the old Hudson's Bay Company held a big public sale to sell off some of its reserve land right in the middle of town. You heard about that? It was a wild time. About 1,500 people lined up around the block, playing cards all night around bonfires, just waiting for a chance to make an offer. In one day that old HBC collected $3.6 million in cash. In cash, sir. I do not lie. Now I wasn't there, but I bought a lot from a fellow, who purchased it from another gentleman for a song, and I'm willing to pass along the savings to you. How much would you be willing to invest in a real hot property? We've got 336 real estate men in this town, with runners on the street, and not one will give you a better deal than me. Remember, the name's Charlie....

EDMONTON BALLOONED from 31,000 people to 50,000 people in 1912—or so said the city's boosters in a delirium of wild land speculation. Cash flew in a thousand directions when a sudden depression hit the West in 1913. Wheat prices tumbled. Worried business investors began to sell off city properties and soon the real estate market was a gloomy bargain basement sale with no buyers. Edmonton had expanded too quickly, spent too heavily on Chicago-sized projects, and the local government was unable to collect $1.2 million in unpaid taxes. Railway construction came to a sudden halt across the province and labourers hitched rides into the city or walked. In January, 1914, 500 unemployed railway workers arrived in Edmonton on the train, desperate for work. The small city's relief department reported 4,000 people without jobs and no way of finding any. Suddenly the boom town was flat busted. On the first Sunday morning in February, 300 men marched through snowy streets to McDougall Methodist Church to protest their impossible situation.[63] Most were young immigrants who had come from Europe and the British Isles a few years before, full of optimism about a new life in a new land.

Soon they would march toward European trenches—or immigrants' internment camps in the Rockies—far away from the town that had welcomed them with its arms wide open.

In Our Own Words

OLD TIMERS

Donald Ross, hotelkeeper

Now New-Comers, welcome, let all have their fling,
  As sung the Old-Timers—let every one sing,
To Alberta so fertile and vast in its might,
  Sure road to contentment with prospects so bright.
Then hurrah, bring them on, take Old-Timer's advice,
  Let your friends pick up stakes and come here in a trice,
They're sure of a welcome, there is room for them all,
  In this new land of ours we Old-Timers recall.[64]

Jim Gibbons, Daddy Osborne and Donald Ross called themselves Edmonton's Old Timers in the early twentieth century. To qualify as an Old Timer, you had to be a fur trader, prospector or settler who had "walked into the country," or arrived on horseback or Red River cart before the arrival of the immigrant trains in 1891.

The Cree of Edmonton

Generations of Cree people have used the word for town, *otinow*, as another name for Edmonton. The city remained their meeting place. In the early 1900s Charles Mathers and Ernest Brown photographed their public gatherings, family portraits, and special occasions such as the Jasper Avenue gathering on Queen Victoria's Jubilee—but rarely identified the people in the pictures. Descendants and archivists are working to restore names to these images through careful research and contributions from private family collections.

Early settlers camped in tents on the river flats while they searched for a homestead in the surrounding district, or a place to live in town. In 1912, some 2,600 people were reported to be living in a tent city along the river.

"We are here" from America ⤙ Ellen Hopkins, descendant

In 1890 my grandfather Lewis Ervin and his bride of one year…decided that times were too hard and chances of making a living too slim to remain in their childhood home of Mount Pleasant, Michigan U.S.A. Having heard wonderful tales of land here, and chickens running wild for the taking in midwestern Alberta, they packed their belongings along with great grandmother and grandfather Archer, Uncles Zeke and Jonah, and their household effects and moved to what is now the city of Edmonton.

On a chill November day the Ervins and Archers arrived into the little settlement in search of a house in which to rest their travel weary bones. The gentlemen of the party left the ladies in charge of the baggage while they [left] to find the said dwelling. The first gentleman questioned informed them that there was a dandy frame house empty for anyone's use who cared to move in and best of all, no rent was required. Upon questioning the good man further the ancestors found that a man had lived in it some time ago with his flighty wife. This man had been ill and every night his wife would go out to meet a lover and leave him walking the floor and moaning piteously in his agony until she returned. Then suddenly one day the wife packed in a hurry and left, saying only that her husband had died and was buried on the hill.

Soon after a family had moved into the vacant house and moved out after a brief stay of two days, saying that the house was haunted. Grandfather scoffed at the tale and though the rest of the family were rather skeptical had them moved in before they knew it. The first night the travellers slept well and the next day much time was spent in scoffing at superstitious neighbours and their grandmothers' tales. But alas, the following night at 12 a.m. sharp...thud, thump! thud, thump! across the attic floor. It was a windy evening and eerie moans were heard interspersed by clanking as of chains being drawn across a floor! Thud, thump! eee! clank! clank! The spirit was abroad.

Grandmother shot bolt upright in bed and clawed the air wildly, her elbow winding up in Grandpa's solar plexus which aroused him out of a deep sleep and set him grasping for air. "Sure, and what is it that ye be knockin' me brea...." Thud thump clank, eee! Grandpa slid like an eel into the feather tick, burrowing in it up to his ears. "Wh-wh-what was that?"

Grandfather was too frightened to answer and the rest of the night was spent in listening to the noises overhead until the wind went down and the sun arose in all its glory. That morning a group of white-faced Irish Americans, after exchanging "Did you hear it?" hit upon a plan. That afternoon Grandpa took a bag of flour and went upstairs. He sprinkled the flour on the floor and left feeling quite smug. That night the wind came up again howling about the house shutters and tearing through the barren branches of the big trees behind the little cottage on Mount Pleasant. And soon to the waiting ears of the settlers again came the weird sounds as of a man in agony dragging chains across the upper floor and moaning in agony all the while. This continued until 3 a.m. and suddenly to the already terrified listeners, although I fancy Grandpa's Irish blue eyes were twinkling with fun, came sounds of the piano in the parlor being played! Uncle Zeke could almost see the ghostly fingers trailing up and down the keys.

Thump! The music stopped. Another morning rolled around and it was with some difficulty that grandfather persuaded the family to stay but another day. That evening the men were returning from town when Uncle Jonah happened to turn and look back down the hill. Rolling up the hill toward them were three balls of fire glowing vividly in the dark. That was enough! Jonah threw up his hands and told his brothers, "Boys 'tis a warnin' sure and I'm sure of it." The next morning the frame house was again vacant but not for long. An English family by the name of Bisset moved in at noon and at night they moved out, after summoning Lewis Ervin to board up the windows. This he did and as they were about to leave asked Mrs. Bisset why they were leaving so soon. For answer she took him inside the house and opened the cellar door. From out the cellar came an unholy stench. Grandpa Ervin was never a superstitious man but for some reason that smell made the hair raise straight up on his scalp.

No one ever lived in that house again but perhaps the restless spirit.[65]

"Nous sommes ici" ⟿ Lucile Tellier Hittinger

Emery and Clara Tellier from Ste-Mélanie, Québec, had heard of the westward migration of people to what was then known as the Northwest Territories. The popular slogan of the time was "Go west, young man, go west." Dieudonné [Emery's father] had twelve children and felt that they would have a better chance at obtaining their own land if the family moved west. So, in March of 1891, my father Emery and his brother Tancrede accompanied their father Dieudonné as he joined a contingent of some sixty-five French Canadians bound for the West.

Headed by Father Jean-Baptiste Morin, they embarked on a seven-day journey on the CPR to Calgary. They had three train cars filled with farm machinery, household goods, a sewing machine, a spinning wheel and other necessities to start a new life on an unknown frontier. Horses, cattle, pigs, sheep and chickens were part of the trek. There was no railroad from Calgary to Edmonton at that time, so they traveled in covered wagons. They forded the Red Deer River while the cattle and horses swam across the swollen spring river.

When they arrived in Strathcona, all of their belongings were ferried across the North Saskatchewan River at a point a little west of the present Low Level Bridge. They disembarked below Fort Edmonton. The escarpment was high so all of their possessions including animals were loaded on a lift to be raised to the top....

The three Telliers, Dieudonné, Emery and Tancrede arrived at Fort Edmonton to the sound of mission bells. It had taken them a month to come from Québec. They immediately filed for homesteads and with their belongings, followed a trail to an area five miles northwest of the present town of Morinville in an area known as le grand brûlé. There they each chose adjoining homesteads. There were no roads other than a few paths, and of course, no fences, farm buildings, water wells, schools or churches. So the first thing they did was to cut down trees for logs. Each of them built a log house, a barn and then cleared a few acres of land....

The settlers quickly discovered that this was not going to be the land of milk and honey which they had been promised. They had acquired fertile lands but they had to contend with no roads, no stores, no doctors and no schools. They survived, raised their families and tilled the soil. They broke the land and became as self-sufficient as possible. They worked very hard, were happy and eventually prospered.[66]

"Wir sind hier" ⟿ Emma Mohr, speaking of Catherine Hennig of Josephsburg

Mother decided to earn a bit of extra money to help buy the many necessary household items which were still needed. She got a part-time job as maid for the Johnstone Walkers, owners of the first Johnstone Walker store in Edmonton. Her usual mode of transportation was on foot, and in order to save her shoes she walked barefoot and carried her shoes. She stayed in Edmonton three or four days a week, then walked home to see how things were progressing there. Occasionally she was able to catch a ride home on the wagon with a neighbour or pioneer farmer who had gone to Edmonton for supplies. While she was away her mother...helped to look after the children and housework. Wages were very low, and were taken out in merchandise in some cases. She often talked about the time she worked for days to earn a fairly large tin box with a tight-fitting lid in which to store flour or any perishable food, as the house had no screen doors to keep our flies or insects. The Johnstone Walker store got its supplies packed in these tin boxes. This particular one had contained tea.[67]

RIVAL CITIES: EDMONTON VS. SOUTH EDMONTON

Frank Oliver

Edmonton is usually a quite place, a very quiet place. There are people who say that it is positively dull. On Saturday last it was, if possible, more quiet than usual—up to about three o'clock in the afternoon. After that hour and until late midnight it was undoubtedly the most alive, lively, excited, exciting and generally interesting place in all Canada, or its colonies in North or South Dakota, or Washington. There was the biggest kind of a circus on. There was more fun than could be furnished by a barrel of monkeys. Five hundred men with blood in both eyes were engaged in demonstrating that even in this dull town, in this peaceful country, physical force as a means of maintaining public right is not played out....

In a few minutes they and an angry crowd of citizens had gathered around the office while the alarm was sent all over town. While the main crown was gathering the nuts were taken off the wagon axles and the horses unhitched, so that the stuff already loaded could not be moved. In a very short time not less than 200 men were around the land office determined to know why the promises made so definitely by the government were broken and their interests so wantonly attacked. Mr. Anderson drove

When the Dominion Land Agent "Timber" Tom Anderson sent wagons to move the land office to the south side of the river in 1892, 200 Edmonton men quickly gathered in a vigilante action to stop the move.

An unidentified child takes a pony ride down Jasper Avenue in the homestead era.

to the police barracks for assistance and two policemen arrived promptly on the scene, but under the circumstances were unable to do anything as they could not move the wagons without horses, and other horses were not to be had. Telegrams were sent to all the members of the cabinet, to Davis, Davin, Macdowall, Senators Lougheed, Girard, and Sir Donald A. Smith, stating the facts of the case and asking an explanation. A mass meeting of citizens was assembled in front of the land office, about 8 o'clock. Inspector Piercy arrived about the same time. Just then, four teams from the South side, who had been telephoned for by Mr. Anderson, arrived. The horses were taken from the wagons by the crowd, and the drivers informed that they must not interfere. Finally horses and wagons were driven across the river and tied up on the other side. There was some slight disturbance while this was going on, but nothing serious occurred....

Sunday passed quietly, the police guard remaining in charge of the wagons, and a citizens' guard remaining as well.

This (Monday) morning Supt. Griesbach arrived from Fort Saskatchewan with twenty policemen. He left the police at Rat Creek, outside the town limits, and came in alone. As soon as the arrival of the police was known the supposition became general that the intention was to forcibly remove the office. To meet this possibility Mayor McCauley, councillor Cameron and J.A. McDougall, J.P.'s, issued an order calling out the home guards organized in '85 by General Strange, to keep the peace—that is the land office. At 1 p.m. nearly every able bodied man in town—most of them armed—appeared at the town clerk's office, ready for any event.[68]

KLONDIKE DAYS

William Griesbach

In 1898 one of the biggest things happened, up to that time at all events, to Edmonton. The rush to the Klondyke gold fields had set in. The hardships of the Pacific Coast-Whyte Pass route profoundly effected the rush and many prospective prospectors were induced to look at the map and consider what we called the "Edmonton" route. The Honourable Frank Oliver in his newspaper, the *Edmonton Bulletin*, wrote glowingly of the ease with which people could get to the Klondyke by travelling via Edmonton. We had two routes to offer. One was the over-land route by pack horse. In a general way it could be said that this route followed the present Alaska Highway but nobody was quite sure of that. We could give them a good start, however, from Edmonton to Fort St. John. After that, no one really knew. The water route, however, did make sense. One could travel over land from Edmonton to Athabasca Landing one hundred miles. There, boats and barge could be built, and the rest of the journey was down stream practically to the mouth of the Mackenzie River, and then by going up a small river, known as the Rat River, the height of land could be crossed and the Klondyke area approached from the east by utilizing streams in that locality.

An American named Mrs. Garner left Edmonton for the Klondike in August 1897. About 1,560 hopeful prospectors rushed through Edmonton in 1897 and 1898 with little or no idea of the punishing wilderness ahead. About half of the Klondikers turned back and an estimated 70 people and 2,000 horses died en route.

Col. O'Brien's party packed champagne for a luxurious trip to the Yukon.

Savvy little Edmonton found a get-rich scheme during the Yukon gold rush of 1898. As William Griesbach remembered it, Edmonton collected the treasure. Few prospectors who reached the Yukon made much money.

In due course the rush came upon us. The town was shortly filled with prospectors who arrived on every train. Many of them were wild-eyed individuals with preconceived notions. They refused to take any advice from us at all. I remember several of the proposals that were actually attempted. One man arrived with barrels of salt pork. He proposed to put an axle through each barrel, to link the barrels together by side-bars, to follow the frozen streams of the north country, the contraption being hauled by team of horses, each barrel revolving on its own axis. On top of the barrels was a box which would carry hay and oats camping equipment and the like. This outfit started out one day and came to grief in the outskirts of Edmonton when one of the barrels was [destroyed] by a bump in the road. This convinced the inventor that he was off on the wrong foot.

Another ingenious contrivance merely illustrated that the inventor had been born thirty years too soon. It was simply this: that a steam engine be installed on a set of sleigh runners with a large cogged wheel in the centre shod with heavy spikes, drawing several cabooses in which the adventurers would live in comparative comfort.

Here again the route was to be down the frozen rivers. The engine burned wood which could be cut as the party moved along.... Everybody turned out to see this party start. I think these men came from Michigan. The smoke poured out of the stoves in the cabooses in which the men were warm and comfortable as long as they kept the fires going. The locomotive whistled, everybody shook hands with everybody else and wished the adventurers bon voyage, the throttle was opened and the big driving wheel began to revolve. It tore a hole in the frozen ground but the train did not move. Indeed, it never moved.

The engine simply was not strong enough for the job. Finally, the whole train was dismantled and bought up by some of the local boys for some other purpose....

It need scarcely be said that these thousands of prospectors left a great deal of money and property in Edmonton. All sorts of local people opened offices to sell pack saddles, maps and the like. The maps were largely imaginary as to data and were frequently based upon the stories told by old fur traders who professed to have travelled the area at one time or another in their careers. Any oldtimer who had ever been in the north country was invited to join these offices and, in a new suit of clothes and smoking a cigar, could be seen for a price. Some of these prospectors never left Edmonton and for many years could be seen around Edmonton following various sorts of more or less legitimate and sometimes illegitimate business.

By the end of 1898, the "Edmonton" route to the gold fields had died a natural death. I remember one incident that sticks in my memory. I was watching one of these parties packing their ponies and getting ready for the start. Everything seemed to be packed up and one pony remained without a pack. A bewhiskered individual approached me and said, "Sonny, do you want to buy a horse?" I said, "How much?" He replied, "Ten dollars." I happened to have ten dollars that day, for some reason or other. The transaction was completed and I led the horse away. A hundred yards or so down the street was another party getting ready to leave. All their pack horses were packed but a good deal of stuff was still lying around. I led the pony into this "layout" and asked several men if they wanted to buy a horse. They said they did, "How much?" I said, "Twenty-five dollars." The deal was made and I walked off, fifteen dollars to the good.[69]

THE FLOOD OF 1899

Olive Kathleen Heathcote Murdoch

In the early part of August in the year 1899, Mother went to town in the buggy with Elsie. The Saskatchewan River was very high when she went over on the ferry, and for safety the ferry was taken off that same night.

The next morning when she went to the edge of the hill to see if she could cross that day, the river was a roaring flood. The days dragged by, days of misery for Mother, wondering how we were getting along out on the farm. Eveline, the eldest, was not quite fourteen and ranging down to

Winnie, who was three and a half, were the five of us. [Their father had died.] Instead of receding, the river rose, and tore away trees, barns and houses. Mother tells how she could see houses tied to trees all along the banks with a rope through the door and one window, for in those days more people built down on the flats near the water line. Nowadays most of Edmonton is built on high ground. Piers for the first bridge to span the Saskatchewan here, had been completed, but the water completely covered these. The Hudson's Bay boat, the "North West," a pretty, little white two-decker was as moored just beyond the piers.

One morning while Mother stood and watched on the hill where the Macdonald Hotel now stands, she saw this little boat break away from its moorings and go careening down the river. Would it miss the piers save itself, or would it strike them? It sailed gaily along, when crash, it hit one of the piers, knocking out its boilers and with a bad list went wobbling woefully down the current. And day after day, that boiling caldron raged on.

High up on the bank where Mother stood, and our North Saskatchewan has very high banks, you had to shout to make yourself heard. The 22nd of August came along, Eveline's fourteenth birthday, and Mother was still stranded across that raging river.

Meanwhile, out on the farm were we five girls with our woe. When Mother did not come back the day after she left, we were frankly puzzled. Then it rained, and we at times forgot Mother with our own troubles.

Everywhere was rain and water. We would dress up in old coats and bring the cows home, milk them, set the milk in pans, do the chores around the house, and try to dry our wet clothes. We would set out to fetch the cows home at night in clothes not the least bit dry, and this happened day after day, and still it rained, and rained, and rained.

In the Bible, it had also rained, forty days and forty nights, and then there was a floods. And where was Mother and why had she not told us her reason for not coming home? ...We began to feel that Mother was lost—shortly before this a horse and buggy had been lost from the ferry on account of the horse becoming frightened—and this must have happened to Mother, and there we were—five little orphans. I don't know what we lived on. I was only ten and details about eating do not linger long in the memory of a child, but there was always the milk and butter and we would have some vegetables by August....

They managed to get a little boat over the river on the ferry cable to carry the mail across, and Mother with her baby went over on one of the first

boatloads. She hired a rig in Strathcona to drive her home, and reached
her poor, frightened daughters in a
happy reunion.[70]

MORE ARRIVALS

"Our search led us to Michael Gowda" ⤏ Peter Svarich

We arrived in Strathcona—that's
how southern Edmonton was called
then—on April 14, 1900, on the eve
of Thomas' Sunday, happy at last to
have reached the end of the railway

and our destination. We went to the Immigration Hall, which we called
the "Emigrant." There we found many of our people who had come to
Edmonton to meet us and to find out whether there were any of their
fellow countrymen from their villages in the Old Country. Few were
disappointed; they soon found whom they wanted, greeted them enthusiastically and, forming groups, began to talk about the Old Country, their
travelling experiences, and the new life on the farms. The women got busy
preparing meals, washing their clothing, linen, and sheets....

After consulting with my family and some acquaintances, we decided
to stay in town for a few days, either at some boarding place or at the
"Emigrant." We were reluctant to stay at the latter for fear that we might
once more be eaten alive by the vermin. So, one man and I went into town
to see if we could find some of our people who could direct us to a place
where we could stay for a few days.

Our search led us to Michael Gowda who had already lived in Edmonton for two years and who was an interpreter for a farm implement dealer.
Michael greeted us warmly and asked many questions. Upon hearing my
story, he said that he felt sorry for me that I had come to Canada, because
I could expect nothing beyond a miserable existence. He pointed out that
life on the farm was very hard, and employment in town was practically
unavailable without knowledge of the English language. Back home he
had completed his divisional school and cantor's training, but here it was
worth nothing. He had picked up a little English, but neither one of us
could understand the other.

*By day Michael Gowda
worked as a Ukrainian
interpreter at a farm
equipment store on Jasper
Avenue. In his spare time,
and at his own expense, he
guided hundreds immigrants
like Peter Svarich through
their first difficult days in
Edmonton. He also wrote
moving poetry about his
new homeland.*

The vocalization of English words was very difficult for me, for, really, I had heard little of the language spoken. I only knew it from the books which I had brought with me. I knew many words and could read with comprehension, but I could not sound out the words, nor could I understand them when they were spoken to me. The English spoke so rapidly that I could not catch individual words or phrases. When it was necessary for me to know what was spoken, I quickly took my notebook out, wrote what I wanted to say and asked for a written reply, or begged the speaker to speak more slowly, sounding each word out slowly and distinctly.

Michael Gowda undertook to look after me. On his recommendation we found a large building which we could have for five dollars a week; the building was a skating rink and provided accommodation for ten families. We agreed that the men would go out to look for farms, and the women and children would remain behind. Whoever found a suitable homestead would get a neighbour to drive back to town with him and a wagon and bring the rest of his family. Of course, this applied to those who had some money with them. My father and Wasyl Cherniawsky had the most, $1500 and $2000 respectively, which was sufficient to begin farming operations in earnest. They decided to buy horses, a wagon, a plough, harrows, and some kitchen and household items at once and set out with their families eastward where, they were told, was the best land.[71]

"I cursed my husband and his Canada" ⌐ Maria Yureichuk

It was towards the end of September [1899] when our group of eight families, five from Bukovina and two from Galicia, arrived at Strathcona in Alberta. The Bukovinians visited with their acquaintances here, and on the third day, they hired a wagon for fifteen dollars per family to take them to Ihlyky, now the district of Andrew, in Alberta. We could have gone with them, but we did not have enough money. All we had was $7.50 and we needed it to buy food.

Our husbands then decided to look for homesteads closer to Edmonton. They tramped all over the country for a whole week, famished and exhausted, trying to find a homestead in the woods, in the sandy areas, and in the muskegs, but they could not find any good land. All the good land had already been taken....

I was left alone with my children, lodged in a livery barn in Strathcona. As long as there were other people around, I was not lonely, but as soon as my husband departed and I was left alone with the children, my heart

broke with loneliness. I almost died of boredom. I wept, my children wept, and my despair almost drove me crazy. We could, of course, have gone to Victoria, but we could find no one who would transport us there, to Pasichny's place (we had his address), for less than twenty dollars. We did not have that kind of money, but there was still no point in our staying at Strathcona with winter coming if we had no money to live on.

To solve the problem, my husband decided to build a raft which would take us the 120 miles east down the river to Pasichny's...on the bank of the North Saskatchewan. My husband was strong and healthy, but he was a clumsy *hutsul*. We were called *hutsuls* because we had lived in the Carpathian Mountains of Galicia. My husband had worked there driving log booms down the Cheremosh River as far as Moldavia. In Bukovina, he had heard that people were leaving for Canada, and all of a sudden, without giving any thought to the problem of how to make a living there, he, too, had taken a notion to pull up stakes and go to Canada.

As soon as he had put a raft together on the river at Strathcona, we carried our luggage down and loaded it on. Everything went well until we started to move our chest, which contained all our most precious belongings and weighed around 400 pounds. Spectators began to congregate to

Ukrainian immigrants arrived in the first wave of a mass immigration. If they walked to Market Square, they might have encountered another immigrant, John Liss, trying to find his compatriots: "It was very colourful crowd. One could hear a variety of languages spoken. I listened for awhile and suddenly realized that one of the languages sounded very familiar. It was neither Belorussion, nor Russian, nor Polish...."

watch our stupidity and have fun at our expense. My husband could not speak English and did not know how to ask someone to cart the chest to the raft. As our luck would have it, someone happened to come by with a wagon. Seeing us struggle as we rolled the chest along the street, he drove up to us and asked us to load the chest onto the wagon. My husband then walked ahead of the wagon to lead the way to the raft. When the wagon reached the river, the driver chuckled to himself, and the kids from town came running down to the river to watch us float away. Everyone had a good laugh, and we heard someone say, "Galician go homestead." The kind man who had helped us did not want to accept any pay for carting the chest; he only waved to us and said, "Bye-bye."

It was already afternoon when we launched our raft and shoved off from the shore. The water in the river was very shallow, and the raft drifted sluggishly. Toward evening of the next day we docked at Fort Saskatchewan.... We met some German people who could speak Russian, and we learned from them that Victoria was still a long distance away and that it would take us a whole week to reach it.

We had just enough food to last us a couple of days, so my husband dashed to the store at the Fort and bought some potatoes, pork fat, and bread. On the raft, we had a pan in which we built a fire and baked potatoes. We smeared them with the pork fat, and that was our meal.

To shelter us from rain and storm, and to provide a place for the children to sleep at night, my husband built a hut on the raft. As the raft floated at night, one of us would nap while the other kept watch lest we founder on the shoals or smash up against the riverbank.

On the third night, heavy snow began to fall. We wrapped ourselves in blankets and huddled in the hut. We failed to notice that our raft had run aground on a sandy shoal and come to a dead stop. To free it, we had to get down into the water with our bare feet, but no matter how hard we pushed the raft and struggled with it, in no way could we dislodge it from the sandbar. Morning found us there, crouched at the entrance of our shelter. And the snow came down like an avalanche, as though it were trying to bury us alive. To pitch a tent was out of the question, for the snow that had fallen during the night was over twenty inches deep. The firewood that my husband had picked up in Edmonton got soaked and would not burn. We were so cold our teeth chattered, and we were afraid that by morning it would be the end of us. I wept bitterly over my fate and cursed my husband and his Canada.

It was already late morning when some Indians who lived near the river noticed a strange object sitting on top of the sandbank and came down to investigate. They took us into their home (an old shack), made some tea, gave us some dry biscuits to eat, and we gradually thawed out. Our children were not as cold as my husband and I. They had slept all through the night tucked in a featherbed that I had brought from the old country. But we had both caught severe colds as we waded in the icy water trying to free the raft from the sand.

I will not forget that incident as long as I live. Just picture what it was like to be out there on a river in the middle of nowhere, surrounded by water, wading in the mud, heavy snow beating down on you without a letup. You don't know where you are or how far from your destination, and no people around to help you push the raft back into the water. It was a great blessing from God that the Indians caught sight of our raft, for without their help we would have perished there.[72]

"Mir zeinen doh" ⌐ Mozanne Baltzan Dower, granddaughter of the Cristalls

My grandfather met my grandmother on his way west in Oxbow, Saskatchewan and they got married. Rebecca Levitt was her name.... My grandmother came from Odessa originally. She loved to sing and dance and there wasn't very much entertainment here and so the only way that she could get the entertainment was going with the Salvation Army when they were on parade and sing with them....

My grandfather and grandmother were very friendly with Father Lacombe. My grandfather was in the hotel business so he met many, many people from across Canada, the furriers, the prospectors going up north.... Grandfather explained he came over from Russia as a young immigrant. He first became a pedlar, and then he was able to buy a small piece of property, which first became a small store, then a larger store, and which later became the Royal George Hotel. He also said that he had even done a little bootlegging along the way....

[My grandmother] was a most unusual woman with a wicked sense of humour.... I remember my mother telling me when they were little kids, they were the first Jewish family here. [People here] didn't know about Jewish traditions or anything and all their friends at school were having Christmas. They couldn't understand why the family couldn't have Christmas. The kids, two sisters and three brothers, thought they'd give

Abraham and Rebecca Cristall are believed to the first Jewish immigrants to settle permanently in Edmonton in 1893.

it a chance anyways, so they all hung up their stocking on Christmas Eve only to wake up the next morning to find that their mother had filled their stockings with potatoes. That was the end of Christmas for them.

I think at this point my grandfather thought that he should do something with his children to let them know they were Jewish. Therefore he got in touch with Mr. Goldstick, Tiger Goldstick's father, and he came to give them Hebrew lessons or Jewish lessons and to sort of introduce some bit of religion into their lives.[73]

Rabbi Hyman Goldstick

During the year 1906 the Jewish people of Edmonton and Calgary made inquiries to the rabbis in Montreal to seek a young rabbi to organize the scattered Jewish people of Edmonton and Calgary, providing he possessed all the qualifications...to provide kosher meat; a mohel to perform circumcisions; to serve as a Hebrew teacher and to serve as cantor; that is, to conform to all Jewish tradition....

I arrived in Edmonton, August 6, 1906.... I was referred to a Mr. A. Cristall, Mr. Diamond and Mr. Jack Berkman.... On my advice it was agreed to name the congregation the Edmonton Hebrew Association and was registered under that name.

Now came the important question of providing kosher meat. We selected a committee consisting of Mr. A. Cristall, Mr. Wm. Diamond and myself, to interview a Mr. Gallagher who operated a retail butcher shop and packing plant. He agreed to give us a corner in his shop with a new block and new utensils for the use of kosher meat only of course. I had to be in the shop every morning. It was very successfully carried out for a few years.

By this time it was close to our High Holidays, I was given permission to order a Torah and prayer books and other necessary things required for the service. Everything arrived in plenty of time for the holidays and we held services in the International Order of Foresters Hall on Jasper Avenue, Surprisingly we had a large turnout for the service. People came from Calgary and from all corners of the country. At that time the Poderskys and the Goldbergs were homesteading in the district....

Now, another problem arose in the community, a child was born to Mr. and Mrs. Berkman the latter part of December, 1906. Unfortunately the child only lived a few days. It was a very cold winter and it was our problem to bury the child. As we did not have a place of our own, we went to the City authorities to ask if they would give us permission to bury the child in some corner in their cemetery with the understanding that we would remove the remains as soon as we could procure a place of our own. Soon after we bought a place and removed the remains as soon as possible. Today we possess a cemetery to be proud of.

By this time the community was well organized. Soon it became known to the Jewish people that they were able to get all Jewish services. It wasn't long before they came from the east and west and from all corners. In 1908 they were considering the building of a synagogue. Mr. Diamond donated a corner lot south of Jasper Ave. on 95th St. in 1910. This synagogue was built and although it was not quite finished, it was good enough in which to hold our High Holidays services that year.[74]

Arthur Hiller, movie director

My father and mother immigrated from Poland to New York in 1904. Two of their brothers came from Poland to Montreal and became news agents on the Canadian Pacific Railway—carrying sandwiches and magazines across the country. Well, they came to visit our family in New York, and they reported that the streets of Fort Edmonton were "paved with gold"... and so the whole family picked up and moved to Edmonton. Well, nobody found gold, shall we say, but everybody liked living here—except my father's brother and sister, who moved back to New York. My father wanted to become a doctor. They wouldn't let him into the Polish university because he was Jewish.... He had to support everybody, and he became a barber. He set up a barbershop here on 101st St. around 103rd Avenue. I think it was called the American Barber Shop and he worked there...and across the street he set up "Harry Hiller's Exchange Shop." Basically men's clothing, but he loved musical instruments and such, so he had those, too. My father loved culture. He introduce me to reading, to literature. He helped to start a Yiddish theatre. He loved their heritage. Once or twice a year they would do a play—and the same was true in Calgary. They would do a play and bring it to Edmonton—do it at the shul. We would do a play and go to Calgary. I had good involvement...at seven or eight years old I would help build and paint sets. By the time I was eleven I was acting. You know, with a beard and Payes. It really started my love of theatre.[75]

LOST AND FOUND

"He led me to Market Square" ⤳ M. Kotyk

I came to Canada when I was twelve years old. At the farm there was nothing to eat, so my parents took me to the immigration building in Edmonton. I wanted to find a job as a housemaid. Some English-speaking women who came to hire me took one look and concluded, "She still needs someone to look after herself." No one hired me. I stayed there three days, and then I could no longer afford to buy any food. Besides, I had to pay for my overnight accommodation.

On the fourth day, I left Edmonton and headed for home on foot. But instead of setting out toward the east as I should have done, I set out toward the north where even an adult would have got lost, for it was total wilderness, and there was not a single settler there yet.

My route took me past a tipi, a rather fine-looking dwelling alongside the road. I began to hurry in order to get past it quickly, for I had been warned at home to be on guard against a tribe of black people in Canada who were called Indians and who killed and ate our people. Just as I was about to pass by the tipi, an old Indian with braided hair rushed out of it, grabbed me by the hand, and began to drag me inside. Although I struggled and resisted him with all my might, he had me inside the tipi in no time and made me sit on an animal skin which was spread out on the ground. I was seized by fear. "There is no question; he is going to kill me right here and now."

Meanwhile, his wife was busying herself by the fire. She poured some soup into a cup, handed it to me, and gave me a biscuit. I was terribly frightened and trembled like a leaf. In sign language, I tried to tell her that I was not hungry.

The old man opened some boxes and took out of them several pairs of moccasins. He sat down beside me and proceeded to take off my shoes. "This is it," I said to myself. "He is getting me ready for the knife." I had on my old-country shoes, and I wore the stockings that mother had knitted for me, with designs on them. He examined them, shook his head, and tried a pair of moccasins on my feet. That pair was too large. He searched and found another pair. They were just the right size for my feet. He put them on and laced them up tight. Then he rummaged through his boxes once again. He took some bread and meat out of one box, made up a package of food, handed it to me, took me by the hand, and gently led me out of the tipi.

Back to Edmonton! Once in the city, he led me to Market Square. There were many Ukrainians there who had come from different places, and he released me right into their midst.

"Here," he spoke, "these are your people."

Truly, that kindhearted old Indian saved me from a disastrous end in that northern wilderness.[76]

COMMUNITY NEWS

Born in a Blizzard ⌁ **Helen Learmonth, daughter of Mrs. McQueen**
Mother's second baby was born on a night of blizzard when the thermometer dropped to 57 below zero, and father had quite a time to keep the house reasonably warm. Lights were of course candles and coal oil lamps, the latter needing to be cleaned and filled every day....

Although the community was small, there was no lack of variety in its people. They had come west for every sort of reason, and in an isolated spot like Edmonton then everybody knew everybody else's business, income, and skeletons-in-the cupboard. There were many interesting people here, and no lack of mental stimulation. There were several good musicians, who gave generously of their talents at the many entertainments. There were amateur theatricals of no mean order. There was also a Shakespeare club, where the members read parts. It makes one wonder looking back, where they found the time for all this activity.

Robbie Strong and his dog.

Edmonton had a dignity, small as it was, and things were nicely done. Mother remembers that when the women went downtown there was no rushing out in housedresses—they dressed in street clothes—even although there was only half a block of sidewalk between the houses and main stores. Nearly everyone had a flower garden, and one or two were show places. Many of the women had brought fine china and good silver from home, and entertaining could be a gracious thing in spite of the limitations of a frontier community....

No account of Mother's early days would be complete without reference to the Indians. Her acquaintance with them began on her second Sunday in Edmonton, Father was out conducting a service at one of the country points and Mother was alone.

She was surprised to see three Indian women drift silently in through the kitchen door in moccasins, and sit down on the floor, wrapping their blankets around them. Mother tried to welcome them, but although they understood English, they were too shy to say a word to her. She gave them tea and they stayed all afternoon, talking in Cree to each other. One of them, whose name Mother later learned was Star, walked around and around the room waving a handful of feathers—Mother did not know whether this was some kind of charm, or what its significance was. One of the others was Cecile, whose husband had been the last chief of the [Papaschase] tribe. At the end of the afternoon they silently left, but after that they came often and Mother grew to know them all well, also many others who came.

Through many years they came to the Manse—indeed some of their children still come to see Mother. We used to buy beaded moccasins and gauntlets from them and berries in season. They came to the Manse for help in all sorts of situations and we all grew up with a most friendly feeling towards them and were always highly amused at our friends who were afraid of them....

One vivid memory Mother has is of Cecile coming in to the Manse at the time the Edmonton, Yukon & Pacific Railway was being built. The men were digging along near the hill in front of the Fort. Years before a child of Cecile's had been buried in this location. She knew the exact spot, and when the men left, went and took the bones, which she brought wrapped in her apron to Mother, and asked her to fix a little coffin.

She showed she wanted the box covered with black, like the dress she wore, and lined, with white, like her apron, on the inside. Mother did this for her, and the little coffin was taken out to the burying place on the [Enoch] Reserve at Stony Plain.[77]

Eye-Opener Bob in Edmonton ⌐ Bob Edwards

Edmonton now estimates that it has a population of over 4,000. Estimates are easy to make. Calgary with her bona fide population of 11,000 is seriously thinking of estimating her population at 25,000 just to prove that its imagination is not inferior to Edmonton's.

The scenery round Edmonton is lovely. It doubtless inspired the bard who sang "Ye Banks and Braes of Bonny Rat Creek." The view from the Edmonton Club is superb, looking down the valley of the Saskatchewan on to the dilapidated gold dredges and battered grizzlies of days that are no more. After a few horns inside, the gorgeousness of the scene becomes more and more impressive. It looks especially fine after two stiff Collinses.

The one redeeming feature of Edmonton is its old-time spirit of hospitality, friendliness and camaraderie. This has always been Edmonton's most lovable trait.

And when you want a drink, you can get it. What, ho![78]

Bob Edwards, the hard-drinking satirist, lampooned Edmonton's gentry in *The Alberta Sun* from a cubby-hole office on Whyte Avenue. He had wanted to call his paper *The Strathcolic.* He described Edmontonians as cliff-dwellers who decorated their homes with "enlarged pictures of deceased Ontario relatives." In a whiskey-soaked huff, he left town and later founded the *Calgary Eye-Opener.*

"I played 'lady' with some little friends" ⌐ Dorothy May King

People were very formal and polite in conversation compared to the present time. The ladies "bowed" and the gentlemen raised their hats on meeting: I remember well my mother telling my father or some other adult after returning home from shopping perhaps: "I saw Mrs. Blank in Johnstone Walker's and we bowed," or "I caught a glimpse of Mr. So-and-so; he raised his hat and I bowed to him."

Most ladies had calling days, for instance, the 1st Monday or the 3rd Wednesday, or whatever day in the month was suitable; or perhaps they chose a day which coincided with the one other ladies near them and that saved time and walking.... They had little notebooks in which they put down the calling days of all the women they should call on and when they went calling they carried their card cases, I think in their purse, but my memory doesn't carry me this far and I may be wrong. If relatives lived with them and could not come themselves, the lady would put their cards with her own, theirs' turned down at one corner, which meant they sent apologies or salutations. My mother's day, I recall, was the 3rd Thursday, and in the afternoon tea and little cakes were ready to be passed on to the visitors, and a card tray was left in the hall on which visitors left their cards.

There was an expression I used to hear: "Mrs. Blank received today," or "Mrs. Blank is not receiving today." The ladies usually went calling in pairs, or a mother would be accompanied by her grown daughters. Most people walked, unless one came from a distance, and that was unlikely in the little city of Edmonton. If a lady had to cross a street, she would gather up her skirts in one hand an inch or two off the ground, which would show off her figure nicely, I should think. Whenever I "played lady" with some little friends, we had to find some adult skirts and pin them up so that they came just to our ankles, and I used to practice this maneuver....

Quite often, when the weather was suitable, we went for drives. In winter, my mother, or sometimes my Aunt Jessie, who lived with us, would take us children in a roomy wooden sleigh, built close to the ground with wide runners. It was called a "jumper" and was painted red. We had a big, warm buffalo robe which covered the main seat and hung over the back, and another fur robe to cover our knees....

In summer we drove in the "surrey," which was a two seated rig with a flat top with a fringe all around it, like "The Surrey with the Fringe on

Top." We had some lovely drives in this with a horse which succeeded Dave, called "Fred." He was a sorrel. One day we drove west on Jasper Ave. along a pretty, woodsy trail leading to what is now 124th St., tied the horse and had a little picnic on the grass by the side of the road. I remember that we had raspberry vinegar to drink.[79]

Mr. Collins, known as "Muchias," with Percy Hardisty, Henry LaRoche and Fred Young.

"MUCHIAS"

A.F. Dreger

As a boy he hung around the fort helping wherever and whenever he could. He was a skilled hunter with a bow and arrow. Many a table at the fort bore a gift from the little hunter with a big smile.

"Little John" Collins found a friend in "Big John" Walter. They were drawn to one another from the start. John Walter felt the boy's need for a friend and Muchias was quick to grasp the friendship offered. He adopted the Walter family as his own and as a result when the Walters moved to the south side of the river in 1873, Muchias moved too. He built a little house in the shade of the high river bank on John Walter's property. Here he used to cook in a big iron kettle which hung from a tripod over an open fire. His house was tiny and it seemed as though it was made for a child. You could touch the ceiling with your hands.

Little John was a great favorite with the kiddies. He used to weave a magic spell over them as he told them many tales about the birds and the animals of the forests. He was also well liked by the adults of the community. Although he was only four feet high, weighing 175 pounds, he was nearly as wide across his shoulders as he was tall. He could lift a three hundred and fifty pound barrel and walk away with it while others would still be straining to grab a hold of it....

It seems that one time he was walking down the board sidewalk in the town and a loose board flew up with a nail in it and it caught in his trousers and tore them. So, John immediately sued the town for neglect and golly if he didn't get a new pair of trousers.[80]

Anna Laura Robertson Harrison

While I am telling you about these days, I must mention a [man] that worked about the Fort, known as Muchias, a very powerful man and a wonderful swimmer though not much more than four feet tall, if that. After many years I saw Muchias in a store and spoke to him, and asked if he remembered me, that I was one of the little girls that played at the Fort long ago. His remark was not flattering. He said, "All the same, like mosquitoes!"[81]

Grace Matthews

He had a very large head and almost repulsive to look at, but a very kind and good natured [man] and we children used to like to ride on his two-wheel cart with the water barrel from which he supplied all the water used in the Fort, hauling it with his old horse named Friday. We had a little shack where he lived and used to have many visitors, played the accordion and lively times went on in his little shack.[82]

PIONEER PHOTOGRAPHERS

"I had a job!" ⌐ Gladys Reeves

I had no intention of starting photography as early as I did. I was still going to school but my mother had sent me up to Mr. Brown to apologize for my sister, who had asked him for a job earlier and he had nothing. He had phoned for her. In the meantime she had another position. We hadn't a phone and my mother sent me up to make apologies. He looked at me and said, "Well what do you do?" I said, "I go to school." "Well aren't you too big to go to school?" I was a big gawky girl. I said my size had nothing to do with it, I'm not very old and I may be going into school work. "Well what are you doing now?" "I'm just having holidays which I'm sick and tired of holidays and there is nowhere to go." In England we had the seaside of families out in the country we could go to and we have no one here. "Would you like to come up and answer the phone and the door and let me get my work done?" I went skipping home to mother to tell her I had a job. I started at $15.00. This was the fall of 1905 or in the summer holidays....

[Ernest Brown] came here in 1903.... He had a studio in Newcastle and he left there because things were bad during the Boer War or following the war and a lot of young fellows were looking toward the Colonies. He had a studio of his own. As I told you he had seven years apprenticeship in England and just before, the year before, he left, he had a travelling studio which was quite an innovation. Then he came out to Toronto and while he was in Toronto, the photographic dealers there told him that there was a man out West that wanted somebody to look after his studio while he took a trip to the Arctic....

Gladys Reeves was the first woman to run her own portrait studio west of Winnipeg. A lifelong friend of Ernest Brown, she described how the young Englishman captured the spirit of pioneer town and prospered until his business collapsed in the 1913 recession. Evicted from his Jasper Avenue studio, he moved to Vegreville but returned in 1929 to open his Pioneer Days Museum. In 1947 the province purchased his 50,000 negatives, a rich treasure later catalogued by Gladys Reeves.

He brought his wife and came to Edmonton. He said "with a wife, a big trunk and a $5 bill"; that was in 1903. He took over the management of the studio for the 12 months while Mathers was away. When Mathers came back he decided to open up a souvenir shop and keep his new collection, He sold Ernest Brown the portrait studio: the property, 66 feet on Jasper, and the studio and the business. Ernest Brown had his eye on that view collection and thought some day "I'm going to have it." In the course of time Mathers moved to Vancouver and he got mixed up very seriously in real estate and forgot all about his photographic store, so Ernest Brown offered to buy the collection of this trip to the North particularly and the early days of Edmonton. It cost him more for those negatives than 66 feet on Jasper had cost him....

After the war of 1914, the loan companies had robbed him and I'm going to say robbed because it was robbery, of his property and literally had put him out on the street. Just as much an eviction as the people who were evicted in Belgium but he lost everything he had. He was even reduced to going to the different stores, Hudson's Bay and different stores, with some of his photographic results to get his next meal.... The only thing they left him was a pile of junk which they thought was no use and which turned out to be the Ernest Brown Collection. The only place he could put it was

Ernest Brown created an enduring image of Edmonton in the early twentieth century with his rich photographic collection. He died in 1951.

in an old shack at the back of the building he used to own. It wasn't even waterproof. He put the most valuable ones up on shelves but he had no money to do much. Some of them were in boxes on the floor, and you can see today about two or three inches of the plate has got watermark where they had been standing in water.... I was the first woman west of Portage la Prairie or Winnipeg that owned and operated my own studio.[83]

Icicle Cigars ⌐ Ernest Brown, photographer

Talking about chinooks, there has not in 40 years ever been one in Edmonton; quick thaws, yes, but never the chinook wind, and very rarely ever a "blizzard" correctly called. But Boy, oh Boy, wc uscd to have 60 below. I recall one such night, five of us left Jasper Ave. for Whyte Ave. to install the officers of a lodge—chief pastime in those days. We crossed the Low Level Bridge—the only one—and up the hill; no street cars or autos of course. It was 60 degrees below when we left Jasper—milkman said it was only 59—anyway it was cold, no wind; wind has not been known in this district at that low temperature, tho' I believe it does blow in the Arctic. Our breathing sounded like a buzz-saw. Talking was out of the question when walking; worse still, smoking was also impossible, you took your pipe or cigar out of your mouth for one, two, three seconds to get your breath and you replaced an icicle.[84]

A NEW CITY, A NEW PROVINCE

Frank Oliver

Ottawa,
8 February 1905

To the Right Honorable Sir Wilfrid Laurier,

Sir... With the extension of the limits of the present district of Alberta to the north and east, as I assume is contemplated, the propriety of locating the capital of the province at Edmonton cannot be fairly questioned. I am prepared to submit facts and figures in support of the location of the capital at Edmonton on its merits as against any other point in the proposed province whenever opportunity is offered, but for the present I merely wish to emphasize the fact that submission of the Government to the dictation of Calgary in this matter would necessarily act as a slap in the face to the large majority of friends of the government in the district of which Edmonton is now the center and commercial capital and cause the exultation of the opponents of the government which constitute a majority in the district of which Calgary is the commercial capital.

When the new province is organized, I take for granted that your government will desire to be able to act in harmony with the government of the new province, this is more likely to be possible if the government of the new province holds the same political views as your government in Ottawa. If this is to be, dependence must be placed upon the vote of the northern part of the new province, which went so overwhelmingly Liberal at the recent elections, while the southern part went the other way. I do not admit for an instant that the conditions are equal between north and south in the respective claims of Edmonton and Calgary for the location of the capital of the new province. The claims of Edmonton are entirely superior to those of Calgary; but supposing the conditions were equal otherwise, I submit that your government is still in honor bound to give the preference to where your friends are in the large majority, as compared with the place where your opponents are in the majority.

Hoping for the favorable consideration of yourself and colleagues, and for an opportunity to place the facts of the case more fully before you, I am,

Yours respectfully,
Frank Oliver[85]

Sir Wilfrid Laurier

Ottawa, 9 February 1905

My dear Oliver,

Sir:—I have your favour of yesterday. I will be very glad, if tomorrow afternoon, you will, immediately after the routine business has been disposed of, come to my room. I would like to discuss with you not only the question of the selection of the capital, but several other matters as to which I have been anxious to have your views.

Yours very sincerely,

[Wilfrid Laurier][86]

Top hats and frock coats ⌐ William Griesbach

Inauguration Day was set for September 1st, 1905, in Alberta and a few days later for Saskatchewan, since the Mounted Police and all the "big shots" had to attend on both occasions. I suggested in the council that the aldermen should turn out with top hats and frock coats, which were then worn. Some of the aldermen bucked and declared with oaths and curses that they would not wear such a contraption. However, a certain amount of pressure was applied and J.I. Mills, the clothier, came up to the next council meeting and measured everybody for top hats and frock coats....

There were bands, floats from patriotic societies and contingents from various sporting clubs marching in the procession. This part of the procession was concluded by a very excellent float advertising Ochsner's Beer. Bottles of cold beer were handed out to any thirsty individual who held up his hand in the crowd.

In those days all orders or announcements for processions concluded with the words "citizens in carriages." I observed, however, that for this procession the closing words were "citizens on foot, on horseback and in carriages...."

So the procession trundled on down McDougall Hill to the Exhibition Grounds, which were then located near the Edmonton Power Plant; in fact, the sedimentation basin now occupies a piece of the old race track. Here in front of the grandstand another stand had been erected with a canvas canopy. There were carpets on the floor and a certain number of chairs for distinguished visitors. Sir Wilfrid Laurier spoke, easily and fluently. I must confess that our local speakers hummed and hawed and appeared

to be distinctly uncomfortable.... In the afternoon there were horse races and foot races. Dancing pavilions had been built, roofed with recently cut trees still wearing their foliage. The floor was ordinary one-inch boards, planed on one side, and the music might consist of a small organ and one or two fiddles.

In every case there was a Master of Ceremonies who called off the dances. There were the usual number of fights, which were really only the finishing up of a fight that had been interrupted at the last sports meeting. The Ladies' Aids of various churches also had booths at which meals were served. These devoted women worked themselves to a frazzle and sweated profusely to turn in an amazingly small amount for the assistance of their churches.

There was a Grand Ball in the Thistle Rink, at which all the men wore tails and the women wore imported costumes. This Ball was designed to be the very latest thing in entertainments of that sort. There were programmes with rendezvous stations; both men and women wore gloves and there was a state set of Lancers. In fact, nothing was left undone that anybody had ever heard of as being done in the most, fashionable centres of the east. Supper was served at midnight which looked more like a square meal than a cold collation. The orchestra was a local outfit with some imported players. The rink was lavishly decorated and everyone voted the Ball a bang-up show.

On the night after the Ball there was a grand concert, at which Vernon Barford was the conductor. The orchestra played selections of high-class music and a chorus of mixed voices performed. This also was voted a first-class performance.

We felt that we had definitely been launched as a social centre.[87]

Dressed in their best clothes, the children of McKay Avenue School walk across the river flats on September 1, 1905 to hear Prime Minister Wilfrid Laurier declare Alberta a province. "I see everywhere hope," he told them. "I see everywhere calm resolution, courage, enthusiasm to face all difficulties, to settle all problems."

Gertrude Balmer Watt

Gertrude Balmer Watt stayed longer in Edmonton than she anticipated on her long journey across the prairies with her happy son. The pioneer journalist wrote columns and reviews for several newspapers in the Edmonton area and was a charter member of the Canadian Women's Press Club, organized in 1904. She wrote two books, *A Woman in the West* (1907), and *Town and Trail* (1908). Her husband, Arthur Balmer Watt, was an early editor of The *Edmonton Journal*.

Six days before last Christmas I started out on my journey for my future home—Edmonton. How well I remember the long trip out, the sitting day after day, gazing out at the dead-level prairie, snow-covered, desolate. Across from me sat a wee boy, merry of face and intensely, oh so intensely, enjoying the situation. With him there was no looking backward. All life lay before him and half of mine I had left behind me.

While he stretched himself out, eagerly watchful for a stray coyote or lone deer—"for you do see them sometimes you know Mother"—I remember repeating over and over again to myself, as women will: "I won't, oh I won't, be buried in this God-forsaken country!"...Would Edmonton be anything like this or that? Should I like the life? Would the people appeal to me? In such fashion the days passed by. We were at Strathcona.

During the drive over I learned that a new venture had first seen the light of day that morning. That was enough. All Christmas forenoon, seated in two straight-backed chairs in a room in a lodging house, we discussed the probable fortunes of the modest, little sheet. Rushing out to the restaurant for dinner we discovered the door of the hospitable shack locked. We were "after hours." Visions of turkey and plum pudding vanished like a dream in the face of that stubborn barrier, so we went dinnerless. And that was how I celebrated my first Christmas in sunny Alberta.

This year the paper is firmly established. Kind friends are legion. Edmonton has become the dearest place in all the world. I no longer utter a mental protest against the prairie as a final resting place. Our Western life is too real, too vital, to waste time in gloomy speculation. It is enough that you are alive, and can take your chances in the great future that lies just at hand....

Motheree! But a journalist's life is no sinecure! And yet how you love it![88]

A PIONEERING UNIVERSITY

Henry Marshall Tory

Because of the intensity of the rivalry between Calgary and Edmonton, and the bitterness of the controversy over the site chosen for the university, I decided that the best thing for me to do was to get an institution started as soon as possible. I therefore began by visiting all the high schools of the

Province, canvassing to see to what extent a new university would receive the patronage of the schools. Here I ran into an exceedingly interesting situation. The high schools were all manned by teachers from the East, men trained at Toronto, Queen's and McGill universities and a few from the Maritimes. These teachers had their own loyalties to the universities from which they came and gave little encouragement at the beginning to any of their pupils to become associated with the University of Alberta. As a matter of fact, in the southern part of the Province, an outstanding citizen of Calgary went so far as to canvas the schools in order to prevent the pupils going to the university. After a full enquiry, however, I found that there were between thirty and forty students available for freshmen, and three or four would like to enter the second year.[89]

Edmund Kemper Broadus

On a day in June, 1908, the president of a university not yet in being, in a province which I had never heard of, in a country which I had never visited, came to Harvard and offered me the professorship of English.

The offer sounded like midsummer madness. I think that what I accepted was, not the position or the salary, but the man. There was something about him that made me feel that to whatever no-man's land he went, there—somehow—the kind of university I should like to have a hand in would get to be. When I came to Edmonton in September of that year, I found him ensconced in the attic of a small brick public-school building. There assembled the four of us who were to constitute the faculty—veritable *philosophes sous les toits*—and he, and we, and it, were for the nonce the University of Alberta.... It is with no sense of shame that I confess that there were compromises in those days. The only wonder is that there were so few; and if some of the forty-five students who gathered on those attic benches had not been subjected to too rigid an entrance standard, certainly no efforts were spared to help them make up their

Edmund Kemper Broadus accepted a position at the new University of Alberta on a whim. The visionary Henry Marshall Tory had convinced the Boston graduate that the tiny university had a future. "The people demand that knowledge shall not be the concern of scholars alone," Tory told the first convocation. "The uplifting of the whole people shall be its final goal."

deficiencies. In an attic, then, with a president, a faculty of four, and a student-body of forty-five, the University of Alberta began its work.[90]

R.K. Gordon

We were a small, light-hearted company, hardly more than a score of us; and all of us were young. We lived in a clearing in the poplar bush on the south bank of the North Saskatchewan River. On the sloping sides of the great valley, and on the flats below, the coyotes barked and howled at night, but on top of the bank we taught mathematics and physics, Greek and history, English literature, and biology. Along with some four hundred students and two red brick buildings, we were the University of Alberta; and we felt sure that the future belonged to us, not the coyotes.[91]

Edmonton was determined to win the Stanley Cup in 1908 and lured Montreal hockey stars Lester Patrick and Tom Phillips to play with the local team. In the days before radio, fans had to wait at the CNR station for the telegraph operator to decipher the play-by-play. Sadly the Montreal Wanderers won the Cup.

THE TELEGRAPH PLAYOFFS

Face Deeton gets it . Gardner takes it gives to Glass shoots and misses. Glass crosschecked Miller and is put off . Deeton passes to Vair to Miller who loses to Gardner passes to Smith who score eighth game for Wanderers, in 2 mins by Smith. Edmonton 4 Wanderers 4. Face Smith gets the draw Deeton takes it from him passes to Whitcroft to Smaill now Vair rushes down and shoots wild. Miller is put over with body check face Deeton gets draw passes to Vair who shoots wild Ross rushes loses to Pitre who loses to Smaill . Miller gets it rushes to Deeton who runs down and scores.

A FRIENDSHIP IN CHINATOWN

"Two-Gun Cohen and Sun Yat-sen" ⟿ Cedric Mah

In 1908, revolutionary leader Sun Yat-sen toured western Canada raising money for his fight to overthrow the Chinese warlords and unite the country. Out of earnings from their stores, cafés, laundries and market gardens, western Chinese-Canadians made systematic contributions to the Chinese Nationalist League.

In 1919, the league sponsored the Keng Wah (Victorious China) flying school in Saskatoon, which operated three years and trained 17 pilots. In 1928, Sun's successor Chiang Kai-shek united China with one-time Edmonton character-about-town Morris "Two Gun" Cohen as general in his army and recruited pilots from Canada.[92]

"I didn't forget my Chinese friends" ∽ Morris "Two-Gun" Cohen

I'd begun to think that there were better ways of earning one's coffee and doughnuts than sitting over a pile of poker chips. It struck me too that I might do better in a bigger town and I'd heard that things were pretty good around Edmonton, a place away west in Alberta that, not long before, had been proclaimed the provincial capital....

In fact the place was just ripe for a real estate boom. I had a few hundred dollars, so I packed my valise and took them there to try my luck. And my luck was in....

There was good money to be made in city building lots at $250 a time. I often sold four lots in a day and once or twice I handled as many as twenty in a week; at ten per cent commission that made five hundred smackers for Morris.... I rented an office on First Street. I put in a big, solid safe to hold the cash and I recruited ten salesmen. They were all sorts, shapes, and sizes, but the youngest of them was more than twice my age. (I was still only twenty, remember.) Some of them I'd known as rounders and I was scared they might try to dodge vagrancy charges by working for me as an alibi and go back to their old games again. The day we opened I had them all in together and gave my first pep-talk:

"Now, boys, if you wanna work here, you gotta show results. I don't want any of you lads using this office as a cover for a poker school and me finding the cops in here asking about some producer you've trimmed. If you can't sell a coupla lots a day, I just don't want you around. Now get cracking...." I went out selling myself too. "High, dry, level, and a good building lot" was my motto. At first I sold nothing that was more than a mile from the center of the town. Later on we started buying land from the nearest farmers, subdividing it, putting in roads, and selling that too. Sometimes I made a thousand a week....

I didn't forget my Chinese friends, or rather they didn't let me forget them. If any Chinese in the West thought of a deal in real estate, he'd come and consult me about it. That meant more business and good business too. I went on attending their lodge meetings as regularly as I could manage and presently I found myself giving sizeable sums, say fifty or a hundred dollars, to various revolutionary funds. I began asking other people for contributions, and that in turn started me speaking at their lodge meetings. I'd always had a pretty good line of sales talk, but to stand up and address a regular seated audience was something that I'd never tried before. Presently I got good at that too. I even started to learn

Morris Cohen was a gun-toting gambler when he came to Edmonton seeking his fortune in 1909. His life took a dramatic turn when he struck up a lifelong friendship with local Chinese immigrants. They introduced him to people who hired him as a bodyguard for revolutionary leader Sun Yat-sen who was touring North America. Cohen later moved to China and became a general in the Chinese military. Here he describes how his adventure began in a real estate office in downtown Edmonton.

one of the many local Cantonese dialects, but I must admit that I never got very far with that. Another thing I did at this time was to try my hand at recruiting and training a few amateur soldiers, again with the forthcoming Chinese Revolution always in mind....

That was a good time for me—lots of work, lots of fun, not too much worry or responsibility, and making money hand over fist. And it went on for a couple of years. Then one day there was a rumor that Dr. Sun had arrived in Canada. He was said to have landed at Vancouver and to be coming our way....

[Later, Cohen met the Chinese leader.]

"This is Morris Cohen," said Mah Sam, "a great friend of our revolutionary party."

"Pleased to meet you," said Dr. Sun. That was all.

It is tempting for me to start in now and tell you all that I was to learn about him in the next fifteen years—his statesmanship, his patriotism, his idealism and all the rest of it. But to do that wouldn't give you the right picture at all. You must remember that I was still only a boy and a good deal of a roughneck at that. I'd met plenty of people of all kinds and I'd learned to look after myself, but at that time I'd never met any great men and I'd no means of judging one—that is, except for my instinct for anything that's good quality....

Then came my big surprise. A couple of my own friends and two others I didn't know came up to me and, without beating about the bush in the usual Chinese way, they asked me straight out if I was willing to accompany Dr. Sun on his tour of Canada and the United States and look after his safety.

My first reaction was just the same as when old Mah Sam took me to that Tong meeting in Calgary—I felt a bit scared. Don't mistake what I mean. I was big and I was tough. In those days I literally feared no man and I'd learned how to handle a rod. But when it came to watching over the safety of a man like Sun with a million dollars on his head, I could see that there was more to the game than that....

The tour came to an end, Dr. Sun went off to Japan and I found myself back in my branch office of the National Land Company again. But I'd changed. I was older and wiser and a lot more serious. I'd started out a happy-go-lucky rounder who thought the Chinese were a good bunch of scouts and the Chinese Revolution something vague and exciting a long way away. I came back a devoted follower of Dr. Sun, convinced that the Revolution was something vitally important and just around the corner.

I'd not only met a great man, I'd enjoyed his confidence and got to know him and to see—just a little bit—how the mind of a great man works. For the first time in my life I'd met something that was right outside myself and my own people and yet had to be lived up to.

I plunged into my real estate sales again, but I gave my spare time—all my spare time—to the Chinese cause. I gave interviews on Dr. Sun to the Edmonton papers; I organized a proper Chinese cadet corps and brought its numbers up to four hundred and fifty—nearly every young Chinese man in the town.

By this time my standing with the local Chinese was real high and they brought all their troubles to me. The Chinese cooks in Alberta were having difficulties with the local labor unions and also with their employers who thought that they were just cheap Chinese labor and wouldn't pay them a fair living wage. I tried this and that and in the end I got in touch with Samuel Gompers, the organizer of the American Federation of Labor—who was the second great man I met in my life. He negotiated for them and got them admitted to the local unions. After that the hotels would come to me to find them cooks, and, as long as the wages were right, I'd help the hotels as well.... When I left England I was 16 and I had five pounds in cash and my first fedora hat. [Now] I was 22, I had a four-carat diamond ring, a diamond stickpin in my tie and a letter of credit for ten thousand dollars.[93]

THE ARRIVALS CONTINUE

"All five of us slept in a double bed" ⌐ Charles Anderson

We arrived in Edmonton the night of December 18, 1911. Maybe a Monday.

On arrival, at Edmonton the night of December 18, we of course did not have any prearranged reservations. Unless you had a lot of money in those days you would never do that.

My father searched the downtown area of Edmonton and could not locate a place for us to sleep until he stumbled on a new rooming house—two stories—with some rooms available on the second floor on the block which is now north of 102nd A Ave on 101st St. They weren't known by those names in that day, they were all named. Upstairs there was one bed in this unopened room, and all five of us slept in the one double bed. There were no dressers or anything else, just the double bed there....

The reason we had to stay overnight in Edmonton was that we had to transfer our baggage from the Grand Trunk Pacific in the location where

In 2002, at the age of 101, Charles Anderson described in perfect detail his first day in Edmonton in 1911. The Andersons were on their way to the United States when another Scottish immigrant convinced the family to stay.

Three of the quadruplets born to the Robertson family to Edmonton's delight in 1907.

the CN station used to be on 101st St. You had to arrange for this transfer yourself which was done through John McNeil's Twin-City transfer at the southwest corner of 104th Avenue and 101st Street.

They loaded baggage onto a dray pulled by a team of horses and travelled south on 101st Street to the riverbank and there was an escalator there which loaded horses and wagons and took them down to an area just south of the Low Level Bridge, and this to Strathcona, as it was named in those days. It was, as I remember, about plus five Fahrenheit, which was colder than Celsius.

Now on the morning on which we went to arrange transfer of the baggage with McNeil's outfit we entered the store or office that they used on 101st Street. My mother and we three children stayed back while my father approached the counter about 40 feet away and as he did so, a man who then appeared to be quite elderly (probably about thirty) said to my father, "Good God John! What brings you here?"

John McNeil had been an egg merchant in Glasgow and had done business with my father in Paisley, selling him eggs. As a result of this, my father explained to Mr. McNeil that we were on our way to Seattle. Mr. McNeil started to convince my father that he should stay in Edmonton and advised him that if he did so he would put us up—if I can use that language—in his home.

This is now an historic designation on the 112th block on 97th St.—a large brick house. And that he had a job for him through a friend who owned Sturrock's department store—that is, in the grocery department of it—at Kirkness St. and Norwood Blvd. (now 95th St. and 111th Ave.), on the northeast corner.

We just decided to stay.[94]

THE AFRICAN-AMERICANS FROM OKLAHOMA

John Bell Bowden

There was a man called Mitchell who was quite a businessman. He was one of the leading men in real estate; he had a real estate office, a grocery store and a vinegar factory. His business was located at 98 Street and 105 Avenue. The vinegar factory building is still there; don't think it is being used. But a colored man established that—he started that vinegar factory. He had a maid and a chauffeur.

He had one of the best cars there was; throughout those times, I dare say, there wasn't a half-dozen cars in Edmonton. These old cars had the chain drive—if you went out to the museum you'd see one out there.

This Mr. Mitchell had ordered one of the latest model cars. He lived about six houses west of 95 Street, on 106 Avenue; on the south side of the Avenue....

You've seen stagecoaches—I used to drive one of those over the Low Level Bridge, bringing passengers from the south side to the north side C.P.R. station. There were no tracks for the C.P.R. train to come from the south side to the north side.

It was quite a chore; but I always had a desire and belief that there was a wonderful future in this part of the world and I haven't regretted sticking it out.[95]

Thomas Mapp

In 1912 we dug the basement of the Macdonald Hotel. There were about twenty-two teams of mules and horses working on it. I had a team of

African-American immigrants came north from Oklahoma after 1910 to homestead at Amber Valley near Athabasca and at other small farming settlements; many decided to work in Edmonton, where they formed a strong community around Shiloh Baptist Church.

mules. I had team working on the Fresno. Two colored fellows loaded the Fresno and two guys dumped the soil dug out, over the river bank. Quite a few horses went over that bank, but you couldn't push a mule over the bank.

The building that's there now is the same Macdonald Hotel—only they've built on to it. It took us about a month to dig the basement.[96]

A petition to the Prime Minister, signed by 3,400 Edmontonians

We, the undersigned residents of the city of Edmonton, respectfully urge upon your attention and upon that of the Government of which you are the head, the serious menace to the future welfare of a large portion of Western Canada, by reason of the alarming influx of negro settlers.

This influx commenced about four years ago in a very small way, only four or five families coming in the first season, followed by thirty or forty families the next year. Last year several hundred negroes arrived in Edmonton and settled in surrounding territory. Already this season nearly three hundred have arrived; and the statement is made, both by these arrivals and by press dispatches, that these are but the advance guard of hosts to follow.

We submit that the advent of such negroes as are now here was most unfortunate for the country, and that further arrivals in large numbers would be disastrous.

We cannot admit as any factors the argument that these people may be good farmers or good citizens.

It is a matter of common knowledge that it has been proved in the United States that negroes and whites cannot live in proximity without the occurrence of revolting lawlessness and the development of bitter race hatred, and that the most serious question facing the United States today is the negro problem.

We are anxious that such a problem should not be introduced into this lawlessness as have developed in all sections in the United States where there is any considerable negro element. There is not reason to believe that we have here a higher order of civilization, or that the introduction of a negro problem here would have different results.

We therefore respectfully urge that such steps immediately be taken by the Government of Canada as will prevent any further immigration of negroes into Western Canada.

And your petitioners, as in duty bound, will ever pray....[97]

Edmonton's first unions

Skilled trades workers and labourers poured into the city in the first wave of immigration, looking for jobs in a booming economy. Carpenters organized Edmonton's first trade union local in Edmonton in 1902.

Women at the Great Western Garment Company, which opened in 1911, were the first factory seamstresses in Canada to belong to a union.

GUNFIRE AT THE COMMERCIAL

A.F. Dreger

Let me tell you about the biggest celebration for the Dominion Day of 1912. As you will remember, 1912 was the boom year so as a result money was plentiful and great preparations were made to make that year's sports day a big one. But unfortunately, nature didn't see it that way, for she rained down for two days. Real heavy rain which lasted till the morning of the celebration. The grounds and streets were seas of mud. The celebrations were cancelled. The city was crowded with strangers as a boom city would be. Hotel accommodation was at a premium. Of course, these type of affairs always seemed to attract toughs who drifted in from outside of the city and province. Since the celebrations were cancelled there wasn't too much for them to do but frequent the hotel bars.

So, they staged a celebration of their own with very disastrous results, to say nothing of the excitement it caused for a short time.

The bars were crowded and about 1:00 p.m. I happened to drop into the Commercial Hotel to see a friend who had come in from out of town. While visiting my friend we heard a hot argument in progress in the bar. We had no more gotten into the bar when a shot was fired and we saw a man at the back of the bar drop to the floor. The man who fired the shot fled out the back door of the hotel. The whole crowd took after him. About two blocks south of the hotel there was a thick poplar bluff covering about two blocks. When the man got to the edge of the bluff, he looked around and saw the crowd chasing him. He took a step into the bluff and pulled the gun on himself, the bullet entering his head and he died instantly.

After this we all ran back to the hotel to notify the police and also to find out how the man was who had been shot at. We found him with three or four other chaps all standing up at the bar enjoying a drink. He had dropped to the floor in case he would be shot at again, but it did hit his bowler hat and left a hole in it.[98]

THE HIGH LEVEL BRIDGE

High Jinx ⤙ Grace Duggan Cook

In 1913 the city had the marvel of the opening of the new High Level Bridge. It was said to be the only one of its kind in the world. On the upper level it had streetcar tracks on each side with the railway track running down the middle. But there were no side railings. Definitely there were not streetcar stopping stations allowed up there. On the lower level there were, and still are, a road way and a sidewalk on each side of it.

The bridge was just two short blocks from our house. A ride on the streetcar was as thrilling as on a roller coaster.

We travelled on it frequently, and we could look out the window, and down, and see nothing but the river or trees, 157 feet below.

On one occasion my father and I were on the streetcar when the electric power went off. We had to step out and walk on the railway tracks, through which we could see the traffic on the lower level, to the end of the bridge.

How scary for an eight year old, but how comforting to be walking with Father. My sister Frances had a more unpleasant experience. One morning, at three years of age, she started out to walk the top of the bridge with her four year old boy friend.

Fortunately, or unfortunately, depending on the point of view of the father or the daughter, Dad was on his way to work. He saw them. He caught up with them, and in no uncertain terms, ordered them to go home.

When he returned in the evening he gave her a spanking.[99]

Tobogganning across the High Level ⤳ Reg Lister

The High Level Bridge was finished in 1913. At the initiation ceremonies that year the [university] students broke down the barrier and crossed the bridge, led by a student named Sandy Carmichael riding on a donkey.

They were the first people to use the bridge. In later years a student drove a car right across the top level of the bridge. And another time two students were going tobogganing and arrived at the street car tracks just as the street car came along.

Students on the car helped tie the toboggan to the back of the car in order to give their friends a tow across to the hills on the north side of the river.

All went well until the street car stopped just before it started across the bridge. The toboggan slid under the back of the car. However, when the car started again, they managed to get the toboggan free and they rode along very well. But the street car gathered speed and this made the toboggan sway from side to side so much so that the boys could see over the edge of the bridge with each outswing.

Construction workers needed three years to build the High Level Bridge; four labourers died on the job before it was finished. When it opened in 1913, The *Edmonton Journal* declared: "Stupendousness of High Level Bridge is Amazing!" Engineer P.M. Motley and his colleagues claimed it was the highest streetcar crossing over a river in the world. Kids have terrified their elders with wild antics on the bridge since the day it opened. Young nurses used to throw their shoes over the railings as a graduation tradition. The last regular streetcar rattled across the bridge on September 2, 1951.

You may remember there was no railing. Both students managed to roll off and remain on the bridge; and finally recovered enough to crawl the rest of the way; but they were too badly scared to go tobogganing that evening. The students in the street car thought it was a good joke. No one ever tried it again.[100]

THE BOOM GOES BUST

A.F. Dreger

With the coming of the famous 1912 real estate boom, many "Paper Millionaires" were made who, when the bottom fell out of the business, were without a penny to bless themselves with. All had gone down the drain. People just weren't buying. Looking back over the years, today the 1912 boom seemed like an epidemic....

I recall that in the lumber business I put in long hard hours, seldom getting home until around 7 p.m. I was only a block away from my boarding house so that by the time I got home they would all be finished eating supper. I would have to gulp mine down, clean up a bit, then hurry down to Whyte Avenue.

It should be stated here that the real estate offices stayed open as long as there were any customers around. I was known to all of them so they would often phone me at the lumber yard to say they had a good buy. I'd make my rounds for the Company and invariably I'd put a deposit on a piece of property. Then the next night I would go down to sign the documents and make a down payment.

Just a peek or two at some of the unusual deals. The real estate salesman had just received a listing on four lots in the Ritchie district which in those days was known as the Irvine Estate at a price of $300 each.

I was not too impressed and was going to shop around a bit, but the salesman was so persistent, making me an unheard of proposition. He asked for a deposit of $10 swearing he would have the lots sold by the next night at $400 each....

A few days after the previously mentioned deal, I received a phone call from another salesman informing he had just received another good listing. So that night I went down to see him. He had a listing of a five acre block in the Hazeldean subdivision at $3,000; half cash, balance in six and twelve months. In a few days he sold half of tile block for the same figure I paid for the whole block....

The first investors if they weren't too greedy, made themselves a good profit through selling part of their purchases and re-investing in more. This was like an endless chain, it just kept on going....

By the spring of 1914 everything had almost come to a standstill...by that time World War I had broken out, so it was impossible to sell anything—even gold bricks.[101]

The Emerging City

1914 to 1946

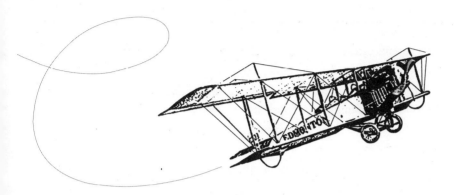

Bound for home, a young traveller leaves Frankfurt on the 3 p.m. flight. For nine hours she travels over the top of the world with no sense of motion, altitude or the international boundaries she is crossing. As the jet begins its easy descent into Edmonton, she adjusts her digital watch to 5 p.m. local time. She looks down at a curling twist of river and the skyline of a city at peace with the world. Everything is familiar. She doesn't see the dirigibles and hot-air balloons, open cockpit biplanes and bush planes, Spitfires and Lancasters that once soared through the same wide, blue sky.

⚊⚊

The sky is the canvas for an emerging city after 1914. The first sparks of Edmonton's passion for aviation ignited in 1911 when two stunt flyers, "Lucky Bob" St. Henry and Hugh Robinson, assembled their odd plane—with birch propellers and a rocking chair for a seat—in a horse barn at Edmonton's racetrack. The quirky aircraft reached a cruising altitude of 60 metres to the amazement of 1,800 people who were seeing a flying machine for the first time.[1] Among the spectators was a 15-year-old boy known as Wop May. His real name was Wilfrid, but he became "Wop" because a two-year-old cousin had trouble pronouncing his name. As a student May preferred tinkering with auto engines to classes at Victoria High School.[2] Like many boys of his generation, Wop May saw the First World War as an opportunity to learn how to fly.

The Great War began as a summer parade. On the evening of August 4, 1914, hundreds of people gathered to sing "Rule Britannia" and "The Maple Leaf Forever" outside the offices of the *Edmonton Bulletin* and the *Edmonton Journal*. The next night the Edmonton Scottish Pipe Band and the Citizens' Band led more than 1,000 volunteer soldiers from the CPR Station at 109th Street, along Jasper Avenue and into an unknown, unimaginable chaos.

Helen Boyd recalls going to the Exhibition Grounds with her brother and parents early in the war to watch the recruits march past: "Fred and I cheered and clapped as the crowd was doing, but father just looked sad. Then mother whispered to us: 'Your father says many of these men will be killed. It's nothing to be happy about.' We thought father must be mistaken. How could these happy young men, striding along, winking at the girls, be marching to their deaths?"[3]

Jean G. Côté joined the cheering crowd at the CPR Station to wave goodbye to the soldiers. "When the train began to move I remember one coach, apparently newly painted, had its windows stuck shut," he recalled. "The boys burst the glass with their rifle butts and waved to their families through the broken glass, all set for a breezy ride to Calgary."[4]

Soldiers were recruited in local regiments, so a single defeat on a battlefield would wound a city's heart. In January 1915, Lt.-Colonel William Griesbach, once called Edmonton's boy mayor, recruited 1,000 local men for the 49th Battalion in a single week. With a coyote named Saskatchewan as a regimental mascot and the motto "Fear No Foe," Griesbach led the Albertans into battle. Of the 4,000 men who served with the regiment through the First World War, 1,000 were killed and 2,300 wounded.[5] Alberta maintained one of the highest enlistment rates in Canada: One in every three men between 18 and 45 joined up. Of the 45,136 Albertans who served overseas, 6,140 men were killed and thousands more were wounded.[6] John Groat, a son of one of Edmonton's oldest fur trade families, died in the mud of France and was buried in a heap of corpses in a common grave. His father, Malcolm, was one of the first Fort Edmonton employees to build a farm outside the stockade. His Métis mother, Margaret Christie Groat, was the daughter of the chief factor who wrote the letter for Sweetgrass in 1870, asking for Treaty 6. His great-grandfather, Alexander McKay, reached the Columbia River before David Thompson in 1811. His Métis wife, Adelaide Fraser, was the granddaughter of Colin Fraser, the personal bagpiper to the governor of the old Hudson's Bay Company.

Could any of these ancestors have foreseen a war so terrible?

The Emerging City 1916

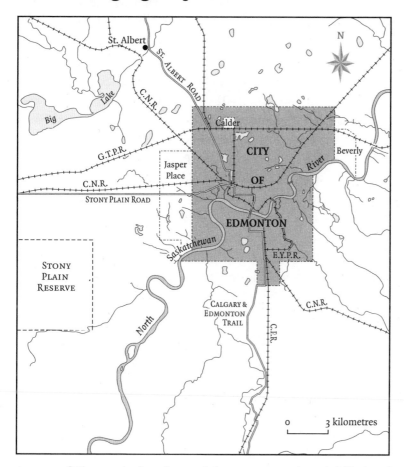

Any map of Edmonton in the early twentieth century creates the optical illusion of a large western Canadian community. The city had claimed a large district within its boundaries in the 1912 real estate boom that crashed a year later. Scattered neighbourhoods were surveyed, but sparsely occupied and separated by huge tracts of empty land. By 1916 Edmonton and Strathcona had amalgamated and North Edmonton had been annexed. The communities of Calder, Jasper Place and Beverly were still independent. Residents relied on a network of new railway and streetcar lines and new bridges for transportation.

One dead soldier, one grieving family, is not the entire story of a war. A city grieved for sons and brothers, husbands and lovers, all with achingly familiar surnames: Anderson, Belcourt, Belcher, Bird, Clarke, Donald, Ducharme, Fraser, Halchuk, MacDonald, Matheson, Melnichuk, Pestrnek, Poitras, Pruden, Ross, Shute, Sinclair, Ward, Whyte....

The First World War memorial on Jasper Avenue lists the names of 2,386 men.

Consider the slaughter of a single day. On October 30, 1917, 558 members of the 49th Battalion climbed out of the trenches at Passchendaele. Before nightfall, 443 were dead. Alex Decoteau died in the dark hell of that day. He was 29 years old, Edmonton's hero. A Cree from the Red Pheasant reserve, Decoteau had moved to Edmonton in 1909 to live with his married sister Emily Latta and her large family on Jasper Avenue. He was a champion marathon runner who won every long-distance race in Alberta until the prizes were acknowledged as his exclusive property. In 1911 he became the first aboriginal police officer in Canada. He competed for Canada in the 1912 Olympics in Stockholm and in military competitions after he enlisted in the army. King George V awarded him a gold watch after one race in England. According to the Latta family story, Decoteau's friends found the watch in the pocket of a German soldier who also died in the fighting. They returned the prize to the athlete's relatives.[7] Soldiers who survived the battle returned with mustard gas burns, bullet wounds and emotional trauma that was barely recognized or treated. The 49th Battalion—later known as the Loyal Edmonton Regiment—suffered more casualties in this single battle than on any other day of the two world wars.

Sitting at a writing desk in the heart of Garneau, a university professor contemplated the small city's evolution during the war. His name was Edmund Broadus. In 1908 Henry Marshall Tory had convinced the young Harvard graduate to leave Boston for a new university in the unknown north.[8] Broadus had never heard of Edmonton, or Alberta, but he took a position as the first English professor at the newborn University of Alberta and quickly learned to love this "town at the edge of the silent places." At first, he wrote,

> the war seemed a grand game, a splendid triumphant thing that
> would be over in three or four months. The Fairgrounds, with
> the long rows of horse- and cattle-sheds and the big exhibition

pavilion became a barracks. Everywhere in the streets squads were drilling.... They went to the front, with the tragedy which nobody dreamed of already hanging over their heads."

Broadus was startled at the number of men "coming by ones and twos and threes, with their traps left to rust on wilderness trails, or their reapers left to rust on hard-won acres—men hungry to know and hungry to go.[9]

By 1916 the daily casualty list sickened him. "Any human life, and particularly any young life full of the promise of fine things, is a big thing to waste in the casual way in which war wastes it. I think that those of you who live in great cities cannot realize that quite as vividly as we do. With us in a little town, death is somehow a more intimate thing."[10] The dead were his students, colleagues and friends. Grieving parents were his neighbours. "I am no longer capable of commercing with the skies as I think of the war," Broadus wrote. "More and more it is getting to mean to me nothing but a tragedy of thwarted lives."[11]

The professor was silent about thwarted lives closer to home. Some of Edmonton's men were marching into prison camps in Jasper and Banff. The Canadian government imprisoned more than 8,579 men, 81 women and 156 children from the Austro-Hungarian empire and other European nations during the war. They were held in 24 internment camps, without charges, without trials, on the unproven assumption that they were a security risk.[12] Pioneers once recruited as the stalwart men in sheepskin coats were suddenly called enemy aliens. The Edmonton district had a high concentration of Ukrainians, Germans, Austrians, Poles, Croatians, Hungarians, Czechs and Slovaks without citizenship papers. Police rounded up hundreds of these men. Unemployed labourers and radical labour organizers were the most vulnerable to arrest. Sometimes their wives and children went with them. Across Canada more than 100 interned men died from disease, accidents and suicides during the war years; 10 were killed or wounded while trying to escape.[13]

As if casualty lists and internment camps were not demoralizing enough, the North Saskatchewan River delivered a punishing flood on Sunday, June 27, 1915. Thousands of people watched from the high riverbanks as large houses, stables, shacks and fences crashed into the bridges below. To save the Low Level Bridge, city workers loaded sand on a long string of CNR freight cars, then sent the train on to the bridge to hold it down. Street superintendent Dan Alton organized large crews of volunteers to save whatever could be salvaged. The disaster left 800 families homeless, destroyed businesses and painted thousands of homes in layers of caked mud. The only citizen who died was a tiny infant who fell from a mother's arms as she struggled across a flooded street.[14] With most of the young men away at war, the families left behind worked for months to clean up the wreckage and rebuild small homes and businesses on the river flats.

"One never knows what can be accomplished until a trail is made," Edna Kells told her *Edmonton Journal* readers in an attempt to boost their spirits. "Nothing is impossible to women with brains, ambition and a sense of humour." She urged Edmonton's women to become wartime soldiers, too, "not to fight in the trenches, but to do equally necessary work for the nation."[15]

At first women volunteered for the Red Cross and the Patriotic Fund and knit soldiers' socks until their fingers were numb. Soon younger women entered the workforce as clerks, factory workers, farm labourers and lumber mill workers to replace the missing men. Annie Jackson worked in Edmonton as Canada's first female police officer. Bessie Nichols, the first woman to win a local election, became a school trustee. Gladys Reeves, an assistant to the pioneer photographer Ernest Brown, became the first woman west of Winnipeg to open her own photo studio.[16] And in 1915—true to the athletic spirit of the city—young girls at McDougall Commercial High School began to play basketball with a passion and skill that would make them world champions within a decade. Watching the Grads, a generation of local children learned they could aspire to achievements beyond the city's horizons.

Two dynamic social reformers met in the city in the early years of the war. Emily Murphy and Nellie McClung shared firm convictions and a love of writing; both were married to middle-class professionals who supported their endeavours. The two friends formed a reading circle in a Jasper Avenue bookstore and began spirited discussions with like-minded activists on their verandahs. These women demanded the vote for women, equal property rights, better health care, better public education, prison reform, new child welfare legislation and minimum wage laws for women. The provincial government listened, and acted, with a decade of reform legislation.

McClung and Murphy were only one element of a larger Alberta reform movement that included farmers' protest groups, temperance organizations, social gospel advocates and the growing labour movement. Together, they upset the status quo before Edmonton's soldiers marched home.

The reformers fought an early battle against prostitution and the hypocrisy that surrounded it. In private, successive mayors told police chiefs to leave the 100 brothels alone; in public, they fired the same police chiefs for failing to rid the town of vice. By 1914 brothel owner Billie Morton estimated that 500 prostitutes were working in Edmonton. Rumours circulated that police officers were consorting with the women, warning them of raids and taking protection money. After an inquiry Mr. Justice D.C. Scott reported that city council had kept the city wide open to the flourishing trade. Angry citizens demanded Mayor McNamara's resignation and an upstart alderman named Joe Clarke championed their cause. "I'll mop the earth with you!" Clarke yelled at the mayor at one meeting. "You haven't got the courage of a rat!" McNamara shouted back. Both gentlemen suffered black eyes and bruises in the legendary fistfight that followed in council chambers and out on the street. Fightin' Joe Clarke was subsequently elected to two terms as mayor. Prostitutes kept working. Reformers moved on to their next crusade: the battle against the bottle.[17]

Demanding a total ban on liquor sales, more than 10,000 temperance advocates marched through Edmonton streets on July 19, 1915. The parade stretched for two miles, the largest protest march that the city had seen. Children carried a huge banner: "Give us a chance! Clear the Road for Us! Old King Alcohol is no friend of ours." Two days later 58,295 Alberta men voted for prohibition in a plebiscite, while 37,509 men voted "Wet." The Edmonton Equal Franchise League had asked that women be allowed to vote, but the province refused. Prohibition continued from 1915 to 1923, but Edmonton's drinking citizens and bootleggers found easy detours around the law.

Women continued to demand the right to vote and to serve in government. Murphy and McClung were the Edmonton suffragettes that history remembered, probably due to their popularity as authors and public speakers, but other women were also active. About 200 women in the Edmonton Political Equality League walked into the legislature to petition Premier Arthur Sifton for the vote. He told them to go home and wash their dishes, but his patronizing tone did not last long. The premier appointed Emily Murphy and Alice Jamieson as the first female magistrates in the British Empire in 1916; their assignment was to rule on criminal cases involving women and juveniles in Edmonton and Calgary. That same year, Alberta women became the first in Canada to vote in a provincial election. Far away, each Alberta soldier was eligible to cast two votes in the upcoming provincial election. An Edmonton war nurse named Roberta MacAdams, stationed in Britain, agreed to run for office in absentia. "Give one vote to the man of your choice, and the other to the sister," her campaign poster suggested. The appeal worked. MacAdams and Louise McKinney of Claresholm were the first women elected to any legislature in Canada or the British Empire.[18]

The new social reformers reflected the prevailing morality and the uglier prejudices of their generation and social class. Although McClung taught her maids how to read at night, the new women's organizations did not try to raise the monthly wages of domestics above $15 a month, or limit their work hours. They did organize charity for immigrant women from eastern Europe, but they did not invite these newcomers to join their organizations. Louise McKinney was convinced that the improvement of the Anglo-Saxon race in Canada required limits on immigration. McClung and Murphy promoted eugenics: a theory of social "improvement" that would justify the forced sterilization of hundreds of mentally-handicapped Albertans and result in a serious abuse of human rights. When the suffragettes joined with Protestant churches to enforce Prohibition, they lost credibility with younger men and women, who were weary of war and the righteous morality of their elders. "We were in deadly earnest, and our one desire was to bring about a better world for everyone," McClung wrote in explanation. "Ours was not a rage, it was a passion."[19] It was anything but a universal passion. Embittered and matured by war, First World War soldiers balked at any zealous effort to change their drinking habits, or social attitudes.

Far away, Edmonton's flying aces lived for the moment. Wop May was a trained pilot in England waiting for his first assignment in March 1918 when he was suddenly dismissed from his squadron after a raucous graduation party. With luck he ran into a Victoria High School pal, Captain Roy Brown, on the same day. Brown was a squadron leader and requested that May be put under his command. On April 21, on his second combat flight in the sky, May found himself trapped among German flyers during a dogfight. His machine guns jammed and he raced away, only to see a red tri-plane chasing him. Baron von Richthofen, the legendary Red Baron, pursued May through valleys, over hills, until the trapped Edmonton pilot prepared to plunge into the Somme River. From above Roy Brown suddenly appeared to shoot at the German plane. An Australian gunner on a nearby hill took aim at the same time. May remained convinced he owed his life to Brown's surprise rescue. Later he brought home a wooden strut from Richthofen's downed Fokker aircraft. Edmonton's newspapers proudly listed the accomplishments of the hometown heroes: Wop May shot down 13 aircraft; John Manuel, 10; Roy Brown, 9; Stanley Puffer of Lacombe, 9; and W.J. Gillespie, 5.[20]

The city's spirits began to lift. The final summer of the war brought a light-hearted giddiness—a few hours of pure relief—to a town that craved some fun. Early on the evening of July 3, 1918, aviator Katherine Stinson carried Edmonton's first airmail toward the city. The Texan was already a world-famous aviator at 22: the first woman to fly over China and Japan; a stunt flyer who thrilled audiences with twirling, spiralling, diving and soaring sky tricks. Her plane, with its 90-horsepower radial engine, was a modern miracle. As she flew over each rural railway station on her way north, telegraph operators tapped excited messages to Edmonton. Stinson caught up to an Edmonton-bound train at Lacombe. To the delight of railway passengers waving madly at the woman in the sky, the train began to race the plane. The engineer cranked up the speed to a whirlwind 60 km an hour, but lost the contest at the Morningside station when the biplane soared overhead at 92 km an hour. Cheering farmers waved from fields near Wetaskiwin, Millet and Leduc. A crowd gathered at the Edmonton Exhibition grounds at Rossdale Flats to wait for the visitor.

Looking down through her aviation goggles, Katherine Stinson saw nothing that told her an HBC trading post had once dominated the riverbank. Fort Edmonton was gone. Early in the war local politicians had broken their promise to save the historic trading post and ordered a quick demolition. When wrecking crews pulled down the palisades on October 11, 1915, young people hauled away souvenir logs, and farmers used the old planks to build barns. Two new prairie castles—the Alberta Legislature and the Hotel Macdonald—replaced the old fort as Edmonton's signature buildings on the riverbank.

From the sky the pilot saw the scattered bits and pieces of a prairie city. The HBC still owned a large island of grass and low bush north of the river. Although Edmonton had annexed a huge circle of territory around the HBC reserve, almost all of this surveyed land remained empty. A worldwide recession and four years of war had not just interrupted the city's growth, but reversed it. Edmonton was shrinking. To the dismay of the old-timers,

20,000 people abandoned the town between 1914 and 1916. Grassland and bush reclaimed subdivisions. Most people lived around two commercial districts, Whyte Avenue on the south side of the river; and Jasper Avenue on the north side. Clusters of families lived in small houses in the river valley; in older neighbourhoods north of Jasper; around the railway yards in Calder, the meat-packing plants in North Edmonton; the coal mines in Beverly; and in the newer developments of Groat Estates, Westmount and the Highlands. These neighbourhoods looked like islands from the air. The city's pride, Portage Avenue—paved to perfection in 1911 with its own streetcar track—was an embarrassing strip of asphalt that connected nowhere to nowhere.

In early July, sunlight stays in the sky over Edmonton long after it has disappeared in other places. At 8.30 p.m. Stinson circled over her admirers at the Exhibition Grounds and bracing against the wind, brought her biplane to a bumpy halt in the infield of the baseball diamond, just short of a fence. A small figure, 5 feet 3, 105 pounds, wearing breeches, a leather jacket and aviation helmet, she climbed out of the open cockpit with a bundle of letters and a big smile. A northern city was falling in love with the aeroplane.

EDMONTON WAS HOME TO 54,000 PEOPLE in 1918, not counting the young soldiers, war nurses and airmen still fighting a distant European war. Within four months of Stinson's visit, another 445 people in Edmonton died in the Spanish influenza epidemic. Schools, theatres and churches closed as the medical crisis deepened. Exhausted doctors, nurses and nursing students risked their lives to care for thousands of infected people. Businesses shut down every morning to allow volunteers in surgical masks to tend to the sick and bury the dead. Amid hundreds of grieving families in the grip of a harsh winter, a six-year-old girl named Nellie Hrynuk waited for a postman to deliver hot soup every day so she could spoon-feed her parents and siblings, who were too ill to get out of bed. Other children remember the masks they wore and their fear of the hearses on the streets.

At 2 p.m. on November 11, 1918, Edmonton's factory whistles and church bells rang out the joyful news that the war was over. Edythe and Pauline Maloy jumped out of their beds in Riverdale, dressed and ran up the hill to celebrate. "By golly we went wild," Edythe told her neighbour Allan Shute many years later. The Maloy sisters lit one of Edmonton's traditional bonfires at the corner of Jasper and 101st Street. "We had to do something desperate to know that the war was over, you see."[21]

Five months later a train carrying the surviving soldiers of the 49th Battalion rattled across the High Level Bridge to the CPR station. More than 30,000 people lined Jasper Avenue to welcome them home. Weary soldiers returned to a city with high unemployment, low wages and rising ethnic tensions. Veterans suspected Canadian businessmen and affluent farmers had profited from the war, sometimes at their expense. Immigrants, particularly Germans and Ukrainians, were forced out of jobs to make way for returning soldiers and they resented it. Urban leaders of the Ukrainian Labour Farmer Temple Association included Senefta Rybka, a waitress in the Hotel and Restaurant Employees Union, and her husband, Gregory Kizyma, a coal miner and union organizer. In the bitter aftermath of war, the Winnipeg general strike sparked a sympathy strike in Edmonton. The city witnessed the first appearance of radical political movements on the left and right and angry social divisions in a city too small to accommodate them.[22]

The sky offered welcome diversions. Flying aces returned home in 1919 to thrill crowds with their spectacular stunts. Wop May and George Gorman dove at a local bandstand one day just as a startled John Philip Sousa was leading his musicians in a rousing patriotic march. The famous visitor was not amused. On another flight May swooped under the High Level Bridge to drop a baseball to Mayor Fightin' Joe Clarke at an opening game at Diamond Park. Barnstormers and balloonists flew over the city all summer. Gladys Walker, Marjorie Chauvin and Elsie McLean watched the horizon longingly until at the end of the 1920s they became Edmonton's first female pilots.

TONY CASHMAN GREW UP AT A TIME when the city's children worshipped the bush pilots. His superheroes lived right around the corner. "While Charles Lindbergh was a distant mythic figure to all the world," he writes, "stars like Punch Dickins, Wop May and Grant McConachie, all local boys from well-known families, could be seen close up and in person going about the ordinary business of daily living."[23] His own uncle, George Gorman, made the first commercial flight in Alberta in an open biplane, delivering a bundle of *Edmonton Journal* papers to the Wetaskiwin fairground in 1919. Cashman's comprehensive account of Edmonton's aviation history, *Gateway to the North*, offers far more detail on the stories described here as well as a careful explanation of the early successes and failures of the industry. Early bush pilots did not launch the northern aviation industry on their celebrity status alone, he says. "Geography certainly offered opportunity but they couldn't have made Edmonton Gateway to the North if the business community hadn't been committed participants."[24]

Edmonton's bush pilots and their willing backers kept exploring the commercial potential of northern aviation despite many setbacks. In 1928 Punch Dickins suggested the possibility of an Arctic air route to Europe when he flew 1,350 kilometres between Baker Lake and Lake Athabasca without radio contact, maps or weather reports. Grant McConachie overcame similar risks when he began to deliver airmail to remote northern locations. Edmonton was soon licensing more bush pilots than any other city in Canada and its pilots here were flying more hours. Local business leaders quickly recognized that Edmonton's bush pilots were creating a vigorous image for the city. They were savvy about attracting more publicity with impressive air shows, a proposal to develop Blatchford Field, and free flights for visiting businessmen, celebrities and journalists.

Edmonton's early fascination with radio added to the bush pilots' mystique at home and it strengthened the city's connection to the North. Kids gathered on 101st Street in the spring of 1922 to gawk at the odd tangle of wires and metal masts on the roof of the *Edmonton Journal* building. A young broadcaster, Dick Rice, was constructing northern Alberta's first radio studio in a corner of the *Journal's* newsroom. Around the city families were reading bewildering instructions and piecing together the $3 radios they had bought from mail-order kits. Rice and his colleagues planned the first local programs: the *Igloo Hut* radio club, *Radio Ramblers* and a program called *Calling the North* that invited city residents to send messages to loved ones in remote settlements. On May 1, all was ready. Mayor David Duggan stepped up to the microphone and signed off with the unforgettable words: "Edmonton leads the way in all Alberta! Calgary and others follow! That is all! Goodnight!"[25] The mayor's daughter, Grace, recalled her father's excitement. "Later Dad exclaimed: 'My family could hear my voice all the way to the south side of the river!'"[26]

Radio sets pulled the distant North into the city's imagination and created a new urban identity for many people who had never ventured as far as Athabasca Landing. When an Edmonton bush pilot was lost, or late,

Dick Rice offered snappy bulletins that kept listeners spellbound. This was the first generation to listen to live news broadcasts and it was not a skeptical audience.

Edmonton's most famous radio report—the hour-by-hour account of a mercy flight in the winter of 1929—enthralled audiences across North America. The story began when a fur trader named Alfred Logan died of diphtheria in remote Little Red River four days before Christmas. His wife, a nurse, sent for help, knowing the community had been exposed to the virus. Dr. Harold Hamman wrote out the terse message: "Diphtheria. Fear Epidemic. Send Anti-Toxin." Two northerners, Willie Lambert and Joe Lafleur, travelled by horse and sleigh, and dog team, through wilderness for 12 days to bring the message to the nearest telegraph office in Peace River. Edmonton answered the call. Flying north in an open biplane for two terrifying days, without instruments or radio contact, Wop May and Vic Horner carried the vaccines to Fort Vermilion through strong head-winds, blinding snow and -33°C temperatures. Radio bulletins alerted northerners up ahead to clear landing strips on lakes. Trappers lit smudge fires along riverbanks to show the pilots the way. Up above, May and Horner coped with two threats of fire, an engine that quit three times, and frostbite. They carried the vaccine supply inside their trousers to keep it from freezing. At Peace River they swooped under the railway bridge as the townspeople waved goodbye. When they delivered the serum to Dr. Hamman and turned around for the return trip, the news flashed across the continent. An estimated 10,000 citizens welcomed the bush pilots home to Edmonton with delirious enthusiasm.[27] Edmonton's promoters dusted off a booster slogan—always spelled out with capital letters—and declared the city the Gateway to the North.

WHEN ABE AARON OR ALI AHMED ABOUCHADI left Edmonton to buy furs, their gateway to the north was the front door of a railway station. They travelled on rattling, swaying trains that frequently tumbled off the tracks into the muskeg. They shipped their furs on river scows; travelled into the bush with city merchandise on dogsleds and learned to speak Cree and Dene with foreign accents. With no public fanfare, no bonfires of celebration, Jewish and Arab immigrant fur traders returned to narrow, little shops on 101st Street with profit margins as slim as their storefronts. They, too, opened the north to commerce.

Through the 1920s, city trains carried nurses and doctors, farmers and trappers, missionaries and bootleggers back and forth from the city to the north country. The returning trains carried increasing numbers of children to the Edmonton Indian Residential School at St. Albert as the federal government expanded its doomed attempt to erase aboriginal culture. New federal laws required compulsory attendance in the residential schools, penalizing parents who refused to part with their offspring, although some families and communities found detours around the rules. Children at the boarding school were forbidden to speak their language or practise their spiritual beliefs; some grew up to report childhood beatings, food shortages and sexual abuse. Aboriginal youngsters with tuberculosis also came to the city for treatment at the Charles Camsell hospital. Travelling through Edmonton's gateway was a frightening and lonely journey for many northern children.

Historians Donald Wetherell and Irene Kmet conclude that, ultimately, aviation did not transform the north in the interwar years as much as the public's fascination with bush flying would suggest. Railways and rivers were still more economical travel routes. In an echo of Edmonton's earlier frustration with central Canada, northern Albertans often resented railway routes and freight rates in the 1920s. Some northerners considered Edmonton's business class "remote, exploitative and self-interested,"[28] although they were grateful for emergency access to hospitals and airmail. Métis northerners witnessed a new threat to their livelihood as trains and bush planes slowly eliminated their traditional jobs as river freighters and mail carriers. Edmonton's export of new technology and settlers also disturbed the hunting and trapping territory they considered their own. All northerners watched the region's resource wealth flow south to the cities while their towns, settlements and reserves remained undeveloped and underfunded.

Edmonton was sometimes blind to these resentments. With so much drama in the north, the city also underestimated its reliance on three other gateways. Most residents had far more contact with farmers south through Red Deer, west through Stony Plain to Edson, or east through Vegreville and St. Paul than they did with anyone in Aklavik. The city owed its increasing prosperity as much to progressive farmers near Onoway as it did to successful trappers near Kinuso.

Grain prices were rising by the end of the 1920s and farmers spent much of their money in the provincial capital. Edmonton's population grew steadily until it finally returned to its 1912 levels. Volunteers improved the quality of life for city-dwellers with summer camps and playgrounds, carnivals and sports activities. The Gyro Club built eight city playgrounds through public fundraising. Edmonton's unique system of community leagues—a vigorous network of neighbourhood volunteers—organized free recreation activities for children and adults as the small city expanded in an era of modest prosperity.

The children of Alberta's homestead era were now ambitious young adults. Many moved to Edmonton to pursue an education, to marry, to find a factory job with higher pay or to enjoy the small pleasures of city life. Their hopes were high at the end of the 1920s. They arrived to a nightmare.

⁕⁓

You're hungry? You want a job? Sorry, buddy, this is Edmonton in 1931. Line up at the relief office if you're desperate. Fight the other guys for a place in line. Do you have a family? You have to be married for this relief job and you need a city address because the mayor has just banned transients from coming into town. Take this paper out to Blatchford Field. They'll give you a shovel. They'll let you work a day a week so you can qualify for a few lousy bucks of relief. You'll dig the new airstrip by hand, scrape the surface flat, and haul the dirt way in wheelbarrows. You and the other men will compete for the 10,000 workdays it takes to finish the job. You'll need every measly nickel you earn. Single guys in Edmonton get $2.50 a week on relief, and you can barely eat on that. The city is scooping hundreds of farm boys off the trains in Calder and shipping them out to relief camps so nobody has to look at them. If you don't have citizenship papers, you can get deported. Where were you born? Poland? Let's see your papers.

⁕⁓

"Edmonton's streets are made of glass,"[29] Wilma Stevenson whispered to her sisters in wonderment in July, 1933. The seven-year-old country girl had just caught her first glimpse of city lights on wet pavement. She rode in the back of a cattle truck with her father, her siblings and all of the family's possessions; her mother and little brother were sitting up front. Hundreds of rural families arrived in Edmonton every month in the early years of the Depression. Wilma's parents ran a small gas station and confectionary on the old Fort Road until bankruptcy sent them on their way again. They were luckier than many. Roughly 14,600 out of Edmonton's

79,200 people were on subsistence relief by 1931. Thousands more were unemployed and somehow hanging on without assistance. In 1932 more than 20,000 men and women in the city applied for temporary relief jobs and pittance pay. Many were turned away. The city could neither collect taxes, nor pay its bills and by 1934 it was $2.5 million in debt. City council raised its mill rate by 64 per cent in a single year. Families lost homes, and many drifted out of town. The average per capita income in Alberta in 1933 was $212 a year, less than half what it had been in the 1920s.

The unemployed generation—those who were already adults in 1931—are in their nineties today, if they are still alive. Their children are in their seventies. The younger ones love to tell family stories about endurance and ingenuity in Edmonton during the Depression: how Lillian Pawlyk's sister bought a brick house in Strathcona for $100; how a Chinese immigrant grandfather planted a market garden in the valley just east of the Le Marchand Mansion; how brothers dug coal from the riverbank in Beverly at night until the cops stopped them; how a Latvian immigrant mother smuggled a cow behind the bushes on the Hudson's Bay reserve and delivered cheap milk at night to her Norwood neighbours. They describe what they witnessed with their own eyes at the Hunger March in Market Square before Christmas in 1932. They forget the doctrinal differences of the Social Credit; the left-leaning Cooperative Commonwealth Federation; the old mainstream parties and the more radical political groups of the era. They remember a rattling ride on the streetcar to the Edmonton Exhibition on July 6, 1935, where in the blistering heat of an election campaign, William Aberhart hosted the Big Northern Alberta Social Credit Picnic to promise their parents a $25 a month dividend. They remember children's races, ring-toss games, acrobatic dancers and a comedy race in which the Social Credit stallion won the day. They recall singing "What a Friend We Have in Jesus" at the urging of Bible Bill. They can remember parents paid in Social Credit Prosperity Certificates, the funny money that flopped.

They were observant witnesses, these little ones. They can remember the faces of the unemployed drifters as if they met them in the Mill Creek ravine this morning. They can tell you exactly where their gang scavenged for crates near Market Square, how they tore the crates apart and sold the firewood. They can recite the cost of every kind of plain food, down to the penny, and tell you exactly how juicy and delicious, how perfect, the orange from the Bon Ton Grocery tasted at Christmas. They will tell you how Edmonton Public Schools always kept the heat up high in winter, and why. They can describe how it felt to wake up in a cold-water flat near Boyle Street in January. They talk repeatedly about their shoes: pinched at the toes, worn at the heels, patched and mended. Listen to pauses between sentences and you learn even more. What do they leave out? What have they forgotten? What hardships and fears did their parents hide from them? It is hard to know. Their stories end with the same cheerful sentences: It wasn't so bad. We were all in it together. We helped one another. We made our own fun.

~

THEY DID NOT ALWAYS make their own fun. Sometimes the Edmonton Commercial Grads made it for them. As Gradettes graduated to Grads and the faces on Edmonton's champion basketball team changed over the years, the winning streak continued under the leadership of a gifted teacher. J. Percy Page became the coach by default. He and another teacher at McDougall Commercial High School, Ernest Hyde, could not decide who should teach physical education to the 60 girls in the school. Page lost the toss. He remained coach until their final game in 1940. His advice to the Grads was simple: "You must play basketball, think basketball and dream basketball."[30]

The Grads' record remains unbroken. Between 1915 and 1940, they played 502 games in Edmonton, across the United States, and all over the world; they lost only 20 of them. They played 147 games between 1915 and 1922 and never lost a single game. They played in the Paris Olympics, the Amsterdam Olympics, the Los Angeles Olympics and the Berlin Olympics, and never lost an Olympic contest. They played exhibition games with 10 men's teams and beat seven of them.[31] In the most humiliating years of the Depression, the Grads gave Edmonton the pride of a world-class achievement. Could there be a finer gift? So why is it that Edmonton has a Wayne Gretzky Drive but not a freeway, not a stadium, named after the Grads?

In the best of times—our times—people in Edmonton share a passion for competitive sports and the arts. In the worst of times, these passions repaired the city's torn spirit.

Fans filled the bleachers all over town to watch John Ducey and his friends play baseball. They found the money to build Clarke Stadium for the Edmonton Eskimos. They watched the wild ski jumpers on Connor's Hill, then lined up with battered wooden skis for lessons from the Rault brothers. They played fierce hockey on outdoor rinks, with no uniforms or equipment, through the coldest winters. They competed or caddied at Canada's first public golf courses for next to nothing.

In summer, readers enjoyed novels beside the open windows of the Edmonton Public Library and felt the breeze from the river valley. They listened to the home-grown radio plays of Elsie Park Gowan or Gwen Ringwood on CKUA. The Edmonton Symphony Orchestra went broke in 1932, but its musicians continued to play for the love of music. Singers organized the Edmonton Civic Opera in 1935. Children who once saw Charlie Chaplin in person at the old Empire Theatre on 101st Street—or joined Ukrains'ka Ditocha Hromoda on stage at the Ukrainian National Home on 108th Avenue—grew up to act in their own plays with the help of an inspired director named Elizabeth Sterling Haynes. With limitless energy, she could make the most awkward teenagers feel like John Barry-more or Carole Lombard by opening night. Unemployed adults took their nickels to the Dreamland and dreamed away the Depression.

One unforgettable night Edmontonians tuned their radio dial to CJCA and the latest news about Albert Johnson, the Mad Trapper, and his 15-hour shootout with the Mounted Police in the high Arctic. They listened to the announcer read the latest messages from Aklavik to the Calder tele-graph office: Johnson's wild escape across the snow, the police pursuit over 9,600 kilometres in 29 days, and the emergency call to Edmonton's hero Wop May. They listened to the hourly radio reports as May and his mechanic, Jack Bowen, tracked the escapee over the Yukon mountains, rescued the wounded sergeant in a blinding blizzard and returned to pick up the stranded RCMP officers and the corpse. Edmonton was flat busted in the winter of 1932, but the radio transmitted reassurance over the air-waves. Wop May was flying home. Everything would be all right.

Every Depression story in Edmonton concludes with the same words: As soon as the war started, we had work again.

PROSPERITY RETURNED TO EDMONTON in planes, of course. Thousands and thousands of war planes.

A city craned its neck to look up at the sky. Between sunrise and sunset on a single day—September 29, 1943—860 American pilots flew combat planes into Edmonton.

The Allies invaded the city during the Second World War for some sensible reasons. They chose Edmonton as a staging and training centre for pilots and a repair centre for planes because of the city's aviation expertise, location, secure airspace and ideal weather conditions. Winters were cold, but the skies were usually clear and bright. The city supplied the Northwest Staging Route, became an important base for the British Commonwealth Air Training Plan, and served as the engineering headquarters and supply depot for the Canol Pipeline. Edmonton's airport workers were the busiest on the continent at times, flagging through American planes on their way to Alaska and shipments of bombers to a wartime ally, the Soviet Union. Thousands of soldiers, pilots, officers, construction workers and civilian workers poured into the city from all over Canada, the United States, Britain, Australia and New Zealand. The military spent millions of dollars in Alberta and hired every available local adult in an all-out effort to win a distant war.

Edmonton learned to contend with the contradictions. The war picked up a broken prairie city and put it on its feet again, while it sent Edmonton's youth to their deaths in southern Italy or the skies over Germany. Children in the city waved a happy welcome to foreign pilots while citizens in Berlin and Dresden, Tokyo and Hiroshima, looked to the same approaching aircraft with terror. The Allies brought good jobs, marriage proposals and fresh beginnings to Edmonton during the war; and a new wave of European immigrants who fled the war's worst consequences after 1945.

Edmonton thrived through the accident of its geography, yet it mourned, too. The city's per capita enlistment was among the highest in Canada: more than 15,000 citizens eventually went to war. Altogether Alberta sent 78,000 men and 4,500 women; half the adult men in the province were in the armed forces. Casualties were not nearly as high as in the First World War, but they were still devastating for a small city with 90,000 people. Of the 840 students of Strathcona High School who enlisted, 108 were killed in action and more returned with serious wounds.

Altogether 666 Edmonton men were killed in the Second World War. Almost all were in their early twenties.

The first men to enlist were the unemployed veterans of the Depression, eager for three square meals a day and army pay. When the Loyal Edmonton Regiment—the Loyal Eddies—left the CNR station on December 15, 1939, the first 450 city recruits were on the train. Thousands of people gathered to see them off. Parents forced smiles as they waved goodbye, hiding their secret dread.

Family names on the recruitment lists reflected the generational transition in the city's population. Children and grandchildren of east European and German homesteaders were well-represented in the ranks. The Métis, the Cree, and the Nakoda fought beside men whose pioneer families had been in Edmonton for decades.

The casualty lists of the Loyal Eddies were a reminder that they died together: Calder, Fraser, Boyarchuk, Buehler, Campion, Cardinal, Cohen, Christie, Demchuk, Dietrich, Diebold, Fediuk, Feschuk, Fehr, Flett, Kerek, Letendre, MacDonald, Novodvorski, O'Neill, O'Donnell, Probizanski, Rasmussen, Ritchie, Taylor, Wabisca, Weisgerber, Whitford, Wittenberg, Wityshyn, Wychopen, Zilnec, Zuber, Zulauf. Every family's heartbreak was a city's loss.

At home, the invasion was overwhelming at times, but also invigorating: Mackenzie Air Service hired 3,000 local workers to work at Aircraft Repair; the United States built the Canol pipeline from Norman Wells to a refinery at Whitehorse. After Pearl Harbor, the United States decided to protect Alaska with an inland road through Canada and new airfields along the route. In 1942, 1,400 American troops came through the city to build 2,400 kilometres of road through the bush and muskeg in eight months; Edmonton shipped the construction equipment to the north. The Stars and Stripes flew over an army base on 127th Street and the Americans leased 52 downtown buildings, including the Tegler, the McLeod and the Empire Theatre. The Americans built another military base at Namao in 1943.

Wop May was no longer a pilot. He ran one of three air training schools in Edmonton. One day Marie Silvester walked into his office and told him she wanted to be a pilot. She insisted she was as qualified as any man. May had known Silvester since she was two years old. He told her about a training program for women in Moose Jaw. She was one of nine Canadian women accepted, and one of two who graduated. Through the winter of 1944–45, she flew Lancaster bombers and Hurricane and Spitfire combat planes from factories to distant air squadrons. She remembers the shock of seeing the severely injured airmen returning from combat. "You never cried where the crews could see you," she recalled. "No matter what, you would never let them see you cry."

While Marie Silvester was the only female pilot from Edmonton to transport planes, many local women joined the military. "When I decided to join up I did so because I only had two choices," recalled Mary Cardinal. "I was not interested in becoming a nun, so I became a soldier." Her father, one sister and two brothers also joined the army, reflecting a common family pattern among First Nations and Métis Albertans. Cardinal says military service changed the character of Canadians: "It taught us all to get along with others, no matter what their race or creed. I believe we can make a better world to live in if everyone has respect for each other."[32]

Work was so plentiful that the city's population grew by 21,000 over the war years, not counting the foreign military. Edmonton's high school enrolment fell 30 per cent as students abandoned classes to join the armed forces, or local war industries. Construction workers, truck drivers, cooks and cleaners, waitresses and secretaries, garment workers, mechanics, plumbers and carpenters—and everyone else—could work for the Americans for double Canadian wages. After work they gathered at George Spillios' café, American Dairy Lunch, for the best food in town. Hotels, restaurants, dance halls and beer parlours were full to overflowing. Musicians played every weekend for foreign airmen and their local girlfriends at a converted HBC warehouse called The Barn. Late-night bootleggers and prostitutes could name their price. In a town where a laughing couple could stash a mickey in a slot under the table and kick it across the floor when the cops arrived, Social Credit liquor laws meant nothing.

Overnight, a startled Edmonton found itself located at precisely the right place on the map. Always on the lookout for a hyperbolic slogan, business boosters began to describe a celestial city at "The Crossroads of the World." When Igor Gouzenko, a future Russian defector in Ottawa, flew into the city, he strolled downtown and wrote in his diary: "Edmonton is built on the prairie and prides itself on being the Gateway to the North. I was impressed by the order and cleanliness of it; the wide streets and homes with space around them. Major Romanov asked: 'I wonder where the workers live?' It seemed surely unthinkable that ordinary workers should live in such a setting."[33]

A few blocks away Assunta Dotto was boarding with the Cicciarelli family. Tired of cleaning houses for $1 a day in Cadomin, she had come to wartime Edmonton to work as a seamstress at the Great Western Garment factory on 97th Street. As an Italian immigrant, and officially an enemy alien, she reported every month to an RCMP officer. She worked long hours at her sewing machine, stitching together army coveralls and shirts for piecework wages. Yet for the first time in her life she felt free and independent.[34] The GWG workers, almost all women, were considered essential workers. The plant ran three shifts, 24 hours a day, seven days a week and produced 25,000 articles of military clothing a week. Employees at the city's four meat-packing plants worked similar shifts as essential war workers.

Women in Edmonton suddenly had more economic freedom than their mothers or grandmothers had ever experienced. They worked as aircraft mechanics, streetcar operators and truck drivers for wages that would have been a fantasy five years earlier. An estimated 1,000 of the 2,400 workers at Aircraft Repair in 1943 were female. They had severe difficulties finding care for their children as babysitters were in short supply and Edmonton had only one "creche" or early daycare centre, with room for only 130 children. In 1943, the president of GWG reported that 100 workers had quit in two months because they were unable to find child care.[35]

Edmontonians moved into high gear as volunteers. Families planted Victory Gardens in more than 4,000 vacant lots. Neighbourhood by neighbourhood, block captains collected 20 million kilograms of salvaged metal, glass, rubber and car tires in the city's first recycling effort. Children won a free theatre ticket for every two pounds of fat they collected. Civilians raised enough money to send 750,000 quarts of milk to bombed-out British children. YWCA volunteers met trains and helped travellers make connections. Even the female prisoners at Fort Saskatchewan jail knit 500 donations in the first two years of the war. Families welcomed foreign airmen into their homes, packed Bundles for Britain, raised money for the Red Cross, and sold Victory Bonds and war savings stamps. Despite all the opportunities for well-paid work and social activity, the war years were a lonely and anxious time for many Edmonton women. Any day a delivery boy on a bicycle could arrive at the door with a black-rimmed letter or telegram. "Our instructions were not to leave the customer alone until they had read the message," remembers Dennis Mahoney. "Because it was wartime most of the telegrams dealt with the tragedy of young people dying far away."[36]

Edmonton's soldiers, sailors and pilots fought and died across Britain and Europe and Asia, but one word, the name of an Italian seacoast town, brought the war into focus at home: Ortona. When the Allies began to refer to the town as a "second Stalingrad," Adolf Hitler decreed that his forces should hold it at any cost. House-to-house fighting began on December 21, 1943. Canadian soldiers quickly learned that the houses had been mined, and that snipers were everywhere. Private Norman Letendre of Lac Ste. Anne described the horrors of the battle to CBC war correspondent Matthew Halton, then added: "I used to like hunting but when I get home I never want to see another rifle again."[37] In 19 days of fighting, Canada suffered 2,339 casualties. One explosion killed an entire platoon of the Loyal Edmonton Regiment, with the exception of one soldier, Lance Corporal Roy Boyd, who was buried for three-and-half days before he was rescued. Edmonton's weariest soldiers ate Christmas rations in shifts in the battlefield, then resumed the fighting until they took Ortona on December 28.

In early January the painful letters started filtering home.

A winter of mourning passed and Edmonton began the long wait for the end of the war. On V-J Day, the last day of the Second World War, young men and women crowded into Market Square to celebrate the peace. They knew nothing yet about a mysterious gift of nature, buried deep beneath Mike and Pearl Turta's farm near Leduc, or about the subterranean fields of fortune that would sustain their families for the next half-century. They danced under a wide, empty sky, feeling lucky for more important reasons.

In Our Own Words

"THIS INFERNO OF WAR" 1914

A parent's view ⟿ Nellie McClung

This morning we said goodbye to our dear son Jack at the C.N.R. station where new snow lay fresh and white on the roofs and on the streets, white, and soft, and pure as a young heart. When we came home I felt strangely tired and old though I am only forty-two. But I know that my youth has departed from me. It has gone with Jack, our beloved, our first born, the pride of our hearts. Strange fate surely for a boy who never has had a gun in his hands, whose ways are gentle, and full of peace; who loves his fellow men, pities their sorrows, and would gladly help them to solve their problems. What have I done to you, in letting you go into this inferno of war? And how could I hold you back without breaking your heart?[38]

An immigrant's view ⟿ Ignaty Kreway

I came to Canada with about twenty-five dollars in my pocket. I found it very difficult to get by, because I knew no English, nor the value of Canadian money. I soon found that I was being taken advantage of.... I heard that there was a railway being built from Edmonton north.... I did get a job on the railway hauling dirt with a wheelbarrow. For every cubic yard of dirt I hauled, I got fifteen cents. I made a dollar and a half a day, from which seventy-five cents was deducted by the railway for my room and board.

After this job ended, I went back to Edmonton. The money I made on the railroad didn't last too long and soon I found that I was broke and hungry again. I asked the authorities for relief. When they checked me over they found a dollar hidden in my wallet. Since I had not admitted having a dollar, I was sentenced to jail for eight days at Fort Saskatchewan. A barber there shaved my head and I was given khaki prison clothes with the numbers 777 on them. I unloaded coal and dug ditches with a pick and shovel for eight days.

After release from jail, I walked back to Edmonton. I was completely broke, as was everyone else. The city of Edmonton was in a state of turmoil. No jobs were available and every man was encouraged to join the army. I had no other alternative since I was near starving; I joined up! At least as a soldier I would be able to have food and a place to sleep.[39]

Edmonton's families say goodbye to departing soldiers in the 101st Battalion in 1914. Lt.-Col. George Roy Stevens recalled: "In the cities men formed long queues at the armouries; in the countryside they handed over their uncut crops and livestock to their neighbours, locked the door and headed for the nearest railway station."

Scapegoats at home ⤳ N. Olynik, interned Ukrainian Canadian, in a letter to his wife

28 OCTOBER 1915

I am glad to have received your welcome letter. I am very glad to hear from you that you are back from hospital and that you are in better health though you say you are very weak. I believe you but I cannot help you. As you know yourself, there are men running away from here every day. The conditions here are very poor, so that we cannot go on much longer. We are not getting enough to eat—we are hungry as dogs. They are sending us to work, as they don't believe us, and we are very weak. Things are not good. The weather has changed for some time past and it is wet and muddy. Also in the tents in which we sleep, everything is wet. We get up at 5 o'clock in the morning and work till 10 o'clock at night. Such conditions we have here in Canada, I will never forget. Men have escaped from here—28 now.

Nick Mudry ran away yesterday. You might tell his wife. But I must wait till the end because I have been here 10 1/2 months already. I don't wish to lose the money I have earned here. My dear wife, please try to find somebody to help you because you are not able to go to work. I am sure you are very weak, and I would advise you to write a letter to the Camp Commandant asking for support. If they refuse to give it to you, ask them to release me so I could support you as you need. I have nothing else to write you, only to wish you better health.[40]

"NOI SIAMO QUI"

Assunta Dotto, Italian immigrant

My husband's parents came to Canada from Italy in 1914. Everything they owned was in two suitcases. Gus' mother was expecting a baby; it turned out to be twins. His father, thinking it might help his wife during the trip, had hidden a bottle of wine in a suitcase, forgetting that one sister-in-law in the family was an alcoholic. During the night she took advantage and drank half the wine, filling the bottle with water. Who knows? The lady might have prevented the boys being born with fetal alcohol syndrome. Mr. Dotto was not amused.

It took a special kind of courage to undertake such a trip under those conditions. Arriving in Edmonton, they rented a furnished room. Mr. Dotto worked for the railroad. I always went with mother when she visited Mrs. Dotto; she would tell us about her life in Canada, not with a "poor me" attitude, and yet it had to be as hard as it gets. The twins were born at the General Hospital on March 19, 1915; St. Joseph's Day, the Patron Saint of the worker. One twin was named Guiseppe-Augustino; the other Augustino-Guiseppe. Guiseppe is the Italian version of Joseph; Augustino is their grandfather's name.

I can only imagine the stress. Two babies. One rented room. How could they manage? The foreman from work made a proposition to Mr. Dotto: he would give them $1,000 for one of the boys. Poor Mr. Dotto. For

one minute he might have been tempted: $1,000 in 1915 had to be a lot of
money and they were really in a bind. Visiting his wife in the hospital he
told her about the offer and asked her what she thought. In her own quiet
way she said, "Dear, I gave birth to the boys and we will keep them." She
added: "When you give birth to yours, you can sell them."[41]

MIKE'S NEWS

Francis Winspear

John Michaels had a rather obscure boyhood as a newspaper vendor on the
sidewalks of New York. He never lost his Brooklyn accent and expressions.
("Dem guys is bugs, Winspear!") When he first came to Edmonton it is
reputed that he carried on his newspaper operations at the corner of 101st
Street and Jasper Avenue.

This grew into a fabulous store. Mike's not only sold newspapers, magazines, books, all types of candies, cigarettes, cigars and tobacco, but also
developed an associate business to wholesale newspapers, magazines and
books. At Mike's store you could get your hometown newspaper from any
part of Canada, the United States, or England, or practically anywhere
else in the world, and the Provincial News Co. Ltd. maintained a massive
subscription business. Mike was a real entrepreneur. Not educated in the

formal sense, he nevertheless had a discerning and courageous mind, and built up a loyal and forceful organization. He went into many other enterprises—bowling alleys, mines, aircraft. For a period there were few capital ventures in Edmonton of which Mike was not a part.

But this was not the only respect in which he was a great citizen. He had a heart as big as a barrel, and took a special interest in young people. The Newsboys' Band, which in time became the Edmonton Boys' and Girls' Band, was sponsored by Mike, even to the point where he married the charming girl who trained the band and was his solo cornetist. This, however, was only one example of his many altruisms, and his interest in Edmonton. Sponsoring boxing tournaments, other athletic events, and an annual dinner on Christmas Day for homeless ex-servicemen, he could always be relied upon to use his imagination and skill in the service of his community.[42]

THE GREAT FLOOD OF 1915

Fred Barns

We used to play down around the river bank down here. We played at the old fort.... Us kids played cowboys and Indians you know. Dug caves in the bank down there. Come down and scramble over the old City of Edmonton steel rail used to be docked right here. Things like that. Lots of bush around....

Well, I'll always remember the flood. When the 105th Street Bridge here nearly went out, and all this sawmill stuff went all the way down the river, we had a ball then. We went down on the flats and used the wooden sidewalks. We were floating around. We'd pull ourselves over in front of a house, and then holler for help, and they'd come and rescue us. We spent all day getting rescued.[43]

Elsie Lloyd, as collected by Amos Skinner

My Dad and some others were measuring the river in front of our house, but as Bertha lived around the riverbend south of our place, she said there was a real loud roar of water, coming along with it carrying chicken coops, barns, etc., also some houses, some animals like cows, chickens were in the buildings, which was a sad sight. Well, when it hit the bend it flooded

the flats before it reached where Dad was measuring.... It didn't take long for them to realize the danger, so Dad saved his papers, books, etc., by putting them in the attic. Our furniture was completely ruined, of course, except the sideboard, which just floated around making holes in the walls. He tied the house to the trees in front, got out of his motor boat and helped people to get out safely. By nightfall, it was over our window tops.... We went back, it was sure a mess, the City firemen hosed the house out, but as long as I live I'll never forget that awful caked clay all over everything. I felt so sorry for Grandma. She looked so unhappy to see everything gone. All the gardens were destroyed, but I'll always remember my Dad's sweet williams all down the walk. They bloomed better than ever that year.[44]

A child wades across a street in Rossdale during the 1915 flood.

VOTES FOR WOMEN: "OUR PLEA IS NOT FOR MERCY BUT FOR JUSTICE"

Tom Wilson, MLA

The Edmonton Political Equality League organized a meeting with [Premier] Sifton. They came down to the Legislature and there must have been 150 or 200 women. They gave a spiel, both Nellie [McClung] and Janey [Emily Murphy] spoke because they were both good speakers, but Sifton wouldn't let them go up the front steps to the Legislature. He stood on the second step and kept them standing around the well in the approach and he said to them: "Did you ladies wash up your luncheon dishes before you came down here to ask me for votes?" He said, "If you haven't you'd

The Edmonton Equal Franchise League presented a 12,000-name petition to Premier Arthur Sifton in 1914. Nellie McClung, Emily Murphy and other activists continued to argue for the vote until the provincial law was changed on April 19, 1916.

better go home because you're not going to get any votes from me." He was most ungentlemanly. So the next session of the legislature was in February [1914], a regular session, and I suggested to Mrs. Ferris that a better way would be to infiltrate the government so to speak, and get possession of the building. So when two or three women appeared I took them in to see the interior of the building, and then two or three others came along casually and the first thing we knew we had the legislative hall filled with women. And they were sitting in the members' seats.

Sifton couldn't call the police but he certainly gave them a piece of his mind. Anyway, they had won a point on him.[45]

Nellie McClung, speaking at the Alberta Legislature

Our plea is not for mercy, but for justice. I ask no boon, no favour, no privilege. I am just asking for plain, old-fashioned, unfrilled justice. A man considers himself honest if he pays his debt the first time he gets the bill. This is the second time you have got it. Therefore, in view of the fact that you are honest men, you must recognize the justice of our claim and there is nothing for you or your colleagues to do but come across.[46]

Lucien Boudreau, dissenting MLA for St. Albert

You believe you are elevating women by giving them the vote. I say, "No, you are ruining them." You cannot undo what Providence has done. You are making a mistake when you say it is time for them to share the responsibility.... The woman who is against the measure is not here. She is at home. The duty of her home is more important than public life. We are going back when we put such a measure on our statute books.[47]

Dorothy Bowman Barker

The day that women's suffrage became "un fait accompli" in Alberta, Mrs. [Alice] Jamieson was in Edmonton. When the news came through that the women of the province had been granted the franchise, she rushed to the phone and called up two of her friends, both very prominent women in Canada and tireless workers for suffrage, Judge Emily Murphy and Mrs. Nellie McClung. The trio held a caucus and decided that they must celebrate in some way.

"Being women," says Jamieson, "we couldn't very well express our joy and satisfaction by going out and getting a bottle, so as we walked down Jasper Avenue with our arms interlocked.

Some women in Edmonton would have voted 20 years before most Canadian women if Alderman Charlie May had not put his foot down. In 1906, city council voted 4–3 against voting rights for female property owners after Alderman John Boyle convinced his wavering colleague that the proposal was a socialist notion. Local suffragettes resumed the struggle.

Mrs. Murphy suggested that the most rash things we could do would be to have our pictures taken.[48]

A prisoner named Margaret, Fort Saskatchewan jail, in a letter to Magistrate Emily Murphy

I have come to the conclusion I had been a bad girl but will be a good girl when I get out. Mrs. Murphy please don't order any more whippings for me. Sargent gave me such hard whipping I shall never forget it. I like the matrons very much. I am crocheting a yoke for one.... Well, Mrs. Murphy I must say goodbye hoping to hear from you soon with lots of love from your little girl Margaret.[49]

Emily Murphy to the prisoner named Margaret

I was glad to get your letter of June 5th and to hear that you were being a good girl.

I did not order you that whipping which you mentioned; but if you got one, I have no doubt in the world but that it was well deserved as apparently you are behaving yourself better. Dr. Orr was speaking to me about you the other day and said you were giving no trouble. I am wondering why you are so bad in Edmonton and so good at the Fort.... At any rate you will be back here shortly and we will hear all about it.[50]

In 1917, Emily Murphy overheard lawyer E.E. Jackson say in her courtroom: "To hell with women magistrates; this country is going to the dogs because of them." She demanded an apology. When other lawyers challenged her authority because she was not a "person" by legal definition, she began spirited debates with them, "the thing appealing to my fancy immensely." The fight was on.

An early homesteader, Alwyn Bramley-Moore, was an Edmonton businessman and former MLA when the war began. He had already published a book to advocate the revolutionary idea that Alberta should control its own natural resources. He could have qualified as a commissioned officer, but enlisted as an ordinary soldier at the age of 37. Bramley-Moore wrote faithful letters to each of his five children in turn, including this note to his eldest son, Alfred. The family kept the letters and eventually historian Ken Tingley collected them in a book, *The Path of Duty*.

Alwyn Bramley-Moore

27 SEPTEMBER 1915

My dear Alfred:

We are just leaving the base for the front so I shall soon have news for you about the actual fighting line. I have heard a lot of stories but they all seem different, so one must see for oneself.

You won't mind me giving you a few tips, will you, as I may not get the chance again? If I don't come back, you will be more or less left in charge of your younger brothers and sisters; that will mean that you must help them, and when they make mistakes must try to put them right. Children may quarrel among themselves, but the one in charge must not quarrel with them, so you won't do that. They will soon all be grown up, so it won't take much of a slice out of your life looking after them.

Over here they are always clamouring that the youngsters should go and get killed and leave their fathers comfortably at home, but I think that is a rotten view. You are too young at present anyway, but if you were older, it would be proper that I should go first, not you.

But you must be ready to take my place for a while and get the younger ones started; I know you will try. We older men have more or less had our innings and have not got so much to lose, and we want our children to take our places and then we shall live. I don't believe in any life after this one, but all you children are part of me so that I am still alive in a sense.

You will soon have to make up your mind what you are going to be; if you mean to be good one, it pays to put up with some discomforts and stick to the schools and take law or medicine; but other callings are just as honourable. Farming is all right if you like it, but no profession is any good if you are ashamed of it. You are inclined to be easy, but make up your mind that you are going to be as good as the best.

Stick to Alberta and be an Albertan and then it won't be your business whether Serbia or Bulgaria becomes larger.

Lots of love, my dear boy,
from your loving Father[51]

Alfred Bramley-Moore

2 April 1916
624 Hardisty Avenue
Edmonton, Alta.

My dear Father:

Many thanks for your letter. We are having a play. The name of it is Macbeth, and I am taking Macduff's part while Ted is Macbeth.

I have just started to wear long pants. I only wear them on Sundays yet. Ted wears them all the time now.

The weather is fine now. The few roses that were brought in are all right. Two of them have got buds on. The others that were left outside are not uncovered yet, as the weather can not be depended upon yet.

I most likely will go to Ashworth's this summer. A regiment left here Saturday for the front. It was the 51st.

William went out to Fort Sask. with Duncan and his father to-day.

I am sending a book called *Chronicles of England, France and Spain* etc. This book was written by Sir John Froissart, who lived during Edward III's time. That is the time the book deals with.

Did you hear about the coins dug up at the front?

I hope you got the parcel which was sent to you.

I was at the [Legislature] Session Wednesday night.

We are all well and I hope you are the same. I send my best wishes.

From your affectionate Son

Alfred
P.S. Letters are welcomed.[52]

Alfred Bramley-Moore was a student at Victoria School. His last letter to his father, on this page, was returned from the Boulogne hospital in France with the envelope marked "Deceased." He did "stick to Alberta," as his father had advised and became an Edmonton lawyer.

Alexander Wuttunee Decoteau
with his mother, Mrs.
Pambrun, and a nephew,
before the First World War.
Alex wrote this final letter
from the trenches to his sister,
Emily Latta, who lived with
her large family on Jasper
Avenue. Six weeks later the
champion was dead.

Alex Decoteau's last race

France,
10 SEPTEMBER 1917

My Dear Sister,

Received your very welcome letter yesterday and was very glad to know that you were all well. I also received the parcel some time ago and you may be sure the contents were very welcome....

I have met quite a lot of Edmonton men since I came to France. We do such a lot of moving about, that we run across someone we know almost every day.... It sometimes seems as if Edmonton had moved over here, and left all the woman folk behind, one meets so many from home. Every once in a while someone would come up to me and say, "Do you remember the time you chased me on your motorcycle?" Many an hour we pass away talking of old times, and wishing we were all back home again.

Well, sis, in spite of the fact that we are used decently by the French people, there's no use denying the fact that we are all aching and longing for our own beloved Canada. Of course there's work to be done yet and I 'spose will stay here till it is finished. A man has lots of time to think of his people and home out here, and one does get awfully lonesome at times. I know in my last trip to the front line, I dreamed of home, and about "all the mothers, sisters and sweethearts" I ever had.

Of course we have lots of fun too. It isn't all hardships and loneliness out here. Most of the boys turn (Fatalists). I don't know if I've got it spelled right, after a few months of fighting. They believe that everything is prearranged by the Divine Power, and if it one's time to die no matter what one does, one has to die. Their motto is "If my turn comes next, I can't do anything to avoid it, so I shouldn't worry." They don't worry either. Of course there are lots who suffer from shell shock or nervous breakdown, and they can't fight against fear, but most of the boys have a keen sense of humor, and laugh at almost anything. I know of one in particular, a corporal. He is the life and wit of our party. A shell landed close to him one night and the concussion threw him on his head several yards away. The shock stunned him for a minute and when he came to, the first question he asked was "Is my head still on?" That sent the rest into a roar, and only a minute before, they were all ready to beat it to the nearest dugout. It's the likes of him that make army life bearable, and the army is full of such as he. Then we have our sports and games, concerts and picture shows where one may forget his troubles awhile. But best of all for cheering a soldier's heart is a letter from "Home." There's always a scramble when the mail is being given out....

I am laying on the ground trying to finish this letter before dark. I hope I do for I don't know when I'll have another opportunity. I wish mother understood English and could read.

I had a tough day the day before yesterday. I don't know whether it was the gas that sickened me or the berries that I ate. Some of the gas that "Fritz" is using now does not affect one till 24 hours after. I was taken ill while on the march, vomiting, and later, *sapoosowin* very severe. I wasn't able to hold down anything for two meals after. However I'm completely over it now, so there's nothing to worry about. Well sis, I don't know what else to tell you so I better close now. I'm enclosing a picture taken just after my attack of "shin-fever." I was rather shaky in the legs, as the boys got me out of bed to have it taken.

Give my love to Grannie when you see her. Love to the children. Remember me to what few friends I've left. For yourself, good wishes, love and affection, from,

Your brother

Alex.[53]

An Olympic runner and Canada's first Cree police officer, Alex Decoteau was killed in France in 1917. The athlete's pocket watch was returned to his mother from the battlefield. It had been a prize from King George V.

Lieutenant-Colonel William Griesbach

28 OCTOBER 1916

Dear Mrs. Waring...

Your husband was a very gallant soldier and died very bravely with his face to the foe. The Battalion was, at the time, delivering an attack on the enemy which was designed to take the pressure off neighboring Battalions which were being hard pressed. The 49th Battalion was called upon to sacrifice itself for the benefit of others and every man who died that day in that undertaking undoubtedly I come with in the meaning of that passage in Scripture which says—"Greater love hath no man than this that he lay down his life for his friend." Your husband's death must be a severe blow to yourself and your children. I trust that you will never forget to tell your children just how and why he died. It is because we have had so many men

Lt.-Col. William Griesbach led the 49th Battalion, primarily soldiers and officers from Edmonton and district, through the First World War. His letters to families in praise of fallen husbands and sons were treasured across the city.

W.A. Griesbach, a former mayor, posed for this portrait as the war began. Recruiting posters around the city read: "The present war is the Greatest War in History. We are fighting in the defence of Weaker Nations to overthrow a political and military system which THREATENS the FREEDOM of the world and the very EXISTENCE of the British Empire."

in this Regiment like your husband that it has in France the reputation that it has. I trust that, if I should be spared to return to Edmonton, I may have the honour of meeting you and of saying to you what I find very difficult to say on paper.[54]

Widow of man under W.A. Griesbach's command

SPRING 1917 I have your letter of March 2. I was so glad to get it. But I do not feel able to answer so kind a letter and so noble of you, a man in your position in life, to write to a poor broken-hearted woman. As long as I have memory I shall never cease to ask God that your life may be spared and that after victory is achieved you may be returned to your wife.[55]

My Encounter with the Red Baron ⌐ Wilfrid "Wop" May

21 APRIL 1918 Engaged 15–20 tri-planes. Claimed one. Blue one. Several on my tail. Came out with red tri-plane on my tail. Guns were jammed. Tripe on my tail all the time. Got several bursts into me but didn't hit me. When we got across the line he was shot down by Capt. Brown. I saw him crash into side of hill. Came back with Capt. We afterward found out that the tri-plane (red) was famous German airman Baron Richthofen. He was killed.[56]

THE SPANISH INFLUENZA

"There was nobody to dig graves" ⌐ Charles Anderson, aged 102, remembering the Spanish influenza

In the winter of 1918, November, when the flu epidemic swept the world, I went on a skating party to Borden Park. It was just a slough that they fixed up for skating in the wintertime; there was a bathroom there, and it was free. There were several people in that party, girls and boys, and my recollection is that two of the boys caught the flu there that night and died. Two others, including myself, got very light attacks of it. One of the girls of the party also died. My mother caught a very severe attack of it and we summoned the family doctor—he came to houses in those days—and he advised us of the cure he was using which was to pour 26 ounces of

Mr. Engel and his children, Gerry and Molly, like most people in Edmonton, wore masks in the fall of 1918 during a deadly epidemic of Spanish influenza.

Scotch whiskey into the patient over a very short period of time. He had found that the poison from the overdose of liquor counteracted the flu. He informed us at about 10 o'clock at night that my mother would have a crisis at about 3 o'clock in the morning, after which she would either live or die. Sure enough, the crisis came and my mother lived. We had poured the alcohol into her. It worked in her case—the doctor said it doesn't work in every case, but it worked in my mother's case. People were dying like flies around here. The undertakers couldn't keep up with it.[57]

Grace Duggan Cook

Three weeks after the first case was diagnosed, 2,000 more had been reported. Already, as a precaution, all schools, theatres, and churches were closed, and public meetings banned. Further, health officers ordered everybody to wear gauze masks in public.

The authorities divided Edmonton into districts, each under the supervision of a trained nurse. As many volunteers as were available were allotted to each district. Dad and Kit both acted in this capacity, Dad as a driver for the "soup kitchens" and Kit as a volunteer nurse's aid. Although entire families came down with it, and in some cases it claimed mother, father and children, our entire family escaped unscathed.

How thankful we were.

During the epidemic, [my husband] Alex Cook, a young man in his early twenties, acted as an orderly in Pembina Hall, the university women's residence which was functioning as a temporary hospital. He had the task of removing seven bodies in one night. In contrast to this traumatic experience, on several occasions he had the satisfaction of being mistaken for a doctor. On November 6th, 54 people died in the city, the highest mortality in any one day. By Armistice Day, November 11, the total number of deaths stood at 262, but, thankfully the number of fatalities was falling off. Finally, over the whole province, 30,000 had caught the disease and over 3,000 had died. As the flu gradually subsided, with grateful hearts, all Edmonton turned to celebrating the Armistice.

On November 11, 1918, the war to make the world safe for democracy was over and the allies had won.[58]

THE 1919 STRIKE

Superintendent Wroughton, commanding officer of RCMP in Edmonton, to Regina Headquarters

I am taking all precautions with regard to our own arms and our men and horses are being trained for emergencies. Revolvers have been fired in the stable to accustom the horses to the sound. I have also had the horses out on the range with carbine and revolver, also machine gun, which has worked admirably. I was in consultation with the premier the other day and informed him that should the province need our assistance in the event of not being able to maintain protection of life and property, they would have to requisition through the federal authorities before we could interfere.[59]

Superintendent Wroughton to Regina, in code

Contain re sweetly weed reassured approves panegyrized. Offending earache overheard arrowy lathe. Swarming recommended oozing sceptical. Mechanics signatory sprat fitting oozing jet. Schedules approves mammak dump telephones oozing Fanny. Automatic Fanny ineffable collect. Panoply carbonic oozing neutral sprat fitted.

Decoded message:

Strike quiet and orderly; streetcars not running but mail service continuing; the rural and long distance phone systems out of commission but city's automatic phones unaffected and ordinary business not much dislocated so far.[60]

In an era of labour activism and radical political movements, disillusioned citizens in Winnipeg began a general strike on May 15, 1919. A sympathy strike began in Edmonton a week later. City employees and many trades workers, clerks and labourers walked off the job. Streetcars stopped. Electricity was shut off. Police warnings of violence proved wrong. The strike ended in June, but by the end of the year, Edmonton's teachers had gone on strike for the first time; provincial civil servants had organized a staff association; and printer Elmer Roper and others had founded the first labour newspaper, *The Edmonton Free Press*, which was published under various names until 1953.

REBUILDING THE COMMUNITY

A river's gifts ⟿ **Peggy Holmes, mourning the loss of twin infants, early 1920s**

Returning from the hospital to a tidy house, I found every tiny reminder of the expected babies had been spirited away. I wrapped myself in a mental cocoon and proceeded to "forget" the whole incident. In fact, I forgot most things. I just sat and sat, gazing at the frozen river.

Everything seemed grey to me at that time, the lowering sky, the unemployed men slowing walking up the frozen riverbank, the bare winter trees with their arms stretched beseechingly toward the sky. Even my parents seemed to move silently around in a grey fog.

People were very kind and endeavored to interest me in the happenings on the Flats. Neighbors regularly popped in and out with baking and preserves, and Mrs. MacOwen came every day with news of interesting happenings. Truly, I did try to respond.

Watching the river turned out to be good therapy, for it was such a busy place. On the opposite bank, where there was a surface coal seam, young

Elchanon Hanson in front of his store in 1917; immigrant storekeepers opened narrow shops all along 101st Street where customers could buy just about everything.

boys cut the coal out, loaded it up on sleighs and took it home to their families, a very welcome addition to the budget.

Sad, old men scratched around in the snow, picking up loose pieces and stuffing their pockets. Where the river had overflowed and frozen solid and smooth, the ice skaters glided by in colorful toques, mitts and long, flowing scarves. The frozen riverbank was a favorite place for weekend recreation.

In the days before refrigerators, Edmontonians relied on river ice to keep their food cold. Workers for the Arctic Ice Company cut ice chunks out of the North Saskatchewan and hauled it away on horse-drawn sleighs to the ice house on the Rossdale Flats.

The Arctic Ice Company worked near our house on the riverbank. Employees cut huge blocks of ice out of the river. These were sold to houses and stores around the city and stored in cold rooms for refrigeration.... Flood stories ran rampant on the Flats, especially toward the end of the winter. As the weather got warmer most Edmontonians began to look forward to the break-up. Not on the flats, however. Our people would wander down to the river bank and try to size up the amount of ice that had to melt and estimate how high up the river would come....

Understandably, anxiety about the spring break-up colored my thoughts, and every day I would walk to the edge of our garden and look at the river. The pressure from the ice slabs made them rear up on end in great pinnacles, the scene resembling a crazily iced cake. I'd look from the great floes to the bridge and wonder how it could possibly withstand the vicious strength of the ice, let alone the meltwaters. But despite my fears, as the temperature rose so did my spirits.

The roaring and cracking of the ice became incredible. You could hardly hear yourself speak. Lottery tickets were sold so people could bet both on the day and time of the actual break-up. My sleep became punctuated with nightmares of our being drowned in our beds, and I found myself listening for the creaks and groans of the ice. Each day a bigger crowd gathered on the banks to watch. Finally, under a blue sky and bright sun, the river gave a great roar and started to move again. An answering cheer went up from the waiting crowd and hats were thrown up in the air.

Spring was truly on its way. One cannot grieve forever.[61]

"They deserve a lot of credit" ↦ Bing K. Mah

I went to Chinese school during evenings. It was a privately-organized school. My father was the one who organized and promoted it, because our teacher had been his teacher in the Old Country. He came over here when he was fairly old and wasn't able to work much any more. So, he taught quite a number of us kids to speak, write, and read Chinese. We were very busy, what with regular school too, but we loved it. He taught us the Chinese classics. To me that was very, very interesting....

In those days the employment opportunities for Chinese immigrants were very, very limited; so, they either set up a laundry or a café. They deserve a lot of credit, because they looked after themselves. They'd hire you as a second cook for twenty-five dollars a month, with accommodation and food included. Workers would live above the restaurants. Thank God, Chinese society stressed perseverance and fortitude. They were thrifty, hard workers: that's how they survived and some got ahead.[62]

In 1922, Bing K. Mah emigrated from Toi Shan, China, to join his father, Joe Mah, at the Union Café. He attended public school and later initiated the first English language program for Chinese at Alberta College. A mentor, advocate, scribe, and interpreter for all Chinese immigrants to Edmonton for over 70 years, Bing's many contributions included the establishment of a visible Chinatown and the vision for a Chinese Elders' Mansion.

A child's ravine ↦ Peace Cornwall Hudson

As a child, the centre of my world was the ravine. Our house was perched on the edge of Groat Ravine at the end of Villa Avenue, and our nearest neighbours were the squirrels and chipmunks who lived in the woods.

Early morning was a time of enchantment, with the sounds of many birds and the sighing of the breeze in the trees. Luckily my bedroom windows overlooked the green expanse below, and the long sloping roof was easily accessible. Being caught on this favorite spot brought certain punishment so I felt most wildly daring.

There is nowhere better to take favorite books than the shelter of a leafy tree on a warm day. The ravine offered many lovely spots where *Treasure Island*, *Little Women*, *Alice In Wonderland* and *The Secret Garden* could be devoured.

Every girl and boy in our neighborhood loved the ravine as a wonderful place for games. We never tired of Hide and Seek, Run Sheep Run, and Paper Chase, and of course picnics by the brook at the deep centre of the ravine. We could follow the brook down to the river on special hikes that had to be approved by parents, and were exciting occasions.

Norah and Peace Cornwall, with a young pal, centre, on the porch at Villa Avenue.

With the first fall of snow our ravine became a most thrilling place, as sleighs and toboggans of all sizes gave us joy rides on McKenzie Hill. The ravine seemed vast and mysterious on winter nights and tales of bears in hidden caves caught our vivid young imaginations. As a setting for our Halloween pranks it was made to order, with spooks and ghosts and wild cowboys and Indians howling and whooping to our heart's content and then bobbing for applies at everyone's houses.

Far from being the forest we felt it was, Groat Ravine is a lightly treed hilly place that made our part of Edmonton a peaceful and happy place to grow up in.[63]

How to love an Edmonton winter ⤙ Isobell Crook Dittrich

We had little hand sleighs, close to the ground, that were fun on the rink—hold the sleigh to your stomach, run and fall on the sleigh or some-one would take the rope, tied to the front of the runners, run pulling you then stop and spin you around trying to unseat you.... Large fox and goose circles were made and played in—there were three or four neighbour children. Snow angels were fun to make—lie down on your back, move your arms and legs back and forth, then get up and look at the angel you'd made. And snowmen of course, with coal for eyes and teeth, carrot for a nose.

Cross-country skiing was nice—the Indian Reserve was just across the railway tracks, half a block from us, which was untouched land, mostly willow bushes, as I recall and no one questioned us when we skied there....

The foot-gear for skiing was a lot different than now. We wore moccasins. To hold the feet in the cross-strap over the toe, we would cut a narrow, one inch cross section out of an old car tire inner tube—they were made of rubber and stretched—now slip this over your foot before you put your foot through the strap, then stretch the piece of inner-tube under your toes. This held your foot from slipping out of the strap as it was behind your heel too. We couldn't afford ski poles, so did without—still had fun, lucky to be able to buy the skis.

Downhill skiing didn't appeal to me—we went a few times to the hills of the Saskatchewan riverbanks. Our ski pants were riding breeches. My jacket was an old cut-off coat.[64]

FAMILY LOYALTIES

Bedtime radio ⟿ Edward Jordan

In December of 1928, or perhaps it was 1929, it became known that the British Broadcasting Corporation was going to put on the first, Christmas Day round-the-world broadcast, with segments originating in different parts of the British Empire.

As a member of the CNR radio network, CKUA would air this special in Edmonton. The broadcast would begin in London with Christmas Day greetings from the King and Queen, followed by a musical program, after which the segments would follow from Montreal, Vancouver, and then other different parts of the British Empire. Because of the time difference, the program opened in Edmonton at six a.m., which meant someone had to get up at 4:30 a.m. to arrive at the studio in time to check out the circuits and equipment.

Mr. Brown asked me if I would handle the assignment, including the opening and sign-off announcements. I accepted with alacrity, as I was most pleased to be allowed to participate in this historic event.

It was a thrill, indeed, to be on the line to hear the London engineer checking the circuits with "Hello Montreal? Are you there, Montreal?" and to hear Montreal respond. When the time came, I opened in Edmonton with the CKUA announcement, switched lines through to the station, and monitored the two-hour program, which proceeded without a hitch. At the end of the program, BBC signed off, then Montreal signed off, and finally yours truly signed off for CKUA, the radio station of the University of Alberta. It was an experience I would never forget. When I returned home, I learned that my mother and dad had sat up in bed listening to the program on the radio set I had made. Mother told me that, when Dad heard me make the final sign-off announcement, he stood up in bed with his arms above his head and shouted: "That's my boy!"[65]

"We are born optimists" ⌐ E.A. Cobbs, African-American immigrant

I have to remind you that the immigration laws in Canada were not always lily-white. Non-Whites were not allowed into the country unless they were needed to do the dirty jobs that the white man didn't want to do....

We lived on 101 Street and 106 Avenue when I was very young. I remember soldiers marching from the armories to the CNR station to go overseas. I saw my first plane and balloon at that time.

The war started in 1914 and several of our people felt that Canada had given them chance for a new life so this country was worth fighting for. So off they went to join the army. They were told this was a White man's war and they were not wanted. This was their first taste of a racial problem. Later, the year conscription came into force, many of our people we compelled to enlist. The names Fay Carothers, Boots McNeil, and Lummy Bowen come to mind.

In the 1920s racial feelings were running very high in America and pressure was put on the Black people to leave.... There were a fair number of Black people in Edmonton at that time, the largest group west of Toronto. There were rooming houses run by Mrs. Sales and Mrs. Dolly Smith on the south side. There was by this time a Methodist Church. Reverend Slater was one of its pastors. Reverend Henry Brooks was the pastor of the Baptist Church. Like any other ethnic group we all lived in a district, 97th Street and 111 Avenue. We mostly went to Queen's Avenue School and McCauley and had a fight every few days.

Around 1925 several families moved out of the city. The Adams family went back to Oklahoma: the Brooks, the Bells, and the Griffiths moved to Vancouver. Earlier, the Thompsons went back to the States.

Then came the Depression. Our people were used to such hardships and we survived. Employment was always a problem, only we got the job that no one else wanted. There was the railroad for a few. My brother, my

E.A. Cobbs, the younger
teenager in the picture, grew
up in central Edmonton,
the son of immigrants from
Oklahoma. The Cobbs family,
left to right: Doc, Harry,
Hattie, E.A., and Clara.

grandfather, and my brother-in-law, Andy Henderson, worked for the CNR
shops for years, then; in the coal mines and packing plants. Several drove
drays and worked on construction jobs. Several worked in poultry pools,
killing and dressing poultry....

There was no encouragement to finish school, for there were no jobs
opened for our people. Several made a living shining shoes. After ten years
of hard times came the Hitler war. Many moved from Edmonton to Calgary,
Vancouver, and Winnipeg, and started to work on the railroad which paid
$80 a month.

As I look back on my life in Edmonton, I see one big, loving, caring
family. There were no divisions that you might expect. Christmas time,
every Black child in Edmonton was at the Shiloh Church Christmas concert
and received a present....

When I think of how those presents were secured, I have to laugh.
The Women's Group would form a committee of two and on the 15th of
December would start out. First the manager of the Bay. They gave him
a real sob story. I'm sure, after twenty minutes of that, he would be willing to part with the store, just to get rid of those gals. So he would come
through with candy, oranges, and presents, after which the old gals would
call down a whole flock of blessings on the man.

Then they would go to Eaton's and do the whole process all over again.
After that, Woodward's, James Ramsey's, and finally to the Jewish merchants, who usually gave money.

A Ku Klux Klan gathering on March 25, 1932 attracted hundreds of Edmontonians to Memorial Hall. The KKK had between 5,000 and 7,000 members in Alberta in the early 1930s. They campaigned against Catholic businesses, the French language, racial intermarriage and non-white immigration. Imperial Wizard John Maloney called on "Exalted Cyclops" to study the Klan's "wholesome teaching and to morally profit thereby." He was jailed for fraud, theft and vandalism in 1932, and the organization withered away.

I have often wondered where the prejudice came from. You must realize that most of the white Anglo-Saxons came from the British Isles where you had no Black people. The others came from the northern states like Minnesota and the Dakotas where there were a few Black people.

But it was here in Edmonton that we were barred from the city pool at Borden Park. The old Pantages Theatre would only allow us to sit in the balcony.

This bias was good because it caused the Blacks to fight and as a result changes were made. You were encouraged to get an education even though you couldn't see where it was going to help. You still had to buck the system. We had students going to high school and today they would be honour students: Kay Henderson, Agnes and Velma Leffler, Rhumah Utendale, just to name a few.

Later, I remember Rhumah making an application to enter the Royal Alex Hospital and being told that the other girls would not want to live with her.

When God made Black people, in His foreknowledge, He knew the many problems that we would be faced with, so He gave us the ability to take the punches of race hatred and still not stay down. We are born optimists. The sun will shine in my back door tomorrow, I know, so I want to see it tomorrow, and that is what Martin Luther King could see in his dream.... I am thankful there are two classes of man, good and bad. The good works to change the injustices of the world.[66]

Living above the St. Louis Café ⌁
William Chee Kay

My brothers and sister and I were rarities in Edmonton in the 1930s and 1940s because of our background. We are of Chinese and Ukrainian descent. This was a time in our history, the first part of the 20th century, when the union between our mom and dad was not looked upon favorably. They were among three or four couples of similar backgrounds in this city that had married.

We are proud of our heritage. If you think only of the food, who else would have the best of both worlds as we do? We experienced the joys of helping our Ukrainian grandmother decorate eggs for Easter, make pyrohies and sauerkraut. Some of these we continue to make today. On the other hand we learned first-hand how to make traditional vegetarian soup Lohan Jain for New Year's, and many traditional home style Chinese dishes including shark's fin and bird's nest soup.

Gee Soon Kee, known as Slim, and Jessie Natasia Skedaniuk about the time of their marriage in 1934.

Our Dad, Gee Soon Kee, known as Slim, passed away in 1980. He was born in China, raised in Malaya, but moved back to the family village in Toishan in the 1890s. One of his brothers went back to Malaya, and another to Cuba, to help the family finances. He came to Canada in 1911 at the age of 17 on one of the CPR Empress ships to earn sufficient funds to help out the rest of his family back in China. This was difficult as he had to repay a loan of $500, the head tax, which Canada applied as a deterrent to all Chinese entering the country to live and work.

Dad worked as a cook and pastry chef in Vancouver. After a period of time he headed east to find work and new opportunities. On the way he worked in lumber camps as a bull cook, barber and labourer among other things. He told us of his time working on the CPR railroad, preparing and building rock slide and avalanche sheds in the Rogers Pass, and on the way from Vancouver through the mountains. Dad said he was very fortunate that he was not killed at one shed site... Dad and the rest of the Chinese labour crew were the first to go to lunch while the Japanese crew

"Many men wandered in looking for a decent meal, any meal at times. People with enough pride would not beg for a handout. In our café, as with many cafés of the period, my Mom and Dad set out soda crackers, bottles of ketchup, sugar cubes and salt and pepper. Men would come in, and ask for a bowl of hot water, and they would proceed to make soup out of these ingredients. Mom said this happened on many occasions in the Depression. Dad was always willing to help others within his ability to do so."

—Bill Kay.

continued to work until after the return of the Chinese. When Dad and his crew returned they found a rock slide had buried and killed the Japanese... This work was during the construction of the Connaught Tunnel in the Rogers Pass.

From here he gravitated to Edmonton where he partnered up with a friend to own the St. Louis café on Jasper Avenue. This period is vague in my memory but I do know that like all businesses in Canada and the United States prosperity reigned in the 1920s. Dad went back to China, around 1929, to visit family and marry. While he was there the stock market crashed and everything went awry. He received a message from his partner that the business was in trouble and to come back to Edmonton as soon as possible.... The business lost the building to taxes, but the City of Edmonton rented the building back to him so it could continue. Dad's wife in China died in childbirth, leaving a little girl to be raised by her family. Dad never saw her, or met her, until the year he passed away, 50 years later. But that is another story.

My mother's family came to Canada from Ukraine in the early 1900s. My great-grandparents and grandparents came to take up land offered to the people of Ukraine in hopes of opening up the country. Their land was at Wastau, now Wostok, northeast of Edmonton. My mother, Jessie Nastasia Skedaniuk, was born there in 1910. Not long after they moved into Edmonton. Grandma did housekeeping for other people to help earn money for food, clothing and lodging. Grandfather went to work with the CNR after serving some time in the Canadian Army in World War I. He was an engine cleaner, the dirtiest job on the railroad, a job he worked at until he retired in 1952.

Mom and three brothers and fours sisters all attended Highlands School, now a junior high school. Mom only went to Grade Six, and because she was the oldest she had to quit early to help the family.

Our family lived in the St. Louis café at 9695 Jasper Avenue. This building at the time of my birth was not only a café on the main floor, but also a rooming house with a dozen sleeping rooms on the second floor. During my first three years, we lived in the back of the café in a lean-to section...

The small three-room converted apartment that we eventually lived in upstairs was heated by a small gas heater and sometimes an electric radiant heater. The windows frosted over in the cold weather, and we would melt into the ice, and scratch pictures and scenes in the heavy, white frost. I recall on some evenings looking out over the activity across the river at

Connor's Hill, and the ski jump at the Edmonton Ski Club. They had some sort of celebration with what appeared to be fireworks. We were fascinated at the time. It wasn't until many years later that I found out that they were having ski-jumping demonstrations, and some of the more daring jumpers such as Bruce McGavin, John Hougan and Ole Hovind had mounted railroad flares on their backs, and on their skis...

Living above the St. Louis café up to June of 1945 was an education of sort. Since my Dad had contracted to feed the World War One veterans who were on relief, I gained an appreciation of the world events unfolding before and during World War Two. While these veterans had the radio turned on to the CBC, with Lorne, the Voice of Doom, Greene, we followed the course of the war.... Our family became good friends with many of these men, and it was a sad event when we had to close the café in 1945....

It wasn't until after 1947, when the Chinese Exclusion Act of 1923 was repealed, that our father was permitted to become a citizen of Canada. Our mother, who lost her Canadian citizenship because she married a Chinese man, was able to recover her standing as a Canadian citizen. The world was changing rapidly and the lines between different backgrounds began to blur and our unique situation was going away. The story of the Kay family continues to be written as new generations come along.

"In McKernan, we look out for each other" ⌁ Marion Robinson

My parents were on a soldier settlement farm in Entwistle in 1921. On March 20th, a neighbor shot and killed my father over a pitchfork that belonged to my father. My father had fought for four years in World War I. Two weeks later, my mother lost her eighteen-month-old daughter to pneumonia. The Red Cross moved my mother and her children to Edmonton. They put them up in the Ritz Hotel on 97th Street.

Five weeks later on April 27th, I was born. Old Dr. Baker delivered me. We moved to Norwood and lived there for three years. By this time, the older children moved out to work. My mother and I moved to McKernan. Mrs. Manning had a rooming house and we rented a room for $3 a month. My mother had a $10 a month mothers' allowance.

In about 1933, my mother traded her sewing machine for a 12 x 14 wall tent. It was put up in the bush on a shiplap floor and three foot shiplap wall. We had no stove, only a round heater. It was used to heat and cook. We lived here in 40 degree below weather for six years. When it stormed in summer, we ran the half block to Mrs. Manning's barn and slept with the sow.

Anne Sztyk, the Carnival Queen of McKernan, and her attendants.

We ate a lot of bread fried in lard. Once a month we might have a little stew. In the summer we ate a lot of berries. We couldn't can anything because it would freeze, as did everything else. We used to take things into bed if we didn't want it to freeze. We didn't know you could freeze vegetables and eat them. We gathered wood out of the bush and in winter we had to buy coal. We had a coal oil lamp and carried water a half block. Christmas was special. The Rotary Club always brought us a box of groceries, it was so special.

The Knights, May and Fred, lived on 76th Avenue between 114th and 115th Street. The Toonerville Trolley ran right past their door. Mary Knight used to bake buns and buy hot dogs. Every Tuesday in summer she would gather 12 to 14 girls in the neighborhood and take us to Whitemud Creek. There was always fried onions and relish; she gave us a good time. We carried water and all our equipment draped over two bikes, which we took turns pushing. Another neighbor had Sunday school in her home.

We attended Normal Practice School, which is now Corbett Hall. We played basketball and baseball, which we enjoyed. There was a cafeteria and we could buy a scoop of mashed potatoes and gravy for five cents. In the winter, McKernan always had a nice Winter Carnival complete with Carnival Queens.... McKernan has changed a lot, as most areas have. University Avenue was a narrow, dirt road then, wide enough for two cars. When it rained, it was a mud hole; 76th Avenue was the same, 114th Street was just a trail wide enough for a car.... Another landmark was the Old Chinese market gardens between 115th Street to 118th Street, 76th Avenue to 78th Avenue. These two great gentlemen worked so hard all summer. That's what people did in those days. Our community was made up of good, hard-working people. When the war came, all the young men joined up. Some never came home. May they rest in peace. A lot of us have been close friends all our lives and we go out for lunch quite regularly. They are real friends, always there for each other....[67]

"Pow—everything was gone" ⌐ Clare Botsford

My father was a business man. He gambled on the grain exchange and in '29. Pow, everything was gone. Shot.

My father's broker killed himself and a lot of his associates went that way. We were very poor after that. My father left, because he thought they wouldn't take our house if the man of the house was gone. Well that didn't happen. We lost everything. My mother worked for a time as housekeeper. My father and family got back together again. He looked for us. We looked for him. We got back together again. Then we lived in Edmonton, in poor surroundings of course. We lived in "cold water flats," as everybody did in those days. In North Edmonton there was a place called the Martell Block. Very poor people lived there. Everybody on relief. It was sort of a converted hotel. There were wood stoves. You actually had to haul your wood up. The Hope Mission bought us food. As I said, the head of the family did not get welfare relief. Only the mother and children.

Really dark days. We went out to the dump, we kids, and we found a bunch of wheels. We had four different wheels and we made up a wagon. We went all through the city and picked up wood boxes and broke them down and made kindling and sold it. We were enterprising little devils. Poor, but always on the go. Street kids, but with a very strong background of family values. My mother said: "You stay honest. Whatever happens, you stay honest. This family is that way."

Oh yes. We fought kids. We stayed behind Eaton's and Woodward's and places like that. That's why I was at the market when the 1932 Hunger March happened, because we were there picking up boxes, beating the heck out of the other kids who were there ahead of us. You had to get the stuff to sell it. It was terrible.

I just happened to be there. My father was there as well and I lost him and I worried. I was terrified. It was winter. I was nine.

You never forget the sound of heads being clubbed. You never forget that sound, I can say that. To this day I sort of get a little tremble in the lip when I think about it, because I never forgot that. At the start it seemed innocent enough. There were people gathered. People wanted jobs. People wanted decent conditions for their families. None of us could understand why people were starving in a big beautiful, half-empty country. We couldn't understand. Then all of a sudden the police were there on the horses.

Fleeing drought and farm foreclosures, more than 10,000 prairie refugees moved to Edmonton during the Great Depression. Few found jobs. The city and the province were bankrupt and could do little to assist a destitute population. On December 20, 1932, thousands of people from across Alberta gathered in Market Square—now the site of the Stanley A. Milner Library in downtown Edmonton—to march to the legislature in protest. Mayor Dan Knott refused to authorize the parade, but the crowd began to march anyway.

RCMP officers and Edmonton police, many on horseback, met the demonstrators with guns in holsters and batons ready. A riot began. Protesters would later say they ran to hide under a pyramid of Christmas trees, but were chased and clubbed. Police reported that the marchers used the tree trunks as weapons.

I stood against the building, the fish market. I was against the building, cringing. Just like a bad dream. I couldn't believe it.

First, there were speeches, that was all. There was singing, but mostly it was speeches that I remember. And looking for my father. Suddenly this happened: the police got down off their horses. People ran for shelter in the pyramids of Christmas trees that were on sale. The clubbing went on. The heads were being clubbed inside the shelter of these trees. Some of it you saw, some of it you heard. But certainly a lot of people were injured.

The pyramid of Christmas trees was almost like a tipi. The protesters thought they'd be sort of half safe in there, but they weren't. Because that's when the real nastiness went on inside this shelter.

These were police on horseback. It's pretty scary. You always thought of the policemen as your friend.

Then I found my father and of course he said, "Let's get out of here, let's go."

When I was twelve or thirteen I went to work as a waitress. And you know what? I told them I was 18 of course. We worked ten hours. That was allowed. And we got a dollar. Then we worked another two hours and that was just to hold your job. You cleaned the restaurant after that. Then you were released to go home at two in the morning. Can you imagine a thirteen or fourteen year old at two in the morning with no streetcars running? You had to walk home. Some of the toughest streets in this city. I tell you, I was like a windmill. I went down those streets, about a mile to walk home. 95th Street or 96th Street or 97th Street. I went like a windmill, flinging my arms out, defending myself, fending off guys, arms reaching out of doorways. It was terrifying. Your employer had no responsibility to see that you got home safely. If you got hurt on the job, just don't bother coming back. There was no workers compensation. There was nothing.

Quite often you had to quit because your employer just took it for granted that you'd be his next sexual victim. Many, many times I walked off a job. I knew how to walk. I walked fast.[68]

Orval Griggs

There were hundreds of onlookers and I was one of them. The police charged the head of the parade hitting the men with truncheons. Some tried to pull the police off their horses. Panic broke loose and I was almost swept under the crowd. I was lucky to get away from that.[69]

Ben Swankey, protest organizer

I was secretary of the Young Communist League in northern Alberta at the time. We had about 1,000 members in the area. My job was to help organize the youth contingent of the Hunger March.

The organization of the march was no small job. Meetings had to be held with various organizations throughout the province on the sending of local contingents. Food and lodging had to be arranged for the many hundreds of farmers, unemployed workers, and others coming in from points outside the city. We had to find halls in which to hold meetings. In this we had the full cooperation of the Ukrainian Labour Temple on 96th Street, operated by the Ukrainian Labour Farmer Temple Association. We also had at our disposal the facilities of the Youth Centre next door, an abandoned church that had been taken over by the Young Communist League and other youth groups.

The main demands raised by the Hunger March committee in consultation with local organizations were: non-contributory unemployment insurance (there was at this time no unemployment insurance of any kind); the closing of the 20-cents-a-day relief camps called "slave" camps by their inmates; cash relief instead of bags of groceries or scrip; relief for farmers; and an end to evictions and foreclosures in both city and country. An even more difficult problem was getting farmers into Edmonton.

Ben Swankey, secretary of the Young Communist League in northern Alberta, was arrested after the Hunger March.

The RCMP, acting on the orders of the Brownlee government, not only issued warnings to farmers not to come to the city for the March, they stopped cars and trucks, turning back any they suspected of going to Edmonton for that purpose. The result was that farmers had to slip into the city at night, by side roads not patrolled by the police. The fact that some 2,000 made it into the city despite the obstruction of the police was proof of their determination to air their grievances and take their demands direct to the government.

There was the added problems that labour mayor Dan Knott and his labour majority on city council, in cooperation with Premier Brownlee, had refused to grant a permit for a parade from the Market Square to the provincial legislature. Had the parade permit been granted, the parade would undoubtedly have been peaceful and without incident. It appeared, however, that the provincial government, the city fathers, and the police were determined not to allow any parade and to teach the "Reds" a lesson.

On Monday morning, Dec. 19, the day before the demonstration, a squad of 20 RCMP and 50 city police raided the Ukrainian Labour Temple and the Youth Centre next door while the early arrivals for the march were having their noon meal.

The police claimed they were searching for firearms, but we understood quite well that it was an act aimed at trying to intimidate us and to prejudice the public against us. No firearms were found, of course, nor any clubs. But they did find that the halls were well stocked with food, enough to feed 3,500 people for five days....

Contingents of marchers were already in from Drumheller, Smoky Lake, Radway, Vilna, Willingdon, Myrnam, Two Hills, Mundare, and many other points in the province. When the demonstration convened on the Market Square on the afternoon of Dec. 20, the huge crowd overflowed into the streets and sidewalks surrounding the square.

A. Irvine and a half a dozen other speakers addressed the meeting and a committee was dispatched to see Premier Brownlee in a last minute attempt to secure permission to parade. It reported back within the hour that permission was still refused. The speakers then stressed that the people had the right to use the streets to appeal to their elected government and urged that the march be kept orderly.

"They are waiting," warned one of the speakers, "and they will use agents to try and start trouble, but don't be intimidated. We have a constitutional right to use the King's highway to petition parliament."

"All right, comrades, let's go," said the last speaker and the meeting began to move. More banners were raised, that people had concealed on their persons, to join the already colorful array of banners and placards that dotted the huge gathering.

We began to move off the south-east corner of the square and although many of us had expected the police to step in, we were unprepared for the fierceness of their attack. The RCMP on horseback and the city police on foot attacked everyone within reach, bystanders and marchers alike. People were knocked down and many pushed over and trampled on by the horses of the RCMP. The number of police involved ran into the hundreds. Some 150 RCMP reinforcements alone had been brought in from Regina. We were told that police machine guns were stationed on the roof of the post office, just across from the square.

When the police attacked there was momentary panic as people ran for cover. Then anger set in and marchers picked up anything they could lay their hands on to fight back. A number of Christmas trees on sale for the holidays were quickly grabbed and used as clubs or weapons of defence. Several dozen people climbed the roof of one of the market square buildings and showered the police with gravel and stones. But the unarmed crowd was no match for the well planned battle tactics of the police. The march was broken up before it could get started. Within two hours it was

Police wait on horseback as the Hunger March begins. Later they chased more than 500 men down Jasper Avenue; some marchers were subsequently arrested and jailed.

all over. Only two men were arrested on the square, John Gager and Peter Yakerowski.... Most of the arrests took place the next day at the Ukrainian Labour Temple and the adjacent Youth Centre. In both places meetings of the marchers were in progress discussing the lessons and results of the march and the police attack. I was addressing a youth meeting in the Youth Centre when the RCMP broke in. Everyone was asked his or her name and notes were made by the police. Constable Keeler, a former RCMP stool pigeon who had been expelled from the Communist Party some years before as a police spy, was in charge of the operation. On his instructions people were released or arrested. When it came my turn and I gave my name, he said simply: "Young Communist League. Take him away!"

We were forcibly taken to paddy wagons and then to the city police station where we were interrogated and placed in cells. Arraigned in court later, we were charged with unlawful assembly under Section 87 of the Criminal Code. Then we were whisked off to jail in Fort Saskatchewan, some 25 miles away.... For me the trial was quite an eye opener and from first hand experience I learned something about class justice. The fact was that we were on trial for trying to protest the intolerable conditions people lived under during the Hungry Thirties and the failure of governments, all governments, to do anything about them.[70]

George B. McClellan, RCMP officer on duty at the Hunger March

I had read of the awesome sound of an angry mob, but now I felt its actual physical impact. The adrenalin poured into my blood stream; my guts retreated up my backbone and the hair of some atavistic ancestor crawled up the back of my neck and scalp.

Under direct, uncompromising orders, our revolvers were already unloaded, safe in their holsters. We were further ordered on no account to draw a truncheon without orders. No mounted man struck a blow that day, but we prevailed.

Came the order to wheel the troop into line to face the oncoming mob.

I saw Assistant Commissioner "Spike" Newson, commanding the Force in Alberta, watching us from a vantage point. I had no inkling at that time that I would one day succeed to his rank and command. At that particular time, my only concern was with my immediate well-being. As the troop wheeled into line like a closing fan, I glanced along the line to see how my comrades were taking it. To my surprise, their features were composed and seemingly at rest. They looked straight ahead, displaying no emotion. As calmly as a riding school manoeuvre, they kneed their horses into line and the whole moved forward at a slow, unflappable, deliberate walk towards the shouting, surging mob.

In sudden relief, I realized that I was displaying the same composed exterior as my comrades, and reacting to the hand signals of Inspector Irvine as routine. I suspect it was there that I first began to really comprehend that special discipline which is the Force's own. Some disgruntled ex-member, writing in a publication or on radio, referred to the "mindless discipline" of the Force. What I saw and felt that day, as a recruit Constable, was no mindless discipline.

That group of men, from all walks and conditions of life, many of us scoured by the winds of Depression and discouraged by deadening economic conditions, had come together as a cohesive, disciplined body. As the day was just about to show, they had reserves of initiative, self-reliance and mutual reliance. These qualities would take some of us through even greater risks than we faced that day—risks we usually had to face alone—and there lies the true test of a man and his training.

As for the riot, the mob broke for the sidewalks just an instant before they would have reached the horses. The composure of the quiet force, slowly but inexorably approaching, broke its nerve. True, we were showered with missiles from the rooftops. I was fortunate but some of the men took some nasty face cuts and lumps. There were some brisk encounters with the foot police; but the mounted troop broke into sections of fours and gradually we separated large groups into small groups, quietly shepherding them to egress streets which had been deliberately kept open for easy crowd dispersal. Some of us heard our ancestry traced back in several foreign languages, interspersed with good solid Anglo-Saxon encouragement to commit amazing and intricate acts of physical dexterity.

Today my office overlooks that same Square and its magnificent Centennial Library. I look across it sometimes and reflect that perhaps here, 40 years ago, I found the way of life I was meant for.

My motives for joining the Force were the purest—anticipated hunger. They might not pass the test to-day, where great concern is directed to a man's motivation toward a career in the Force. However, I was a product of my time, and the search for a bed, three meals a day, some clothing and a few bucks, went on throughout the land, and was understood for the desperate need behind it. I had no real sense of purpose or career. I needed a stopping place until the winds of want blew over. I found both.[71]

Men shovel snow from city streets for subsistence pay.

Dolly Freeman had a gift for prophecy and self-sufficiency. In 1933, her husband was injured on the job. To support her family Dolly read tea leaves in downtown cafés for three cents a cup, raised to five cents when she found work at Log Cabin café, later called the Silk Hat. "She never read my cup or my sisters', " said her daughter, Velma Logan, "but then we knew our future was in pretty safe hands."

PULLING THROUGH THE THIRTIES

Curly ⟿ Alex Latta

During the Depression years of the 1930s, there were many itinerant people living in cardboard and packing crate shacks along the river banks and in the bush east of the Dawson bridge. It was a life of bare survival. Each spring the shanties were searched for those that did not survive the long hard winter and after the bodies were removed, the structures were burned to the ground by the fire department, probably for health reasons. As our home was the last one on the south side of Jasper Avenue, going east, we had a very good view of these annual proceedings.

About the mid-thirties, when I was about seven years old, my father took me and my brother David, down in the bush behind our house, and in a small protected grove of poplar trees, we came upon one of these shacks, where we were introduced to the lone occupant, who I only know as "Curly." Curly was a survivor, in those tough years, and earned his way in a unique manner. He foraged for used, discarded car tires from local service stations, or wherever. These tires were to provide him with a bare subsistence income until economic circumstances improved.

In his little grove of trees, he cut down a large poplar, and left the stump about two feet high. On this he secured an anvil, which I think was made of a short piece of railway track. On another stump, he secured a home made knife. On another tree, he fastened a punch and lever contraption. With these crude tools, Curly went to work on his used tires. Using the knife, he cut the tires into long strips, of a predetermined width. He then took them to the punch apparatus, and made holes in the strips about one and a half inches apart over their entire length. He also used the punch to make rubber washers from the sides of the tires. With the wire from coat-hangers, he secured the whole lot together to produce his final product, a hard wearing, long lasting rubber door mat.

Curly must have made a great many of these mats. I know that our house had them for many years, as did many businesses, which had traded goods and services for them. Many years later, I returned to the area, but could find little evidence of its existence as a home or workplace. I do not know what eventually became of Curly, but I hope that he was rewarded for his endeavours and survived a long time. His industriousness should surely be an example for all.[72]

A Cop Who Cared ⤳ John Reid

For those who lived in northeast Edmonton anywhere near the Exhibition Grounds at that time, one in all probability knew Jack. He was an officer with the Edmonton Police Department. If you went to the Arena to a hockey game, he was there. The Edmonton Grads all knew him. He was at every one of their games held in Edmonton. As boys we went to mainly hockey games. We didn't always have quite enough money to pay our way into the Arena, and most of the time we had none. Mr. Driscoll, a man we did not seem to like, would always chase us kids away from the gate, but he would see that we always ended up where Jack was stationed. Jack would then usher us up to the place where he wanted us to sit and behave ourselves. There were many spirited hockey games seen in this manner. I can also remember seeing quite a number of Grads games, probably courtesy of Mr. Driscoll and Jack.[73]

The Boys' Bands of Edmonton ⤳ Alex Mair, former band member

The Edmonton Newsboys Band gradually faded from the local musical scene, but they were replaced in the fall of 1935 when a new organization appeared. It was called the Edmonton Schoolboys Band, under the direction of T.V. Newlove. There were forty-two players in that first band but it didn't take long to grow. The rules in 1935 stayed with the band all the years that it played. A young man didn't even have to own an instrument to become a member. He just needed to want to play. The instrument and instruction were provided at a nominal cost if the student could afford them, and free if not. Two years later the band had grown to sixty members, and Newlove took them all to Banff for a two-week vacation.

It was a playing vacation, in that the band would parade up and down Banff Avenue to draw a crowd and then stage a small concert in the park adjacent to the Bow River. Newlove would address the crowd at some point, telling them how much the band boys ate, and then a collection would be taken to help offset the cost of the trip. The Banff trip proved to be such a successful climax to a year of rehearsing and playing that it was repeated in 1938 and again in 1939.

A high percentage of the band members were from what, today, we would refer to as inner city schools. McCauley School was the band's base. That's where Newlove was a full-time teacher and many of the members were students at McCauley. They didn't think of themselves as being from an inner city school. They just came from families that didn't have a lot of disposable income.

Newlove would scrounge what he could in the way of free groceries, he would arrange for the band to march in the Calgary Stampede parade for a fee, and he would make a deal with the CPR and Edmonton Motors for rail and truck transportation from Edmonton to Banff. The band boys would go to Banff for two weeks, travelling by rail. The princely sum of $5 per member covered transportation, all the food they could eat, and accommodation in tents in Banff. And if your family didn't have the $5? Looking back on it now, one comes to the realization that Newlove always found the money somewhere. Nobody was left behind.... Over the years, some 1,300 young Edmontonians, including 50 young ladies, were members of this unique Edmonton organization. The band went out of existence in 1969, but all those old horn blowers still gather and reminisce about the golden days of the Edmonton Schoolboys Band.[74]

Bible Bill comes to Edmonton ⌁ Elsie Park Gowan, teacher and playwright

In July 1932, I was marking Grade Ten Departmental History papers in the Normal School (Corbett Hall). Our history team shared a large classroom with an Arithmetic group, separated only by a dividing wall of lockers.

As the days went by, we were increasingly bothered by a penetrating voice from the other side. History in those days had essay answers; we had to read every word. Arithmetic had more time to chat. Little notes thrown over had no effect. The VOICE went on.

Coffee time gossip revealed that the Voice belonged to Mr. William Aberhart, of Calgary, who was explaining a book he had read about a monetary theory called Social Credit.

One hot afternoon, exasperated by the distracting offstage noise, I completely lost my cool and shouted over the lockers, "Shut up over there! OR HIRE A HALL!"

The joke was on me. Mr. Aberhart hired a hall, and how!

We were marking past history. He went on to make history.[75]

Funny Money ⌐ Sterling Haynes

My father died poor. My legacy was a safety deposit box full of Alberta's Prosperity Certificates.

A customer pays for merchandise with a Prosperity Certificate at the Army & Navy Store in 1936. Alberta's own currency lasted until the Supreme Court of Canada disallowed the Social Credit experiment.

My dad had been a dentist and later in his career had received a Master of Dental Surgery degree. He spent a lifetime repairing maxillas, mandibles and fractured zygomas, removing impacted wisdom teeth as well as doing general dentistry. He and the Dean of Dentistry at the University of Alberta were the only two dentists in Edmonton doing this type of work until much later when plastic surgeons started doing it.

Dad was one of the first to have an x-ray machine. The wide scattered rays of the cathode tube gave him exfoliative dermatitis of the hands and later lymphatic leukemia.

Horses were plentiful on Alberta farms in the 1920s and 30s. Iron cranks were used to start cars and tractors. Those were hazardous times—if a shod hoof didn't hit your jaw, the kick-back from the crank could strike you in the face during motor start-ups. Facial fractures were common.

In the days before endo-tracheal anesthesia, it was safer to do these facial surgical repairs under local anesthetic. Dad performed surgery at night and I was the teenage assistant. He taught me the anatomy of the head and neck while he did the three hour surgery. After placing arch wire splints for fractured mandibles, reducing and immobilizing broken maxillas, he was exhausted and the patient was worn out.

On July 6, 1935, in a summer of
drought and blistering heat,
William Aberhart hosted the
Big Northern Alberta Social
Credit Picnic at the Edmonton
Exhibition Grounds. Eager
for the promised $25 a month
dividend, 10,000 people
turned out to enjoy an election
campaign extravaganza. On
election night, Social Credit
won 56 of 63 seats; Edmonton
elected four of the seven
Opposition members. The
Social Credit party won nine
successive elections and
governed Alberta until 1971.

Dad was usually paid in kind—chickens, sauerkraut, salt pork. Sometimes, if he was unlucky, the farmers paid him with Alberta funny money.

Funny money was produced under Social Credit premier Bill Aberhart in 1936. Aberhart was a Calgary high school principal and a disciple of God and an English civil engineer, Major C.H. Douglas. Bible Bill adopted Douglas's dictates: the A plus B theorem....

Bible Bill, citing The Statute of Westminster, declared that Alberta was a sovereign entity, and could control credit and produce Alberta currency to pay for all Alberta made goods (part B of the theorem). These theories were promoted by the farmers of Alberta.

As an election incentive in 1935, Bible Bill promised all adult Albertans twenty-five dollars. It was no wonder the Socreds were elected. Bible Bill put purchasing power in the hands of the people.

The Alberta Treasury Branches were established and funny money put into circulation. A discount of five percent was given by ATBs for goods and services made in Alberta. "What Alberta Makes, Makes Alberta" was the battle cry of the Socreds.

Everything was to be paid for in Prosperity Certificates of one-dollar denominations. The kicker was that every time the certificates were cashed a very small one cent stamp was to be glued to the back of the certificate, which was marked into one hundred small grids. The stamp glue was poor and the bills large. Over time, with flour and water depression glue, the stamps and bills developed a patina of flour. As these 'certs' became heavier and heavier, the stamps became loose and straight pins and small gold safety pins were taken from women's lingerie to secure the stamps. After two years, (the declared life of the bill) they could weigh six ounces. As the glue aged, the certificates became brittle and the funny money could break and shower the floor with stamps.

In Edmonton, the money could be cashed in only a few places—the ATB, Alberta liquor stores, the University of Alberta Tuck Shop and the Army and Navy Department Store. Nobody wanted cracked money, that had to be carried in a shoe box, or to give change in good Canadian coin. Finally the Supreme Court declared the monetary system illegal.

Part of the money my Dad received for difficult dental surgery remained in his safety deposit box until he died, a reminder from Bible Bill that Dad's skillful work, performed in the Dirty Thirties had been paid for with illegal money produced and signed by Aberhart and the Social Credit fundamentalists. My father never recouped his losses.[76]

The *Journal* vs. Aberhart ⟿ John Imrie

My heart is full to overflowing as I accept tonight on behalf of the *Edmonton Journal* this plaque of bronze and on behalf of other Alberta newspapers these certificates of co-operation with my own. I am deeply grateful for the recognition thus given to the struggle of Alberta newspapers to preserve the freedom of the press within that province. That struggle is for much more than a free press. It is a struggle for democracy itself.

It is of the very essence of democracy that the people should have opportunity to know and freedom to discuss the activities and policies of their government. That is essential to the formation of intelligent public opinion which in the final analysis is alike the motivating force and the effective safeguard of true democracy. Over the centuries the struggle for freedom of the press has been linked at almost every step with the struggle for freedom of speech, of assembly, of access to the courts. It is a lesson of history that these several forms of freedom must stand or fall together.

Government control of the press is an indispensable instrument of dictatorship. On the other hand, a free press is both an essential and an evidence of democratic institutions.

It seems to me, sir, that this occasion of recognition tonight might well be made an occasion of re-dedication also. This past quarter century has witnessed the setting up of one dictatorship after another. Even in some of the few remaining democracies a strange and dangerous infiltration is in process. It is not for me, coming from another country, to suggest to you the form and nature of your own re-dedication. But speaking for myself and I believe for my fellow-publishers of Alberta, I give you this pledge:

Humbly, but without fear, not for ourselves alone but for our province, not simply for the press as such but for democracy, we will continue with unabated vigor, without equivocation or surrender, and notwithstanding whatever sacrifice may be involved, the struggle to preserve inviolate in Alberta those fundamentals of liberty and freedom that are the common and glorious heritage of your people and of mine.[77]

> Most of Alberta's newspapers denounced the policies of the new Social Credit government. Fed up with the criticism, Aberhart introduced the *Accurate News and Information Act* to gag the press. The *Edmonton Journal* led five dailies and 90 weeklies in a spirited fight against the bill, and for this effort, they won a Pulitzer Prize. *Journal* publisher John Imrie accepted the award in New York in 1938 with a timely call for courage.

THE DREAMLAND AND OTHER DIVERSIONS

The Grads in flight ⟿ Edith [Stone] Sutton, Edmonton Grad

As you have probably heard, our team—The Edmonton Grads—travelled about a bit. And when we travelled, we did so by train. Travelling by train you get to see a great deal of your country firsthand, and at ground level.

Edmonton Grad Edith Stone Sutton waits with her twin sister, Helen (left), and Babe Belanger before their first flight to a basketball game in Calgary.

We have a great big wonderful, beautiful, magnificent country to see. You may think that travelling by train is a slow way to go. The trains didn't trundle—they hurtled! We crossed the entire width of Canada many, many times as well as a good portion of the U.S.—down to the Olympic games in California and all up the Coast to Seattle. Went from there to Victoria, Vancouver and Prince Rupert—obviously by cruise ship.

Even here in Alberta—in defending our Provincial title we went back and forth to Calgary by train. That trip took about six hours—not because it was a slow train, but because it was necessary to service all of the towns and hamlets between here and Calgary—and there are quite a number of them. I personally loved train travel. We were a closely knit group, and always seemed to find plenty to talk about. The time went pleasantly, and you could move about, walk the length of the train and to the dining car. The dining car was a real treat and I guess we were always ready to go there.

But one time, this train travelling routine was interrupted. Late in May 1932, we were scheduled to meet Harry Wilson's Red Devils from Chicago, for the International title. The Chicago team was always very strong and we had to be at our best to "take" them. The competition was to take place on a Saturday evening and a Monday evening. (Sunday was for the relaxing and socializing of the two teams and friends—a barbeque perhaps.) At our last practice before the series, we were informed that—win, lose or draw, we would be playing the same team in Calgary on the Tuesday, as an exhibition game for The Shriner's charity fund, and in order to make the date, we would be flying. We looked at our captain in disbelief and complete misunderstanding. Nobody *flew*! The only people who flew were the bush pilots like Punch Dickins, Wop May, Paul Caulder. It was their work. They flew in wealthy entrepreneurs who owned mining interests or transportation businesses in the far north country and had stratospheric amounts of money. They could own their own planes or at least hire daring young flyers to take them up there. No passenger flights, of course. No need. Nobody flew. And here we were told we were about to fly!

The reason for this ground-breaking arrangement was that we were all office workers and our respective firms would not allow us to take time off for any reason, so we must needs put in our eight hours before we could take off. Even then there was some discussion as to whether or not we would take to the air, since the day was somewhat stormy. But of course, we had to go.

The Chicago team had already arrived in Calgary, having gone ahead by train—a special floor had been put down, special lighting had been installed in the building, and tickets had been sold. We were picked up at work and rushed over to the Municipal Airport, loaded into two Fokker 14's. Seats had been hastily installed into the two small planes—six passengers each, and took off over a grass field. No need for paved runways, the planes were so light.

Pilot Wop May kept fragments of Baron von Richthoven's plane as a memento of his encounter with the Red Baron. When the Edmonton Grads left for the 1936 Olympics in Berlin, May asked the Canadian Olympic Committee to return one fragment to the dead pilot's family. He sent an accompanying telegram to Hermann Goering, the head of the German airforce, and Goering replied with this telegram.

Commercial Grads Yell:

Pickles, ketchup,

chow, chow, chow,

Chew, 'em up, eat, 'em up,

bow, wow, wow;

Hannibal, cannibal,

sis, boom, bah,

Commercial Graduates,

rah, rah, rah!

It was quite a rough plane ride, and two hours and 200 miles later we put down at the Calgary airport—also on a grass field. We were offered supper—for those who could manage it, and played our game—which we won. The Chicago girls had had a leisurely train trip to Calgary arriving around noon, so had all the afternoon and early evening to rest up. We, on the other hand, had done a day's work and had experienced that rough two-hour plane ride before taking to the floor.

After the game we took the midnight train to Edmonton, arriving in time to clean up in the train washroom, have breakfast at the station lunch counter, and get to work. This meant, as you can see, that we left home at 7:30 a.m. to get to work Tuesday morning, and did not get back until supper time Wednesday evening. It was quite an experience and we enjoyed it all. We were the first basketball team—men or women—to fly to keep an engagement.[78]

Play ball! ⌐ John Ducey

We'd play games in North Edmonton, you see. And we'd go out in the Gainers' trucks...and we'd draw the truck up behind the grandstand in North Edmonton. They had very rabid fans out there in North Edmonton. Good fans, very intense.... As we'd get to the last inning, particularly if we were in the lead, we'd turn the motors on, and get them revved up.... With the last out...we'd make a beeline for the trucks and just get out of there quick because those fans are after you, I tell you.[79]

"Someday, perhaps, we'll build our own theatre" ⌐ Elizabeth Sterling Haynes

The one thing I'm sorry about is that they always have to go away: Alberta must export her acting talent because, as yet, there's no employment here. Some day, perhaps, we will truly build our own theatre. Alberta playwrights will create drama—as strong and colourful and moving as the province itself—and Alberta actors will translate it into life, all over Alberta, for thrilled Alberta audiences....

I remember the first theatrical production I ever saw advertised in Edmonton. I had just come here from Toronto—back in the early Twenties—and it was forty-five below on that dark winter's morning. The little villages, which I had glimpsed through holes scratched in the frost on the train windows, had seemed so stark and naked and uninhabited in the dirtied snow that I felt very disconsolate and uprooted. Then, as we turned into the old Barootes cafe for coffee, I saw this playbill announcing a first-rate English company's production of Galsworthy's *The Skin Game*. I went, and I have never forgotten the performance.

It was Galsworthy at his best—the story of an uncouth, ruthless and ambitious mill-owner who discovered that his whole material success had been earned at the cost of a spoiled and neglected family. It was superbly played, magnificently spoken; and throughout, it drew low chuckles and pithy comments from a bespectacled gentlemen next to me.

"Who is he?" I whispered to my husband. I got my answer from the man himself.

"I'm Joe Clarke, Edmonton's recurrent mayor!" he chuckled. "Galsworthy should have been here through the real-estate boom of 1911. He'd have seen what a real skin game was!...."[80]

Elizabeth Sterling Haynes inspired a generation of Albertans to look beyond the frustrations of the Depression to the magic of the stage. The University of Alberta's Faculty of Extension hired the young director to train actors in amateur theatre. Haynes helped to found the Edmonton Little Theatre, the Alberta Drama League and the Banff School of Fine Arts.

Barbara Villy Cormack

Elizabeth Haynes and her magic wand of theatre swept across rural Alberta like a strong, healing wind. In her work with the university's extension department she travelled an incredible number of miles, adjudicating, giving lectures and courses, assisting groups of local actors in production, extending the ever-warm helping hand, lighting or rekindling the spark of theatre in many a lonely and discouraged heart. For all the rural folk who were touched directly or indirectly by that magic wand which for a moment replaced the grim saga of drought, grasshoppers and hard times, with visions of something fine and beautiful, thank you Elizabeth Haynes. We shall never forget you.[81]

Joe Shoctor, founder of The Citadel Theatre

Thirty years ago, I acted under Mrs. Haynes' direction in *Ten Cents a Copy* (in Talmud Torah Hall), and in Maxell Anderson's war play *The Eve of St. Mark* (in Westglen School). Theatre became as important to me as breathing. I'm doing nothing these days but raising the five million dollars to build the new Citadel in Edmonton Centre. This will have three stages, a library and a first-class lecture hall. Elizabeth made me want to be in theatre.[82]

Hilwie Hamdon helped the fund-raising campaign to build Canada's first mosque. The Al-Rashid Mosque was built in 1938 at 101st Street and 108th Ave. It was moved in 1946 to a new site near the Royal Alexandra Hospital. The original mosque is now at Fort Edmonton Park.

Canada's first mosque ↪ Sid Hamdon

My mother Hilwie Taha Jomha was born in the village of Lala, in the Bekaa Valley of Lebanon, in 1917. At the age of sixteen, she met and married Ali Hamdon who was visiting from Canada. Together they crossed the Atlantic on the Queen Mary and then travelled here on the train.

Ali Hamdon was an established fur trader in Fort Chipewyan where they lived for the next nine years. It was there my mother gave birth to her six children and had many rich experiences.

In 1933 she moved to Edmonton because she wanted her children to have wider educational opportunities. At that time there were only a few Lebanese families here. They would gather in one another's homes for the comfort of familiar food and language. A few people wanted to build a centre for the Lebanese Muslims. When this suggestion was made, two people in the group, my mother and Najeeb Ailey said: "If we can build a hall, we can build a Mosque."

The first task was to acquire land on which to build the Mosque. A delegation was chosen to approach Mayor Fry. There were several men in the delegation and they asked my mother to join them. She was very reluctant because her English was poor. But they insisted so she went and as it turned out, she became the primary spokesperson! The Mayor agreed to provide the community with the land on the condition that they raise a significant portion of the building cost first.

Hilwie Hamdon never shied away from a challenge and thus began an exciting and busy time for my mother and the entire community. They raised the required amount of money and went back to the Mayor who, true to his word, donated a piece of land at 104th Street and 108 Avenue.

The next challenge was to find a builder. They hired Walter Kostiuk, a local contractor. I recall my mother speaking to Mr. Kostiuk regarding the building of the Mosque. The small community did not have enough funds to start and complete the job so she told Mr. Kostiuk to begin the project and when the current funds were used up, he was to advise her, which he did. The job would then stop and the members of the community would go on a fundraising drive.

They would seek funding from any and all individuals and businesses. With the newly acquired funds, she would contact Walter Kostiuk and the building would once again begin. On several occasions, when the group was seeking funds, my mother with other members of the community, would drive to Saskatchewan and seek donations from the Arabs living in that province. We had great support from both Muslim and Christian Arabs in Edmonton and elsewhere.

This cycle of fundraising and building continued until the Mosque was completed. For the official opening of the first Mosque in North America, our Master of Ceremonies was the Mayor of Hanna, Alberta, Mr. I.F. Shaker, a Christian Arab. He was selected for this role as he was fluent in both English and Arabic and was a close friend and supporter of our community. There were several other dignitaries on hand for the opening, including Mayor Fry of Edmonton, and Imam Youssef Ali, a well respected Qu'uranic translator and scholar, who was traveling across Canada at the time and who dedicated our new Mosque. What a day it was!

This Mosque, which was the result of the efforts of a small but determined community, now sits proudly at Fort Edmonton Historical Park and is symbolic of the pioneering spirit of these new Canadians.[83]

The King and Queen and Uncle Mike ⌐ Harley Reid

It was during the Royal Visit of 1939 that I accidentally invented "The Wave," so popular at today's sporting events. I was eight years old in Grade Three at John A. McDougall School and one of many school kids waiting for the arrival of the Royal Family. We were seated on the wooden bleachers that lined both sides of Edmonton's Portage Avenue that Friday, June 2, 1939. Our school of approximately 250 kids, in Grades One to Eight, had walked over from the school yard some three blocks away. A small army of excited children were buzzing with activity and waving the miniature Union Jacks they were given at school. After we had settled down in our seats we watched hundreds of children and adults milling about and seating themselves on the bleachers around us.

There were two or three false alarms as we waited when some excited person would holler "Here they come!" and much moaning when they didn't. A police motorcycle approached our location from the east. As it came closer, I thought I recognized my Uncle Mike Kelly seated in the sidecar. Hoping it was him, I jumped up and hollered, "Uncle Mike! Uncle Mike!" but he was too far away to hear. Disappointed, I sat down

More than 68,000 people lined Edmonton's streets to welcome King George VI and Queen Elizabeth to Edmonton. Portage Avenue was renamed Kingsway Avenue in honour of the royal visit.

but told all my classmates that Uncle Mike was an Edmonton policeman and he was guarding the King and family. Time passed and no Royal Family motorcade showed up. Then some person called out, "Hey kid, here comes your Uncle Mike. You'd better wave."

Sure enough, a motorcycle was coming on my side of the avenue and there he was sitting in the side car. Several classmates joined me and leaping up we hollered "Uncle Mike! Uncle Mike!" at full volume. The motorcycle was now right in front and he looked towards the bleachers, but he did not acknowledge our calls. They passed by and, terribly disappointed, I sat down. Soon my credibility was under fire and comments came doubting this uncle existed.

My classmate seated next to me tugged at my sleeve and said, "Look! The motorcycle is turning around down there and they're coming back." The vehicle passed us again on the far side of the road. Then it made a second U turn and it was now approaching our bleachers.

The entire packed bleacher full of students seemed to rise as the two policemen came abreast of us. A deafening shout of "Uncle Mike! Uncle Mike!" filled the air. As I stood there hollering my lungs out, Uncle Mike half rose in the sidecar and both police officers smiled and waved at the excited young school kids.

The Royal motorcade came by later.[84]

TWO LONELY CHILDREN

"If I look hard enough, maybe I will see our house" ᴔ **Kathleen Steinhauer, student at the Edmonton Indian Residential School**

My father took sick when I was five. I am not sure what was wrong with him. They thought he might have TB. We suddenly found out that we couldn't go to District School. They had wanted the three of us to go because my youngest sister was a baby. They thought that if the three of us were in school all day it would be easier. I think the teacher was quite willing, but we weren't allowed to go and the only alternative was the residential school.... So my mother took us to the Edmonton Indian Residential School....

One thing, I can remember looking out the window from the dormitory and crying my eyes out. My aunt came in and I said to her, "If I look hard enough, maybe I will be able to see our house." She told me I was looking in the wrong direction.

I was beaten by the supervisor and the matron for various things, for speaking Cree. I was not someone who sat in the corner and hid. I played with the other children. There was nobody around watching us at the time so some of them couldn't speak English, so we spoke in Cree.

My grandmother lived in Edmonton, my mother's mother. I don't remember how many times she came to visit but one visit I remember was this one: I don't know if it was a Church Service upstairs or concert, sometimes the CGIT girls group would come and do a concert and distribute these oranges, one to each child. I didn't know she was there and we were coming out and we had to line up and walk out and weren't to get out of line and we weren't allowed to talk. As I was a little girl, we went out first. I noticed my grandmother sitting at the very back, right inside the door and the doors were open. The Matron, girls supervisor, was standing just right outside the door and as soon as the last of her charges went out she would follow us. I saw my grandmother. I whispered, "Grandmother." The supervisor heard me and just as soon as I got outside the door she whacked me across the head. I fell into the other child. I didn't dare cry out loud because, it would be worse.

Another day, after my mother left, at breakfast, I was sitting right next to the cement wall and we got our Sunny Boy and cut of skim milk, cold, and I asked the supervisor for brown sugar. She whacked me, and my head bounced off the cement wall. She hit me on the other side and she said, "Stop crying or I'll hit you again," and I bounced into poor Sarah and Sarah started to cry. Oh! Terrible old lady.

There was a girl in our dorm who was enuretic, she was a bed wetter, and she had a terrible time. Every morning she would be beaten through her wet nightie. Big welts and she would be screaming. I didn't dare wet my bed. I did a couple of times and was whacked.

After that, you find there is no way out of this. This went on and on. I remember being totally overcome by the most devastating sense of despair. Just total despair and I was just a kid. Nobody should feel that way, especially not a little kid. I just had no hope of anything....

I went in at the age of five and came out at the age of eight. My sister, Doreen, got very, very ill. She had pneumonia and she almost died. My parents were never notified. I vaguely remember, I went to the infirmary with a scratch because I wanted to see her and I peeked my head in there, and I was caught, and Wham. I remember, in the middle of the night an awful lot of excitement. She was still in the infirmary, people going up and

Kathleen Steinhauer entered the Edmonton Indian Residential School in 1937. Her father, Ralph Steinhauer, a leader of the Saddle Lake Cree, later became Alberta's first aboriginal Lieutenant-Governor. Kathleen is among the former students who have sued the Canadian government and the United Church in a case that alleges physical, emotional and cultural abuse of students at the school.

down the hallway and voices up and down the stairs. What happened was, they called the doctor in the middle of the night and they put her in an oxygen tent. There was a teacher there, named Miss Spence, and she knew grandmother quite well. She was a substitute teacher.... Miss Spence happened to be there when Doreen was very sick and she wrote to my mother and told her what she thought of the place and what had happened to Doreen and that she was very concerned.

My mother had met Miss Spence and when she came to get us she had a row with the principal. I was standing up at the top of the stairs, just inside because I knew my mother was in the office and I could hear this. My mother was a very reserved person, but when she was angry, I was sure I had done something wrong. I could hear these voices and I was terrified of the principal. We never had to go back.[85]

This was a heart-rending time ⌁ Peter Owen

About 1937 it became evident to us that something had to be done to get us out of Germany.... The gates had shut all over the world. Finally in early 1938 through a distant relative my parents learned that it was possible to obtain an emigration visa to Bolivia. They applied, and were ready to leave, when suddenly and unexpectedly some correspondence arrived from a place called Edmonton.

Mr. Friedman had a very close friend in Edmonton named Julius Erlanger, an optometrist. They had roomed together when they were bachelors. By 1937 the conditions of the Jews in Germany had become pretty widely known. Mr. and Mrs. Friedman made up their minds that they would like to bring to their home a young Jewish boy to give him the opportunity of an education, to help him make something of himself.... They asked Mr. Erlanger to help them find a boy....

This was a heartrending time for us, my mother in particular. She never quite got over it because they had to leave me behind without any assurance that Canada would issue a visa. I stayed behind with my aunt and her husband and three children, with whom I'd been really close. My parents left in the summer of 1938, with my young brother. I stayed with Uncle Max and Aunt Hannah and their three children, constantly waiting for some positive word from Canada....

Then came Kristallnacht on November 9, 1938. On the morning after Kristallnacht I hadn't heard of the events when I left for school. When I

CANADIAN PACIFIC
TELEGRAPHS

DIRECT CONNECTION WITH
POSTAL TELEGRAPH - CABLE CO.
COMMERCIAL CABLES - - IMPERIAL CABLES

MONEY TRANSFERRED
BY TELEGRAPH

W. D. NEIL, General Manager of
Communications, Montreal.

STANDARD TIME

2 WN CW 27 DL

OTTAWA ONT NOV 28 1938 940 AM

H A FRIEDMAN
BANK OF COMMERCE BLDG
EDMONTON ALTA

PETER ARRIVING STEAMER COLUMBUS NEWYORK SCHEDULED TO ARRIVE DECEMBER 2ND
IF YOU REQUIRE ANYTHING TO BE DONE HERE LET ME KNOW PERSONAL REGARDS
TO YOU ALL

SAM

812AM

Peter travelled to Edmonton alone, but the Friedmans' friends met him at every railway station along the route and sent telegrams ahead to Edmonton to reassure his sponsors.

biked past the synagogue where I had had my bar mitzvah the year before, it was a smoking ruin. A crowd of citizens was jeering and taunting an old man with a beard who was in the gutter trying to retrieve the Torah scrolls. They'd been taken out before the place burnt down, and they'd been thrown out in the street. About 10 days before, my uncle had been arrested. My aunt was terribly distraught; she had her three children and a nephew to look after, and all the while wondering what happened to her husband.

So I came home on that 10th of November, I related what I'd seen. Within a day or two I received word that the visa had been granted, and I could go to Edmonton.

On December 2, 1938 my poor aunt, who still hadn't heard from her husband, and I got on a train to Bremen. She left me there in a sort of boarding house for émigrés, to wait to board ship. On the cold day of December 3, I got on the ship by myself and sailed to America....

[Peter travelled alone across the continent by train.]

The trip was long. It seemed like forever. I arrived in Edmonton at the old CNR Station at six a.m. on a snowy day. Mr. Erlanger drove me straight to the Friedmans' house. It was very bewildering at first. The Friedmans were always very careful to be loving and kind, but not to replace my own parents, or to give me that impression.[86]

"What lies ahead for us all?" ⤳ Dolly Lone

Riding the bus one morning, at the start of World War II, I was thinking of all the young men from Jasper Park, my home town, who were missing and presumed dead. The most recent one was on my mind as the bus stopped in traffic in front of the General Hospital. I glanced at the statue of our Lord and gave a silent prayer—"Please God bring him home!" A hand touched my shoulder and a voice said "Hi! How are you?" I raised my eyes and could not speak, the tears welling up in my eyes. There was my answered prayer. The most unforgettable moment of my life.

I am 82 and still cry at the memory of the moment.[87]

Guardian Angels ⤳ Norah Plumley Hook, worker at Aircraft Repair

Shortly after the outbreak of World War II, Aircraft Repair Ltd. evolved out of McKenzie Air Services. It was a facility to overhaul, repair and assemble a variety of military aircraft used as part of the British Commonwealth Air Training Plan. Records show that in April 1941, the first 25 employees moved to No. 1 Plant which was only partially completed. They were primarily employed in the assembly of Fairey Battle aircraft, which were British-made bombers.

At that time, I was employed at GWG, a garment factory, sewing coveralls and jeans. After 10 months of work, I was not enjoying the routine, the experience, or the pay. A fellow worker had heard that Aircraft Repair was hiring women, so we decided to apply. On a hot July afternoon, after our shift at the garment factory, we walked from 97th Street to the Aircraft Repair office. There we put in an application and crossed our fingers hoping for a new job.

I was hired on July 12, 1941, expecting that with sewing experience, I would be working in the fabric department. That was not meant to be. My acceptance slip read "MISC" and the starting pay 30 cents per hour. On my first day of work, I was given a badge #881, and a handbook of rules. Another girl and I were escorted to the Sheet Metal Dept. As the first girls in that department, we were being tested, "to see if girls could do Sheet Metal work." Our first job was filing—not fingernails or documents!

Seated on high stools at a wooden bench, we were each given some different sized files with teeth ranging from very fine to coarse. Beside us was a box of large metal washers. They had been stamped out by machine

With so many men on overseas duty women found jobs as mechanics and factory workers in Edmonton's wartime aviation industry.

but had to have the rough edges smoothed. Then they were sent to the inspection department, tried on a "jig," and either passed, or rejected and returned for more filing. Routine job again! ...but that was only the beginning. Large metal parts that had been repaired by welding needed to be smoothed down before being sent to the paint shop and on to assembly—more filing!

In due time, we went on to many different aspects of sheet metal work. We took out dents and straightened ailerons, cowlings, flaps and under-carriages and all metal parts with equally strange names. Surprise...girls could do the job! We bucked rivets for the men and ended up using rivet guns, drill presses and huge metal sheers, as well as all small tools. We wore white coveralls and had to keep our hair tied up in a kerchief, and our sleeve cuffs taped in order to keep them from being caught in machinery. The day was divided into three eight-hour shifts: day shift, swing shift, and night shift.

As time went on, the variety of planes and jobs changed. Added to the Fairey Battles were planes with such exotic names as, Anson, Harvard, Air Speed Oxford, and the odd Bolingbroke. At times we could see on the tarmac American fighters—P51s, Mustangs and P39s, and B29 bombers—on their way to Alaska and the Aleutian Islands. I was finally given the job of making sure that the right metal parts—by number—were repaired for the particular aircraft waiting on the assembly line. Quite a responsibility! My whole Aircraft Repair experience was never boring, sometimes challenging, and always rewarding. In August 1943, I married Jack Hook, one of the dreaded inspectors, and I left Aircraft Repair in 1944. By that time there were many girls working in the sheet metal department as well as other departments. They were excellent welders as they could do more delicate repairs. Women of all ages worked in the paint shop, radiator department, machine shop, wood working shop, and wherever else they were needed. My own mother worked in electrical accessories, rewiring engine harnesses...and surprise again...women could do the job!

In September 2000, I was invited to a ceremony at the Aircraft Museum. It was the dedication of the "Angels Memorial" to honour the women in aviation. We were each presented with a lapel pin in the shape of an angel. As Marie (Silvester) Wright, a pilot behind the project, said in her speech, "We, in the repair field, were their Guardian Angels."[88]

Yanks ∽ Helen I. Mahoney

When the Commonwealth Air Training Plan started sixty years ago our family lived at 11004–108 Street, north of MacDougall Elementary-Commercial School. Our parents had rented rooms to graduate nurses from the Royal Alexandra Hospital. Soon we were renting these rooms to the young wives of the Canadian trainees. The girls went door to door in our neighbourhood for a place to live. They wanted to spend time with their husbands before they were posted overseas.

Our Dad was unable to say "No" to anyone. The first two girls were welcomed at the door with a smile.... "Of course we have room. Don't we Isabel?" he asked our mother. Willingly we all doubled up again....

Nine people and a baby shared one small bathroom and kitchen. No arguments. How did our mother remain sane? Fred and Harold were posted and Lois and Elva and Linda returned home. We were all sad, Mum and young brother Calvin especially. Our cousin Jack trained in Edmonton. One day he told his Aunt Belle (Mom) that they used our home as a turning point to return to base. As the noisy, yellow planes clumsily came around. Mother would rush out the back door waving a tea towel. Jack would kindly tell her that everyone appreciated her enthusiasm.

Our quiet neighbourhood was no more as men from Canada, Australia, New Zealand and other countries trained on Tiger Moths, Harvards and Avro Ansons. Were there other types of aircraft? I don't know.

It wasn't long before Dad filled the empty rooms again. We remember Anne with affection. Anne worked at the base canteen. She was very pretty and friendly. I was impressed with the parade of young airmen who dropped by to visit and take our roomer out. My Dad wasn't pleased when the military police arrived to break up a fight over Anne and suggested that Dad and Mom should look for another tenant, especially since we were impressionable youngsters....

Edmonton handled the influx of Commonwealth young men with ease. They were invited into homes for dinner, taken roller skating and dancing. How we enjoyed watching the Australians and New Zealanders learn to skate with help from their girl friends; 112th Street and Jasper Avenue had the largest open air rink. Central Rink owned by Mr. Barnes. Sundays there was a live band playing waltzes etc. Mixed in with the whizzing speed skaters, figure skaters and us ordinary skaters were the red-faced airmen jerking along with terror stricken faces.

Another influx of foreigners claimed our small city's attention. This time it was Americans billeted here as the building of the Alaska Highway started. I remember 109th Street plugged with convoy trucks from Kingsway down to the small "Rathole" tunnel.... Complete with sheepskin flight boots and jacket, a drawl and a new bride of eighteen years—plus the most important item—a JEEP—our American descended on us. What a time that was. If our young Captain wasn't rushing off in his jeep—with driver—he was bouncing up the stairs to see his lonesome girl. How my brothers wanted a ride in that jeep. Both Mom and Dad said: "Don't you dare ask." I think we were all relieved when they found roomier accommodations. The boys never did get their ride. Overlooked in all the confusion of strange accents and uniforms were the Canadian soldiers barracked at the Prince of Wales Armoury next to Victoria High School. They did not have the new accents, uniforms and extra pay of the newcomers. I wonder if they were a little upset at the lack of attention they received—or if they were also treated well by Edmontonians?[89]

Blizzard of '42: The worst snowstorm in Edmonton's history ⌐
Nan Morrison

As an eleven year old, I woke up being told there had been a very heavy snowfall the previous night and the schools were closed. Dad was using a gravel shovel to shovel his way from our back door to 76 Street, a distance of 100 feet. From there, he intended to shovel from 110 Ave to 112 Ave in order to take the streetcar to work. However, after shovelling some more, he came to the conclusion the street cars were not running. I remember walking in the narrow path with, what it seemed, the snow as high as my waist. My father, George Clark, decided he must get to work and keep the boilers stocked. While this was not his regular job, being one of the owners of Clark Lumber he realized the pipes in the factory, warehouse and office would freeze if the boilers went out.

Dad had a pair of 1926 era skis which came with a leather harness. He tied the metal lunch bucket around him, and with his bamboo ski poles, he skied to work on 109 Street and 104th Avenue. He remained on the business site, stocking the boilers for two full days and two full nights catching up on a little sleep in an old oak chair that stayed in the boiler room. The odd employee arrived at work if they lived nearby.

Around eight o'clock, on the second night of the heavy snow storm, we heard a loud noise outside in the dark. It was a massive grader, plowing out the snow on the road in front of our home. Edmonton simply did not have graders like this! The grader belonged to the Americans who were in Edmonton for the building of the Canol Pipeline and Alaska Highway. We later found out the only reason we were fortunate in getting 110th Ave snowplowed was the urgent need for the University Hospital to receive their daily coal deliveries from the coal mines in Beverly.[90]

"How's Joe?" ⌐ Igor Gouzenko, junior Russian officer, 1943

Now, as our transport plane came in for the landing and I fastened my safety belt, the houses of Edmonton, seen through a starboard window, caused little shivers of uncertainty. I had been lectured to and drilled in the procedure to follow, yet this seemed different.

When the aircraft bumped slightly, then finally rolled to an easy stop by a hangar, I unbuckled my belt slowly—actually loath to leave this last contact with my familiar Russia and step onto this strange, threatening, foreign soil. Zabotin, however, showed no hesitation. He was the first out of the plane. As I emerged into the bright sunlight a group of young men on a truck whisked over to the plane, apparently to unload baggage and mail sacks. They were in uniform, which I did not recognize at the time as that of the Royal Canadian Air Force. I must have been staring at them because one laughed outright and yelled:

"Hiya, chum—how's Joe these days?"

I glanced uncertainly at Romanov, who shook his head almost imperceptibly. The English words were understandable but I didn't know what was meant by "Joe." Both Romanov and I would have been flabbergasted if we had realized the query referred to Joseph Stalin. As it was, we merely followed our instructions: "When in doubt simply act as if you do not understand, and keep silent." Our ideas about Canada were soon hopelessly confused. We had read, of course, all the official articles in encyclopedias and brochures.... We were not prepared for the wealth of food in the Edmonton hotel where we stayed, nor the abundance of clothing, candies and luxuries of all kinds in such windows as those of the huge Hudson's Bay store on the main street. The hundreds of automobiles, carrying people who certainly didn't seem to have an official hearing, left us gaping in astonishment. We continued our journey to Ottawa aboard a Canadian National Railways' transcontinental train. The swaying fields of wheat extending endless miles from the tracks, the rich soil, the forests, the lakes, the gardens beside homes in towns and villages, reflected a prosperous and colorful country.[91]

Ortona

Dear Mrs. Vass:

It is with deep regret that I confirm the news of the death of Sgt. D.P. Vass who died of wounds on Dec. 21, 1943. He was with us in the battle of Ortona and having advanced with his company was helping to lift a wounded man on to a stretcher outside a ruined factory when a burst of Jerry Machine Gun fire hit him in several places. He was in bad shape so we loaded him into the waiting ambulance and sent him to the hospital. We have been in action ever since so had no news of him. A couple of days ago I visited the Military Cemetery at San Vito and found his grave there. We fixed it up with a nice cross, bordered it with white stones and planted some narcissus bulbs on it. His loss will be a great blow to you and the officers and men of the regiment send sincere sympathy to you. He died fighting in a great army for a great cause. He was a good leader of men and we honour his memory.

    May God Bless and Comfort you

    Yours Sincerely

    Edgar J. Bailey. H/Major.

    Loyal Edmonton Regiment

P.S. I hope I am writing to the right person; one of the men gave me this address as his pay book went with him. Please convey our sympathy to other members of the family.[92]

Edmonton's soldiers died across Europe and Asia in the Second World War, but the Battle of Ortona in December 1943 defined the city's sacrifice for a generation. The Loyal Edmonton Regiment suffered 172 casualties in the Italian town, including 63 killed. In the bitter January of 1944, the letters of consolation began to reach Edmonton.

Soldiers in the Loyal
Edmonton Regiment help
a wounded comrade walk
through the ruins of San
Leonardo di Ortona.

Soldiers gather to read their
mail from Edmonton, two
days before Christmas, 1943.

**A sharp salute and a surrender ∾ William Ziegler,
one of Canada's youngest brigadiers, 1945**

On the 4th and 5th of May, I took the surrender of two German
Corps commanders. The first one was in the north. I rendez-
voused with a German vehicle, which took me to Leiden, a little town in
the middle of tulip country. I drove with my staff captain, interpreter and
driver, in a Jeep flying a white flag. When we arrived at the town centre I
was told, "The General is upstairs, sir."

I was a bit apprehensive because my captive outranked me. He was a
Lieutenant-General and I was merely a Brigadier. At the top of the stairs,
I took a deep breath, entered the room, gave him a sharp British salute,
and said, "Brigadier Ziegler." In reply, he snapped his heels together and
thrust his hand up: "Heil Hitler!" I turned on my heel and stormed straight
back down to my Jeep. The bugger wasn't going to "Heil Hitler" me. However, the whole street was packed with Dutch people and we couldn't
drive away.

The General's aide came running after us and said, "The General would
like to see you again, sir." I replied, "You go back and tell the General that
I will see him when he learns how to salute properly." He said, "The General has already learned how to salute properly."

So I went back up, and this time I did not salute him. I just stood there
and waited. Sure enough, he gave me a smart British salute. I felt that was
a victory![93]

*Members of the city's Chinese
community marching in
the victory parade through
downtown Edmonton on
August 15, 1945.*

*With the war over, a little
girl tells her soldier father to
report for active service on
76th Avenue.*

The New City

1947 to 2004

Go to almost any corner of Edmonton and you will hear the staccato rhythm of hammers, the whine of electric saws, the low-gear growling of bobcats in motion. Carpenters perched on high rafters shout instructions as a crane operator edges a roofline into position. From dawn until dusk the hammers pound away, providing the soundtrack for a city that is a perpetual building site. If Edmonton needed a new motto to replace allusions to sports champions and Alberta's capital, the sign might say: "Under Construction—Again."

Some new neighbourhoods offer hints of the city's past, but only in name. Prospective home buyers can tour show homes in Henday Village, or Lacombe Park Estates, The Village at Griesbach or Rutherford in Heritage Valley, without knowing the story of a fur trader, a pioneer priest, a military leader or a first premier. They can buy a condominium in a development called The Trails, The Homesteads, The Brickyard or Railtown without knowing the location of the original trails, homesteads, brickyards or railway stations. They can move into an uptown urban loft in the old warehouse district and remain oblivious to the gritty origins of a chic address.

The names of other urban developments evoke the nostalgia of a commodified generic past: Victorian Village, The Chateaux, California Casa, Sierras on the Lake or Devonshire Mews. The homes here are immensely comfortable by the standards of every previous Edmonton generation, although not all citizens can afford them. The average new house has two storeys, three bedrooms, two or three bathrooms, a living room, a family room, a well-equipped kitchen, a double garage, and a spacious lower level. Edmonton's new homes and condominiums—like the surrounding subdivisions, shopping malls and big-box retail parks—are mirror images of others across North America. In the words of historian Gerald Friesen, the urban environment in western Canada is becoming "just another neighbourhood of a single, homogenous global metropolis."[1]

If this is true, Edmonton is one of the world's most spacious neighbourhoods. It has a small population by international standards—with one million residents in the city and its satellite communities—but its metropolitan area expands over 850 square kilometres. This means that the Edmonton metropolitan region covers more land than Bangkok, Cairo, Delhi, Moscow, Beijing or Rome do.

Edmonton has the lowest population density among Canada's 10 largest cities, but this might soon change. Listen carefully and you will hear workers tapping out a new character for the city. The hammering stops only on the coldest days of winter. Use the lull to reflect on the prospering city's changing character.

***

LIKE THOUSANDS OF RURAL ALBERTANS, Bill and Pearl moved to Edmonton after the Second World War in search of a more agreeable life. For years Pearl had been after Bill to leave the farm, and finally he consented. They borrowed Mike Shandro's farm truck, packed up the last of their belongings at Wasel, and turned towards Edmonton. Jeannette, their only daughter, sat between them. At 30, Bill did not look like the type of guy who quoted Tennyson, but he began to recite aloud when he saw Edmonton on the horizon: "*For I dipped into the future, far as human eye could see, Saw the Vision of the world, and all the wonder that would be....*" In his first business venture, he had paid $2,500 for a quarter-interest in Prairie Rose Manufacturing, a soft drink bottling company. He steered the truck up Scona Hill, turned left on 86th Avenue, and stopped at the curb opposite a small, stucco bungalow. The couple had scraped together a $1,500 down payment for this $9,000 home. It was the first house they had ever owned: two bedrooms on the main floor and a picture window facing south. Edmonton had 111,745 residents, plus three, on November 12, 1945. The Hawrelaks were home.

The New City 1950

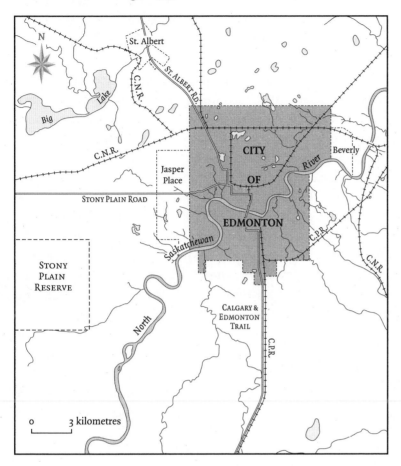

The oil strike at Leduc No. 1, south of the city, brought prosperity and new residents to the Edmonton area. Post-war citizens began their exodus from older homes in the city's inner core to new planned neighbourhoods like Westmount and Parkallen and to the independent communities beyond city boundaries such as St. Albert, West Jasper Place, Leduc, Devon, Fort Saskatchewan and Stony Plain. Sherwood Park did not exist until 1955.

The most dramatic change in western Canada after the war was the mass migration to cities. Rural Albertans who had moved to Edmonton to work in war industries appeared reluctant to return to the countryside. The rural prairies lost 750,000 people between the end of the war and 1981, meaning that the population, and the number of farms, dropped by half.

On a spring Saturday in 1948 young couples looked wistfully at tiny boxes in the basement of Eaton's. They peered into miniature windows, and touched the small sidewalks and front steps, wondering if these "scale models of prize-winning designs"[2] at the Canadian Small Homes Exhibition were beyond their reach. A new house might cost an astronomical $4,700, but perhaps they could rent a basement suite to a tenant if they built a separate entrance? The little boxes on the table tantalized them with fantasies of a new kind of family life: the infinite privacy of a home without parents or in-laws. They craved every ingredient of the dream: the stucco exterior walls studded with bits of glass that would reflect the winter sunlight; the potted fern in the picture window; the L-shaped living room; the kitchen with a Frigidaire; and two or three small bedrooms. This was Edmonton's post-war dream home. Warm and bright, a bungalow was easily large enough for a young war veteran, his pregnant wife and the four or five children they would welcome in the decade ahead. The dreamers touched the little boxes and waited.

All Canadian cities struggled to provide affordable housing after the Second World War, but Edmonton's problems were acute. Few houses had been built during a decade of Depression and through six years of war. Alberta soon discovered that it lacked skilled workers in the construction trades, building materials for new subdivisions, and real estate developers with the capital to meet the housing demands of 24,500 returning veterans and their young families.

Rural westerners were accustomed to space. They preferred single-family homes with vegetable gardens to the rented row houses and apartments acceptable in Montreal, Ottawa and Toronto. The Canadian government offered housing and education grants to veterans and substantial assistance to the developers of new subdivisions. With some ingenuity, the city salvaged building materials from an abandoned American army base in Dawson Creek, B.C. to construct a few hundred houses. The city also converted existing army huts into temporary shelters. For all their combined efforts, governments could not begin to meet the demand. In 1947 more than 2,000 Edmonton families applied for the 250 new homes available from the Wartime Housing Corp. Everyone in town, it seemed, had a name on a waiting list.

In *Homes in Alberta*, Donald Wetherell and Irene Kmet conclude that "the existing housing crisis was aggravated by the high expectations for post-war life held by many people." They suggest that new homes, no matter how small or similar, quickly became the outward symbol of individuality and upward mobility, "the focus for a reunited family, a family that would find contentment and purpose through its material possessions."[3] The deprivation of Depression childhoods in the West and the sacrifices of war and separation, encouraged post-war couples to crave a new home with new furnishings, a new Chevrolet in the driveway, and new furniture to replace wartime mattresses and orange-crate bedside tables. Every stucco bungalow in a subdivision was a declaration of independence, a repudiation of Alberta's hardest times.

A boomtown can be a dream home, too. The front door of the new Edmonton swung wide open at 3:55 p.m. on February 15, 1947 when oil gushed from the subterranean depths and sent a perfect cloud of smoke into the winter sky above Leduc No. 1. A long-delayed fantasy—new houses, neighbourhoods, schools, parks, shopping districts, bridges and paved roads—suddenly became affordable. The post-war generation wanted a city that would express its energy and confidence, not a hand-me-down town from a shabbier era. Post-war Edmonton would look nothing like the dusty prairie city it replaced. Everything had to be new.

◆〜

TODAY EDMONTON'S ELEMENTARY SCHOOL CHILDREN explore Internet sites about the Leduc oil strike or visit the Leduc No. 1 Interpretive Centre on the southern edge of the city. With knowledgeable grandparents looking over their shoulders, they draw careful diagrams of the Devonian oil reefs. They know their pump jacks from their oil derricks; and they understand that a barrel is the oil industry's standard unit of measurement. A few can recite the names of the familiar heroes in the Alberta legend: Vern Hunter of Imperial Oil, the driller who endured 133 consecutive failures before his lucky day on Mike and Pearl Turta's farm; Ben Owre, the driver who brought the drilling rig through the mud on a workhorse truck they called Big Bertha; George McClintock, the head geologist, who first noticed the porosity in the samples, and gave the final order to set the fire to the flare line; John Funk, the crew's youngest worker, who found a rag in the diesel house, soaked it in fuel, tied it around a rock with binder twine, then threw the torch "and ran like hell."[4]

This is the creation story of the new city. It is an exciting tale, worthy of retelling, but the early discovery and extraction of the oil and gas wealth in the territory around Edmonton depended on hundreds of thousands of hard-working people. They had names and stories, too.

"The discovery opened the door to potential treasure beyond anyone's wildest imagination,"[5] writes Bea Hunter, Vern's widow, who interviewed early oilpatch workers for her oral history, Last Chance Well. Jobs flowed faster than oil. Through 150 rainy spring days in 1950, 1,500 workers with welding equipment and backhoes built the Interprovincial Pipe Line in an 1,800-kilometre line from Edmonton to Superior, Wisconsin. Survey crews and labourers built the TransMountain Pipe Line from Edmonton to Jasper and over the Rockies to Burnaby, B.C. in 21 months. Labourers and truckers dismantled the old Imperial refinery in Whitehorse, Yukon and brought it down the Alaska Highway in pieces so it could be rebuilt as the first refinery in Edmonton's old Clover Bar district. Local construction workers built two refineries in the next three years and then built petrochemical plants. More than 1,000 people found jobs at the first plant, Canadian Chemical Co., later Celanese Canada, while construction crews built new ones.

Edmonton's young men signed up by the hundreds for new jobs in the oilpatch. Rig workers learned quickly that the job was dirty, exhausting and dangerous. They worked without hard hats, protective eyewear or flame-retardant clothing at a time when training and safety regulations were minimal.

"Everyone wanted to get into the act," recalled Doug Gibbs, an Edmonton safety inspector, "so you had inexperienced men working with very powerful machinery, often under high pressure, extreme weather conditions and at considerable heights."[6] Fifteen rig hands died on the job in Alberta in 1955 and severe injuries were common.

Edmonton learned its first lesson in the ecological cost of a barely-regulated industry when Atlantic Oil took shortcuts in its drilling exploration. The Atlantic No. 3 blowout spewed oil over the surrounding countryside and ignited a firestorm that cast an orange glow over the city's southern horizon. The infamous blowout resulted in tougher regulations on exploration and extraction methods, but city residents could taste oil in their drinking water for months. It would be years before they questioned the petrochemical industries' air emissions. In the early days, they called it the smell of money.

A roughneck could earn 90 cents an hour in the first oilfields around Edmonton and $1.10 an hour after the raise in 1949. In post-war Alberta this was a miracle wage. The majority of oilpatch workers expressed little interest in collective bargaining or union membership. "They'd found a gold egg down here and they weren't going to allow any union representative to spoil it,"[7] remembered Neil Reimer, who came to Edmonton in the early 1950s as Canadian director of the Oil, Chemical and Atomic Workers Union. To this day Reimer contends that the Social Credit government had an understanding with the American companies that their heavy investment would be rewarded with a union-free environment. A small group of oil well drillers at Leduc tried to organize a union local in 1948. Before the vote was taken, Reimer says, Imperial Oil transferred half the drillers to the Northwest Territories, half to northern B.C., and hired a new crew which voted against the union. When Reimer attempted to organize Edmonton refinery workers in the early 1950s, he says company representatives stood outside meetings, jotting down the names of people who attended. "It was illegal, but who was going to stop them?"[8] Reimer said oil workers who did express an interest in organizing a union local quickly encountered the brick wall of Alberta's labour legislation. Oil companies set up company associations to handle grievances. In the end the energy industry kept the unions out of the Alberta oilpatch, with the exception of some refinery workers in Edmonton and Lloydminster.

It was a confining decade for women with ambitions to be geologists or technologists in the new industry. Only two female geologists graduated from the University of Alberta in 1948. "I was ecstatic when I was offered a job with Great Plains Oil and Gas Company," Jean McLaws recalled. "A few days later my joy turned to devastation. A company representative informed me they had changed their minds."[9] Women did find good jobs in the clerical ranks of the energy industry, thanks to the trailblazing efforts of Edmonton's Mary Dawe who in 1948 successfully challenged Imperial Oil's rule that married women had to resign. In the 1950s Edmonton women contended with the social expectation that they quit their jobs to raise a family; some welcomed the unwritten rule, others tolerated it, and a few challenged it. The University of Alberta did not produce a single female geology graduate in 1958, and few interested women found promising positions outside the clerical sector until the 1970s.

Thousands of Edmonton women worked in the oilpatch, however, and supported the industry with their labour. Moving every few months, they created homes out of skid shacks, the small cabins that could be moved on a truck. They transformed rough camps in the muck into communities. "Trying to keep things halfway civilized and the babies quiet, so husbands on night shift could sleep, was quite a challenge," remembered Dorothy Morris, who lived in the Imperial Oil camp at Leduc. "A few had battery radios, but there was no TV, no electricity, no running water, no heat other than the cookstove."[10] Young women washed diapers on scrubbing boards and watched them freeze solid on clotheslines; they hauled water for cooking and bathing; and sometimes they had to thumb their noses at the snobbery of disapproving townspeople. They fed the men who searched for oil and they helped one another's families when their husbands were away. Like the countrywomen in Edmonton's fur trade a century earlier, they contributed their sweat and optimism to a multi-million dollar industry and to an expanding Alberta economy.

Catherine Cavanaugh has investigated the impact of western Canada's rapid economic development on women and children over time. She and other historians contradict the widely-held notion of steady social progress in *Telling Tales: Essays in Western Women's History*. The truth is more complicated, says Cavanaugh, because economic expansion sometimes affected men and women differently. "For example, the boom-and-bust economic cycles associated with resource-dependent western economies created unstable and transient communities," she suggests. "The instability and disorder of 'bonanza frontiers' increased women's domestic responsibilities, particularly when they were forced to relocate or to re-establish the family home." She cautions contemporary readers to look beyond the uniform heroic myths of western Canadian history: "Changing who tells the story can change the tale itself and, with it, the whole way the world is seen."[11] Historian Nanci Langford adds that few accounts of Alberta's history give adequate credit to the women who volunteered their labour to improve hospitals, schools and community services at a time when their political and economic priorities were often ignored or marginalized.[12]

Many community workers improved the quality of life in post-war Edmonton, usually without pay. Winnifred Stewart insisted on better education for handicapped children; Arlene Meldrum organized skating lessons for children across the city; Joyce Buchwald baked homemade bread for school children and started community kitchens in poorer neighbourhoods; Georgina Donald helped aboriginal newcomers get settled in the city; Tiger Goldstick and Gordon Russell introduced thousands of kids to athletics; Bing Mah worked on behalf of Chinese immigrants; and Henry Shimizu advocated for Japanese-Canadians who sought redress for wartime losses. Thousands of other volunteers quietly shaped the character of a growing city with a renewed emphasis on equal opportunity and human decency. Sometimes their contributions were taken for granted.

The oil boom of the early 1950s brought a new wave of post-war European immigrants and young job-seekers from every corner of Canada. Families searched for homes in new satellite communities such as Devon, Sherwood Park and West Jasper Place. The city's population almost doubled in the decade after 1948 to 252,000. Edmonton had plenty of land, if not houses, for the newcomers. The city had repossessed entire subdivisions after the crash of 1913 and hundreds of small houses during the Depression for unpaid taxes. It owned half the empty lots after the Second World War and could develop them in an orderly way.

An inventive Englishman, Noel Dant, arrived as the first full-time city planner in 1949, bringing fresh proposals that blended well with an older local tradition. Edmonton had been the first city in Canada to develop community leagues: a network of neighbourhood volunteers that built hockey rinks, meeting halls and playgrounds and organized inexpensive recreational activities after 1917. In response, Dant and his staff designed a new kind of neighbourhood—built around a park or playing field, beside an elementary school—with family homes and low-rise apartments forming a protective circle around the green space. Heavy traffic was kept out. Community leagues, in turn, built small halls beside these parks for neighbourhood gatherings and indoor recreation. In 1951, Parkallen became the first planned neighbourhood. The enduring pattern still lures residents to the city's early post-war neighbourhoods. Today Edmonton, with its 460 parks, has more green space than any other city in Canada.

The city's architects were eager to prove their talent after the Leduc strike. The University of Alberta had a School of Architecture between 1914 and 1940, but its graduates found few creative opportunities until the first oil boom. They worked beside young immigrant architects from Britain, Belgium, Holland and Germany to introduce the modern movement to the urban landscape. The city gave architects Jean Wallbridge and Mary Imrie a three-month leave to complete a study tour of post-war reconstruction and community planning in Europe and the team returned to build some of Edmonton's first walk-up apartment buildings. Immigrants remember these small apartment blocks as their first homes in Edmonton. Other architects created new recreation centres, a hospital, churches and synagogues, an expansion to the university, a planetarium and the first downtown office towers and commercial buildings. Edmonton's citizens were never shy about expressing opinions about unfamiliar architectural styles. They loved the glamorous Paramount Theatre built in the International Style on Jasper Avenue in 1952 and the first shopping mall, Westmount, which welcomed huge crowds three years later. They loathed the 300-room addition stuck like a barnacle to the Hotel Macdonald. The ugly, grey box was eventually removed.

The oil boom quickly became a real estate boom. Young developers became millionaires because they supplied a treasure more valuable to families than all the black gold in Alberta: an affordable home. Sandy Mactaggart and Jean de La Bruyere were roommates at the Harvard Business School who combined the first three letters of each of their surnames to invent a company name, and then looked around for the best place to make money. Alberta's oil boom beckoned. Maclab Construction Company built 44 houses in Dovercourt in 1954 and lost $393.91 in its first year of operation; by 2004 Maclab Enterprises was the largest privately held residential rental property holder in Alberta and a major developer in an industry with many similar success stories. In the early 1950s, William Hawrelak, the young man of Prairie Rose Manufacturing, was turning his soft drinks profits into real estate holdings and his firm handshake into votes.

"THE TIME IS NOT FAR AWAY when no Edmontonian will remember the glory of Bill's finest moments, nor the tragedy of his worst,"[13] concluded Diane King Stuemer in Hawrelak, her detailed, if partisan, biography of her grandfather. Perhaps it has already happened. Mention the word Hawrelak today to any city dweller under the age of 55 and you will receive helpful directions to a beautiful city park. Ask anyone older and be prepared to listen to an impassioned argument.

Bill Hawrelak was either the finest mayor Edmonton ever had or the worst scoundrel ever kicked out of office twice. He was either a man of the people, a true populist, a generous and decent man or he was a corrupt demagogue who used his position to get rich and allowed goons to intimidate his opponents. He was either the proud son of Ukrainian homesteaders, standing up to the affluent Anglo-Saxon business elite on behalf of Edmonton's new immigrants and the working class or he was a canny politician who exploited class and ethnic tensions in the city to promote his interminable political career. Those who remember the man are never neutral.

"Fan or foe, both sides are partly right," concludes Olive Elliott, the retired *Edmonton Journal* city hall columnist who observed the city's most controversial mayor through his later political reincarnations. "He had the ambition, energy and ability to become a wealthy businessman and an effective mayor," she suggests, but he approached politics like a nineteenth century American party boss, and "he never understood that serving his own interests didn't necessarily serve the city's interests."[14]

Behind the curtain of open democracy in Edmonton, small cliques recruited candidates and financed their campaigns through much of the twentieth century. There were no political parties at the local level, only influential committees behind the scenes. In the 1920s and 1930s, informal coalitions of socialists and union leaders had succeeded in electing several left-leaning mayors and councillors who appealed to the political views of lower-income citizens, trades workers, and the first wave of European immigrants. A coalition of business and financial leaders—most often known as the Citizen's Committee—challenged the labour groups for political supremacy as the Depression ended. Between 1934 and 1960, the Citizen's Committee slate produced 87.5 per cent of the successful candidates for city council. After the Second World War a new wave of more conservative European immigrants and an influx of rural and southern Albertans tipped the political balance. The anti-communist hysteria led by Senator Joseph McCarthy in the United States, and nurtured by Alberta's Social Credit government, did not help Edmonton's labour candidates. Voters preferred candidates who combined progressive social views with business smarts—the perfect example was a socialist businessman like Elmer Roper—or they shifted their allegiance to the pro-business slates. Between 1945 and 1959 every city councillor had the Citizen's Committee prior stamp of approval.

Bill Hawrelak was one of them. With vast appeal among the city's newcomers, he entered politics as a Citizen's Committee candidate for city council in 1949 and entered his first race for mayor in 1951. For the rest of the decade, the mayor found a way to put his own supporters on the committee. City council's self-appointed watchdog, Ed Leger, began to suspect a conflict of interest in the mayor's profitable and continuing land deals. Nipping at Hawrelak's heels for years, he sniffed the trail of every real estate transaction and eventually succeeded in his demand for a judicial inquiry into the mayor's wrongdoing. Justice M.M. Porter confirmed that Hawrelak tried to influence the rezoning of land he owned for personal gain and cited evidence of "gross misconduct." Pleading his innocence, the mayor resigned in 1959.

Disgrace did not mean discomfort. By 1960 the Hawrelak family had moved from the post-war bungalow in Mill Creek to a larger house in Windsor Park. The mayor's share of Prairie Rose Manufacturing was worth $125,000; his real estate development company, Metropolitan Investments, had $400,000 worth of land and buildings and $200,000 in bank loans; and he had $60,000 in the bank. As for his political career, Bill would bounce back.

·~

IN THE EXHILARATING DECADE after the discovery of oil, people in Edmonton sometimes forgot they also owed their increasing prosperity to the slow, steady growth of Alberta's civil service and its relatively high wages. Safety inspectors and stenographers in the provincial capital may not have had the mystique of roughnecks and toolpushers in Alberta's oilpatch, but their hard work and their pay cheques built the local economy, too.

Another spark to the city's growth was the post-war baby boom. No one knew that better than a hard-working educator named Ross Sheppard. An Olympic athlete and brilliant scholar in his youth, Sheppard was the capable superintendent of Edmonton's public schools at the end of the war. As early as 1946, Sheppard warned school trustees about the migration of families from the city's core to the suburbs and the need to prepare for an influx of children in all neighbourhoods. Sheppard worked nights and weekends to oversee school construction through an exhausting decade. As architects and construction crews worked overtime to build new schools, children studied in hallways, school basements, gym stages, church basements and rough, portable classrooms nicknamed "chicken coops." Under Sheppard's leadership, the number of public schools doubled and enrolment increased by 1,000 children a year.

Both Edmonton Public Schools and Edmonton Catholic Schools struggled to keep pace. The city was welcoming new families, many with four or five children. Alberta's fertility rate was higher than the national average. The situation at Donnan Elementary School was typical of a city-wide emergency. The school opened in 1949 with 12 rooms. By 1955, it had a 10-room addition, six portable classrooms, and ran 10 Grade 1 classes in double shifts. At McKernan School some classes ran in triple shifts.

Schools also coped with a critical shortage of teachers. Edmonton had always insisted the new teachers have a minimum of three years experience in other districts before working in the city. In 1947, for the first time in the city's history, the school superintendent requested permission to hire inexperienced teachers. One obvious problem was that Edmonton's female teachers were quitting to have their own babies and the number of teachers with university degrees declined steadily in the 1950s.

When Edmonton's baby-boomers entered adolescence, construction crews began to build some of Canada's largest composite high schools. Enrolment at the University of Alberta tripled in the 1960s and the modern campus took shape. New post-secondary institutions also met the growing demand for higher education: the Northern Alberta Institute of Technology enrolled its first students in 1962, followed by Grant MacEwan Community College in 1971.

"The large youth population and the affluence of the times created a climate that was particularly suitable for an assertion by the young of their own values and attitudes," observed historian Doug Owram in his analysis of the phenomenon that swept across North America.[15] This clash of values shocked a small, conservative city that was still recovering from the social divisions of the Hawrelak years.

◆◆～◆

WILLIAM HAWRELAK RETURNED from his comfortable purgatory to run for office again in 1963.

The mayoralty race was the dirtiest, most violent and most divisive political campaign in Edmonton's history. Stan Milner, the oil company executive and city councillor who was Hawrelak's main opponent, confirms he carried a gun for self-protection on the advice of the city's police chief and sent his family out of town after receiving death threats. Milner challenged his opponent privately about the threats to his children, and the trouble stopped.[16] For their part, the Hawrelaks reported a shotgun blast that shattered the front window and similar telephone threats to their children from unknown sources. On the night before the election, in a raucous election meeting at Alberta Avenue Community League Hall, all candidates faced 600 hollering citizens, with another 100 yelling through the windows. The crowd shouted down Hawrelak's opponents. Milner believed some men at the back of the hall had locked the doors, and on the advice of a police officer, he made his exit out a back window. The next day Bill Hawrelak won his eighth term as mayor.

The city was bitterly divided, partly along ethnic and class lines. Residents with Ukrainian and Polish family backgrounds—roughly 15 per cent of the city's population at the time—resented what they saw as the establishment's exaggerated attack on the integrity of the mayor. When three University of Alberta lecturers attempted to disrupt a council meeting, Hawrelak called the police and ordered them arrested. University students marched to City Hall in a peaceful protest. An angry crowd of 500 waited for them downtown. One student was punched while others were shoved, kicked and spat upon and heckled as "Cubans," "communists" "fascists" and "university punks."[17] Police cleared Winston Churchill Square to protect the young people.

Mayor Hawrelak began another descent on his roller coaster. In 1965 Alberta Chief Justice C.C. Laurin disqualified him from holding office and declared the mayor's chair vacant after finding another conflict of interest on a land deal. Hawrelak lost one subsequent election and returned to his life as a wealthy businessman. By his own calculation his net worth doubled between 1958 and 1968; it doubled again before 1973. Returning to politics on a whim, he soared to the sky again in 1974 when he defeated Ivor Dent in one last race for the mayor's office. Not only did Hawrelak take every poll in Ukrainian-Canadian neighbourhoods, he won almost every poll in the city by a wide margin. He died in office the following year. More than 10,000 mourners paid their respects at City Hall before the funeral, and thousands of citizens lined the streets to wave goodbye to the funeral cortege. Why had they forgiven him so often? Perhaps Bill Hawrelak personified Edmonton's ambitions in the whirlwind decades after the oil strike. He was one more self-made millionaire in a rags-to-riches town.

⁓

FAR AWAY FROM MINOR POLITICAL CONTROVERSIES in a northern Canadian city, Sheik Ahmed Zaki Yamani led the Organization of Petroleum Exporting Countries toward a momentous decision in 1973. The oil cartel quadrupled oil prices to $11.16 a barrel in one year. In a series of aftershocks prices rose as high as $32.50 U.S. a barrel by 1979.[18] Consumers and international governments called it an energy crisis. In Edmonton, the second oil boom began.

Young Canadians from recession-torn provinces; immigrants from every corner of the world; aboriginal families from isolated reserves all arrived in the city in a new influx through the 1970s and early 1980s. While Ottawa and Alberta wrestled over the rights to oil wealth, these newcomers began their own quest for a microscopic piece of the action. They were mostly young and like their predecessors who came to Edmonton after the Leduc strike in 1947, they were barely aware of the city's history or traditions when they arrived.

These young migrants quickly learned that it was easier to find a job than an apartment. Edmontonians measured the vacancy rate in decimal points through the 1970s and early 1980s and the city swallowed some of Alberta's richest farmland to accommodate the new arrivals. In an innovative response to the population influx, the city assembled 18 square kilometres of woods and farmland beyond Edmonton's southeast boundary in 1970. The development of Mill Woods was the largest publicly sponsored land assembly ever undertaken in North America. More than 83,000 people eventually moved into the new area and a large proportion were recent immigrants to Canada from India, Pakistan, China and Vietnam, and Central and South America.

Citizens who had lived in the city for a longer time took a new approach to the second oil boom in their lifetime. They were living with the consequences of Edmonton's earlier decisions and they began fierce debates about how to manage this second wave of prosperity.

Their first battle was over freeways. By 1970, Edmonton was surrounded on all sides by relatively large, confident and independent communities, some on their way to city status: St. Albert, Sherwood Park, Spruce Grove, Stony Plain, Leduc and Fort Saskatchewan. Every morning their citizens joined commuters from Edmonton's suburban neighbourhoods on narrow roads to the city's downtown core. When the city administration decided to build five major freeways through the wooded ravines, and six new bridges across the North Saskatchewan River, community protest groups and many individual citizens challenged what they saw as a destructive and expensive plan. To their surprise, they succeeded in their public battle, although the freeway plan collapsed as much because of its expense as its potential to ruin the landscape.

Across North America, through a period of intense social upheaval, haphazard freeway construction became a symbol of haphazard urban growth. In Edmonton, the controversy over the MacKinnon Ravine freeway mobilized many people to question the city's often distant and autocratic decisions on other matters. Citizens demanded more public transit. People in Rossdale, Riverdale and Cloverdale fought the city's plan to flatten their historic neighbourhoods. Like the citizens who defended Old Strathcona, they eventually succeeded in preserving their communities. Some neighbourhoods demanded a stronger voice in city planning; others organized new social services to alleviate the urban poverty. Political leaders like Harold Cardinal, Stan Daniels and Eugene Steinhauer, and community leaders like Chester Cunningham, Jenny Margetts, Muriel Stanley-Venne and Ralph Bouvette demanded a new deal for Edmonton's growing aboriginal population and more respect for indigenous language and culture. Nellie Carlson remembers her sense of accomplishment when a small group of Edmonton women helped to win treaty rights for tens of thousands of aboriginal Canadians: "We must have been strong to put up with that hassle. You know what? I'm not going to say I'm proud. I will just say I'm thankful that we were blessed with the energy that we used to correct this mess."[19]

If people in Edmonton welcomed "the smell of money" after Leduc No. 1, this time their children sniffed the air and demanded stronger emissions standards in the petrochemical industry and a cleaner river. While grateful for the city's economic growth, many people asked why Edmonton's heritage buildings had to collapse like dominoes to make way for sterile Jasper Avenue skyscrapers. What about the city's character? What about its soul? Over their objections the well-loved Tegler Building crumbled to the ground as Edmonton's old-time town crier, Pete Jamieson, lamented into his megaphone: "Thar she blows!"[20]

Voters began to demand more open government at City Hall, more public hearings and fewer private decisions. Returning to Edmonton's earlier political tradition, they elected councillors on new slates like URGE, the Urban Reform Group of Edmonton, and EVA, the labour-oriented Edmonton Voters Association. For a time community-minded councillors like Bettie Hewes and Una MacLean Evans challenged the perspectives of business interests that had dominated Edmonton's public life for two decades.

Looking back on the city's decisions in the 1970s, two former mayors take opposite positions on their consequences. Cec Purves points to enduring transportation problems in the absence of freeways; the residential enclaves in the river valley that should have been preserved as parks for everyone; and the growth of expensive city social services that did not relieve urban poverty, but did employ the middle class.[21] Jan Reimer lists the achievements of the period and their lasting impact: more responsive city planning and open government; the development of the Light Rapid Transit system; river valley trails; the Safer Cities initiative to improve the quality of life; and a new environmental consciousness that led to the city's significant recycling and waste management reforms and a cleaner river.[22]

Watching the vigorous debates at City Hall in the late 1970s and taking the measure of them were the Ghermezian brothers. The sons of Iranian immigrants, Eskander, Raphael, Nader and Bahman Ghermezian had been acquiring land on the city's western edge for a project beyond the scope of Edmonton's imagination. They were planning the Eighth Wonder of the World, right here in river city, and they could cite their great expectations faster than a city councillor could blink.

The Ghermezians wanted city council to rezone a large parcel of land on Edmonton's western boundary. They wanted high-speed detours around planning rules; tax concessions; more land; more tax concessions. They practised their political lobbying until they were the world-class masters in the art of pleading, pleasing and cajoling. In 1974 a city councillor named Alex Fallow called police and reported that he has been offered a $40,000 bribe during a meeting with Raphael Ghermezian. After an exhaustive judicial inquiry, Justice William Morrow concluded that city councillors had not requested, or accepted, bribes although some had been close to the line of impropriety in their relationships with the developers. Tantalized by the promises of world-class tourism and heavy employment, the city eventually agreed to the Ghermezians' requests. Within a decade, people in Edmonton could go anywhere in North America—and many places in the world—and hear the same excited question: "Don't you have that big mall up there?"

Big, it was. Sometimes West Edmonton Mall seemed bigger than the city itself.

From the beginning West Edmonton Mall attracted international tourists and startled debate among Canada's architects and city planners about the evolution of urban space in a materialist culture. Commercial enterprises and their customers began another exodus from the city's downtown core; homebuyers followed them to the new suburban housing developments in the city's southwest corner. West Edmonton Mall eventually employed 23,500 people directly and thousands more indirectly in the local hospitality, tourism and construction industries. The mall put an overwhelming commercial stamp on Edmonton's urban identity. With a reputation as a shoppers' paradise, the city became a testing ground for North American retailers who built some of the first and largest big-box stores in Edmonton and huge retail parks on acres of asphalt parking lots. Thousands of visitors came only to shop in Edmonton. The local reaction to the phenomenon was definitely mixed. People in Edmonton loved or hated Canada's largest mall and its concrete offspring, but they soon learned to live with the galumphing elephants in their midst.

Huge shopping malls were the consequence of rapid suburban growth in post-war Edmonton, not the cause of it. More than half of Edmonton's residents lived in suburban neighbourhoods. Long before the Ghermezians arrived in town, Edmontonians had embraced Westmount Shopping Park, one of Canada's first prototype shopping malls, and Southgate Mall, the largest mall west of Toronto when it opened in 1970. The city redesigned itself to serve drivers and their cars, not pedestrians or bus passengers. Public transit did not keep up with suburban growth. Suburban residents became impatient with Edmonton's limited public transit to their neighbourhoods, not to mention winter waits at outdoor bus stops. They preferred to drive across a wide city to indoor shopping malls where they could park for free.

In a city where January can bring wind-chill temperature of -45°C, all residents embraced the warmth of indoor gathering places. Most people accepted without question that this meeting space would be privately owned as a commercial endeavour—not that they had much choice. They enjoyed Saturday excursions to the Strathcona Farmers Market and the boutiques and nightclubs on the restored Whyte Avenue, but the majority of downtown office workers evacuated the city centre at the end of the working day. They spent their money in their own neighbourhoods. For a time Edmonton's suburban malls became the new Jasper Avenue, the new Market Square.

EDMONTON CONTENDED WITH A DOUBLE WALLOP to the provincial economy in the early 1980s.

In 1980 the Liberal government in Ottawa began its doomed experiment with the National Energy Policy. The stated purpose was to regulate oil prices, restrict exports, raise corporate taxes and redirect development to the Arctic for the benefit of Canadian consumers. The unstated purpose was to transfer a larger portion of Alberta's resource wealth to the federal treasury in Ottawa through taxation; and to focus exploration in the Northwest Territories, a region under federal control, in order to funnel more resource wealth to the federal government. The policy had vast public support in many parts of the country; in Alberta, it was loathed. Across Alberta, the giants in the oil and gas industry drastically cut production; small companies went bankrupt and mass layoffs and unemployment sparked a wave of political fury against Pierre Trudeau's government that has dogged the Liberals ever since. "It was a nightmare," remembers Stan Milner, then president of Chieftain Development, a home-grown oil company. "All projects came to a grinding halt."[23] Premier Peter Lougheed began tug-of-war negotiations with Ottawa with firm support from Albertans and the clout of the multinational giants behind him. By 1985, a new Conservative government in Ottawa and four western provinces had negotiated a new deal: the National Energy Policy was dismantled and free trade in national and export markets was restored.

Edmonton's economy had no time to recover before the international energy sector delivered the second punch. In 1986 OPEC's unity disintegrated and oil prices plunged.[24] More than 50,000 jobs disappeared in a province still reeling from an earlier setback. By April 1987, the provincial unemployment rate stood at 11.1 per cent and Edmonton had more people out of work than all of Alberta had seen in 1980. Concerned citizens had invented the Edmonton Food Bank by then—the first in Canada.[25] Volunteers fed 16,900 people that month and reported that one in five children in the city relied on groceries from the food bank.

"In my opinion, the National Energy Policy was a virus that destroyed our immune system," recalled Milner. "So many companies didn't have the financial strength to go into another period of decreased prices. It was like we had two depressions in a row."[26]

Two for Calgary, perhaps. Edmonton confronted a third unexpected setback. In the early 1990s the energy sector in both cities recovered quickly with Alberta's expansion of natural gas exports and the subsidized development of mega-projects in the oil sands near Fort McMurray, and at the heavy-crude upgrader at Lloydminster. Meanwhile Alberta poured millions of dollars into a series of risky private ventures—hazardous waste treatment, magnesium, telephone technology—and subsidized one collapse after another. In response, a new provincial government led by a Calgarian, Ralph Klein, reduced Alberta's substantial public debt with deep cuts to public spending over four years. People across Alberta lost valuable public services and good jobs in a whirlwind of political fervour, but the capital city and its public sector employees paid the greatest price. Pointing to Calgary's growing political influence, Jan Reimer, the mayor of Edmonton at the time, suggested that her city was punished out of proportion because its voters had elected New Democrats and Liberals to the provincial legislature.[27] The Alberta government's budget cuts happened so rapidly, and with so little advance planning, that Edmonton found itself demoralized and defensive and at times very angry. When the new Grey Nuns hospital was threatened with sudden closure in 1994, 15,000 citizens gathered to object in the largest protest demonstration in the city's history.

The Edmonton capital region sometimes underplayed the economic penalty of its internal divisions. Four emerging cities and four heavily-populated counties surrounded Edmonton; more than two dozen local governments were locked in a costly competition. Edmonton had less than 75 per cent of its regional population within its city boundaries; in comparison, Calgary had 90 per cent. In a comparative study in 1997, political scientist Jim Lightbody found that citizens in Edmonton spent roughly 10 per cent more for public services than Calgarians because of this splintered development. "What also seems clear is that Edmonton must spend more because its suburbs spend less," Lightbody observed. "At the same time the suburbs are bleeding away Edmonton's population base."[28]

The city's last four mayors—Cec Purves, the late Laurence Decore, Jan Reimer and Bill Smith—have challenged these arrangements with limited success. Their questions echoed over the decades: Wouldn't all citizens benefit if two dozen municipalities pooled resources with one regional economic plan? Shouldn't satellite communities share the responsibility for tough urban problems and expenses if their residents earn incomes in the city? While their perspectives differed on many other issues, Purves, Reimer and Smith agreed in 2004 that the splintered metropolitan area remained one of Edmonton's greatest challenges. "We have a tremendous opportunity to market ourselves as one region," said Smith. "If we miss that opportunity, it will be a huge loss. My concern is that we'll make huge planning mistakes if we don't work together. We still have so much opportunity here."[29]

Edmonton's neighbours listened to the city's arguments and rejected every annexation bid. Several communities, like St. Albert and Fort Saskatchewan, argued that their decision was necessary to protect their historic identities and character. They pointed out that Edmonton doubled in size between 1960 and 1980—not just in population, but in land—through 20 annexations. Did Edmonton not have enough empty space without another annexation? Satellite communities insisted on friendly boundaries.

Personal connections crossed boundaries, of course. Just as the Métis families of Lac Ste. Anne and St. Albert celebrated Christmas with the Orkney fur traders and Cree families at Fort Edmonton, their successors created a unified community when it counted. The people of Edmonton and their neighbours shared a single heartbeat many times in the postwar period. In an emergency—the polio epidemic of 1953, the tornado of 1987—people grieved together and comforted one another.

Together they celebrated the delirious first victories of the Edmonton Eskimos in the 1950s and the Edmonton Oilers in the 1980s, in a breathless city of champions. They cheered the roof off the old Northlands Coliseum on unforgettable winter nights and huddled under blankets together for football games at Commonwealth Stadium. They volunteered as hosts for the Commonwealth Games, the Universiade, the World Track and Field competition and the Canadian Finals Rodeo. The city's children embraced amateur sports, in part, because they worshipped the gifted athletes in their midst, heroes like Jackie Parker and Wayne Gretzky, as well as local amateur athletes who competed in the Olympics and Commonwealth Games. When a local team won a sports competition, municipal boundaries on the map became invisible. The Stanley Cup and Grey Cup came home to one ecstatic community, not many.

Together Edmontonians and their neighbours stood apart slightly from other Albertans at election time, electing the majority of the Opposition members. Together they argued about Peter Pocklington's treatment of the strikers at the Gainers meat-packing plant in 1986—the most violent and divisive labour dispute in the city's history's—and they lamented Pocklington's sale of Wayne Gretzky to an American franchise.

They took pride in what might be Edmonton's greatest achievement: North America's longest urban park. They walked, cycled, jogged or skied along river valley trails that wound along both sides of the North Saskatchewan River, up and down three major ravines and 19 secondary ravines, for almost 200 kilometres. Conceived by landscape architect Frederick Todd and protected by law since 1915, the river valley park system eventually protected 7,400 hectares of natural landscape for public enjoyment in all seasons. The trails linked ski hills, outdoor skating rinks, picnic areas, public golf courses and playgrounds in a spectacular landscape that remains a wildlife sanctuary, a meeting place and a haven for contemplation. The river tied the communities together.

Edmontonians and their suburban neighbours reinvented the city as a cultural capital of the prairies, an edgy town in love with theatre, books, music, art and design; a place with imagination. They soaked up avant-garde theatre at The Fringe, and late-night improv comedy in Old Strathcona; raced for the best spot on Gallagher Hill at the Edmonton Folk Music Festival; ate together at the Heritage Festival and Taste of Edmonton; and rescued the listener-supported radio station, CKUA. They organized The Works, a visual arts festival; Dreamspeakers, an aboriginal arts festival; the Jazz City festival; the Labatt Blues Festival; the International Children's Festival; a freezing-but-fun First Night Festival. They never abandoned old Klondike Days even though Henry Singer once said it was as exciting as a Saturday night bath.

Other Canadians may have suspected the city owed its returning affluence and confidence to yet another resource windfall in the late 1990s, but people in Edmonton were as likely to cite individual accomplishments in the arts, sciences and technology. When local publisher Mel Hurtig and editor James Marsh gave the *Canadian Encyclopaedia* to Canadians; when Anne Wheeler or Tom Radford captured the community's eclectic character on film; when Dr. Ray Rajotte and a team of medical researchers at the University of Alberta produced a breakthrough treatment for diabetes; when ecologist David Schindler won global recognition for ground-breaking scholarship on water quality; when writers like Rudy Wiebe, Greg Hollingshead, Ted Blodgett and Gloria Sawai won the Governor-General's Award for Literature, Edmontonians took pleasure in a reflected sense of achievement. They looked in the mirror and liked what they saw—most of the time.

Some people in Edmonton confronted the city's shortcomings in the 1990s and questioned its new certainties. On March 18, 1999, the Edmonton Task Force on Homelessness took a one-day snapshot of a growing social problem. Researchers found 836 homeless people: 313 people with no place at all to live, and 523 people in emergency shelters. Among the homeless were 112 children. In 2002, amid a new wave of unprecedented prosperity, city researchers counted again. This time they found 1,915 homeless people and 65 per cent of them had no shelter at all. The number of homeless children had doubled in two years. The city identified the lack of affordable housing in Edmonton as a much larger problem with severe personal consequences for thousands of citizens. Waiting lists for public housing increased from 300 to 4,300 households between 1997 and 2003; 6,500 low-rent homes were demolished, or transformed into expensive condominiums.

As a new century began, Edmonton confronted the social divisions that afflict every North American city when the affluent and poor live too far apart to encounter one another. At times Edmonton seemed to contain the characteristics of two distinct cities: casual affluence beside deepening poverty; good-natured citizenship beside alienation and racism; artistic ingenuity beside banal materialism. Conscientious citizens asked their own questions. How could people be homeless in a city so blessed? If life was so good here for most of its citizens, why was it not so for more of them? What was the environmental price of new wealth and unchecked urban growth? How could Edmonton maintain a sense of its best self?

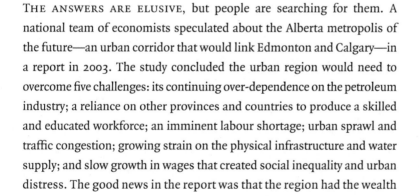

THE ANSWERS ARE ELUSIVE, but people are searching for them. A national team of economists speculated about the Alberta metropolis of the future—an urban corridor that would link Edmonton and Calgary—in a report in 2003. The study concluded the urban region would need to overcome five challenges: its continuing over-dependence on the petroleum industry; a reliance on other provinces and countries to produce a skilled and educated workforce; an imminent labour shortage; urban sprawl and traffic congestion; growing strain on the physical infrastructure and water supply; and slow growth in wages that created social inequality and urban distress. The good news in the report was that the region had the wealth and flexibility to overcome all five challenges, if it could find the collective will. Alberta's urban corridor offered a quality of life that beckoned newcomers and market opportunities and low taxes that appealed to new investors. The urban region had a gross domestic product per capita that was 10 per cent above the U.S. average and a striking 40 per cent above the Canadian average.

Once again Edmonton looked north for its good fortune. Canada's richest petroleum resource, the Athabasca oil sands near Fort McMurray, became the site of new, multi-billion-dollar projects in the development of synthetic crude oil. The economic benefits of oil continued to flow through Edmonton, creating jobs in the energy and construction sectors and financing a $300 million trust fund that supports the Alberta Heritage Foundation for Medical Research. Economist Mike Percy has suggested that Edmonton's future well-being will depend on the success of its efforts to diversify its economic base as Alberta's energy resources decline and the world moves beyond fossil fuels to protect the environment. The city will need a highly-skilled workforce in the information and technology sectors, he said, adding that it is capable of reaching every goal it sets for itself.[30]

◦⌣

EDMONTON'S PROMOTERS HAVE ALWAYS WORKED OVERTIME to capture the city's potential in hyperbolic shorthand. *Gateway to the North. City of Champions.* Each time the city's boosters invent a new catchphrase, its residents roll their eyes and respond with good-natured nicknames of their own: *E-Town. Emminton. The Big Eddy. Redmonton. Deadmonton. Edmonchuk.* Outsiders try to convey the city's character with wacky metaphors. Charles Lynch, a national newspaper columnist, once called it "Baghdad on the North Saskatchewan"; novelist Mordecai Richler described it in the *New Yorker* as "the boiler room of Canada." Edmontonians bristle at outsiders' judgements and talk about the city's undiscovered qualities: the spirit of voluntarism and community; the creative impulse in the arts scene; the streak of political independence; the refuge of the river valley; the shared tradition of athletics; the warmth and comfort of a hometown that looks winter in the eye, and defies it.

The true Edmonton has never been quite as large as its superlative slogans, or as small as its self-deprecating nicknames. It has outgrown a single definition of its character.

Historian Doug Owram suggests that the oil boom of the 1970s transformed the city's character in a fundamental way: "Alberta became a complex urban society in the late post-war period, and in some ways, the politics of the province haven't caught up with that," he said. "As Edmonton's population approaches one million, the city is entering a new metropolitan phase of existence, creating the potential for a much richer culture...and that implies a certain cultural diversity, and a certain pride."[31] The maturing of the community comes at a cost: new environmental and social problems, the disappearance of the small-town atmosphere and the loss of strong family ties with rural Alberta. The benefit is that the city becomes more complicated, more interesting, more connected to the surrounding world.

In 2004 about one million people live in the city and its surrounding urban communities. Almost half of these citizens were born outside Alberta and about 18 per cent were born outside Canada. As with all Canadian cities, the origins of the population have changed markedly. About 45,000 people moved to Edmonton from other countries in the 1990s alone; more than half came from Asia and the Middle East. More people in Edmonton in 2004 were born in the Philippines than in Germany; in Vietnam than in Italy; in Lebanon than in Ukraine. The number of Edmonton's inhabitants born in China and Hong Kong, counted together, is roughly the same as the combined number born in the United Kingdom and the United States. If the ethnic diversity of the immigrant population is one dramatic change, so is the resurgence in Edmonton's aboriginal population—now almost five percent of the city's total, which makes it the second largest urban aboriginal population in Canada, per capita, after Winnipeg. This is due not only to migration from rural reserves and a younger aboriginal population with a higher birth rate, but also the increasing tendency of Edmonton families to identify themselves as aboriginal out of pride in their ancestry.

In 2004 Edmonton's children can clamber up family trees to find the first Cree, Blackfoot, Nakoda and Métis inhabitants of this river valley; French-Canadian voyageurs and Scottish fur traders; Ukrainian homesteaders, Welsh coal miners and Hungarian refugees; ancestors in China, India and Pakistan, Vietnam, the Philippines, or the Sudanese and Somali grandparents who arrived on last night's plane. The city's children can belong to a single extended family that includes any of these people. Their mixed families will shape their understanding of Edmonton, but they live in a global culture, and in an urban landscape of their own invention. What do they have in common with the children who lived here 10,000 years ago, 500 years ago, or a century ago? Perhaps they share only the common imprint of their humanity; the sight of their breath in the air on a cold, winter day and a beautiful river that connects them to one another, and to the children of the distant future.

Who can claim the right to tell the story of this place? Everyone who has ever lived here. Everyone who ever will.

In Our Own Words

LEDUC NO. 1

Vern Hunter, toolpusher

After drilling a series of dry holes in Saskatchewan and earning the name "dry hole" or, affectionately, "salt water" Hunter, we moved the rig (Wilson #2) to Provost, Alberta....

We drilled two wells in Provost, one of which was a short-lived oil producer, the other a fair gas well and then early in October of 1946 Charlie Visser informed us we were to go to Leduc. We were quite happy to move as we were getting itchy feet from staying too long in one town, but fully realized that no oil could possibly be found within 20 miles of a city like Edmonton.

I made a trip up to Leduc where I met Walt Dingle and together we went out to stake the rig site which Walt had already surveyed. Walt drove the stake, and being of little faith, left immediately for South America. A short time later we moved the rig, shacks and trailers, into Leduc and began to settle down in the town park right next to the Curling Rink.

The rig was located on Mike Turta's farm just outside his barnyard. Mike refused to let us go around his yard, for some reason, and I am afraid that with the constant traffic some of his chickens and ducks came to an untimely end. I was always afraid that it would be one of his kids. Walking through his yard was too dangerous, with the ganders snapping at your

On February 12, 1947 the new city of Edmonton was born with the turn of a valve. After drilling 133 dry holes, toolpusher Vern Hunter and a crew of 35 men hit oil on Mike and Pearl Turta's farm near Leduc.

Vern Hunter, centre, with Walker Taylor, right, of Imperial Oil and N.E. Tanner, Alberta's Minister of Mines, on the day of the Leduc oil strike. It was a nerve-wracking day for Hunter: "Shortly before 4 p.m. the well started to show signs of life, greatly to my relief."

heels like the hounddogs after little Eva. However, we had very good relations with the Turtas and were always welcome for a cup of tea or a meal. The whole crew made a point of buying their cream, eggs and chickens and Mike Turta seemed to thoroughly enjoy the company the crew provided.

The weather turned very cold the night we spudded in and "Mousie" McIntyre, who had just been set up as driller, on the graveyard shift, had the misfortune of the stand-pipe and Kelly hose freezing up on his first tour. Mousie was a pretty sorry looking fellow when he brought the reports in that morning. No hole and lots of trouble. I don't imagine he thought it portended a great future for Leduc #1....

Well, we cut a core and on visual examination it didn't look too hot. The porosity was so good that the washing action of the mud had removed all the oil. However, we ran in with the tester, hooked up to the flare line and dropped the dart. Without any hesitation there was action. Air from the empty pipe started to flow, to be followed by gas and mud and then oil, flowing by heads. We lit the flare and all stood around it, grateful for the heat even though we were frying on one side and freezing on the other. After about an hour we shut it in, let the pressure build up for information purposes and then pulled out of the hole, little realizing that this event was changing the whole economy of Western Canada.

Several cores and drillstem tests later, on instructions from Calgary, we called it deep enough and ran casing.

I have forgotten the exact date, probably about February 10, the two Taylor boys—Walker and Vern—told me that a celebration was to be held on the day the well was to be brought in with invitations being sent to the Government and Industry officials. They wanted me to name the day which I did under protest, as so many things can happen when fooling with temperamental oil wells. Another thing that scared me was that the crew, including myself, were experts at abandoning wells, but didn't know too much about completing oil wells. However, I named February 13 and started praying.

Shortly before 4:00 p.m., the well started to show some signs of life, greatly to my relief, as I was having trouble dodging Walker Taylor, [the western production manager]. He was at least as concerned as I was and possibly more so as he had to face the invited guests. Then, with a roar, the well came in, flowing into the sump near the rig. We switched it to the flare line, lit the flare and the most beautiful smoke ring you ever saw went floating skywards. Shortly after that, Campbell Aird turned the production through the separator to the tank, and my day was over. I didn't even go to the reception in Edmonton as bed looked more inviting to me.

If I ever learned a lesson that day it was this: never predict when a well will come in.[32]

John Funk, floorman

How did members of the crew feel that cold Thursday in February 1947? I'd say we were all pretty excited. We knew we'd struck oil, but we hadn't yet brought in an oil well. It was a big event for us.

I was the floorman on the crew that was working the four-to-midnight shift. George Tosh was our driller. When we got to work, we had to park our trucks about a mile down the road and walk to the well site because the roads were clogged with cars. Invitations had been sent to the media and to VIPs in government and the city, but word had also gotten out. By noon that day, crowds of spectators had gathered.

Everything had been made ready the night before. Although the official activities were scheduled to take place about 1 p.m., during the early morning, the line broke, leaving the swab stuck several hundred feet down the hole. The crew was frantically trying to free the swab while the crowds were milling about, stomping their feet, blowing on their hands to keep warm, and getting in the way.

By 4 p.m., crews had fixed the swabbing unit, and the well began to show signs of life. The earth trembled and you could hear it coming. With a roar like a freight train, mud, water, natural gas and oil gushed into the sump pit. After some of the mud and water had run off, the stream was switched to the flare line. My big moment had arrived.

I'd practiced the day before, so I swung the burning, oil-soaked sack around my head and let it fly. Up it soared up to the top of the flare line. Whoosh! Flames and black smoke shot into the air. The well belched a few times as it cleared itself, then a perfect smoke ring formed and floated off in the clear, cold air. People said that was a good omen. Other rings

The Leduc oil field produced 200 million barrels of oil, considerable wealth for the energy companies and the province, and new prosperity for thousands of people in Edmonton. Bea Hunter, Vern's widow, collected the stories of oilpatch workers who participated in the Leduc strike in an excellent anthology called Last Chance Well.

Fern Smith, Dorothy Morris and Rose Desnoyers settled into their skid shacks at the Imperial Oil Ltd. Camp in the Leduc fairgrounds in 1947. "We helped each other with our babies, shared our meagre utensils and got together every other day or so for morning coffee," recalled Morris. "We were like a big family."

on other wells followed over the years but none as perfect as that first one. Then N.E. Tanner, the Minister of Lands and Mines, turned the valve and oil flowed into the storage tank. Leduc No. 1 produced 41 barrels of oil in its first hour of operation.

It was an accident that the company struck oil. We were actually circulating mud to pull out and cement the well in. George McClintock, the well-site geologist, said to George Tosh, the driller, "Aw heck, let's take a chance and drill another five feet." We did and when McClintock pulled a core, oil oozed out of it. "Look at this," he exclaimed, and off he went to Edmonton to show it to the head geologist, Fred Keller.

"Keep quiet about this until Calgary is notified or somebody will get shit," Keller warned. Imperial was tough about doing things without permission. We weren't supposed to drill an inch without their approval. Reports may differ about what really happened all those years ago, but that's how I remember it.[33]

Dorothy Morris, wife of oilfield worker

We were like a bunch of gypsies and the local residents were not pleased to see us. The hotel [in Leduc] said they only accepted decent people. The restaurant wouldn't serve us. I was down to my last can of milk for my baby daughter's formula. The storekeeper said I had to have a doctor's prescription to buy more. Part of the hostility had been caused by the seismic crews—young, single guys who lived like there was no tomorrow. Those of us with trailers or skid shacks were allotted space in the ball park. The others scrambled for what they could find.

Then they struck oil. Yes! There was a lot of excitement among the crew. We had been afraid we'd have to go back fanning if the company didn't find something soon—and we were happy for Vern—he'd drilled so many dry holes. Bud took me out to see the well brought on stream. It was cold and the dignitaries in their city clothes were shivering. I remember Bud heated Denna's bottle in the boiler house.[34]

Dorothy Pickard, city worker

It was early 1947 when oil was discovered in Leduc. I was young and very much in love with the man I later married. We both worked for the City of Edmonton.

When the oil discovery was made in Leduc, close to Edmonton, nearly every truck driver around those parts equipped their trucks with "oil tanks." You see, there were no pipelines then to get the oil to the refineries.

One such truck driver was a fellow named Walter who had worked for the City and knew Ralph. He asked him if he would take his truck to Leduc to get two fill-ups of oil per night and truck it to Edmonton. I went along for the ride, of course, and what an experience to be in on the ground floor of the big discovery!! We'd take Walter's truck around 5 p.m. after work, go to Leduc and line up at the wellhead.

As I recall, the wellhead was a little east of the town of Leduc. There was always a line-up at the wellhead. We'd wait our turn, talking with the other truckers, eat our lunch etc., load up, then leave for Edmonton....

Little did Ralph and I know, back in 1947, that we would become one of those "oil patch couples." We came after the original oil riggers and drillers and we were the pipelines who worked jobs as they became available.[35]

Andrew Turta, farmer's son at the Leduc oil site

We were pleased about the discovery but when you don't have the mineral rights it doesn't mean that much. Stories have been told and printed stating that after the discovery my father drove to Calmar with a sleigh to pick up a load of beer for the crew. That's not true, nor is it true that he stood at his gate and collected 25 cents from everyone who came to see the well. My father was a proud, but friendly man who liked people. He would never have done that—more likely he would have welcomed them.

After oil was discovered a lawyer came to see my dad and explain that, since my parents had signed the surface lease in the presence of each other,

Ben Owre and his famous truck, Big Bertha, hauled skid shacks and oilfield equipment to local camps; this granary became a temporary home for the Desnoyers family. "Our wives coped with babies, washing on a scrubbing board, cooking on a woodstove, a husband on shift work and moving every three or four months," recalled Ben. "It was a rough life, but in those days we were thankful to have a job."

Workers at Leduc No. 1 collect souvenir samples after the dignitaries have gone home.

it was not valid. A new contract was drawn up, which increased the payment to $3,000 and they were paid $500 annually for the surface rights.

My grandfather, whose farm was two miles west, owned the mineral rights on his place [because he was a homesteader]. At least he thought he did, but the Canadian Pacific Railway claimed them.

An Edmonton lawyer, George Steer, represented my grandfather and after a long legal battle, which lasted from 1949 to 1954, they won the case. In the meantime oil had been discovered on grandfather's farm—eight producers in all, and he collected 12 per cent royalty, which he gave to his children and grandchildren. Less than one quarter of the local farmers had mineral rights. If you had them you were lucky. That's all there was to it.[36]

ATLANTIC NO. 3

Andrew Turta

Atlantic No. 3, the famous well that blew wild for six months, was located one mile straight east of Leduc No. 1 on the Rebus farm. If the wind was blowing our way my mother's washing would be speckled with oil. On Sept. 6, 1948, my dad and I were cutting grain when we saw Atlantic No. 3 catch fire. At night you could see the glow in the sky in Edmonton, 20 miles away. About three days after it caught fire it was brought under control, leaving an incredible mess to clean up. The rig and the draw works had fallen into the giant crater—it's still down there somewhere. Reclaiming the land meant removing all the oil-soaked earth and replacing it with fresh top soil. For years they planted alfalfa to refresh the soil. The land is only now getting back to the way it was.[37]

EDMONTON'S OILPATCH KIDS

Karen Bower

When you are five years old bed time comes early, whether you like it or not. When I was five I remember being put to bed one day for a very long afternoon nap. The evening was to be special, because Mom, Dad, and I were doing something unheard of, going for a drive after dark.

I don't remember what I was told would happen, but I knew it had to be special for me to be allowed to stay up so late. The sun had long since gone when we piled into the car and drove for what seemed like hours. Today I know the distance was less than five miles. We stopped on a height of land with a clear view of the western sky. Today that spot is at 75th Street and 45th Avenue overlooking the far northern edges of the Mill Woods area of Edmonton. That spot is nowhere near the "country," which was where we felt we were.

The entire southwestern sky was alight with a pulsing orange-red glow. The horizon was dotted with dozens of fires, all of them flares from the Leduc oilfield. I had no idea what an oil well was, but what the flares did to the sky was mesmerizing to my young eyes. I remember Dad saying this was going to create huge changes in the world we knew. I had no idea what that meant, but anything that could make the night sky dance had to be exciting.

He was right about the magnitude of change and I was to feel the impact too. We moved to Leduc in the summer of 1949. We went from living in the city of Edmonton, close to my grandparents, with tree shaded streets and paved roads, to a town that ended almost before it began and streets of nothing but mud.[38]

Ian Archibald

Coming to Edmonton in 1950 was a dramatic but not a too traumatic change. Dad was working further and further north during that period and with the travel conditions this meant more long-change time wasted traveling to and from the well site. So we were to move north to a place I had

City people drove to the edge of Edmonton to stare at the orange glow in the night sky, the sign of prosperity on its way. Elsie Garstad-Rosenau collected these memorable stories in an oral history of the period, *Oil Patch: Recollections of the Way Things Were.*

never heard of, having just completed Grade I. I remember asking an older neighbor kid about Edmonton and he gave me a typical 10 year old's line of BS, not knowing a thing about which he spoke.

It was not really like moving into a city when we moved to the far west end of Edmonton just north of McKinnon Ravine. Consequently the move was easy: new friends, new surroundings, new and more varied things to do while still being close to the countryside.

Never mind the fuzzy reception and the awkward bunny-ears antenna. Tune into Edmonton's first television broadcast on CFRN in October 1954. Stay tuned for early local productions, such as Don Brinton on the kids on Kiddies' Korner in 1958.

The intent of the move was to allow Dad to spend more time at home. In those days they worked six weeks in the bush and had 12 days out. The drilling contracting companies would send their crews in for the entire winter, from freeze up until the road bans were off in the spring!.... For Mom and Dad it meant weeks of loneliness and longing with no supporting mate. Then a hectic reunion followed by a review of the activities of the kids and homey issues of the last 6 weeks.

One thing that an oil patch kid learns very early in life is the complete absurdity of the phrase "Wait 'til your father gets home!" I never heard of a father who wants to lay a lickin' on a youngster for teasing his or her sibling for some vaguely recalled incident after an absence of about five weeks. However, the count-down to Dad's return was always filled with mixed emotions. It was nice to have this semi-stranger around but he had trouble remembering that he wasn't on the job at home too. I would be given an assignment of jobs as if I were a floor hand, and I should add, without floor hand pay.

The lifestyle did have a profound effect on the family. This is not a whimper, just a statement that there must certainly be some mostly negative consequences of continual, periodic absences of the father from the otherwise traditional family unit of the forties and fifties. My Mother became increasingly affected by Dad's absence, perhaps as most mothers were. The kids had their friends and school to keep them busy; they got by. As a teenager it became apparent to me that my parents were having more and more difficulty relating to each other because of the continual physical distances between them.[39]

Satchmo ⌐ **John Stefanyk**

Through the hardest years of the 1930s and a stint as a wartime entertainer, John Stefanyk had earned his living as a trumpet player. Louis Armstrong was his lifelong inspiration. When the American jazz trumpeter came to Edmonton in 1956, the Calder railwayman decided he was going to the concert—money or no money—to meet his musical soulmate.

I wanted to play, my brothers and I, and so I sent away for a record by Louis Armstrong, I didn't know who he was, but a trumpet soloist. I sent from Edmonton to Winnipeg. One side was St. Louis Blues and the other side was Sweet Sue by Louis Armstrong and I played that. We slowly got together, my brother and I practiced. And I got a horn. This guy, this Polish fella, sold me his trumpet....

From then on my biggest desire was to see Louis Armstrong. There was an ad I saw in Vancouver, he was playing in Vancouver that year but I had no money to go there. But when he was playing in Edmonton I bought the tickets right away. They were $2.50....

My wife was kind of against that because we had orange boxes for cupboards, a house 8 feet wide and 17 feet long, we were crowded and she said: "You're spending money on Louis Armstrong?" So anyways she went with the struggle....

I had my book with me... and I put it to my chest and I'm trying to sneak among the crowd to the stage. When I got a little close, he beckoned to me, he says, "Hi Cat" and we start talking. He says, "I'll be by the door" and he kept on playing.

So after he finished we walked to the place by the door, next place that he was signing autographs. He signed autographs for everybody fast and went along. But when I got to his place he got up, shook hands with me, took this book, looked at it and asked me: "How'd you like it?" I said: "It's kind

Tommy Harries

of hard." "Yeah, but it's good," he says. Then he says: "Where would you want me to sign it?" So he signed it in the index here. Then he also told me, "I always use a green pen when I sign." But I didn't know what it was about you know, I didn't care. So then he shook hands with me and wished me good luck and we separated— and that was my day![40]

The Polio Epidemic of 1953 ⌐ Joyce Harries

A little boy of almost four and a half. Getting a cold, perhaps, but tonight is Hallowe'en. We'll let him go out with his younger brother. Baby Jody is too young to go.

My mother made the clown suits. One's still in the costume box. We took pictures of the two little clowns.

Next morning, there they all were: Tommy and Brucie in Jody's crib, all trading licks of suckers.

That night Tommy cried—he was so sick. Doctors told us that flu symptoms, especially pain when lowering the head to chest, must be watched.

My husband out of town. Doctor at the house. "Yes, it's polio."

My parents with us. Hu back home.

I sleep in the room with Tommy. He's quiet and looks puzzled. For six days we nurse him at home. On the sixth night he breathes too hard. Nanny and Gramp babysit the others. We take him to the hospital. Quarantine, so we had to leave him. Went home to bed.

Middle of the night, doorbell. Our doctor, who is a friend, in tears. "We lost him."

My first thoughts: Poor little boy, we weren't even with him. Then: What about Bruce and Jody? Hu has had enough sadness—his father, his mother, his friends—I've only had sunshine.

My first tragedy—at twenty-five.[41]

A day's work ⌐ Lois Hole

One sunny morning, I had just come back from picking the year's very first pail of cucumbers. I was about to go out and pick more, because there were so many of them. It had been a glorious spring and early summer. Just then, a car pulled into the yard and two men got out.

They had been driving by and spotted my huge, thriving garden. They didn't speak much English, but they managed to ask if I would sell them some fresh cucumbers. So I brought out my pail, and they looked at the cucumbers I had just picked.

They were the firmest, most beautiful cucumbers you ever saw in your life. The fellows tried their best to look nonchalant, in order to get a good price. I could tell by the gleam in their eyes, however, that I could charge them just about anything I wanted.

Still, when they asked me "How much?" I had no idea what to answer. I had never sold vegetables before. We didn't even have a scale. I looked at this big five-gallon pail of cucumbers and tried to decide how much it weighed.

I said, "I really don't know how many pounds this might be." One of the men frowned and said, "Ooooh, I'd say maybe six or seven pounds." Of course, I knew they were kidding me. There had to be a good 25 or 30 pounds in there.

So I said to them, "I'll tell you what: I'll let you have the whole pail for two dollars." And that was when I learned my first lesson in marketing. I should have said three, because now they started to bargain with me. I ended up selling those cucumbers for a dollar!

Of course, about a week later, those fellows were back for more. As soon as they got out of their car, I told them, "This time it's going to cost you more than a dollar."

But those two fellows started it all. Ted and I figured that if they were so interested in our vegetables, maybe other people would be too. We put a tiny ad in the Edmonton Journal.

It cost us $2.50 for one full week. All the ad said was "Hole's Farm—Vegetables for Sale," and our phone number. Well, our phone just rang off the hook.

Before long, we were dealing with twenty or so customers every day. At that time, Edmonton had a lot of recent Italian immigrants, and they were just dying for home-grown garden produce. People would phone us up and we would tell them what we had that day.

We were lucky that it had been such a good growing year. Our production was about twice what it would be in an ordinary summer. Even so, we couldn't come close to keeping up with the demand.

In the early 1950s Lois Hole—later know with affection as Alberta's Lieutenant-Gardener —struck gold in a cucumber patch.

One evening, after the last car had pulled out of our yard, I counted up the day's receipts: $36! The total was staggering. I just couldn't believe it. "Ted," I said delightedly, "we've struck gold!"[42]

The Town Crier ⌐ Ed Wigmore

One night, walking along 97th Street, much to our delight we spotted Pete Jamieson striding purposefully but rather tipsily on the other side of the street carrying his megaphone. Well, we couldn't resist. It was Street Urchins versus Pete.

Let me explain: Pete was one of Edmonton's great characters. He was the unofficial town crier. Every morning he would sweep the sidewalks in front of Mike's Newsstand and other businesses. With his commanding manner, megaphone and ramrod-straight posture he would order people around in the long lineups outside the downtown movie theatres. He and his megaphone seemed omnipresent at downtown outdoor events. He was also a mystery: nobody seemed to know where he lived or whether he had any family. It was rumoured that he liked his booze. But to us kids, he was pompous and grandiose, somehow a comic character. I realize now there was a strangely vulnerable

Pete Jamieson strolled through the downtown streets, shouting into his megaphone year after year.

man behind this supercilious veneer and I think we as kids unconsciously tapped into that. He was an irresistible target.

The taunting began. "Hey Pete, where you goin'?" "Hey Pete, you're walking funny." "Hey Pete, come and line us up." It was mild stuff, really, no swearing, no obscenities. It went on for about a block. Then Pete, with great dignity, raised his megaphone to his mouth and began to let us have it. His voice resonating up and down the street, he boomed out: "Here, ladies and gentlemen, you have an example of what is wrong with Edmonton today. You have an example of this younger generation which has turned into a pack of juvenile delinquents." He said a bit more and we yelled a few other things across the street, but we knew when we were beaten.

Our heart was no longer in it. The *Reader's Digest* would have called it "the perfect squelch." And I think maybe we realized, at some level, that there *was* something obscene about a gang of boys taunting an old man on a street late at night. We slunk around the next corner and headed back to Boyle Street.[43]

"We knew that Christmas would be difficult" ⌐ Inge Vermeulen

I don't eat cornflakes anymore. They remind me of the first few months in Canada when we were so poor that we couldn't afford much else. My husband, Henry, and I had come from Germany and arrived in Edmonton's Immigration Hall in May 1952, along with our two little girls—Philine and Charlotte, two and a half, and one and a half years old.

Within a week Henry had been accepted as a medical intern at the University Hospital. He was paid $40 a month, and room and board. That wasn't quite enough to feed us, so I got a job as a maid at the Aberhart Hospital for $175 a month—enough for the girls' room and board, a furnished room for me, and a bit of food, mostly cornflakes! These were grim times, and I really don't want to talk about them. I'd rather tell about a very special event, our first Christmas in Edmonton.

We knew Christmas would be difficult. We'd be homesick and we would feel very strange in a country where we had heard about Christmas customs that were quite different from the familiar German ways. So we expected to feel very lonesome.

To have no money for buying Christmas presents didn't make things easier. But Henry had made friends with the carpenters at the University Hospital. They found a discarded wooden barrel for him in the shop and helped him put in a floor and outside skids. After he had painted it bright red and wallpapered the inside it looked great—a truly original crawl-in dollhouse for the girls!

The Christmas parcel from Germany had arrived in time and we were looking forward to opening it, but not before Christmas Eve! In Germany they call it "Heilige Nacht" which means "Holy Night," and this is the evening when Christmas happens. There is nothing "Ho, Ho, Ho" about Holy Night. There is no Santa, only the Baby Jesus and angels in the crèche under the tree, and the joyous get-together of family members for a celebration with Christmas music, special foods, and of course the exchange of gifts under the beautifully decorated tree glowing with the lights of candles.

"You can't use wax candles on the tree in Canada. It's against the law!" we were told. And we could see that a fire could be disastrous in a wooden building. Since we didn't have enough money for a nice big tree, we waited until the afternoon of December 24th and bought a leftover little tree for 50 cents. It was a terrible, terrible tree! And it didn't improve with our single string of cheap lights that worked only sporadically. When one bulb jiggled, the whole thing went dead.

So it was mostly dark. But Henry played his guitar out and we sang our familiar songs of "Silent Night" and "O Tannenbaum" while the little girls had a wonderful time crawling in and out of their dollhouse.

We were about to open the Christmas parcel from home when somebody knocked on the door, really loud. This was strange—who would go around on Christmas Eve visiting? This was a night for staying home, for being with family! I got up to open the door, and my misgivings were forgotten in a second.

Our visitors were friends! Dr. Donald, his wife Peggy, and his three daughters were the first and dearest friends we had made in Edmonton. They had come to wish us Merry Christmas and bring doll carriages for the girls, and food and drink for us.

They had barely sat down when there was more knocking at the door. Rodney Pike, the man who had sold Henry life insurance, arrived with his family. And two of the hospital carpenters came. And more of Henry's hospital friends. One of them brought a parcel with two dolls for the girls. His mother had bought them and knitted all their outfits. It was absolutely overwhelming, and it went on for a long time. The living room was full of people. We sat on the floor, and we laughed and talked for hours.

After everybody had left, Henry and I sat hand in hand on the chesterfield. We knew that this had been the happiest Christmas of our lives. We no longer felt like strangers in this country. People had gone out of their way to make us feel welcome and liked. I think it was that night, in Edmonton, that we became Canadians at heart.[44]

Welcome to Muddington ⤙ Mary Spencer

In 1953, I arrived in Edmonton to look for a job. It turned out that my taxi driver had just done the same. After checking his map of the city, he decided that the shortest route to the University campus was over the Groat Bridge. We found our way to the appointed place on the riverbank without difficulty, but lo and behold, either the bridge had sunk, or it had not yet been built. The latter proved to be true. I eventually did manage to cross the North Saskatchewan River and became a U of A faculty member.

After spending five-and-a-half years in the San Francisco Bay area, coming to Edmonton was like entering a different world. Early in the oil boom days, the overwhelming impression was of mud (*Muddington*, a visiting friend from Sweden called it!). As the residential and industrial areas rapidly expanded, construction of paved roads and sidewalks could not keep pace, and there was little in the way of sod or landscaping to cope with the gumbo.

In those times, Edmonton's ballet performances were held in the Sales Stock Pavilion, for lack of a better venue. The makeshift platforms "whomped" with every graceful landing, and long, lonesome train whistles created melancholy discords within the music.

I remember being in Eaton's basement one Saturday, during our first November back in Canada, and being almost overwhelmed with nostalgia for the fresh daffodils that would have been blooming in our California garden. Grey November, with its bare deciduous trees and no snow cover, was (and is) surely Edmonton's bleakest month.

Nevertheless, even though our California employers had offered to keep our jobs open for a year, my husband and I decided to stay in Canada. For all of the most important things in life, we made the right move.[45]

Book burglars ⤳ Mel Hurtig

Who steals books?

Alas, a lot of different people. Over the years I narrowed the list down to the following categories: ministers, priests, and rabbis; doctors, dentists, lawyers, engineers, and architects; students, teachers, and professors; clerks, farmers, and homemakers; men, women, and children.

Just as I cannot explain why so many men in the book trade drink so much, I cannot, for the life of me, explain why so many normally law-abiding citizens steal books. At my store businessmen with briefcases, mothers with baby carriages, and students with clipboards had to be asked to step back into the store after departing with books they hadn't paid for.

One day the long and eagerly awaited Webster's Third International Dictionary arrived. It was huge, selling for $79.95, the equivalent of well over $300 today. We had ordered ten copies. I asked the staff to put nine copies in the storage room at the back of the store and to put one copy on display near the cash register. Fifteen minutes later, I went to show the

Mel Hurtig opened a tiny independent bookstore on 103rd Street in 1956 for a city that loved to read. Hurtig would later become a successful local publisher, the visionary who convinced Peter Lougheed to back the *Canadian Encyclopedia*, and Canada's best known economic nationalist.

new dictionary to a teacher-librarian; it was gone. I called the police and told them to look for someone walking down Jasper Avenue listing heavily to one side. No luck.

We had in the store a magnificent four-volume boxed set of the nature writings and art of Ernest Thompson Seton, *Lives of Game Animals*, published in Boston and selling for $150. It was one of my prized book sets, one I wished I could afford for my own library. One day a staff member glumly reported to me that the first volume in the set was missing. Blast! I asked Gordon Elbrond to get on the phone to Boston and order a replacement. No luck again. The publisher advised that they sold only the four-volume set.

Two weeks later volume two was gone. I was furious. Now, nothing else mattered; I was determined to catch the rotten son of a bitch, no matter what! The next morning I called a meeting of the staff. "I don't care what else you do, I want you to keep a close eye on the nature section. Don't leave the floor without passing the responsibility on to another member of the staff." Ten days later volume three was gone. That night when the store closed, I did something I had never done before and have never done since. I gathered the staff together in the alley behind the store and burned a book—volume four. There was no bloody way in the world I was going to allow the thief a crack at the last volume.

On another occasion a staff member phoned back to my office from the front of the store. "Mel, we've just caught a man going out of the store with eleven books on archaeology under his raincoat."

"Send him back here," I said.

In all the years I was a bookseller, I never once called the police when we caught someone stealing books. However, I usually tried very hard to scare the heck out of him or her.

Theft was a great problem for us; it cost us lost sales and had a substantial impact on our fragile bottom line. Dozens of times I would walk to a particular bookshelf in response to a customer inquiry, reach for a book, only to find it wasn't there even though I knew it hadn't been sold. So not only had the book been stolen, but the sale had been lost and it was often weeks before a replacement arrived.

Back to the office came the man, the raincoat, and the eleven books on archaeology. Immediately one thing became apparent. This was one very big man—perhaps six foot four, 240 pounds. As he climbed the four steps up to my office, he banged his forehead on the top of the door frame. If he had been unhappy as he was escorted back to my office, now he was bridling with hostility. I asked him to have a seat. As I put my hand on the telephone, here's how the conversation went:

"Is there any reason why I shouldn't call the police?"

"No."

(Wait a minute, this wasn't what I expected. That was the wrong answer. What do I say now? I stuttered and improvised.)

"Have you ever been charged with a crime before?"

His eyes narrowed. "Yes, I have."

"Do you mind my asking what for?"

His eyes narrowed further, he leaned closer, fixed me with his gaze, and growled: "Assault with a dangerous weapon."

"I see." Gulp.

What I almost said was, "Are there any other books you'd like to have, sir?" We let him go and he never came back. However, I can still see his scowling, menacing face today.[46]

SPORTING CITY

The Waterloo Mercurys brought Edmonton's passion for hockey to the World Championships in London in 1950 and to the Oslo Olympics where they won gold in 1952—Canada's last gold medal in hockey until 2002. Their benefactor was Jim Christiansen, a local car dealer who paid all expenses for the 51-game tour of Europe that preceded the Games and who hired players to work at his car lot to assist with expenses.

Praying for touchdowns ⤙ Preston Manning

One of the first times that both forms of faith—my faith in the West and in God's providence—were simultaneously tested occurred on the occasion of the 1954 Grey Cup game, when I was twelve years old.

The Edmonton Eskimos, representing the West, went into the game as underdogs. In those days, the winner of the Western Conference was decided by a best-of-three playoff, whereas the winner of the Eastern Conference was decided by a two-game total-point playoff. Obviously, this arrangement would not have withstood the test of regional fairness because it was heavily biased in favour of the East. To get to the Grey Cup, Western teams often had to play three playoff games, late in the fall on frozen fields, whereas the Eastern teams only had to play two playoff games in the milder November climate of the St. Lawrence basin. In 1954, the Eskimos had advanced to the Grey Cup after a brutal three-game play-off with the Winnipeg Blue Bombers, in which the Esks had suffered many injuries on the frozen turf.

The Montreal Alouettes, on the other hand, had advanced after their two-game semifinal almost injury free. To make matters worse, the Alouettes outweighed the Eskimos by more than ten kilograms (twenty-five pounds) per man along the line. The oddsmakers favoured the Alouettes to win by two or more touchdowns, and some Eastern commentators hinted that it would be less embarrassing if the Eskimos simply didn't show up for the big game.

The situation was so desperate for committed Eskimo fans like me that extraordinary measures had to be considered to increase the Eskimos' chances of victory. I therefore inquired of my father, Christian layman and the premier of the province whose capital city the Eskimos represented, whether it was theologically permissible to pray for an Eskimos victory. After all, the Eskimos were the underdogs, and was not God always on the side of the underdogs? Even more important, the Eskimos were representing the West, and surely there was no question as to where God stood when it came to West versus East. My father advised that it was always a good idea to pray for God's will to be known and done in every situation. But he also said that I should be aware that in great contests there are often devout believers on both sides, so that God must take into account the prayers of both. Sometimes the prayers of neither can be answered fully (as Mr. Lincoln had observed in his Second Inaugural Address). No doubt there would be devoted fans in Montreal praying for an Alouette victory just as earnestly as I would be praying for an Eskimos victory, and when it came to the teams, it was quite likely that there would be Christian brothers on both sides.

In any event, I prayed fervently for an Eskimos victory, and when the day of the Grey Cup came, November 27, 1954, I was expecting not only a superhuman effort by the Eskimos but, if necessary, divine intervention on their behalf.

Throughout the first three quarters, the Eskimos played ferociously, and they were trailing by only five points early in the fourth quarter. But their injuries and the greater size and weight of the Montreal line were beginning to take their toll. With only three and a half minutes left in the game, the Alouettes were moving inexorably down the field to score the touchdown that would drive a stake through the Eskimos' heart. Then, suddenly, it happened!

Theologians and other students of the game are still divided over exactly what happened, and how it happened, but the authorized Edmonton version of the events is as follows. Montreal had marched to within one foot of the Eskimos' ten-yard line. In the Alouette huddle, Brother Etchevery, the Montreal quarterback, called for a sweep to the left, with Brother Hunsinger, the Montreal halfback, carrying the ball. In the defensive huddle on the other side of the line of scrimmage, desperate measures were being discussed, as the Eskimos' only hope was to stop the Montreal advance and somehow get the ball back. The referee whistled the ball into play and Etchevery handed it off to Hunsinger, who proceeded to run the halfback sweep to the left.

Now there are those who maintain that at precisely that moment Hunsinger heard a still, small voice whispering in his ear, "Lateral the ball, lateral the ball." There are others who maintain that Hunsinger heard no such thing. It is generally agreed, however, that for whatever reason, Hunsinger was not gripping the ball as tightly as he should have. As he moved to his left, Brother Tulley, an Eskimos linebacker, burst through the line hitting him low, just as Brother Prather, the Eskimos' defensive end, hit him high—and, wonder of wonders, the ball came loose. For Eskimos fans watching the spectacle, it was as if time stood still. That ball, propelled by Hunsinger's forward momentum, was destined by the law of gravity to hit the ground, but how would it hit the ground? If it hit the ground and rolled, there would be a free-for-all to regain possession. But if it hit the ground and bounced, a miracle was possible.

The football was now on its own. Slowly, oh so slowly—or so it seemed to Eskimos fans—it descended, hitting the ground. But instantly it bounced up and forward again, straight into the arms of Jack Dickerson "Spaghetti Legs" Parker. Brother Parker was the Eskimos' star offensive halfback, playing the same position on offence as Brother Hunsinger. (Oh, the symmetry of it all.) But as the Eskimos' defence tired late in the game, Parker had been called upon to play defensive halfback as well—and he needed no still, small voice to tell him what to do once he got his hands on the pigskin. He took off like a bat out of Hades for the Montreal goal line, which he crossed untouched by any Montreal tackler.

The game was now tied. (In the 1950s, a touchdown was worth only five points, not yet having been adjusted for inflation.) The contest of underdog versus favourite, West versus East, justice versus injustice, faith versus skepticism, now hung in the balance, the outcome depending on whether the Eskimos could kick the winning convert. Brother Bob Dean, the Eskimos' kicker, trotted out on the field, beads of sweat standing out on his brow.

Normally the convert would have been a foregone conclusion, but Brother Eagle Keys—from Turkeyneck Bend, Kentucky, the Eskimos' all-star centre—had broken his leg earlier in the game and was unable to hobble onto the field. Brother Bill Briggs, the backup centre, was also hurt, so it was the third-string centre, Brother Don Barry, who would have to make the all-important snap for the convert.

No time now for advice or instruction. The Eskimos were out over the ball. Straight as an arrow came the snap from Brother Barry to Brother Ray Wilsey, the Eskimo holder. In one deft motion, Wilsey pinned the ball, spinning it on its longitudinal axis so that the laces faced away from the kicker and towards the goalposts. "Thud" was the sound as Dean's toe connected with the ball—a "thud" that reverberated across the country, from the shores of Lake Ontario to the Rocky Mountains and back. High and clean flew the football, straight through the uprights. One more defensive stand, and the game was over.

Final score: 26 to 25 for the Edmonton Eskimos!

Philosophers and theologians have argued for centuries as to whether there is definitive proof of divine intervention in the affairs of men. But for a small boy in Edmonton, Alberta, what further evidence was required than that provided by that miraculous bounce of the football on November 27, 1954.[47]

"Cold enough for you?" ⌐ Abdul Kamal

Over tea one lovely autumn afternoon, Avadh [Bhatia] gave me some advice that would make my first day in Edmonton memorable: "Don't do what the Canadians do. You will see them go out in minus thirty-degree weather in shirt sleeves. At that temperature, exposed flesh freezes in a matter of a few seconds! Wrap yourself up well, even at the risk of looking a tad overdressed."

Meanwhile, a Canadian graduate student had been filling my head with far-fetched tales of Canada. "Out west," he assured me, "when people kiss, sparks really do fly!" And, "You can get quite a charge off the doorknobs." I laughed. Something literally as dead as a doorknob would suddenly come to life and zap me with a bolt of lightning! Yeah, very likely.

By the time my wife and I left England, we had formed an image of an Edmonton where grizzlies roamed the streets alongside gun-toting cowboys wearing Stetsons at a jaunty angle, chewing on blades of grass, swaggering bow-legged in their pointy boots with spurs and spitting like lizards in heat. In fact, when I informed my father, in what is now Bangladesh, that I was going to Canada, he sent me some advice, as any caring father would. "Watch out for bears and wolves when you go to the outhouse. And don't answer the call of nature after dark, even if it means doing some extra laundry the next day."

We arrived in Edmonton at 3 a.m. on the last day of October 1963, by a Trans-Canada Airlines' Viscount on a milk run from Montreal. The airport building only helped to reinforce our image of Edmonton as a frontier town. As we walked through the ramshackle hangar, I was summoned to the Trans-Canada counter on the PA system. There I was handed a message from Harry. The missive was brief: "Welcome to Edmonton. Take a limo to Athabasca Hall."

Now, coming from England, where the longest car was all of eight feet, taking a limousine seemed the height of wasteful extravagance. Instead, we took a bus to the Park Hotel on the south side and a taxi from there to the campus.

That morning we woke up late. We drew the curtains warily, fearing to see the ground covered in snow. Instead, to our surprise, we were greeted by a stunningly clear day. Limpid sunshine bathed the trees as I had never seen. It looked like a crisp, cold day. As I entered the bathroom, I was liter-

Abdul Kamal was a graduate student in Liverpool in 1963 when he decided to move to Canada. After hunting for Edmonton in an atlas, he met Avadh Bhatia, a visiting physics professor from the University of Alberta, who offered some fateful advice about winter clothing in the city.

ally shocked when the seemingly inert doorknob delivered its promised bolt of charge to my unsuspecting hand.

It was too late for breakfast and too early for lunch in Athabasca Hall, so we decided to go downtown for brunch. Paying heed to Avadh's advice, I wasn't about to take any chances. I wrapped my head and upper torso in my Liverpool University Science Faculty scarf, a veritable blanket in bold blue and white stripes designed for survival in emergencies such as being marooned on the Hebrides. Thus mummified, I put on my thick tweed jacket and a pair of grey flannel pants (the kind that only the English seem to know how to make, which last you a lifetime). Having fortified myself thus, I donned a thick dark blue winter coat as a final defensive measure against the flesh-freezing weather. A pair of leather gloves completed my accoutrements. Only my eyes were exposed to the harsh outside world.

As I took my first few tentative steps outside, I attracted bemused looks from the locals, who were indeed walking about in their shirt sleeves—just as Avadh had told me! Good job that I was forewarned, I thought to myself.

We walked to the bus stop to go downtown, and, lo and behold, there were more of the crazy Canucks in their shirt sleeves! "Cold nuff fo' ya?" one of them said to me. As I felt the sweat beginning to course down my body in runnels, I have to admit that I was beginning to doubt the wisdom of Avadh's advice.

By the time the bus reached Jasper Avenue, I could feel my soaked shirt clinging uncomfortably to my body. I was swimming in my own sweat and on the verge of drowning. Just as we found a restaurant (well, actually more of an eatery, as there were no memorable restaurants on Jasper Avenue), we saw a neon sign flash the time and the temperature: 11:30 a.m. and 63°F!

You can imagine my embarrassment as I laboriously unswathed myself, layer by woolen layer, much to the amusement of the motley crowd assembled in the restaurant for their morning coffee.

I came to Edmonton for a two-year stint and stayed a lifetime.[48]

"I had a strong mind" ⟿ Alvena Strasbourg

In February 1958, Wilfred came to see me. He said, "If you want to go to Edmonton and make a fresh start, Eleanor and I'll keep your kids until school is out in June. By then you should have a job and a place to keep them." I agreed, but I was so scared. I had no experience in anything besides cleaning. I had no faith in my abilities, certainly no self-esteem. Momma gave me a warm coat and boots plus enough money for train fare.

I left Fort McMurray, sad about leaving the north, worried about my future and afraid of being truly alone, for the first time in my life. It's a good thing I had a strong mind. Through it all I never became depressed or suicidal, just lonely.... Every morning I checked out newspaper ads and looked at Help Wanted signs in store windows but felt too afraid, too unsure, too shy to go in. I'd think, "I have no experience and I'm Native. I can't do it...." One day, as I walked along the street I came to a dry cleaner's with a Help Wanted sign in the window. I took a deep breath and walked in. An old man sat behind the counter watching me as I stumbled over my questions about the sign. He looked at my old coat, faded pants and thin legs. I was nothing but skin and bone by then. He asked, "Ever pressed clothes before?" and I managed a "Yes. At home with an iron." He invited me into the back room, introduced me to a girl pressing shirts and asked her to teach me how to use the pressing machines. I was determined to learn and I did. At noon he returned and said, "You have the job, starting at 65 cents an hour." I was so excited, I wanted to hug him.

That first month I had nothing. My clothes consisted of one old black skirt, two pairs of slacks and a few tops. I had neither furniture, dishes, pots, nor linens, nothing for a home. I walked everywhere because I could not afford bus fare. Eventually I found a place on 107th Avenue and 102nd Street for $12.50 a week. It fit my budget.... The single room barely had space for a bed next to the tiny kitchen, but I was in heaven.[49]

"We had $100 and two suitcases" ∾ Scarlett Gonzalez

We were at university during the years of terror under Pinochet's military rule. When the terror touched Patricio and me personally, we knew we had to leave Chile.

I was studying physical education. Patricio had finished four years of engineering and was studying architecture. We were right in the centre of the student protests against the terror of the Pinochet regime. One day, the police blindfolded and interrogated me because they were looking

Alvena Strasbourg's Métis grandparents—the Laboucanes and Cardinals—had once lived and worked in Edmonton and central Alberta, but moved north during the First World War. At 37 Strasbourg retraced their steps. Within two decades she was an employment recruiter with Syncrude, but her first years here were challenging.

Scarlett Gonzalez
was among the 6,000
Chileans who came to
Alberta as political refugees
after the military coup
in Chile in 1973.

for Patricio. He was warned that he should quit his studies and leave the country. A week after we left, the police came to Patricio's house looking for him. We were lucky to escape when we did or we might be dead.

We became government-sponsored refugees. We had $100 and two suitcases and didn't know anyone. When the airplane landed in Edmonton, I remember telling Patricio that we were on the moon. Everything was all white and flat; it was so depressing. Nobody was on the street, just cars and buses. There were no trees, the buildings were like warehouses. It was so ugly compared to Chile.

At that time there were many jobs and we had the opportunity to choose. I held a sales jobs at Woolworth's, The Bay and at a jewelry store. Patricio worked as a cleaner, at a window and door company and in sales. After seven years, he finally got a job in an architectural department. Unfortunately, the company closed down. He then took some university courses and got a job with the City of Edmonton's engineering department.

Our three children were all born here. We sponsored Patricio's parents and his sister to Edmonton, as well as all of my immediate family. Our oldest daughter, Karin, found that the kids in her elementary school were really intrigued to hear about our family. But when she got to junior high school, they weren't interested in her Chilean background. Three other children in her school were hiding the fact that they were Latinos. She thought that was wrong so she put together a multicultural day.

So many people don't appreciate what Canada is. I want my kids to know the value of what they have here and not to take it for granted. We would like them to go to Chile and see the difference. We have never wanted to go back, except to visit. I'd like to go to the beaches—I still miss the ocean.

We have liberty, security, peace, and freedom here. We are free to try and accomplish our own goals. Here, my kids have everything. Here, you can take it for granted that when you leave in the morning you'll probably be back at night. That wasn't the case when we were in Chile.[50]

CITY OF CHAMPIONS

Oil Kings ⌐ Bill Hunter

Oil Kings wasn't just a name. We carried ourselves like junior hockey royalty. After all, there wasn't a lot else in Edmonton in the late 1960s.

After the Oil Kings and the Eskimos, there wasn't much. There weren't a lot of other sports on TV, either. In winter the Oil Kings were pretty much the only show in town. There wasn't much to think about other than hockey. Despite its prosperity and growth, Edmonton really was an overgrown small town back then with a small-town homogeneity to it. Most people had similar backgrounds. They'd either grown up in Edmonton or had recently moved from the farm or from a smaller town somewhere else in western Canada. Everybody knew hockey; everybody had hockey in common. It was a language everyone spoke and an atmosphere everyone breathed. That made it easy to focus everyone's attention on the Oil Kings, and it was a perfect atmosphere in which to promote a team....

When I was trying to buy the Penguins, Clarence Campbell came to Edmonton to speak to the Alberta Medical Association. While he was in town, he took me to dinner. Clarence had been born and raised in Edmonton. He'd played hockey in Edmonton, had refereed there and had graduated from the University of Alberta. But he sat across from me at a restaurant table and said, "Bill, you must be smoking something to think Edmonton could support a National Hockey League team. I don't want to see you wasting your time and energy in pursuit of this impossible dream. It'll never happen."

I was angry. I felt as if Clarence thought he could come out here to visit a rube in his hometown, pat me on the head, tell me to go away and I would.

He thought he was being kind, but I wouldn't be patronized. "Clarence, you've lost touch," I said. "You've buried your head in the sand. This is great hockey country. Hockey isn't reserved for just the Montreal Canadiens and the Toronto Maple Leafs like you think it is. It isn't the size of the city—it's the size of the heart of the city. Your old big six. Hell, we'll outdraw all of them when we get started up." Clarence laughed. "I knew I wasn't going to talk you out of it, Bill," he said, and we parted on friendly terms.[51]

"Welcome to the Big Time" ⌐ Wayne Gretzky

I landed in Edmonton with my hockey stuff, the clothes I was wearing, an extra pair of pants and a toothbrush. Welcome to the big time. When we got out of the plane, there was nobody there, no press, no Oilers people, zip. Turns out we landed at the wrong airport. Back in the plane. When we finally got to the right airport and the right press conference, you could hardly understand our answers. We were so hungry we stuffed ourselves with the appetizers they had sitting out for the press.

The next morning, the head coach, Glen Sather, called me into his office and told me I could live with him until I got settled. I thought that

Joey Moss and Wayne Gretzky became friends when the Edmonton Oilers' superstar was dating Joey's sister, Vicky. "When I first met Joey, he was 17 years old, and working for a bottle depot in Edmonton. Every day he would be out there at -40 below taking the bus to work." At 21 Moss became the Oilers' dressing room attendant: folding towels, collecting water bottles, vacuuming, joking, offering advice—and earning the admiration of the team, and the city. "The best part is hanging out with all the guys," he said. "I work hard every day keeping the room clean. It's important." Moss and Gretzky stood together when the Oilers retired the Great One's sweater.

was very nice and I accepted. I stayed about three weeks. He also told me another thing that made my eyes bug out.

"One day, we're gonna be in the NHL and one day you're going to be captain of this hockey team," he said. "Remember I told you that."[52]

How we won the Commonwealth Games ⌁ Ivor Dent, former mayor

On June 13, 1972, I left Edmonton to begin the most hectic fourteen and one-half days I'd ever experienced.

By the time it was finished, we were assured that Edmonton, with the proper follow-up work, would win the bid in Munich. Before it began we were confident we had thirteen to fourteen votes nailed down; by the time it ended, we had twenty-five to twenty-six votes—sufficient to win!...

At three in the morning I rolled up to my hotel in Johannesburg, went quickly to my room and climbed into the bed I'd left twenty-four hours earlier, satisfied that one man alone, with proper back-up and planning, could woo Africa over to our side in Canada's pursuit of the Games.

I am grateful to the Kensington Close Hotel in London for having notepaper which is just the right size for keeping track of expenses.

By the time I reached home those three small sheets, used front and back, contained every expenditure—large and small—made on the African trip. Each of the 105 carefully recorded entries, totalling $709.20, is written in Canadian funds. That means 105 transpositions from 14 different currencies into Canadian dollars. What a chore! But it did keep me occupied on airplanes.

At least my shoes were kept well shined. There are entries showing costs for that service ranging from forty cents to ninety-five. Taking a guest to lunch in Manzini is certainly cheaper than hiring a taxi. The former cost $4.05, while the ride ran to nine dollars. After running out of City of Edmonton cuff links, which were presented to the major personalities that I met along the way, I purchased a bottle of Canadian Club in the airports of the centres I was leaving. This I would present to the next representative I met. The Games leaders must have thought I had left Edmonton with a couple of cases

of whiskey, for they always assumed that, because of its name, the liquor had been carried from home. My choice of the beverage rather than some other gift was forced upon me as it was the only clearly identifiable Canadian product that one could be certain of buying in any part of the world.[53]

Graham Smith won a record six gold medals at the Commonwealth Games in 1978, swimming in the pool named after his father, Don Smith, who had died shortly before the opening ceremonies. He set two world records during his swimming career.

"For the fans, it was paradise" ⟿ Rod Phillips, recalling the Oilers' first Stanley Cup victory, May 24, 1984

The game began at a torrid pace. The 17,498 fans made more noise than I ever heard Edmonton fans make. Wayne Gretzky scored on a break away, and it was a mad house. Moments later, a three on one, with Jari Kurri, Dave Semenko and Wayne. Kurri took it in across the Islander blue line. Semenko broke for the net. Kurri dropped it back to Gretzky. He took a couple of strikes and ripped a "howitzer" between the legs of Billy Smith (the Edmonton fan's villain). It was 2–0 and crazy. In the second period, Ken Linseman scored to make it 3–0 and then Kurri made it 4–0. Now the entire building sensed what was happening. The Edmonton Oilers were about to make history.

Pat Lafontaine of the Islanders tried very hard to spoil Edmonton's biggest ever party. He scored twice early in the third period. But the Oilers tightened up and with only 13 seconds remaining Dave Lumley fired the puck into an empty Islander net. It was 5–2 and all over. Northlands was a sea of emotion.

My own emotions were running high. When Lumley scored we knew it was over. The feeling was like nothing I ever experienced at any sporting event I have covered. Two people I admired and respected very much came to mind seconds after Lumley scored. Hal Pawson, the former Sports Editor of the *Edmonton Journal*, and Henry Singer, the greatest sports fan Edmonton has ever had. I mentioned that I wished they could have been there that night. It was a proud evening for our city. I will always have the feeling that they were watching from up above.

Our post game show from the Oilers dressing room was a very emotional scene. For those of us who watched the team from the beginning, it was more than special. When we signed off the air, I spent a few moments sipping champagne with Lee Fogolin. I admire him as a man and a player. We both enjoyed a good cry. It was the same with Kevin Lowe, Wayne Gretzky, Barry Fraser and just about everyone in the room.

After that we had a party at the Agricom. [My wife] Debby left for home at about 1:00 a.m. I stayed and celebrated with assistant coach, John Muckler. At 3:00 a.m. we were standing on Jasper Avenue watching thousands of people whoop it up. It was incredible. After John drove me home I spent the rest of the night watching the replay of the game on my video cassette recorder. Sleep came after 6 a.m., on May 20, 1984. It was "ENORMOUS!"[54]

CREATIVE CITY

Music from the sixth floor ⤙ Holger Petersen

CKUA's legendary, sixth-floor record library is probably the most extensive one in Canada. When I started hanging around the station in 1969, it completely filled a very large room. Since then, this collection has expanded into an adjoining control room, and also invaded a large, fourth-floor

The sounds of summer in Edmonton, 1975: a bluegrass jam session on a front porch in Garneau. The housing co-op was nicknamed the Heartbreak Hotel. The musicians, left to right, James Hay, unknown, Calvin Cairns, Don Leckey, Allan Stein, Paddy Byrne and Don McVeigh, with his back to the camera. "The Hovel was happening then, so a lot of these musicians would have played there," said the photographer Cathy Roy.

office. In this library, you'll find every kind of music, including approximately 428 discs of Beethoven music and 190 by Duke Ellington. In this sixtieth year, the total count approaches 55,000 items. No wonder the announcers—not DJs, thank you—have a tradition of being knowledgeable music freaks, vinyl junkies, and eclectic-music experts.

CKUA is where most of us heard Frank Zappa, Wynton Marsallis, Glenn Gould, Miles Davis, Robert Cray, and k.d. Lang for the first time. The station continually discovers and broadcasts quality new recordings, overlooked obscurities, and music with an historical perspective, thanks to that incredible library. Contacts from many listeners over the years have confirmed that their musical knowledge and tastes—indeed, careers—have also been influenced by CKUA's music.

I first discovered how special CKUA is in the mid-sixties. As a high school student into "British Invasion" bands, I remember accidentally tuning into a blues program hosted by Sev Sabourin—an hour of music and discussion on the merits of Buddy Guy and Junior Wells! Then it was Tony Dillon-Davis pioneering the province's first album rock on weekends. In short order, Bill Coull, Studs Terkel, Dekoven, and The Old Disc Jockey opened new worlds to me.

With the support and encouragement of then program director Ed Kilpatrick, I started working regular shifts that led to the series "Natch'l

CKUA opened in 1928 as a campus radio station for the University of Alberta and quickly became Canada's first public radio station on a shoe-string budget. Through good times and hard times, CKUA nurtured the city's artistic soul with fine music and a sense of community.

Blues," and "H.P. Sauce," heard on Saturday afternoons. Starting in 1971, Bob Chelmick, Marc Vasey, and I produced on CKUA a locally-recorded weekly music series called "The Acme Sausage Company." For years, the series helped support live music throughout the province, won international awards, and released in 1972 perhaps Canada's first, regional-radio compilation album. In retrospect, this programming seemed to encapsule an unspoken CKUA philosophy: treat every kind of quality music with equal respect.

CKUA's influence touches people differently from any other radio station. Listeners are treated as intelligent, open-minded adults. The content has substance. The music is presented for enjoyment and cultural enrichment by an announcer who probably knows the name of every musician on the session and who tells you something about the music instead of the sponsor. The process is a lifelong education for announcer and listener alike.

CKUA's influence stretches even farther than its airwaves. The station offers the type of climate and offers the kind of encouragement that sees current staff playing key, and in some cases, founding roles in organizations like Jazz City, Edmonton Folk MUSIC Festival, Grant MacEwan Community College, the Banff Centre for the Performing Arts, the City Media Club, the Calgary Olympics and many others throughout the province.

Hopefully, these cultural influences will carry on at least another sixty years, and a few more generations of Alberta children will have a chance to discover just how valuable eclectic music can be. Although we'll probably have to tear down another wall or two on the sixth floor.[55]

Tommy Banks

Just ask any reasonably successful Alberta recording artist where their record first got played, and the answer is CKUA, always, just always.... Most of them would lie down in front of a train for CKUA.... It was the first place that many, many Alberta artists got their first substantive airplay to a discerning audience that understands what's going on and who will either like it or not with some reason to their opinion....

It's been important to everybody who has been involved in the arts in Alberta.... [CKUA created] a fertile base on which other things have been able to grow. It's in no small measure responsible for the happy existence of the sort of reasonable infrastructure of arts support and knowledge about the arts in Alberta.[56]

Edmonton on the Fringe ↬ Brian Paisley

Dissect the beast. Move aside the technicians, the administrators, the hundreds of community volunteers, the enormous audience, the funders and the sponsors, the food merchants and the craftspeople... They're all necessary, of course, all intricate, living, lovely parts of this huge event, but we're looking for its heart....

There it is, still beating....

At the heart of the Fringe is the theatre artist. Be they professional or student or amateur, young or old, writer, producer, director, designer, musician, dancer, singer or just plain ol' actor, the theatre artists who have created the hundreds of shows that have swept (or stumbled) across ten years of Fringe stages are the people who continue to provide the basic, driving, joyous rhythm of the festival.

Imagine being asked to write a script or devise a scenario, gather the necessary people and equipment and funds, rehearse when you can in whatever space you can find, and, eventually, put this essentially untested (but heartfelt) piece of work out on a stage—or more likely, onto a hastily constructed plywood platform in an old brick building disguised as a theatre. For a mere nine days. For no pay—no guarantee of any remuneration whatsoever. In fact, let's be honest here, you actually have to pay Chinook Theatre for this somewhat dubious privilege.

That's art in the raw.... Naked, unadorned desire to speak and be heard, to move and be watched, to play and be listened to. The rest will take care of itself.

Just give 'em a stage and the artist will come. And they'll make the journey not for fame or fortune (though either would be a welcome bonus) but for the one thing every performer wants and needs—an audience. An incredible audience that spends nine long days and nights prowling the streets of Old Strathcona eagerly, voraciously, searching for something called risky theatre.

Carol Shaben remembers the beginnings of the Fringe: "Truth is, nobody knew what madness the idea would hatch—least of all Brian Paisley. But artists, disgruntled with the lack of space or opportunity to produce their own work, were willing to give it a go."

And sooner or later they find it, we all do.... The play that makes you laugh and cry and wonder how that long silent heartstring was gently plucked, the juggler who astounds you even though you've probably seen thousands of airborne bowling pins during the past decade, the young and nervous and gloriously ambitious actor/playwright/director who takes the stage with sheer audacity and just a tiny, tiny sprout of undernourished talent, full of promise....

The pulse of the Fringe, the heart of the beast....

Still beating.[57]

"The room was vibrant with energy" ⌐
Laura Roald

The first day I walked into the *ihuman* studio, I was overcome by a sense of possibility. In the messy basement of a run-down building in downtown Edmonton, groups of youth were painting, drawing,

Klondike Days may have had a slender link to the city's history, but the annual fair in July was everyone's favourite dress-up party in the 1980s—and the first hint of summer festivals to come.

arguing and hanging out. Every inch of wall space was hung with art works in progress, every table and empty space was covered with graffiti. The colours and images were overwhelming. The room was vibrant with the energy of twenty-odd young people determined to find their voice and to shout out loud. I had never seen a place like it. Gail Olmstead, the musician/composer who had been volunteering her time, had asked me to come in to help out with this new project, helping untrained actors to create a musical based on their life experiences. I had recently completed my MFA in Directing, was trying to write my thesis, and needed some hands-on work to get me away from my computer. I walked into the adventure of my artistic life to avoid my homework.

I knew the youth at the studio came from a wide variety of backgrounds, but I was unprepared for the marked differences. As the other volunteer coaches arrived that first afternoon, I observed as mosaic of youth, each wearing the marks of their community, slowly gathered together and began working on improvised scenes. Girls with multicoloured hair worked with tough looking older boys wearing expensive track suits, heavily made-up girls in tight jeans were doing scenes with long haired young men in ripped skateboarding gear. Before I knew their names, I recognized the physical appearance choices actors were making to place themselves, to belong. But in this strange studio, they were all thrown together. Over the next year, I came to know these young people very well, and heard horror stories of drugs, violence, abuse and the dark side of Edmonton's streets. But on that first afternoon, I was simply astonished by their potential....

No matter what background, what baggage they carry, in that theatre they were working together.[58]

Coming home ⌐ Mieko Ouchi, as told to Vivian Giang

I never imagined that I would stay in Edmonton. I thought I would jet off to Toronto or New York, or live somewhere more glamorous, but I started working right away after I got out of school, and was offered some shows quite quickly. I just really fell in love with theatre community here, and they really embraced me. I felt like they offered me a community, that after awhile, I felt really loathe to leave. As it turns out, I travel a lot in my work now, and I spend maybe half a year outside of Edmonton, but I really love having Edmonton as my home base....

I think the Edmonton arts community is really unique, and you discover that when you travel. I've been lucky to travel to film festivals across Canada; to see plays in all different corners of Canada; and I have been able to travel across the U.S. as well to international film festivals. All of those experiences made me appreciate Edmonton all that much more. I think it's because we have a really strong base of people who love the arts. They are not necessarily wealthy people who get corporate tickets, but they are people who have passionately grown up on the Fringe, the Folk Festival, Heritage Days. There are so many events the city has to offer. People just really love the arts, and it's a part of their everyday life. They go to the theatre. They go to the opera, World at Winspear, all of these things. It's just part of their life...

I would love to see more immigrant stories celebrated.... That's always been a passion of mine in my work, and in my films. It's interesting. I met a fellow the other day who was a famous broadcaster in Romania. He came over to Edmonton to cover the World Track and Field Games. He immigrated here. He's working in a liquor store in south Edmonton and obviously not doing what he was doing in Romania. He was working there at such a high level, and yet he has chosen to live here. That's a great endorsement. Maybe those are the kinds of stories we need to find, and celebrate too. Just the people who do a great thing.[59]

A bitter labour dispute at the Gainers' meatpacking plant in 1986 quickly became the most violent strike in Edmonton's history, an exception to the rule in local labour relations.

THE WAR ON 66th STREET

Andrew Nikiforuk

The strike began on June 1, 1986, on the corner of 66th Street where the barbed wire fence ringing the Gainers' meat packing plant meets the dust and diesel fumes of the Yellowhead Highway. The worst battles took place right outside the main gate, in front of Sunshine Chick Hatchery Supplies, Fred's New and Used Luggage, and the rented ATCO trailer that served as strike headquarters for the United Food and Commercial Workers. Some days the police scuffled with pickets as far afield as Angie's Lounge: it's a block north of Gainers, near the rapid transit tacks where strikers collected debris to hurl at the busloads of replacement workers. During the war—and that's what the strike became—Angie's "no minors allowed" sign was altered to read "no scabs." It still reads that way.

The Gainers plant occupies a whole block in the heart of Edmonton's northeast. The red-brick central office, which used to be owned by Swift and Company, has been a landmark for fifty years. Most people in the neighbourhood work at Gainers or have friends or relatives who do. With a work force of 1,100 it's the city's eighth largest employer as well as the third largest meat packing company in the country, after Canada Packers and Schneiders. The average wage is $12 an hour; the strike didn't change that.

In the northeast the average resident is middle-aged, has raised two or three children, owns an $80,0000 bungalow, drives an American car, enjoys Canadian beer, and does not question the existence of God. Many north-easterners also speak English with accents that reflect distant origins: Poland, Italy, the Ukraine, Germany, Portugal, Chile, Vietnam, Korea, rural Alberta or the Maritimes. They are hard-working and law-abiding—the kind of people who, if the police laid a yellow tape down a road, wouldn't cross it. Robert Claney, the superintendent of the local police station says, "We may argue and fight verbally, but we don't do it toe-to-toe, hand-to-hand. We don't hammer the hell out of each other and threaten to kill each other, and throw rocks and bottles and glass and pieces of metal. We don't deal with disputes that way."

The Gainers' strike bloodied this community and polarized Alberta. Before Premier Don Getty intervened and a settlement was reached, after six and a half months, the whole raw, class struggle from which the labour movement was born seemed to have been re-enacted. The overt issue was parity with workers at Canada Packers, but the confrontation and the events leading up to it touched every Albertan with eyes and ears. Righteousness and an army of unemployed youth fuelled management's intransigence while impotence and a new labour solidarity fuelled the strikers' fury. The northeast grew familiar with the military thump of riot police beating shields like Zulu warriors as they marched up 66th Street. The war left no heart untouched, no pocketbook unruffled, no ideals unsullied. [60]

Strikers and replacement workers fought on the streets in a divided and troubled city. The strikers stayed out for seven months, but the economic fallout continued for years after the province intervened to end the dispute.

Fred Pester, neighbour

It was wild, all right. I stayed neutral because I wanted to stay out of trouble. You just sit your bum-sa-daisy down on that chair, and I'll tell you…. They went crazy. They went haywire.

They didn't act like humans. It's hard to believe human nature can change so fast, within a few days. [61]

Wolfgang Plath, neighbour

So one day I'm standing at my door, and this cop puts his billy club against my stomach, and says, "Get out of here." And I say, "But I live here." And he says, "Go inside or I'll arrest you." [62]

Brian S., replacement worker

None of us had ever been members of their stupid union so we weren't scabs and I think that was the one thing that always stuck in my craw the most, being called a scab. I was not a scab; I was just a guy out trying to get a job and make some money. [63]

Bill V., striker

We won a little bit. Everybody knew about the injustices to workers in Alberta. Pocklington, he won because he never had to pay us benefits back. But the amount he lost? Respect.[64]

Dave Werlin, president of the Alberta Federation of Labour

You know it was a very little strike at a very little plant...but it took on that kind of significance. They realized they had to win it just as badly as we realized we had to win it.[65]

Peter Pocklington, Gainers owners

I'm a winner because I proved that in a free society you don't have to be pushed around by anyone, that you can stand your ground and demand that they negotiate.[66]

Robert Claney, police superintendent

The labour dispute kind of made us as a community, dirty. It reduced our humanity, you know, our ability to deal with problems in a rational, reasonable way.[67]

Neil Farrell, Edmonton Power worker

It was awful. I'll just never get those scenes out of my mind. There had been a hundred strikes before in this city, and there have been a hundred strikes since then, but nothing like this had ever happened in Edmonton.... Everybody lost.[68]

BLACK FRIDAY, 1987

Darla Quinlan was living at the Evergreen Mobile Home Park when the tornado hit. Her sons, Michael McMullan and Greg Buteau, her daughter, Angela Buteau, and her niece, Jamie McGaughey were with her that day.

Darla Quinlan: It seems like a lifetime ago, but it has only been just over sixteen years. The images and feelings are easy to conjure up from the midst of that tragic day. We had just brought our first home in May 1987 at Evergreen Mobile Park. In July of 1987 we lost our home. In time we endured the loss of our marriage, went into bankruptcy and questioned our spirituality.

My first memory was that the sky was very, very brilliant blue. It was so hot that day, and you were playing in the park.

Angela: We were asking what was going on. It was changing so quickly, from being totally blue, gorgeous day, then raining and the power going out.

Greg: I remember going into the kitchen and looking out the kitchen window, it would have been looking at the neighbors' place and seeing the swirl.... I was looking out and just seeing all the leaves blowing and windows popping, and then all of us we were behind the couch. How did you arrange us? It was Michael, then Jamie, Angela, and then you were kind of cradled over us, behind the couch.

Angela: The windows were smashing and you went on top of us. I remember going down, and a window smashing, and that's how I ended up with the cuts.

Greg: We got up and did a walk around the house and everybody just said, "What the heck just went on?" Oh it was just chaos. The doors were blown off the trailer next to us. The trailer behind us was on its roof.... Insulation everywhere. Our trailer actually did okay, minus the windows and doors and a little of this and that. We all went outside and walked across the street, the water was up to your waist....

A tornado survivor is rushed to an ambulance after being rescued near 64th Avenue and 27th Street.

Mayor Laurence Decore struggles with his emotions as he tours a devastated neighbourhood after the tornado.

Angela: I remember you saying: "Don't look back. Just get out, and don't turn around. Just keep going."

Greg: The tornado defined my personality and who I am. After that happened you and Dad separated and times were really tough. I was just hitting that age where I was getting into trouble at school and being defiant because I didn't know how to handle everything and then all of a sudden, boom, the family's gone, no more happiness. Things had been awesome—going to Parks and Rec, everything was going so well. Then after everything transpired, things turned upside down. My fascination for storms is unbelievable.

Angela: I have a fascination with them as well.... One thing is that it really put a value on life. I know some of the kids that we hung out with at Parks and Rec did not survive. Looking back at a family that lost their kids—and for us to be in a trailer with four kids and not be touched with all the devastation around us—you can't help but think, "Why us?" So many people have different views on what happened, but to be one of those lucky few...provides a different outlook. We faced death, we were there, and we came so close. We walked away from it. So many people didn't.[69]

"Rule 1: Start with a hug" ⌐ Heather Airth, director, Edmonton Emergency Relief Services

On the afternoon of the tornado I was working at our warehouse. When we realized a disaster had occurred, I immediately called my [four] colleagues. We had a short conference call and decided, "Damn the torpedoes, full speed ahead."

The marvelous thing about our organization is that we're very small, very dedicated and not encumbered by rules or policies we have to follow. We just got together on a conference call and said: "Yes, let's do it." We had no idea at that time what "it" might be.

I called Alberta Public Safety Services and told them who we were and that we had a warehouse with clothing, furniture and household items available, and that we also would be accepting donations to be held in trust and turned over to families in need. They said: "Thank God." We also called the media.

In a short time our phone started ringing off the hook. Meanwhile water was pouring in and we were trying to move our supplies and mop up to prevent water damage. We began receiving donations from people arriving at our front door even before they were told it was safe to drive again.

During the next hour the other directors arrived. Next began what was probably the longest 48 hours of our lives. When it was declared safe to drive, it was as if floodgates had opened up. People lined up at our door... people who came to help...people who came with donations.

At about 0200 hours on Saturday, we had 50 volunteers inside sorting the donations that were being constantly delivered. People were lined up in the rain 20 deep bringing donations in. The volunteers ranged from teenagers to senior citizens. Some stayed 24 to 35 hours. We didn't shut down until Sunday at midnight when we couldn't handle it any more, and had to go home to get two or three hours of sleep.

On Saturday it was still raining outside but marvellous things were happening inside the warehouse. People kept arriving to help. The large parking lot beside the warehouse was full and cars were parked for a block on either side. A hundred more cars had commandeered the park opposite the warehouse. People who came in, didn't look around for direction. They just looked around, saw what needed to be done and did it. ...One fellow realized there was a lot of perishable food coming in so he went home and came back with his freezer. Another asked if he could call Safeway to get some refrigerated trucks. It was a beautiful meshing of people and ideas combining with work that had to be done.

By noon there was no place to park for people coming in with donations. There were two lanes of cars lined up for a couple of blocks in either direction. A relay team was set up. They had shopping carts, and runners ran back and forth, carrying donations from the parking lot to the warehouse. By afternoon we realized there was no room left to stack anything. The mayor [Laurence Decore] arrived and arranged for an old airplane hangar to be made available to us. On Sunday afternoon the Mayor's office asked for a head count so they could send food for the volunteers. At 1400 hours we had over 500 people working. We had over 10,000 names in all on our assignment sheets for August....

Throughout the week donations arrived from farther and farther afield. Sometimes there was a three-hour wait to unload the semis, the line was so long.... To summarize, what I think is important: Our organization is comprised of very dedicated people who care very much and very deeply for what we do. None of us has a Master's degree or PhD. We are just caring people.

Our organization is very flexible. It is not hampered by rules, regulations, bureaucracy or red tape. I think that was important to the people who came. [Tornado victims] were frightened, confused. So much had happened to them, and they had lost so much so fast. We had just two rules...

1. Start with a hug.

2. Make damn sure those people have enough.[70]

WHERE ARE YOU FROM?

More than 7,500 refugees arrived in Alberta from Southeast Asia in 1979 and 1980.

"I owned nothing except some clothing" ⤳ Jeffrey Chan

I successfully escaped from Vietnam by way of a small, overcrowded sailboat. After spending thirty-three days on the sea I arrived in the Macau refugee camp in December, 1978. In February, 1980, sponsored by a church, I came to Canada....

Three weeks after my arrival in Edmonton, I found a job and worked as a break press and punch operator in a furniture factory—Superior Steel Desk. I worked eight hours a day, five days a week. I could now go to adult school at night or on Saturdays with little effort. A few months later, the working hours were changed to ten hours a day and four days a week. I worked from half past seven in the morning until six at night. My class started at seven o'clock and it took a little more than forty minutes to travel from work to home and from home to school. When I got home from work, I had to take a shower (after long day of hard working, I had a mixed smell of sweat, oil, and grease) and finish my supper in less than twenty minutes. If there was a traffic jam, especially in winter, I would not even have the time for my supper.

A thoughtful grandchild sits quietly through speeches about the political crisis in India at a Sikh conference in Edmonton in 1985. A new wave of immigrants from India and Pakistan arrived in the city in the 1970s and 1980s. Alberta is home to more than 40,000 Sikhs.

In 1984, most of my family had settled down in Canada and all of them could earn a living on their own, I did not have to support them any more. I became financially free and my goal to further my education seemed more attainable than ever. Thus, I decided to quit my job and spent seven months as a full time adult student to complete all the grade-twelve courses which were required to enroll in Engineering or other faculties at the University.

By the time I came back to school as a full-time student, I was twenty-seven and had been out of school for ten years. It was extremely difficult for me to get back to the proper studying habit after working for so many years. Because English was not my mother tongue, I had to concentrate more and study long hours every day. With strong determination and high motivation, I worked hard to overcome all these problems and difficulties. After several years of hard work, I finally completed my Bachelor of Science degree in Computer Engineering at the University of Alberta in 1989.[71]

Thanh L. Hua

Sometimes, on a quiet Sunday morning, I think back to the small river that meanders through my native town, and I recall the music of the rains which tapped on the roof of my parents' home during the long rainy season. But I also find spectacular the Rockies at dawn I contemplated a few years ago on a camping trip. All those images, sounds and sensation, old and new, form the basic ingredients of our emotional life. Those sensations do not exclude one another, rather each of them makes us a little bit richer as a whole person. And that enrichment, I believe, makes us more and more tolerant towards people of backgrounds that are different from ours. And that tolerance contributes its part to the harmony of this society and to the mutual understanding between its members.[72]

"I will live like them, too" ↶ Mary Kur

Mary Kur fled to Kenya as a child to escape the war in southern Sudan. After five years in a refugee camp, she arrived in Edmonton in 2001. At 16 Mary learned to speak English with the help of Joanna Foster, a youth worker from the Mennonite Centre for Newcomers. She is beginning to like her new city. "The scariest thing for me here," she says, "is the snow."

Did you choose Edmonton?

We didn't know where we would be going. We just applied to go. Whoever accepted us, we would go. We waited there for five years, and then in 2000, they called us for an interview. On July 24, we went to Nairobi for an interview. On November 11, we went for a medical check. We stayed there until September 11, 2001. We were supposed to leave that day. That was the day of the bombing in America. They cancelled our flight. Oh my gosh, I thought, we're not going to go anymore. We stayed until October 9 in Nairobi, and we arrived here on October 11, 2001 at 3.30 p.m.

Did you want to come to Canada?

They didn't ask people: "Where do you want to go?" When the Canadian embassy decided they needed people, they took them and brought them to Canada. You don't choose.

I thought it was a good thing. There is no war here. We thought it would be great to live in Canada.... When we came here the winter was really, really cold for us.

I was on the plane. When I got off the plane I didn't see any black person. I'm not with my people anymore. I'm with different people. This guy came to pick us up, to take us to the reception house. We stayed there for a month. They found a house, and we moved to the house....

It was really cold. One week I didn't go outside. I thought to myself: "Oh my gosh, I can't take this cold." Then I told myself: "Okay. It is not that bad." Last year was my second winter. It wasn't cold like the first time. I'm getting used to it.

Was it the first snow you'd ever seen?

Yes. I was wondering: "What is this white thing? Ice or what? No, this is called winter. Where did this come from? It just came by itself. People didn't bring it." I stood at the window, and I thought: "Who made this?" And then I said to myself: "Nobody made it. It just came by itself." I was confused. I thought it would stay like that.

How did you imagine snow when you were a child?

Before we came here, we had some friends in Canada. They would call us and tell us about winter and snow. And I would ask: "What is this snow? Is it something like ice?" I thought it would be like ice that would never go away. Why do those people live here, I thought. I will live like them, too.

What are the hard parts of being here?

I feel at home here. At the same time I don't really feel at home because my family is not all here. My mother is in Sudan. I am a twin. My sister, Adit, is not here. She lives in a place where there are no phones so I can't talk to her. I don't think my Mom wants to come here. I think sometime I may go back to visit, but I am not really sure.

Mary Kur, a student at
Queen Elizabeth High School

Do you know what kind of job you would like?

When I finish high school and go to college, I want to be a nurse....

Do you have favourite places in the city?

Usually I don't go out. I stay at home. I watch movies.

Have you made friends?

It's not easy. The first time I came here I didn't know anybody. I didn't speak English. When I came to Queen Elizabeth High School I met these two girls from Ethiopia and they always took care of me. They took me to the cafeteria, and everywhere. Their names are Rahel and Tadelech. They were really kind to me. Everybody at the school helped me....

Do you feel like a Canadian yet?

Yes. At first when I came here I didn't know anything about Canada or its people. When I came to Camp Warwa [a Rotary Club summer camp] in May I felt welcome. When I needed help, I found some. The first time, when I came to the summer camp, I thought: "Oh my gosh, why did they choose me to come here? This is something beautiful. I didn't even do any-thing, or say anything, to make people say: 'Mary is a good person.' People are friendly to each other here. People help each other. It is so good. I like it. I was climbing at the summer camp." I said: "Let me tell my body to keep going." The others were calling out to me: "You can do it Mary. Come on. You can do it!" I feel strong. I can do it.

What do you miss about your life in Sudan?

Canadian parties are not the same as our parties.... In Sudan, there are not the same kinds of parties. There people are dancing all the time. Last week I went to help my friend Rebecca and her Mom. We were working the night shift, cleaning offices downtown. Early, early in the morning, we were waiting for the LRT at Churchill Station and we just started dancing on the platform. People were looking at us, and maybe saying: "Are those women crazy?" We didn't care. We just danced![73]

...Papaschase ↝ Dwayne Donald

"Where are you from?" The question is always asked with a tone of famil-iarity and camaraderie that distracts me and leaves me not wanting to answer. "I'm from Edmonton," I reluctantly reply, and then I wait for the response that I know is coming. This response is rarely verbal. Mostly, I get nonverbal responses to this answer—looks of confusion, wonder-ment, the slow nodding of the head. These responses give one message: "I thought this guy was an Indian, but I guess he's not...."

When Aboriginal people meet each other for the first time, the most common question is: "Where are you from?" The question is directed towards finding out your roots, your family, your ancestors, your rela-tions, your home, your place, your tribe, your Reserve. When a person can say that they are "from" a particular Reserve, then there seems to be a certain comfort, a common understanding that makes Aboriginal people with similar backgrounds, histories, and memories feel a unique kind of solidarity. Although one may be Cree and the other Blackfoot, they seem to identify with each other through their similar experiences and world-views.

I don't come from a reserve, nor do any of my immediate relatives. I don't have a place in the Aboriginal sense of traditional territory or sacred land. I may have distant relatives on reserves, but my family must have lost contact with them a long time ago. That was before the time "where it went wrong...."

My ancestors were late in signing an adhesion to the conditions of Treaty 6. In August of 1877, Chief Papastayo agreed to the terms of Treaty 6 at Fort Edmonton on behalf of his band of about 241 followers. Papastayo selected an area for their Reserve approximately four miles south of the North Saskatchewan River, directly across the river from the original site of Fort Edmonton. Soon after making this decision, trouble started. A large and vocal group of settlers and citizens of the Edmonton area did not want the Papaschase Indian Band Indian Reserve No. 136 to be anywhere near the growing settlement of Edmonton. They argued that the Reserve would impede the growth and development of the town and deny the settlers access to valuable resources and fertile land. A newspaper of the time, the *Edmonton Bulletin*, advocated that the Papaschase Band "be sent back to the country they originally came from."

In the end, the settlers got their wish. The members of the Papaschase Band, forced to wait while their Treaty rights hung in limbo, were left destitute and hungry for several years after the signing of Treaty 6 and the disappearance of the buffalo. Eventually, the members either took Métis scrip and lost their Treaty status or simply moved to other reserves in the Edmonton area. On November 19, 1888, three adult males who were living on the Enoch Reserve surrendered the rights of the Papaschase Band to Reserve No. 136.

Rose Lameman, left, great-great-granddaughter of Chief Papastayo, is the chief of the Papaschase First Nation.

Rosalind Callihoo, right, great-granddaughter of Chief Michel Callihoo, is the chief of the Michel First Nation.

My parent's home is located on the very land that was surrendered on that day. I grew up in that part of the city of Edmonton, went to school, played in the parks, rode my bike on the streets, threw rocks in the river, shovelled snow, kissed girls, walked my dog, went to the movie theatre, visited my grandparents, shopped at the farmers' market, studied at the University of Alberta (which, ironically, has a Papaschase Room in its Faculty Club), and no one ever said a word about it. No one knew about it. How do these things get swept under the carpet so completely? How do people's lives get expunged from collective memory so easily?

My Mom has been diligently digging up fragments of the history of my Dad's family. It is a process that she and I started together when we both started scouring Hudson's Bay Company records and Métis land scrip lists looking for familiar names. Gradually, we pieced together an extensive and detailed family tree with names, dates, and places of birth. The next task was to uncover the life stories and memories to these people, these relatives we only knew on paper, by talking to relatives and friends who might remember and provide us with a closer connection to the past. My Mom, working with my Dad's sister, has dug deepest and discovered three things of significance: our connections to the Papaschase Band, Grandma Ward's rocking chair from the cabin on Hastings Lake, and a Bible written in Cree syllabics. She gave the Bible to me.

Sometimes I take the Bible out of the cedar chest where it is stored, unwrap the cloth that surrounds it, and hold it in my lap while I sit. The Bible was a prized possession of Emerance Charland, my great grandma's sister. Both sisters received identical prayer books from the St. Albert mission where they were raised and educated. My great grandma, Madelaine Ward, couldn't read, and I am told that she would sit and rock in her chair while holding her Bible on her lap. When I do the same, I somehow feel connected to her and wonder what she would think of her family today. Would it bother her that so few remember what happened to them back then?

The current leaders of the re-established Papaschase Band have filed court documents outlining their case against the Canadian government in which they are seeking compensation for the wrongful removal of Treaty and land rights. My Dad, his family, and our relatives are considered Papaschase members, and we stand to benefit from any court decisions that favour the Papaschase case. In all likelihood, they will win some form of compensation. This raises the possibility that my family and I could receive some form of 'official' recognition as Indians with membership in the Papaschase Band. Finally, I could answer the question that has been plaguing me for so many years with a clear and definite answer:

"Where are you from?"

"Papaschase."

"Where's that?"

"Edmonton."[74]

The Edmonton Region 2004

Edmonton and its neighbouring communities have more than one million residents in 2004. The majority of people live in suburban neighbourhoods, and in independent satellite communities and acreages. They depend on an expanding network of freeways and roads to reach the downtown business district by car. This map does not indicate that Sherwood Park is one of the largest communities in the metropolitan area, as its boundaries flow into Strathcona County. The city annexed West Jasper Place and Beverly in the early 1960s; the Michel reserve west of St. Albert ceased to exist in 1958 when a majority of band members voted for enfranchisement.

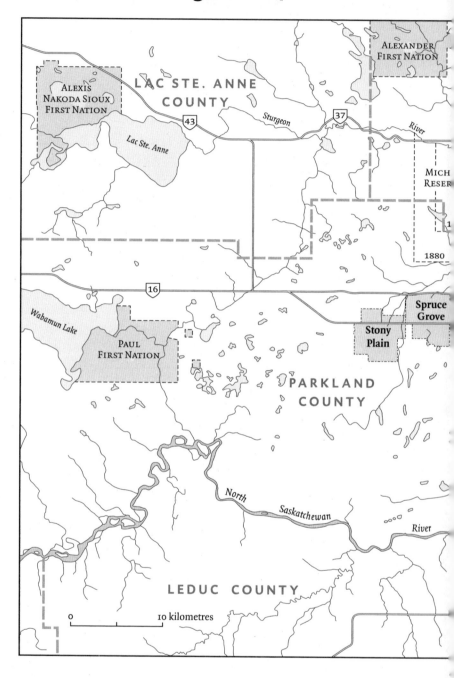

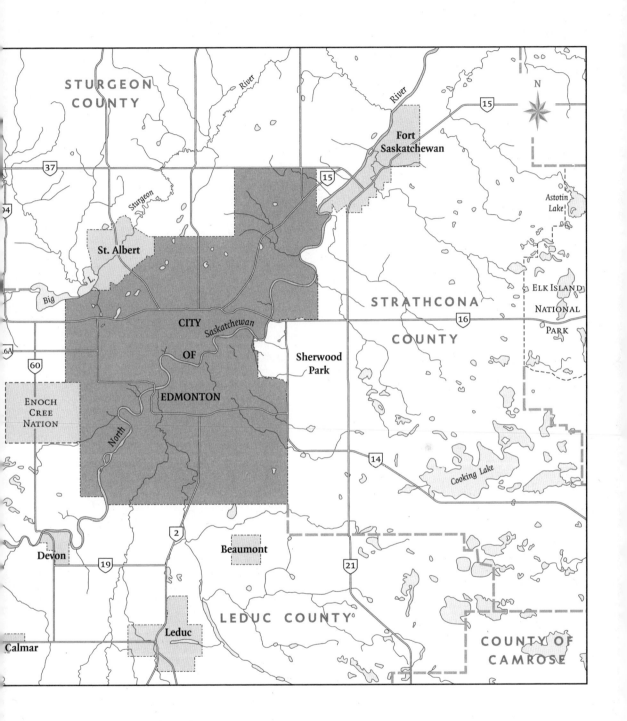

Edmonton: A City Called Home—
A Centennial Project

THE EDMONTON: A CITY CALLED HOME PROJECT began with an intriguing question. An updated narrative history of the city seemed overdue as it had been more than 30 years since the publication of J.M. MacGregor's *Edmonton: A History*. Should one author tackle the assignment, or should the project be a collaboration?

In the spirit of the place, we decided to work together.

Tougher questions came next. How could we honour the overlooked contributions of thousands of citizens who are rarely, if ever, acknowledged by name? How could we combine personal stories with the latest scholarship from urban historians? How would we contend with competing versions of the same events?

We wanted to reach the city's children, and document the history of a childhood in Edmonton in a way they would enjoy. Should we create a picture book, or a book of true stories for older children?

We knew we could not include every citizen's contribution in a single volume. How could we preserve the full collection of original stories, interviews and photographs, and publish them in an affordable format?

Like the city itself, the project grew beyond original expectations. The result is this book, *Edmonton In Our Own Words*; a nonfiction chapter book for children, *Kidmonton: True Stories of River City Kids*, published by Brindle & Glass; www.edmontonhistory.ca, a new urban history web site, created by Chinook Multimedia Inc., and co-hosted by the University of Alberta

Libraries and the Edmonton Public Library; and The Edmonton: A City Called Home Collection [CCH], a compilation of original stories and photographs in the City of Edmonton Archives.

━◦◦∽

THE EDMONTON: A CITY CALLED HOME PROJECT owes special thanks to Mayor Bill Smith, who decided in 1999 it was time for a new investigation of the city's history and refused to take "no" for an answer. His steadfast support for the larger education project for the city's centennial in 2004 will be appreciated for many years to come.

The Edmonton Public Library is the perfect place is to write a book. For two years Director of Libraries Linda Cook and her staff offered us a warm welcome and continuing encouragement, while former Associate Director Keith Turnbull provided the administrative leadership for a complex project.

Alva Shewchuk and the Education 2004 committee organized community support on behalf of the City of Edmonton, City of Edmonton Archives, Concordia University College of Alberta, Conseil scolaire Centre-Nord, Edmonton Catholic Schools, Edmonton Historical Board, Edmonton Public Library, Edmonton Public Schools and Metro Continuing Education, Grant MacEwan College, NorQuest College, Northern Alberta Institute of Technology, TELUS and the University of Alberta Libraries. Ernie Ingles, Chief Librarian and Associate Vice President of the University of Alberta, provided generous assistance at every stage of the project.

Edmontonians from all walks of life began to arrive at the library in 2002 with handwritten stories, family photographs, scrapbooks, letters, wartime ration books, Social Credit funny money, research tips, old maps and documents—even a copper pot from Edmonton's fur trade era. We started regular coffee sessions where these citizens could read—or tell—their original city stories to one another. Regrettably only a representative selection of their contributions could appear in this book. I hope that future editors, anthologists and historians will consider publication and that researchers and students will explore the collection. Listening to these storytellers for two years has been a privilege and an inspiration. I thank them for their friendship and trust.

I am particularly grateful to many members of Alberta's founding families, especially elders, for their willingness to share some of the oral history of the First Nations and Métis in their traditional territory: Nellie Carlson, Gordon Lee, Gilbert Anderson and Kathleen Steinhauer, Calvin Bruneau and Joyce Bruneau, Rose Lameman, Rosalind Callihoo, Leroy Ward, Duane Good Striker, Terry Lusty, Liliane Coutu-Maisonneuve and Philip Coutu, Pamela Cunningham, Francis Alexis, Kathleen Alexis, Gerald Delorme, Lewis Cardinal, Muriel Stanley-Venne, Mary Cardinal, Clara Woodbridge, Marge Friedel, Margaret McGilvery, Shirley Gladue, Doreen Wabasca, Fran Gosché, Darlene and Dwayne Donald, and Ron Maurice deserve special thanks, along with many other individuals in the Papaschase, Enoch, Michel, Alexander, Alexis, Paul, Saddle Lake and Ermineskin First Nations, the Confederacy of Treaty Six First Nations, the Métis Nation of Alberta and the Canadian Native Friendship Centre.

My colleague Carolina Jakeway Roemmich not only supplied research to the project, but also organized 62 volunteers who generously transcribed and edited hundreds of citizens' stories, and entered them in a database. We thank them for their hard work.

The City of Edmonton Archives deserves wider recognition for its preservation of the city's collective story. City Archivist Leslie Latta-Guthrie and her colleagues, Bruce Ibsen, Kim Christie-Milley, Susan Stanton, Glenys Smith and Laurette Miller enthusiastically shared their intimate knowledge of the city's collections with us. We would also like to express our respect and appreciation to Edmonton's Archivist Emeritus, Helen LaRose, who continues to set an example for us in her lifelong commitment to historical preservation and community service.

We appreciate the encouragement of Edmonton 2004 Chair Ralph Young; the Mayor's Advisory Committee, and the Edmonton Urban Aboriginal Affairs Committee. Lorraine Wadel of the Office of the Mayor, and Chris McLeod, Tiffany Nelson and Cindy Lieu of the City of Edmonton offered substantial administrative support; many other city employees provided research support.

I also appreciated the guidance of faculty and staff at the University of Alberta, in particular Rod McLeod, Frank Tough, Doug Owram, Ian MacLaren, Gerhard Ens, Heather Zwicker, Mike Percy, Jim Lightbody, Merrill Distad, Fern Russell and Peter Binkley; France Levasseur-Ouimet and Frank McMahon of the Faculté St. Jean; provincial archaeologists Heinz Pyszczyk, Jack Ives and Jack Brink; and historians Susan

Berry of the Provincial Museum of Alberta; Alvin Finkel, Jeff Taylor, Nanci Langford of Athabasca University; and Bob Hesketh of Chinook Multimedia Inc.

Julaine Scott and the rest of the Chinook team deserve special thanks, as do editor Laura Sproule; researchers David Ryning, Samantha First Charger and Magnolia Unka; and volunteers Jean Crozier, Vivian Giang, Charlene Wiebe, Susan Godwin, Phyllis Johnson, Blanka Kaiser, Darla Quinlan and Kira Goyette Dreimanis.

Carolina and I would also like to acknowledge the contributions of Edmonton Public Library staff members who offered daily support in research and community outreach work: Heritage Librarian Joseph Rek; Multilingual Services Librarian Najma Karmali, Judy Moore, manager of the Centre for Reading and the Arts, Iolanni Domingo, Joan Paton, Yvonne Footz, Sylvia Hertling, Dianne Szlabey, Aline McDonald, Therese Gavignan, Chris Bezovie, Jean Stefiuk, Shara Rosko, Sarah MacDougall, David Huggett, Louise Luk, Susan Thomson and the dedicated staff of the Library Access Division. We appreciated the administrative support of Pat Jobb and Norm Ouellet; and the technical support of Peter Schoenberg, Lachlan Bickley, Jamie Moxam and especially John Sylvestre who rescued many a lost computer file. The Edmonton Public Library Board and the Edmonton Historical Board also offered invaluable support, as did storytellers with the Edmonton Lifelong Learning Association.

We also relied on the expert guidance of the staff at the Provincial Archives of Alberta: the late Sandra Thomson, Claude Roberto, Diane Lamoureux, Dennis Hyduk and Jonathan Davidson; Ann Ramsden of the Musée Héritage in St. Albert; Debbie Shoctor and Dan Kauffman of the Jewish Archives and Museum of Edmonton and Northern Alberta; Nashir Karmali and Larry Shaben of the Edmonton Council of Muslim Communities; Sharon Morin of the Michif Institute; Jim Bowman of the Glenbow Museum and Archives; the staff at the University of Alberta Archives; Lori Clark and Mike Kostek at the Edmonton Public Schools Archives; Tim Marriott and Larissa Stedzenko at Fort Edmonton Park; Sherry Haley and Bruce Macdonald of the Edmonton Artifacts Centre; David Haas of the Loyal Edmonton Regiment Museum; social studies consultants Ian Kupchenko, Randy Lyseng and Marie Settle; Kristina Nygren of the Fort Saskatchewan Museum; Michael Dawe of the Red Deer and District Archives: the Ukrainian Cultural Heritage Village and other regional museums and historic sites.

Many of the city's community historians and writers—especially Ken Tingley, Lawrence Herzog, Jars Balan, Marianne Fedori, Judy Berghofer, Kathy Ivany, Bert Yeudall, Alan Vanterpool, Catherine Cole, Olive Elliott and Edmonton's historic tour guide extraordinaire, Cameron Malcolm—offered generous advice and support, as did Don Bouzek and his colleagues in the Alberta Labour History Institute; Frank Norris and the Edmonton and District Historical Society; Ed Liss of the Lac Ste. Anne Historical Society and Adrienne Lamb of CBC Radio. I gratefully acknowledge the encouragement of Tony Cashman and the late Alex Mair, who have delighted readers with their Edmonton stories for decades.

In the summer of 2003 I submitted a draft manuscript that was more than double the length of this book to Linda Cameron of the University of Alberta Press. I am grateful to editor Mary Mahoney-Robson and a gifted copy editor, Peter Midgley, for helping me to shape this early draft into a book that could be lifted, let alone read. Cathie Crooks, Alan Brownoff, Alethea Adair, Laraine Coates and Yoko Sekiya provided generous assistance at the Press. We especially thank designer Kevin Zak, cartographer Wendy Johnson, indexer Judy Dunlop and photographer John Ulan for their creative contributions to the book. The University of Alberta Press would like to thank Dick Harrison and John Taylor for their careful reading of the manuscript.

We gratefully acknowledge the financial support of the Department of Canadian Heritage, Canada Council for the Arts, Alberta Lottery Fund, Alberta Community Development, Alberta Foundation for the Arts, Alberta Historical Resources Foundation, the Office of the Mayor, the Clifford E. Lee Foundation and the Friends of the Edmonton Public Library in the development of all aspects of the Edmonton: A City Called Home project. George and Elizabeth Jakeway, Carolina's parents, offered the gift of a new series of historic maps, a contribution we truly appreciate.

Finally, Carolina and I thank our husbands, Mike Roemmich and Allan Chambers, and my children, Peter and Kira Goyette Dreimanis, for their loving support and patience.

To Edmonton's storytellers, and storykeepers, I offer one last thank you. This has been a labour of love for all of us.

Notes

How a City Remembers

1   William Newton, *Twenty Years on the Saskatchewan, N.W. Canada* (London: Elliot Stock, 1897), 35.

2   Anthony Henday, *A Year Inland: The Journal of a Hudson's Bay Company Winterer*, ed. Barbara Belyea (Waterloo: Wilfred Laurier University Press, 2000), 3.

3   George Melnyk, *New Moon at Batoche: Reflections on the Urban Prairie* (Banff: Banff Centre Press, 1999), 90.

A Bend in the River to 1700

1   B. Newton, J. Pollock, J.W. Ives, and H. Pyszczyk, *Strathcona Site (FjPi-29) Excavations 1978, 1979 and 1980* (Edmonton: Alberta Culture, Historical Resources Division, 1985), 89.

2   Roger D. Morton, "The Edmonton Region Through Time," in *Edmonton Beneath Our Feet: A Guide to the Geology of the Edmonton Region*, ed. John D. Godfrey (Edmonton: Edmonton Geological Society, 1993), 5.

3   Ibid., 10.

4   Ibid., 13.

5   Ibid., 16.

6   James A. Burns, "Ice-Age Fossils," in *Edmonton Beneath Our Feet*, 19.

7   John Shaw, "Geomorphology," in *Edmonton Beneath Our Feet*, 28.

8   Ibid., 31.

9   Ibid., 32.

10 Ed Struzik, "Monster prehistoric bear's bone plucked from a conveyor belt," *Edmonton Journal*, 30 May 1993, A1.

11 Jim Burns in discussion with Linda Goyette, 18 February 2003.

12 Olive Dickason, "A Historical Reconstruction," in *The Prairie West: Historical Readings*, eds. R. Douglas Francis and Howard Palmer (Edmonton: Pica Pica Press, 1985), 39.

13   Richard T. Price, ed., *The Spirit of the Alberta Indian Treaties*, 3rd ed. (Edmonton: The University of Alberta Press, 1999), 117.

14   Jack Brink in discussion with Linda Goyette, February 2003; Jack Ives in discussion with Linda Goyette, February 2003; Heinz Pyszczyk in discussion with Linda Goyette, 23 October 2003; and Elaine Dewar, *Bones: Discovering the First Americans* (New York: Caroll and Graf, 2002).

15   See Ruth Gruhn, "Linguistic Evidence in Support of the Coastal Route of Earliest Entry into the New World," in *The Native Imprint: The Contribution of First Peoples to Canada's Character, Volume 1: To 1815*, ed. Olive Patricia Dickason (Athabasca: Athabasca University, 1995), 33.

16   Pyszczyk, in discussion.

17   See Newton et al., *Strathcona Site Excavations*.

18   Ibid.

19   Heinz W. Pyszczyk, *Archaeology Guide and Tour of Greater Edmonton Area* (Edmonton: Strathcona Archaeological Society, Provincial Museum of Alberta, 1999).

20   Pyszczyk, in discussion.

21   Scace and Associates Ltd., *Elk Island National Park: A Cultural History* (Calgary: Parks Canada, Department of Indian and Northern Affairs, 1976).

22   This version of the story is taken from Canada's First Nations, "Antiquity: A. Native Creation Myths; Cree—World Parent," The University of Calgary, http://www.ucalgary.ca/applied_history/tutor/firstnations/world.html (accessed 14 March 2003). It has been adapted from James R. Stevens, *Sacred Legends of the Sandy Lake Cree* (Toronto: McClelland and Stewart Ltd., 1971). The dated and anglicized Cree spellings have been replaced with the Plains Cree spellings from Nancy LeClaire and George Cardinal, *Alberta Elders' Cree Dictionary: Alperta ohci kehtehayak nehiyaw otwestamâkewasinahikan*, ed. Earle H. Waugh (Edmonton: The University of Alberta Press and Duval House, 1998).

23   *The Syncrude Gallery of Aboriginal Culture*, The Provincial Museum of Alberta, Edmonton.

24   *The Syncrude Gallery*.

25   Eleanor Brass, "Origin of the Moon," in *Medicine Boy and Other Cree Tales* (Calgary: Glenbow-Alberta Institute, 1979), unpaginated.

26   Pyszczyk, *Archaeology Guide*, 4–5.

27   Catherine Reininger in discussion with Linda Goyette, March 2003.

The Meeting Place 1700 to 1869

1   Jennifer S.H. Brown, *Strangers in Blood: Fur Trade Company Families in Indian Country* (Vancouver: University of British Columbia Press, 1980), 157; Sylvia van Kirk, *"Many Tender Ties": Women in Fur-Trade Society in Western Canada, 1670–1870* (Winnipeg: Watson and Dwyer, 1980), 97.

2   William Moorman, in discussion with Jacqueline Pelletier, 27 November 2003, in The Rossdale Flats Aboriginal Oral Histories Project Research Team, "Rossdale Flats Aboriginal Oral Histories Project: Report Findings, Part 2 of 2; The Appendices" (report prepared for the City of Edmonton, 10 February 2004), unpaginated; Sir Henry Lefroy, "Sir Henry Lefroy's Journey to the North-West in 1843–4," in *Proceedings and Transactions of the Royal Society of Canada, Third series, Volume XXXII*, ed. W.S. Wallace (Ottawa: The Royal Society of Canada, 1938), 93.

3   The Rossdale Flats Aboriginal Oral Histories Project Research Team, "Rossdale Flats Aboriginal Oral Histories Project: Report of Findings, Part 1 of 2" (report prepared for the City of Edmonton, 10 February 2004), 97.

4   See Scace and Associates Ltd., *Elk Island National Park: A Cultural History* (Calgary: Parks Canada, Department of Indian and Northern Affairs, 1976).

5   Mildred Stefiszyn, ed., *Land Among the Lakes: A History of the Deville and North Cooking Lake Area* (Deville: Deville-North Cooking Lake Historical Society, 1983), 11, 263.

6   Scace, *Elk Island National Park*, 25.

7   Alexander Henry the Younger, *The Journal of Alexander Henry the Younger, 1799–1814*, *Vol. II*, ed. Barry M. Gough (Toronto: The Champlain Society, 1988), 546.

8   See Olive Patricia Dickason, *Canada's First Nations: A History of Founding Peoples from Earliest Times* (Toronto: McClelland and Stewart, 1992), 123, 176; and Gerald Friesen, *The Canadian Prairies: A History* (Toronto: University of Toronto Press, 1987), 24.

9   See Friesen, *Canadian Prairies*; and Dickason, "A Historical Reconstruction," in *The Prairie West: Historical Readings*, eds. R. Francis Douglas and Howard Palmer (Edmonton: Pica Pica Press, 1985).

10   Friesen, *Canadian Prairies*, 25.

11   See Anthony Henday, *A Year Inland: the Journal of a Hudson's Bay Company Winterer*, ed. Barbara Belyea (Waterloo: Wilfrid Laurier University Press, 2000); and Glyndwr Williams, "The puzzle of Anthony Henday's journal, 1754–55," *The Beaver* 309, no. 3 (Winter 1978): 41–56.

12   See James MacGregor, *Edmonton: A History* (Edmonton: M.G. Hurtig Publishers, 1967) and Arthur S. Morton, *A History of the Canadian West to 1870–71, Second Edition* (Toronto: University of Toronto Press, 1973).

13   See Henday, *A Year Inland*.

14   Alice M. Johnson, *Saskatchewan Journals and Correspondence: Edmonton House 1795–1800; Chesterfield House 1800–1802* (London: Hudson's Bay Record Society, 1967), xxviii.

15   Arthur S. Morton, ed., *The Journal of Duncan M'Gillivray of the North West Company at Fort George on the Saskatchewan, 1794–5* (Toronto: MacMillan, 1929), 77.

16   The Autobiographical notes of John McDonald of Garth, 1859, John Macdonald of Garth fonds, MG-19-A17, vol. 1, National Archives of Canada; and 5 October 1795, Edmonton House Post Journal.

17   23 November 1795, Edmonton House Post Journal.

18   William Tomison, 29–31 October 1795; William Tomison to James Spence, 12 November 1795, Edmonton House; and William Tomison to George Sutherland, 20 December 1795, Edmonton House, Edmonton House Post Journal.

19   William Tomison to George Sutherland, 12 February 1796, Edmonton House Post Journal.

20   Angus Shaw to Joseph Colen, 10 May 1797, Fort Augustus, York Factory Correspondence Books, B.239/b/59, fo. 27d, Hudson's Bay Company Archives, Winnipeg, quoted in Johnson, *Saskatchewan Journals*, xxxii.

21   Johnson, *Saskatchewan Journals*, lxxvii.

22   Ibid.

23   See James G. MacGregor, *Blankets and Beads: A History of the Saskatchewan River* (Edmonton: Institute of Applied Art, 1949), 166.

24   Johnson, *Saskatchewan Journals*, lxxvii.

25   29 October 1821, Edmonton House Post Journal.

26   Johnson, *Saskatchewan Journals*, lxxvii, n4.

27   London Office to Depots on Hudson and James Bay, 1800, 152–93, London Office Post Records, A.6/16, Hudson's Bay Company Archives, Winnipeg, quoted in Johnson, *Saskatchewan Journals*, lxxvii.

28   See Johnson, *Saskatchewan Journals*, xxxi; David Thompson, *David Thompson's Narrative: 1784–1812*, ed. Richard Glover (Toronto: The Champlain Society, 1962), 311; and Sir George Simpson, *Journal of Occurrences in the Athabasca Department by George Simpson, 1820 and 1821, and Report*, ed. E.E. Rich (Toronto: The Champlain Society, 1938), 415.

29   See the cover of the Edmonton House Post Journal for the season of 1832 to 1833.

30   19 October 1807, Edmonton House Post Journal.

31   16 December 1796, Edmonton House Post Journal.

32   Gerhard Ens in discussion with Linda Goyette, 23 October 2002.

33   Ibid.

34   London Office to depots on Hudson and James Bay, 1800, p. 213, London Office Post Records, A.6/16, Hudson's Bay Company Archives, Winnipeg, quoted in Johnson, *Saskatchewan Journals*, lxxvii.

35   Gail Morin, "Métis Family of James Curtis Bird," http://www.televar.com/~gmorin/bird.htm (accessed 24 February 2004); and van Kirk, *Many Tender Ties*, 189.

36   Lefroy, "Sir Henry Lefroy's Journey," 93; "William Gladstone's Diary—III: Rough Times in the North, copied from the Rocky Mountain Echo by Freda Graham Bundy," *The Lethbridge Herald*, 29 April 1958; and "William Gladstone's Diary—IV: By Portage to Cedar Lake, copied from the Rocky Mountain Echo by Freda Graham Bundy," *The Lethbridge Herald*, 6 May 1958.

37   John Rowand to James Hargrave, 8 July 1840, York Factory, in James Hargrave, *The Hargrave Correspondence 1821–1843* (Toronto: The Champlain Society, 1938), 316.

38   John Rowand to Donald Ross, 24 February 1849, Edmonton House, John Rowand clipping files, City of Edmonton Archives, Edmonton.

39   John Rowand, Edmonton House, D.5/18, fo. 308, Hudson's Bay Archives, Winnipeg, quoted in van Kirk, *Many Tender Ties*, 111.

40   Macpherson, *The Sun Traveller: The Story of the Callihoos in Alberta* (St. Albert: Musée Héritage, 1998), 6–7.

41   Ibid., 25–27, 41.

42   Kenneth James Tyler, "A Tax-Eating Proposition: The History of the Passpasschase Indian Reserve," Master's thesis, University of Alberta, Spring 1979, 31–32. Tyler.

43   Paul Kane, *Wanderings of an Artist Among the Indians of North America: From Canada to Vancouver's Island and Oregon through the Hudson's Bay Company's Territory and Back Again* (London: Longman et al., 1859. Reprint, Edmonton: M.G. Hurtig Publishers, 1974), 263.

44   Ibid., 265.

45   I.S. MacLaren, "Paul Kane and the Authorship of Wanderings of an Artist," in *From Rupert's Land to Canada: Essays in Honour of John E. Foster*, eds. Theodore Binnema, Gerhard J. Ens, and R.C. Macleod (Edmonton: The University of Alberta Press, 2001), 225–47.

46   I.S. MacLaren, "'I came to rite thare portraits': Paul Kane's Journal of his Western Travels, 1846–1848," in *The American Art Journal XXI*, no. 2, (1989): 57.

47   Ibid.

48   Ian MacLaren in discussion with Linda Goyette, September 2002.

49   Heinz W. Pyszczyk, *Archaeological Investigations, Fort Edmonton V, 1992: Alberta Legislature Grounds; A Synopsis* (Edmonton: Provincial Museum of Alberta, 1993), ii.

50   Ibid., 10.

51   See Nancy Saxberg, Claire Bourges, and Brian Reeves, *Rossdale Unit 11 Historical
      Resources Impact Assessment 2000 Field Studies Final Report* (Edmonton: Lifeways of Canada
      Limited, 2001); Philip Coutu, *Appendix A: Fort Edmonton Cemetery and Native Burial Ground
      Burial Records* (Edmonton: Métis Nation of Alberta, 2003).

52   *Impact and Assessment Monitoring: Developments at the Rossdale Generating Station Permit No.
      77–47* (Calgary: Aresco Ltd., 1977), plate 4.

53   Sheila J. Minni, *Impact and Assessment Monitoring: Developments at the Rossdale Generating
      Station Permit No. 77–47* (Edmonton: Aresco Ltd., 1981), summary and interpretation.

54   Ibid., 29.

55   *Impact and Assessment Monitoring* (1977), 9.

56   Geoff McMaster, "Conflict over Ancestors' Remains," *Express News*, University of
      Alberta, 27 Sept. 2000. http://www.expressnews.ualberta.ca/expressnews/articles/
      news.cfm (accessed 16 December 2003).

57   Gerald Delorme, "Report of the Amiskwaci-Waskhikan Burial Grounds," unpublished
      report submitted to the City of Edmonton, 4 December 2000.

58   See Saxberg et al., *Rossdale Unit 11*; Coutu, *Appendix A*.

59   Steve Simon, *Healing Waters: The Pilgrimage to Lac Ste. Anne* (Edmonton: The University
      of Alberta Press, 1995), 8–9.

60   Henday, *A Year Inland*, 159–73.

61   Vern Wishart, "Edmonton: A City Called Home," Edmonton: A City Called Home
      Collection; and in discussion with Linda Goyette, 30 July 2002.

62   Autobiographical notes of John McDonald of Garth.

63   12 and 17 March 1796, Edmonton House Post Journal.

64   Thompson, *David Thompson's Narrative*, 229–33.

65   Liliane Coutu-Maisonneuve, in discussion with Linda Goyette, 1 April 2003; George
      Dugas, *The First Canadian Woman in the Northwest; or, the Story of Marie Anne Gaboury, Wife
      of John Baptiste Lajimoniere, Who Arrived in the Northwest in 1807, and Died at St. Boniface at
      the Age of 96 Years* (Winnipeg: The Manitoba Free Press Company, 1902), 13–14.

66   Alexander Henry the Younger, *Journal*, 414.

67   Francis Heron, Reports on the State of Edmonton District during the Year 1820–21,
      Edmonton: Report on District, 1820–1821, reel 1M777, B.60/e/4, Hudson's Bay
      Company Archives, Winnipeg.

68   Francis Heron, Reports on the State of Edmonton District for the Year 1818–19,
      Edmonton: Report on District, 1818–1820, reel 1M777, B.60/e/3, Hudson's Bay
      Company Archives, Winnipeg (microfilm, University of Alberta Library).

69   John Rowand to Peter Pruden, 12 October 1826, Edmonton, John Rowand clipping
      file, City of Edmonton Archives, Edmonton.

70   *Revue Légale (Decisions des Tribunanx)*, vol. 1 (Montreal: Wilson and Lafleur, 1869),
      185–86.

71   Edna Rowand Cramer and E.J. Don Rowand, interview notes, John Rowand
      clipping file, City of Edmonton Archives, Edmonton.

72   2 April 1824, Edmonton House Post Journal.

73   5 June 1828, Edmonton House Post Journal.

74   Alexander Ross, *Fur Hunters of the Far West*, vol. 2 (London: Smith, Elder and Co., 1855),
      210–11.

75   1–2 January 1828, Edmonton House Post Journal.

76 A.D. Pambrum, "Autobiography of A.D. Pambrum," unpublished MS by R.E.S. Clark, 1968, Research Material for Fort Edmonton Park, Box 1: Miscellaneous interviews and reports, City of Edmonton Archives, Edmonton.

77 Fran Gosché in discussion with Linda Goyette, 10 March 2003.

78 John Rowand to Donald Ross, 21 December 1844, Edmonton House, Donald Ross fonds, MS-0635, Reel 6/A00833 196, British Columbia Archives, Victoria.

79 John Rowand to Sir George Simpson, 20 December 1844, Edmonton House, Sir George Simpson Governor's Records, D.5/12, Reel 3M68, fos. 569–570d, Hudson's Bay Company Archives, Winnipeg.

80 Robert Terrill Rundle, *The Rundle Journals: 1840–1848*, ed. Hugh A. Dempsey (Calgary: Alberta Records Publications Board, 1977), 54.

81 Albert Lacombe, Personal Papers, Memoirs, 30, Oblats de Marie Immaculée, Records of the Alberta-Saskatchewan Oblate Province, 1842–1983, accession 71.220, Box 157, File 6575, fols. 140, Provincial Archives of Alberta, Edmonton.

82 Hargrave, *Correspondence*, 441.

83 Lacombe, Memoirs, 174–75.

84 "William Gladstone's Diary—VII: Making Hay at Fort Edmonton, copied from the Rocky Mountain Echo by Freda Graham Bundy," *The Lethbridge Herald*, 27 May 1958.

85 Katherine Hughes, "John Norris, Pioneer," *Alberta Historical Review* 9, no. 4 (Autumn, 1961): 11–13.

86 Frank Norris in discussion with Linda Goyette, 25 March 2002.

87 Lacombe, Memoirs, 97, 100–103.

88 Peter Erasmus, *Buffalo Days and Nights: As Told to Henry Thompson* (Calgary: Fifth House, 1999), 43–48.

89 Henry John Moberly, *When Fur Was King* (London and Toronto: J.M. Dent and Sons Limited, 1929), 71–75.

90 "William Gladstone's Diary—IX: Trading with the Red Men, copied from the Rocky Mountain Echo by Freda Graham Bundy," *Lethbridge Herald*, 10 June 1958.

91 "William Gladstone's Diary—III."

92 "William Gladstone's Diary—VII."

93 "William Gladstone's Diary—XIII: Battle of Brigade 'Bullies,' copied from the Rocky Mountain Echo by Freda Graham Bundy," *The Lethbridge Herald*, 8 July 1958.

94 "William Gladstone's Diary—XIV: The End of One-Pound-One, copied from the Rocky Mountain Echo by Freda Graham Bundy," *The Lethbridge Herald*, 15 July 1958.

95 George Simpson to Alexander Rowand, 29 July 1856, Hudson's Bay House, Lachine, Simpson's private outward correspondence, D.4/83, reel 3M40, fo. 785, Hudson's Bay Company Archives, Winnipeg.

96 6 October 1856, Edmonton House Post Journal.

97 July 1859, Edmonton House Post Journal.

98 9 February 1861, Edmonton House Post Journal.

99 Erasmus, *Buffalo Days*, 38–45.

100 Lacombe, Memoirs, 139–40.

101 Thomas Woolsey, *Heaven Is Near the Rocky Mountains: The Journals and Letters of Thomas Woolsey, 1855–1869*, ed. Hugh A. Dempsey (Calgary: Glenbow Museum, 1989), 26.

102 Walter B. Cheadle, *Cheadle's Journal of Trip Across Canada, 1862–1863*, ed. F.P. Grove (Ottawa: Graphic Publishers Limited, 1931), 141.

103 Anne Anderson, *The First Métis... A New Nation* (Edmonton: Uvisco Press, 1985), 333–36.

104 Drouin, *Lac Ste-Anne Sakahigan* (Edmonton: Editions de l'Hermitage, 1973), 27.

105 Ibid., 31–32.

106 Ibid., 30.

107 Soeur Zoé Leblanc-Emery to Mère Deschamps, 3 April 1860, 35, quoted in Janet Ross Kerr and Pauline Paul, "The work of the Grey Nuns in Alberta—1859–1899: A feminist perspective," 28 June 1990, 2, Soeurs Grises de Montreal, Musée Héritage Museum, St. Albert.

108 Sister Zoé Leblanc-Emery to Mother J.H.-Deschamps, 25 December 1860, GNRC Archives, quoted in Thérèse Castonguay, *A Leap in Faith* (Edmonton: Grey Nuns of Alberta, 1999), 30.

109 James Carnegie, Earl of Southesk, *Saskatchewan and the Rocky Mountains: a Diary and Narrative of Travel, Sport, and Adventure during a Journey through the Hudson's Bay Company's Territories in 1859 and 1860* (Toronto, Edinburgh: J. Campbell, Edmonston and Douglas, 1875), 158–59.

110 Woolsey, *Heaven*, 67.

111 Cheadle, *Cheadle's Journal*, 144–45.

112 Colin Fraser, "Reminiscences of Colin Fraser Free Trader of Fort Chipewyan, as related to George Pendleton of the Hudson's Bay Company, Oct. 1938," 1–3, Alberta Folklore and Local History Collection, 96–93–835, University of Alberta.

113 Lacombe, Memoirs, 140, 55–57.

114 Hippolyte Leduc, O.M.I., newspaper article on Christmas 1867, City of Edmonton Archives, Edmonton.

115 Mark Sweeten Wade, *The Overlanders of '62*, ed. John Hosie (Victoria: King's Printer, 1931), 75.

116 Victoria Belcourt Callihoo, "Our Buffalo Hunts," *Alberta Historical Review*, 8 no. 1 (Winter 1960): 24–25.

117 Richard T. Price, ed., *Spirit of the Alberta Indian Treaties*, 3rd ed. (Edmonton: The University of Alberta Press, 1999), 122.

The Manitou Stone 1870 to 1891

1 See Viscount William Fitzwilliam Milton and Walter Butler Cheadle, *The North-West Passage by Land: Being the Narrative of an Expedition from the Atlantic to the Pacific* (London: Cassell, Petter, and Galpin, 1865), 166–67; John Chantler McDougall, *George Millward McDougall: The Pioneer, Patriot and Missionary* (Toronto: William Briggs, 1902), 141–42; and *The Syncrude Gallery of Aboriginal Culture*, The Provincial Museum of Alberta, Edmonton.

2 Alexander Henry the Younger, *The Journal of Alexander Henry the Younger, 1799–1814. Vol. 1: Red River and the Journey to the Missouri*, ed. Barry M. Gough (Toronto: The Champlain Society, 1988), 467.

3 Thomas Woosley, *Heaven Is Near the Rocky Mountains: The Journals and Letters of Thomas Woolsey, 1855–1869*, ed. Hugh A. Dempsey (Calgary: Glenbow Museum, 1989), 94.

4 Woosley, *Heaven*, 94.

5 Milton and Cheadle, *North-West Passage*, 166.

6 McDougall, *George Millward McDougall*, 104.

7 Ibid., 140.

8 Ibid.

9 Ibid., 142.

10 William Francis Butler, *The Great Lone Land: A Tale of Travel and Adventure in the North-West of America* (Toronto: MacMillan of America, 1872), 304–5.

11 The Manitou Stone was apparently transferred to Red River and then to Victoria University, the Methodist's college in Ontario, sometime before this school joined the University of Toronto in 1890. See Phyllis de Luna, "Rendezvous with a Legend," *The ATA Magazine* 61, no. 4 (May 1981): 11.

12 Gerald Friesen, *The Canadian Prairies: A History* (Toronto: University of Toronto Press, 1987), 149–50, 137.

13 Gilbert Anderson in discussion with Linda Goyette, 13 January 2003.

14 John Chantler McDougall, *In the Days of the Red River Rebellion* (Edmonton: The University of Alberta Press, 1983), 50.

15 *Canadian Encyclopedia Online*, s.v. "Rupert's Land," (by Shirlee Anne Smith), http://www.thecanadianencyclopedia.com/index.cfm?PgNm=TCE&Params=A1ARTA0007006 (accessed 13 February 2004).

16 Ibid.

17 McDougall, *Red River Rebellion*, 171.

18 Joseph F. Dion, *My Tribe the Crees* (Calgary: Glenbow-Alberta Institute, 1979), 67–69.

19 McDougall, *Red River Rebellion*, 130.

20 McDougall, *George Millward McDougall*, 161–66.

21 William J. Christie to George W. Hill, "Messages from The Cree Chiefs of The Plains Saskatchewan, To His Excellency Governor Archibald, Our Great Mother's Representative at Fort Garry Red River Settlement," 26 April 1871, Edmonton House, #272, Adam G. Archibald Papers, Correspondence and Papers, 1869–1873, reel M2, MG 12 A 1, Archives of Manitoba, Winnipeg.

22 Alexander Morris, *The Treaties of Canada with the Indians of Manitoba and the North-West Territories Including the Negotiations On Which They Were Based* (Saskatoon: Fifth House, 1991), 352.

23 *Canadian Encyclopedia Online*, s.v. "Oliver, Frank," (by Eric J. Holmgren).

24 P.H. Belcher and John A. McDougall to Sir John A. Macdonald, [1881], Edmonton, Indian Affairs, RG 10, volume 3737, reel C-10129, file 27596, finding aid 10–13, National Archives of Canada, Ottawa.

25 *Edmonton Bulletin*, 17 January 1881.

26 Ibid., 3 February 1883.

27 Ibid., 28 July and 4 August 1883.

28 Ibid., 14 June 1884.

29 [Tahkoots to W. Anderson], [1884], Indian Affairs, RG 10, volume 3576, reel C-10101, file 309 part B, finding aid 10–13, National Archives of Canada, Ottawa.

30 Bob Beal and Rod Macleod, *Prairie Fire: The 1885 North-West Rebellion* (Edmonton: M.G. Hurtig Publishers, 1984), 11.

31 Cited from James MacGregor, *Edmonton: A History* (Edmonton: M.G. Hurtig Publishers, 1967), 100. Unsubstantiated by other sources.

32 McDougall et al. to Strange, 7 April 1885, MG29 E40, National Archives of Canada, Ottawa, quoted in Beal and Macleod, *Prairie Fire*, 209.

33 Blair Stonechild and Bill Waiser, *Loyal Till Death: Indians and the North-West Rebellion* (Calgary: Fifth House, 1997), 18; and Beal and Macleod, *Prairie Fire*, 209.

34 D'arcy Jenish, *Indian Fall: The Last Great Days of the Plains Cree and Blackfeet Confederacy* (Toronto: Viking, 1999), 212.

35 Quoted in Beal and Macleod, *Prairie Fire*, 46.

36   Frank Tough in discussion with Linda Goyette, 14 May 2002. See also "Métis Aboriginal Title MatriX Research Initiative," University of Alberta, School of Native Studies, http://www.ualberta.ca/NATIVESTUDIES/matrix.htm (accessed 29 February 2004).

37   *Edmonton Bulletin*, 20 June 1885.

38   Ibid.

39   W. Anderson to the Superintendent General, August 26, 18856, Canada, *Sessional Papers for 1886*, Vol. XIX (No. 4), 70–72, quoted in Kenneth James Tyler, "A Tax-Eating Proposition: The History of the Passpasschase Indian Reserve" (master's thesis, University of Alberta, Spring 1979), 84.

40   L. Vankoughnet to Sir John A. Macdonald, 3 April 1886, Indian Affairs, RG 10, volume 3723, file 24,303–2, National Archives of Canada, Ottawa.

41   *Edmonton Bulletin*, 10 July 1886.

42   W. Anderson to E. Dewdney, 7 July 1886, Indian Affairs, RG 10, volume 3724, reel C-10190, file 1239, part 12, National Archives of Canada, Ottawa.

43   Tyler, "A Tax-Eating Proposition," 124.

44   "Edmonton Agency—Surrender and Sale of the Passpasschase Reserve and its Amalgamation with Enoch's Band," 19 November 1888, Indian Affairs, RG 10, volume 3582, reel C-10102, file 1023 ½, finding aid 10–13, National Archives of Canada, Ottawa.

45   D.I.N.A., "Reserve Land Sales Register," Sales Book No. 2, file 774/32–1–2 in the possession of the Department of Indian and Northern Affairs, Ottawa, quoted in Tyler, "A Tax-Eating Proposition," 144.

46   Margaret McGilvery in discussion with Linda Goyette, 12 March 2003.

47   Rod Macleod in discussion with Linda Goyette, 18 April 2003.

48   Ibid.

49   John McLean, *The Indians: Their Manners and Customs* (Toronto: William Briggs, 1889), 203.

50   de Luna, "Rendezvous," 10–11.

51   *The Syncrude Gallery.*

52   Ibid.

53   8–10 December 1862, Edmonton House Post Journal.

54   Edward Ahenakew, *Voices of the Plains Cree*, ed. Ruth M. Buck (Toronto: McClelland and Stewart Limited, 1973), 37–39.

55   Hugh Dempsey, ed., *The Early West* (Edmonton: Historical Society of Alberta, 1957), 22–23.

56   Harrison S. Young, "Impressions of Fort Edmonton," *Alberta Historical Review* 14, no. 1 (Winter 1966): 22–25.

57   James Gibbons, "The Narrative of James Gibbons (part 2)," ed. W.A. Griesbach, *Alberta Historical Review* 6, no. 4 (Autumn 1958): 11.

58   Marius Barbeau, *Indian Days on the Western Prairies* (Ottawa: [Queen's Printer], 1960), 59–60.

59   Colonel Frederick C. Jamieson, "The Edmonton Hunt," *Alberta Historical Review* 1, no. 1 (April 1953): 21–22; 27–29.

60   Angelique Nault, land claim declaration, 7 October 1891, Department of the Interior (1881–1929), William Pearce fonds, University of Alberta Archives, Edmonton.

61   McDougall, *George Millward McDougall*, 161–64.

62   Ibid., 158–60.

63   Ibid., 161–64.

64 Paul and Audrey Grescoe, eds., *The Book of Letters: 150 Years of Private Canadian Correspondence* (Toronto: Macfarlane Walter and Ross, 2002), 17.

65 Dr. Anne Anderson, *The First Métis... A New Nation* (Edmonton: Uvisco Press, 1985), 333–36.

66 Soeur Emery a Mere Slocombe, St. Albert, 27 novembre 1870, Archives des Soeur Grises de Montréal, 231–39.

67 William Francis Butler, *Report by L. Lieutenant Butler (69th Regiment) of his journey from Fort Garry to Rocky Mountain House and back: under instructions from the Lieut.-Governor of Manitoba, during the winter of 1870–71* (Ottawa: s.n., 1871), 12–15.

68 McDougall, *George Millward McDougall*, 179–80.

69 W.J. Christie to George W. Hill, 26 April 1871, Edmonton House, Saskatchewan District, Adam G. Archibald Papers, Correspondence and Papers, 1869–1873, reel M2, MG 12 A 1, Archives of Manitoba, Winnipeg.

70 Ibid.

71 Samuel B. Steele, *Forty Years in Canada: Reminiscences of the Great North-West with Some Account of His Service in South Africa*, ed. Mollie Glen Niblett (Toronto: McClelland, Goodchild and Stewart, 1915), 88–89.

72 Richard T. Price, ed., *The Spirit of the Alberta Indian Treaties*, 3rd ed. (Edmonton: The University of Alberta Press, 1999), 115.

73 John Brown, interview, *T.A.R.R. Background Papers* (Edmonton: Treaty and Aboriginal Rights Research of the Indian Association of Alberta, 1974).

74 Alexander Morris, *The Treaties of Canada with the Indians of Manitoba and North-West Territories Including the Negotiations on Which They are Based, and Other Information Relating Thereto* (Toronto: Willing and Williamson, 1880), 352–53, 361.

75 Steele, *Forty Years*, 84–85.

76 Brian M. Owens and Claude M. Roberto, eds., *The Diaries of Bishop Vital Grandin 1875–1877*, Vol. 1, trans. Alan D. Ridge (Edmonton: The Historical Society of Alberta, Amisk Waskahegan Chapter, 1989), 28.

77 Canada, Parliament, *Sessional Papers of the Dominion of Canada XIV*, no. 14 (Ottawa: Hunter, Rose, 1881): 102–4.

78 Oral tradition, quoted in Thérèse Castonguay, *A Leap in Faith* (Edmonton: Grey Nuns of Alberta, 1999), 39.

79 McDougall, *Red River Rebellion*, 146–47.

80 Jean D'Artigue, *Six Years in the Canadian North-West* (Toronto: Hunter, Rose and Company, 1882), 132–33.

81 Gibbons, "The Narrative of James Gibbons (part 2)," 14.

82 Elizabeth M. McCrum, ed., *Letters of Lovisa McDougall, 1878–1887* (Edmonton: Alberta Culture, Historical Resources Division, 1978), 40.

83 D'Artigue, *Six Years*, 131.

84 Calvin Bruneau in discussion with Linda Goyette, 17 March 2003.

85 Canada, Parliament, *Sessional Papers of the Dominion of Canada XIV*, no. 14 (Ottawa: Hunter, Rose, 1881), 108–10.

86 *Edmonton Bulletin*, 31 January 1881.

87 Jerry Quinn, interview by Richard Lightning, 20 March 1975, *T.A.R.R. Background Papers*.

88 Charles John Brydges, *The Letters of Charles John Brydges, 1883–1889, Hudson's Bay Land Commissioner*, ed. Hartwell Bowsfield (Winnipeg: Hudson's Bay Record Society, 1981), 240–43.

89   *Edmonton Bulletin*, 3 February 1883.

90   Anna Laura Robertson Harrison, Memoirs of life in Edmonton, 1883–1964, p. 3–4
      and 10–12, Alberta Folklore and Local History Collection, 96–93–502, University of
      Alberta Libraries.

91   Clare Matthews, "Happy memories of my childhood," 14 August 1962, Henry Samuel
      Casey fonds, MS 294 C1 F1, City of Edmonton Archives, Edmonton.

92   Michael Kostek, *A Century and Ten: The History of Edmonton Public Schools* (Edmonton:
      Edmonton Public Schools, 1992), 20–21.

93   W.A. Griesbach, *I Remember* (Toronto: Ryerson Press, 1946), 47–48.

94   John Walter, Northern Alberta Pioneers' and Oldtimers' Association fonds, MS 56.14,
      City of Edmonton Archives, Edmonton.

95   J.R. McPhaden, interview by Ella May Walker, fall 1944 and 1945, Ella May Walker
      fonds, MS 52, file 12, City of Edmonton Archives, Edmonton.

96   *Edmonton Bulletin*, 23 April 1885.

97   Harry Long, "Diary of Harry Long," in Bertha M. Speers, ed., *A Cameo of the West: A Story
      of the Pioneers of the Present Namao School District No. 24* (Namao: Namao U.C.W. and
      the Namao F.U.A. Local 539, 1968), 58–59.

98   Kate Maloney, "The St. Albert Mounted Rifles, Volunteers of 1885, being the personal
      reminiscences of an Old Timer," Musée Héritage, St. Albert.

99   Annie (McKernan) Turnbull, interview by Ella May Walker, Ella May Walker fonds,
      MS 52, file 15, City of Edmonton Archives, Edmonton.

100   Jenish, *Indian Fall*, 212.

101   "The Wisdom of Papasschayo, A Cree medicine man" in James Brady fonds, 1895–
      1967, [M125/19] Glenbow Archives, Calgary.

102   Lazarus Roan, interview by Eric Stamp, 12 March 1973, T.A.R.R. *Background Papers*.

103   Father A. Blanchet, Codex historicus, Riviere Qui Barre 1886–1889, Oblates of Mary
      Immaculate, Records of the Order, 71.220/5383, Provincial Archives of Alberta, quoted
      in Elizabeth Macpherson, *The Sun Traveller*, 62–63.

104   *Edmonton Bulletin*, 10 July 1886.

105   Ibid., 4 September 1886.

106   Newton, *Twenty Years on the Saskatchewan*, 35, 86–87.

107   Frank Oliver, address given by Honourable Frank Oliver, P.C. on the occasion of
      the official opening of the 50th anniversary of the Edmonton Exhibition on Monday,
      15 July 1929, Frank Oliver clipping file, City of Edmonton Archives, Edmonton.

108   Brydges, *Letters*, 82.

Newcomers 1892 to 1913

1   *Edmonton Bulletin*, 23 May 1892.

2   Ibid., 1 August 1891.

3   "Canadian Confederation: National Policy," National Library of Canada,
      http://www.nlc-bnc.ca/2/18/h18-2986-e.html (accessed 22 February 2004).

4   *Edmonton Bulletin*, 4 July 1910.

5   Ibid., 28 July 1910.

6   Ibid., 21 July 1910.

7   Ibid., 5 July 1910.

8   Ibid., 18 July 1910.

9   Ibid., 27 June 1910.

10   Ibid., 5 July 1910.

11   Ibid., 10 January 1906.

12   Ibid., 26 May 1910.

13   Ibid., 30 July 1910.

14   Howard Palmer, with Tamara Palmer, *Alberta: A New History* (Edmonton: M.G. Hurtig Publishers, 1990), 76–86.

15   *Edmonton Bulletin*, 4 August 1892.

16   Palmer, *New History*, 90.

17   Ibid., 91.

18   Vladimir J. Kaye (Kysilewsky) and Francis Swyripa, "Settlement and Colonization," in *A Heritage in Transition: Essays in the History of Ukrainians in Canada*, ed. Manoly R. Lupul (Toronto: McClelland and Stewart, 1982), 36–37.

19   Ivan Pylypiw, interview by I. Bobersky, Ukrainian Cultural Heritage Village.

20   Yar Slavutych, "Ukrainian Literature in Canada," in *Heritage in Transition*, 297.

21   Jars Balan, Biography of Michael Gowda, Edmonton: A City Called Home [CCH] Collection, 2003.

22   Palmer, *Alberta: A New History*, 92.

23   Brian Evans in discussion with Linda Goyette, March 2004.

24   Brian Evans, in discussion.

25   John Brian Dawson, *Moon Cakes in Gold Mountain: From China to the Canadian Plains* (Calgary: Detselig Enterprises, 1991), 173.

26   Colin A. Thomson, *Blacks in Deep Snow: Black Pioneers in Canada* (Don Mills: Dent, 1979), 77.

27   Ibid.

28   Ibid., 78.

29   Ibid., 80. See also "Petitions Remonstrating Against Negro Immigration Are Circulated," *Edmonton Capital*, 25 April 1911.

30   Thomson, *Deep Snow*, 82.

31   Uriel Rosenzweig, ed., *The First Century of Jewish Life in Edmonton and Northern Alberta, 1893–1993: The First and Second Generations* (Edmonton: Jewish Archives and Historical Society of Edmonton and Northern Alberta, 2000), 8–10.

32   Edmonton Board of Trade and Edmonton City Council, *The Edmonton District in Central Alberta* (Edmonton: n.p., 1923), 8, quoted in Gilbert A. Stelter, "What Kind of City is Edmonton?" in *Edmonton: The Life of a City*, eds. Bob Hesketh and Francis Swyripa (Edmonton: NeWest Press, 1995), 5.

33   Ron Newton, "Two Viewpoints on Alberta's Beauties: Don't bother to come, warned American visitor. It's cold, there's no work, and no facilities for immigrants," *Edmonton Journal*, 21 November 1978, Immigration Hall clipping file, City of Edmonton Archives, Edmonton.

34   Myrna Kostash, *All of Baba's Children* (Edmonton: M.G. Hurtig Publishers, 1977), 24.

35   *Edmonton—Souvenir of the Alberta Inaugural Ceremony, Friday September First, Nineteen Hundred and Five* (Edmonton: Edmonton Printing and Publishing Co. Ltd., 1905), unpaginated, quoted in Brock Silversides, *C.W. Mathers' Vision: 1893–1905* (Edmonton: Alberta Culture and Multiculturalism, 1989), 27.

36   Anna Laura Robertson Harrison, "Memoirs of life in Edmonton, 1883–1964," 16–17, Alberta Folklore and Local History Collection, 96–93–502, University of Alberta Libraries.

37   "Mme. Bernhardt's Art Moves Many of Audience To Tears," *Edmonton Journal*, 14 January 1913.

38   "A Capsule History," Edmonton Public Library, http://www.epl.ca/EPLCapsuleHistory.cfm (accessed 20 February 2004).

39   Katherine Hughes, 21 September 1908, Katherine Hughes Papers, 74.340/81, Provincial Archives of Alberta, Edmonton, quoted in Padraig O Siadhail, "Katherine Hughes Irish Political Activist," in Hesketh and Swyripa, *Edmonton: Life of a City*, 87.

40   Vernon Barford, "Music in Alberta," in *The Alberta Golden Jubilee Anthology*, ed. William G. Hardy (Toronto: McClelland and Stewart, 1955), 222–23.

41   Jars Balan, Ukrainian Theatre: Showtime on the North Saskatchewan," in Hesketh and Swyripa, *Edmonton: Life of a City*, 5.

42   Canadian Encyclopedia Online, s.v. "Oliver, Frank," (by Eric J. Holmgren) http://www.thecanadianencyclopedia.com (accessed 17 February 2004).

43   "Patriotic Orations at the Inaugural," *Evening [Edmonton] Journal*, 5 September 1905.

44   Canada, Alberta Act, 1905: An Act to Establish and Provide for the Government of the Province of Alberta, 20 July 1905, 4–5 Edward c. 3, http://www.solon.org/ Constitutions/Canada/English/aa_1905.html (accessed 20 February 2004).

45   R. Newton, "I Passed This Way (Memoirs)" quoted in R.G. Moyles, *The University of Alberta: 1908–1983* (Edmonton: The University of Alberta Press, 1982), facing title page.

46   A.C. Rutherford, *Budget Speech Delivered by Hon. A.C. Rutherford, Prime Minister and Provincial Treasurer of Alberta, May 7, 1906* (Edmonton: Jas. E. Richards, 1909), 6.

47   O.K.M., "John Walter and Mrs. John Walter," 17 January 1939, Northern Alberta Pioneers and Old Timers Association.

48   Tyler and Wright Research Consultants, "The Alienation of Indian Reserve Lands during the Administration of Sir Wilfrid Laurier, 1896–1911: Michel Reserve #132" ([Alberta]: Indian Association of Alberta, 1978), 88.

49   Rod Macleod in discussion with Linda Goyette, 18 April 2003.

50   Ibid.

51   Peggy Martin-McGuire, *First Nations Land Surrenders on the Prairies* (Ottawa: Indian Claims Commission, 1998), 173–35, 341–43.

52   Tyler and Wright Research Consultants, "The Alienation of Indian Reserve Lands," 167.

53   Martin-McGuire, *Land Surrenders*, 180–82.

54   Ibid., 192.

55   Ibid., 361–63.

56   Ibid., 363.

57   Lynda Harris, "Revillon Frères Trading Company Limited: Fur Traders of the North, 1901–1936," Vol. 1, Historical Planning and Research Branch, Ministry of Culture and Recreation, Province of Ontario, Toronto, 1976, quoted in Arthur J. Ray, *The Canadian Fur Trade in the Industrial Age* (Toronto: University of Toronto Press, 1990), 92.

58   Ray, *Canadian Fur Trade*, 131.

59   Allan Shute and Margaret Fortier, *Riverdale: From Fraser Flats to Edmonton Oasis* (Edmonton: Tree Frog Press, 1992), 59–60.

60   Warren Caragata, *Alberta Labour: A Heritage Untold* (Toronto: James Lorimer and Company, 1979), 17.

61   Ibid., 25–27, 47.

62   Ibid., 9–51.

63   Ibid., 53.

64 Donald Ross, "Toll of the Years," Christina McKnight fonds, MS 131, City of Edmonton Archives, Edmonton.

65 Ellen Hopkins, "The Haunted House," 24 December 1945, Alberta Folklore and Local History Collection, 96-93-508, University of Alberta Libraries.

66 Lucile Tellier Hittinger, "Memories of Lucile and Tony Hittinger," 23–24, acc. no. 93.216 SE, Provincial Archives of Alberta, Edmonton; see also *Edmonton Bulletin*, 4 April 1891.

67 Linda Redekop and Wilfred Gilchrist, *Strathcona County: A Brief History* (Edmonton: W. Gilchrist, 1981), 27.

68 *Edmonton Bulletin*, 20 June 1892.

69 W.A. Griesbach, *I Remember* (Toronto: Ryerson Press, 1946), 184–88.

70 Olive Kathleen Murdoch, "When you are very green, being the true experience of the Heathcote family, coming from the city of London, England, to a homestead in Alberta, Canada," Heathcote family fonds, MS 258, C1, F1, City of Edmonton Archives, Edmonton.

71 Peter Svarich, *Memoirs: 1877–1904*, trans. William Kostash (Edmonton: Ukrainian Pioneers' Association of Alberta and Huculak Chair of Ukrainian Culture and Ethnography, 1999), 110–13.

72 Maria Yureichuk and M. Kotyk, "Encounters with the Indians," in *Land of Pain, Land of Promise: First person accounts of Ukrainian Pioneers 1891–1914*, trans. Harry Piniuta (Saskatoon: Western Prairie Books, 1978), 79–82.

73 Mozanne (Baltzan) Dower, interview by Becky, 7 June 1999, JAHSENA Oral History Project, JAHSENA Oral History Project fonds, JOH.03.1, Jewish Archives and Historical Society of Edmonton and Northern Alberta, Edmonton.

74 Hyman Goldstick, History of the Birth of Edmonton and Calgary Jewish Communities, Rabbi Hyman Goldstick fonds, GSK.02.1, Jewish Archives and Historical Society of Edmonton and Northern Alberta, Edmonton.

75 "Arthur Hiller: interviewed for JAHSENA Historical Documentary Project," *Heritage: The Journal of the Jewish Archives and Historical Society of Edmonton and Northern Alberta* 4, no. 4 (Summer 2002): 3.

76 Yureichuk and Kotyk, "Encounters," 82–84.

77 Mrs. Charles Learmonth, "'Women Pioneer: Mrs. McQueen,' Mrs. Charles Learmonth's pioneer experience and life in Edmonton," Alberta Folklore and Local History Collection, 96–93--859, University of Alberta Libraries.

78 Hugh Dempsey, ed., *The Best of Bob Edwards* (Edmonton: M.G. Hurtig Publishers, 1975), 232, 233, 236.

79 Dorothy May King, "Childhood memories of Edmonton, Alberta, 1902–1911," CCH Collection. 2002.

80 A.F. Dreger, *A Most Diversified Character* (Edmonton: Co-op Press, 1971), 115–16.

81 Harrison, "Memoirs," 16.

82 Grace Matthews, Henry Samuel Casey fonds, MS 294, C1 F1, City of Edmonton Archives, Edmonton.

83 Gladys Reeves, interview by Helen LaRose and Maida Scott, 5 June 1970, A70–75 oral history binder, City of Edmonton Archives, Edmonton.

84 Ernest Brown, 26 March 1945, Alberta Folklore and Local History Collection, 96–93–425, University of Alberta.

85 Frank Oliver to Sir Wilfrid Laurier, 8 February 1905, Sir Wilfrid Laurier fonds, MG26 G, C819, vol. 355, 94623–94637, National Archives of Canada, Ottawa.

86　Sir Wilfrid Laurier to Frank Oliver, 9 February 1905, Sir Wilfrid Laurier fonds, MG26 G, C819, vol. 355, 94623–94637, National Archives of Canada, Ottawa.

87　Griesbach, *I Remember*, 325–28.

88　Gertrude Balmer Watt, "Christmas in the West," *A Woman in the West* (Ottawa: National Library of Canada, 1978), 26–27.

89　E.A. Corbett, *Henry Marshall Tory: Beloved Canadian* (Toronto: Ryerson Press, 1954), 94.

90　Edmund Kemper Broadus, *Saturday and Sunday* (Toronto: Macmillan Co. of Canada, 1935), 20–21.

91　R.K. Gordon, "University Beginnings in Alberta," University of Alberta Alumni Association, University of Alberta, http://www.ualberta.ca/~alumni/history/founding/52Sprbegin.htm (accessed 22 February 2004).

92　Tony Cashman, *Gateway to the North* (Edmonton: Duval House, 2002), 91.

93　Charles Drage, *The Life and Times of General Two-Gun Cohen* (New York: Funk and Wagnalls, 1954), 34–42.

94　Charles Anderson in discussion with Linda Goyette, 22 March 2002.

95　John Bell Bowden, "John Bell Bowden," in *The Window of Our Memories*, eds. Velma Carter and Wanda Leffler Akili (St. Albert: B.C.R. Society of Alberta, 1981), 46–47.

96　Thomas Mapp, "Thomas Mapp," in Carter and Akili, *Window of Our Memories*, 19.

97　"Petitions Remonstrating Against Negro Immigration Are Circulated," *Edmonton Daily Capital*, 25 April 1911, front page.

98　A.F. Dreger, *Diversified Character*, 117–18.

99　Grace Duggan Cook, *Roots and Romance: The David and Marian Duggan family* (Edmonton: G. Cook, 1981), 24–25.

100　Reg Lister, *My Forty-five Years on the Campus* (Edmonton: University of Alberta, 1958), 19.

101　A.F. Dreger, *Diversified Character*, 65–68.

The Emerging City 1914 to 1946

1　Tony Cashman, *Gateway to the North* (Edmonton: Duval House, 2002), 2–4.

2　Information collated from Sheila Reid, *Wings of a Hero: Canadian Pioneer Flying Ace Wilfrid Wop May* (St. Catherines: Vanwell Publishing Limited, 1997) and discussions with Denny and Marg May.

3　Helen Boyd, "Early Alberta Politics: Memories of J.R. Boyle," ed. T.A. Crowley, *Alberta History* 30, no. 3 (Summer 1982): 15.

4　Jean G. Côté, "When Edmonton was a Small Town: Memoirs of an old timer, a talk given at the Alberta Historical Society at the Provincial Museum Theatre," 2 October 1985, Jean G. Côté fonds, MS 446, 5, City of Edmonton Archives, Edmonton.

5　"Loyal Edmonton Regiment History," National Defence, Minister of Publiuc Works and Governement Services Canada, http://www.army.dnd.ca/Land_Force_Western_Area/41_Canadian_Brigade_Group/Loyal Edmonton Regiment/History/history.htm (accessed 23 February 2004).

6　R. Francis Douglas and Howard Palmer, eds., *The Prairie West: Historical Readings* (Edmonton: Pica Pica Press, 1985), 167.

7　"Alex Decoteau Edukit," Heritage Community Foundation, http://www.edukits.ca/decoteau/index.html (accessed 20 February 2004).

8　Edmund Kemper Broadus, *Saturday and Sunday* (Toronto: Macmillan Co. of Canada, 1935), 46.

9　Ibid., 49.

10　Ibid., 58.

11   Ibid.

12   *Canadian Encyclopedia Online*, s.v. "Internment," (by Patricia E. Roy),
      http://www.thecanadianencyclopedia.com (accessed 17 February 2004).

13   Lubomyr Luciuk, *In Fear of the Barbed Wire Fence: Canada's First National Internment Operations
      and the Ukrainian Canadians, 1914–1920* (Kingston: Kashtan Press, 2001), 137–38.

14   "Tens of Thousands Watched Flood From Vantage Points on Hillside," *Edmonton Daily
      Bulletin*, 29 June 1915.

15   Linda Rasmussen et al., eds., *A Harvest Yet to Reap: A History of Prairie Women* (Toronto:
      The Women's Press, 1979), 114.

16   "Interview with Gladys Reeves," 5 June 1970, A70–75 oral history binder, City of
      Edmonton Archives, Edmonton.

17   "Commissioner's Report on Police Investigation," *Edmonton Official Gazette* 1, no. 15
      (25 June 1915): 303–6.

18   Nellie McClung, address to the Strathcona Local of the United Farmers of Alberta,
      typescript, McClung Papers, quoted in Candace Savage, *Our Nell* (Saskatoon: Western
      Producer Prairie Books, 1979), 122; Rasmussen et al., *Harvest*, 194, 203.

19   Nellie McClung, *The Stream Runs Fast: My Own Story* (Toronto: Thomas Allen, 1945), 134.

20   Denny May in discussion with Carolina Roemmich, 17 November 2003.

21   Allan Shute and Margaret Fortier, *Riverdale: From Fraser Flats to Edmonton Oasis*
      (Edmonton: Tree Frog Press, 1992), 319.

22   Edmonton Labour History Timeline, Edmonton: Alberta Labour History Institute, 2004.

23   Tony Cashman, *Edmonton: Stories From the River City* (Edmonton: The University of
      Alberta Press, 2002), 172.

24   Ibid.

25   *Edmonton Journal*, 2 May 1922.

26   Grace Duggan Cook, *Roots and Romance: The David and Marian Duggan Family* (Edmonton:
      G. Cook, 1981), 64.

27   Reid, *Wings of a Hero*, 41.

28   Donald Wetherell and Irene Kmet, *Homes in Alberta: Building Trends and Design*,
      (Edmonton: The University of Alberta Press, 1991).

29   Wilma Stevenson, "Edmonton Streets Are Made of Glass," Edmonton: A City Called
      Home [CCH] Collection, 2002.

30   Trent Frayne, "The Edmonton Grads: a quarter century of utter destruction," eds.
      Trent Frayne and Peter Gzowski, *Great Canadian Sports Stories: A Century of Competition*
      (Toronto: Canadian Centennial Publishing Company, 1965), 54.

31   See *Edmonton Grads: 25 Years of Basketball Championships* ([Edmonton]: Royal Bank of
      Canada, 1975).

32   Ginny Belcourt Todd, *Our Women in Uniform*, ed. Muriel Stanley Venne (Calgary: Bunker
      to Bunker Publishing, [2003]), 72.

33   Igor Gouzenko, "Wartime Canada: A Soviet View," in *First Drafts: Eyewitness Accounts
      from Canada's Past*, eds. J.L. Granatstein and Norman Hillmer (Toronto: Thomas Allen
      Publishers, 2002), 282–83.

34   Assunta Dotto, GWG Factory, CCH Collection, 2002.

35   Catherine Cole, "'Every Kitchen is an Arsenal': Women's War on the Home Front
      in Northern Alberta," in *For King and Country: Alberta in the Second World War*, ed. Ken
      Tingley (Edmonton: Provincial Museum of Alberta, Reidmore Books Inc., 1995), 266;
      Bob Gilmour, "The Homefront in the Second World War," in *Edmonton: The Life of a
      City*, eds. Bob Hesketh and Francis Swyripa (Edmonton: NeWest, 1995), 212–25.

36   Denis Mahoney, Memories of a Northern Alberta Telegraphs Messenger, CCH Collection, 2002.

37   Fred Gaffen, Canadian Battle Series: Ortona, Christmas 1943 (Ottawa: Canadian War Museum, 1988).

38   Nellie McClung, *The Stream Runs Fast: My Own Story* (Toronto: Thomas Allen Limited, 1945), 155.

39   "The Trapper: Reminiscences of Ignaty (Ike) Kreway," in *Shadows of the Past*, ed. Bohdan I. Shulakewych (Edmonton: St. Michael's Extended Care Centre, 1986), 103–4.

40   N. Olynik, 28 October 1915, RG 24, vol. 4729, file 3, National Archives of Canada.

41   Assunta Dotto, CCH Collection, 2002.

42   Francis Winspear, *Out of My Mind* (Victoria: Morriss Printing Co., 1988), 59–60.

43   Fred Barns, interview, 4 October 1970, A70–75 oral history binder, City of Edmonton Archives, Edmonton.

44   Shute and Fortier, *Riverdale*, 48, 50, 51.

45   Rasmussen et al., *Harvest*, 194.

46   "Women's Suffrage Before Legislature Next Year," *Edmonton Bulletin*, 26 February 1915.

47   Eleanor Mac, "Large Gathering of Alberta Women See Vote Bill's Passage," *Calgary Herald*, 2 March 1916.

48   Dorothy Bowman Barker, newspaper report, quoted in Rasmussen, *Harvest*, 196.

49   Margaret Garrison [McKee] to Murphy, 5 June 1921, Emily Murphy Papers, MS 2, City of Edmonton Archives, Edmonton.

50   Emily Murphy to Margaret Garrison, Provincial Gaol, Fort Saskatchewan, 15 June 1921, Emily Murphy Papers, MS 2, City of Edmonton Archives, Edmonton.

51   Ken Tingley, ed., *The Path of Duty: The Wartime Letters of Alwyn Bramley-Moore, 1914–1916* (Calgary: Alberta Records Publication Board, Historical Society of Alberta, 1998), 58–59.

52   Ibid., 124–25.

53   Alex Decoteau to Emily Latta, 10 September 1917, Izola (Latta) Mottershead private collection.

54   W.A. Griesbach to Mrs. R. Waring, 28 October 1916, The Loyal Edmonton Regiment Museum, http://www.lermuseum.org/ler/mh/wwi/flanders.html (accessed 20 February 2004).

55   Griesbach papers, Loyal Edmonton Regiment, Militia (Third Battalion Princess Patricia Canadian Light Infantry), quoted in Max Foran, "W.A. 'Billy' Griesbach and World War One," *Alberta History* 32, no. 3 (Summer 1984): 1–8.

56   Reid, *Wings of a Hero*, 18–20.

57   Charles Anderson in discussion with Linda Goyette, 22 March 2002.

58   Cook, *Roots and Romance*, 24–25.

59   Records of the Department of Labour, vol. 313, file 153, National Archives of Canada, quoted in Warren Caragata, *Alberta Labour: A Heritage Untold* (Toronto: James Lorimer and Company, 1979), 73–74.

60   Caragata, *Alberta Labour*, 74.

61   Peggy Holmes and Andrea Spalding, *Never a Dull Moment* (Toronto: Collins, 1984), 21–26.

62   J. Brian Dawson, *Moon Cakes in Gold Mountain: From China to the Canadian Plains* (Calgary: Detselig Enterprises, Ltd., 1991), 171.

63   Peace Cornwall Hudson, "The Ravine," Eirene Hebb fonds, MS 621, 1–2, City of Edmonton Archives, Edmonton.

64 Isobell (Crook) Dittrich, "My Memoirs," CCH Collection, 2002.

65 Edward Jordan, "Recollections of CKUA," in *A Sound for All Seasons: CKUA's 60th anniversary* (Edmonton: ACCESS Network, 1987), 22.

66 E.A. Cobbs, "E.A. Cobbs," in *The Window of Our Memories Volume II: The New Generation*, eds. Velma Carter and Wanda Leffler Akili (St. Albert: B.C.R. Society of Alberta, 1981), 65–68.

67 Marion Robinson, "Memories of My McKernan Home," CCH Collection, 2003.

68 Clare Botsford, Interview by Alberta Labour History Institute, CCH Collection, 2002.

69 Orval Griggs, "The Dirty Thirties," CCH Collection, 2002.

70 Ben Swankey, "Reflections of an Alberta Communist: the Hungry Thirties," *Alberta History* 27, no. 4 (Autumn, 1979): 8–12.

71 Geo. B. McClellan, "Personal experiences of an R.C.M.P. officer," *Canadian Geographical Journal* LXXXVI, no. 5 (May 1973): 184–86.

72 Alex Latta, "Curly," CCH Collection, 2003.

73 John M. Reid, *All Those Other Guys and Me* (Edmonton: self-published, 2003), 31–35.

74 Alex Mair, *Gateway City* (Calgary: Fifth House, 2000), 127–29.

75 Elsie Park Gowan, "He took me at my word," in *History Made in Edmonton*, ed. Edith Rogers (Edmonton: Rogers, 1975), 105.

76 Sterling Haynes, "Funny Money," in *Bloody Practice: Doctoring in the Cariboo and Around the World* (Prince George: Caitlin Press, 2003).

77 John Imrie, Pulitzer Prize acceptance speech, 2 May 1938, Columbia University, New York.

78 Edith Sutton, CCH Collection, 2002.

79 John Ducey, "Interview with Mr John Ducey, Edmonton's 'Mr. Baseball' conducted by John McIsaac, 1979," Edmonton Parks and Recreation, City of Edmonton Archives, Edmonton.

80 Elizabeth Sterling Haynes, "Stardust in their Eyes," in *The Alberta Golden Jubilee Anthology*, ed. W.G. Hardy (Toronto: McClelland and Stewart, 1955), 230–35.

81 Barbara Villy Cormack, "...Like a Strong Healing Wind," in *Remembering Elizabeth*, ed. Elsie Park Gowan (Edmonton: Committee for Elizabeth Haynes Theatre Event, 1974), unpaginated.

82 Joe Shoctor, "She Made Me Want to be in Theatre," in Gowan, *Remembering Elizabeth*, ed. Elsie Park Gowan (Edmonton: Committee for Elizabeth Haynes Theatre Event, 1974), unpaginated.

83 Sid Hamdon, "Hilwie Taha Jomha," CCH Collection, 2004.

84 Harley Reid, "The Wave," CCH Collection, 2003.

85 Kathleen Steinhauer in discussion with Linda Goyette, 13 January 2003.

86 Peter Owen in discussion with Linda Goyette, 29 December 2003.

87 Dolly Lone, "Dolly Lone—A surprise encounter," in *The Women's Canadian Club of Edmonton Remembers: World War II Vignettes*, comp. Hazel Burn, ed. Heather Northcott (Edmonton: Purple Wolf Publishing, 1996), 78.

88 Norah Plumley Hook, CCH Collection, 2004.

89 Helen I. Mahoney, CCH Collection, 2002.

90 Nan Morrison, CCH Collection, 2002.

91 Igor Gouzenko, "Wartime Canada: A Soviet View," in *First Drafts: Eyewitness Accounts from Canada's Past*, eds. J.L. Granatstein and Norman Hillmer (Toronto: Thomas Allen Publishers, 2002), 282–83.

92 Edgar J. Bailey to Mrs. Vass, 31 January 1944, The Loyal Edmonton Regiment Museum, http://www.lermuseum.org/ler/mh/wwii/ortona.html (accessed 20 February 2004).

93   William Ziegler, "Why?" in *Echoes in the Halls: An Unofficial History of the University of Alberta*, eds. Mary Spencer, Kay Dier, and Gordon McIntosh (Edmonton: Duval House and The University of Alberta Press, 1999), 263–64.

The New City 1947 to 2004

1   Gerald Friesen, *The Canadian Prairies: A History* (Toronto: University of Toronto Press, 1987), 418.

2   Donald Wetherell and Irene Kmet, *Homes in Alberta: Building Trends and Design*, (Edmonton: The University of Alberta Press, 1991), 223.

3   Wetherell and Kmet, *Homes in Alberta*, 221.

4   Bryant Avery and Jim Farrell, "The strike that changed Alberta: Leduc #1 began gushing oil 50 years ago," in *Leduc #1: 1947–1997*, 50 (Edmonton: The Edmonton Journal, 1997), 3.

5   Bea Hunter, *Last Chance Well: Legends & Legacies of Leduc No. 1* (Edmonton: Teddington Lock, 1997), 20.

6   Doug Gibbs, "Doug Gibbs," in Hunter, *Last Chance Well*, 113.

7   Warren Caragata, interview with Neil Reimer, 1988, Alberta Archives, quoted in Warren Caragata, *Alberta Labour: A Heritage Untold* (Toronto: James Lorimer and Company, 1979), 133.

8   File LR 807, Alberta Board of Industrial Relations, Edmonton, quoted in Caragata, *Alberta Labour*, 136.

9   Jean McLaws, "Jean McLaws," in Hunter, *Last Chance Well*, 168.

10   Dorothy Morris and Elsie Owre, "Dorothy Morris and Elsie Owre, Oil Wives," in Hunter, *Last Chance Well*, 174.

11   Catherine A. Cavanaugh and Randy R. Warne, eds., *Telling Tales: Essays in Western Women's History* (Vancouver: UBC Press, 2000), 3–15.

12   Nanci Langford in discussion with Linda Goyette, 13 March 2004.

13   Diane King Stuemer, *Hawrelak: The Story* (Calgary: Script: the writers' group inc., 1992), 234.

14   Olive Elliot, "The Invincible Mayor: Edmonton's Roller Coaster Ride with William Hawrelak," prepared for the CCH Collection, Edmonton, August 2003.

15   Doug Owram in discussion with Linda Goyette, 21 May 2003.

16   Stanley Milner in discussion with Linda Goyette, August 2003.

17   Stuemer, *Hawrelak: The Story*, 161–62.

18   "Spot Oil Price: West Texas Intermediate," Stock Market Data, Dow Jones Energy Service, http://www.forecasts.org/data/data/OILPRICE.htm (accessed 12 January 2004).

19   Nellie Carlson in discussion with Linda Goyette, 2 October 2002.

20   *Edmonton Access Catalogue: 1984* (Edmonton: Tree Frog Press, 1984), back cover.

21   Cec Purves in discussion with Linda Goyette, 23 June 2003.

22   Jan Reimer in discussion with Linda Goyette, 24 June 2003.

23   Milner, in discussion.

24   "Spot Oil Price: West Texas Intermediate," Stock Market Data.

25   "Food for Thought: History," Edmonton's Food Bank, http://www.alocalchoice.com/listings/s-non/edmontonfoodbank/edfood.htm (accessed 3 March 2004).

26   Milner, in discussion.

27   Reimer, in discussion.

28   James Lightbody, "The Comparative Costs of Governing Alberta's Metropolitan Areas," Western Centre for Economic Research Bulletin 48, December 1997–January

1998, 12. http://www.bus.ualberta.ca/CIBS-WCER/WCER/wcer.htm (accessed 12 January 2004).

29   Bill Smith in discussion with Linda Goyette, 6 June 2003.

30   Mike Percy in discussion with Linda Goyette, 12 May 2003.

31   Doug Owram, in discussion.

32   Paul and Audrey Grescoe, eds., *The Book of Letters: 150 Years of Private Canadian Correspondence* (Toronto: Macfarlane, Walter, and Ross, 2002), 88–90.

33   John Funk, "John Funk," in Hunter, *Last Chance Well*, 31–33.

34   Dorothy Morris and Elsie Owre, "Dorothy Morris and Elsie Owre, Oil Wives," in Hunter *Last Chance Well*, 174.

35   Dorothy Pickard, "Dorothy Pickard," in *Oil Patch: Recollections of 'The Way Things Were'*, ed. Elsie Garstad-Rosenau (Edmonton: Lifelines, Etc., 1997), 222.

36   Andrew Turta, "Andrew Turta," in Hunter, *Last Chance Well*, 192.

37   Ibid., 193.

38   Karen Bower, "Karen Bower," in Garstad-Rosenau, *Oil Patch*, 246.

39   Ian Archibald, in Garstad-Rosenau, *Oil Patch*, 243–45.

40   John Stefanyk in discussion with Linda Goyette, August 2002.

41   Joyce Harries, *Girdles and Other Harnesses I Have Known* (Edmonton: Lone Pine, 2000), 101.

42   Lois Hole, *I'll Never Marry a Farmer: Lois Hole on Life, Learning, & Vegetable Gardening* (St. Albert: Hole's, 1998), 21.

43   Ed Wigmore, "Growing up on Boyle Street—a personal memoir," CCH Collection, 2002.

44   Inge Vermeulen in discussion with Linda Goyette, 29 July 2002.

45   Mary Spencer, "Learning to love Muddington," in *Echoes in the Halls: An Unofficial History of the University of Alberta*, eds. Mary Spencer, Kay Dier, and Gordon McIntosh (Edmonton: Duval House and The University of Alberta Press, 1999), 35–36.

46   Mel Hurtig, *At Twilight in the Country: Memoirs of a Canadian Nationalist* (Toronto: Stoddart, 1996), 43–45.

47   Preston Manning, *Think Big: Adventures in Life and Democracy* (Toronto: McClelland and Stewart, 2002), 9–12.

48   Abdul N. Kamal, "Braving the Frontier: Remembrance of my arrival in Edmonton," in eds. Mary Spencer, Kay Dier and Gordon McIntosh, *Echoes in the Halls* (Edmonton: Duval House and The University of Alberta Press), 24–26.

49   Alvena Strasbourg, *Memories of a Métis Woman: Fort McMurray Yesterday and Today* (Alberta: n.p., 1998), 59–60.

50   Scarlett Gonzalez, "Here, My Kids Have Everything: Security, Peace, Freedom," in *Canadian By Choice*, ed. Liza Linklater (Ottawa: Citizenship and Immigration Canada, 1994), 7.

51   Bill Hunter, *Wild Bill: Bill Hunters' Legendary 65 Years in Canadian Sport* (Calgary: Johnson Gorman Publishers, 2000), 179–80.

52   Wayne Gretzky with Rick Reilly, *Gretzky: An Autobiography* (Toronto: HarperCollins Publishers Ltd., 1990), 35–36.

53   Ivor Dent, *Getting the Games* (Alberta: Ardent Enterprises, 1977), 120–21, 194.

54   Rod Phillips, "Stanley Cup Game," in Gary W. Zeman, *Alberta on Ice* (Edmonton: Westweb Press, 1985), 101–2.

55   Holger Petersen, "CKUA's Music," in *A Sound for All Seasons: CKUA's 60th Anniversary* (Edmonton: ACCESS Network, 1987), 30–31.

56   Marylu Walters, *CKUA: Radio Worth Fighting For* (Edmonton: The University of Alberta Press, 2002), 365.

57   Brian Paisley, "Heart of the Beast," in *Edmonton's Fringe Theatre Event*, 17.

58   Laura Roald, "The Avenue: a director's journey creating theatre with youth at risk," *Theatre Alberta Newsletter*, Fall 2002, <http://www.theatrealberta.com/newsletter/Fall2002/TheAvenue.htm> (3 June 2003).

59   Mieko Ouchi in discussion with Vivian Giang, 2 February 2004.

60   Andrew Nikiforuk, "The War on 66th Street," in *Running on Empty: Alberta After the Boom*, eds. Andrew Nikiforuk, Sheila Pratt, and Don Wanagas (Edmonton: NeWest Press, 1987), 129–30.

61   Fred Pester in discussion with Linda Goyette, 6 June 1996.

62   Wolfgang Plath in discussion with Linda Goyette, 6 June 1996.

63   Nikiforuk, "The War on 66th Street."

64   Ibid.

65   Ibid.

66   Ibid.

67   Ibid.

68   Neil Farrell in discussion with Linda Goyette, 6 June 1996.

69   Greg Buteau and Angela Buteau in discussion with Darla Quinlan, 25 February 2004.

70   Heather Airth, "Edmonton Emergency Relief Services Society," in *Tornado: A Report, Edmonton and Strathcona County* ([Edmonton: [Alberta Public Safety Services], 1990), 143–44.

71   Jeffery Chan, "Back to School," in *Chia-na-ta Ya-sheng Ai-cheng Yüeh-nan Hua ch'iao lien i hui ch'eng li shih chou nien chi nien t'e k'an (Boat People 10 Years in Edmonton)* (Edmonton: Vietnamese Association of Edmonton, 1991), 17–18.

72   Thanh L. Hua, "Multicultural Society and the Newcomers," in *Chia-na-ta Ya-sheng Ai-cheng Yüeh-nan (Boat People 10 Years in Edmonton)* (Edmonton: Vietnamese Association of Edmonton, 1991), 16–17.

73   Mary Kur in discussion with Linda Goyette, 16 September 2003.

74   Dwayne Donald, CCH Collection, 2003.

A Note on Aboriginal Names

THE ABORIGINAL PEOPLES of the Edmonton area, both First Nations and Métis citizens, have different traditions in the naming of tribal groups and communities. In this book, we respect the preference of the speaker. For Cree words, our reference is the *Alberta Elders' Cree Dictionary*.

Spelling of tribal names and family names also vary over time in English and French. Historical texts from the nineteenth century mention tribal names that are no longer in use. The following list provides some of the known naming variants that occur:

Cree: The Cree people refer to themselves in their own language as *nehiyawak*. Historic texts written in English and French use Cree, Krees, Kinistinaux, Kilistinos; or Nehathawas, Nahathaways, Ne-heth-aw-as; Southern, Southerd and South Indians.

Variations on the English spelling for Chief Papaschase and his band in the Edmonton area include: Pahpastayo, Passpasschase and Papastew; the chief was also known in Edmonton by an English name, John Gladu Quinn.

The founding chief of the Enoch Cree, had his name spelled Lapotac, Laputigue, Lapotack, or Lapatac in English and French references. His son, known in Cree as Mahminahwatah, and to English speakers as Tommy Lapotac, died in 1883 after bringing the band into Treaty 6. Enoch Lapotac's brother, Lazarus, adopted the surname Morin, which was passed down to descendants.

The Alexander Cree Nation west of Morinville is also named for its founding chief. Cree place names for Edmonton include *amiskwaciwaskahikan*, meaning Beaver Mountain House, or Beaver Hills; or informally, "*otinow*" which means town.

Iroquois-Cree: Louis Callihoo, a Mohawk from Ganawake, near Montreal, came west as a voyageur in 1800. His family intermarried with western aboriginal people. His son, Michel Callihoo, gave his name to the Michel band, which settled west of St. Albert. The Iroquois-Cree founding families of the band were known in English and French documents as: Kwarakwante or Karaconti; Calihue, Kalliou, Calahoo, Calliou, and Callihoo.

Nakoda: The Nakoda Sioux were known in English as the Stony or Stoney, and in the early nineteenth century as the Assiniboines. Variations in fur trade journals and other historic records include: Assinae Poets, Usinnepwats, Assinipualaks, Sinepoets and Poets. Chief Alexis signed Treaty 6, and until 1890, was hereditary chief of the community that takes his name. The Nakoda Sioux live at *Waka Mne*, translated as God's Lake, and known in English and French as Lac Ste. Anne. The Paul First Nation also has Nakoda Sioux roots, with the community known as *Whihne mne*.

Blackfoot: The Blackfoot peoples of southern Alberta refer to themselves as the *nitsitapii*. First Nations within the Blackfoot Confederacy include the Kainaiwa, known in English as the Bloods; Siksika, or Blackfoot; and Pikanii, known in English as the Peigan or Piegan. In the early documents of the fur trade, they were sometimes called Archithinues and Plains Indians.

Tsuu T'ina: The Tsuu T'ina are also known in early English and French language texts as the Sarcees, Sarsis, Circees, Susssus or Sussews.

Métis: The Métis define themselves as aboriginal people of mixed ancestry who trace their lineage to First Nations and Euro-Canadian families, and who identify and are recognized as Métis.

Comment on Sources

The *Edmonton: A City Called Home* education project collected more than 250 original stories and more than 500 photographs from citizens of the city and surrounding area. It also commissioned historical and cultural essays from local historians, creative writers, photographers and videographers. We conducted many interviews for the project which have been transcribed and edited. Researchers will find the full collection online at www.edmontonhistory.ca and in a printed format at the City of Edmonton Archives (CEA).

The best way to learn about Edmonton is to explore it on foot, and talk to its people. Researchers might begin with a canoe trip down the North Saskatchewan, through the heart of the city; or an historical walking tour with an informed guide along the riverbank. We made extensive use of the rich archival collections, libraries, museums and historical parks in the Edmonton area as well as the historical records of community organizations. For a full list of these resources, contact the City of Edmonton or Alberta Community Development, or visit their web sites.

The CEA has assembled the most comprehensive collection of primary resources about Edmonton, including oral histories, photographic collections, city records, historic maps and family and business fonds. The Glenbow Museum and Archives in Calgary, the Provincial Archives of Alberta in Edmonton (PAA), the Heritage Room of the Edmonton Public Library, the University of Alberta Libraries and Archives, and the Musée

Heritage in St. Albert also offer extensive primary materials, highlighted in the bibliography that follows. Major photographic collections include the Ernest Brown and Alfred Blyth collections at the PAA; the McDermid Studio Fonds at the Glenbow Archives; and the Hubert Hollingworth collection at the CEA. The National Archives of Canada and the Canadian Broadcasting Corporation Archives contain many primary materials related to Edmonton and district. Researchers can review primary resources online by visiting the *Peel's Prairie Provinces* site at the University of Alberta Libraries and following the links:

Peels Library: http://peel.library.ualberta.ca

The *Archives Network of Alberta* data base: www.archivesalberta.org

Early Canadiana Online (http://www.canadiana.org)

The National Archives of Canada (http://www.archives.ca)

The National Library of Canada (http://www.nlc-bnc.ca

The Alberta Heritage Digitization Project (http://ahdp.lib.ucalgary.ca/ home.htm)

The National Aboriginal Documents Database (http://collections.ic.gc.ca/aboriginaldocs)

Alberta Source, the online collection of the Heritage Community Foundation, offers exciting materials for general readers and students at http://www. albertasource.ca. Back issues of the city's daily newspapers, *The Edmonton Bulletin* (1880–1951); *The Edmonton Journal* (1903–); and *The Edmonton Sun* (1978–) exist in microfiche format, but can also be consulted online; other valuable periodicals include *Legacy*, Alberta's cultural heritage magazine and *Alberta History*.

The aboriginal peoples of the Beaver Hills and North Saskatchewan River territory preserve their history in the oral tradition. To learn more, contact the Enoch, Alexander, Alexis, Paul, Ermineskin, Samson, Louis Bull, Montana or Saddle Lake First Nations; the Descendants' Societies of the Papaschase and Michel First Nations; or the Confederacy of Treaty Six First Nations. The Métis Nation of Alberta can direct researchers to several local resource centres and informed elders. Communities and individual historians have collected and published aboriginal oral history from the area, and new publishing projects were underway in 2004. For further information on local history from aboriginal perspectives, see: Richard Price, ed. *The Spirit of Alberta Indian Treaties* (Edmonton: University of Alberta Press, 1987); Anne Anderson, *The First Metis, A New Nation* (Edmonton: Uvisco Press, 1985); and Elizabeth MacPherson, *The Sun Traveller: The Story of the Callihoos in Alberta* (St. Albert, AB: Musée Héritage, 1998). Phyllis Cardinal has written two books for young people, *The Cree People* (Edmonton: Duval House Publishing and Tribal Chiefs Institute of Treaty 6, 1997) and with Dale Ripley, *Canada's People: The Metis* (Edmonton: Plains Pub., 1987). A visit to the Syncrude Gallery of Aboriginal Peoples at the Provincial Museum of Alberta provides a vivid introduction to Edmonton's founding peoples.

Primary sources in local aboriginal history include the Edmonton House post journals, correspondence books and district reports of the Hudson's Bay Company, as well as records relating to the Department of Indian Affairs, Government of Canada [RG–10, black series, B–3–6]. Copies are available on microfiche at the University of Alberta Libraries. Other primary documents include the *T.A.R.R. Background Papers* (Edmonton: Treaty and Aboriginal Rights Research of the Indian Association of Alberta, 1974); Métis scrip records, and *The Rossdale Flats Aboriginal Oral Histories Project* commissioned by the Edmonton Aboriginal Urban Affairs Committee, with research by Pamela Cunningham, Jacqueline Pelletier, Dianne Stretch-Strang, Melanie Poole and Crystal Davidson.

Edmonton's writers have explored the history and character of the city in historical studies, short story collections, novels, plays and poetry. Researchers and general readers will find a comprehensive guide to western Canadian resources in Ernie B. Ingles and N. Merrill Distad, eds., *Peel's Bibliography of the Canadian Prairies to 1953* (Toronto: University of Toronto Press, 2003). Joseph Rek is currently updating and digitizing his helpful guide, *Edmonton: an annotated bibliography of holdings in the Canadiana Collection* (Edmonton: Edmonton Public Library, 1996.)

For an interpretive analysis of aboriginal history in the West, see Olive Dickason, *Canada's First Nations: A History of Founding Peoples from Earliest Times* (Toronto: McClelland and Stewart, 1992). For another excellent overview, see Arthur J. Ray, *I Have Lived Here Since the World Began: An Illustrated History of Canada's Native Peoples* (Toronto: Lester Pub., Key Porter Books, 1996.) See also L. Barkwell, Leah Dorion and Darren Prefontaine, eds., *Métis Legacy: A Métis Historiography and Annotated Bibliography* (Saskatoon: The Gabriel Dumont Institute of Metis Studies and Applied Research, co-published with the Louis Riel Institute in Winnipeg, 2001).

Most published histories of the Edmonton area have explored community life only after the arrival of the North West Company and Hudson's Bay Company. For a comprehensive overview, see Bob Hesketh and Frances Swyripa, eds, *Edmonton: The Life of a City* (Edmonton: NeWest Press, 1995); and James MacGregor, *Edmonton: A History* (Edmonton: M.G. Hurtig Publishers, 1967).

For an interpretive analysis of the history of Alberta and western Canada, see: Gerald Friesen, *The Canadian Prairies: A History* (Toronto: University of Toronto Press, 1987); and Howard Palmer and Tamara Palmer *Alberta: A New History* (Edmonton, M.G. Hurtig Publishers, 1990).

Journalists have also explored the popular history of the city and province, through an overview, notably in *Alberta in the 20th Century: A Journalistic History of the Province in Eleven Volumes*. (Edmonton: United Western Communications, 1991) and Marc Horton and Bill Sass, with research by Patricia Beuerlein, *Voice of a City: The Edmonton Journal's First Century* (Edmonton: Edmonton Journal Group Inc., 2003).

Selected Bibliography

A Bend in the River to 1700

Archaeological Survey of Alberta. *Archaeology in Alberta*. Edmonton: Alberta Culture, Historical Resources Division, [19–].

Battiste, Marie. *Reclaiming Indigenous Voice and Vision*. Vancouver: UBC Press, 2000.

Cruden, D.M., Bruce Rains and Stanley Thomson. *The Valley Beneath Our Feet: An Earth Science Walk Across Edmonton's River Valley*. Edmonton: Edmonton Geological Society, 1998.

Dewar, Elaine. *Bones: Discovering the First Americans*. New York: Caroll and Graf, 2002.

Dickason, Olive Patricia. *Canada's First Nations: A History of Founding Peoples from Earliest Times*. Toronto: McClelland and Stewart, 1992.

———. *The Native Imprint: The Contribution of First Peoples to Canada's Character, Volume 1: To 1815*. Athabasca: Athabasca University, 1995.

Godfrey, John D., ed. *Edmonton Beneath Our Feet: A Guide to the Geology of the Edmonton Region*. Edmonton: Edmonton Geological Society, 1993.

Hardy, W.G., ed. *Alberta: A Natural History*. Edmonton: M.G. Hurtig Publishers, 1967.

Helgason, Gail. *The First Albertans: An Archaeological Search*. Edmonton: Lone Pine, 1987.

Huck, Barbara, and Doug Whiteway. *In Search of Ancient Alberta*. Winnipeg: Heartland Publications, 1998.

Ives, John W., Alwynne B. Beaudoin, and Martin P.R. Magne. "Evaluating the Role of a Western Corridor in the Peopling of the Americas." Paper presented at the Circum-Pacific Prehistory Conference, Seattle, Washington, August 1–6, 1989.

Kidd, Robert S. "Archaeological Excavations at the Probable Site of the First Fort Edmonton or Fort Augustus, 1795 to early 1800s." Alberta Culture and Multiculturalism, Historical Resources Division, Human History Occasional Paper No. 3, 1987.

Milholland, Billie. *North Saskatchewan River Guide*. Edmonton: North Saskatchewan Watershed Alliance, 2002.

Pyszczyk, Heinz W. *Archaeology Guide and Tour of Greater Edmonton Area*. Edmonton: Strathcona Archaeological Society, Provincial Museum of Alberta, 1999.

Pyszczyk, Heinz W., Ross W. Wein, and Elizabeth Noble. "Aboriginal Land Use of the Greater Edmonton Area." Unpublished paper, Edmonton, 2002.

Ray, Arthur J. *I Have Lived Here Since the World Began: An Illustrated History of Canada's Native Peoples.* Toronto: Lester Publishing, Key Porter Books, 1996.

Roed, M.A. *A Guide to Geologic Features of Edmonton, Alberta.* Ottawa: Geo-Analysis Ltd., 1978.

Scace and Associates Ltd. *Elk Island Park: A Cultural History.* Calgary: Parks Canada, Department of Indian and Northern Affairs, 1976.

Vickers, Roderick J. *Alberta Plains Prehistory: A Review.* Edmonton: Alberta Culture, 1986.

The Meeting Place 1700 to 1869

Ahenakew, Edward. *Voices of the Plains Cree.* Toronto: McClelland and Stewart, 1973.

Anderson, Anne. *The First Métis… A New Nation.* Edmonton: Uvisco Press, 1985.

Archives of the Missionary Oblates of Mary Immaculate, Provincial Archives of Alberta, Edmonton. [Papers: Albert Lacombe, Constantin Scollen, Jean-Marie Lestanc, Hippolyte Leduc]

Binnema, Theodore. *Common and Contested Ground: A Human and Environmental History of the Northwestern Plains.* Norman: University of Oklahoma Press, 2001.

Binnema, Theodore, Gerhard Ens and R.C. Macleod, eds. *From Rupert's Land to Canada: Essays in Honour of John E. Foster.* Edmonton: The University of Alberta Press, 2001.

Brown, Ernest. *From Fort to Capital: Edmonton, Alta.* Edmonton: E. Brown Ltd., 1927.

Brown, Jennifer S.H. *Strangers in Blood: Fur Trade Company Families in Indian Country.* Vancouver: University of British Columbia Press, 1980.

Callihoo, Victoria Belcourt. "Our Buffalo Hunts." *Alberta Historical Review* 8, no. 1 (Winter 1960): 24–25.

Castonguay, Thérèse. *A Leap in Faith.* Edmonton: Grey Nuns of Alberta, 1999.

Charette, Guillaume. *Vanishing Spaces: Memoirs of Louis Goulet.* Trans. Ray Ellenwood. Winnipeg: Editions Bois-Brûles, 1976.

Cheadle, Walter Butler. *Cheadle's Journal of Trip Across Canada, 1862–1863.* Ottawa: Graphic Publishers, 1931.

Cole, Jean Murray, ed. *This Blessed Wilderness: Archibald McDonald's Letters from the Columbia, 1822–44.* Vancouver: UBC Press, 2001.

Commonwealth Historic Resource Management Ltd. *Rossdale Historical Land Use Study* Edmonton: City of Edmonton, Planning and Development Department, 2004.

Coutu, Philip. "Fort Edmonton Cemetery and Native Burial Ground." Unpublished Report, Philip Coutu and the Métis Nation of Alberta, 2003.

Dalheim, K. *Calahoo Trails: A History of Calahoo, Granger, Speldhurst-Noyes Crossing, East Bilby, Green Willow: 1942–1955.* [Alberta]: Calahoo Women's Institute, [1975].

Delorme, Gerald, "Report on the Amiskwaci-Waskahikan Burial Grounds." Unpublished report submitted to the City of Edmonton, 2000.

Dempsey, Hugh. *Big Bear: The End of Freedom.* Vancouver: Douglas and McIntyre, 1984.
———. *Crowfoot: Chief of the Blackfeet.* Edmonton: M.G. Hurtig Publishers, 1972.

Dion, Joseph F. *My Tribe, The Crees.* Calgary: Glenbow-Alberta Institute, 1979.

Drouin, E.O. *Lac Ste-Anne Sakahigan.* Edmonton: Editions de l'Hermitage, 1973.

Dugas, George. *The First Canadian Woman in the Northwest; or, the Story of Marie Anne Gaboury, Wife of John Baptiste Lajimoniere, Who Arrived in the Northwest in 1807, and Died at St. Boniface at the Age of 96 Years.* Winnipeg: The Manitoba Free Press Company, 1902.

Dumont, Gabriel. *Gabriel Dumont Speaks.* Trans. Michael Barnholden. Vancouver: Talonbooks, 1993.

Edmonds, W. Everard. *Brief History of Edmonton*. Edmonton: Edmonton Technical School Printing Dept., 1921.

Edmonton: The First Fifty Years. Edmonton: The City of Edmonton, 1954.

Edmonton House Post Journals, Correspondence Books, and Reports on the District. Hudson's Bay Company Archives and Provincial Archives of Manitoba, Winnipeg.

Erasmus, Peter. *Buffalo Days and Nights*. Calgary: Glenbow-Alberta Institute, 1976.

Foster, John E. "The Metis and the End of the Plains Buffalo in Alberta." In *Buffalo*, edited by John E. Foster, Dick Harrison and I.S. MacLaren. 61–77. Edmonton: The University of Alberta Press, 1992.

Francis, R. Douglas, and Howard Palmer, eds. *The Prairie West: Historical Readings*. Edmonton: Pica Pica Press, 1985.

Friesen, Gerald. *The Canadian Prairies: A History*. Toronto: University of Toronto Press, 1987.

Gladstone, William. "William Gladstone's Diary [I-XXX], copied from the Rocky Mountain Echo by Freda Graham Bundy." *The Lethbridge Herald*, 15 April to 27 May, 1958.

Glover, Richard, ed. *David Thompson's Narrative, 1784–1812*. Toronto: Champlain Society, 1962.

Gough, Barry M., ed. *The Journal of Alexander Henry the Younger, 1799–1814. Vol. II*. Toronto: The Champlain Society, 1988.

Grandin, Vital. *The Diaries of Bishop Vital Grandin*. Edited by Brian M. Owens and Claude M. Roberto. Edmonton: Historical Society of Alberta, Amisk Waskahegan Chapter, 1989.

Grey Nuns. Papers. The Grey Nuns Regional Centre Archives, Edmonton.

Hart, Edward John. *Ambition and Reality: The French-Speaking Community of Edmonton: 1795–1935*. Edmonton: Salon d'histoire de la francophonie albertaine, 1980.

———. *The Franco-Albertan Community*. Edmonton: Association canadienne-française de l'Alberta, 1996.

Hawker, Peter D. *Fort Edmonton: Fur Trade Entrepôt, 1795–1870*. Edmonton: Hawk Productions, 1995.

Henday, Anthony. *A Year Inland: the Journal of a Hudson's Bay Company Winterer*. Edited by Barbara Belyea. Waterloo: Wilfrid Laurier University Press, 2000.

Hopwood, Victor G. *David Thompson: Travels in Western North America 1784–1812*. Toronto: The Macmillan Company of Canada, Ltd., 1971.

Hunter, Robert, and Robert Calihoo. *Occupied Canada: A Young White Man Discovers His Unsuspected Past*. Toronto: McClelland and Stewart, 1991.

Jackson, John. *Jemmy Jock Bird: Marginal Man on the Blackfoot Frontier*. Calgary: University of Calgary Press, 2004.

Jenish, D'arcy. *Indian Fall: The Last Great Days of the Plains Cree and the Blackfoot Confederacy*. Toronto: Viking, 1999.

Johnson, Alice M. *Saskatchewan Journals and Correspondence: Edmonton House 1795–1800; Chesterfield House 1800–1802*. London: Hudson's Bay Record Society, 1967.

Kane, Paul. *Wanderings of an Artist Among the Indians of North America: From Canada to Vancouver's Island and Oregon through the Hudson's Bay Company's Territory and Back Again*. London: Longman et al., 1859. Reprint, Edmonton: M.G. Hurtig Publishers, 1974.

Lamb, W. Kaye, ed. *The Journals and Letters of Sir Alexander Mackenzie*. Toronto: Macmillan, 1970.

LeClaire, Nancy and George Cardinal. *Alberta Elders' Cree Dictionary: Alperta ohci kehtehayak nehiyaw otwestamâkewasinahikan*. Edited by Earle H. Waugh. Edmonton: The University of Alberta Press and Duval House, 1998.

Levasseur-Ouimet, France. *Saint-Joachim, La Première Paroisse Catholique d'Edmonton: 1899–1999*. Edmonton: F. Levasseur-Ouimet, 1999.

MacDonald, George Heath. *Edmonton: Fort, House, Factory*. Edmonton: Douglas Printing, 1959.

MacDonald, Janice E. *The Northwest Fort: Fort Edmonton*. Edmonton: Lone Pine, 1983.

Macdonald of Garth, John. Fonds. National Archives of Canada, Ottawa.

MacLaren, I.S. "'I came to rite thare portraits': Paul Kane's journal of his Western travels, 1846–1848." *American Art Journal* XXI, no. 2 (1989): 4–93.

Macpherson, Elizabeth. *The Sun Traveller: The Story of the Callihoos in Alberta*. St. Albert: Musée Héritage, 1998.

Mandelbaum, David. *The Plains Cree: An Ethnographic, Historical and Comparative Study*. Regina: Canadian Plains Research Centre, University of Regina, 1979.

McDougall, John. *Forest, Lake, and Prairie: Twenty Years of Frontier Life in Western Canada, 1842–2*. Toronto: William Briggs, 1895.

———. *George Millward McDougall: The Pioneer Patriot and Missionary*. Toronto: William Briggs, 1902.

———. *In the Days of the Red River Rebellion: Life and Adventure in the Far West of Canada*. Toronto: William Briggs, 1903.

———. *On Western Trails in the Early Seventies: Frontier Pioneer Life in the Canadian North-West*. Toronto: William Briggs, 1911.

———. *Opening the Great West: Experiences of a Missionary in 1875–6*. Calgary: Glenbow-Alberta Institute, 1970.

———. *Parsons on the Plains*. Don Mills: Longman, 1971.

———. *Pathfinding on Plain and Prairie: Stirring Scenes of Life in the Canadian North-West*. Toronto: William Briggs, 1898.

———. *Saddle, Sled and Snowshoe: Pioneering on the Saskatchewan in the Sixties*. Toronto: William Briggs, 1896.

McDougall and Secord Limited Fonds. City of Edmonton Archives, Edmonton.

McNaughton, Margaret. *Overland to Cariboo: An Eventful Journey of Canadian Pioneers to the Gold Fields of British Columbia in 1862*. Vancouver: J.J. Douglas, 1973.

Miller, J.R. *Skyscrapers Hide the Heavens: A History of Indian-White Relations in Canada*. Toronto: University of Toronto Press, 1991.

Milloy, John S. *The Plains Cree: Trade, Diplomacy and War, 1790 to 1870*. Winnipeg: University of Manitoba Press, 1988.

Milton, William Fitzwilliam, and Walter Butler Cheadle. *The North-West Passage by Land*. London: Cassell, Petter, and Galpin, 1865.

Minni, Sheila. Final Report, Fj-pi-63, [Rossdale] Archaeological Monitoring, Consultant's Report, Archaeological Survey of Alberta, Edmonton.

Morin, Gail St. Joachim, Fort Auguste: Baptisms, Marriages, Burials, 1858–1890. Pawtucket: Quinton Publications, 2000.

———. *Métis Families: A Genealogical Compendium*. Pawtucket: Quinton Publications, 1996.

Morton, Arthur S. *A History of the Canadian West to 1870–71*. 2nd ed. Toronto: University of Toronto Press, 1973.

———. ed. *The Journal of Duncan M'Gillivray of the North West Company at Fort George on the Saskatchewan, 1794–5*. Toronto: Macmillan Co. of Canada, 1929.

Morton, W.L. *The West and Confederation: 1857–1871*. Ottawa: Canadian Historical Association, 1958.

Palliser, John. *The Papers of the Palliser Expedition, 1857–1860*. Edited by Irene M. Spry. Toronto: Champlain Society, 1968.

Palmer, Howard, with Tamara Palmer. *Alberta: A New History*. Edmonton: M.G. Hurtig Publishers, 1990.

Pannekoek, Frits. *The Fur Trade and Western Canadian Society 1670–1870*. Ottawa: Canadian Historical Association, 1987.

Peterson, Jacqueline and Jennifer S.H. Brown, eds. *The New Peoples: Being and Becoming Métis in North America*. Winnipeg: University of Manitoba Press, 1985.

Ray, Arthur J. *The Canadian Fur Trade in the Industrial Age*. Toronto: University of Toronto Press, 1990.

———. *Indians in the Fur Trade: Their Role as Trappers, Hunters, and Middlemen in the Lands Southwest of Hudson Bay, 1660–1870*. Toronto: University of Toronto Press, 1974.

Research Material for Fort Edmonton Park. City of Edmonton Archives, Edmonton.

Ross, Alexander. *The Fur Hunters of the Far West a Narrative of Adventures in the Oregon and Rocky Mountains*. London: Smith, Elder, 1855.

Rossdale Flats Aboriginal Oral Histories Project Research Team. "Rossdale Flats Aboriginal Oral Histories Project: Report of Findings." Edmonton: City of Edmonton, 2004.

Rundle, Robert Terrill. *The Rundle Journals: 1840–1848*. Edited by Hugh A. Dempsey. Calgary: Alberta Records Publications Board, 1977.

Russell, Dale A. *Eighteenth-Century Western Cree and Their Neighbours*. Hull: Canadian Museum of Civilization, 1991.

Saxberg, Nancy, Claire Bourges, Scott Haddow and Brian Reeves. "Fort Edmonton Burial Ground: An Archaeological and Historical Student." Report prepared for EPCOR by Lifeways of Canada Ltd. Calgary, 2003.

Simpson, George. *Fur Trade and Empire: George Simpson's Journal Entitled Remarks Connected with the Fur Trade in the Course of a Voyage from York Factory to Fort George and Back to York Factory 1824–25, with Related Documents*. Edited by Frederick Merk. Cambridge: Belknap Press of Harvard University Press, 1968.

———. Governors' Records. Hudson's Bay Company Archives and Provincial Archives of Manitoba, Winnipeg.

———. *Narrative of a Journey Round the World During the Years 1841 and 1842*. London: Henry Colburn, 1847.

Southesk, James. *Saskatchewan and the Rocky Mountains: A Diary and Narrative of Travel, Sport, and Adventure, During a Journey through the Hudson's Bay Company's Territories, in 1859–1860*. Edinburgh: Edmonston and Douglas, 1874. Reprint, Edmonton: M.G. Hurtig Publishers, 1969.

Thomas, Lewis H., ed. *Essays on Western History: In Honour of Lewis Gwynne Thomas*. Edmonton: The University of Alberta Press, 1976.

van Kirk, Sylvia. *"Many Tender Ties": Women in Fur-Trade Society in Western Canada, 1670–1870*. Winnipeg: Watson and Dwyer, 1980.

Woodcock, George. *Gabriel Dumont*. Don Mills: Fitzhenry and Whiteside, 1978.

Woosley, Thomas. *Heaven Is Near the Rocky Mountains: The Journals and Letters of Thomas Woolsey, 1855–1869*. Edited by Hugh A. Dempsey. Calgary: Glenbow Museum, 1989.

The Manitou Stone 1870 to 1891

Banski, E., Russell, F., eds. *A Guide to the Alberta Folklore and Local History Collection*. Edmonton: University of Alberta Libraries, 2001.

Beal, Bob, and Rod Macleod, eds. *Prairie Fire: The 1885 North-West Rebellion*. Edmonton: M.G. Hurtig Publishers, 1984.

Bell, Keith. *Edmonton: The Way it Was*. Edmonton: Fort Edmonton Historical Foundation, 1977.

Bowsfield, Hartwell, ed. *The Letters of Charles John Brydges, 1883–1889, Hudson's Bay Land Commissioner*. Winnipeg: Hudson's Bay Record Society, 1981.

Butler, William Francis. *The Great Lone Land: A Tale of Travel and Adventure in the North-West of America*. Toronto: MacMillan of America, 1872. Reprint, Edmonton: M.G. Hurtig Publishers, 1968.

———. *Report by Lieutenant Butler (69th Regt.) of His Journey from Fort Garry to Rocky Mountain House and Back: Under Instructions from the Lieut.-Governor of Manitoba, During the Winter of 1870–71*. Ottawa: Times Print. and Pub. Co., 1871.

Cashman, Tony. *The Best Edmonton Stories*. Edmonton: M.G. Hurtig Publishers, 1976.

———. *Edmonton Exhibition: The First Hundred Years*. Edmonton: Exhibition Association, 1979.

———. *Edmonton: Stories From the River City*. Edmonton: The University of Alberta Press, 2002.

———. *The Edmonton Story: The Life and Times of Edmonton, Alberta*. Edmonton: Institute of Applied Art, 1956.

———. *More Edmonton Stories: The Life and Times of Edmonton, Alberta*. Edmonton: Institute of Applied Art, 1958.

Christensen, Jo-Anne. *An Edmonton Album: Glimpses of the Way We Were*. Toronto: Hounslow Press, 1999.

d'Artigue, Jean. *Six Years in the Canadian North-West*. Toronto: Hunter, Rose and Company, 1882.

Department of Indian Affairs, Government of Canada, Annual Reports and Correspondence, 1864–1990. http://www.collectionscanada.ca/indianaffairs.

Denney, Charles. *Métis Genealogical Collection*. Glenbow Museum and Archives, Calgary.

———. *Charles Denney Papers*. Glenbow Museum and Archives, Calgary.

Edmonton '75: 75 Year History of Edmonton. Edmonton: Provost, 1979.

Garneau, R.D. "Canadian History: A Distinct Viewpoint." Garneau family history, genealogy, photographs http://www.agt.net/public/dgarneau.

Gilpin, John F. *Edmonton: Gateway to the North, An Illustrated History*. Burlington: Windsor Publications, 1984.

Griesbach, W.A. *I Remember*. Toronto: Ryerson Press, 1946.

Hildebrant, Kate. *Edmonton: The New Best West, A Contemporary Portrait*. Burlington: Windsor Publications, 1991.

Indian Association of Alberta. "The Alienation of Indian Reserve Lands During the Administration of Sir Wilfrid Laurier: Michel Reserve #132." Edmonton: Tyler and Wright Research Consultants, 1978.

———. *T.A.R.R. Background Papers*. Edmonton: Treaty and Aboriginal Rights Research of the Indian Association of Alberta, 1974.

Kostek, Michael. *A Century and Ten: The History of Edmonton Public Schools*. Edmonton: Edmonton Public Schools, 1992.

Leonard, David. *A Builder of the Northwest: The Life and Times of Richard Secord*. Researched and compiled by David Leonard, John McIsaac and Sheilagh Jameson, under the direction of Richard Y. Secord, ed. Edmonton: Richard Y. Secord, 1981.

MacGregor, James Macleod, R.C. *The North West Mounted Police, 1873–1919*. Ottawa: Canadian Historical Association, 1978.

———. *Edmonton Trader: The Story of John McDougall*. Toronto: McClelland and Stewart, 1963.

———. *Senator Hardisty's Prairies, 1849–1889*. Saskatoon: Western Producer Prairie Books, 1978.

Macpherson, Elizabeth. *The Sun Traveller: The Story of the Callihoos in Alberta*. St. Albert: Musée Héritage, 1998.

Mair, Alex. *Gateway City*. Calgary: Fifth House, 2000.

MacDonald, Jac. *Historic Edmonton: An Architectural and Pictorial Guide.* Edmonton: Edmonton Journal and Lone Pine, 1987.

McCardle, Bennett. *The Michel Band: A Short History.* Edmonton: Treaty and Aboriginal Research, Indian Association of Alberta, 1981.

McCrum, Elizabeth M., ed. *Letters of Lovisa McDougall: 1878–1887.* Edmonton: Alberta Culture, Historical Resources Division, 1978.

McGuire, Peggy. *First Nation Land Surrenders on the Prairies: 1896–1911.* Ottawa: Indian Claims Commission, 1998.

Morin, Gail. *Métis Families.* http://www.televav.com/~gmorin.index.html.

Morris, Alexander. *The Treaties of Canada with the Indians of Manitoba and the North-West Territories Including the Negotiations On Which They Were Based, and Other Information Relating Thereto.* Toronto: Willing and Williamson, 1880.

———. *The Treaties of Canada with the Indians of Manitoba and the North-West Territories Including the Negotiations On Which They Were Based, and Other Information Relating Thereto.* Saskatoon: Fifth House, 1991.

Newton, William. *Twenty Years on the Saskatchewan, N.W. Canada.* London: Stock, 1897.

O'Riordan, Terance. *Straddling the Great Transition: The Hudson's Bay Company in Edmonton During the Transition from the Commons to Private Property, 1854–1882.* PhD diss., University of Alberta, 2001.

Owram, Doug. *Promise of Eden: The Canadian Expansionist Movement and the Idea of the West, 1856–1900.* Toronto: University of Toronto Press, 1980.

Pearce, William. *Papers.* University of Alberta Archives, Edmonton.

Person, Dennis. *Edmonton: Portrait of a City.* Edmonton: Reidmore, 1981.

Price, Richard T., ed. *The Spirit of the Alberta Indian Treaties.* 3rd ed. Edmonton: The University of Alberta Press, 1999.

Steele, Samuel Benfield. *Forty Years in Canada: Reminiscences of the Great North-West with Some Account of His Service in South Africa.* Edited by Mollie Glen Niblett. Toronto: McClelland, Goodchild and Stewart, 1915.

Stefiszyn, Mildred, ed. *Land Among the Lakes.* Edmonton: Deville-North Cooking Lake Historical Society, 1982.

Stonechild, Blair, and Bill Waiser. *Loyal Till Death: Indians and the North-West Rebellion.* Calgary: Fifth House, 1997.

Turner, John Peter. *The North-West Mounted Police.* Ottawa: King's Printer, 1950.

Tyler, Kenneth James. "A Tax-Eating Proposition: The History of the Passpasschase Indian Reserve." Master's thesis, University of Alberta, Spring 1979.

Walker, Ella May. *Fonds.* City of Edmonton Archives, Edmonton.

Wiebe, Rudy, and Bob Beal, eds. *War in the West: Voices of the 1885 Rebellion.* Toronto: McClelland and Stewart, 1985.

University of Alberta Libraries. *Alberta Folklore and Local History Collection,* http://folklore.library.ualberta.ca.

Newcomers 1892 to 1913

Borgstede, Arlene. *The Black Robe's Vision: A History of St. Albert and District.* Edmonton: Inter-Collegiate Press, 1985.

———. *St. Albert: A Pictorial History.* St. Albert: St. Albert Historical Society, 1978.

Broadus, Edmund Kemper. *Saturday and Sunday.* Toronto: Macmillan Co. of Canada, 1935.

Carter, Velma, and Wanda Leffler Akili, eds. *The Window of Our Memories.* St. Albert: B.C.R. Society of Alberta, 1981.

Carter, Velma, and Leah Suzanne Carter, eds. *The Window of Our Memories Volume II: The New Generation*. St. Albert: B.C.R. Society of Alberta, 1990.

Cashman, Tony. *Singing Wires: The Telephone in Alberta*. Edmonton: Alberta Government Telephones Commission, 1972.

Chalmers, John W. *Looking Back: King Edward Park and District*. Edmonton: King Edward Park Community League, 1985.

City of Edmonton Archives, Oral History Collection, Edmonton.

Côté, Jean Gustave. *Senator Jean Léon Côté: Pioneer Land Surveyor and Early Legislator; A Personal Biography*. Edmonton: n.p., 1992.

Dawson, John Brian. *Moon Cakes in Gold Mountain: From China to the Canadian Plains*. Calgary: Detselig Enterprises, 1991.

Dreger, A.F. *A Most Diversified Character*. Edmonton: Co-op Press, 1971.

Early History of Calder School and District. Edmonton: n.p., 1977.

Farnell, Peggy O'Connor. *Old Glenora*. Edmonton: Old Glenora Historical Society, 1984.

Fjestad, Dennis P., ed. *South of the North Saskatchewan*. Fort Saskatchewan: Josephburg History Book Committee, 1984.

Griesbach, W.A. *I Remember*. Toronto: Ryerson Press, 1946.

Hanon, Stephen. *The Steel Ghost*. Edmonton: Film and Video Arts Society of Alberta, 1998. Documentary.

Hatcher, Colin. *Edmonton's Electric Transit: The Story of Edmonton's Streetcars and Trolley Buses*. Toronto: Railfare Enterprises, 1983.

Herzog, Lawrence. *Built on Coal: A History of Beverly, Edmonton's Working Class Town*. Edmonton: Beverly Community Development Society, 2000.

———. *The Life of a Neighbourhood: A History of Edmonton's Oliver District, 1870 to 1950*. Edmonton: Oliver Community League, 2002.

The Highlands: Edmonton Historical Walking and Driving Tour Alberta. Edmonton: Alberta Community Development, Historical Sites and Archives Service and Highlands Historic Foundation, 1993.

Historical Guide to Groat Estate, Westmount, Inglewood. Edmonton: n.p., 1980.

Johns, Walter H. *A History of the University of Alberta, 1908–1969*. Edmonton: The University of Alberta Press, 1981.

Kostash, Myrna. *All of Baba's Children*. Edmonton: M.G. Hurtig Publishers, 1977.

Levy, Daniel S. *Two-Gun Cohen: A Biography*. New York: St. Martin's Press, 1997.

Lister, Reg. *My Forty-five Years on the Campus*. Edmonton: University of Alberta, 1958.

Lowe, Shirley Ann. *Beverly Walking Tour: A Presentation of the Beverly History Committee, Beverly Towne Community Development Society and the Beverly Business Association*. Edmonton: Beverly Business Association, 1998.

Macdonald, John. *The History of the University of Alberta, 1908–1958*. Toronto: W.J. Gage [for the University of Alberta], 1958.

MacGregor, James. *The Klondike Rush through Edmonton, 1897–1898*. Toronto: McClelland and Stewart, 1970.

Martin-McGuire, Peggy. *First Nations Land Surrenders on the Prairies*. Ottawa: Indian Claims Commission, 1998.

Masson, Jack K. with Ed C. LeSage, Jr. *Alberta's Local Governments: Politics and Democracy*. 2nd ed. Edmonton: The University of Alberta Press, 1994.

Memory Trails of Winterburn. Edmonton: Winterburn Women's Institute, 1977.

Minde, Emma. *kwayask ê-kî-pê-kiskinowâpahtihicik/Their Example Showed Me the Way: A Cree Woman's Life Shaped by Two Cultures*. Edited and translated by Freda Ahenakew and H.C. Wolfart. Edmonton: The University of Alberta Press, 1997.

Monto, Tom. *Strathcona: The End-of-Steel*. Edmonton: Crang Publishers, 1989.

Moyles, R.G. *The University of Alberta, 1908-1983*. Edmonton: University of Alberta, 1982.

Old Strathcona Foundation. *Walk through Old Strathcona*. Edmonton: The Foundation, 1987.

Piniuta, Harry, trans. *Land of Pain, Land of Promise: First Person Accounts of Ukrainian Pioneers 1891–1914*. Saskatoon: Western Prairie Books, 1978.

Ream, Peter T. *The Fort on the Saskatchewan: A Resource Book on Fort Saskatchewan and District*. Edmonton: Metropolitan Print, 1974.

Redekop, Linda, and Wilfred Gilchrist. *Strathcona County: A Brief History*. Edmonton: W. Gilchrist, 1981.

Shute, Allan, and Margaret Fortier. *Riverdale: From Fraser Flats to Edmonton Oasis*. Edmonton: Tree Frog Press, 1992.

Rosenzweig, Uriel. *The First Century of Jewish Life in Edmonton and Northern Alberta, 1893–1993: The First and Second Generations*. Edmonton: Jewish Archives and Historical Society of Edmonton and Northern Alberta, 2000.

Sharek, Walter and Anne. *Mostly Pleasant Memories*. Edmonton: Ukrainian Pioneers' Association of Alberta and Canadian Centre for Ukrainian Culture and Ethnography, 2001.

South Edmonton Saga. Edmonton: South Edmonton, Papaschase Historical Society, 1984.

Spencer, Mary, Kay Dier, and Gordon McIntosh, eds. *Echoes in the Halls: An Unofficial History of the University of Alberta*. Edmonton: Duval House and The University of Alberta Press, 1999.

Stinson, Margaret. *The Wired City: A History of the Telephone in Edmonton*. Edmonton: Edmonton Telephones, 1980.

Supernault, Esther. *Many Faces—One Heart: Stories of Stony Plain*. Stony Plain: Heritage Agricultural Society, 1999.

Svarich, Peter. *Memoirs: 1877–1904*. Translated by William Kostash. Edmonton: Ukrainian Pioneers' Association of Alberta and Huculak Chair of Ukrainian Culture and Ethnography, 1990.

Swyripa, Frances. *Wedded to the Cause: Ukrainian-Canadian Women and Ethnic Identity, 1891–1991*. Toronto: University of Toronto Press, 1993.

Through the Years: Alberta Avenue. Edmonton: n.p., 1995.

Tingley, Kenneth W. *The Best of the Strathcona Plaindealer: 1977–1998*. Edmonton: Old Strathcona Foundation, 1999.

Tyler and Wright Research Consultants. "The Alienation of Indian Reserve Lands during the Administration of Sir Wilfrid Laurier, 1896–1911: Michel Reserve #132." [Alberta]: Indian Association of Alberta, 1978.

University of Alberta Alumni Association. "History Trails." http://www.ualberta.ca/~alumni/history/index.htm.

Watt, Gertrude Balmer. *Town and Trail*. Edmonton: News Pub. Co., 1908.

———. *A Woman in the West*. Ottawa: National Library of Canada, 1978.

Wetherell, Donald, and Irene R.A. Kmet. *Alberta's North: A History, 1890–1950*. Edmonton, The University of Alberta Press, 2000.

Vant, J. Ross. *More Than A Hospital: University of Alberta Hospitals 1906–1986*. Edmonton: The University Hospitals Board, 1986.

Vanterpool, Alan. *The Railways of Edmonton*. Calgary: British Railway Modellers of North America, 1997.

Yanish, Lori. *Edmonton's West Side Story: The History of the Original West End of Edmonton from 1870*. Edmonton: 124 Street and Area Business Association, 1991.

Yedlin, Tova and Joanna Matejko, eds. *Alberta's Pioneers from Eastern Europe: Reminiscences*. Edmonton: Division of East European Studies, University of Alberta, 1976.

The Emerging City 1914 to 1946

Awid, Richard Asmet. *Through the Eyes of the Son: A Factual History About Canadian Arabs*. Edmonton: Accent Printing, Ltd., [2000].

Buck, William. *In My Charge: The Canadian Internment Camp Photographs of Sergeant William Buck*. Kingston: Kashtan Press, 1997.

Burn, Hazel, comp. *The Women's Canadian Club of Edmonton Remembers: World War II Vignettes*. Edited by Heather Northcott. Edmonton: Purple Wolf Publishing, 1996.

Callaghan, William J. *How I Flew the Forties*. Edmonton: NeWest Press, 1984.

Caragata, Warren. *Alberta Labour: A Heritage Untold*. Toronto: James Lorimer and Company, 1979.

Cashman, Tony. *Gateway to the North*. Edmonton: Duval House, 2002.

Cavanaugh, Catherine, and Randi Warne, eds. *Standing on New Ground: Women in Alberta*. Edmonton: The University of Alberta Press, 1993.

———. *Telling Tales: Essays in Western Women's History*. Vancouver: UBC Press, 2000.

Dempsey, James. *Warriors of the King: Prairie Indians in World War I*. Regina: Canadian Plains Research Centre, University of Regina, 1999.

Dempsey, Lotta. *No Life for a Lady*. Don Mills: Musson Book Company, 1976.

Doskoch, Walter H. *Straight from the Heart: Biography of W. (Bill) Doskoch, 1893–1941*. Edmonton: W.H. Doskoch, 1985–1993.

Ducey, Brant E. *The Rajah of Renfrew: The Life and Times of John E. Ducey, Edmonton's 'Mr. Baseball'*. Edmonton: The University of Alberta Press, 1998.

Edmonton Grads: 25 Years of Basketball Championships, 1915–1940. [Edmonton]: Royal Bank of Canada, 1975.

Elliott, David R., ed. *Aberhart: Outpourings and Replies*. Calgary: Historical Society of Alberta, 1991.

Ells, S.C. *Recollections of the Development of the Athabasca Oil Sands*. Ottawa: Department of Mines and Technical Surveys, Mines Branch, 1962.

Gray, James. *Red Lights on the Prairies*. Saskatoon: Fifth House, 1971.

———. *Booze: When Whiskey Ruled the West*. Saskatoon: Fifth House, 1972.

Griesbach, William. Papers. City of Edmonton Archives, Edmonton.

Haynes, Sterling. *Bloody Practice: Doctoring in the Cariboo and Around the World*. Prince George: Caitlin Press, 2003.

Hebb, Eirene. Fonds. City of Edmonton Archives, Edmonton.

Hesketh, Bob, ed. *Three Northern Wartime Projects*. Edmonton: Canadian Circumpolar University and Edmonton and District Historical Society, 1996.

Hillenbrand, Laura. *Seabiscuit: An American Legend*. New York: Random House, 2001.

Holmes, Peggy and Andrea Spalding. *Never a Dull Moment*. Toronto: Collins, 1984.

Huser, Beatrice Daily. *The Big Gate*. Highland: B. Daily Huser, 199–.

Irving, John A. *The Social Credit Movement in Alberta*. Toronto: University of Toronto Press, 1959.

Kordan, Bohdan S. *Enemy Aliens Prisoners of War: Internment in Canada During the Great War*. Montreal: McGill-Queen's University Press, 2002.

Luciuk, Lubomyr. *In Fear of the Barbed Wire Fence: Canada's First National Internment Operations and the Ukrainian Canadians, 1914–1920*. Kingston: Kashtan Press, 2001.

McClung, Nellie L. *In Times Like These*. Toronto: University of Toronto Press, 1972.

———. *The Stream Runs Fast: My Own Story*. Toronto: Thomas Allen Limited, 1945.

McPherson, C.B. *Democracy in Alberta: Social Credit and the Party System*. Toronto: University of Toronto Press, 1962.

Murphy, Emily F. *Janey Canuck in the West*. Toronto: McClelland and Stewart, 1975.

Myers, Patricia. *Sky Riders: An Illustrated History of Aviation in Alberta, 1906–1945*. Saskatoon: Fifth House, 1995.

Myles, Eugenie Louise. *From Tarpaper Shack Twice to Watch Royalty Disrobe in Westminster Abbey*. Victoria: Elm Editions, 1995.

Now That We Are Persons. Edmonton: University of Alberta, Museums and Collections Services, 1990.

Official Records of the Edmonton 'Grads', World Champions: Covering 466 games, 23 Years of Play and Over 100,000 Miles of Travel. Edmonton: Commercial Printers, 19–.

Rasmussen, Linda, et al. *A Harvest Yet to Reap: A History of Prairie Women*. Toronto: The Women's Press, 1979.

Reid, John M. *All Those Other Guys and Me*. Edmonton: n.p., [200-].

Reid, Sheila. *Wings of a Hero: Canadian Pioneer Flying Ace Wilfrid Wop May*. St. Catherines: Vanwell Publishing Limited, 1997.

Savage, Candace. *Our Nell*. Saskatoon: Western Producer Prairie Books, 1979.

A Sound for All Seasons: CKUA's 60th Anniversary. Edmonton: ACCESS Network, 1987.

Stevens, George Roy. *A City Goes to War*. Brampton: Charters Publishing Co., 1964.

Tingley, Ken. *The City of Champions: Highlights from Edmonton's Sport History*. Edmonton: n.p., 2003.

———. *For King and Country: Alberta in the Second World War*. Edmonton: Provincial Museum of Alberta and Reidmore Books Inc., 1995.

———. *The Path of Duty: The Wartime Letters of Alwyn Bramley-Moore, 1914–1916*. Calgary: Alberta Records Publication Board, Historical Society of Alberta, 1998.

Todd, Ginny Belcourt. *Our Women in Uniform*. Edited by Muriel Stanley Venne. Calgary: Bunker to Bunker Publishing, 2003.

Waiser, W.A. *Park Prisoners: The Untold Story of Western Canada's National Parks, 1915–1946*. Saskatoon: Fifth House, 1995.

Walters, Marylu. *CKUA: Radio Worth Fighting For*. Edmonton: The University of Alberta Press, 2002.

Waugh, Earle H., Baha Abu-Laban, and Regula B. Qureshi, eds. *The Muslim Community in North America*. Edmonton: The University of Alberta Press, 1983.

Winspear, Francis. *Out of My Mind*. Victoria: Morriss Printing Co., 1988.

Zeman, Gary W. *Alberta on Ice*. Edmonton: Westweb Press, 1985.

The New City 1947 to 2004

Boothe, Paul, ed. *Alberta and the Economics of Constitutional Change*. Edmonton: The Western Centre for Economic Research, 1992.

Campbell, Douglas. *Looking Back: As Recalled by Douglas and Margaret Campbell*. Edmonton: D. Campbell, 1994.

Campbell, Maria. *Halfbreed*. Edmonton: Alberta Education, 1973.

Chambers, Edward J., and Michael B. Percy. *Western Canada in the International Economy*. Edmonton: The University of Alberta Press, 1992.

Dent, Ivor. *Getting the Games*. Alberta: Ardent Enterprises, 1977.

Diotte, Kerry, ed. *Black Friday: Ten Years After*. Edmonton: The Edmonton Sun, 1997.

Dumont, Marilyn. *A Really Good Brown Girl*. London, Ont.: Brick Books, 1996.

Elves, Douglas. *Love Song on the North Saskatchewan and Other Poems*. Edmonton: n.p., 1996.

Garstad-Rosenau, Elsie. *Oil Patch: Recollections of 'The Way Things Were'*. Edmonton: Lifelines, Etc., 1997.

Gillespie, Curtis. *Someone Like That: Life Stories*. Edmonton: Rowan Books, 2000.

Glenfield, Mary. *The Growth of Theatre in Edmonton from the early 1920s to 1965*. Master's thesis, University of Alberta, 2001.

Grescoe, Paul, and David Cruise. *The Money Rustlers: Self-made Millionaires of the New West*. Markham: Viking, 1985.

Gretzky, Wayne, with Rick Reilly. *Gretzky: An Autobiography*. Toronto: HarperCollins, 1990.

Gzowski, Peter. *The Game of Our Lives*. Toronto: McClelland and Stewart, 1982.

Herrington, Kate. *Sherwood Park: The First Twenty-five Years*. [Alberta]: Josten's / National School Services Ltd., 1983.

Hole, Lois. *I'll Never Marry a Farmer: Lois Hole on Life, Learning, & Vegetable Gardening*. St. Albert: Hole's, 1998.

Hunter, Bea. *Last Chance Well: Legends and Legacies of Leduc No. 1*. Edmonton: Tree Frog Press, 2002.

Hunter, Bill. *Wild Bill: Bill Hunter's Legendary 65 Years in Canadian Sport*. Calgary: Johnson Gorman Publishers, 2000.

Hurtig, Mel. *At Twilight in the Country: Memoirs of a Canadian Nationalist*. Toronto: Stoddart, 1996.

Jensen, Agnes Jelhof. *Hello Canada*. Translated by Bodil Jelhof Jensen. Edmonton: Danbooks, 1998.

Kepley, Dan. *Inside the Dynasty*. Toronto: Methuen, 1983.

Laxer, Gordon, and Trevor Harrison, eds. *The Trojan Horse: Alberta and the Future of Canada*. Montreal: Black Rose Books, 1995.

Leduc #1: 1947–1997. Commemorative series, Edmonton: Edmonton Journal, 1997.

Lisac, Mark. *The Klein Revolution*. Edmonton: NeWest Press, 1995.

Lowe, Kevin. *Champions: The Making of the Edmonton Oilers*. Scarborough: Prentice-Hall Canada, 1988.

Major, Alice. *Tales for an Urban Sky*. Fredricton: Broken Jaw Press, 1999.

Manning, Preston. *Think Big: Adventures in Life and Democracy*. Toronto: McClelland and Stewart, 2002.

Mansell, Robert L., and Michael B. Percy. *Strength in Adversity: A Study of the Alberta Economy*. Edmonton: The University of Alberta Press, 1990.

Nikiforuk, Andrew, Sheila Pratt, and Don Wanagas, eds. *Running on Empty: Alberta After the Boom*. Edmonton: NeWest Press, 1987.

O'Callaghan, William J. *Great Balls of Fire, or, How I Grew to Love Rock and Roll Under the Shadow of the A-bomb*. Edmonton: Plains Publishers, 1988.

Redmond, Gerald. *Forty Years of Tradition*. Edmonton: ESP Marketing and Communications, [1990].

Shaben, Carol, ed. *Edmonton's Fringe Theatre Event: The 1st Decade 1982–1991*. Edmonton: Chinook Theatre Society, 1991.

Strasbourg, Alvena. *Memories of a Métis Woman: Fort McMurray Yesterday and Today*. [Alberta]: n.p., 1998.

Stuemer, Diane King. *Hawrelak: The Story*. Calgary: Script: the writers' group inc., 1992.

Taylor, Russell Frederick. *A Memorial for Russell Frederick Taylor: Polio '53*. Edmonton: The University of Alberta Press, 1990.

Tornado: A Report, Edmonton and Strathcona County. Edmonton: Alberta Public Safety
  Services, 1990.

Wetherell, Donald G. and Irene R.A. Kmet. *Homes in Alberta: Building Trends and Design*.
  Edmonton: The University of Alberta Press and Alberta Culture and Multiculturalism and
  Alberta Municipal Affairs, 1991.

von Hauff, Donna. *Everyone's Grandfather: The Life & Times of Grant MacEwan*. Edmonton: Grant
  MacEwan Community College Foundation, 1994.

Permissions

Pages 12–13: Excerpts from *The Syncrude Gallery of Aboriginal Culture* at the Provincial Museum of Alberta. Used by permission of the Provincial Museum of Alberta, *The Syncrude Gallery of Aboriginal Culture*.

Pages 13–14: Excerpt from Eleanor Brass, "Origin of the Moon," in *Medicine Boy and Other Cree Tales* (Calgary: Glenbow-Alberta Institute, 1979), unpaginated. Used by permission of the Glenbow Museum and Archives.

Page 14: Excerpt from Heinz W. Pyszczyk, *Archaeology Guide and Tour of Greater Edmonton Area* (Edmonton: Strathcona Archaeological Society, Provincial Museum of Alberta, 1999), 4–5. Used by permission of Heinz W. Pyszczyk.

Pages 14–15: Excerpt from an interview with Catherine Reininger by Linda Goyette, March 2003. Used by permission of Catherine Reininger.

Pages 38–39: Excerpt from Francis Alexis, quoted in Steve Simon, *Healing Waters: The Pilgrimage to Lac Ste. Anne* (Edmonton: The University of Alberta Press, 1995), 8–9. Used by permission of Francis Alexis and The University of Alberta Press.

Pages 39–40: Excerpt from Anthony Henday, *A Year Inland: The Journal of a Hudson's Bay Company Winterer*, ed. Barbara Belyea (Waterloo: Wilfrid Laurier University Press, 2000), 159–73. Used by permission of Wilfrid Laurier University Press.

Pages 40–41: Excerpt from Vern Wishart, CCH Collection. Used by permission of Vern Wishart.

Pages 41–42: Excerpt from The Autobiographical Notes of John McDonald of Garth, 1859, John Macdonald of Garth fonds, MG-19-A17, vol. 1, Library and Archives Canada. Used by permission of the Library and Archives Canada.

Pages 42–43: Excerpt from 12 and 17 March 1796, Edmonton House Post Journal, 1795–1798, reel 1M48, B.60/a/1, Hudson's Bay Company Archives, Archives of Manitoba (microfilm, University of Alberta Library). Used by permission of Hudson's Bay Company Archives, Archives of Manitoba.

Pages 43–45: Excerpt from David Thompson, *David Thompson's Narrative: 1784–1812*, ed. Richard Glover (Toronto: The Champlain Society, 1962), 229–33. Used by permission of The Champlain Society.

Page 45: Excerpt from an interview with Liliane Coutu-Maisonneuve by Linda Goyette, 1 April 2003. Used by permission of Liliane Coutu-Maisonneuve.

Pages 46–47: Excerpt from Alexander Henry the Younger, *The Journal of Alexander Henry the Younger, 1799–1814. Vol. 1: Red River and the Journey to the Missouri*, ed. Barry M. Gough (Toronto: The Champlain Society, 1988), 414. Used by permission of The Champlain Society.

Page 47: Excerpts from Francis Heron, Reports on the State of Edmonton District during the Year 1820–21, Edmonton: Report on District, 1820–1821, reel 1M777, B.60/e/4, Hudson's Bay Company Archives, Archives of Manitoba. Used by permission of the Hudson's Bay Company Archives, Archives of Manitoba.

Page 48: Excerpt from John Rowand to Peter Pruden, 12 October 1826, Edmonton, John Rowand clipping file, City of Edmonton Archives. Used by permission of the City of Edmonton Archives.

Page 49–50: Excerpt from Edna Rowand Cramer and Mr. E.J. Don Rowand, interview notes, John Rowand clipping file, City of Edmonton Archives. Used by permission of the City of Edmonton Archives.

Pages 50–51: Excerpt from 2 April 1824, Edmonton House Post Journal, 1796–1826, reel 1M49, B.60/a/4–23, Hudson's Bay Company Archives, Archives of Manitoba. Used by permission of the Hudson's Bay Company Archives, Archives of Manitoba.

Page 51: Excerpt from 5 June 1828, Edmonton House Post Journal, 1796–1826, reel 1M49, B.60/a/4–23, Hudson's Bay Company Archives, Archives of Manitoba. Used by permission of the Hudson's Bay Company Archives, Archives of Manitoba.

Pages 52–53: Excerpt from 1–2 January 1828, Edmonton House Post Journal, 1796–1826, reel 1M49, B.60/a/4–23, Hudson's Bay

Company Archives, Archives of Manitoba. Used by permission of the Hudson's Bay Company Archives, Archives of Manitoba.

Page 53: Excerpt from A.D. Pambrum, "Autobiography of A.D. Pambrum," unpublished MS by R.E.S. Clark, 1968, Research Material for Fort Edmonton Park, Box 1: Miscellaneous interviews and reports, City of Edmonton Archives. Used by permission of the City of Edmonton Archives.

Pages 54–55: Excerpt from an interview with Fran Gosché by Linda Goyette, 10 March 2003. Used by permission of Fran Gosché.

Page 55: Excerpt from John Rowand to Sir George Simpson, 20 December 1844, Edmonton House, Sir George Simpson Governor's Records, D.5/12, reel 3M68, fos. 569–570d, Hudson's Bay Company Archives, Archives of Manitoba. Used by permission of the Hudson's Bay Company Archives, Archives of Manitoba.

Page 56: Excerpt from Albert Lacombe, O.M.I., Personal Papers, Memoirs, English version, typed, 30, Oblats de Marie Immaculée, Records of the Alberta-Saskatchewan Oblate Province, 1842–1983, accession 71.220, Box 157, File 6575, fols. 140, Provincial Archives of Alberta. Used by permission of the Missionary Oblates, Grandin Archives at the Provincial Archives of Alberta.

Page 57: Excerpt from Albert Lacombe, O.M.I., Personal Papers, Memoirs, English version, typed, 174–75, Oblats de Marie Immaculée, Records of the Alberta-Saskatchewan Oblate Province, 1842–1983, accession 71.220, Box 157, File 6575, fols. 140, Provincial Archives of Alberta. Used by permission of the Missionary Oblates, Grandin Archives at the Provincial Archives of Alberta.

Page 58: Excerpt from Katherine Hughes, "John Norris, Pioneer," Alberta Historical Review 9, no. 4 (Autumn, 1961): 11–13. Used by permission from the Historical Society of Alberta.

Pages 58–59: Excerpt from an interview with Frank Norris by Linda Goyette, 25 March 2002. Used by permission of Frank Norris.

Pages 59–60: Excerpt from Albert Lacombe, O.M.I., Personal Papers, Memoirs, English version, typed, 97, 100–103, Oblats de Marie Immaculée, Records of the Alberta-Saskatchewan Oblate Province, 1842–1983, accession 71.220, Box 157, File 6575, fols. 140, Provincial Archives of Alberta. Used by permission of the Missionary Oblates, Grandin Archives at the Provincial Archives of Alberta.

Pages 60–63 and 69–71: Excerpts from Peter Erasmus, Buffalo Days and Nights: As Told to Henry Thompson (Calgary: Fifth House Publishers, 1999), 43–48. Reprinted with permission from Buffalo Days and Nights. Copyright © 1999, Fifth House Publishers. Published by Fifth House Ltd., Calgary, Canada.

Pages 67–68: Excerpt from George Simpson to Alexander Rowand, 29 July 1856, Hudson's Bay House, Lachine, Simpson's private outward correspondence, D.4/83, reel 3M40, fo. 785, Hudson's Bay Company Archives, Archives of Manitoba. Used by permission of the Hudson's Bay Company Archives, Archives of Manitoba.

Page 68: Excerpt from 6 October 1856, Edmonton House Post Journal, 1825–1864, reel 1M50, B.60/a/23–33, Hudson's Bay Company Archives, Archives of Manitoba (microfilm, University of Alberta Library). Used by permission of the Hudson's Bay Company Archives, Archives of Manitoba.

Pages 68–69: Excerpt from July 1859, Edmonton House Post Journal, 1825–1864, reel 1M50, B.60/a/23–33, Hudson's Bay Company Archives, Archives of Manitoba (microfilm, University of Alberta Library). Used by permission of the Hudson's Bay Company Archives, Archives of Manitoba.

Page 69: Excerpt from 9 February 1861, Edmonton House Post Journal, 1825–1864, reel 1M50, B.60/a/23–33, Hudson's Bay Company Archives, Archives of Manitoba (microfilm, University of Alberta Library). Used by permission of the Hudson's Bay Company Archives, Archives of Manitoba.

Page 71: Excerpt from Albert Lacombe, O.M.I., Personal Papers, Memoirs, English version, typed, 139–40, Oblats de Marie Immaculée, Records of the Alberta-Saskatchewan Oblate Province, 1842–1983, accession 71.220, Box 157, File 6575, fols. 140, Provincial Archives of Alberta. Used by permission of the Missionary Oblates, Grandin Archives at the Provincial Archives of Alberta.

Pages 71–72: Excerpt from Thomas Woolsey, Heaven Is Near the Rocky Mountains: The Journals and Letters of Thomas Woolsey, 1855–1869, ed. Hugh A. Dempsey (Calgary: Glenbow Museum, 1989), 26. Used by permission of the Glenbow Museum and Archives.

Pages 73–74: Excerpts from E.O Drouin, O.M.I., Lac Ste-Anne Sakahigan (Edmonton: Editions de l'Ermitage, 1973). Used by permission of the Grey Nuns Regional Centre Archives, Edmonton.

Page 75: Excerpt from Soeur Zoé Leblanc-Emery to Mère Deschamps, 3 April 1860, 35, quoted in Janet Ross Kerr and Pauline Paul, "The work of the Grey Nuns in Alberta—1859–1899: A feminist perspective," 28 June 1990, 2, Soeurs Grises de Montreal, Musée Héritage Museum, St. Albert. Used by permission of the Grey Nuns Regional Centre Archives, Edmonton.

Page 75: Excerpt from Sister Zoé Leblanc-Emery to Mother J.H.-Deschamps, 25 December 1860, GNRC Archives, quoted in Thérèse Castonguay, A Leap in Faith (Edmonton: Grey Nuns of Alberta, 1999), 30. Used by permission of the Grey Nuns Regional Centre Archives, Edmonton.

Page 75: Excerpt from Thomas Woolsey, Heaven Is Near the Rocky Mountains: The Journals and Letters of Thomas Woolsey, 1855–1869, ed. Hugh A. Dempsey (Calgary: Glenbow Museum, 1989), 67. Used by permission of the Glenbow Museum and Archives.

Pages 76–77: Excerpt from Colin Fraser, "Reminiscences of Colin Fraser Free Trader of Fort Chipewyan, as related to George Pendleton of the Hudson's Bay Company, Oct. 1938," 1–3, Alberta Folklore and Local History Collection, 96–93–835, University of Alberta. Cited from the Alberta Folklore and Local History Collection, University of Alberta.

Pages 77–78: Excerpt from Albert Lacombe, O.M.I., Personal Papers, Memoirs, English version, typed, 140, 55–57, Oblats de Marie Immaculée, Records of the Alberta-Saskatchewan Oblate Province, 1842–1983, accession 71.220, Box 157, File 6575, fols. 140, Provincial Archives of Alberta. Used by permission of the Missionary Oblates, Grandin Archives at the Provincial Archives of Alberta.

Pages 78–80: Excerpt from Hippolyte Leduc, O.M.I., newspaper article on Christmas 1867, City of Edmonton Archives. Used by permission of the City of Edmonton Archives.

Pages 80–82: Excerpt from Victoria Belcourt Callihoo, "Our Buffalo Hunts," Alberta Historical Review 8, no. 1 (Winter 1960): 24–25. Used by permission from the Historical Society of Alberta.

Pages 82–83: Excerpt from John Buffalo, quoted in Richard T. Price, ed. *Spirit of the Alberta Indian Treaties*, 3rd ed. (Edmonton: The University of Alberta Press, 1999), 122. Used by permission of Richard Price and The University of Alberta Press.

Page 107: Excerpt from 8–10 December 1862, Edmonton House Post Journal, 1825–1864, reel 1M50, B.60/a/23–33, Hudson's Bay Company Archives, Archives of Manitoba (microfilm, University of Alberta Library). Used by permission of the Hudson's Bay Company Archives, Archives of Manitoba.

Pages 110–11: Excerpt from Hugh Dempsey, ed., *The Early West* (Edmonton: Historical Society of Alberta, 1957), 22–23. Used by permission from the Historical Society of Alberta.

Page 111: Excerpt from Harrison S. Young, "Impressions of Fort Edmonton," *Alberta Historical Review* 14, no. 1 (Winter 1966): 22–25. Used by permission from the Historical Society of Alberta.

Page 112: Excerpt from James Gibbons, "The Narrative of James Gibbons (part 2)," ed. W.A. Griesbach, *Alberta Historical Review* 6, no. 4 (Autumn 1958): 11. Used by permission from the Historical Society of Alberta.

Pages 113–14: Excerpt from Colonel Frederick C. Jamieson, "The Edmonton Hunt," *Alberta Historical Review* 1, no. 1 (April 1953): 21–22, 27–29. Used by permission from the Historical Society of Alberta.

Pages 115–16: "Letter of 12 September 1870 to S.G. Mgr Taché from Alb. Lacombe ptre," taken from *The Book of Letters: 150 Years of Private Canadian Correspondence*, by Paul and Audrey Grescoe. Used by permission of McClelland and Stewart, Ltd., *The Canadian Publishers*.

Pages 116–17: Excerpt from Sister Emery to Mother Slocombe, Grey Nuns correspondence, Ancien journal vol. 1 (1863), Les soeurs grises de Montrèal, Prov. St-Albert Archives. Used by permission of the Grey Nuns Regional Centre Archives, Edmonton.

Pages 119–20: Excerpt from W.J. Christie to George W. Hill, 26 April 1871, Edmonton House, Saskatchewan District, Adam G. Archibald Papers, Correspondence and Papers, 1869–1873, reel M2, MG 12 A 1, Archives of Manitoba, Winnipeg. Used by permission of the Archives of Manitoba.

Pages 120–21: Excerpt from W.J. Christie to George W. Hill, 26 April 1871, Edmonton House, Saskatchewan District, Adam G. Archibald Papers, Correspondence and Papers, 1869–1873, reel M2, MG 12 A 1, Archives of Manitoba, Winnipeg. Used by permission of the Archives of Manitoba.

Pages 122–23: Excerpt from Lazarus Roan, quoted in Richard T. Price, ed. *The Spirit of the Alberta Indian Treaties*, 3rd ed. (Edmonton: The University of Alberta Press, 1999), 115. Used by permission of Violet Rowand, daughter of Lazarus Roan, and The University of Alberta Press.

Pages 125–26: Excerpt from Brian M. Owens and Claude M. Roberto, eds. *The Diaries of Bishop Vital Grandin 1875–1877, Vol. 1*, trans. Alan D. Ridge (Edmonton: The Historical Society of Alberta, Amisk Waskahegan Chapter, 1989), 28. Used by permission from the Historical Society of Alberta.

Page 127: Excerpt from Thérèse Castonguay, *A Leap in Faith* (Edmonton: Grey Nuns of Alberta, 1999), 39. Used by permission of the Grey Nuns Regional Centre Archives, Edmonton.

Pages 128–29: Excerpt from James Gibbons, "The Narrative of James Gibbons (part 2)," ed. W.A. Griesbach, *Alberta Historical*

Review 6, no. 4 (Autumn 1958): 14. Used by permission from the Historical Society of Alberta.

Page 130: Excerpt from an interview with Calvin Bruneau by Linda Goyette, 17 March 2003. Used by permission of Calvin Bruneau.

Pages 133–34 and 157: Excerpt cited from Charles John Brydges, *The Letters of Charles John Brydges, 1883–1889, Hudson's Bay Land Commissioner*, ed. Hartwell Bowsfield (Winnipeg: Hudson's Bay Record Society, 1981), 240–43.

Pages 137–38: Excerpt from Anna Laura Robertson Harrison, Memoirs of life in Edmonton, 1883–1964, pp. 3–4 and 10–12, Alberta Folklore and Local History Collection, 96-93-502, University of Alberta Libraries. Cited from the Alberta Folklore and Local History Collection, University of Alberta.

Pages 138–39: Excerpt from Clare Matthews, "Happy memories of my childhood," 14 August 1962, Henry Samuel Casey fonds, MS 294 C1 F1, City of Edmonton Archives. Used by permission of the City of Edmonton Archives.

Page 139: Excerpt from Michael Kostek, *A Century and Ten: The History of Edmonton Public Schools* (Edmonton: Edmonton Public Schools, 1992), 20–21. Used by permission of Michael Kostek.

Page 140: Excerpt from John Walter, Northern Alberta Pioneers' and Oldtimers' Association fonds, MS 56.14, City of Edmonton Archives. Used by permission of the City of Edmonton Archives.

Page 141: Excerpt from J.R. McPhaden, interview by Ella May Walker, fall 1944 and 1945, Ella May Walker fonds, MS 52, file 12, City of Edmonton Archives. Used by permission of the City of Edmonton Archives.

Pages 143–44: Excerpt from Kate Maloney, "The St. Albert Mounted Rifles, Volunteers of 1885, being the personal reminiscences of an Old Timer," Musée Héritage. Cited from the St. Albert Heritage Society fonds, 2003.02.62, Musée Héritage Museum.

Pages 145–46: Excerpt from Annie (McKernan) Turnbull, interview by Ella May Walker, Ella May Walker fonds, MS 52, file 15, City of Edmonton Archives. Used by permission of the City of Edmonton Archives.

Pages 147–49: Excerpt from "The Wisdom of Papasschayo...", James Brady fonds, 1895–1967 [M125/19] Glenbow Archives, Calgary. Used by permission of the Glenbow Museum and Archives.

Pages 150–51: Excerpt from Lazarus Roan, interview by Eric Stamp, 12 March 1973, T.A.R.R. Background Papers. Used by permission of Violet Rowand, daughter of Lazarus Roan.

Pages 151–53: Excerpt from [Father A. Blanchet], Codex Historicus, Riviere Qui Barre 1886–1889, from the Missionary Oblates, Grandin Archives at the Provincial Archives of Alberta. Accession 71.220, File 5383, (translated from French). Also quoted in Elizabeth Macpherson, *The Sun Traveller: The Story of the Callihoos in Alberta* (St. Albert: Musée Héritage, 1998), 62–63.

Page 156: Excerpt from Frank Oliver, "Address given by Honourable Frank Oliver, P.C. on the occasion of the official opening of the 50th anniversary of the Edmonton Exhibition on Monday, 15 July 1929," Frank Oliver clipping file, City of Edmonton Archives. Used by permission of the City of Edmonton Archives.

Page 182: Excerpt from Donald Ross, "Toll of the Years," Christina McKnight fonds, MS 131, City of Edmonton Archives. Used by permission of the City of Edmonton Archives.

Pages 184–85: Excerpt from Ellen Hopkins, "The Haunted House," 24 December 1945, Alberta Folklore and Local History Collection, 96–93–508, University of Alberta Libraries. Cited from the Alberta Folklore and Local History Collection, University of Alberta.

Pages 191–93: Excerpt from Olive Kathleen Murdoch, "When you are very green, being the true experience of the Heathcote family, coming from the city of London, England, to a homestead in Alberta, Canada," Heathcote family fonds, MS 258, C1, F1, City of Edmonton Archives. Used by permission of the City of Edmonton Archives.

Pages 193–94: Excerpt from *Peter Svarich, Memoirs: 1877–1904*, trans. William Kostash (Edmonton: Ukrainian Pioneers' Association of Alberta and Huculak Chair of Ukrainian Culture and Ethnography, 1999), 110–13. Used by permission of Mary Kostash.

Pages 197–98: Excerpt from Mozanne (Baltzan) Dower, interview by Becky, 7 June 1999, JAHSENA Oral History Project, JAHSENA Oral History Project fonds, JOH.03.1, Jewish Archives and Historical Society of Edmonton and Northern Alberta. Used by permission of the Jewish Archives and Historical Society of Edmonton and Northern Alberta.

Pages 198–99: Excerpt from Hyman Goldstick, History of the Birth of Edmonton and Calgary Jewish Communities, JAHSENA. Used by permission of the Jewish Archives and Historical Society of Edmonton and Northern Alberta.

Pages 199–200: Excerpt from "Arthur Hiller: interviewed for JAHSENA Historical Documentary Project," *Heritage: The Journal of the Jewish Archives and Historical Society of Edmonton and Northern Alberta* 4, no. 4 (Summer 2002): 3. Used by permission of the Jewish Archives and Historical Society of Edmonton and Northern Alberta.

Pages 201–2: Excerpt from Mrs. Charles Learmonth, "'Women Pioneer: Mrs. McQueen,' Mrs. Charles Learmonth's pioneer experience and life in Edmonton," Alberta Folklore and Local History Collection, 96–93–859, University of Alberta Libraries. Cited from the Alberta Folklore and Local History Collection, University of Alberta.

Pages 203: Excerpt from Hugh Dempsey, ed., *The Best of Bob Edwards* (Edmonton: M.G. Hurtig Publishers, 1975), 232, 233, 236. Used by permission of Hugh Dempsey.

Page 204: Excerpt from Dorothy May King, "Childhood memories of Edmonton, Alberta, 1902–1911," CCH Collection. Used by permission of Denny May.

Page 206: Excerpt from Anna Laura Robertson Harrison, Memoirs of life in Edmonton, 1883–1964, pp. 3–4 and 10–12, Alberta Folklore and Local History Collection, 96–93–502, University of Alberta Libraries. Cited from the Alberta Folklore and Local History Collection, University of Alberta.

Page 206: Excerpt from Grace Matthews, Henry Samuel Casey fonds, MS 294, C1 F1, City of Edmonton Archives. Used by permission of the City of Edmonton Archives.

Pages 206–8: Excerpt from Gladys Reeves, interview by Helen LaRose and Maida Scott, 5 June 1970, A70–75 oral history binder, City of Edmonton Archives. Used by permission of the City of Edmonton Archives.

Page 208: Excerpt from Ernest Brown, 26 March 1945, Alberta Folklore and Local History Collection, 96–93–425, University

of Alberta. Cited from the Alberta Folklore and Local History Collection, University of Alberta.

Page 209: Excerpt from Frank Oliver to Sir Wilfrid Laurier, 8 February 1905, Sir Wilfrid Laurier fonds, MG26 G, C819, vol. 355, 94623–94637, Library and Archives Canada. Used by permission of the Library and Archives Canada.

Page 210: Excerpt from Sir Wilfrid Laurier to Frank Oliver, 9 February 1905, Sir Wilfrid Laurier fonds, MG26 G, C819, vol. 355, 94623–94637, Library and Archives Canada. Used by permission of the Library and Archives Canada.

Page 212: Excerpt from Gertrude Balmer Watt, "Christmas in the West," *A Woman in the West* (Ottawa: National Library of Canada, 1978), 26–27. Used with permission of the Gertrude Balmer Watt Estate.

Page 217–18 and 264–65: Excerpt from an interview with Charles Anderson by Linda Goyette, 22 March 2002. Used by permission of Charles Anderson.

Page 219: Excerpt from John Bell Bowden, "John Bell Bowden," in *The Window of Our Memories*, eds. Velma Carter and Wanda Leffler Akili (St. Albert, AB: B.C.R. Society of Alberta, 1981), 46–47. Used by permission of Junetta Jamerson, niece of Velma Carter, and Wanda Leffler Akili.

Pages 219–20: Excerpt from Thomas Mapp, "Thomas Mapp," in *The Window of Our Memories*, eds. Velma Carter and Wanda Leffler Akili (St. Albert, AB: B.C.R. Society of Alberta, 1981), 19. Used by permission of Junetta Jamerson, niece of Velma Carter, and Wanda Leffler Akili.

Pages 222–23 and 265–66: Excerpt from Grace Duggan Cook, *Roots and Romance: The David and Marian Duggan Family* (Edmonton: G. Cook, 1981), 24–25. Used by permission of David Duggan, Grace Duggan Cook's nephew.

Pages 252–53: Excerpt from "The Trapper: Reminiscences of Ignaty (Ike) Kreway," in *Shadows of the Past*, ed. Bohdan I. Shulakewych (Edmonton: St. Michael's Extended Care Centre, 1986), 103–4. Used by permission of Bohdan I. Shulakewych and the St. Michael's Extended Care Centre.

Pages 253–54: Excerpt from N. Olynik, 28 October 1915, RG 24, vol. 4729, file 3, Library and Archives Canada, quoted in Kordan, *Enemy Aliens Prisoners of War*, 70. Used by permission of the Library and Archives Canada.

Pages 254–55: Excerpt from Assunta Dotto, CCH Collection. Used by permission of Assunta Dotto.

Page 255: Excerpt from Francis Winspear, *Out of My Mind* (Victoria: Morriss Printing Co., 1988), 59–60. Used by permission of Harriet Winspear, wife of Francis Winspear.

Page 256: Excerpt from Fred Barns, interview, 4 October 1970, A70–75 oral history binder, City of Edmonton Archives. Used by permission of the City of Edmonton Archives.

Page 256: Excerpt from Allan Shute and Margaret Fortier, *Riverdale: From Fraser Flats to Edmonton Oasis* (Edmonton: Tree Frog Press, 1992), 48, 50, 51. Used by permission of Allan Shute.

Page 259: Excerpt from Margaret Garrison [McKee] to Emily Murphy, 5 June 1921, Emily Murphy Papers, MS 2, City of Edmonton Archives, Edmonton. Used by permission of the City of Edmonton Archives.

Page 259: Excerpt from Emily Murphy to Margaret Garrison, Provincial Gaol, Fort Saskatchewan, 15 June 1921, Emily

Murphy Papers, MS 2, City of Edmonton Archives, Edmonton. Used by permission of the City of Edmonton Archives.

Pages 262–63: Excerpt from Alex Decoteau to Emily Latta, 10 September 1917, Izola (Latta) Mottershead private collection. Used by permission of Izola Mottershead and the Latta family.

Page 263: Excerpt from W.A. Griesbach to Mrs. R. Waring, 28 October 1916, Loyal Edmonton Regiment Museum. http://www.lermuseum.org/ler/mh/wwi/flanders.html. Used by permission of the Loyal Edmonton Regiment.

Page 264: Excerpt from Griesbach papers, Loyal Edmonton Regiment, Militia (Third Battalion Princess Patricia Canadian Light Infantry), quoted in Max Foran, "W.A. 'Billy' Griesbach and World War One," Alberta History 32, no. 3 (Summer 1984): 1–8. Used by permission from the Historical Society of Alberta.

Page 264: Excerpt from Sheila Reid, Wings of a Hero: Canadian pioneer flying ace Wilfrid Wop May (St. Catherines, ON: Vanwell Publishing Limited, 1997), 18–20. Used by permission of Denny May, son of Wilfrid May.

Pages 267–68: Excerpt from Peggy Holmes and Andrea Spalding, Never a Dull Moment (Toronto: Collins, 1984), 21–26. Used by permission of Andrea Spalding, Brandywine Enterprises Limited.

Page 269: Excerpt from J. Brian Dawson, Moon Cakes in Gold Mountain: From China to the Canadian Plains (Calgary: Detselig Enterprises, Ltd. 1991), 171. Used by permission of Liliane Mah and Brian Dawson.

Pages 269–70: Excerpt from Peace Cornwall Hudson, "The Ravine," Eirene Hebb fonds, MS 621, 1–2, City of Edmonton Archives. Used by permission of the City of Edmonton Archives.

Pages 270–71: Excerpt from Isobell (Crook) Dittrich, "My Memoirs," CCH Collection. Used by permission of Isobell Dittrich.

Page 271: Excerpt from Edward Jordan, "Recollections of CKUA," in A Sound for All Seasons: CKUA's 60th Anniversary (Edmonton: ACCESS Network, 1987), 22. Used by permission of CKUA.

Pages 272–74: Excerpt from E.A. Cobbs, "E.A. Cobbs," in The Window of Our Memories Volume II: The New Generation, Velma Carter and Leah Suzanne Carter, eds. (St. Albert, AB: B.C.R. Society of Alberta, 1990), 65–68. Used by permission of Junetta Jamerson, niece of Velma Carter.

Pages 275–77: Excerpt from William Kay, "The Kay Family As Told By William Chee (Bill) Kay," CCH Collection, 2004. Used by permission of William Kay.

Pages 277–78: Excerpt from Marion Robinson, "Memories of My McKernan Home," CCH Collection. Used by permission of Marion Robinson.

Pages 279–81: Excerpt from an interview with Clare Botsford, interview by the Alberta Labour History Institute. Used by permission of Clare Botsford.

Page 281: Excerpt from Orval Griggs, "The Dirty Thirties," CCH Collection. Used by permission of Orval Griggs.

Pages 281–84: Excerpt from Ben Swankey, "Reflections of an Alberta Communist: The Hungry Thirties," Alberta History 27, no. 4 (Autumn, 1979): 8–12. Used by permission from the Historical Society of Alberta.

Pages 284–85: Excerpt from Geo. B. McClellan, "Personal experiences of an R.C.M.P. officer," Canadian Geographical Journal LXXXVI, no. 5 (May 1973): 184–86. Used by permission of the Canadian Geographical Journal.

Page 286: Excerpt from Alex Latta, "Curly," CCH Collection. Used by permission of Alex Latta.

Page 287: Excerpt from John M. Reid, All Those Other Guys and Me (self-published, 2003), 31–35. Used by permission of John Reid.

Pages 287–88: Excerpt from Alex Mair, Gateway City (Calgary: Fifth House, 2000), 127–29. Reprinted with permission from Gateway City: Stories from Edmonton's Past. Copyright © 2000, Estate of Alex Mair. Published by Fifth House Ltd., Calgary, Canada.

Pages 289–90: Excerpt from Sterling Haynes, "Funny Money" in Bloody Practice: Doctoring in the Cariboo and Around the World (Prince George, B.C.: Caitlin Press, 2003). Used by permission of Sterling Haynes.

Page 291: Excerpt from John Imrie, Pulitzer Prize acceptance speech, 2 May 1938, Columbia University, New York. Used by permission of the Red Deer Archives.

Pages 291–94: Excerpt from Edith Sutton, CCH Collection. Used by permission of Edith Sutton.

Page 294: Excerpt from John Ducey, "Interview with Mr John Ducey, Edmonton's 'Mr. Baseball' conducted by John McIsaac, 1979," Edmonton Parks and Recreation, City of Edmonton Archives. Used by permission of the City of Edmonton Archives.

Page 295: Excerpt from Joe Shoctor, "She Made Me Want to Be in Theatre," in Remembering Elizabeth, ed. Elsie Park Gowan (Edmonton: Committee for Elizabeth Haynes Theatre Event, 1974), unpaginated. Used by permission of Debby Shoctor, daughter-in-law of Joe Shoctor.

Pages 296–97: Excerpt from Sid Hamdon, "Hilwie Taha Jomha," CCH Collection, 2004. Used by permission of Sid and Faye Hamdon.

Pages 297–98: Excerpt from Harley Reid, "The Wave," CCH Collection. Used by permission of Harley Reid.

Pages 298–300: Excerpt from an interview with Kathleen Steinhauer by Linda Goyette, 13 January 2003. Used by permission of Kathleen Steinhauer.

Pages 300–301: Excerpt from an interview with Peter Owen by Linda Goyette, 29 December 2003. Used by permission of Peter Owen.

Pages 302–4: Excerpt from Norah Plumley Hook, CCH Collection. Used by permission of Norah Plumley Hook.

Pages 304–5: Excerpt from Helen I. Mahoney, CCH Collection. Used by permission of Helen Mahoney.

Pages 305–6: Excerpt from Nan Morrison, CCH Collection. Used by permission of Nan Morrison.

Page 307: Excerpt from Edgar J. Bailey to Mrs. Vass, Loyal Edmonton Regiment Collection. Used by permission of the Loyal Edmonton Regiment.

Page 309: Excerpt from William Ziegler, "Why?" in Echoes in the Halls: An Unofficial History of the University of Alberta, eds. Mary Spencer, Kay Dier, and Gordon McIntosh (Edmonton: Duval House Publishing and The University of Alberta Press, 1999), 263–64. Used by permission of the Association of Professors Emeriti, University of Alberta.

Pages 339–41: Excerpt from Paul and Audrey Grescoe, eds. The Book of Letters: 150 Years of Private Canadian Correspondence (Toronto: Macfarlane, Walter & Ross, 2002), 88–90. Used by permission of McClelland & Stewart Ltd., The Canadian Publishers.

Pages 341–42: Excerpt from John Funk, "John Funk," in Beatrice Hunter, *Last Chance Well: Legends & Legacies of Leduc No. 1* (Edmonton: Teddington Lock, 1997), 31–33. Used by permission of Beatrice Hunter.

Page 342: Excerpt from Dorothy Morris and Elsie Owre, "Dorothy Morris and Elsie Owre, Oil Wives," in *Last Chance Well: Legends & Legacies of Leduc No. 1* (Edmonton: Teddington Lock, 1997), 174. Used by permission of Beatrice Hunter.

Page 343: Excerpt from Dorothy Pickard, "Dorothy Pickard," in *Oil Patch: Recollections of 'The Way Things Were'*, ed. Elsie Garstad-Rosenau (Edmonton: Lifelines, Etc. 1997), 222. Used by permission of Elsie Garstad-Lambert.

Pages 343–45: Excerpt from Andrew Turta, "Andrew Turta," in Beatrice Hunter, *Last Chance Well: Legends & Legacies of Leduc No. 1* (Edmonton: Teddington Lock, 1997), 192. Used by permission of Beatrice Hunter.

Page 345: Excerpt from Karen Bower, "Karen Bower," in *Oil Patch: Recollections of 'The Way Things Were'*, ed. Elsie Garstad-Rosenau (Edmonton: Lifelines, Etc. 1997), 246. Used by permission of Karen Bower.

Pages 345–46: Excerpt from Ian Archibald, in *Oil Patch: Recollections of 'The Way Things Were'*, ed. Elsie Garstad-Rosenau (Edmonton: Lifelines, Etc. 1997), 243–45. Used by permission of Ian Archibald.

Page 347: Excerpt from an interview with John Stefanyk by Linda Goyette, August 2002. Used by permission of John Stefanyk.

Page 348: Excerpt from Joyce Harries, *Girdles and Other Harnesses I Have Known* (Edmonton: Lone Pine Publishing, 2000), 101. Used by permission of Joyce Harries.

Pages 348–50: Excerpt from Lois Hole, *I'll Never Marry a Farmer: Lois Hole on Life, Learning, & Vegetable Gardening* (St. Albert: Hole's, 1998), 21. Used by permission of Earl Woods, representative of the Hole family.

Pages 350–51: Excerpt from Ed Wigmore, "Growing up on Boyle Street—a personal memoir," CCH Collection. Used by permission of Ed Wigmore.

Pages 351–52: Excerpt from an interview with Inge Vermeulen by Linda Goyette, 29 July 2002. Used by permission of Inge Vermeulen.

Page 352: Excerpt from Mary Spencer, "Learning to love Muddington," in *Echoes in the Halls: An Unofficial History of the University of Alberta*, eds. Mary Spencer, Kay Dier and Gordon McIntosh (Edmonton: Duval House Publishing and The University of Alberta Press, 1999), 35–36. Used by permission of the Association of Professors Emeriti, University of Alberta.

Pages 353–55: Excerpt from Mel Hurtig, *At Twilight in the Country: Memoirs of a Canadian Nationalist* (Toronto: Stoddart, 1996), 43–45. Used by permission of Mel Hurtig.

Pages 356–58: Excerpt from Preston Manning, *Think Big: Adventures in Life and Democracy* (Toronto: McClelland and Stewart, 2002), 9–12. Used by permission of Preston Manning.

Pages 359–60: Excerpt from Abdul N. Kamal, "Braving the Frontier: Remembrance of my arrival in Edmonton," in *Echoes in the Halls*, 24–26. Used by permission of the Association of Professors Emeriti, University of Alberta.

Pages 360–61: Excerpt from Alvena Strasbourg, *Memories of a Métis Woman: Fort McMurray Yesterday and Today* (Alberta: s.l.: 1998), 59–60. Used by permission of Alvena Strasbourg.

Pages 361–62: Excerpt from Scarlett Gonzalez, "Here, My Kids Have Everything: Security, Peace, Freedom," in *Canadian By Choice*, ed. Liza Linklater (Ottawa: Citizenship and Immigration Canada, 1994), 7. Used by permission of Scarlett Gonzalez.

Pages 362–63: Excerpt from Bill Hunter, *Wild Bill: Bill Hunters' Legendary 65 Years in Canadian Sport* (Calgary: Johnson Gorman Publishers, 2000), 179–80. Used by permission of Johnson Gorman Publishers.

Pages 363–64: Excerpt from pages 35–36 from *Gretzky: An Autobiography* by Wayne Gretzky with Rick Reilly. Copyright © 1990 by Wayne Gretzky. Reprinted by permission of HarperCollins Publishers Inc.

Pages 365–66: Excerpt from Rod Phillips, "Stanley Cup Game," in Gary W. Zeman, *Alberta on Ice* (Edmonton: Westweb Press, 1985), 101–2. Used by permission of Rod Phillips.

Pages 366–68: Excerpt from Holger Petersen, "CKUA's Music," in *A Sound for All Seasons: CKUA's 60th Anniversary* (Edmonton: ACCESS Network, 1987), 30–31. Used by permission of Holger Petersen.

Page 368: Excerpt from Tommy Banks, quoted in Marylu Walters, *CKUA: Radio Worth Fighting For* (Edmonton: The University of Alberta Press, 2002), 365. Used by permission of Tommy Banks and The University of Alberta Press.

Pages 369–70: Excerpt from Brian Paisley, "Heart of the Beast," in *Edmonton's Fringe Theatre Event*, 17. Used by permission of Brian Paisley.

Pages 370–71: Excerpt from Laura Roald, "The Avenue: a director's journey creating theatre with youth at risk," *Theatre Alberta Newsletter*, Fall 2002, <http://www.theatrealberta.com/newsletter/Fall2002/TheAvenue.htm> (3 June 2003). Used by permission of Laura Roald.

Page 371: Excerpt from an interview with Mieko Ouchi by Vivian Giang, 2 February 2004. Used by permission of Mieko Ouchi.

Pages 372–74: Excerpts from Andrew Nikiforuk, "The War on 66th Street," in *Running on Empty: Alberta After the Boom*, eds. Andrew Nikiforuk, Sheila Pratt, and Don Wanagas (Edmonton: NeWest Publishers Ltd. 1987), 129–30. Used by permission of Andrew Nikiforuk.

Pages 374–76: Excerpt from an interview with Greg Buteau and Angela Buteau by Darla Quinlan, 25 February 2004. Used by permission of Greg Buteau, Angela Buteau and Darla Quinlan.

Pages 380–82: Excerpt from an interview with Mary Kur by Linda Goyette, 16 September 2003. Used by permission of Mary Kur.

Pages 382–85: Excerpt from Dwayne Donald, CCH Collection. Used by permission of Dwayne Donald.

NOTE: All material is properly cited in the Notes. The author has made every effort to contact the copyright holders of the excerpts included in the book. Please contact the author if you have further information concerning copyright materials. If additional information is received after publication, it will be included in future editions of the book.

Photograph Credits

Front cover and Frontmatter

Front cover: Hockey players. Glenbow Museum and Archives, NC–6–11932 (b).

Front cover: Edmonton Grads: Helen Stone, Edith Stone and Babe Belanger. Courtesy of Edith Sutton.

Front cover: Papaschase, also known as John Quinn, with his granddaughter Nancy Quinn. (The man in the photograph has been identified as Papaschase, but others suggest that it might be his brother.) Courtesy of Joyce Bruneau and Papaschase First Nation.

Page ii: Oceania and Kehew Bellerose. Photographer: John Ulan. Courtesy of Louis Morris and Theresa Bellerose, parents, and John Ulan.

Page v: "I LOVE YOU" written in the snow. City of Edmonton Archives, EA–160–1972.

A Bend in the River to 1700

Page 1: Canoes on riverbank. Photographer: John Ulan. Courtesy of John Ulan.

The Meeting Place 1700 to 1869

Page 16: William Gladstone and his granddaughter, Nellie. Glenbow Museum and Archives, NA–184–23.

Page 16: Julie Daignault. Courtesy of Fran Gosché.

Page 17: Rossdale cemetery. Photographer: John Ulan. Courtesy of John Ulan.

Page 41: John MacDonald of Garth. Alberta Folklore and Local History Collection, Bruce Peel Special Collections Library, University of Alberta, 96–93–529.

Page 43: Louis Callihoo's contract with the North West Company. Archives nationale du Québec.

Page 46: Marie-Anne Gaboury Lagimodière. Glenbow Museum and Archives, NA–3694–1.

Page 48: John Rowand. City of Edmonton Archives, EA–10–2773.

Page 49: Margaret Harriott Rowand. City of Edmonton Archives, EA–10–1651.

Page 50: Extract from the June 5, 1828 entry in the Edmonton House Post Journal, 1828–1829. HBCA B. 60/a/26 fo. 3 (N15573); and extract from the June 5, 1828 entry in the Edmonton House Post Journal, 1828–1829. HBCA B. 60/a/26 fo. 3d (N15574).

Page 53: Jimmy Jock Bird. Glenbow Museum and Archives, NA–360–21.

Page 55: Depiction of a Cree buffalo pound. Artwork by Lt. George Back. Glenbow Museum and Archives, NA–1344–2.

Page 57: William Gladstone and his granddaughter, Nellie. Glenbow Museum and Archives, NA–184–23.

Page 59: Albert Lacombe. Glenbow Museum and Archives, NA–4209–2.

Page 61: Peter Erasmus. Glenbow Museum and Archives, NA–319–1.

Page 64: Fort Edmonton, with nearby camps. Artwork by Paul Kane. City of Edmonton Archives, EA–10–3249.

Page 72: Milton and Cheadle's party. Glenbow Museum and Archives, NA–1240–1.

Page 76: Canada's earliest industry. Colin Fraser, trader at Fort Chipweyan, sorts fox, beaver, mink and other precious furs, 189–. Ernest Brown collection. Library and Archives Canada, C–001229.

Page 77: Julie Daignault. Courtesy of Fran Gosché.

Page 79: Graphic of a pemmican recipe of Louisa Bellcourt, Métis descendant. Louisa Bellcourt, interview, April 1968, 3, Research Material for Fort Edmonton Park, Box 1—Miscellaneous Interviews and Reports, City of Edmonton Archives.

The Manitou Stone 1870 to 1891

Page 84: The Land Reserved for the Band of Chief Papaschase. Library and Archives Canada, LAC, RG 10, volume 3786, reel C–10192, file 42010.

Page 84: Cree family in camp with tipis and Red River cart close-up. Provincial Archives of Alberta, B 3.

Page 85: Manitou Stone. Photographer: John Ulan. Courtesy of John Ulan and Provincial Museum of Alberta.

Page 108: Maskipiton. Glenbow Museum and Archives, NA–4169–1.

Page 108: Letter by Maskipiton written in Cree syllabics. Glenbow Museum and Archives, Letter 1844, M–1083 f. 4.

Page 113: Victoria Belcourt Callihoo. Courtesy of the Lac Ste. Anne Historical Society.

Page 115: George McDougall. Glenbow Museum and Archives, NA–589–1.

Page 118: Elizabeth Chantler McDougall. Glenbow Museum and Archives, NA–1010–22.

Page 119: Samuel Trott at Fort Edmonton. Photographer: Charles G. Horetzky. City of Edmonton Archives, EA–128–5.

Page 121: Sweetgrass. Glenbow Museum and Archives, NA–1677–10.

Page 126: OB. 1942—St. Albert, Youville Convent and Orphanage. Convent opened in 1863. Photograph date 1884. Photographer unknown. Missionary Oblates, Grandin Archives, Provincial Archives of Alberta.

Page 130: Papaschase, also known as John Quinn, with his granddaughter Nancy Quinn. (The man in the photograph has been identified as Papaschase, but others suggest that it might be his brother.) Courtesy of Joyce Bruneau and Papaschase First Nation.

Page 131: The Land Reserved for the Band of Chief Papaschase. Library and Archives Canada, LAC, RG 10, volume 3786, reel C–10192, file 42010.

Page 135: Bobtail. Provincial Archives of Alberta, P 131.

Page 137: Fort Edmonton families. City of Edmonton Archives, EA–13–3.

Page 140: The Walter family. City of Edmonton Archives, EA–10–1677.

Page 141: Edmonton's first telephone conversation. Edmonton Bulletin, 10 January 1885. Courtesy of the City of Edmonton Archives.

Page 142: Samuel Cunningham. Musée Héritage Museum, St. Albert, St. Albert Heritage Society fonds, 974.185.01. Photograph owned by the Cunningham family.

Page 144: Kate Maloney. Musée Héritage Museum, St. Albert, St. Albert Heritage Society fonds, 981.05.03. Photograph courtesy of Margaret Victoor.

Page 145: Christine Lacombe and Leon Harnois. Glenbow Museum and Archives, NA–518–7.

Page 146: Mayor Matthew McCauley with Chief Ermineskin. Provincial Archives of Alberta, B 6897.

Page 147: Laurent and Eleanor Garneau. Digitally reconstructed. Glenbow Museum and Archives, PA–2218–6.

Page 149: Agathe, Archange and Charlotte Garneau with Placide Poirier. Glenbow Museum and Archives, PA–2218–2.

Page 150: Elizabeth Brass Donald. Courtesy of Fran Gosché.

Page 152: Chief Michel Callihoo and his family. Musée Héritage Museum, St. Albert, 995.03.07.

Page 153: Hudson's Bay Company receipt. Musée Héritage Museum, St. Albert, 991.28.01.

Page 154: Scrip cartoon. Alberta Folklore and Local History Collection, Bruce Peel Special Collections Library, University of Alberta, 96–93–425.

Page 156: Frank Oliver. City of Edmonton Archives, EA–10–689–45.

Newcomers 1892 to 1913

Page 158: Nellie Engley. Photographer: John Ulan. Courtesy of John Ulan and Nellie Engley.

Page 158: Homesteaders. Provincial Archives of Alberta, B 671.

Page 158: Ukrainian child with man at railway station. Provincial Archives of Alberta, B 10473.

Page 159: Nellie Engley. Photographer: John Ulan. Courtesy of John Ulan and Nellie Engley.

Page 182: Old Timers. City of Edmonton Archives, EA–10–1074.

Page 183: Cree couple in blanket coats, on horseback. City of Edmonton Archives, EA–10–2356.

Page 183: Cree couple with baby, 1910. Provincial Archives of Alberta, B 910.

Page 183: Jasper Avenue scene, June 22, 1897. Provincial Archives of Alberta, B 821.

Page 183: Cree family in camp with tipis and Red River cart close-up. Provincial Archives of Alberta, B 3.

Page 184: Homesteaders. Provincial Archives of Alberta, B 671.

Page 188: Child on pony. Provincial Archives of Alberta, B 6380.

Page 189: Mrs. Garner on horseback. City of Edmonton Archives, EA–10–2761.

Page 190: Col. O'Brien's party. City of Edmonton Archives, EA–10–813.

Page 193: Michael Gowda. Courtesy of Jars Balan.

Page 195: Ukrainian children at railway station. Provincial Archives of Alberta, B 10464.

Page 198: Abraham Cristall. City of Edmonton Archives, EA–250–9a.

Page 198: Rebecca Cristall. City of Edmonton Archives, EA–600–584.

Page 202: Robbie Strong and his dog. Provincial Archives of Alberta, B 6252.

Page 205: John Collins (Muchias). City of Edmonton Archives, EA–13–4.

Page 207: Gladys Reeves. Provincial Archives of Alberta, A 14–076.

Page 208: Ernest Brown. Provincial Archives of Alberta, B 4241.

Page 211: Kids on Inauguration Day. City of Edmonton Archives, EA–10–798.

Page 213: Edmund Kemper Broadus. Artwork by Grandmaison. University of Alberta Archives, 74–27.

Page 214: Telegraph playoffs, December 1908. City of Edmonton Archives, EA–572–13.

Page 218: Robertson quadruplets. Provincial Archives of Alberta, B 3805.

Page 219: African-American construction crew. Provincial Archives of Alberta, B 1322.

Page 221: GWG garment workers at sewing machines. Glenbow Museum and Archives, NC–6–3270.

Page 221: Carpenters working on an Edmonton home. Provincial Archives of Alberta, A 4665.

The Emerging City 1914 to 1946

Page 226: Women working in Clark's lumberyard. Glenbow Museum and Archives. NC–6–3311.

Page 226: Alwyn Bramley-Moore. Courtesy of Gladys Bramley-Moore.

Page 226: Orval Griggs, Cecil Boggiss, and Harvey Griggs, with Prince. Courtesy of Orval Griggs.

Page 227: Pilot in the sky. Photographer: John Ulan. Courtesy of John Ulan.

Page 253: 101st Battalion leaves CPR Station. Glenbow Museum and Archives, NC–6–1208.

Page 255: John Michaels and Bob Wright in front of Mike's News. City of Edmonton Archives, EA–10–1587.

Page 257: Child in Rossdale during 1915 flood. City of Edmonton Archives, EA–10–884.

Page 259: Nellie McClung, Alice Jamieson, and Emily Murphy. City of Edmonton Archives, EA–10–2070.

Page 261: Alfred Bramley-Moore. Courtesy of Gladys Bramley-Moore.

Page 262: Alex Decoteau with his mother, Mrs. Pambrun. City of Edmonton Archives, EA–302–68.

Page 264: William Griesbach. City of Edmonton Archives, EA–10–1545.

Page 265: Engel family, during the 1918 flu epidemic. Courtesy of Gerry Engel.

Page 267: Elchanon Hanson in front of his store, 1917. Provincial Archives of Alberta, A 75.195.200.

Page 268: Harvesting ice on the North Saskatchewan River. City of Edmonton Archives, EA–10–1403.

Page 269: Bing Mah. Courtesy of Lillian Mah.

Page 270: Cornwall children. Provincial Archives of Alberta, A 3806.

Page 271: Wop May and Vic Horner after the 1929 Mercy Flight. City of Edmonton Archives, EA–10–3181–26–1.

Page 273: The Cobb family, from The Window of Our Memories Volume II: The New Generation, eds. Velma Carter and Wanda Leffler Akili (St. Albert: B.C.R. Society of Alberta, 1981), 67. Courtesy of Junetta Jamerson and Wanda Leffler Akili.

Page 274: Ku Klux Klan, 1932. Provincial Archives of Alberta, BL 102.

Page 275: Gee Soon Kee and Jessie Natasia Skedaniuk. Courtesy of William Kay.

Page 278: Anne Sztyk, McKernan Lake Carnival Queen. Courtesy of William Sztyk.

Page 280: Hunger March. Glenbow Museum and Archives, NC–6–13014 (e).

Page 282: Ben Swankey. Glenbow Museum and Archives, NA–3634–23.

Page 283: Hunger March. Provincial Archives of Alberta, A 9025.

Page 286: Men on relief, clearing sidewalks. City of Edmonton Archives, EA–160–1053.

Page 286: Dolly Freeman. Courtesy of Velma Logan.

Page 289: Store offering sales by Prosperity Certificates. City of Edmonton Archives, EA–10–2198.

Page 292: Edmonton Grads: Edith and Helen Stone, with Babe Belanger. Courtesy of Edith Sutton.

Page 293: Wop May telegram to Hermann Goering. City of Edmonton Archives, EA–10–3181–5–3.

Page 295: Elizabeth Sterling Haynes. City of Edmonton Archives, EA–600–291a.

Page 296: Hilwie Hamdon. Courtesy of Sid and Fay Hamdon.

Page 301: CP telegram to H.A. Friedman. Jewish Archives and Historic Society of Edmonton and Northern Alberta.

Page 301: Peter Owen, waiting to leave Germany. Jewish Archives and Historic Society of Edmonton and Northern Alberta.

Page 303: Guardian angels, mechanics in cockpit of plane. Provincial Archives of Alberta, BL 529/2.

Page 308: Personnel of Edmonton Regiment during street fighting in San Leonardo di Ortona, Italy, December 10, 1943. Photographer: Frederick G. Whitcombe. Library and Archives Canada, PA–114487.

Page 308: Men of Edmonton Regiment gathered around mailbags, Ortona, Italy, December 21, 1943. Photographer: Terry F. Rowe. Library and Archives Canada, PA–163924.

Page 309: "Daddy, come home." Letter by Arlene May Wells, November 11, 1945, Edmonton Remembers fonds, MS 669. 10, City of Edmonton Archives.

Page 309: VJ Parade. Provincial Archives of Alberta, BL 965.

The New City 1947 to 2004

Page 310: An unidentified grandfather and granddaughter at the International Sikh Youth Federation of Canada conference, September 1985. Mike Pinder, Journal photographer. Courtesy of the Edmonton Journal.

Page 310: Firefighter Ray Bock rescues Hugh Auigbelle from a house fire, December 22, 1988. Rick McWilliam, Journal photographer. Courtesy of the Edmonton Journal.

Page 311: Carpenter on site. Photographer: John Ulan. Courtesy of John Ulan.

Page 340: Vern Hunter, with Walker Taylor and N.E. Tanner. Courtesy of Bea Hunter.

Page 342: Fern Smith, Dorothy Morris and Rose Desnoyers. Courtesy of Bea Hunter.

Page 343: Ben Owre and Big Bertha. Courtesy of Bea Hunter.

Page 344: Worker taking a sample from Leduc No. 1. Courtesy of Bea Hunter.

Page 346: Kiddies Korner. Courtesy of CFRN.

Page 347: John and Satchmo. Courtesy of John Stefanyk.

Page 348: Tommy Harries. Courtesy of Joyce Harries.

Page 350: Pete Jamieson, the town crier, at an Edmonton Eskimos game. Richard Siemens, Sun photographer. Courtesy of the Edmonton Sun.

Page 355: Hockey heroes. City of Edmonton Archives, EA–600–2228a.

Page 361: Alvena Strasbourg. Courtesy of Alvena Strasbourg.

Page 364: Joey Moss and Wayne Gretzky. Steve Simon, Journal photographer. Courtesy of the Edmonton Journal.

Page 365: Graham Smith, 1978 Commonwealth Games. City of Edmonton Archives, ET–14–173.

Page 367: Front-porch jam session. Courtesy of Cathy Roy.

Page 369: Brian Paisley. Brian Gavriloff, Journal photographer. Courtesy of the Edmonton Journal.

Page 370: Alexander and Carolina Jakeway watching a Klondike Days parade. Courtesy of the Jakeway family.

Page 372: Street conflict, Gainers' meatpacking plant, 1986. Chris Schwarz, Journal photographer. Courtesy of the Edmonton Journal.

Page 375: Emergency workers carrying stretcher, 1987 tornado. Larry Wong, Sun photographer. Courtesy of the Edmonton Sun.

Page 375: Mayor Lawrence Decore at tornado scene. Jack Dagley, Sun photographer. Courtesy of the Edmonton Sun.

Page 375: Graffiti at Evergreen Mobile Home Park, 1987 tornado. Gorm Larsen, Sun photographer. Courtesy of the Edmonton Sun.

Page 377: Heather Airth, tornado emergency services. Peter Cutler, Sun photographer. Courtesy of the Edmonton Sun.

Page 379: An unidentified grandfather and granddaughter at the International Sikh Youth Federation of Canada conference, September 1985. Mike Pinder, Journal photographer. Courtesy of the Edmonton Journal.

Page 381: Mary Kur. Photographer: Dianne Szlabey. Courtesy of Mary Kur and Dianne Szlabey.

Page 383: Rosalind Callihoo. Courtesy of Rosalind Callihoo.

Page 383: Rose Lameman. Photographer: Terry Lusty. Courtesy of Rose Lameman.

Edmonton: A City Called Home

Page 389: Jim Walls, delivering Christmas parcels for Canada Post, 1938. Courtesy of Gladys Nagel.

Index

Page numbers in **bold** *refer to photographs and illustrations.*

Brady, James, on Garneau, 147–49

Bramley-Moore, Alwyn and Alfred
letters during WWI, 260–61, **261**

Brass, Eleanor, on sun and moon, 13–14

Brazeau, Mr., 77, 107

Briggs, Bill, 358

Brinton, Don, 346, **346**

British Commonwealth Air Training Plan, 247, 304–5

British newcomers (after 1890), 164–66, 217–18, 247, 304–5,
359–60

Broadus, Edmund Kemper
as first English professor at U of Alberta, **213**, 213–14
on WWI soldiers, 232–33

Broken Arm *See* Maskipiton (Broken Arm)

Brooks, Henry, 272

Brown, Ernest, photographer, xxix, 103, 154, 183, 206–8, **208**
on Edmonton winters, 208

Brown, Jennifer, 30

Brown, John, on talks before Treaty 6, 123–24

Brown, Roy, 236–37

Brownlee, Premier, xxxiii, 282

Bruneau, Calvin and Joyce, on land claims, xv, 130–31

Brydges, Charles John
on land speculation and railways, 133–34, 157

Buchwald, Joyce, 320–21

buffalo
buffalo hunts, 27, 55, **55**, 80–83, 113–14
disappearance, xxv, 82–83, 90, 92, 96, 105, 120
before disappearance, 22–23, 26, 45–46

Buffalo, John, on the buffalo, 82–83

Buffalo Lake, 23, 33

Bulyea, George, first lieutenant-governor, 173

Bulyea Park, 10

Burns, Jim, 15

Buteau, Greg and Angela, on the tornado, 374–76

Butler, William Francis, xxv
on Manitou Stone, 90
on smallpox epidemic, 117

Byrne, Paddy, **367**

Cairns, Calvin, **367**

Calder, xxxii, 231

Calgary and Edmonton Railway, xxviii

Calgary/Edmonton rivalry, xxvii, 173–74, 203, 209, 212–13

Callihoo, Louis (Kwarakwante; Mohawk), xxiii, 32, **43**, 43, 418

Callihoo, Michel and Marie Savard, xxiv, **152**
about names, 418
ancestors and descendants, 32, 91, 113, 383, **383**, 418
on treaty rations, xxviii, 151–53
Treaty 6 signator, xxvi, 94, 123–25
See also Michel band

Callihoo, Philomene, Sévère, and Jean Baptiste, **152**

Callihoo, Rosalind, **383**

Callihoo, Victoria Belcourt, **113**
on buffalo hunts (1860s), 80–82
on smallpox epidemics, 113–14

Cameron Mine, xxix

Campbell, Clarence, on NHL, 363

Camp Warwa, 381–82

Canada, government of, before 1915
Alberta as new province (1905), xxix, 173, 209–11, **211**
criminal and civil court actions (1880s), xxvii, 139–40, 149
Edmonton as provincial capital, xxx, 156, 172–73, 209–11
protests from Cree (1870s and 1880s), xxix, 93–94, 98,
119–21, 134–36, 151–53, 176
See also North West Mounted Police; North-West Rebellion of
1885; Rupert's Land; scrip for land titles; Treaty 6

Canada Packers, xxxiii

Canadian Broadcasting Company, first broadcasts, xxxiv

Canadian National Railway, xxx

Canadian Northern Railway, xxx, 177

Canadian Pacific Railway (CPR)
Chinese labourers, 167–68, 275–76
as national railway, xxvii, 104–5, 288, 344

Canadian Women's Press Club, xxx, 212

Canol Pipeline, xxxiv, 247, 248

Caragata, Warren, 178

Cardinal, Harold, xxxvi, 328

Cardinal, Mary, on military service, 248–49

Cardinal families, 361, **361**

Carey, Ed, 105

Carlson, Nellie, on treaty rights, 328

Carnegie, James, on children (1859), 75

Carothers, Fay, 272

carpenters, first labour union, xxix, 178, 221, **221**

Cashman, Tony, on aviation history, 239–40

Catholic missionaries *See* Roman Catholic missionaries

Caulder, Paul, 293

Cavanaugh, Catherine, on social progress, 320

Celanese Canada, 318

Centennial Library, xxxvi

CFB Edmonton, xxxviii

CFRN, first television broadcast (1954), 346, **346**

Chan, Jeffrey, on being a newcomer, 378–79

Charland, Emerance, 384

Charland, Louis, 77

Chastellaine, Louis, on land claims, 141–42

Chauvin, Marjorie, first female pilot, 239

Cheadle, Dr. Walter B.
on Manitou Stone, 88
on missionary life, 72, **72**, 76

Chelmick, Bob, 368

Cherniawsky, Wasyl, 194

Chevraux, Sharleen, 106

Chieftain Development, 331

child labour, 280–81

Chilean newcomers (1970s), 361–62

Chinese community, 164–65, 167–68, 214–17, 269, **275**,
275–77, 278, **309**

Chipewyan names for Edmonton, 26

Christiansen, Jim, 355

Christie, Margaret, 230

Christie, William J., Chief Factor
as HBC company man, 77, 93–94, 112, 123
on protest re hardships (1871), 119–20